THE OXFORD HANDBOOK OF

THE POLITICAL ECONOMY OF INTERNATIONAL TRADE

THE OXFORD HANDBOOK OF

THE POLITICAL ECONOMY OF INTERNATIONAL TRADE

Edited by
LISA L. MARTIN

OXFORD
UNIVERSITY PRESS

OXFORD
UNIVERSITY PRESS

Oxford University Press is a department of the University of Oxford. It furthers
the University's objective of excellence in research, scholarship, and education
by publishing worldwide. Oxford is a registered trade mark of Oxford University
Press in the UK and certain other countries.

Published in the United States of America by Oxford University Press
198 Madison Avenue, New York, NY 10016, United States of America.

Library of Congress Cataloging-in-Publication Data
The Oxford handbook of the political economy of international
trade / edited by Lisa L. Martin.
pages cm
Includes bibliographical references.
ISBN 978–0–19–998175–5 (hardback : alk. paper); 978–0–19–007783–9 (paperback : alk. paper)
1. International trade. 2. Commercial policy. I. Martin, Lisa L., 1961–
HF1379.O9965 2015
382—dc23
2014039333

Contents

PART III   INDUSTRY-LEVEL PROTECTION

PART IV   DOMESTIC INSTITUTIONS

PART V   INTERNATIONAL NEGOTIATIONS AND INSTITUTIONS

PART VI ISSUE LINKAGES

About the Contributors

Susan Ariel Aaronson is a research professor in the Elliott School of International Affairs at George Washington University.

Jennifer Bair is an associate professor of sociology at the University of Colorado, Boulder.

J. Samuel Barkin is a professor in the Department of Conflict Resolution, Human Security, and Global Governance at the McCormack Graduate School of Policy and Global Studies at the University of Massachusetts Boston.

Gordon Bannerman is a tutor at International Correspondence Schools.

Chad P. Bown is lead economist at the World Bank in Washington, DC, and a research fellow at CEPR in London.

Marc L. Busch is Karl F. Landegger Professor of International Business Diplomacy at the School of Foreign Service, Georgetown University.

Tim Büthe is an associate professor of political science and public policy, as well as a senior fellow for the Rethinking Regulation Project at the Kenan Institute for Ethics at Duke University.

Kerry A. Chase is an associate professor of politics at Brandeis University.

Mark S. Copelovitch is an associate professor of political science and public affairs and Trice Faculty Scholar at the University of Wisconsin-Madison.

Christina L. Davis is a professor of politics and international affairs at Princeton University.

Erik Gartzke is a professor of political science at the University of California, San Diego.

Lucy M. Goodhart is a lecturer at Brandeis University.

Joanne Gowa is William D. Boswell Professor of World Politics of Peace and War at Princeton University.

Walter Hatch is an associate professor of government and the director of the Oak Institute for Human Rights at Colby College.

Günter Heiduk is a professor in the East Asian Center at the Warsaw School of Economics.

Raymond Hicks is a statistical programmer at the Woodrow Wilson School of International Affairs, Princeton University.

Leslie Johns is an assistant professor of political science at the University of California, Los Angeles.

Soo Yeon Kim is an associate professor of Political Science at the National University of Singapore.

Daniel Yuichi Kono is an associate professor of political science at the University of California, Davis.

Jason Kuo is a PhD candidate in the Department of Political Science at the University of California, San Diego.

Mark S. Manger is an associate professor of political economy and global affairs in the Munk School at the University of Toronto.

Lisa L. Martin is a professor of political science at the University of Wisconsin–Madison.

Bumba Mukherjee is an associate professor of political science at the Pennsylvania State University.

Megumi Naoi is an associate professor of political science at the University of California, San Diego.

Erica Owen is an assistant professor of political science at Texas A&M University.

Krzysztof J. Pelc is an associate professor of political science and William Dawson Scholar at McGill University.

Lauren Peritz is a PhD candidate in the Department of Political Science at the University of California, Los Angeles.

Margaret E. Peters is an assistant professor of political science at Yale University.

Timothy M. Peterson is an assistant professor of political science at the University of South Carolina.

Jon C. W. Pevehouse is a professor of political science at the University of Wisconsin–Madison.

Michael Plouffe is an assistant professor of international political economy in the Department of Political Science at University College London's School of Public Policy.

Stephanie J. Rickard is an associate professor in the Department of Government at the London School of Economics.

B. Peter Rosendorff is a professor of politics at New York University.

Kenneth C. Shadlen is a professor in development studies at the London School of Economics.

Cameron G. Thies is a professor and the director of the School of Politics and Global Studies at Arizona State University.

Meredith Wilf is an assistant professor in the Graduate School of Public and International Affairs at the University of Pittsburgh.

Jiakun Jack Zhang is a PhD candidate in the Department of Political Science at the University of California, San Diego.

....

CHAPTER 1

INTRODUCTION

....

LISA L. MARTIN

Introduction

International trade offers opportunities and risks to countries, groups, and individuals. Opening an economy up to trade with other economies provides potential advantages for all, as it allows for specialization that leads to higher levels of productivity and efficiency, enlarges the markets available to firms, and increases the scope for consumer choice. However, the process of specialization entails redeployment of assets that is costly for some actors, and exposure to the global economy can create new sources of risk. For these reasons, trade is highly politicized. No government in the modern state system has ever pursued an entirely hands-off approach to trade policy.

This volume features chapters that view the politics of international trade from a wide variety of angles. It considers the concepts that have driven trade policy, the interests that compete over it, and the institutions that channel these interests. The actors that care about trade policy range from individuals and firms to interest groups, government agencies, and international institutions. Economists have made great strides in understanding the factors that create a demand for international trade and the economic consequences of trade for various actors. Many of the approaches studied in this volume build on such economic models. However, the focus here is very much on politics: who wins and who loses from different policies, who is able to organize and to influence governments, and thus how politics influences actual patterns of trade.

In this introductory chapter I provide some historical and conceptual background to the more advanced theoretical perspectives and sophisticated empirical work showcased in the rest of the volume. The next section looks at the progression of eras of trade policy, from the mercantilism that emerged along with the modern state system to today's landscape of global, regional, and bilateral trade institutions. The third section turns to theories, providing an overview of economic models of trade that help us understand the interests that go into making trade policy and the domestic and international institutions that aggregate these interests. Finally, I briefly discuss the organization of this volume.

HISTORICAL OVERVIEW

In a very broad-brush sense, the history of the politics of international trade is about movement from extensive government intervention and control of trade, to an appreciation of the potential value of freer trade, to a search for mechanisms that liberalize trade while providing some basic protections against the pressures of international competition. However, within this big picture of long-term trends there is a tremendous amount of variation. Pressures for protection ebb and flow with business cycles, political trends, and new ideas. Some countries now have only modest impediments to trade, while others continue with more protectionist policies. Some industries lobby for more openness to trade, while others demand protection. This volume is about explaining such variations. This section highlights some of the major shifts in general trends in trade policy over time.

Prior to 1500, trade between economic and political units was rare, costly, and thus concentrated in luxury goods. However, as European states began conquering and settling the rest of the world at the turn of the sixteenth century, regular patterns of trade emerged within Europe and between European countries and their colonies. European governments engaged in colonization largely because of their desire to assure access to natural resources and markets in the rest of the world. The economic and political doctrine that informed this period of expansion was mercantilism. Under mercantilism, military power and state wealth were understood as opposite sides of the same coin. As Thomas Hobbes famously proclaimed during this era, "Wealth is power, and power is wealth" (Viner 1948, 15). During the mercantilist era, which roughly covered the sixteenth through the eighteenth centuries, imperial governments established monopolies that controlled trade. Governments regulated and intervened extensively in these new trading networks, manipulating the terms of trade (the ratio of the cost of imports to exports) to enrich themselves and their domestic supporters.

Under mercantilism, European monarchies put in place laws and policies that ensured they gained access to resources from their colonies at artificially low prices. Trade between colonies and states other than the colonial power was prohibited or extremely limited. In addition, imperial powers required that their colonies import manufactured goods only from them, thus constraining supply and driving up the prices of their exports. This meant that colonists paid high prices for imported manufactured goods and received low prices for the commodities that they exported to Europe; in exchange, they received military protection from the empire. For example, Thomas (1965) estimated that English restrictions on trade with the thirteen North American colonies cost the colonists approximately $2,255,000 per year, primarily through the artificially low prices the colonies received for exports of tobacco and rice to Britain.

During the three centuries that mercantilism dominated the pursuit of international politics, underlying economic and political interests, as well as the ideas structuring trade, underwent fundamental changes.[1] The next major era of international trade can be dated from 1815, when the Napoleonic wars ended with the defeat of France by Britain and its allies, to 1914 and the outbreak of World War I. Known as the Pax Britannica, this period was characterized by growing economic exchange among European powers—the first era of what we now recognize as globalization. This period saw, in general, more cooperation and less warfare among European states, as well as the spreading Industrial Revolution. Peace and more integrated economies via increased capital flows led to rapidly expanding international trade and substantial economic growth in much of the world. The end of mercantilist doctrines took hold first in Britain, the vanguard of the Industrial Revolution. Industrialists opposed restrictions on the import of food and other resources, as this raised the costs of their workforce and other industrial operations. They also strongly desired the end of protectionism, which blocked them from exporting to other markets. Urban areas of Britain thus became opponents of restrictive devices such as the British Corn Laws (which taxed imported grain) and proponents of free trade. While remaining protectionist interests in Britain, especially farmers, lobbied in favor of maintaining government restrictions on trade, by the 1840s Britain had overturned most of its mercantilist policies.

Other governments, both in Europe and the Americas, followed Britain's lead and began dismantling their systems of trade protection. They built on this unilateral liberalization with bilateral, and then multilateral, agreements to reduce trade barriers. If we focus on the rich countries of the late nineteenth century, we see that their trade over the course of the century grew at a rate that was nearly three times that of the growth of those rich-countries' economies. By 1900 trade represented a much larger share of the global economy than it had in 1800, up to eight times as large (Maddison 1995, 38). Beyond changes in doctrine and spreading industrialization, the growth of trade was encouraged by new technologies, such as telephones and steamships, and the concomitant rapidly declining costs of long-distance trade. In addition, the establishment of the classical gold standard throughout most of the industrialized world and beyond facilitated trade as well as global movements of capital and people.[2]

As the twentieth century began, the relative decline of Britain and rise of Germany, as well as the ongoing collapse of remaining empires within Europe (Ottoman, Austro-Hungarian, and Russian), led to rising tension in Europe and the formation of rigid alliances. These alliances contributed to the outbreak of World War I in 1914, and the growing importance of the United States and Japan meant that this war spread far beyond European boundaries. The war devastated European economies and the trade networks that had grown over the previous century, and neither recovered rapidly when the war ended in 1917. The United States emerged as the major economic power in the world during the war and increased its international trade and investment to a remarkable degree during this time. However, after the war isolationist forces won political battles back home, and the United States pulled back from its participation in European economies.

Lack of leadership and very weak economies during the interwar period meant that trade did not return to prewar levels. This situation was exacerbated by the Great Depression beginning in 1929, which was characterized by competitive devaluations and renewed protectionism that devastated international trade as well as national economies. World War II brought an initially reluctant United States fully back into European politics and economics, and the economic destruction caused by that war left it the undisputed leader in the global economy. With the advent of the Cold War, the Eastern bloc broke nearly all of its economic ties with the West, and the United States set out to create renewed economic integration within the West. One novel aspect of the postwar economic order was its highly institutionalized nature, as the existing network of bilateral and multilateral trade agreements was overlaid with more formal global and regional trade organizations. Attempts to create a far-reaching International Trade Organization (ITO) failed, largely because they were too ambitious and ran into resistance in the United States. However, the failed ITO negotiations left in their wake the General Agreement on Tariffs and Trade (GATT), an informal set of deals to reduce barriers to trade. Under the GATT, impediments to trade fell rapidly over the next decades, and trade flows increased.[3]

While the GATT was intended as simply an interim accord, by default it became the institutional basis for global trade. Rounds of multilateral negotiations greatly expanded its reach, both to new types of trade and to more of the world. The GATT allowed for regional trade agreements (RTAs) that even further liberalized trade, and countries took advantage by creating and strengthening RTAs, especially beginning in the 1980s.[4] Many developing countries, especially in Latin American, initially resisted the trend toward liberalization, following instead policies of import-substituting industrialization (ISI). While the early years of ISI saw some notable successes, such as the establishment of automobile industries in Brazil and Mexico, the debt crises of the 1980s forced most developing-country governments to drop ISI and follow the export-led development strategies that were pioneered in East Asia. Liberalization thus spread beyond the rich world to the developing world and new democracies. By the 1990s, measures of global economic integration including trade flows were back to pre-World War I levels. In 1995 the GATT was replaced by the more formal and institutionalized World Trade Organization (WTO).

The existing trade regime faces a number of challenges. As the WTO has expanded to include economies in which the state plays a major role, such as China, other members worry that these states are breaking the rules and undermining the system. Many worry that the WTO's proliberalization agenda undermines local economies and culture. Ambitious negotiations within the WTO to further expand its scope have not resulted in major new trade deals, although the ongoing dispute resolution mechanisms of the WTO are an essential element of the global trade regime.[5] In the absence of breakthroughs in the WTO, further liberalization has occurred primarily through the proliferation of RTAs and other preferential trade agreements (PTAs). In spite of protectionist pressures, global trade flows have remained surprisingly robust. For example, in the initial stages of the Great Recession in 2008, many expressed concern that the economic downturn would empower protectionist forces and lead to decreased trade. While trade did show a small dip as economies contracted, fears of a surge of protection and collapse of trade proved unfounded.

Global forces, particularly the rise of China, could in the future lead to another fundamental transformation in the pattern and practice of international trade. However, for the medium term the current system seems stable. A network of organizations and agreements promote liberalized trade while offering loopholes that governments use to offer temporary protection to threatened industries.[6] Economic integration, on both global and regional scales, rules the day. The countries that have resisted integration into the modern trade system, such as North Korea, are remarkably rare. Economic integration, in turn, has created vested interests in the current system that are a major source of its stability.

APPROACHES TO THE STUDY OF INTERNATIONAL TRADE

Studies of the politics of international trade aim to explain variation in the demand for and supply of protection over time, across countries, and across sectors. To do so, they build on understandings of economic interests, domestic institutions, and international institutions. The chapters in this volume explore those factors, and their interaction, in great detail. In this section I provide some basic background on the major economic models of interests and types of institutions that go into analyses of the politics of trade.

To understand the interests that go into the making of trade policy, we need to begin with theories of what kinds of goods countries are likely to export or import. This analysis is rooted in the concept of comparative advantage, as explained in 1776 by Adam Smith, the founder of classical economics (Smith 1937). When countries trade with one another, they no longer need to be self-sufficient and can specialize in producing goods that they make more efficiently than other goods; that is, in the goods in which they have a comparative advantage. The process of specialization leads to gains in productivity and improvements in aggregate welfare for all countries. However, to build on this insight to explain the specifics of trade policy, we require a theory of comparative advantage. How do we know what goods a particular country will be able to produce the most efficiently?

The dominant approach to this question was developed in the 1920s by Swedish economists Eli Heckscher and Bertil Ohlin. The Heckscher-Ohlin model focuses on countries' factor endowments: the distribution of resources that go into production of goods and services. Typically we divide these factors into three groups: land, labor, and capital. Many modern analyses further divide capital into capital for investment and human capital. Countries differ in their capital endowments. Rich countries are abundant in capital and relatively scarce in labor compared to poor countries. Heckscher-Ohlin models argue that a country will produce most efficiently the goods that use the endowments that it has in abundance. Thus, rich countries will specialize in producing capital-intensive goods such as complex machinery or high-technology products. Countries abundant in land will tend to be agricultural exporters, while countries abundant in unskilled labor will focus on production and export of consumer goods such as clothing and simple manufactured goods.

In 1941 Wolfgang Stolper and Paul Samuelson built on the Heckscher-Ohlin approach to trade to develop a model of the losers and winners within each country from increased exposure to trade. The Stolper-Samuelson theorem argues that abundant factors within a country will benefit from increased trade, as resources will flow into sectors that use abundant factors as trade opens and new export markets become available. For example, China is abundant in unskilled labor. As China opened to trade, resources poured into the basic manufacturing sector there, benefiting workers in that sector and leading to the massive income gains that China has experienced over the last decades. In contrast, scarce factors will tend to be hurt by increased exposure to trade, as resources leave their sector and returns to the scarce factor decrease. In the United States unskilled labor is a scarce factor, and the wages of unskilled labor have fallen as trade has increased, as resources have left sectors such as textiles and apparel.

The Stolper-Samuelson (or HOSS) model predicts that abundant factors within a country will tend to support freer trade, while scarce factors will prefer protectionist policies. In the aggregate, the HOSS model is a good place to start developing an understanding of domestic interests regarding trade. Labor in rich countries such as the United States does lean toward protectionism, while those who are well educated (endowed with human capital) and rich tend to support free trade. Where land is scarce, for example in much of Western Europe or crowded developing countries, the agricultural sector is highly protectionist. Many models of trade politics thus build on the HOSS approach.

However, empirically we can also identify plenty of situations that don't fit the HOSS predictions, and economists have developed alternative models of interests regarding trade policy. Analysts frequently observe that the predicted split between labor and capital over trade policy does not obtain. For example, HOSS would predict that in debates over protection for the automobile industry in the United States, capital within the industry would lobby for reduction in levels of protection, while labor in the automobile industry would lobby for increased protection. However, most debates over protection for General Motors or Ford have not played out in that manner. Instead, we usually find that both capital and labor within the industry strongly support protection.[7] How do we account for these anomalies?

The HOSS model makes a strong assumption about the mobility of factors of production (their ability to move from one productive activity to another). It assumes that factors are fully mobile within a country (but not at all mobile across countries). So, for example, it assumes that if the US automobile industry is under pressure from imports, capital within that industry can easily deploy to a new use, such as production of pharmaceuticals. So capital's interests are not determined by the specific industry in which it is invested. Obviously factors are not always fully mobile; sometimes they are barely mobile at all, being sunk in a particular industry and very costly to redeploy (Hiscox 2002). An alternative to the HOSS model is thus known as the specific factors approach, or the Ricardo-Viner model. Ricardo-Viner assumes that factors are tied to particular industries. Thus, when that industry is under threat from imports, all factors tied to it will support protection. Likewise, when an industry is highly productive and gaining export markets, all factors within it will favor freer trade. While HOSS predicts cleavages in trade policy based on broad categories of factors (land, labor, capital) (Rogowski 1990), Ricardo-Viner predicts cleavages based on the specific sector in which a factor is invested or employed. In periods, countries, or industries in which factor mobility is limited, Ricardo-Viner may provide a better starting point for understanding economic interests than HOSS.

Modern work in economics has challenged the assumptions of both HOSS and Ricardo-Viner and provides theoretical frameworks that may better fit a globalized world in which capital and other factors freely flow across international borders. New trade theory, which Paul Krugman and others developed in the late 1970s, challenged the assumption of constant returns to scale in production. If instead production exhibits increasing returns to scale—that is, production becomes more efficient when carried out on a large scale—then industries and countries that initially begin production can outcompete new, smaller entrants into the industry (Krugman 1979). This model can provide justification for government protection of new industries, so that they can get a head start on potential competitors and grow in scale to become efficient exporters.[8] In addition, new trade theory assumes that consumers prefer to have choice among a number of brands within an industry; thus, for example, the variety of luxury car brands that we observe. These assumptions lead to models that help to explain why we observe so much trade among countries with similar factor endowments, while HOSS predicts trade among dissimilar countries on the basis of comparative advantage. Under new trade theory, countries specialize in producing a few brands of a given product and will trade these brands with one another. Germany exports BMWs to Sweden, and Sweden exports Volvos to Germany.

While new trade theory drew attention to the industry as the major unit of analysis, the so-called new new trade theory delves even deeper, focusing on variation among firms within an industry (Melitz 2003). Within any industry in a country, firms will vary in their level of productivity. When trade opens up, the most productive firms will become exporters, and the least productive firms will be driven out of business. Thus, even within an industry we expect to observe variation in preferences for protection, with globally competitive, productive firms preferring free trade and less productive firms demanding protection. With international competition, the population of firms changes as the least productive are driven out of business. Within this new, smaller population of remaining firms, the threshold at which firms are productive enough to export rises, so firms that were formerly marginally in support of freer trade can now become protectionist instead. Empirical explorations of new new trade theory are emerging, providing the foundation for a wave of work in political science asking about individual-level preferences for protection.[9]

One additional foundational economic model of trade, this one focused on the political economy of trade, has become essential to the analysis of the politics of trade. Gene Grossman and Elhanan Helpman, in what has become known as the protection-for-sale (PFS) or Grossman-Helpman model, examine the interplay between governments and sectors that demand protection.[10] They assume that the government values both aggregate welfare in the country, which is harmed by trade protection, and contributions from economic actors who demand protection in exchange. Sectors of the economy can be either organized or not. Organized sectors can offer the government a specified contribution in exchange for a particular level of protection. The government chooses to provide protection to some industries, until it reaches a point where further protection would reduce aggregate welfare enough to make the government worse off.

This model offers some clear predictions about the level of protection given to various industries and has received substantial empirical evaluation. Some of the main insights of the PFS model are discussed here. First, governments that more highly value aggregate welfare will provide less trade protection. Political scientists have thus linked the PFS model to variation in domestic institutions that determine the extent to which governments must be responsive to general welfare concerns. Second, organized industries will receive protection, while industries that are not organized will receive no protection or be subject to taxes on exports.[11] Third, government will provide more protection to those industries for which trade distortions will have the smallest impact on aggregate welfare. In this model, that means that protection will be higher for goods for which demand is relatively inelastic. If demand is inelastic—not highly responsive to price—then providing protection will generate lower distortions to the overall economy and have less impact on overall welfare. Empirical tests of the PFS model have generally found support, in that industries where demand is inelastic do tend to receive higher levels of protection (Goldberg and Maggi 1999). However, empirical tests have also led to some surprising results, such as the finding that the US government puts a much greater weight on aggregate welfare than on contributions, to an extent that seems implausible. When connecting economic models of trade interests to the actual provision of protection, many political scientists begin with some version of the PFS model.

Models of economic interests in trade are an essential starting point in studying the politics of trade. They provide insight into the demand for protection. The PFS model provides one way of connecting that demand for protection to its supply by governments, but its model of the government is very simple: just an actor that maximizes some weighted combination of aggregate welfare and contributions from sectors. Where these weights come from is not examined, nor is any other aspect of government. Political scientists probe much more deeply into the institutions, both domestic and international, that channel demand for protection or for freer trade into actual policy outcomes.

As mentioned in discussion of the PFS model, preferences regarding trade policy interact with the organization of economic interests. Interests that are diffuse and so difficult to organize, or that face other obstacles to mobilization such as unfortunate geographical distribution,[12] will find it more difficult to have their preferences reflected in policy outcomes. Protection tends to help more particular, well-organized interests, while harming diffuse interests such as general consumer welfare. Trade policy battles thus often come down to concentrated, particularistic interests demanding protection from international competition against more diffuse, disorganized interests in free trade that reduces distortions to the national economy. Domestic institutions become essential in explaining policy at this point, as they help to determine the degree to which governments are responsive to particularistic versus general interests.

One crucial set of institutions that play into this process are social institutions that organize broad coalitions and effectively present their demands to government. If unskilled labor, for example, is organized through encompassing and effective unions—as in the United States in the mid-twentieth century—labor's interests are more likely to influence trade policy than in the absence of such unions. When interests are narrowly organized, along sectoral or regional lines, they are likely to put less weight on aggregate welfare and be more protectionist. The more narrow the organization of interests, the more protectionist demands are likely to be. Thus it is not surprising that where labor is organized on a country-wide basis, as in much of Western Europe, labor's demands are less protectionist (McGillivray 2004).

Political institutions become linked to the social institutions that organize interests. Some political institutions encourage tight links between narrowly organized interests and government; others create governments that are necessarily more responsive to broad interests. In a very broad-brush sense, democracy is an important factor in this equation. To varying degrees, democratic institutions force politicians to respond to broad constituencies rather than the narrow base of support that we might find in a personalistic dictatorship, for example. This logic suggests that in general, moving toward more democratic institutions should empower broad interests and in many cases support movement toward freer trade. We do observe, again in a very general sense, that recent waves of democratization have gone hand in hand with trade liberalization, although attributing causal mechanisms in this process is difficult. In a more systematic examination, Milner and Kubota (2005) find that developing countries that are more democratic are also more likely to engage in trade liberalization, corroborating the general insight.[13]

Scholars also tie more specific elements of political institutions to patterns of protection. When politicians are elected on a narrow regional basis, they are likely to be highly responsive to the economic conditions of their regional constituency and less responsive to national welfare concerns. We would therefore expect that politicians elected on a broad national basis—such as the president in the United States—would tend to support free trade, while members of the legislature who are elected by a small district would be more protectionist. Lohman and O'Halloran (1994), for example, provide support for this hypothesis about the relationship between the size of the constituency and the politician's stance on trade policy. Similarly, political parties that are organized along broad lines of class are more likely to support free trade than are those that are tied to specific industries or regions. Rogowski (1987) has argued that proportional representation systems, in which voters choose a party rather than an individual candidate, will result in less protectionist outcomes than those in which elections are for a specific individual candidate, as in the United States.[14] Beyond electoral systems, other aspects of domestic institutions will determine trade policy. For example, in the United States a shift in authority to provide protection away from Congress to the president coincided with the move away from very high levels of protection in the interwar period (Bailey, Goldstein, and Weingast 1997; Lohmann and O'Halloran 1994). In many developed countries today, much of the action on trade policy takes place within agencies rather than legislatures, as the agencies are empowered to provide temporary relief from protection through safeguard provisions in international agreements. These agencies can operate without much public visibility and can be captured by narrow interests, perhaps leading to an increased tendency to protect threatened industries.

Studies of domestic institutions tend to examine individual countries in isolation. However, as the previous section of this chapter discussed, over time more and more trade policy is made not by individual governments, but in the process of international negotiation and through the work of international institutions. A complex web of bilateral and multilateral trade agreements, regional and other preferential trade organizations, and the global WTO regime now constrain individual states' trade policies. Governments enter these agreements voluntarily, but once in it is very costly to exit such commitments, and as trade competitors enter agreements, choosing to remain outside of them can become prohibitively expensive. Thus, international bargaining and international institutions are another crucial channel through which interests are aggregated into trade policy outcomes.

Governments that enter into international negotiations on trade or that request admission to a trade organization are typically driven by the desire to gain access to additional markets (driven, in turn, by the interests of exporters and potential exporters back home). While economists focused on comparative advantage decry such language, negotiations therefore take the form of offering reciprocal "concessions" in terms of access to the home market. Reciprocity is central to international trade politics. During initial bargaining, governments offer to lower barriers to specific types of trade in exchange for lower barriers to their exports in other countries. Reciprocity continues to dominate the functioning of agreements and trade institutions after governments reach deals. Countries are often tempted to cheat on trade agreements, providing protection to home industries during hard times (Downs and Rocke 1997). If they do and are caught, enforcement takes the form of retaliating by imposing punitive tariffs on that country's exports in the affected market. Complementing reciprocity, the concept of most-favored-nation (MFN) status extends deals that countries reach bilaterally, or among a small group, to all other members of an organization. Reciprocity and MFN status characterize the agreements and institutions that structure modern international trade, although we increasingly see regional deals offering market access that goes beyond what countries receive through MFN status.

As discussed in the previous section, the modern global trade regime dates to the creation of the GATT in 1947, replaced by the more formalized WTO in 1995. Throughout the history of the GATT/WTO, rounds of multilateral negotiations have led to commitments to reduce barriers to trade. Small groups of states reach deals on the basis of reciprocity and then use MFN to extend these deals to all members of the regime. The WTO also has rules for providing temporary relief to threatened industries and a dispute resolution mechanism for members. While technically all members of the WTO have the same voting power, in practice the process of negotiation among the major trading powers—the United States, European Union, and Japan—has meant that deals have favored the interests of these rich, developed countries, and the concerns of developing countries have not been as high on the agenda (Gowa and Kim 2005).

The WTO launched the latest round of negotiations, known as the Doha Round, in 2001, and over a decade later the round has not yet reached a final deal. Doha Round negotiations have been characterized by confrontation between developing countries who want to see liberalization of agricultural trade in the rich world and developed countries concerned about trade in services and protection of intellectual property. A draft deal in December 2013 renewed hopes that the Doha Round would eventually be completed. But even in the absence of major new trade deals, the WTO dispute resolution mechanism and existing framework of rules provide an institutional structure that sets the foundation for members' trade policies. The WTO also engages in monitoring of members' trade policies and in a variety of ways provides extensive information about trading activities. The provision of information and mechanism for resolving disputes are crucial to the maintenance of multilateral cooperation on trade issues.

As negotiations in the WTO have stalled or failed to address individual states' trade concerns, governments have increasingly turned to RTAs and PTAs. As of 2013, the WTO estimates that there were 379 RTAs in force. Some of the most important RTAs are the European Union (EU); the North American Free Trade Agreement (NAFTA); and Mercosur, an agreement among South American countries in which Brazil plays a leading role. Some RTAs are bilateral, and others are very large—the EU has twenty-seven members and continues to expand. Like the WTO, RTAs operate on the basis of reciprocity. They vary greatly in the extent to which they are formalized and provide institutional mechanisms for dispute resolution, monitoring of trade policies, and so forth. One ongoing debate among economists and political scientists revolves around the relationship between the WTO and RTAs. Does increasing reliance on RTAs as the mechanism of liberalization undermine the multilateral trade regime and introduce distortions into global trade? Or do RTAs allow for more rapid, deeper integration among small groups of countries that will eventually translate into deep multilateral liberalization?[15] Regardless of the answer to this question, in the absence of successful negotiations in the WTO, states will pursue their interests through other international trade institutions.

The chapters in this volume build on these historical and conceptual foundations. Economic models of trade interests provide a starting point. Political scientists focus on aggregation of interests through organization, bargaining, and institutions, on both the domestic and international levels. In the next section I explain how this general framework is reflected in the organization of this volume.

Organization of This Volume

The chapters in this volume are organized into six sections, which loosely follow the conceptual and theoretical framework just discussed. The contributions survey both classic work in the field and new developments. They outline new research agendas and standing puzzles and present new, cutting-edge research on the politics of international trade.

The first section provides an overview of historical, theoretical, and methodological developments in the study of trade. Joanne Gowa explains the GATT/WTO system, both its origins in international negotiations and its effects. She argues that the benefits of the system have largely been concentrated among its large founding members and ties this result to major powers' security concerns. Gordon Bannerman provides a conceptual overview of the idea of free trade. What began as a unilateral, voluntary commitment to removing all restrictions on international exchange has evolved into a much more nuanced understanding of the benefits and costs of trade liberalization. Chad P. Bown focuses on the specific instruments that governments have used in the modern era to limit and channel trade flows. The GATT/WTO has drastically reduced what was previously the major impediment to trade, tariffs (taxes on imports at the border). But that process has revealed, or perhaps even encouraged, the use of administrative means of protection known collectively as nontariff barriers (NTBs). Finally, Raymond Hicks delves into the methodological challenges of testing theories of trade politics by concentrating on the debate over the effects of the GATT/WTO. The availability of new data and the rapid development of new statistical methods have challenged scholars attempting to stay at the frontiers of research. Hicks offers some central lessons of methodological developments for ongoing empirical research.

Parts 2 through 5 consider a particular set of actors in international trade. Part 2 begins by looking at domestic society. Jason Kuo and Megumi Naoi examine what is probably the most micro-level of analysis, the individual. Advances in survey research techniques have opened up the ability to test theories of trade by asking whether the predicted effects obtain at the individual level. Kuo and Naoi survey this new research on individual attitudes and present some new results. Within domestic society—especially in developed countries—the role of labor in debates over trade policy has often been central. Erica Owen looks at the work on whether labor is an important source of protectionist sentiment and how the role and attitudes of labor have changed over time. Finally, B. Peter Rosendorff links the domestic to the international level through the lens of trade disputes. Because domestic actors are subject to economic shocks and put pressure on governments to shield them from these shocks, international trade agreements allow for some flexibility in the enforcement of trade deals. However, governments can be tempted to use this flexibility in unintended ways, creating the need for dispute settlement procedures in international agreements. Rosendorff argues that these procedures are best seen as information-providing devices.

Part 3 turns to firms as the unit of analysis. The five chapters in this section consider the role of the firm in trade policy from different angles. Lucy M. Goodhart begins by looking at efforts to explain variations in the level of protection that different industries receive. She presents a detailed discussion of the PFS model, empirical studies of PFS, and where it falls short of explaining observed variation in levels of protection. She discusses new work that goes beyond PFS to present new models of the demand and supply of protection by industries. Timothy M. Peterson and Cameron G. Thies focus on the role of international trade within industries. A number of analysts have studied the implications of intraindustry trade for domestic outcomes such as lobbying activity. Peterson and Thies expand this discussion to international-level implications, such as political affinity and militarized conflict. Michael Plouffe analyzes the new new trade theory summarized above and its implications for variation in protection. As discussed, the key insight of this body of work is that, even within a given industry, firms are heterogeneous in their levels of productivity. This heterogeneity gives rise to variation in demands for protection or liberalized trade. Tim Büthe examines the interaction of antitrust policies and trade policies. Economists have typically understood these policy areas as substitutes; there is little need for antitrust regulation to keep the domestic market competitive if the market is open to international competition. However, empirical evidence does not support this interpretation. A resolution to this conflict may lie in the recognition that firms lobby regulators not just in their own country, but across national borders. Finally, Hatch, Heiduk, and Bair consider the implications of the growth of multinational corporations (MNCs) for trade policy. Increasingly, MNCs use a model of production that relies on networks—different elements of the productive process are scattered around the globe, building on comparative advantage and variation in legal environments. Focusing on production networks in different regions, Hatch, Heiduk, and Bair show how global production networks fundamentally change the context of international trade.

Part 4 concentrates on domestic political institutions. As mentioned above, studies of newly democratizing states have generally found that democratization and trade liberalization go hand in hand. However, Bumba Mukherjee argues that this generalization misses a great deal of nuance in the pattern of protection in developing countries that undergo democratization. While these governments typically do liberalize trade in low-skill goods, they often maintain or increase protection of skill-intensive industries. In addition, Mukherjee examines the question of whether trade liberalization itself is a contributing factor to democratization. Stephanie J. Rickard turns to political institutions in established democracies, where a major source of variation is in the details of electoral systems. While there is a great deal of work on the effects of electoral systems, there is surprisingly little consensus on those effects. Rickard argues that the lack of robust empirical findings in this literature so far is not a reason to declare the research program a failure and identifies new directions for research. Daniel Yuichi Kono takes on the relatively new and challenging topic of trade policy in authoritarian regimes. As nondemocracies, especially China, play a larger role in the global trade regime, it is crucial that we understand trade politics within these states. Yet we have few generalizations about how trade policy is made in authoritarian states. Kono identifies four elements of authoritarian regimes (economic structure, coalition size, time horizons, and leader's mode of entry into power) as promising bases for developing theories of authoritarian regimes. Finally, Kerry A. Chase looks at the interaction between domestic geography and institutions. Different industries have different geographical organization within countries, which in turn affects their ability to influence government policy. Chase identifies the central questions in this research area, such as whether geographic concentration is helpful or harmful for the pursuit of trade interests.

Part 5 jumps to the international level of analysis. As discussed above, international trade politics is highly institutionalized, and the four chapters in this section look at these international institutions from different perspectives. Leslie Johns and Lauren Peritz focus on the design of trade agreements. They provide insight into why PTAs are designed in particular ways, but also suggest that this literature needs to move beyond examining individual PTAs to take a more systemic view that includes the interaction of PTAs with one another. Soo Yeon Kim studies RTAs, in particular their role in promoting "deep integration" that goes well beyond removing impediments at the border to trade flows. As global trade negotiations stall, this regional promotion of deep integration may represent the future of international trade politics. Christina L. Davis and Meredith Wilf consider the expansion of the WTO over time. What determines the pattern of WTO expansion, and what are its implications? Davis and Wilf argue that noneconomic interests are important in explaining decisions to join the WTO. Finally, Marc L. Busch and Krzysztof J. Pelc focus on the dispute settlement elements of the WTO, which provide ongoing support to liberalization efforts even in the face of stalled negotiations. Busch and Pelc argue that existing political science literature on dispute settlement does not pay sufficient attention to its legal dimensions.

Trade policy does not exist in a vacuum. It interacts with other policy areas, such as national security, human rights, and capital flows. Part 6 examines these issue linkages. Erik Gartzke and Jiakun Jack Zhang take on the perennial topic of the relationship between trade and war, arguing that this literature needs to incorporate better models of domestic politics to make sense of conflicting empirical results. Mark S. Copelovitch and Jon C. W. Pevehouse note the surprising deficit of work linking exchange rate and trade policies, in spite of widespread understanding that these policies are codetermined. They present initial work that bridges these "silos" in the literature. Does international trade harm the natural environment, and how should environmental concerns enter into trade agreements? J. Samuel Barkin argues that these questions are more complex and multilayered than has been appreciated in the literature. Trade policy has always been a central part of governments' development policies, as the discussion above of ISI indicated. Mark S. Manger and Kenneth C. Shadlen provide an in-depth examination of the relationship between trade and development, arguing that the interests of exporters in developing countries weigh heavily in the policy process and force a shift in theories of trade policy. Susan Ariel Aaronson takes on the fraught question of the relationship between trade and human rights. While much of the literature has focused on the introduction of human rights provisions in trade agreements, Aaronson finds that this literature misses the big picture in its focus on personal integrity rights to the exclusion of other, perhaps more relevant, aspects of human rights for trade. Finally, Margaret E. Peters studies the interaction of migration policies and trade policies. She argues that flows of people and goods are to a large extent substitutes for one another, with predictable implications for the policy preferences of firms and individuals regarding immigration and trade protection.

Understanding the politics of international trade requires a grasp of the economics of trade, how economics translates into variation in preferences over trade policy, and how these preferences are aggregated through negotiations and institutions into policy outcomes. The chapters in this volume present foundational and path-breaking research on each stage of this process. Both theories and empirical studies of trade are a thriving area of research in international political economy, and they draw on a wide variety of analytical perspectives. These perspectives are represented in this volume, which we hope will serve as both an introduction to the subject and the impetus for further research.

Notes

1. See Bannerman chapter in this volume.
2. See Copelovitch and Pevehouse in this volume for analysis of the relationship between trade and exchange rate policies; and Peters for the relationship between trade and migration.
3. However, a lively debate rages about the extent to which the GATT itself actually contributed to increased trade flows. See chapters by Hicks and by Gowa in this volume.
4. On PTAs, see the Kim chapter in this volume.
5. See chapters by Rosendorff and by Busch and Pelc in this volume.
6. See the Bown chapter in this volume.
7. As the industry has become dominated by multinational corporations with global production networks, the pattern of lobbying has become more complex. See the chapter by Hatch, Heiduk, and Bair in this volume.
8. Krugman and others acknowledge that the difficulty of guessing which particular industries might succeed often outweighs the potential benefits of government support.
9. See the Kuo and Naoi chapter in this volume.
10. See the Goodhart chapter in this volume for further discussion of the PFS model.
11. Taxes on exports are highly unusual in the modern economy, so this implication of the PFS model has not received empirical validation.
12. See the Chase chapter in this volume.
13. See also the chapters by Mukherjee in this volume on new democracies and by Kono on dictatorships.
14. But see Rogowski and Kayser (2002). The Rickard volume in this chapter studies the impact of electoral systems on trade policy.
15. See Lawrence (1991).

REFERENCES

Bailey, Michael, Judith Goldstein, and Barry Weingast. 1997. The Institutional Roots of American Trade Policy. *World Politics* 49 (3): 309–338.

Downs, George W., and David M. Rocke. 1997. *Optimal Imperfection? Domestic Uncertainty and Institutions in International Relations.* Princeton, NJ: Princeton University Press.

Goldberg, Pinelopi Koujianou, and Giovanni Maggi. 1999. Protection for Sale: An Empirical Investigation. *American Economic Review* 89 (5): 1135–1155.

Gowa, Joanne, and Soo Yeon Kim. 2005. An Exclusive Country Club: The Effects of the GATT on Trade, 1950–94. *World Politics* 57 (4): 453–478.

Grossman, Gene M., and Elhanan Helpman. 1994. Protection for Sale. *American Economic Review* 84 (4): 833–850.

Hiscox, Michael. 2002. Commerce, Coalitions, and Factor Mobility: Evidence from Congressional Votes on Trade Legislation. *American Political Science Review* 96 (3): 591–608.

Krugman, Paul. 1979. Increasing Returns, Monopolistic Competition, and International Trade. *Journal of International Economics* 9 (4): 469–479.

Lawrence, Robert A. 1991. Emerging Regional Arrangements: Building Blocs or Stumbling Blocks? In *Finance and the International Economy 5: The AMEX Bank Review Prize Essays,* edited by Richard O'Brien, 25–35. New York: Oxford University Press.

Lohmann, Susanne, and Sharyn O'Halloran. 1994. Divided Government and U.S. Trade Policy: Theory and Evidence. *International Organization* 48 (4): 595–632.

Maddison, Angus. 1995. *Monitoring the World Economy, 1820-1992.* Paris: Development Centre of the Organisation for Economic Co-operation and Development.

McGillivray, Fiona. 2004. *Privileging Industry: The Comparative Politics of Trade and Industrial Policy.* Princeton, NJ: Princeton University Press.

Melitz, Marc J. 2003. The Impact of Trade on Intra-Industry Reallocations and Aggregate Industry Productivity. *Econometrica* 71 (6): 1695–1725.

Milner, Helen V., and Keiko Kubota. 2005. Why the Move to Free Trade? Democracy and Trade Policy in the Developing Countries. *International Organization* 59 (1): 107–143.

Rogowski, Ronald. 1990. *Commerce and Coalitions: How Trade Affects Domestic Political Alignments.* Princeton, NJ: Princeton University Press.

Rogowski, Ronald. 1987. Trade and the Variety of Democratic Institutions. *International Organization* 41 (2): 203–223.

Rogowski, Ronald, and Mark A. Kayser. 2002. Majoritarian Electoral Systems and Consumer Power: Price-Level Evidence from the OECD Countries. *American Journal of Political Science* 46 (3): 526–539.

Smith, Adam. 1937 [1776]. *An Inquiry into the Nature and Causes of the Wealth of Nations.* New York: Modern Library.

Thomas, Robert Paul. 1965. A Quantitative Approach to the Study of the Effects of British Imperial Policy on Colonial Welfare. *Journal of Economic History* 25 (4): 615–638.

Viner, Jacob. 1948. Power versus Plenty as Objectives of Foreign Policy in the Seventeenth and Eighteenth Centuries. *World Politics* 1 (1): 1–29.

PART I

HISTORICAL, THEORETICAL, AND METHODOLOGICAL DEVELOPMENTS

CHAPTER 2

EXPLAINING THE GATT/WTO

origins and effects

JOANNE GOWA

It has long been conventional wisdom in international relations that institutions can help states cooperate with each other when their decentralized efforts to do so fail. The canonical problem that creates a role for a trade institution arises when more than one state can exert power over its terms of trade—that is, the price of its exports in terms of its imports. In this case, each state has an incentive to impose a tariff to raise its real income. If all do so, however, they are worse off than if they had all adhered to free trade. This creates the familiar "prisoners' dilemma" (PD). An institution has value added in this case because it can help states realize the Pareto-improving equilibrium outcome of open markets.

The institutions that have governed international trade have varied widely over time. During the first golden age of globalization in the late nineteenth century, a network of bilateral trade treaties regulated commerce. Between the world wars of the twentieth century, a now infamous set of trade blocs did so, the legacy of repeated diplomatic failures to establish a liberal regime and of the Great Depression. The interwar system instantiated discrimination and is widely regarded as having wreaked havoc on global trade while exacerbating the political tensions that erupted into war in 1939. In contrast, the second golden age of globalization, which began after World War II, witnessed the emergence of an overarching multilateral organization, the General Agreement on Tariffs and Trade (GATT), and its successor, the World Trade Organization (WTO).

The variation in international economic institutions over time is due partly to shifts in the distribution of power at home and abroad that make the institutions' construction more or less viable. As several detailed histories of trade make clear (e.g., Findlay and O'Rourke 2007; O'Rourke and Williamson 1999), it is also the product of apolitical changes. During the first golden age of globalization, for example, sharply falling transport costs led to a secular increase in trade. Shifts in exchange-rate regimes can also induce variations in the demand for institutions. The same is true of changes in the composition of trade: trade in differentiated products, for example, increases the gains from trade and the appeal of open international markets.

This chapter examines the role of international politics in the creation and operation of the GATT/WTO. Other chapters in this volume address the role that domestic politics plays in world trade. The question I address here is whether political-military alliances influenced trade expansion after World War II. Allies have an especially strong interest in trading with each other and relatively weak concerns about cheating. This biases them toward increasing their trade with each other despite the explicit prohibition against discrimination in the GATT/WTO charter. I show that alliances do exert a positive impact on the trade of contracting parties, effectively embedding discrimination in the postwar regime.

I begin by briefly explaining the value added of trade institutions and the impact on trade of security interests. Then I explain the intended role of the GATT and the extent to which it fulfilled the role that theory assigns to institutions. Finally, I examine the data, showing that alliances do exert a positive influence on trade between GATT/WTO members.

WHY INSTITUTIONS? ECONOMICS AND POLITICS

International institutions arise to solve market-failure problems (Keohane 1984). Their raison d'être in the case of trade inheres in their ability to solve the public-good problem that arises because some states have incentives to use tariffs and other trade barriers. According to standard trade theory, a large state—that is, one capable of exercising market power—can use a tariff to increase its real income at the expense of other states (e.g., Bagwell and Staiger 2002). A tariff increases a state's welfare because it reduces its demand for imports and lowers their price. Although a tariff also imposes costs in terms of foregone trade, a state can always set its tariff to ensure that its net gain is positive. Its trading partner bears the cost of the price drop and the deadweight loss associated with the inefficient income transfer a tariff effects.

In contrast, standard trade theory does not offer a small state—that is, a state that cannot exercise either monopoly or monopsony power over its terms of trade—any incentive to use a tariff. While leaving the state's terms of trade unchanged, its tariff will reduce its demand for imports. The associated loss of consumer surplus exceeds the gains that its producers and the government reap. This means that open markets maximize a small state's welfare regardless of the trade policies of other states. Even if it is the target of a large state's tariff, for example, the small state is better off absorbing the associated cost than retaliating: a tariff will only decrease its real income without reducing the large state's welfare. As such, a small state's deviation will not induce punishment by a large state; the small state only shoots itself in the foot when it uses a trade barrier.[1]

This implies that there is no role for a trade institution when only small states exist or only one large state exists.[2] The same applies when only two large states exist. In this case, the incentive structure of each corresponds to a PD game in which the dominant strategy is defection. Mutual cooperation can emerge in an infinitely repeated PD game. Although an infinite number of equilibria exist, including perpetual defection, the use of a grim-trigger strategy can, for example, enable two large states to realize the Pareto-improving equilibrium of free trade. The strategy mandates that both states defect forever in the event that either deviates.[3] In this situation, each state has an incentive to monitor the other's compliance, because it bears the full cost of the latter's deviation. As long as the discounted sum of payoffs for cooperation exceeds the sum of a one-shot gain from defection and the discounted sum of payoffs from mutual defection, neither state will wander off the equilibrium path of play. Although implicit, this mechanism presumably enabled a network of trade treaties to emerge sua sponte in the late nineteenth century.[4]

When more than two states capable of exercising market power exist, however, a public-good problem arises. Each state has an incentive to free ride on the efforts of others to monitor compliance. While information about defection is excludable in theory, in practice states have incentives to make it common knowledge, because punishment is incentive compatible for each large state when any defection occurs. This means that making private information public leads to harsher punishment for the defecting state and a more effective deterrent. In practice, therefore, the supply of information is a public good. An institution can help in this situation to the extent that it centralizes the monitoring of compliance.[5]

Existing theory is silent about many other aspects of the "rational design" of a trade institution (Koremenos, Lipson, and Snidal 2001). Among these is the set of rules that should govern negotiations under its auspices. The most basic, perhaps, is whether tariff cuts should be extended to all members—that is, whether to adopt most-favored nation (MFN) treatment. While small states have little reason to join an institution absent MFN treatment and nondiscrimination reduces the costs associated with distinguishing imports by country of origin, it may not be welfare enhancing relative to a regime in which tariff cuts apply more narrowly (Horn and Mavroidis 2001). An MFN clause can induce free riding as states reap the benefits of tariff cuts that other members make without lowering their own trade barriers. This can stall the process of trade liberalization as each state waits for others to cut their tariffs.

The literature about the value added of institutions also has relatively little to say about the role that international politics plays in their creation and operation. As Martin and Simmons (1998, 737) note, "distributive consequences" fell rapidly "from the center of consideration." Attempts to integrate international politics into the study of regimes have proved controversial. Some argue that national interests and institutions are isomorphic (e.g., Mearsheimer 1994/95). Others maintain that institutions affect the interests and behavior of even large states, socializing them to respect the norms of the organizations they join (e.g., Johnston 2001; Finnemore 1993). Still others maintain that institutions can be "simultaneously causes and effects"—that is, they are "both the objects of state choice and consequential" (Martin and Simmons 1998, 743).

Perhaps the most basic issue that the politics of regimes engenders is whether states can cooperate with each other in a world in which each is the guarantor of its security. When war is always an option, some argue, states decide whether to cooperate not only on the basis of the gains they stand to realize but also on the basis of the welfare increases that accrue to other states: an asymmetrical distribution of the gains from cooperation, they contend, can place the security of states at risk (e.g., Waltz 1979; Grieco 1988; Mearsheimer 1994/95, Powell 1991). Krasner (1991) claims that the equilibrium outcomes that institutions enforce are themselves endogenous to international politics: the distribution of power among its members determines the choice among equilibria on the Pareto frontier.[6]

That a link exists between trade and security is the premise of the literature about allies and trade. Trade generates both private and social welfare gains (Gowa and Mansfield 1993; Gowa 1995). Trade with an ally generates a positive security externality, raising the real income of both the home state and its ally and increasing the aggregate power of their alliance. Trade with an adversary, on the other hand, produces private gains and social costs: the income that accrues to the adversary, because it increases its potential political-military power, creates a negative security externality. This gives allies stronger incentives to trade with each other than with other states. Although the original claim applied exclusively to large states, because only they can affect their terms of trade, subsequent work shows that it applies to allies of all sizes (e.g., Gowa and Mansfield 1993; Mansfield and Bronson 1997; Long 2003).

Nonetheless, the extent, if any, to which alliances affect the trade expansion that institutions generate has rarely been systematically examined.[7] This is so even though the existence of security externalities generates stronger incentives to lower trade barriers between allies than between other states. Security externalities also reduce the demand for monitoring, because the payoff that accrues to any member of an alliance from defecting also increases aggregate alliance strength. As long as the sum of the payoffs from the temptation to defect and unilateral cooperation is lower than the aggregate gains from cooperation, however, allies retain an interest in monitoring each other, albeit one that is weaker than in the case of other states.

Before asking about the impact international politics exerted on the postwar trade regime, I briefly review the principles and purposes that motivated the creation of the original GATT to make clear the rules that its architects intended to govern its operation.

THE CREATION OF THE GATT

Secretary of State Cordell Hull's belief that trade discrimination generates hostile political relations has become legendary among students of international politics. He and other US officials set out to create a multilateral regime based on nondiscrimination. Intent on eliminating any vestiges of the interwar blocs, they began to work on a blueprint for the postwar era even before the United States entered World War II. Using

Lend Lease aid as leverage, the United States pressed Britain to sign the 1941 Atlantic Charter, which pledged its signatories to "endeavor, with due respect for their existing obligations, to further the enjoyment by all States, great or small, victor or vanquished, of access, on equal terms, to the trade and to the raw materials of the world ... needed for their economic prosperity."[8]

American officials assumed that a reversion to the interwar system was all too likely absent an overarching trade institution. Before 1914 the gold standard had corrected payment imbalances that otherwise might have impeded global trade; privileging exchange-rate stability over domestic output and employment was designed to ensure the automatic reversal of deficits and surpluses. Tariffs had begun to rise before 1914, but it took the Great War to write "an abrupt and fiery coda to the preceding century's unremitting expansion of trade" (Rogowski 1989, 61). The war per se did not, however, produce the trade and currency blocs that would later preoccupy US officials. Rather, they were endogenous to the onset of the Great Depression and the efforts states made to keep intact what Eichengreen (1992) describes as their "golden fetters."[9] If the postwar exchange-rate regime enabled states to sustain growth, it seemed very unlikely that the years after World War II would witness a replay of the interwar experience. But the specter of the interwar blocs nonetheless motivated the construction of a system of rules designed to facilitate the opening of international markets.

The architects of the postwar trade regime envisaged the GATT as "simply a trade agreement" under the aegis of an International Trade Organization (ITO) that would govern not only trade but also policies related to competition, employment, investment, and economic development (Irwin, Mavroidis, and Sykes 2008, 100). In early 1946 the United States prompted the Economic and Social Council (ECOSOC) of the United Nations to appeal for the creation of a regime to establish the "rules and norms by which trade would occur and would provide oversight, through a large administrative structure, of the adherences to these rules" (Barton et al. 2006, 35). Given its domain, the ITO required member states to delegate "far more authority to an international institution than did the GATT" (Barton et al. 2006, 36). The US Congress, however, refused to sanction the creation of the ITO even though the United States "had taken the principal initiative" to develop its charter (Jackson 1989, 34).

Thus, the GATT evolved as a somewhat accidental organization. The bilateral trade agreements that the United States had concluded under the 1934 Reciprocal Trade Agreements Act (RTAA) became its template. Its founding members accepted several provisions included in the RTAA agreements, such as an unconditional MFN clause, regulations about government purchases, and procedures to compensate changes in agreed-upon tariffs. The GATT, as Irwin, Mavroidis, and Sykes (2008, 12) note, "was not created from scratch, but represented a continuation and expansion of US efforts during the 1930s."

Article I of its charter formally established nondiscrimination, expressed as MFN treatment, as the basis of the postwar regime. The charter also, however, allowed states to retain the preferences that they already had in force, including those that Britain had extended to Imperial Preference System (IPS) members. It also condoned the formation of preferential trade agreements (PTAs) that lowered trade barriers among a subset of GATT members as long as their ex post barriers to trade were no higher on average than they had been ex ante. The PTA provision facilitated European integration, a process that had begun with the proposal for a customs union between France and Italy in July 1947 (Odell and Eichengreen 1998, 193).[10]

Despite the lengthy negotiations that produced it, the GATT was ill-equipped to perform the critical role that market-failure theory assigns to institutions. As noted previously, the principal value added of a multilateral trade organization is its ability to solve the public-good problem created by the need to monitor compliance. The contracting parties, however, refused to endow the GATT with the capacity to perform this role. They agreed neither on a budget nor on "a fully fledged secretariat" (Kim 2010, 7). They were unwilling to "create, or pay for, any kind of standing committees" (Barton et al. 2006, 43). The UN Conference on Trade and Employment created the secretariat, formally known as the Interim Commission for the International Trade Organization (Hoekman and Kostecki 2001, 38). Yet it too had neither "direct oversight nor judicial powers" (Barton et al. 2006, 48). The contracting parties' lack of interest in an administrative apparatus, including a mechanism to monitor cheating, reflected a culture that discouraged "the Secretariat form taking a hard line against its own members in anything other than the most diplomatic language" (Daunton, Narlikar, and Stern 2012).

Although several "ad hoc surveillance schemes" existed (Daunton, Narlikar, and Stern 2012), it was only in 1989 that the contracting parties agreed to establish a provisional Trade Policy Review Mechanism (TPRM), tasked with reviewing their policies. The inception of the WTO in 1995 made the TPRM permanent. Although this mechanism might seem to enable the monitoring of compliance, its reports typically review broad economic policies while taking note of "the consistency of certain trade measures with multilateral principles" (Daunton, Narlikar, and Stern 2012). Members repeatedly refused to make the reports an integral element of the dispute-resolution mechanism (DRM). Even now, states subject to a review have the right to approve or revise it prior to its publication.

Rather than being the centralized provider of information about cheating that market-failure theory calls for, the GATT/WTO remains a "fire-alarm" system (McCubbins and Schwartz 1984), one in which enforcement depends on member complaints (Martin 2008). To help its members penetrate the camouflage that states often use to cloak their deviations, the GATT authorizes them to request informal consultations with the alleged offender. Plaintiffs can also opt to request a panel of experts to adjudicate a dispute. The ability of the GATT to do this requires the acquiescence of the prospective defendant. Even if the latter agrees, it retains the option to block the implementation of a panel decision.

The creation of a new DRM was an integral element of the effort to establish the WTO that began with the 1990 suggestion by Canada to replace the GATT (Hoekman and Kostecki 2001, 49). Perhaps the major shift associated with its inception was to make permanent the changes to the DRM that had occurred during the Uruguay Round. Under the new rules, a defendant cannot veto panel formation. It is still the case, however, that the enforcement of panel rulings depends on the willingness of the defendant to change its behavior and of other states to punish it in the event that it refuses to do so.[11] Because the WTO DRM remains a fire-alarm system, it has a public-good problem of its own: each prospective plaintiff has an incentive to let another bear the costs of litigation.

This very brief discussion highlights the role played in the creation of the GATT/WTO of the lessons of the past that its architects had absorbed. In particular, its genesis makes clear their determination to eliminate all vestiges of the discrimination that had sullied trade between the wars. Yet from the outset it sanctioned the trade preferences that some of its members had previously adopted. Moreover, as it evolved, discrimination, albeit of a different type, would reemerge. In the next section I review the existing empirical evidence about the effects of the GATT/WTO on trade between its members.

THE EFFECTS OF THE GATT/WTO

The failure of the GATT/WTO to respond to the market-failure problem that an institution is designed to solve implies that it would exert a distinctly limited impact on trade flows. Yet students of international relations long believed that the secular increase in global trade that occurred after World War II was attributable at least partly to its existence. While some earlier studies of other trade-related issues included a GATT membership variable (e.g., Mansfield and Bronson 1997),[12] it was not until 2004 that a systematic empirical test of the organization's impact on trade appeared.

In a seminal analysis, Rose (2004a) added to the covariates standard in the gravity model two dummy variables to capture the effects of the GATT/WTO. The first assigns a one to dyads that include two of its members; it is zero otherwise. The second takes on a value of unity for country pairs in which one state is a GATT/WTO member and the other is not. Rose examines trade between 1948 and 1999 using an ordinary least squares analysis that includes year fixed effects.[13] He finds that the postwar regime does not exert any significant impact on trade between its members. Although the addition of country or dyadic fixed effects produces a positive and significant coefficient on the GATT/WTO variable, Rose argues that the impact is nonetheless "small compared to other effects (e.g., regional trade associations), the long-term growth of trade, intuition, and the hype surrounding the GATT/WTO" (2004, 204). In another publication Rose (2004b) suggests that the GATT/WTO's lack of impact is due to the fact that trade-policy liberalization does not accompany state entry into it.

Dissent followed quickly. Gowa and Kim (2005) took issue with Rose's assumption that the postwar trade regime exerted uniform effects on its members' trade. They argue that the principal-supplier rule enabled its largest members to dominate the organization. A legacy of US interwar treaty making, the "so-called chief-source, or 'Principal Supplier, rule" arose in response to the US effort "to respect the MFN clause, expand exports, and protect domestic industry" (Hawkins 1951, 81). Harry C. Hawkins, then head of the Trade Agreements Division of the Department of State, advised its adoption because it would allow the United States to lower its tariffs on "particular products [only] to the country that ... supplied the greatest proportion" of its imports of them (Hawkins 1951, 81 n. 16). This would protect the administration against complaints that "other countries were getting something for nothing."[14]

The rule meant that each country would offer to reduce its tariff on a particular good only if the state to which it extended the offer was the principal supplier of the item to its market. Canada, for example, supplied 96 percent of the agricultural goods and 99 percent of the fish and lumber products on which the United States cut tariffs in the 1935 US-Canadian trade accord (Butler 1998, 135 n. 14). Tariff specialization—that is, the "separating or 'ex-ing out' of portions of a tariff item for negotiating purposes"—served the same end (Pomfret 1988, 6). Because Congress insisted on a principal-supplier rule, postwar tariff cuts would take place on an item-by-item basis rather than across the board as the British preferred. Successive trade rounds therefore opened with the exchange of lists of products on which a state was willing to offer concessions and the exports on which it hoped to lower foreign levies.

Although participants in the Kennedy Round formally adopted a linear approach— that is, they agreed to cut their tariffs by a specified percentage across the board—bilateral negotiations continued to play an integral role. As Hoda observes, the "really meaningful discussions" at the Kennedy Round occurred bilaterally between "the major trading partners." Rather than "obviate the need for bilateral negotiation," the linear approach only gave participants "an additional tool" to use in their negotiations (Hoda 2001, 47). Although a linear-tariff cutting process in principle increases the efficiency of negotiating, it was frequently held hostage to the reciprocity that "will always remain the key to any trade bargain, whatever the formula for tariff reduction agreed upon" (Curzon and Curzon 1976, 161).

Gowa and Kim argue that the principal-supplier rule effectively privileged the goods the largest members of the GATT produced and exchanged. They test their idea by comparing trade flows in the years between the wars to trade after the GATT came into existence. They find that the only contracting parties that realized a significant expansion of trade with each other between 1950 and 1994 were what they label core states: the United States, Britain, France, Germany, and Canada. With the exception of some states that had previously been members of the interwar trade blocs, the GATT exerted no other significant effect on trade.

Subramanian and Wei (2007) also dispute Rose's results. Distinguishing between industrial countries and other states,[15] they estimate a gravity model that includes importer and exporter year fixed effects. They find that trade between industrial countries increases strongly and significantly as a consequence of their membership in the GATT/WTO. In contrast, exports of developing countries to industrial countries increase, but their imports from them do not. This is consistent with the steady drop in tariffs on manufactured goods over time and the adoption of import-substituting industrialization in many developing countries.

It is also consistent with the de facto restraints on trade that the core states in the trade regime imposed. These included voluntary export restraints on cars and steel and quantitative restrictions on agriculture and textiles, precisely the sectors in which developing countries were likely to enjoy a comparative advantage (Subramanian and Wei 2007, 153). GATT/WTO rules about agriculture in general were "shaped around" US domestic politics (Davis 2003, 7). The organization also endorsed reverse discrimination: the special and differential treatment it adopted in 1965 released developing countries from the obligation to reciprocate the tariff cuts of other members. Designed to block a Soviet effort to construct a trade regime under the auspices of the United Nations Conference on Trade and Development (UNCTAD), the exemptions ruffled few feathers: because most developing countries could not affect their terms of trade, other contracting parties could afford to be indifferent to the conditions of their participation.

Tomz, Goldstein, and Rivers (2007) take a different tack in their analysis of the effects of the regime. They argue that Rose underestimates the number of GATT members, because he codes states as such only if they had completed the formal accession process. States, they point out, also could and did become members at the discretion of their colonial "parents." Colonies that became independent could remain members on the same terms they had previously enjoyed. "Provisional" members of the organization—that is, states that had begun but not yet completed the formal accession process—were also entitled to the benefits of membership that existing members agreed to provide them. Including dyadic, country, and year fixed effects in their analysis, Tomz, Goldstein, and Rivers find that the GATT/WTO increased trade between its members by about 72 percent.

The existing empirical literature about the postwar trade regime is virtually devoid of efforts to examine systematically whether international politics influenced them.[16] As Irwin, Mavroidis, and Sykes (2008, 197) point out, however, it was the onset of the Cold War that induced the United States to press ahead with the GATT despite the adamant refusal of the British to eliminate imperial preferences. The US State Department opposed a delay over the IPS, fearing that it would empower the Soviets to "exploit fully any such differences between [the] US and UK just as they are now trying to capitalize on British weakness by increasing pressure throughout Eastern Europe and Near East" (cited in Irwin, Mavroidis, and Sykes 2008, 197).

That the problems market-failure theory identifies are insufficient to explain the practices of the postwar trade regime seems clear. From the perspective of the theory, for example, US support for the creation of the European Economic Community (EEC) and the extension of Marshall Plan aid made little sense. The EEC increased the market power that its constituent states wielded, although it would take them several years to converge on a joint bargaining position that would enable them to exploit it. American support of the EEC reflected its willingness to endow other states with the market power that transformed the opening of postwar markets into a PD game. Absent its national-security interests in European integration, US support for the creation of a rival trade bloc is inexplicable.

It seems unlikely, then, that the postwar trade regime operated independently of the political context in which it was embedded. To the extent that it did so, this implies that states were treated differently as a function of the security ties between them, contravening the de jure nondiscrimination embedded in the GATT charter. In the next section I examine the extent to which these interests, expressed as alliance ties, modify existing empirical findings about the impact of the regime.

Effects of Political-Military Alliances on GATT/WTO Trade

To measure the impact of alliance ties on trade, I use the specification of the gravity model that has become the industry standard in empirical studies of trade in the economics literature. The dependent variable is the annual imports of each state in a dyad from the other. This creates two observations in each year for every country pair: one records the imports of A from B, and the other records the imports of B from A. I examine the years between 1946 and 2003, because data about one key variable end in 2003.

I include directed-dyad fixed effects to take into account the unobserved time-invariant heterogeneity that can occur at the country-pair level. I cluster the standard errors at the directed-dyad level to correct for heteroskedascity. I also include importer-year and exporter-year dummy variables to control for time-varying state-level factors that affect trade (Anderson 2010, 24). These "multilateral-resistance" terms proxy for yearly changes that affect a nation's trade but that cannot be easily measured (Mathy and Meissner 2011, 18). They eliminate the omitted-variable bias that might otherwise result, because bilateral trade depends not only on the costs two states incur when they trade with each other, but also on the costs they incur when they trade with other countries. As Felbermayr and Kohler (2010, 1446) note, the country-year dummies are "perfect controls for country-specific policies that apply to all trading partners." Because they control for annual changes in some standard gravity-model variables, it is not necessary to add separately other covariates that the gravity model typically specifies, such as population and gross domestic product (GDP).

The estimates that this model produces measure the change in dyadic trade that occurs between, for example, two states in a "treatment" group relative to the trade of each state with states in the base group.[17] The coefficient on the GATT/WTO variable, then, estimates the effect of joining the regime on trade between two states relative to the trade of each with nonmember states. Existing studies that include only dyad- and year-specific effects instead estimate the shift in trade between states after they join the regime.[18] This risks conflating an increase in trade induced by the GATT/WTO with an overall increase in world trade that could occur, for example, if the cost of transporting goods from some subset of other states drops at the same time or if the volume of trade in differentiated products increases.[19]

As in Gowa and Kim (2005), I distinguish three subsets of GATT/WTO members. In the "core" group are pairs of major trading nations (i.e., Britain, Canada, France, the United States, and West Germany). In the "other-industrial country" group are pairs of industrial states other than those in the core group. Following the designation of the International Monetary Fund (IMF), this group includes Australia, Austria, Belgium, Denmark, Finland, Greece, Iceland, Ireland, Italy, Japan, the Netherlands, New Zealand, Norway, Portugal, South Africa, Spain, Sweden, Switzerland, and Turkey.[20] Finally, in the "developing-country" group are all other member dyads that include at least one developing country.

To construct the variable representing alliance ties, I use the information about alliances that the project on Alliance Treaties and Obligations (ATOP) makes available (Leeds et al. 2002). It includes data on coalitions between 1815 and 2003. I use these data to create a dummy variable that assumes a value of one if when dyads include allied states in a given year. I create three other variables that interact each of the GATT/WTO group variables with the alliance term. These terms indicate pairs of states that are both regime members and each other's allies. For example, the variable labeled "core-state allies" includes the pairs of core states that are each other's allies.

About 16 percent of GATT/WTO member dyads include two allies. The aggregate statistic conceals sizeable differences in the alliance composition of the three groups. Almost 97 percent of country pairs in the core group include two allies. The corresponding statistic is about 52 percent for other industrial country pairs and about 11 percent for member dyads that include at least one developing country. If security concerns do influence trade expansion within the postwar regime, the dispersion in the alliance composition of the different groups suggests that the GATT/WTO may affect different subsets of its members differently, not only on the basis of whether they are industrialized but also on the basis of whether they are allies.

For data on trade and GATT membership, I use the information in the data set that Tomz, Goldstein, and Rivers assembled. It includes information about bilateral trade flows between states. It also codes PTA member states and the signatories of unilateral trade treaties authorized under the GATT. These agreements, collectively labeled the Generalized System of Preference (GSP), provide one-way preferential market access for developing countries to the markets of an advanced industrialized country or countries. The developing countries that receive GSP preferences are chosen at the discretion of the advanced country that extends them. I also include a dummy variable that takes on a value of one if states are members of a currency union.

As a baseline, I first analyze the effects of the GATT/WTO on bilateral trade using the variables that indicate the subsets of core states, other industrial states, and developing-country members. I control for alliance membership separately. Table 2.1, column 1, displays these results. It shows that neither pairs of core-group states nor pairs of states that include one developing country realize a significant increase in their trade relative to their trade with base-group states. Pairs of states in the other-industrial group witness a marginally significant increase of about 10 percent in their trade relative to trade between these states and those in the base group (p-value ≤ 0.08).

Alliances raise trade between their members by about 16 percent, irrespective of regime membership.

Next I examine whether alliances affect trade expansion in the postwar regime. The results of this analysis are presented in Table 2.1, column 2. They show that core-state allies trade about 15 percent more with each other than do other states in the core group, a statistically significant difference.[21] In the case of states that include at least one developing country, dyads that include allies trade about 42 percent more with each other than do other states in the same group, a large and significant difference. Relative to their trade with base-group states, allied pairs of states in the other industrial-country group trade about 18 percent more with each other, a significant increase.

In other respects, the results in Table 2.1 conform to existing studies. States that are GSP members actually experience a small but significant fall in their trade of about 8 percent. This is not surprising given the constraints that the advanced countries impose on

Table 2.1 The Effects of the GATT/WTO and Alliances on Trade, 1946–2003

Core-state pairs	0.01	−0.27
	(0.17)	(0.15)
Core-state allies		0.46***
		(0.13)
Other industrial-country pairs	0.10	0.10**
	(0.06)	(0.06)
Other industrial-country allies		0.12**
		(0.06)
County pairs with at least one developing country	0.05	−0.00
	(0.03)	(0.16)
Country pairs with at least one developing country: allies		0.39***
		(0.04)
Alliances	0.15***	−0.06
	(0.03)	(0.04)
GSP	−0.09***	−0.08***
	(0.02)	(0.02)
PTAs	0.24***	0.23***
	(0.02)	(0.02)
Currency union	0.41***	0.43***
	(0.09)	(0.09)
N	379476	379476

Note: dyadic and import-year and exporter-year fixed effects included; standard errors clustered on directed dyads in parentheses; ** p-value ≤ 0.05, *** p-value ≤ 0.01; t-tests are two-sided.

the countries to which they grant GSP status. Often the rules of origin they specify are so onerous that countries decline to claim preferential access altogether. Other trade agreements have a positive and significant impact on trade: PTAs raise trade between their members by about 26 percent, while members of a currency union realize an increase of about 54 percent in their trade with each other.

The results in the second column of Table 2.1 show that the impact of the GATT/WTO on trade does vary as a function of the alliance ties of its members, embedding discrimination in the postwar regime for large subsets of its contracting parties. Although the discrimination at work in the GATT/WTO differs from that which motivated the formation of the interwar trade blocs, the trade it created nonetheless differed across its members in systematic ways prohibited by Article I of its 1947 charter.

Conclusion

Historical accounts of the origin of the postwar economic regime emphasize the intense and prolonged diplomacy it involved. They amply document extended Anglo-American debates about the rules and procedures that would govern trade and finance. In contrast, the network of trade treaties that existed during the first golden age of globalization emerged as a series of decentralized responses to the signing of the Cobden-Chevalier Treaty in 1860. The interwar trade blocs also arose as a consequence of a decentralized process of response to the advent of the Great Depression and the slow deterioration of the gold standard.

Despite the long negotiations that produced the ITO charter and that of the GATT, gaps quickly emerged between the de jure rules embedded in the charter of the GATT and its operation. As Hoekman and Kostecki observe (1996, 38–39), the "fairly complex and carefully crafted basic legal text was extended or modified by numerous supplementary provisions, special arrangements, interpretations, waivers, reports by dispute settlement panels, and Council decisions." Some of these modifications, as well as de facto practices, torpedoed the most basic provisions that had been so laboriously embedded in the original GATT charter.

Among them was the importance states attached to increasing trade with their allies. Because international politics prompted de facto discrimination among its members, the GATT/WTO represented less of a clean break from the interwar system than is often assumed. In each case, politics motivated discrimination. The "hub-and-spoke" trade that developed between members of the IPS and the Reichsmark bloc bear the imprint of the security interests that drove Britain and Germany, respectively, to create them (Gowa and Hicks 2013). In the postwar era, security interests also drove a substantial amount of trade within the GATT/WTO. Indeed, absent political interests, it is difficult to know what would have become of the GATT, given its lack of ability to monitor the compliance of its members. As noted previously, alliances mitigate the monitoring problem because they reduce the cost of cheating: while it is still true that the deviator gains at the expense of other states, some of its gains nonetheless accrue to the benefit of the alliance as a whole, encouraging more postwar trade expansion than might have occurred otherwise.

NOTES

1. For a discussion of how a system of multilateral enforcement can trigger punishment in this situation, see Maggi (1999).
2. Domestic politics can, of course, induce small states to impose trade barriers even if they reduce overall welfare. In addition, the time-inconsistency problem free trade creates for small states can lead them to join an institution to tie the government's hands if that institution can punish its deviations (e.g., Levy 1999). As this engages domestic politics, I do not discuss it further here.
3. A grim-trigger strategy requires each actor to defect in perpetuity whenever any defects. A less severe punishment regime can also support cooperation (e.g., Gilligan and Johns 2012).
4. The actual effect of these treaties on trade is disputed. See Accominotti and Flandreau (2008) for an argument that they had little impact on trade, and Lampe (2009) for a different view.
5. Punishing all defections is not necessarily optimal, however. See, for example, Downs and Rocke (1997); Koremenos (2001); and Milner and Rosendorff (2001).
6. Some claim that the distribution of gains does not matter (e.g., Gilligan and Johns 2012, 227), based on work showing that war is not profitable under some conditions (Powell 1999). But Powell does not rule out war and makes clear that the security effects of cooperation are irrelevant if and only if neither state allocates all its gains to its military sector. Otherwise, the "distribution of power would shift in favor of the state that obtained a larger gain." Anticipating this, its prospective partner "would refuse to cooperate in the first place" (1999, 76).
7. For an analysis of the impact of alliances on developing-country GATT members, see Gowa (2010).
8. http://www.ssa.gov/history/acharter2.html (accessed June 17, 2013).
9. Although the fall in trade that followed the Great Depression has long been attributed partly to the interwar blocs, recent work shows that they did not on the whole result in trade diversion or contribute to the depression of trade more generally (Gowa and Hicks 2013).
10. All references to the provisions of the GATT charter are to the language of the charter itself, which can be found at wto.org/english/docs_e/legal_e/gatt47_02_e.htm#articleXXVI.
11. For an incisive analysis of the political processes involved in trade disputes, see Davis (2012).
12. Mansfield and Bronson include a GATT variable in their analyses of PTA effects between 1960 and 1990. They find that it did not increase trade among its members (1997, 99).
13. Neither Rose nor his successors control for selection into the GATT/WTO, because no viable instrument exists: any variable associated with selection is also associated with bilateral trade. Baier and Bergstrand (2007) advocate using dyad fixed effects, discussed below, to take into account endogeneity. They assume that the source of the endogeneity is time-invariant unobserved heterogeneity at the dyad level. See Hicks (this volume) for a more extensive discussion of the gravity model.

14. John Leddy, oral history, http://trumanlibrary.org/oralhist/leddyj, 8–9.
15. They assign states to industrial status based on the classification that the IMF uses—that is, those countries, listed below, that have International Financial Statistics (IFS) country codes less than 200.
16. For an exception, see Kim (2010).
17. Some studies argue that estimating the effects of the GATT/WTO on both the extensive and intensive margins of trade requires taking into account dyads with zero trade. Felbermayr and Kohler (2010, 1451) note, however, that estimating effects at the extensive margin rules out the use of a panel-data approach, because doubts exist about "the reliability of time series variation on the extensive margin of trade." Using time-series cross-sectional analyses, they find that accounting for the zeroes does not change the estimate of the trade regime's effects. Here, as in earlier analyses to which we compare our results, we rely on panel-data estimation.
18. Subramanian and Wei (2007) is an exception.
19. Estimating the model in the Tomz, Goldstein, and Rivers article (2007) but adding importer and exporter year fixed effects produces a much smaller coefficient on the GATT/WTO than they estimate. Formal members trading with each other realize about an 8 percent increase in their trade. The corresponding statistic for nonmember participant dyads is about 17 percent. No significant increase in trade occurs between country pairs that include one formal and one nonmember participant. Complete results are available from the author.
20. The IMF also designates as industrial states Luxembourg, San Marino, and Malta. But no trade data exist for them. Data for Belgium exist as of 1997.
21. This is the sum of the coefficients on the core group, core-group allies, and allies (calculated as $e^b - 1$).

References

Accominotti, Olivier, and Marc Flandreau. 2008. "Bilateral Treaties and the Most-Favored-Nation Clause: The Myth of Trade Liberalization in the Mid-Nineteenth Century." *World Politics* 60 (2): 147–88.

Anderson, James E. 2010. *The Gravity Model*. Working Paper 16576. Cambridge, Mass.: National Bureau of Economic Research. Available at http://www.nber.org/papers/w16576. Accessed 20 June 2012

Bagwell, K., and R. Staiger. 2002. *The Economics of the World Trading System*. Cambridge, MA: MIT Press.

Baier, S., and J. H. Bergstrand. 2007. Do Free Trade Agreements Actually Increase Members' International Trade? *Journal of International Economics* 71 (1): 72–95.

Barton, J., et al. 2006. *The Evaluation of the Trade Regime: Politics, Law and Economics of the GATT and the WTO*. Princeton, NJ: Princeton University Press.

Butler, M. 1998. *Visionary: Cordell Hull and Trade Reform, 1933–1937*. Kent, OH: Kent State University Press.

Curzon, G., and Curzon, V. 1976. *The Management of Trade Relations in the GATT* in *International Economic Relations of the Western World* 1959-1971, Vol. 1. Politics and Trade, edited by H. Oliver, 141-283. London: Royal Institution for International Affairs and Oxford Press.

Daunton, M., A. Narlikar, and R. Stern. 2012. *The Oxford Handbook on the World Trade Organization*. New York: Oxford University Press.

Davis, C. 2003. *Food Fights over Free Trade: How International Institutions Promote Agricultural Trade liberalization*. Princeton, NJ: Princeton University Press.

Davis, C. 2012. *Why Adjudicate? Enforcing Trade Rules in the WTO*. Princeton, NJ: Princeton University Press.

Downs, G., and D. Rocke. 1997. *Optimal Imperfection: Domestic Uncertainty and Institutions in International Relations*. Princeton, NJ: Princeton University Press.

Eichengreen, B. 1992. *The Gold Standard and the Great Depression*. New York: Oxford University Press.

Felbermayr, G., and W. Kohler. 2010. Modeling the Extensive Margin of World Trade: New Evidence on GATT and WTO Membership. *The World Economy* 33 (11): 1430–1469.

Findlay, R., and K. O'Rourke. 2007. *Power and Plenty: Trade, War, and the World Economy in the Second Millennium*. Princeton, NJ: Princeton University Press.

Finnemore, M. 1993. International Organizations as Teachers of Norms: UNESCO and Science Policy. *International Organization* 47 (4): 565–598.

Gilligan, M., and L. Johns. 2012. Formal Models of International Institutions. *Annual Review of Political Science* 15: 221–243.

Gowa, J. 1995. *Allies, Adversaries, and International Trade*. Princeton, NJ: Princeton University Press.

Gowa, J. 2010. Alliances, Market Power, and Postwar Trade: Explaining the GATT/WTO. *World Trade Review* 9 (3): 487–504.

Gowa, J., and R. Hicks. 2013. Politics, Institutions, and Trade: Lessons of the Interwar Era. *International Organization* 67 (Summer): 439–467.

Gowa, J., and S. Kim. 2005. An Exclusive Country Club: The Effects of the GATT on Trade, 1950–94. *World Politics* 57 (4): 453–478.

Gowa, J., and E. Mansfield. 1993. Power Politics and International Trade. *American Political Science Review* 87 (2): 408–420.

Grieco, J. M. 1988. Anarchy and the Limits of Cooperation—a Realist Critique of the Newest Liberal Institutionalism. *International Organization* 42 (3): 485–507.

Hawkins, H. C., 1951. *Commercial Treaties and Agreement: Principles and Practice*. New York: Rinehart.

Hoekman, B., and M. Kostecki. 2001. *The Political Economy of the World Trading System*. 2nd ed. New York: Oxford University Press.

Hoda, Anwarul. 2001. *Tariff Negotiations and Renegotiations Under the GATT and the WTO*. NY: Cambridge University Press.

Horn, H., and P. Mavroidis. 2001. Economic and Legal Aspects of the Most Favored Nation Clause. *European Journal of Political Economy* 17 (2): 233–279.

Irwin, D., P. Mavroidis, and A. Sykes. 2008. *The Genesis of the GATT*. New York: Cambridge University Press.

Jackson, John H. 1989. *The World Trading System: Law and Policy of International Relations*. Cambridge: MIT Press.

Johnston, A. 2001. Treating International Institutions as Social Environments. *International Studies Quarterly* 45 (3): 487–515.

Keohane, R. 1984. *After Hegemony: Cooperation and Discord in the World Political Economy*. Princeton, NJ: Princeton University Press.

Kim, S. 2010. *Power and the Governance of Global Trade: From the GATT to the WTO*. Ithaca, NY: Cornell University Press.

Koremenos, B. 2001. Loosening the Ties That Bind: A Learning Model of Agreement Flexibility. *International Organization* 55: 289–325.

Koremenos, B., C. Lipson, et al. (2001). The Rational Design of International Institutions. *International Organization* 55 (4): 761-80.

Krasner, S. 1991. Global Communication and National Power. *World Politics* 43: 338–366.

Lampe, Marcus. 2009. Effects of Bilateralism and the MFN Clause on International Trade: Evidence for the Cobden-Chevalier Network, 1860-1875. *Journal of Economic History* 69 (4): 1012–1040.

Leeds, B., et al. 2002. Alliance Treaty Obligations and Provisions, 1815–1944. *International Interactions: Empirical and Theoretical Research in International Relations* 28 (3): 237–260.

Levy, P. 1999. Lobbying and International Cooperation in Tariff Setting. *Journal of International Economics* 47 (2): 345–370.

Maggi, G. 1999. The Role of Multilateral Institutions in International Trade Cooperation. *American Economic Review* 89 (1): 190–214.

Mansfield, E., and R. Bronson. 1997. Alliances, Preferential Trading Arrangements, and International Trade. *American Political Science Review* 91 (1): 94–107.

Martin, L. 2008. Introduction. In *Global Governance*, edited by Lisa Martin, xi-xxi. Aldershot, England: Ashgate Publishing.

Martin, L., and B. Simmons. 1998. Theories and Empirical Studies of International Institutions. *International Organization* 52 (4): 729–757.

Mathy, G., and C. Meissner. 2011. Trade, Exchange Rate Regimes and Output Co-Movement: Evidence from the Great Depression. NBER Working Paper No. 16925.

McCubbins, M., and T. Schwartz. 1984. Congressional Oversight Overlooked: Police Patrols versus Fire Alarms. *American Journal of Political Science* 28 (1): 165–179.

Mearsheimer, J. 1994/95. The False Promise of International Institutions. *International Security* 19 (3): 5–49.

Milner, H., and P. Rosendorff. 2001. The Rational Design of International Institutions. *International Organization* 55 (4): 829–857.

O'Rourke, K., and J. Williamson. 1999. *Globalization and History: The Evolution of a Nineteenth-Century Atlantic Economy*. Cambridge, MA: MIT Press.

Odell, J., and J. Eichengreen. 1998. The United States, the ITO, and the WTO: Exit Options, Agent Slack, and Presidential Leadership. In *The WTO as an International Organization*, edited by A. Kruger, 181-209. Chicago: University of Chicago Press.

Pomfret, R. 1988. *Unequal Trade: The Economics of Discriminatory Trade Policy*. New York: Basil Blackwell.

Powell, Robert. 1991. "Absolute and Relative Gains in International Relations Theory. *The American Political Science Review* 85 (4): 1303–1320.

Powell, R. 1999. Shadow of Power: States and Strategies in International Politics. Princeton, NJ: Princeton University Press.

Rogowski, R. 1989. *Commerce and Coalitions: How Trade Affects Domestic Political Alignments*. Princeton, NJ: Princeton University Press.

Rose, A. 2004a. Do We Really Know That the WTO Increases Trade? *American Economic Review* 94 (1): 98–114.

Rose, A. 2004b. Do WTO Members Have More Liberal Trade Policy? *Journal of International Economics* 63 (2): 209–235.

Rosendorff, B., and H. Milner. 2001. The Optimal Design of International Trade Institutions: Uncertainty and Escape. *International Organization* 55 (4): 829–857.

Subramanian, A., and S. Wei. 2007. The WTO Promotes Trade, Strongly But Unevenly. *Journal of International Economics* 72: 151–175.

Tomz, M., Goldstein, J. and D. Rivers. 2007. "Do We Really Know that the WTO Increases Trade? Comment. *American Economic Review* 97 (5): 2005-2018.

Waltz, K. 1979. *Theory of International Politics*. Reading, MA: Addison Wesley.

CHAPTER 3

···

THE FREE TRADE IDEA

···

GORDON BANNERMAN

THE success of the free trade idea in attaining scholarly credibility has led one distinguished writer to claim for it an "intellectual status unrivalled by any other doctrine in the field of economics" (Irwin 1996, 217). The powerful ideological resonance of free trade in nineteenth-century Britain led many historians and economists to follow Rostow in adopting a Whiggish historical approach to describing the progressive advance of nations toward commercial liberalism (1959, 7). Underpinning this interpretation was a scholarly tendency, largely emanating from a preoccupation with the scientific basis of economic theory, to describe free trade and open markets as optimal policy for economic growth and wealth creation (Irwin 1996, 217). In fact, free trade never attained unchallenged ideological hegemony, and recently scholars have more readily accepted a growing number of exceptions to its applicability and the limitations of the policy itself (Irwin 1996, 217–230). The development of a more critical, nuanced approach, partly a consequence of the emergence of new academic disciplines, examines commercial policy armed with a methodology concerned with the multiple contexts of policy formation, processes, and outcomes (Krugman 1987, 131–132). This approach considers the evolution of free trade more precisely in terms of historical context, while assessing alternative models of political economy and economic development more closely. Despite a moralistic assumption of natural justice and an economic assumption of equality being made about it, free trade was, and often is, characterized as far from fair and equal, and historically as a policy has seldom been uncontested.

This chapter seeks to trace the evolution of free trade ideas from earlier centuries by reference to the development of economic theory in tandem with the economic organization and activities of nation-states within the context of prevailing political configurations and imperatives. The organization of the chapter is primarily chronological and seeks to chart long-term developments such as ideological influence and policy formation in time and space. This approach is accompanied by the thematic consideration of how the free trade idea was received, assessed, and modulated by states with diverging economic portfolios and sectors, within different stages of economic development. The chapter takes a historicist and quasi-deterministic approach in concluding that the free trade idea was highly mutable, as well as a contested and controversial policy option, because of divergent socioeconomic contexts and the global imbalance of international economic forces. Translated into policy terms, the ideas became entangled within the international state system, and while commerce had always been an integral component of foreign affairs and diplomacy, the cosmopolitanism of free trade ideas, although powerful, could not supplant the vital diplomatic and foreign policy interests of nation-states in the international policy space. Rather, commercial policy became annexed, and in many cases subordinated, to these wider interests.

DEFINING THE "FREE TRADE IDEA"

What is meant by *free trade*? In theoretical terms precision is possible, because a body of work exists widely acknowledged as containing the core theoretical principles of the policy (Smith 2012; Ricardo 1821; J. Mill 1824; J. S. Mill 1848). Broadly speaking, the absence of artificial legislative enactments imposing taxes on exports and imports, as described by Adam Smith and the classical economists, as opposed to natural restrictions or technological limitations on commercial activity, accurately defines free trade. What actually constitutes "free trade" in practice is more difficult to assess. Trade is never really free so long as tariffs are levied for revenue purposes, and no nation has yet been able to dispense with tariffs completely. Yet the incidence, extent, and nature of tariffs have traditionally determined the nature of commercial policy, and tariff portfolios have always been dependent on wider political and economic conditions, relationships, imperatives, and traditions.

The term *free trade* emerged at the end of the sixteenth century, referring to commerce unhindered by exclusionary guild regulations or monopoly privileges. That was "freedom *to* trade," concerned with access to markets, as opposed to the application of wider philosophical principles (Irwin 1996, 46). The first debate about free trade in the modern sense concerned calico imports shipped to England by the East India Company, which damaged the fledgling domestic cotton industry and raised calls for protection. Import restrictions were imposed by a series of Calico Acts early in the eighteenth century, allowing the English cotton industry to develop as an "infant industry" free from foreign competition (Irwin 1996, 53). This series of events included many of the elements and arguments that have since informed the wide-ranging and intricate debate on the purposes, nature, and application of commercial policy both within and between sovereign states.

The idea of unrestricted trade developed from an early period, but before the seventeenth century ethical, religious, and moral beliefs mainly determined economic thought. The intellectual lineage from Aristotle and Aquinas to the moral philosophers of the Scottish Enlightenment and Adam Smith was clearly, if unevenly, delineated (Irwin 1996, 25). By the seventeenth century global trade expansion and the rise of nation-states and empires led to a more favorable view of commerce and a desire to understand the economic distribution of goods and resource allocation facilities. The natural law of Aquinas proved influential in facilitating invocation of the Creation as a means of explaining global resource allocation. More widely, the role of religious thought proved to be enduring, especially in Britain (Viner 1960, 48).

Religious thought underpinned the doctrine of "Universal Economy," which described the providential plan of unequal resource allocation and distribution throughout the world "to promote commerce between different regions" and contained implications of "design" that were influential from the seventeenth century onward (Irwin 1996, 15). Dean Tucker viewed providential design in the distribution and allocation of goods and resources throughout the world as conducive to "an Intercourse mutually beneficial, and universally benevolent" (1763, 32). Into the nineteenth century, "the unerring and clearly revealed will of a beneficent Creator"[1] was transformed into an antiprotectionist and especially anti–Corn Law argument against market intervention. In 1841 Richard Cobden condemned the protectionist Corn Laws on the basis that they were "an interference with the disposition of divine Providence as proved by the revealed word of God and the obvious laws of nature" (Noble 2005, 105; Matthew 1997, 56). Yet the obvious metaphor for the mechanism driving resource distribution and allocation, Smith's "Invisible Hand," was not presented by Smith as "a proof of either providential order or design" (Milgate and Stimson 2009, 94). This omission represented a significant break with the past, as well as providing an indication of the future trajectory of economic theory toward international trade.

Nevertheless, despite theoretical developments relating to the contours of international trade, policy choices remained primarily determined by revenue, employment, and developmental considerations, most notably in mercantilist doctrine (Irwin 2002, 46). Mercantilism was the predominant theory and practical operation of political economy prevailing in Europe after the decline of feudalism. It was based on national policies of accumulating bullion, establishing colonies and strong maritime forces, and developing national industries, all as a means of attaining a favorable balance of trade in commerce; that is, a country would produce and export more products than it would import. The belief that a finite amount of global commerce meant it was vital to secure a favorable trade balance was based on a static view of wealth creation and economic growth, for the concept of increasing global wealth was "wholly alien" to mercantilists (Heckscher 1969, 25–26). Moreover, in the seventeenth century most mercantilists held the conventional contemporary view that self-interest governed human behavior (Child 1681, 29). Mercantilists like Colbert and Child identified commerce as an aspect of national power, with commercial rivalry an element of "perpetual combat in peace and war among the nations of Europe as to who will gain the upper hand" (Economides and Wilson 2002, 36).

Mercantilist doctrine was perhaps the first manifestation of "globalization," and despite a later tendency in Anglo-American historiography, it was not simply crude protectionism. Most mercantilists were critical of commercial restrictions, and many acknowledged that international commerce promoted domestic manufacturing, thus displaying an understanding of reciprocal trading relationships. Some even disparaged excessive domestic consumption as less important and less profitable than foreign trade (Magnusson 1994, 125–128; Irwin 1996, 29–33). Even historians hostile to mercantilism have acknowledged that it was more efficient in practice than in theory, and that mercantilists did not pursue self-sufficiency at the expense of foreign trade (Fay 1928, 24). While it was unclear whether import tariffs could reverse an unfavorable trade balance, by reducing import penetration tariffs almost always increased domestic production and employment in specific sectors. The formula for achieving this outcome—low import duties on inputs and raw materials and high import duties on processed goods—was a crucial point of convergence between mercantilism and modern industrial protectionism (Irwin 1996, 37–41; Viner 1937, 73).

Classical Political Economy and Free Trade

Mercantilism was never an entirely coherent doctrine, and the work of David Hume arguably represented the first substantial erosion of its central tenets, for Hume demonstrated the fallacy of balance-of-trade arguments by describing how the "price-specie flow" mechanism ensured regulation of distribution and exchange of gold, facilitating balance-of-payments equilibrium (1987, 311–312). In *Of the Balance of Trade*, Hume demonstrated how "real world" factors of labor and fixed assets were prime determinants of commercial expansion and wealth creation, and in *Of the Jealousy of Trade* he illustrated how commercial transactions promoted mutual prosperity and enhanced the prospects for long-term economic growth (1987, 316–317, 334). Anticipating Smith, Hume criticized trade restrictions bred by national antagonisms and argued for mutual expansionary gains for foreign trade and domestic manufacturing accruing from free trade (Irwin 1996, 70–72). Despite the rather unsystematic dispersal of economic ideas throughout his works, Hume clearly exercised considerable influence on Smith.

The search for antecedents for Smith's work has produced many ingenious, if not always convincing, connections (Viner 1960, 54). Before *The Wealth of Nations*, there had been considerable exaggeration of free trade arguments, with many proposals advanced for particular political or economic objectives (Viner 1937, 92). The influence of the physiocrats was limited, and though Smith met, through Hume, many leading physiocrats, familiarity with the ideas of Quesnay, Mirabeau, and Turgot did not lead to the doctrine substantially informing his work (Irwin 1996, 67). In fact, Smith criticized the physiocrats for placing too much emphasis on domestic agricultural output, and by thus imposing restraints on manufacturing and foreign trade, indirectly and inadvertently undermining the prospects for agricultural prosperity. In effect, Smith argued that by undervaluing the industry of the towns, the physiocrats made the opposite mistake to that Colbert had made (Smith 2012, 662, 685).

Other writers provided further grist to Smith's mill. The Dutch merchant Pieter de la Court, opposing the trading monopoly of the Dutch East India Company, lauded free competition in *Interest van Holland* (1662) as central to national wealth and prosperity. Despite interested motives, this type of analysis linked previous definitions of "freedom to trade" with broader conceptions of "free trade," a linkage informing Smith's critique of mercantilism (Smith 2012, 629–630). A cross-current of influences, beginning fundamentally from the Hobbesian relationship between self-interest and society, influenced and informed Smithian political economy. Mercantilists had understood the notion of "economic man" responding to the rational stimulus of pecuniary gain, but Smith argued that they subordinated welfare gains from trade to power considerations (Viner 1960, 56–57; Heckscher 1969, 93). Tucker described the harmony of private and public interests in the economic sphere but considered self-love to outweigh benevolence; Frances Hutcheson bridged the gap between moral philosophy and economic behavior by arguing that empathy provided a moral sense to temper self-interest.

Tucker had also convinced Hume that Britain could safely adopt freer trade without risking its prosperity (Crowley 1990, 339–360). It was not a view anticipating hegemonic power, for other nations could exploit their own product advantage, as well as using protective duties if necessary (Fieser 1999, 312–314). Assailing monopolies as early as 1749, Tucker believed government should support commerce by a regulatory framework but attacked the idea that a country could become prosperous by bankrupting its neighbors, thus promoting a reciprocal, not adversarial, view of commerce (1763, 30–32; Williams 1972, 394). All of these policy positions can be found in Smith's work.

Commercial policy debates generally revolve around how policies influence the most effective use of primary factors of production to produce the greatest possible national income. For Smith, mercantilist policies were primarily a misallocation of resources, which endorsed and fortified restrictive practices (Gomes 2003, 4). Nevertheless, Smith shared with mercantilist writers the view that defense was fundamental to wealth creation and "of much more importance than opulence," and that there were other points of convergence (Smith 2012, 454). Smith accepted a case for protective duties for "infant industries" and defense industries, acknowledged the potency of retaliatory duties, and considered countervailing duties appropriate in particular cases. He qualified this position by questioning the efficiency and productivity of protected industries, but this did not prevent protectionists later citing his claims in relation to industrializing economies (Smith 2012, 442, 447, 452–462).

Despite linking mercantilism with international "discord and animosity," Smith rejected the notion of freer commerce promoting international harmony (Smith 2012, 484; Walter 1996, 5–28). Later political economists were more optimistic, with Ricardo describing the moral exemplar of free trade uniting "by one common interest and intercourse, the universal society of nations throughout the civilized world" (1821, 139). The cosmopolitanism of free trade received greater currency in the nineteenth century from Cobden, but earlier, although Hume and Smith had proclaimed the economic efficiency of free commerce, they were essentially "economic liberals but political realists," convinced of the enduring qualities and patriotic attachment of citizens to nation-states (Sally 2008, 40–41).

Smith promoted free trade in terms of economic efficiency rather than international harmony, by demonstrating how international trade was an extension of the international division of labor, with domestic surplus exchanged for foreign surplus promoting mutual prosperity. The natural human instinct to exchange would be facilitated by removing constraints and promoting commercial freedom (Smith 2012, 15, 22–26). With market activity incentivized, individual self-interest would be "led by an invisible hand" toward socially beneficial rather than socially unproductive activities (Smith 2012, 445). Domestic altruism was thus extended, and Britain would gain by exchanging expensive exports for cheap ones (Smith 2012, 453–454). Smith did not pronounce on factor endowments, commodity composition, or stages of economic development, because he did not consider these factors as in any way determinants of policy outcomes. For Smith, the benefits of free commerce were universally applicable, and possessing ethical and moral value in maintaining individual rights and liberties, went beyond commercial transactions (Irwin 1996, 84–86; Viner 1960, 60).

POLITICAL ECONOMY AND COMMERCIAL POLICY

The coherence of Smith's worldview led Hugh Blair to suggest that *The Wealth of Nations* would become the "Commercial Code of Nations" (Mossner and Ross 1987, 187–190). As policy issues of the 1770s and 1780s indicate, Smith's ideas were slow to be adopted. In Ireland, "free trade" agitation, an attempt to participate in the imperial trading system, was a recrudescence of seventeenth-century debates over monopolies and unequal treatment (Cunningham 1886, 285; Davis 1962, 290–291). Proposals to equalize customs duties raised protests from British manufacturers concerned about Irish competition, fears dismissed by Smith in 1779 on account of the underdeveloped Irish economy (Bowden 1924, 655–674; Browning 1886, 309). Nevertheless, the manufacturers received political support, indicating the limits to which even progressive politicians were prepared to go when links between political control and economic dependency were threatened (Kelly 1975, 562).

The 1786 Anglo-French commercial treaty presented a similar picture of commercial policy subordinate to, or supplementary to, other policy issues. The commitment of manufacturers to trade liberalization was questionable, for the predominant emphasis was on particular sectors rather than wider conceptions of commercial policy (Williams 1972, 186). The manufacturers of 1786 were not forerunners of the Anti-Corn Law League, for "it was no consistent economic theory or enlightened social ideal that dictated the attitude of Wedgwood, Garbett, the Ironmasters, and the Manchester manufacturers," but rather self-interest, that fueled their support for a more liberal commercial relationship (Ehrman 1962, 48). Philosophical support for the treaty was best expressed by Pitt and especially Eden, who, like Montesquieu and Kant, referred to the mutual dependence established by trading relationships and anticipated Cobden in linking commerce and peace.[2] Reaction to the treaty was largely dictated by location and sector, welcomed by southern wine-growers and by manufacturers in central and western France, whose products did not compete directly with Britain, but unpopular with northern industrialists facing competition from cheaper British imports (Sloane 1898, 214; See 1930, 308). As a model of reciprocal tariff reductions the treaty was significant, but in the late eighteenth century commercial policy remained largely confined within a mercantilist framework of protective duties and prohibitions.[3]

The Napoleonic and Revolutionary Wars further undermined commercial progress, with the commercial policy of combatants, the Continental System and Orders in Council, used as strategic instruments of war (Williams 1972, 230). Wartime commercial restrictions provoked middle-class radicalism in Britain and calls for commercial freedom, but revolution and war hindered "the practice of an economic doctrine which linked commerce and peace" throughout Europe (Howe 2002, 195). After 1815 quasi-autarkic policies were adopted by most states, and revenue concerns and notions of economic independence, often based on the ideas of Hamilton, Fichte, and List, were pervasive. Even progressive politicians were concerned that "habitual dependence on foreign supply" was dangerous (Huskisson 1827, 8). The passing of the Corn Laws in Britain crushed any hope that protectionism would be easily reformed (Howe 2002, 195–196). Wartime disruption also encouraged industrial protectionism. Most notably, building on the Hamiltonian thesis that technological advances made by industrial nations meant greater efficiency and cheaper manufacturing than in emerging nations, the United States adopted protective policies on the basis of industrial development and revenue accumulation. Similarly, a succession of postwar tariff increases in France imposed a highly protectionist tariff regime (Williams 1972, 223; Levasseur 1892, 23–24).

In an increasingly protectionist world, free trade entered the policy arena more forcefully as a highly contested policy, but the translation of the idea from its scientific economic base to the popular arena took time. During the war Smith's work was widely hailed as inaugurating a new era in political economy, with ideas that were "radical solvents of the old consensus" (Howe 2002, 194). Dugald Stewart's *Life and Writings of Adam Smith* (1793) robustly promoted Smith's theories and exerted a powerful influence on the next generation of classical economists (Milgate and Stimson 2009, 99–101). Smithian political economy was now at least accompanied, if not superseded, by Evangelical, Malthusian, and Ricardian variants (Howe 2002, 194). Most pertinently, Smith's theories were refined and augmented by Ricardo's theory of comparative advantage. It was a major theoretical advance, vital to understanding international trade patterns. Ricardo illustrated that a country was best served by directing labor and allocating resources to the sector where its comparative advantage *was greater* (Sally 2008, 36). Those sectors with greatest *relative* efficiency advantage would export with the greatest success, and the resultant trade would be mutually beneficial. Comparative advantage meant every party to a transaction gained by specialization, and no country was excluded, for purchasing goods from abroad provided foreign countries with necessary purchasing power (Gourevitch 1986, 39; Irwin 2002, 28).

Ricardo was also concerned with domestic economic sectors, and his theory of "diminishing returns" in agriculture was based on a critique of agricultural protection. Influenced by Malthus but drawing different conclusions, Ricardo argued that since higher corn prices meant higher wages for workers and lower profitability for capitalists, only landlords gained by differential rent; that is, the financial return they secured from their possession of land, a return that varied according to the fertility of the land and the productivity and yield. Ricardo thus concluded that "the interest of the landlord is always opposed to the interest of every other class in the community" (1821, 399). This stance placed him in radical ranks in the Corn Laws controversy, and Marx, citing Ricardo's *Principles*, argued that wage-cutting, consistent with Ricardo's "Iron Law of Wages," meant prospective corn imports accounted for manufacturing support for repeal (Hollander 2011, 232–233). Marx thus identified the class basis of support for free trade, a relationship that Cobden later conceded was accurate.

Initially, support for free trade was sluggish. On presentation of the London merchants' petition in 1820 for removal of "injurious restrictions," Ricardo was "astonished" that free trade principles had taken so long to obtain mercantile support.[4] Intellectual support was forthcoming, notably from Benthamites and philosophic radicals incorporating free trade within a broader program of political and social reform, and theoretical advances were made by classical economists, notably McCulloch and Mill, in claiming discovery and formulation of the "laws" of political economy. Mill complacently described these "laws" as tenets of a progressive science, whose application would destroy the remnants of feudalism and monopoly from an aristocratic political system. The "people's edition" of Mill's *Principles of Political Economy*, published for working men, sold more than ten thousand copies, lending credence to the popularity of free trade in mid-Victorian Britain (Mill 1874, 278–279). By the mid-nineteenth century, the theoretical case was well-stated and increasingly popularized as part of the liberal reform agenda. With industrial, financial, and commercial strength facilitating the potential for penetrating global markets, British commercial policy objectives pointed toward an open trading regime.

ECONOMIC DEVELOPMENT AND COMMERCIAL POLICY

Why were free trade ideas more popular in some countries than others, and why were those principles enacted as governmental policy in only a partial and limited way, albeit in a reasonably large number of countries? While classical economists rigidly argued that the principles were applicable to countries at all stages of economic development, in practice fiscal pressures fueled protectionism in "new" countries and in older economies where tariffs were an important source of revenue. The influence, impact, and popularity of free trade ideas varied according to the political and economic dynamics within each nation, and broadly speaking it is possible to agree with a recent writer that while free trade ideas "may have fostered liberalization in the long run . . . they explain little of its timing" (Federico 2012, 181). We might also add "or its location."

Fears raised during the Revolutionary Wars of greater manufacturing capability among Britain's rivals were not assuaged by British industrial preeminence after 1815, for recurrent depressions and rapid American and European industrialization pointed to the need for new markets. Government responded by cautiously ending monopolies, relaxing restraints, and eliminating differential shipping duties through reciprocity treaties (Williams 1972, 446). Gradual tariff reduction was enacted after 1822 with lower import duties on raw materials, to facilitate a better competitive position for British manufacturers. Britain also discarded prohibitions on artisans leaving the country and exporting machinery, mercantilist-type measures that had aimed at defending industrial advantages (Gomes 2003, 210–211).

After 1815 a dichotomous discourse of "free trade" and "protection" emerged, illustrating the contested nature of commercial policy (Matthew 1997, 135; Howe 2013). The influence of political economists in political circles, with McCulloch in particular delivering lectures attended by ministers and officials, extended the popular appeal of political economy, but it was a controversial policy area, and opposition, deeply felt if not necessarily broadly based, attacked "the dismal science and its practitioners" and the "cash nexus" that appeared to be enveloping Britain (Sack 1993, 182). Yet by the 1830s, despite retaining protective duties and imperial preference, Britain was the leading promoter of commercial liberalism. Peel's 1842 budget reduced import duties on raw materials, partly manufactured goods, and export duties, in totality representing a triumph for export-led industries. An additional motive for enacting liberal measures was the wish to "prevent prohibitive enactments in foreign countries" (Williams 1972, 452). However, France, Prussia, Spain, Russia, and the United States resisted moves toward freer trade, and critics increasingly questioned the value of reciprocity treaties, since European nations competed with Britain in other markets (Williams 1972, 454–456). Gladstone was exasperated by prevalent suspicion of British motives:

> When we maintain the restraints we find in existence, they use our conduct as their apology for inventing new ones. When we remove such restraints, they perceive only a deeper plan for bringing about their ruin by cheap production, which requires of them still more imperiously the multiplication of their repressive and prohibitive enactments.
>
> (Gladstone 1845, 60)

This intransigent stance was especially true of France and Prussia, which justified their own protectionism by reference to British wine, timber, and corn duties, but a myriad of cultural, political, and economic differences lay behind the broader policy divergence.

International market position to some degree determined policy options. The "production profile" of nations, encompassing the timing and extent of industrial development, the nature of international economic relationships, and institutional and political configurations within states, convincingly describes the broad range of policy influences (Gourevitch 1986, 55–60, 63–64; Wallerstein 1979, 66–73). It was against this backdrop that the struggle took place between higher costs incurred by consumers under domestic protection and the job losses suffered by producers under a free trade regime of cheaper imports. Pareto's theory of the role of concentrated interests in maintaining protective duties demonstrates the importance of endogenous elements in policy making (Kindleberger 1975, 22). In developmental terms, maintaining protective duties for most European states was greatly overdetermined. Conversely, developmental theory identified free trade as the policy preference of the most-advanced industrial nation in an open trading system (Irwin 2002, 144). That nation was Britain, but as Corn Law repeal demonstrates, ideology as well as economic interests, and the political institutions through which ideas and interests were expressed, provide greater clarity for understanding the necessary conditions for adopting free trade (Schonhardt-Bailey 2006). Most pertinently, the 1832 Reform Act facilitated middle-class agitation for economic reforms, and parliamentary and pressure-group activity was more intensively focused in Britain than elsewhere. Corn Law repeal, the ending of imperial preference, and repeal of the Navigation Acts reconfigured the British state from its mercantilist base toward unilateral free trade. By 1860 import duties were levied only on noncompeting products, and protective duties were effectively removed from Britain's fiscal system. Tariffs remained on high-yielding, noncompeting imports for revenue purposes. In light of this taxation structure, the "optimistic" view of free trade finance promoted by Matthew and Howe in terms of its contribution toward a moralistic minimal "knaveproof" state is perhaps overstated (Matthew, 1997, 171; Howe, 1997, 113).

As the adoption of free trade was dependent on economic development, human agency, ideology, and political culture, it was certainly not easily transferable. The expectation that repeal would stimulate other nations to reduce tariffs and exploit their comparative advantage in noncompeting products to British manufactures stemmed from a belief that the Corn Laws had inhibited commerce and forced European nations to industrialize (Kindleberger 1975, 33–34). Even Cobden regretted European industrial development, fueled by "the fostering bounties which the high-priced food of the British artisan has offered to the cheaper-fed manufacturer of those countries" (1878, 65).

Did such attitudes amount to pursuit of a hegemonic strategy? In Europe, free trade was often viewed inseparably from perceptions of British hegemony, and limited acceptance of free trade presents a convincing refutation of hegemonic power (Nye 2007, 98). The less-obvious "second face" of hegemony, using international market power to influence prices as a means of influencing economic behavior and attitudes, was largely absent after 1846 (James and Lake 1989, 8). Altering investment patterns and factor and sector returns abroad to "ensure complementary production and the free exchange of primary goods for British manufactured goods" may have motivated classical economists and Board of Trade officials, but the idea of a "conscious motivation" for hegemonic leadership appears misplaced (James and Lake 1989, 27). Promoting free trade ideas should not be conflated with the conceptually distinct notion of hegemony. This is especially true given that despite a shift toward lower tariffs between 1846 and 1873, primarily to advance industrial expansion, most European nations remained generally opposed to radical reductions (Irwin 1996, 98).

As Cobden discovered on his European tour of 1846–1847, the constellation of economic interests and political forms meant that ideological commitment to free trade was limited and free trade movements largely ineffectual, at least partly owing to the strength of protectionist financial and industrial interests within monarchical and authoritarian regimes. In France, even after the 1848 Revolution, the political system remained highly conservative, with the Chamber of Deputies dominated by protectionist interests. Despite the efforts of Bastiat and Chevalier and calls from industrialists for lower input costs, French politicians, from Proudhon to Thiers, denounced free trade as a means by which "perfidious Albion" ensured European subservience to Britain (Cain 1979, 243; McKeown 1983, 73–91). Similarly, in the 1830s Palmerston doubted the commitment of the Zollverein to freer commerce, and by 1847, having witnessed the preferential treatment given to Belgian iron, he was convinced it existed "for the purpose of excluding by high duties the importation of British manufactures into Germany" (Howe 1997, 81). Austria resisted further tariff reductions because it was not satisfied with the subordinate role of supplying raw materials (Williams 1972, 211). Successive parliamentary inquiries into foreign commercial policy revealed a similar pattern of organized protectionist strength, widespread perceptions of protection as a "national" policy, and resistance to free trade allied to deep-seated hostility to British economic dominance.

The necessity Britain was under in making the 1860 Anglo-French commercial treaty indicates that "the hegemonic story is virtually turned on its head," for the treaty contradicted any notion of hegemonic power (Howe 1997, 94–95; Nye 2007, 109). The interlocking network of European treaties that followed, underscored by tariff reductions and most-favored nation (MFN) clauses, was not of Britain's making and represented a return to bargaining and negotiation. For some historians, the treaty system was a paradigm shift, appearing to represent the "cornerstone of a new international trading system" (O'Brien and Pigman 1992, 100). However, attempts to provide a comprehensive explanation for this movement to the point of "near free trade" have fallen back on emphasizing specific and unique, and crucially temporary, national factors (Federico 2012, 166).

While undoubtedly a facet of the reality of international commercial relations, British hegemony was more often not coercively exercised or applied. The "soft power" of persuasion and influence was used, with variable success, by British government departments connected with commerce, such as the Board of Trade and the Foreign Office. Wallerstein's broad claim that "non-hegemonic" powers, fearful of larger economic entities, adopted protection, while apparently historically accurate and contemporarily relevant, unnecessarily inserted hegemonic language into the discussion (Wallerstein 1979, 19). Much of the association made between free trade and British hegemony emanated from those, like Thiers and Bismarck, who skilfully reworked traditional prejudices for their own ends. Hegemonic power was a useful concept for the enemies of free trade, and propagation of the idea often acted as a justificatory ideological weapon for protectionism.

ALTERNATIVES TO FREE TRADE

The most influential alternative to free trade came from Friedrich List, whose vehement opposition to "British" free trade was driven by British economic dominance (List 1856, 437). The "infant industry" argument promoted by List, of tariffs fostering industrial development, was based on historical judgments rather than economic analysis (Irwin 1996, 124–126). As the relative absence of the theory in Ireland demonstrated, it was a theory predicated on a preexisting but nascent industrial sector (Collison Black 1960, 140–143). The theory was not new. In the eighteenth century Tucker identified the relationship between protection and economic development (Semmel 1965, 762). More famously, Smith and Mill both cautiously stated that the theory was not inconsistent with the main tenets of classical political economy (Irwin 1996, 118–119). Such qualified acceptance, easily interpreted as approval, combined with scholarly expositions by Torrens and Mill demonstrating how tariffs improved a country's terms of trade, provided intellectual Delete this respectability for protectionist political economy (Irwin 1991, 202).

While Listian analysis provided ideological impetus, the intellectual challenge to freer trade was fundamentally driven by the "great depression" of 1873–1896. In identifying causes for the damage inflicted by cheaper imports, falling prices, and unemployment, freer trade was an obvious target. Across Europe, powerful coalitions were constructed on the basis of economic grievances, incorporating reconciliation of hitherto opposing economic sectors, particularly in Germany (Rosenberg 1943, 65–66; Schonhardt-Bailey 1998, 293–296). Confrontational in form, with incisive arguments, economic nationalism represented for its leading ideologues not just protectionism but a redefinition of the duties and responsibilities of the state (Viner 1969, 64; Heckscher 1969, 93–94). Historical economists developed historical and inductive methods in attacking orthodox political economy for failing to address wider national interests, aside from wealth and individual self-interest (Cunningham 1925, 738). The influence of Listian historicism was transparent in allusions made to British protectionism of earlier centuries and the subsequent inclination of foreign countries "to imitate the steps by which England attained to greatness," with a corresponding reluctance to embrace policies they considered detrimental to their national interests (Cunningham 1925, 869).

Economic nationalism was also aided by a flaw in Ricardian political economy, for there were never any illusions harbored that comparative advantage would ensure even distribution.

The disproportionate gains secured by developed economies provided economic nationalists with a powerful rallying cry. Nor was protectionist revival geographically confined. Australian protectionism drew on populist elements of colonial nationalism, harnessing resources, providing employment, and raising revenue, to promote a "national" economic policy free from imperial control (Gourevitch 1986, 110). Similarly, after a period of lower American tariffs after 1846, protectionist resurgence, propelled by Carey's virulent anti-British rhetoric, enlarged on Hamiltonian themes of self-sufficiency and independence. Developmental theory has been used to explain why Britain, as export leader in an open trading system, retained free trade in the 1870s (Gourevitch 1986, 77). Similarly, Wallerstein described adoption of free trade as "the definitive mark of the self-confident leader in a capitalist market system" (1979, 32). While rational choice interpretations describe the economic imperatives, ideology was also crucial in converging with and articulating national economic interests. In Britain, free trade was a *Weltanschauung*, a worldview revolving around consumer interests and free exchange (Trentmann 1997, 73). Economic theory and the intellectual dominance of free trade ideas in scholarly and political circles made a significant contribution to this process. Significantly, List's work was not translated into English until 1885, more than forty years after its publication in Europe (Gourevitch 1986, 83).

Improvements in international transport and communications and technological developments in industry and agriculture meant Britain faced significant import competition in the domestic market and foreign tariffs overseas. The practical operations and realities of the international economy were increasingly counterposed to abstract theory, and "unequal" or "one-sided" free trade emerged as a critique of a set of dysfunctional commercial relationships.[5] However, reform was problematic because any reimposition of food taxes, even for fiscal or imperial reasons, was politically difficult (Brown 1943, 68). However, in concentrated domestic industries like silk and sugar, the applicability of comparative advantage and the existence of a "self-regulating mechanism" modulating displacement of labor were increasingly questioned (Trentmann 1997, 90; Green 1995, 109–110; Marrison 1996, 110–112).

At the beginning of the twentieth century the fiscal landscape displayed a familiar pattern, with the trenchant protectionism of Russia and the United States accompanied by less severe protectionist regimes in France, Germany, and Austria (Bastable 1923, 106; Matthew 1997, 569–570). The collapse of the treaty system as a mode of extending freer commerce meant policy outcomes were increasingly driven by "economic circumstance" and international position. Internationally, colonial, economic, and national rivalries undermined freer trade; domestically, the emergence of collectivism and socialism had a similar effect by raising fiscal pressures (Gourevitch 1986, 123).

The ideological contours were changing, with the relationship among free trade, wealth, and welfare assuming greater importance, and support for free trade (and opposition to protectionism) increasingly based on different policy assumptions. Socialist thought, giving precedence to the collective standard of living over individual freedom, denied the primacy of consumerism, claiming that free trade was too narrowly materialistic in excluding important societal considerations (Trentmann 1996, 221–223). Similarly, the labor movement promoted a political economy model of regulation and rights, influenced by atavistic notions of "moral economy" and modern economic planning. Politically, accelerating democratization shifted the policy debate from wealth to welfare, and intellectually, from individualism to collectivism (Trentmann 1997, 82, 97–98). While there was clear erosion of the economic case for free trade, Cobdenite internationalism still had advocates, with Hobson fiercely denouncing protectionism and imperialism as "enemies of international morality" destroying "the free self-expression and intercourse of nations" (1903, 374). Cobden's vision of a productive, peaceful, and prosperous "industrial" society, based on Smithian and Spencerian notions, in which "the aggressive instincts of men were sublimated in work," remained influential (Cain 1979, 230). Nowhere was this so more than in Angell's *The Great Illusion* (1911), in which the shift from militant to industrial societies and forging of economic interdependence by commerce was taken as meaning war was virtually impossible, a view completely undermined by the outbreak of war in 1914 (Howe 1997, 296).

DECLINE AND REFORMULATION OF THE FREE TRADE IDEA

The classical case for free trade rested on the assumption of full employment and elastic labor markets, but once undermined, the economic case was weakened. Correspondingly, from the 1930s onward greater state intervention inevitably meant closer political control of economic policy, with economic planning and collectivist social policies the antithesis of free trade ideology (Howe 1997, 273). Wartime developments changed the intellectual and economic landscape, and the absence of European manufacturing products in third markets motivated "infant industry" protectionism in Japan, Australia, and India. After 1918 tariffs were raised by new European states struggling to achieve economic stability, and Western European economies combined intervention, regulation, and fiscal readjustment as a means of restoring equilibrium.

Restoring pre-1914 economic structures was the fundamental aim of many governments, but comparative responses to reconstruction were largely determined by prevailing financial and monetary constraints (Gourevitch 1986, 127–128). Financial instability was exacerbated by the restored gold standard proving unable to operate a balance-of-payments correction mechanism on account of higher tariffs and wage and price rigidity. In pursuit of a better balance between sectors, import tariffs were raised to offset diminishing domestic demand, while seeking protection from external volatility (Landes 1969, 392). The 1930s witnessed a loss of faith in classical political economy, fatally undermined by economic depression and political turmoil. The international financial crisis fundamentally altered financial and economic structures and practices. Extensive state intervention in the form of neo-orthodox policies of economic planning and regulation protecting domestic producers and satisfying domestic demand represented a departure from orthodox deflation (Landes 1969, 399). Symptomatic of these new realities was the highly protectionist American tariff, which exacerbated the decline in domestic incomes and production and prompted a debilitating retaliatory tariff cycle. Despite the implementation of New Deal ideas and the 1934 Reciprocal Trade Agreements Act, the United States showed little inclination to lower tariffs (Gourevitch 1986, 160).

Keynesian demand stimulus accelerated after 1945, but in the 1930s Germany, Sweden, and America all practiced it to some degree as part of a more pronounced protectionist, insular, and autarkic set of policy preferences (Gourevitch 1986, 142). Others remained more cautious. Britain retained orthodox deflation until 1931, when financial crisis forced devaluation and a general tariff. The reimposition of protective duties and imperial preference in 1932 destroyed the notion of a self-regulating, free-market economy (Howe 1997, 296). The tenets of classical trade theory, factor mobility, and price flexibility were held inoperative under high unemployment, and even Keynes, with the zeal of the convert, enthusiastically endorsed protection (Irwin 1996, 200). France followed the same path, via a demand stimulus interlude in 1936–1937, but financial crisis converged with historical policy predilections based on economic composition, for the French economy was predominantly small scale, labor intensive, and protectionist, and opposed to an open, internationalist strategy (Gourevitch 1986, 156).

Tariffs continued on an upward trajectory throughout the 1930s, along with import quotas and controls, potentially more damaging than tariffs in being less influenced by price mechanisms, within economic recovery programs. Wartime intervention only exacerbated existing trends, and after 1945, with the prospect of a liberal international order far removed from contemporary political realities, a formal international and institutional commitment to freer commerce was made with the 1947 General Agreement on Tariffs and Trade (GATT), and in the following decade with formation of the European Common Market (Irwin 2002, 161–165). In containing protectionist pressures and promoting reciprocal tariff reductions, the GATT has been a practical way of advancing freer trade, for wider policy influences continued to be variable in incidence and impact and have necessarily required constant attention, modification, and negotiation on an international basis.[6]

In broad terms, the pace of ideas and pressure of events outstripped the principles and practices of the mid-Victorian world. Historians may accurately refer to a "free trade era" when classical political economy met with less opposition rather than enthusiastic acceptance, but changing patterns of global political authority and economic power meant continual reconfiguration and renegotiation. Nevertheless, the concept of "globalization," fueled by technological and communications revolutions rather than ideological consensus, has revealed some familiar debates, particularly the relationship between policy formation and outcomes and economic development. In place of "hegemonic" Britain stands "the West," and in place of emergent industrial economies stand less-developed countries, where cheap labor supply and rudimentary facilities and resources reflect a wider disparity in wage rates and living standards. Closer identification of commercial policy with national and regional development, diversity, and sustainability, underpinned by ethical and moral imperatives, has been a significant development, resulting in the traditional protectionism of import-competing domestic industries being supplemented by nongovernmental organizations (NGOs) and anti-capitalist protestors in broad-based attacks against open markets (Irwin 2002, 225–228).

The pursuit of free trade remains controversial, for the policy continues to attract criticism on the basis that it is a tool of the major powers to ensure global market domination. Even avid proponents of laissez-faire economics, while considering the free market a great impersonal force in resource allocation, price determination, and product distribution, concede that it was never universally applicable (Viner 1960, 64). Based on short-term static and long-term dynamic gains of comparative advantage, economies of scale, and technology transfer, a strong case for economic efficiency underpinned free trade. However, economically efficient outcomes, while constituting the main consideration for previous generations, are now rarely considered alone. Ethical policy begins for many antiglobalization thinkers and activists by identifying the imperfections of the free-market Smithian Invisible Hand and the inefficient economic and unjust political outcomes it produces (Stiglitz 2002, 4–10).

Conclusion

Even at the height of its popularity, free trade was a contested policy, and by the twentieth century it no longer appeared sufficiently robust to deal with the demands of collectivism and social democracy. Untrammeled, free-market operations had long been deprecated, and after 1945 open markets coexisted with "distributive justice" in mixed economies (Viner 1960, 68). Despite the exalted intellectual status accorded to classical political economy, alternative models always existed. The idea of the universal applicability of free trade was born out of the political culture of an expanding capitalist economy in the late eighteenth and early nineteenth centuries, but ultimately the policy failed to fully encapsulate the economic experience of less-developed nations. While it would be reductionist to attribute too much influence to import/export orientation, it clearly contributed to the range of exogenous and endogenous factors of economic composition, political culture, and perceptions of place within the international economic order influencing commercial policy.

Ricardian political economy became increasingly divorced not only from Smith's original vision but also from practical economic and political experience, for complex welfare and employment issues in an age of political democracy posed unprecedented fiscal and political demands. Even if the economic efficiency argument retained validity, it is now not the only or even primary factor in the policy space. Not only has free trade "irretrievably lost its innocence," but it "can never again be asserted as the policy that economic theory tells us is always right" (Krugman 1987, 131–132). In fact, free trade had never achieved this status. There were always dissenters from the policy and the philosophical view of the world from which it emerged.

Commensurate with the internationalization of governance and regulatory authority, free trade has now cast off any utopian, unilateral, and voluntarist associations, but the complexity of the international economy makes the modern case for free trade appear "too narrow and mechanical" and even "a little unreal" (Sally 2008, 47–48). Smith's observation that it would be "absurd" to expect the restoration of free trade has great contemporary resonance (Smith 2012, 460). As in 1776, free trade remains an aspiration rather than a reality, and the variable success of the free trade idea reveals the disparity between theory and practice in the domestic and international commercial policy environment (Irwin 2002, 161–164).

Free trade remains a powerful idea, with strong associations with "progressive" ideas of freedom, liberty, and democracy, but despite elements of ideological continuity, the greater mobility of capital and labor, fueled by technological innovation and combined with supranational political authority and multinational business organization, has complicated global trading patterns. The free trade/protection dichotomy between nations has been supplanted by a complex configuration of national, regional, and sectorial models, with the result that notions of reciprocity and perceived vital national interests largely determine commercial policy. The cosmopolitanism of the free trade idea, while not totally discarded in its conception of the universal benefits bestowed by commercial liberalization, has been replaced by a more nuanced, practical, and hard-nosed acceptance of trade liberalization based on and subject to negotiation and bargaining.

NOTES

1. *The Anti-Corn Law Almanack for 1842* (Manchester: J. Gadsby), 27.
2. William Eden to Robert Liston, September 27, 1786, Liston Papers, National Library of Scotland, NLS MS 5545 fols. 84–85.
3. Ralph Woodford to Robert Liston, December 29, 1786, Liston Papers, National Library of Scotland, NLS MS 5545 fols. 151–152.
4. Commercial Restrictions—Petition of the Merchants of London, HC Debates, *Hansard*, May 8, 1820, vol. 1. c. 191.
5. "If ever the battle of Free Trade has to be fought over again, it will be decided, not upon its abstract merits, but by the encounter of sundry conflicting interests." *The Graphic*, no. 939, November 26, 1887.
6. For the origins of GATT, see the chapter in this volume by Joanne Gowa and for the contours and configuration of trading relations instigated by GATT, see the chapter by Raymond Hicks.

REFERENCES

Bastable, C. F. 1923. *The Commerce of Nations*. 9th ed. London: Methuen.
Bowden, W. 1924. The Influence of the Manufacturers on Some of the Early Policies of William Pitt. *American Historical Review* 29 (4): 655–674.
Brown, B. H. 1943. *The Tariff Reform Movement in Great Britain, 1881–1895*. New York: Columbia University Press.

Browning, O. 1886. Adam Smith and Free Trade for Ireland. *English Historical Review* 1 (2): 308–311.

Cain, P. J. 1979. Capitalism, War and Internationalism in the Thought of Richard Cobden. *British Journal of International Studies* 5 (3): 229–247.

Child, Josiah. 1681. *A Treatise Concerning the East India Trade*. London: T.J.

Cobden, Richard. 1878. *Speeches on Questions of Public Policy*. Edited by J. Bright and J. E. T. Rogers. London: Macmillan.

Collison Black, R. D. 1960. *Economic Thought and the Irish Question, 1817–1870*. London: Cambridge University Press.

Crowley, J. E. 1990. Neo-Mercantilism and the Wealth of Nations: British Commercial Policy after the American Revolution. *Historical Journal* 33 (2): 339–360.

Cunningham, W. 1925. *The Growth of English Industry and Commerce in Modern Times*. Cambridge, UK: Cambridge University Press.

Cunningham, W. 1886. The Repression of the Woollen Manufacture in Ireland. *English Historical Review* 1 (2): 277–294.

Davis, R. 1962. English Foreign Trade, 1700–1774. *Economic History Review* 15 (2): 285–303.

Economides, Spyros, and Peter Wilson. 2002. *The Economic Factor in International Relations: A Brief Introduction*. London: I.B. Tauris.

Ehrman, John. 1962. *The British Government and Commercial Negotiations with Europe, 1783–1793*. Cambridge, UK: Cambridge University Press.

Fay, C. R. 1928. *Great Britain from Adam Smith to the Present Day: An Economic and Social Survey*. London: Longmans, Green.

Federico, Giovanni. 2012. The Corn Laws in Continental Perspective. *European Review of Economic History* 16 (2): 166–187.

Fieser, James, ed. 1999. *Early Responses to Hume's Moral, Literary and Political Writings II*. Bristol, UK: Thoemmes Press.

Gladstone, W. E. 1845. *Remarks upon Recent Commercial Legislation*. London: John Murray.

Gomes, Leonard. 2003. *The Economics and Ideology of Free Trade: A Historical Review*. Cheltenham, UK: Edward Elgar.

Gourevitch, Peter. 1986. *Politics in Hard Times: Comparative Responses to International Economic Crises*. Ithaca, NY & London: Cornell University Press.

Green, E. H. H. 1995. *The Crisis of Conservatism: The Politics, Economics, and Ideology of the British Conservative Party, 1880–1914*. London: Routledge.

Heckscher, Eli F. 1969. Mercantilism. In *Revisions in Mercantilism*, edited by D. C. Coleman, 19–34. London: Methuen.

Hobson, J. A. 1903. The Inner Meaning of Protectionism. *Contemporary Review* 84: 365–374.

Hollander, Samuel. 2011. *Friedrich Engels and Marxian Political Economy*. Cambridge, UK: Cambridge University Press.

Howe, Anthony. 1997. *Free Trade and Liberal England, 1846–1946*. Oxford, UK: Clarendon Press.

Howe, Anthony. 2013. Popular Political Economy. In *Languages of Politics in Nineteenth-Century Britain*, edited by. David Craig and James Thompson, 118–141. London: Palgrave Macmillan.

Howe, A. 2002. Restoring Free Trade: The British Experience, 1776–1873. In *The Political Economy of British Historical Experience, 1688–1914*, edited by D. Winch and P. K. O'Brien, 192–213. Oxford: Oxford University Press.

Hume, David. 1987. *Essays Moral, Political and Literary*. Rev. ed. Edited by Eugene F. Miller. Indianapolis, IN: Liberty Fund.

Huskisson, W. 1827. *A Letter on the Corn Laws, by the Right Hon. W. Huskisson, to One of His Constituents, in 1814*. London: James Ridgway.

Irwin, D. A. 1991. Retrospectives: Challenges to Free Trade. *Journal of Economic Perspectives* 5 (2): 201–208.

Irwin, Douglas A. 1996. *Against the Tide: An Intellectual History of Free Trade*. Princeton, NJ: Princeton University Press.

Irwin, Douglas A. 2002. *Free Trade under Fire*. Princeton, NJ: Princeton University Press.

James, S. C., and D. A. Lake. 1989. The Second Face of Hegemony: Britain's Repeal of the Corn Laws and the American Walker Tariff of 1846. *International Organization* 43 (1): 1–30.

Kelly, P. 1975. British and Irish Politics in 1785. *English Historical Review* 90 (356): 536–563.

Kindleberger, C. P. 1975. The Rise of Free Trade in Western Europe, 1820–1875. *Journal of Economic History* 35 (1): 20–55.

Krugman, Paul. 1987. Is Free Trade Passé? *Journal of Economic Perspectives* 1 (2): 131–141.

Landes, David. 1969. *The Unbound Prometheus*. Cambridge, UK: Cambridge University Press.

Levasseur, E. 1892. The Recent Commercial Policy of France. *Journal of Political Economy* 1 (1): 20–49.

List, Friedrich. 1856. *National System of Political Economy*. Philadelphia: J. P. Lippincott.

Magnusson, Lars. 1994. *Mercantilism: The Shaping of an Economic Language*. London: Routledge.

Marrison, Andrew. 1996. *British Business and Protection, 1903–1932*. Oxford: Oxford University Press.

Matthew, H. C. G. 1997. *Gladstone, 1809–1898*. Oxford: Clarendon Press.

McKeown, T. J. 1983. Hegemonic Stability Theory and 19th Century Tariff Levels in Europe. *International Organization* 37 (1): 73–91.

Milgate, Murray, and Shannon C. Stimson. 2009. *After Adam Smith: A Century of Transformation in Politics and Political Economy*. Princeton, NJ: Princeton University Press.

Mill, James. 1824. *Elements of Political Economy*. 2nd ed. London: Baldwin, Cradock, and Joy.

Mill, John Stuart. 1874. *Autobiography*. 4th ed. London: Longmans, Green, Reader, and Dyer.

Mill, John Stuart. 1848. *Principles of Political Economy with Some of Their Applications to Social Philosophy*. London: John W. Parker.

Mossner, E. C., and I. S. Ross. 1987. *The Correspondence of Adam Smith*. 2nd ed. Oxford: Clarendon Press.

Noble, David F. 2005. *Beyond the Promised Land: The Movement and the Myth*. Toronto: Between the Lines.

Nye, J. V. C. 2007. *War, Wine, and Taxes: The Political Economy of Anglo-French Trade, 1689–1900*. Princeton, NJ, and Oxford: Princeton University Press.

O'Brien, Patrick K., and Geoffrey Allen Pigman. 1992. Free Trade, British Hegemony and the International Economic Order in the Nineteenth Century. *Review of International Studies* 18 (2): 89–113.

Ricardo, David. 1821. *On the Principles of Political Economy and Taxation*. London: John Murray.

Rosenberg, Hans. 1943. Political and Social Consequences of the Great Depression of 1873–1896 in Central Europe. *Economic History Review* 13 (1–2): 58–73.

Rostow, W. W. 1959. The Stages of Economic Growth. *Economic History Review* 12 (1): 1–16.

Sack, James J. 1993. *From Jacobite to Conservative*. Cambridge, UK: Cambridge University Press.

Sally, Razeen. 2008. *Trade Policy, New Century: The WTO, FTAs, and Asia Rising*. London: Institute of Economic Affairs.

Schonhardt-Bailey, Cheryl. 2006. *From the Corn Laws to Free Trade: Interests, Ideas, and Institutions in Historical Perspective*. Cambridge, MA: MIT.

Schonhardt-Bailey, Cheryl. 1998. Parties and Interests in the "Marriage of Iron and Rye." *British Journal of Political Science* 28 (2): 291–330.

See, H. 1930. The Normandy Chamber of Commerce and the Commercial Treaty of 1786. *Economic History Review* 2 (2): 308–313.

Semmel, B. 1965. The Hume-Tucker Debate and Pitt's Trade Proposals. *Economic Journal* 75 (300): 759–770.

Sloane, W. M. 1898. The Continental System of Napoleon. *Political Science Quarterly* 13 (2): 213–231.

Smith, Adam. [1776] 2012. *An Inquiry into the Nature and Causes of the Wealth of Nations*. London: Wordsworth.

Stiglitz, Joseph. 2002. *Globalization and Its Discontents*. London: Penguin.

Trentmann, Frank. 1996. The Strange Death of Free Trade: The erosion of the Liberal Consensus in Great Britain, c. 1903–1932. In *Citizenship and Community: Liberals, Radicals and Collective Identities in the British Isles, 1865–1931*, edited by E. F. Biagini, 219–250. Cambridge, UK: Cambridge University Press.

Trentmann, Frank. 1997. Wealth versus Welfare: The British Left between Free Trade and National Political Economy before the First World War. *Historical Research* 70 (171): 70–98.

Tucker, Josiah. 1763. *The Case of Going to War, for the Sake of Procuring, Enlarging, or Securing of Trade, Considered in a New Light*. London: R and J. Dodsley.

Viner, Jacob. 1960. The Intellectual History of Laissez-Faire. *Journal of Law & Economics* 3: 45–69.

Viner, Jacob. 1969. Power versus Plenty as Objectives of Foreign Policy in the Seventeenth and Eighteenth Centuries. In *Revisions in Mercantilism*, edited by D. C. Coleman, 61–91. London: Methuen.

Viner, Jacob. 1937. *Studies in the Theory of International Trade*. New York: Harper.

Wallerstein, Immanuel. 1979. *The Modern World System: Capitalist Agriculture and the Origins of the European World-Economy in the Sixteenth Century*. New York: Academic.

Walter, Andrew. 1996. Adam Smith and the Liberal Tradition in International Relations. *Review of International Studies* 22 (1): 5–28.

Williams, J. B. 1972. *British Commercial Policy and Trade Expansion, 1750–1850*. Oxford: Clarendon Press.

CHAPTER 4

TRADE POLICY INSTRUMENTS OVER TIME

CHAD P. BOWN

INTRODUCTION

THROUGHOUT history governments have applied import protection through many different policy instruments. One extreme is an instrument that is widespread, simple, and relatively transparent: most customs authorities currently apply a nondiscriminatory, ad valorem import tariff. Toward the other extreme are dozens if not hundreds of eclectic instruments that are more complex and less transparent and frequently entail additional political-economic distortions. Consider the experience of only one industry in only one country—US steel—even since the 1960s. While being protected by applied, nondiscriminatory, ad valorem import tariffs, US steel has also experienced quotas, minimum price arrangements, voluntary export restraints, antidumping, countervailing duties, suspension agreements, preferential tariffs to NAFTA and other partners, import licenses and monitoring, safeguards, expanded trade adjustment assistance, and local content requirements.

That import protection arises through such a variety of instruments raises fundamental questions for political-economic research. Are there apparent trends in the use and nonuse of particular import protection instruments? Furthermore, what are the political-economic and institutional determinants of, interrelationships between, and implications for government use of these various instruments?

The next section begins by examining historical trends for a number of import protection instruments. Perhaps the most pervasive trend throughout the international trading system since 1947 has been the reduction in applied tariffs and opening of economies to international commerce. Nevertheless, it is worth recalling the analogy from a *New York Times* article that Robert E. Baldwin made famous at the conclusion of the Kennedy Round, by including it in his comprehensive economic analysis of nontariff protection: "The lowering of tariffs has, in effect, been like draining a swamp. The lower water level has revealed all the snags and stumps of non-tariff barriers that still have to be cleared away" (1970, 2).

While individual nations may have drained their swamps by lowering applied tariffs, the more complete story of import protection demonstrates substantial heterogeneity. Sometimes these low applied tariffs have not been accompanied by the legal commitments that "bind" them under the World Trade Organization (WTO). Sometimes the low applied tariffs are not offered to all trading partners but are instead offered only on a discriminatory basis through regional, bilateral, or preferential regimes. Sometimes a low applied tariff on a particular product is then more than offset by application of a new and higher tax through antidumping, safeguards, or countervailing duties. Sometimes even more innovative, nontransparent, and complex nontariff barriers have come into use.

These trends suggest complexities between tariff and nontariff protection that push beyond even Baldwin's substantial foresight. Draining the swamp of tariff protection may have done more than just reveal the existence of previously unobserved nontariff protection. It may have stimulated *growth* in levels of old and new forms of nontariff protection. It also may have resulted in an altered political-economic ecosystem in which governments conduct trade policy.

The third section reviews some of the theories that guide the literature on import protection as well as the implications for the relationship between tariff and nontariff protection. These theories draw from both economic efficiency and redistributive motives for trade policy; many are also informed by the evolution of the multilateral trading system, from the start-up of the General Agreement on Tariffs and Trade (GATT) through the WTO period that began in 1995.

The fourth section turns to major areas of empirical study in light of this theory. Econometric research has begun to provide new insight into the determinants of government application of import tariffs, as well as the forces that influence their negotiated reduction under international trade agreements. An emerging literature also explores empirically how trade agreement commitments, as well as political-economic shocks and incentives, jointly affect governments' resorting to *other* instruments of import protection.

The fifth section touches on recent and promising research innovations, and the last section concludes by considering open questions and future research.

INSTITUTIONS AND TRENDS IN POLICY INSTRUMENTS

This section describes key institutional developments and trends in the use of tariff and nontariff instruments of import protection since the 1940s.

Institutional Influences under the GATT/WTO System

Before the advent of the multilateral trading system in its current form, tariff and non-tariff barriers were very high. The US Smoot-Hawley tariffs of 1930 and the subsequent retaliatory response by the international community led to an accumulation of various instruments of protection that impeded the worldwide resumption of trade in the aftermath of the Great Depression. Irwin, Mavroidis, and Sykes (2008) provide a fascinating account of the political-economic negotiations that led to the GATT's creation in 1947, signed by twenty-three contracting parties, which includes the following in its charter's preamble:

> Recognizing that their relations in the field of trade and economic endeavour should be conducted with a view to raising standards of living, ensuring full employment and a large and steadily growing volume of real income and effective demand, developing the full use of the resources of the world and expanding the production and exchange of goods,
> Being desirous of contributing to these objectives by entering into reciprocal and mutually advantageous arrangements directed to the substantial *reduction of tariffs and other barriers to trade and to the elimination of discriminatory treatment in international commerce.* . . .

> (GATT 1947; emphasis added)

The broad strategy for those working within the GATT system at its inception was two-fold.[1] First get countries to convert their quantitative restrictions and other nontariff barriers into nondiscriminatory, or most-favored-nation (MFN), tariff form. Then get the GATT contracting parties together in periodic negotiating rounds to reciprocally exchange concessions to lower these applied tariffs and legally "bind" the tariffs to prevent them from increasing. For the more industrialized economies, the result was a general downward trend in applied import tariff rates and binding levels over the next fifty years. For developing countries—when they ultimately became GATT contracting parties—the import tariff story evolved differently. Most self-selected out of the reciprocal, multilateral negotiations framework for reducing MFN tariffs. Instead, developing-country reductions to applied tariffs typically occurred much later and frequently resulted from a unilateral liberalization that took place independently or in conjunction with preferential trade liberalization. Furthermore, most developing countries have not immediately "locked in" those tariffs by making legally binding commitments at the similarly low rates at which their MFN tariffs have actually been applied.

While the GATT framework attempted to cajole import protection toward the instrument of applied MFN tariffs, the 1947 agreement also contained a variety of exceptions spelling out conditions under which governments could subsequently resort to *other* instruments of protection. For example, while the GATT's Article XI contained a general prohibition on the use of quantitative restrictions, Article XII permitted governments to use quotas to address balance of payments problems. While the GATT did not allow governments to simply raise their applied MFN import tariffs unilaterally without notice, Article VI (antidumping and countervailing duties) and Article XIX (safeguards) permitted governments to impose higher duties in response to certain economic shocks, provided they went through particular procedural steps.[2] Finally, while the GATT's Article I demanded participants offer nondiscriminatory MFN tariffs to all other contracting parties, Article XXIV provided a fundamental exception by allowing formation of (preferential) free trade agreements and customs unions.[3]

Important Trends in Use of Different Policy Instruments

Beginning from near autarky during the Great Depression, applied MFN import tariff rates have fallen considerably across countries over time. And while they may have fallen during different periods and for different reasons, the resulting simple average of applied MFN tariffs by 2010, for example, was extraordinarily low for a number of major economies: 3.5 percent for the United States, 4.4 percent for Japan, 5.1 percent for the European Union, 9.6 percent for China, 13.0 percent for India, and 13.7 percent for Brazil (WTO 2011).

The remainder of this subsection describes three other important trade policy instruments of the GATT/WTO era: temporary trade barrier policies, voluntary export restraints (VERs), and preferential trade agreements (PTAs).

Policies such as antidumping, safeguards, and countervailing (antisubsidy) duties constitute one major class of nontariff protection that took on greater significance in an environment characterized by low and legally bound applied MFN tariffs. These policies are often jointly referred to as trade remedies, contingent or administered protection, trade defense instruments, or *temporary trade barriers*—the latter stemming from the fact that WTO rules identify maximum specific periods over which these policies are permitted to remain in effect. Antidumping has been the most frequently used of these instruments; the first antidumping law predates the GATT and was enacted by Canada in 1904. Australia, Canada, the European Union, and the United States dominated global use of antidumping until the early 1990s.

Many major emerging economies became important users of antidumping and other temporary trade barriers beginning in the 1990s (Bown 2011). As Table 4.1 reveals, while the United States and European Union continued to have periods in which a significant share of their imports were covered by such import restrictions, comparable and sometimes higher levels of import coverage under these nontariff instruments arose, seemingly out of nowhere, for countries like Argentina, Brazil, China, India, Mexico, and Turkey. Most emerging economies had virtually no experience using these particular instruments before each underwent its own major episode of tariff liberalization in the late 1980s or 1990s.

Table 4.1 Imports Covered by Imposed Temporary Trade Barriers, 1995–2011

Economy	Year of first antidumping law/initiation	Estimated share of non-oil manufacturing imports covered by TTBs in				Peak year, 1995–2011	(Peak year)
		1995	2000	2005	2010		
Argentina	1972/NA	0.7	2.4	1.8	2.6	3.5	(2002)
Australia	1906/NA	0.8	0.4	0.5	0.5	0.8	(1996)
Brazil	1987/1988	0.5	1.0	1.6	1.4	2.1	(2008)
Canada	1904/NA	1.2	1.9	1.0	0.7	1.9	(2001)
China	1997/1997	0.0	0.5	2.9	2.8	4.5	(2003)
European Union*	1968/1968–69	2.7	3.4	2.9	1.8	4.2	(2002)
Indonesia	1995/1996	0.0	1.1	0.2	0.8	1.3	(2001)
India	1985/1992	0.1	2.6	2.4	4.3	6.3	(2011)
Japan	1920/1982	0.1	0.1	0.0	0.0	1.2	(2009)
Mexico	1986/1987	1.7	1.3	0.7	0.3	1.8	(1998)
South Africa	1914/1921	0.3	0.7	0.9	0.4	1.0	(2002)
South Korea	1963/1986	0.2	0.5	0.5	0.5	0.5	(2009)
Turkey	1989/1989	2.4	1.8	2.6	4.2	4.9	(2008)
United States	1916/1922	1.9	5.2	4.3	3.6	5.6	(2001)

Source: Data taken from Bown (2013, Figure 1a) and Bown (2012).
*EU at the time was the European Economic Community; some EU member states have AD laws that predate 1968. Temporary trade barriers (TTBs) include antidumping, countervailing duties, global safeguards, and China-specific transitional safeguards.
NA = not available.

Voluntary export restraints are a second nontariff instrument that experienced a period of proliferation; most of this occurred prior to the more recent turn to temporary trade barriers. They work like an import quota but with one important difference: because the exporters voluntarily agree to restrict their quantities of foreign sales, the exporting country gets the "rents" associated with the consumer price increase above its free trade level. While the economic outcome for exporters is typically not as good as free trade, it is frequently better than under a comparably trade-restricting import tariff or import quota.

At least two related factors took hold in the 1960s that contributed to the proliferation of VERs. The first was Japan's entry into the GATT in 1955 and the integration of its export-led growth model into the trading system. Increased Japanese exports of textiles and related products put adjustment pressure on import-competing industries across many countries, including a number of industrialized economies. Between Japan's accession in 1955 and 1970, roughly fifty GATT contracting parties invoked their Article XXXV rights not to apply MFN tariffs to Japan's exports; many imposed country-specific quotas. The United States, on the other hand, sought to negotiate VERs with Japan. The second factor was pragmatism. In an environment in which governments were committed to imposing some new import protection, VERs were more palatable to exporters than import quotas or tariffs, for with a VER the exporter at least received the rents associated with the trade restriction.[4]

The proliferation of VERs was ultimately headlined by the Multi-Fiber Arrangement (MFA)—a system of VERs and quantitative restrictions that governed global trade in textile and apparel products for thirty years before it was eventually phased-out in 2005. A number of other US-Japanese VERs continued to arise through the 1980s, including in footwear, semiconductors, automobiles, steel, photo paper, and chemicals. In fact, an explicit outcome of the Uruguay Round of GATT negotiations was attempts to rein in VERs; the more recent increase in temporary trade barrier use may be partially related to VERs falling out of favor by the late 1980s.[5]

A third important trend is that applied import tariffs for a number of countries have also fallen *preferentially*, through two main instruments, for a number of countries since 1947.[6] The first are preference regimes offered to developing countries under programs such as the Generalized System of Preferences, Everything But Arms, and African Growth and Opportunity Act. The second are free trade areas (FTAs) and customs unions; important examples include the European Union, the North American Free Trade Agreement (NAFTA), and MERCOSUR, which involves Argentina, Brazil, Paraguay, and Uruguay. Under both arrangements, not only did applied rates fall to different levels for preferential versus MFN tariffs, but the tariff reductions frequently took place during different time periods.

To summarize, the major intertemporal movements in the rates of import protection under these different policy instruments—for example, applied MFN tariffs, preferential tariffs, VERs, antidumping, safeguards, and countervailing duties—suggest common political-economic determinants. The remainder of this chapter highlights formal research examining these questions.

THEORETICAL STUDIES

Before turning to the determinants of import protection *instruments*, an examination of two more fundamental questions is in order. First, why do governments impose import-restricting policies at all? Second, why do governments voluntarily commit to limit their access to certain import-restricting policy instruments by signing trade agreements? Once informed by frameworks that address these questions, this section then turns to the implications of these trade agreement commitments (covering tariffs) for government use of other instruments of import protection.

Theories of Import Restrictions: Tariffs and Everything Else

Research has coalesced around two main government motives to explain policies that interfere with free trade. The first is economic efficiency. If the country is "large"—so that an alteration in its consumption or supply of a product leads to changes in world (or the foreign exporter's received) prices—the government can use trade policy to shift the terms of trade in its country's favor and improve national well-being relative to free trade (Johnson 1953–1954).

The second motive is redistributive. Even if the country is "small"—so that changes to its trade policy do not affect world prices, thus ruling out the terms-of-trade motive by assumption—governments may want to impose a "politically optimal" import tariff if its benefits are greater than the costs. The economic costs of protection are well known; they include the deadweight losses associated with too little domestic consumption and too much induced production by relatively inefficient domestic industries. However, in political-economy models of import protection, political benefits can overcome such costs. For example, in the Grossman and Helpman (1994) workhorse, political-economy model of lobbying for protection, the benefits arising from tariffs can outweigh their efficiency costs if governments value campaign contributions in addition to the economic well-being of producers and consumers.

A long-standing literature has evolved that compares the political-economic implications of various instruments of import protection. Import tariffs are generally inefficient for small countries relative to free trade; furthermore, they are inefficient relative to outcomes whereby governments use domestic policy instruments (taxes, subsidies) to address particular market failures in ways that do not create by-product distortions.[7] Nevertheless, conditional on an outcome wherein a government is committed to imposing *some* form of import protection, a nondiscriminatory ad valorem tariff is typically the least inefficient instrument.[8] To provide one illustrative example, consider a nontariff alternative such as a quantitative restriction, an instrument that theoretically can be structured so as to be exactly as trade distorting as an import tax. Because quotas also require the government to undertake a separate and discretionary decision about how to allocate the licenses, additional opportunities for wasteful rent-seeking (Krueger, 1974) can arise in addition to the potential for discrimination between foreign sources.

Large Countries, Import Protection, and Trade Agreements

Why do large countries sign trade agreements, and what are the implications? To begin, consider a world without trade agreements, in which rational governments thus set optimal (Nash) import tariffs so as to maximize their countries' economic well-being.

One strain of the literature suggests that governments of large countries find trade agreements efficiency-improving if the agreement helps coordinate theirs and another large country's trade policies so as to avoid a "prisoner's dilemma" outcome (Bagwell and Staiger 1999, 2002). For import tariffs, the trade agreement is needed because neither country has an incentive to lower its tariff *unilaterally*; a unilateral reduction for a large country starting from its optimal tariff would lead to an increase in the world price of its imported good, which would make it worse off. Interestingly, the GATT/WTO principle of reciprocity can be interpreted as facilitating a negotiated outcome whereby one country trades off a reduction to its import tariffs (affecting a foreign trading partner's exports) against a reduction to the foreign country's import tariffs (affecting the home country's exports). The trade agreement's *coordinated* reduction of import tariffs improves each country's economic well-being by expanding the total volume of trade while *neutralizing* what would otherwise be an adverse impact on each country's terms of trade, defined as each country's price of exports relative to its price of imports.

One acknowledged limitation of this approach is its abstraction from the complexities of *enforcement*—a particularly acute issue in the context of trade agreements between sovereign states. Thus a related literature examines the self-enforcing nature of trade agreements between large countries. Bagwell and Staiger (1990), for example, examine a repeated game played between governments in which each stage is a prisoner's dilemma, and there is uncertainty over trade volumes. A trade agreement is modeled as the most liberal or "cooperative" trade policy that can be supported without either government having an incentive to "defect" by imposing its unilaterally optimal (noncooperative) tariff. This approach reveals that governments may need to increase their equilibrium levels of import protection to maintain cooperation in response to import surges, because such surges create a new and strong incentive for a government to defect by raising its tariff because it would improve its nation's economic well-being. However, an implication for countries that have taken on commitments to lower and bind their applied MFN tariffs at the WTO is that the government may need to switch to some other policy instrument to increase protection if it hopes to remain consistent with its basic WTO obligations.

To summarize, large countries have a unilateral incentive to impose beggar-thy-neighbor import protection policies that improve their economic well-being by shifting some of the protection's costs onto trading partners. Trade agreements can thus be used to help two or more such large countries coordinate the import tariff reductions that each would not undertake unilaterally. Nevertheless, trade agreements that constrain national use of tariffs come with their own caveats. In particular, a cooperative trade agreement on tariff commitments may be unsustainable in an environment characterized by trade flow volatility if the agreement does not provide governments with the flexibility to sometimes access additional import protection.[9]

Small Countries, Import Protection, and Trade Agreements

A second strain of the literature examines "small" countries that do not have (national) economic efficiency motives to impose tariffs, yet may do so for redistributive purposes. This literature posits that trade agreements may play a "commitment" role for governments to tie their own hands with respect to their private sectors.

Take the classic Grossman and Helpman (1994) political-economy model of a small country. Here the government would not want to sign a trade agreement that would tie its hands and constrain its tariffs, because this would foreclose its ability to extract rents from domestic producers through their lobbying activities and campaign contributions. However, Maggi and Rodríguez-Clare (1998) relax the model's assumption on capital immobility and allow factors to be mobile across sectors in the long run to show that the expectation of import protection can lead unproductive industries to make excessive investment that even a politically motivated government would prefer to avoid. A trade agreement that *commits* the government to impose lower tariffs in the long run can therefore help prevent excessive lobbying for import protection.[10]

There are, however, potential costs for politically motivated governments that seek to sign trade agreements to constrain their use of tariffs, especially when other instruments of protection are available. Copeland (1990) develops a two-staged game in which governments can first negotiate cooperatively over tariffs and then implement nontariff protection noncooperatively in the second stage. If governments are politically motivated and place a high value on the interests of producers, trade agreements that eliminate tariffs can lead governments to substitute policy toward more economically costly forms of nontariff protection in the second stage so that consumers are made worse off.

Overall, this literature identifies a number of trade-offs associated with trade agreements, even for small countries. Politically motivated governments may use trade agreements as a commitment device to help prevent their own excessive application of import tariffs. However, trade agreements with loopholes that make it too costless to replace (once high) applied tariffs with protection through another instrument can undermine the agreement's commitment value. Furthermore, agreements that constrain tariffs too much may risk pushing import protection into nontariff instruments that may be even more distorting.

EMPIRICAL STUDIES

This section turns to the major empirical studies of import protection. It follows a similar organizational structure, first identifying empirical support for the determinants of import tariffs and the role of trade agreements. The analysis then builds from these results to assess their implications for alternative instruments of import protection.

Evidence on Import Tariff Formation Before and After the Signing of Trade Agreements

The first foundational piece from the empirical literature examines why countries impose tariffs in the *absence* of international trade agreements. Broda, Limão, and Weinstein (2008) provide evidence from disaggregated data and export supply elasticities in line with the terms-of-trade theory: governments impose higher import tariffs where they have greater market power. Evidence on the determinants of these optimal tariffs is supported via four different empirical exercises. First is evidence for the applied import tariffs for fifteen *nonmembers* of the WTO. The second and third are evidence from the United States for its "column 2" tariffs (which apply to countries not granted MFN status) and for measures of its nontariff protection. Fourth is the *lack* of statistical evidence for the US-applied MFN tariff rates. This meets the expectation that US-applied tariffs would be statistically unrelated to the theoretically predicted optimal tariff, because these tariffs have been continually reduced after being subjected to successive GATT/WTO negotiating rounds.

A second set of studies provides evidence that the terms-of-trade theory can help one understand the tariff *cuts* that countries take on under trade agreements like the WTO. Bagwell and Staiger (2011), for example, examine determinants of the one-time tariff cuts for sixteen countries that acceded to the WTO between 1995 and 2005. The evidence indicates that negotiated tariff levels are related to prenegotiation levels of tariffs, import volumes, import prices, and trade elasticities. Furthermore, Ludema and Mayda (2013) examine the Uruguay Round negotiations and the resulting MFN tariffs for thirty-six developing and high income economies, including Australia, Canada, the European Union, Japan, South Korea, and the United States. Evidence suggests that the level of the negotiated import tariff is also negatively related to the importer's market power and the Herfindahl-Hirschman index of exporter concentration. The free-rider problem of dispersed export interests can help explain why some products—such as agriculture, prepared food, textiles, and footwear—have experienced much smaller reductions to their applied MFN tariffs under multiple rounds of multilateral negotiations than did more concentrated export interests.

There are two main insights from this empirical literature. First, in the absence of trade agreements, governments impose higher tariffs where they have market power. Second, these and related economic forces affect the negotiation outcomes for WTO member countries and thus implicitly also affect the size of their remaining ("politically optimal") applied MFN import tariffs.

The Decline in Applied Tariffs and the Rise in Other Instruments of Nontariff Protection

Now armed with a better understanding of the political-economic forces behind the different import tariffs that countries apply in the absence of trade agreements and when they are parties to the GATT/WTO, this subsection turns to research on the implications of trade agreements for other instruments of import protection.

The fundamental fact that applied import tariff reductions resulting from GATT/WTO negotiations are at least partially responsible for the levels and patterns of nontariff protection is implicit, if not explicit, in much of the rest of the literature.[11] In the influential empirical studies of the Grossman and Helpman (1994) theory of the political economy of import protection, both Goldberg and Maggi (1999) as well as Gawande and Bandyopadhyay (2000) do not use data on applied US import tariff rates. Instead, they estimate structural determinants of measures of US *nontariff* protection.

Other approaches attempt to more directly examine implications of the terms-of-trade theory for countries that have taken on MFN tariff commitments under the WTO and must then use alternative policy instruments to increase their levels of import protection. For example, Bown and Crowley (2013b) construct measures of nontariff protection from US application of antidumping and safeguards between 1997 and 2006 to investigate the repeated game model of Bagwell and Staiger (1990). Evidence is consistent with the theory that countries in self-enforcing trade agreements increase their levels of import protection in response to positive trade volume shocks, with variation arising according to industry-level trade elasticities. Market power may thus still affect the *levels* of import protection that governments impose, even when applied MFN import tariffs are constrained by trade agreement commitments, provided that measures of import protection reflect the influence of the appropriate additional nontariff instruments.

Studies on different countries and time periods examine other aspects of the relationship between tariff and nontariff protection. Limão and Tovar (2011) examine Turkey's experience during the 1990s, when Turkey signed a customs union arrangement with the European Union and legally bound some of its tariffs under the WTO. Evidence suggests that Turkey's tariff commitments increased the likelihood and restrictiveness of its government's subsequent use of nontariff instruments of import protection.

Another interesting case study is India, which made massive cuts to its applied MFN import tariffs in the 1990s and subsequently became the trading system's heaviest user of antidumping and safeguards. Bown and Tovar (2011) estimate structural determinants of the Grossman and Helpman (1994) political economy model of protection on repeated cross-sections of Indian data—before and after India's unilateral applied MFN import tariff rate cuts associated with its 1991–1992 standby arrangement with the IMF. Changes to India's applied MFN tariffs during this period appear to have resulted in an exogenous, trade-liberalizing shock to India's trade policy. Nevertheless, by 2002 India had unwound much of the applied MFN tariff reductions of the 1990s by accumulating a substantial stock of imposed antidumping and safeguards nontariff restrictions.

Finally, a number of studies provide cross-country evidence that an important determinant of import protection through "new" policies such as temporary trade barriers is the commitments that governments take on that limit their access to "old" instruments of protection. For example, combined evidence from Bown and Crowley (2013a, 2014) for eighteen high-income and emerging economies between 1989 and 2010 finds that as more products' applied MFN tariffs push up against the trade agreement constraints of WTO tariff-binding commitments, governments implement new import protection by turning to instruments like temporary trade barriers.

Preferential Tariff Reductions and Multilateral Tariff Reductions

A separate stream of research examines potential interrelationships between a government's preferential tariffs and its MFN tariffs offered under the WTO. These empirical studies have begun to inform understanding of whether and when preferential trade agreements can be "building blocks" versus "stumbling blocks" for multilateral cooperation in trade policy (Bhagwati 1991). This has been an open empirical question given the conflicting results that arise from the theoretical literature.[12]

The first major empirical study to examine this question used product-level data from the United States (Limão 2006). It considered the impact of US PTAs on the multilaterally negotiated MFN tariff cuts that the United States subsequently made under the Uruguay Round. Evidence suggests a stumbling block effect: US multilateral tariff reductions were smaller for products imported under its PTAs relative to similar products imported only from PTA nonmembers. In a follow-up study of the European Union, Karacaovali and Limão (2008) provide related evidence indicating that this stumbling block effect is not limited to just the United States and its PTAs. Their evidence indicates that the EU reduced its multilateral tariffs on goods not imported under FTAs by almost twice as much as the tariffs imported under its PTAs.

Because the spread of PTAs is so pervasive, there are many opportunities to investigate the extent to which the stumbling block phenomenon extends to other settings. In one important study, Estevadeordal, Freund, and Ornelas (2008) reach the opposite conclusion after examining the experience of ten Latin American countries in the 1990s. For these Latin American countries, the preferential reductions in applied tariffs were, on average, subsequently followed by governments making applied MFN tariff *reductions*. In this context, Latin American PTAs were found to be a building block to future multilateral tariff liberalization.

Can theory help explain the difference in these results across empirical settings, and whether any particular PTA is likely to hinder or promote subsequent multilateral trade liberalization?[13] Part of the explanation for the stumbling block evidence may be the importance of nontrade objectives particular to the US and EU PTAs. Limão (2007), for example, suggests a theoretical motivation that the United States and EU need to maintain preferences with certain partners to compensate for their commitments to higher labor and environmental standards and intellectual property rights protection.

Furthermore, Estevadeordal, Freund, and Ornelas (2008) note an important difference arising in the context of the Latin American countries' liberalization episodes. Unlike the US and EU cases, the Latin American PTA negotiations would have resulted in a given product's "preference margin"—defined as the difference between its applied MFN tariff and its PTA tariff—being quite large. Large preference margins present the opportunity for substantial economic efficiency costs to arise through trade diversion (Viner 1950). One explanation is that Latin American governments were cognizant of this concern and thus minimized the potential negative PTA impact and deliberately reduced preference margins by also cutting their MFN tariffs toward PTA nonmembers.

Additional Influences on Import Protection: Retaliation Capacity and WTO Dispute Jurisprudence

Because trade policy is a repeated game played between sovereign states, the expected trading partner *reaction* to a new import restriction is also likely to endogenously affect how countries implement import protection in the first place. Historical evidence from the Great Depression has long established expectations that retaliation can have important effects; for example, Irwin (2011) argues that trading partner retaliation against the US Smoot-Hawley tariffs in 1930 severely curtailed US exports.

Research on more recently implemented policies shows how the latent threat of meaningful foreign trade retaliation is also likely to affect the channels through which import protection arises ex ante. Blonigen and Bown (2003) use the setting of industry applications for US antidumping to illustrate how the presence of this tailor-made—that is, product-specific and trading partner–specific—instrument presents opportunities for import protection to be funneled toward certain countries and/or industries that lack the capacity to retaliate. Similarly, Bown (2004) provides cross-country evidence that the incentives inherent in the multilateral system's formal dispute settlement procedures affected government choices of whether to implement protection through GATT-consistent instruments during 1973–1994.

Finally, the WTO's dispute settlement system is also likely to influence the instruments of import protection that member governments apply through means other than its ability to authorize retaliation.[14] Sykes (2003), for example, identifies problems stemming from Panel and Appellate Body decisions resulting from legal challenges to national use of import restrictions under the WTO's Agreement on Safeguards. Not only did these WTO rulings strike down virtually all challenged instances in which governments had applied this nontariff instrument, but the resulting jurisprudence failed to provide policy makers with useful guidance on how to actually apply a safeguard in a WTO-consistent manner.[15] In a trading system in which governments have access to relatively substitutable instruments of import protection, discouraging the use of safeguards in isolation may not lead to less protection overall. While such rulings may help explain the decline in safeguard use, they may also help explain the steady increase in use of antidumping.

New Approaches

Notwithstanding the additional questions raised by the burgeoning empirical literature on the determinants of use of different trade policy instruments over time, a number of new theoretical and methodological approaches are also worth introducing.

Ossa (2011) has provided an innovative theoretical approach that identifies an international cost-shifting effect of trade policy that is separate from the terms-of-trade externality found in Bagwell and Staiger (1999, 2002). The approach starts from a monopolistically competitive market of the "new trade theory" models, which feature shipping costs and two-way trade in similar (but differentiated) products. One important result is that a beggar-thy-neighbor motive for trade policy intervention can arise from a "firm-delocation" (or "profit-shifting") effect, as governments have incentives to attract more of the world's firms to locate locally so as to save on transport costs.

Antràs and Staiger (2012) have introduced a new approach that recognizes the global fragmentation of production, offshoring, and the increasing economic importance of trade in intermediate inputs.[16] They conclude that one change to a simple assumption maintained in most prior economic theory on trade agreements—prices being determined not from market-clearing conditions but due to bilateral bargaining between international buyers and sellers—can have profound implications. Intuitively, an international "hold-up" problem can arise when relationship-specific investments are required if contracts between buyers and sellers are incomplete. In such instances, because one party (e.g., the buyer or importer) may be able to hold up the other (e.g., the exporter) and renegotiate the terms of their deal after the exporter has made a sunk investment, the seller will not make the jointly efficient level of investment in the first place. The hold-up problem can thus result in volumes of input trade across countries under free trade that are inefficiently low, suggesting an additional, efficiency-enhancing motive for trade policy intervention.

Such approaches have the potential to affect understanding of not only why governments impose tariff protection, but also why they voluntarily sign agreements to constrain tariff protection, and thus the implications of these agreements for alternative instruments of protection.

Before concluding this section, it is also worth highlighting that one of the fundamental questions arising from the disparate empirical research on different instruments of import protection involves comparability. Any attempt to make comparisons—across countries, industries, and time—is complicated by the variety and complexity of the instruments in use. For example, how does one compare the restrictiveness of the "protection" inherent in one country, which may apply low MFN tariffs but is also a frequent user of nontariff protection, with that of a different country, which has zero nontariff protection but much higher applied MFN tariffs? One important sign of progress in this area is the effort of Kee, Nicita, and Olarreaga (2009) to more accurately aggregate and measure the many different forms of tariff and nontariff protection through application of the theory of trade restrictiveness indices (Anderson and Neary 2005).

Conclusion

This chapter has examined the evolving nature of import protection and research on the political-economic and institutional determinants of various instruments in use over time.

Nevertheless, one chapter on this topic cannot be comprehensive. Omitted areas include the relationship between import protection and pressures stemming from choice of exchange rate regime; Irwin (2012), for example, describes important link-ages between the constraints imposed on monetary policy under the gold standard and the outbreak of protectionism in the early 1930s.[17] A second omission is subsidy instruments. Bagwell and Staiger (2006), for example, provide a theory to help understand WTO rules on subsidies, identifying some of the trade-offs that arise and suggesting somewhat provocatively that the existing rules on subsidy use may be too stringent. Furthermore, this chapter has deliberately avoided many of the instruments that will arise in attempts to address the "twenty-first-century" trade agreement issues, such as state-owned enterprises, foreign direct investment, intellectual property rights protection, labor and environmental standards, technical and health standards, and achieving other forms of "regulatory coherence."

To conclude, it is worth reconsidering Baldwin's original analogy—that applied tariff reductions are like draining a swamp—in light of this chapter's highlighted body of research. Draining the swamp has more than simply revealed the existence of the "snags and stumps" of nontariff protection. Some of the major instruments of nontariff protection to arise were not even present at the initial draining of some national swamps. Perhaps the GATT/WTO institutional framework helped the seedlings for such instruments blow in from somewhere and take root in new locations. Perhaps the newfound exposure to sunshine, alongside the inevitable rain that followed, also triggered the growth of the new, and still-adapting, forms of nontariff protection. However, it is also possible that draining the tariff swamp may have begun to reveal fundamental limits to feasible international cooperation over import protection. A still open question is whether a multilateral system with fully enforceable, time-invariant, free trade would be possible or even desirable in the long run.

For what outsiders may deride as a swamp, earth scientists refer to more fondly as a wetland. And what the process of swamp draining has also revealed, once its broader contributions to areas such as flood control and biological diversity have come to be accounted for and appreciated, is that such wetlands may play unexpectedly critical roles in sustaining a larger ecosystem than had been previously understood.

DATA SOURCES

Only relatively recently have panel data for product-level trade policy instruments for many countries become publicly and freely available and widespread enough for a wide group of political-economic researchers to access.

Important sources for product-level applied and bound tariff data across countries include the WTO's Integrated Database and Consolidated Tariff Schedule; these are available from both the WTO Web site and through the World Bank's free, online World Integrated Trade Solutions (WITS) software platform. Preferential tariff data compiled by UNCTAD (TRAINS) have also been made available through WITS.

Antidumping, countervailing duty, and safeguards policy use data across countries have been freely and publicly available in electronic format since 2005 through the World Bank's *Temporary Trade Barriers Database* (Bown 2012) and *Global Antidumping Database*.

With respect to other, more difficult to measure, nontariff instruments of import protection, other useful sources for data construction include the information collected by the Global Trade Alert, WTO's Trade Policy Reviews, and the WTO Committees on Technical Barriers to Trade (TBT), as well as Sanitary and Phytosanitary (SPS) measures.

ACKNOWLEDGMENTS

Thanks to Petros Mavroidis, Baybars Karacaovali, and Patricia Tovar for helpful comments on an earlier draft. Aksel Erbahar and Carys Golesworthy provided outstanding research assistance. Any opinions expressed in this paper are the author's and should not be attributed to the World Bank. All errors are my own.

NOTES

1. Important treatments of the evolution of the trading system under the GATT and WTO include Hoekman and Kostecki (2009) and Barton, Goldstein, Josling, and Steinberg (2006). Furthermore, Dam (1970), Hudec (1990), and Jackson (1997) are seminal and accessible studies from the perspective of international law. Gowa (1994) provides a comparison of postwar trade developments under the GATT to political-military trends under NATO. See also Gowa (this volume).

2. The GATT's Article XXVIII also allows contracting parties to renegotiate their MFN tariff commitments so long as they compensate adversely affected trading partners. Antidumping requires evidence of injury to domestic competitors of a like product caused by dumped (low-priced) imports. Countervailing duties require evidence of injury caused by subsidized imports. Safeguards require evidence of injury caused by an unexpected surge in imports. Mavroidis, Messerlin, and Wauters (2008) provide a legal-economic introduction to these import protection instruments.

3. There are other important GATT exceptions to Article I that allow for discriminatory treatment. A GATT waiver initially permitted contracting parties to offer tariff preferences to developing countries before this was formalized in 1979 by the "Enabling Clause." Governments can also apply antidumping and countervailing duties on a discriminatory basis.

4. Baldwin (1970, 30–46) also highlights the frequency with which quotas were used during this period in areas unrelated to Japan's GATT entry. While many of the quotas that had been imposed as Article XII (balance of payments) exceptions after World War II were phased out by the mid-1960s, industrial economy quotas continued to affect coal, petroleum, and agricultural products. Furthermore, Baldwin finds that forty industries were covered by quota bills introduced in the US Congress in the fall of 1968 alone.

5. The 1995 WTO Agreement on Safeguards prohibits VERs as the outcome of investigations. Paradoxically, the WTO's Agreement on Antidumping *encourages* investigations being resolved by exporters voluntarily agreeing to "price undertakings." VERs have thus not completely disappeared: in 2005 the EU, the United States, and China negotiated VERs to address China's export surge around the timing of the expiration of the MFA, and in 2013 VERs were considered as a potential solution to address China's large exports of solar panels.

6. Mansfield and Milner (1999) provide a more comprehensive review of the regionalism phenomenon; Hoekman and Ozden (2007) survey the literature on foreign preference regimes facing exporters in developing countries.

7. There are numerous "second-best" motives for import protection to improve economic well-being when more appropriate domestic policy instruments are unavailable. See the seminal work of Bhagwati and Ramaswami (1963).

8. Ad valorem tariffs are frequently preferred to specific tariffs because the restrictiveness of the latter depends also on price levels. For the specific duties found in the US Smoot-Hawley tariffs, for example, Irwin (1998b) shows how the deflation of the early 1930s increased their trade restrictiveness, while Irwin (1998a) attributes more of the 1940s trade liberalization to the period's import price inflation than to trade policy negotiations.

9. Rosendorff and Milner (2001) provide a related approach that extrapolates from a number of the economic market issues and predictions highlighted in Bagwell and Staiger (1990).

10. Maggi and Rodríguez-Clare (2007) construct a "large" country version of the model to illustrate how the key commitment insights are affected by governments that also have terms-of-trade motivations. Staiger and Tabellini (1987) present a related modeling approach for a small country that is concerned with the time inconsistency problem of trade policy announcements in the presence of discretionary policy.

11. Much of the research described here was also informed by Trefler's (1993) critique of the existing state of the empirical literature on the political-economic determinants of import protection. Trefler identified the importance of this endogeneity for *empirical* estimates of the formation of trade policy; his application to US data in 1983 argued that treating trade policy as exogenous underestimated its *actual* impact on trade flows by a factor of ten.

12. One fundamental economic efficiency concern arising from preferential tariffs is the trade diversion identified initially by Viner (1950). For excellent surveys of the theoretical literature on the incentives that can arise under preferential versus multilateral liberalization, see Freund and Ornelas (2010) and Panagariya (2000).

13. A related question is the extent to which multilateral liberalization affects subsequent efforts at preferential liberalization. On the one hand, when focusing on tariffs alone, full multilateral liberalization over tariffs would obviate the need for additional (redundant) preferential tariff reductions. Mansfield and Reinhardt (2003) argue that impediments to further multilateral liberalization may push members to pursue PTAs instead.

14. Surveys of the empirical literature on GATT/WTO dispute settlement include Busch and Reinhardt (2002), Busch and Pelc (this volume), and Bown (2009, ch. 4); the latter includes a discussion of the potential for GATT/WTO disputes to affect the endogenous formation of trade policy and thus choice of instruments of import protection.

15. Goldstein and Martin (2000) offer other examples of ways through which the increased legalization of the WTO system may have unintended consequences for domestic political economy forces and trade liberalization.

16. In their extensive work studying value-added trade, Johnson and Noguera (2012), for example, find that intermediate inputs may account for as much as two-thirds of international trade.

17. See also Copelovitch and Pevehouse (this volume).

References

Anderson, J., and P. Neary. 2005. *Measuring the Restrictiveness of Trade Policy*. Cambridge, MA: MIT Press.

Antràs, P., and R. W. Staiger. 2012. Offshoring and the Role of Trade Agreements. *American Economic Review* 102: 3140–3183.

Bagwell, K., and R. W. Staiger. 1990. A Theory of Managed Trade. *American Economic Review* 80: 779–795.

Bagwell, K., and R. W. Staiger. 1999. An Economic Theory of GATT. *American Economic Review* 89: 215–248.

Bagwell, K., and R. W. Staiger. 2002. *The Economics of the World Trading System*. Cambridge, MA: MIT Press.

Bagwell, K., and R. W. Staiger. 2006. Will International Rules on Subsidies Disrupt the World Trading System? *American Economic Review* 96: 877–895.

Bagwell, K., and R. W. Staiger. 2011. What Do Trade Negotiators Negotiate About? Empirical Evidence from the World Trade Organization. *American Economic Review* 101: 1238–1273.

Baldwin, R. E. 1970. *Nontariff Distortions of International Trade*. Washington, DC: Brookings Institution Press.

Barton, J. H., J. L. Goldstein, T. E. Josling, and R. H. Steinberg. 2006. *The Evolution of the Trade Regime: Politics, Law, and Economics of the GATT and the WTO*. Princeton, NJ: Princeton University Press.

Bhagwati, J. 1991. *The World Trading System at Risk*. Princeton, NJ: Princeton University Press.

Bhagwati, J., and V. K. Ramaswami. 1963. Domestic Distortions, Tariffs, and the Theory of Optimum Subsidy. *Journal of Political Economy* 71: 44–50.

Blonigen, B. A., and C. P. Bown. 2003. Antidumping and Retaliation Threats. *Journal of International Economics* 60: 249–273.

Bown, C. P. 2004. Trade Disputes and the Implementation of Protection under the GATT: An Empirical Assessment. *Journal of International Economics* 62: 263–294.

Bown, C. P. 2009. *Self-Enforcing Trade: Developing Countries and WTO Dispute Settlement*. Washington, DC: Brookings Institution Press.

Bown, C. P. 2011. Taking Stock of Antidumping, Safeguards and Countervailing Duties, 1990-2009. *The World Economy* 34: 1955–1998.

Bown, C. P. 2012. *Temporary Trade Barriers Database*. The World Bank. May. http://econ.worldbank.org/ttbd/ (accessed June 15, 2013).

Bown, Chad P. 2013. Emerging Economies and the Emergence of South-South Protectionism. *Journal of World Trade* 47: 1–44.

Bown, C. P., and M. A. Crowley. 2013a. Import Protection, Business Cycles, and Exchange Rates: Evidence from the Great Recession. *Journal of International Economics* 90: 50–64.

Bown, C. P., and M. A. Crowley. 2014. Emerging Economies, Trade Policy, and Macroeconomic Shocks. *Journal of Development Economics* 111: 261–273.

Bown, C. P., and M. A. Crowley. 2013b. Self-Enforcing Trade Agreements: Evidence from Time-Varying Trade Policy. *American Economic Review* 103: 1071–1090.

Bown, C. P., and P. Tovar. 2011. Trade Liberalization, Antidumping, and Safeguards: Evidence from India's Tariff Reform. *Journal of Development Economics* 96: 115–125.

Broda, C., N. Limão, and D. E. Weinstein. 2008. Optimal Tariffs and Market Power: The Evidence. *American Economic Review* 98: 2032–2065.

Busch, M. L., and E. Reinhardt. 2002. Testing International Trade Law: Empirical Studies of GATT/WTO Dispute Settlement. In *The Political Economy of International Trade Law: Essays in Honor of Robert Hudec*, edited by D. M. Kennedy and J. D. Southwick, 457–481. Cambridge, UK: Cambridge University Press.

Copeland, B. R. 1990. Strategic Interaction Among Nations: Negotiable and Non-Negotiable Trade Barriers. *Canadian Journal of Economics* 23: 84–108.

Dam, K. W. 1970. *The GATT: Law and International Organization*. Chicago: University of Chicago Press.

Estevadeordal, A., C. Freund, and E. Ornelas. 2008. Does Regionalism Affect Trade Liberalization toward Non-Members? *Quarterly Journal of Economics* 123: 1531–1575.

Freund, C., and E. Ornelas. 2010. Regional Trade Agreements. *Annual Review of Economics* 2: 139–166.

GATT. 1947. *The Text of the General Agreement on Tariffs and Trade.*

Gawande, K., and U. Bandyopadhyay. 2000. Is Protection for Sale? Evidence on the Grossman-Helpman Theory of Endogenous Protection. *Review of Economics and Statistics* 82: 139–152.

Goldberg, P. K., and G. Maggi. 1999. Protection for Sale: An Empirical Investigation. *American Economic Review* 89: 1135–1155.

Goldstein, J., and L. L. Martin. 2000. Legalization, Trade Liberalization, and Domestic Politics: A Cautionary Note. *International Organization* 54: 603–632.

Gowa, J. 1994. *Allies, Adversaries, and International Trade*. Princeton, NJ: Princeton University Press.

Grossman, G. M., and E. Helpman. 1994. Protection for Sale. *American Economic Review* 84: 833–850.

Hoekman, B. M., and M. M. Kostecki. 2009. *The Political Economy of the World Trading System: The WTO and Beyond*. 3rd ed. New York: Oxford University Press.

Hoekman, B. M., and C. Ozden. 2007. Introduction to *Trade Preferences and Differential Treatment of Developing Countries*, edited by B. M. Hoekman and C. Ozden, xi–xlii. Cheltenham, UK: Edward Elgar.

Hudec, R. E. 1990. *The GATT Legal System and World Trade Diplomacy*. Salem, NH: Butterworth Legal Publishers.

Irwin, D. A. 1998a. Changes in U.S. Tariffs: The Role of Import Prices and Commercial Policies. *American Economic Review* 88: 1015–1026.

Irwin, D. A. 1998b. The Smoot-Hawley Tariff: A Quantitative Assessment. *The Review of Economics and Statistics* 80: 326–334.

Irwin, D. A. 2011. *Peddling Protectionism: Smoot-Hawley and the Great Depression*. Princeton, NJ: Princeton University Press.

Irwin, D. A. 2012. *Trade Policy Disaster: Lessons from the 1930s*. Cambridge, MA: MIT Press.

Irwin, D. A., P. C. Mavroidis, and A. O. Sykes. 2008. *The Genesis of the GATT*. Cambridge, MA: Cambridge University Press.

Jackson, J. H. 1997. *The World Trading System: Law and Policy of International Economic Relations*. 2nd ed. Cambridge, MA: MIT Press.

Johnson, H. G. 1953–1954. Optimum Tariffs and Retaliation. *Review of Economic Studies* 21: 142–153.

Johnson, R. C., and G. Noguera. 2012. Accounting for Intermediates: Production Sharing and Trade in Value Added. *Journal of International Economics* 86: 224–236.

Karacaovali, B., and N. Limão. 2008. The Clash of Liberalizations: Preferential vs. Multilateral Trade Liberalization in the European Union. *Journal of International Economics* 74: 299–327.

Kee, H. L., A. Nicita, and M. Olarreaga. 2009. Estimating Trade Restrictiveness Indices. *Economic Journal* 119: 172–199.

Krueger, A. 1974. The Political Economy of the Rent-Seeking Society. *American Economic Review* 64: 291–303.

Limão, N. 2006. Preferential Trade Agreements as Stumbling Blocks for Multilateral Trade Liberalization: Evidence for the U.S. *American Economic Review* 96: 896–914.

Limão, N. 2007. Are Preferential Trade Agreements with Non-trade Objectives a Stumbling Block for Multilateral Liberalization? *Review of Economic Studies* 74: 821–855.

Limão, N., and P. Tovar. 2011. Policy Choice: Theory and Evidence from Commitment via International Trade Agreements. *Journal of International Economics* 85: 186–205.

Ludema, R., and A. M. Mayda. 2013. Do Terms-of-Trade Effects Matter for Trade Agreements? Theory and Evidence from WTO Countries. *Quarterly Journal of Economics* 128: 1837–1893.

Maggi, G., and A. Rodríguez-Clare. 1998. The Value of Trade Agreements in the Presence of Political Pressures. *Journal of Political Economy* 106: 574–601.

Maggi, G., and A. Rodríguez-Clare. 2007. A Political-Economy Theory of Trade Agreements. *American Economic Review* 97: 1374–1406.

Mansfield, E. D., and H. V. Milner. 1999. The New Wave of Regionalism. *International Organization* 53: 589–627.

Mansfield, E. D., and E. Reinhardt. 2003. Multilateral Determinants of Regionalism: The Effects of GATT/WTO on the Formation of Preferential Trading Arrangements. *International Organization* 57: 829–862.

Mavroidis, P. C., P. A. Messerlin, and J. M. Wauters. 2008. *The Law and Economics of Contingent Protection in the WTO*. Cheltenham, UK: Edward Elgar.

Ossa, R. 2011. A "New Trade" Theory of GATT/WTO Negotiations. *Journal of Political Economy* 119: 122–152.

Panagariya, A. 2000. Preferential Trade Liberalization: The Traditional Theory and New Developments. *Journal of Economic Literature* 38: 287–331.

Rosendorff, B. P., and H. V. Milner. 2001. The Optimal Design of International Trade Institutions: Uncertainty and Escape. *International Organization* 55: 829–857.

Staiger, R. W., and G. Tabellini. 1987. Discretionary Trade Policy and Excessive Protection. *American Economic Review* 77: 823–837.

Sykes, A. O. 2003. The Safeguards Mess: A Critique of WTO Jurisprudence. *World Trade Review* 2: 261–295.

Trefler, D. 1993. Trade Liberalization and the Theory of Endogenous Protection: An Econometric Study of U.S. Import Policy. *Journal of Political Economy* 101: 138–160.

Viner, J. 1950. *The Customs Union Issue*. New York: Carnegie Endowment for International Peace.

World Trade Organization (WTO). 2011. *World Tariff Profiles 2011*. Geneva: WTO, ITC, and UNCTAD.

CHAPTER 5

....

METHODOLOGICAL ISSUES

....

RAYMOND HICKS

POLITICAL science has long lagged behind economics in the methods used to analyze trade, usually following innovations or advances made a few years earlier. The focus of research also differs between the two disciplines. While economists examine why countries trade, the welfare effects of trade, and the effect of institutions on trade, political scientists generally focus on the political aspects, especially the effects of institutions. By their nature, trade institutions such as the General Agreement on Tariffs and Trade (GATT)/World Trade Organization (WTO) or preferential trade agreements (PTAs) are political. Political factors such as democracy and veto players influence selection into and ratification of PTAs as well as the choice of members (Gray 2013; Mansfield, Milner, and Rosendorff 2002; Mansfield, Milner, and Pevehouse 2007, 2008; Mansfield and Milner 2012).

Whether these institutions have an independent effect on trade arouses heated debates among observers. In part, the lack of consensus results from the use of different methods to analyze the questions. As the methods used to examine trade advance, the estimated effects of institutions also change. From its beginning as a cross-sectional method, the gravity model has grown from a panel method that includes dyadic and year fixed effects to a panel method that includes dyadic fixed effects and controls for multilateral resistance. As the gravity model has evolved, I argue, the questions that we can ask about the effects of institutions have also changed.

This chapter focuses on the gravity model to address several issues. First, how do the methods affect the questions we can ask? We can consider two separate questions about the GATT/WTO's effects on trade: Does the GATT/WTO increase trade among its members compared to their pre-GATT/WTO trade? Second, do countries in the GATT/WTO trade more with each other than they do with non-GATT/WTO countries? In other words, what comparison do we want to make to determine whether the GATT/WTO increases trade? Interpretation of coefficients with dyadic and year fixed effects is different than when including dyadic fixed effects and country-year fixed effects, which influences the questions we can ask with each method. Also, how do the different methods used to control for multilateral trade resistance compare to one another? A few methods have been advocated to incorporate multilateral trade resistance, but their findings have not been compared with real-world data. Finally, using the most recent methods from the economics literature, what effects has the GATT/WTO had on trade?

A brief history of the gravity model is presented in the next section. The relationship of "the bilateral barrier between [two regions] relative to average trade barriers that both regions face with all their trading partners" (Anderson and Van Wincoop 2003, 176), or the various methods economists have incorporated to control for multilateral trade resistance, are reviewed in the second section. I then review the literature on the trade effects of the GATT/WTO in the third section, focusing on differences in the methodology used. In the fourth section I estimate the effects of the GATT, controlling for multilateral trade resistance. I also discuss reasons for the differences in results. Finally, I offer some suggestions for "best practice guidelines."

Gravity Model

It is axiomatic that studies refer to the gravity model as the "workhorse" model of trade. Although it has been around for decades,[1] economists have only recently provided its microfoundations.[2] Political scientists are less concerned about its foundations and more interested in using the model to determine the effects of institutions on trade. Thus, we as a field rely on the specification that is au courant in economics.

The basic gravity model in trade is similar to the gravity model in physics: trade is a function of the size of countries, their wealth, and the distance between them. That is, just as gravity has a stronger effect on larger and closer objects, so should larger and more proximate countries trade more with one another.[3] Because the marginal propensity to import is positive, trade should increase with income. An inverse relationship exists with distance because trade costs increase across space. Mathematically,

$$T_{ij} = (Y_i * Y_j) / D_{ij} \tag{1}$$

where T_{ij} is trade between countries i and j; Y_i is the gross domestic product (GDP) of country i; Y_j is the GDP of country j; and D_{ij} is the distance between countries i and j.

To estimate the gravity model with ordinary least squares (OLS), we log both sides of (1) to derive the log-linear equation:

$$\ln(T_{ij}) = a + b_1 * \ln(Y_i) + b_2 * \ln(Y_j) - b_3 \ln(D_{ij}) + e_{ij} \tag{2}$$

where e_{ij} is an error term.

Equation (2) is the cross-sectional form of the model and lacks a time dimension. Cross-sectional models assume that trade is relatively constant from year to year—that is, the coefficients on the different variables should have similar values in each year—but this is probably not the case. Rose's cross-section results, for example, show that the GATT/WTO effect varies across time (2004, 105). Given the ease of computing capacity now, most studies use panel data that utilize changes over time and changes within the dyad. Equation (2) can be extended to panel data by adding a time subscript and including a term for year-specific factors (G_t).

$$\ln\left(T_{ij}\right) = a + b_1 * \ln\left(Y_{it}\right) + b_2 * \ln\left(Y_{jt}\right) - b_3 \ln\left(D_{ijt}\right) + b_4 * G_t + e_{ijt} \tag{3}$$

Equation (3) is the specification typically used now. If trade were dependent only on GDP and distance, then we would not have to worry about other variables. But there are a host of other dyadic and monadic factors that may influence trade, so we can think of D_{ij} as the set of dyadic factors and Y_i and Y_j as the set of monadic factors that determine trade. The dyadic factors include, for example, contiguity, distance, common language, combined area, and number of islands, variables that generally do not vary within a dyad, as well as colonial status and membership in trade institutions such as the GATT or trade agreements, which may vary over time. The monadic components include country-level factors such as GDP, population, exchange rates, and tariff and nontariff barriers that influence trade and trade costs.

The use of logged trade values has consequences for interpretation of the coefficients. Because GDP, population, and distance are also logged, their coefficients measure the percentage change in trade when they increase by 1 percent (see Goldstein, Rivers, and Tomz 2007, 47). The effect of a dummy variable is a little different. We use the formula $e^\beta - 1$ to estimate the percentage change in trade when a dichotomous variable changes from 0 to 1.

A second consequence of using the logged value of trade is that trade values of zero are dropped from the analysis, because the log of 0 is undefined. Some studies attempt to accommodate missing trade values by adding a small value to trade before logging it (e.g., $\ln(T_{ij} +1)$), which ensures that zero values are included in the analysis while not affecting actual trade values. Santos Silva and Tenreyro suggest, however, that both this procedure and ignoring zero values are likely to "lead to inconsistent estimators of the parameters of interest" (2006, 643). Instead, they advocate the use of Poisson models with nonlogged trade values, showing that it works as well as log-linear OLS.

The choice of trade flows is also important. We could examine total bilateral trade flows (imports plus exports), exports alone or imports alone, or average trade. Because imports from country A to country B should equal exports from country B to country A, using bilateral trade flows or average trade as the dependent variable involves non-directed dyads, or only one observation per dyad-pair. On the other hand, focusing on either imports or exports entails a directed-dyad approach, or two observations for each dyad-pair, T_{ij} and T_{ji}. Imports are typically viewed as more reliable than exports, because countries have an incentive to track them more closely to maximize tariff revenues; Baldwin and Taglioni, however, suggest that because exporters receive a rebate for correctly announcing exports in the European Union (EU), exports are now equally reliable (2006, 13).

In the standard gravity model, researchers attempt to directly estimate the monadic and dyadic components by including observed variables. The effect of institutions such as the GATT/WTO or PTAs is estimated with a dichotomous variable indicating the presence of the institution in the dyad-year. As Baier and Bergstrand (2007) point out, though, endogeneity is possible when estimating the effects of these institutions with a standard gravity model. The same factors that lead to greater dyadic trade may also lead them to form a trade agreement. Failing to account for this will bias the trade agreement coefficient upward. To control for selection into institutions, Baier and Bergstrand advocate the use of dyadic fixed effects, assuming that "the source of the endogeneity bias in the gravity equation is unobserved time-invariant heterogeneity" (2007, 84). That is, specific unobserved attributes both cause dyads to trade and enter into a PTA and are not accounted for by the standard dyadic variables. Including dyadic fixed effects will control for any unobservable dyadic effect as well as the observable dyadic effects represented by contiguity, distance, or colonial status. Any dyadic variable that does not change over the sample will be dropped from the model. This also means that for the trade institution variables, we need at least one year in the sample when a country was not in an institution. If both countries in a dyad are in an institution for the entire sample, their data will not be used to estimate the institution's effect. Specifically for the GATT, we need at least one year of data before 1948, or trade between founding members does not contribute to the both-in coefficient.

The number of dyads in most data sets is too large to allow the use of dummy variables for the dyadic fixed effects. For example, there are almost 17,500 dyads in the Goldstein, Rivers, and Tomz (2007) analyses that cover the years 1946 to 2003. Rather than dyadic dummy variables, we condition the fixed effects out of the data and then adjust the standard errors appropriately. The coefficient for each dyadic fixed effect is the average trade value for the dyad. We can partition out this effect by subtracting the mean dyadic value of every variable from each observation. For variables that do not change over time within the dyad, such as distance or contiguity, the mean will equal the value for each observation. The time-invariant dyadic variables will drop from the model, making it impossible to estimate how contiguity or distance affects trade. Fortunately, these variables are typically a second-order concern, especially in political science.

The coefficient on the trade institution variable in a model with dyadic fixed effects shows the change in dyadic trade when both are members compared to their trade when at least one is not.[4] This will be the *trade-creating* effect of the institution. This trade-creating effect does not rely on the use of dyadic fixed effects. Instead, it is the coefficient on the variable indicating that both dyad members are in a trade institution. Without dyadic fixed effects, the comparison is not to preinstitution trade, but to trade among the base, or excluded, group, which includes all dyads where at least one country is not a member.

At the same time, the institution may have a *trade-diverting* effect; that is, the institution may shift a member's trade away from nonmembers (Viner 1950; Ghosh and

Yamarik 2004). To measure this effect, we include a variable that takes a value of 1 if only one of the dyad members belongs to the institution. (We will call the trade-creation variable "both-in" and the trade-diversion one "one-in" for short.) With dyadic fixed effects, the one-in variable measures the change in dyadic trade when one of the countries is in an institution.[5] Trade institutions are not necessarily trade-diverting. It is possible that they have no effect on one-in trade or actually exert a positive effect on trade.[6] We want to compare the both-in and one-in coefficients to determine the relative effects of trade-creation and trade-diversion.

Since the year-specific factors (G_t) in panel data are common to all countries, most studies include year fixed effects. One benefit of the year fixed effects is that we do not need to worry about converting trade flows into constant dollars. The coefficients on the right-hand side variables will be the same if we use current or constant values for trade. Since the conversion is usually done using the US GDP deflator or US consumer price index, which is constant for all countries in a given year, it will be collinear with the year fixed effects.[7]

MULTILATERAL TRADE RESISTANCE

For a long time, aside from GDP, population, and maybe exchange rates, researchers ignored the monadic factors affecting trade. Despite the recognition that trading costs play an important role in trade, they were largely consigned to the error term. Trading costs include not just the cost of shipping goods, but also factors such as tariffs and nontariff barriers, which affect the prices at which goods trade. Largely, these costs were ignored because time-series data on tariff and nontariff barriers are sparse. In the mid-1990s, however, McCallum identified a "border puzzle" in his comparison of trade within Canadian provinces to trade between Canadian provinces and US states in 1988. He finds that "trade between two provinces is more than 20 times larger than trade between a province and a state" (1995, 616). Anderson and Van Wincoop (2003) argue that McCallum's large border effect results from the omission of what they label "multilateral trade resistance" (MTR) or the fact that "trade between two regions depends on the bilateral barrier between them relative to average trade barriers that both regions face with all their trading partners" (2003, 176). Multilateral trade resistance includes any policies at the country (or monadic) level that potentially affect trade with all partners and may "include trade policy and tariffs, exchange controls, the effective multilateral exchange rate regime, fiscal policies, financial crises and so forth" (Mathy and Meissner 2011, 13). Anderson and Van Wincoop derive MTR separately for each region in the analysis, and separate terms are estimated for both the importing region and the exporting region.[8] Because they include ten Canadian provinces, thirty US states, and the rest of the United States, they solve forty-one equations to calculate the MTR for each region. If more countries are added, the number of equations to be solved would also increase.

As Baldwin and Taglioni (2006) show, the Anderson and Van Wincoop method is suitable only for cross-sectional data. For panel data, Baldwin and Taglioni suggest including country-year fixed effects, or dummy variables for each importer-year and for each exporter-year, as an alternative solution. Just as the dyadic fixed effects control for any unobserved dyadic factors, the importer-year and exporter-year fixed effects account for any unobserved monadic factors that may influence trade in a year.

As a formula, we incorporate MTR as

$$\ln\left(T_{ij}\right) = a + b_1 * \ln\left(Y_{it}\right) + b_2 * \ln\left(Y_{jt}\right) - b_3 \ln\left(D_{ijt}\right) + b_4 * \ln\left(G_t\right)$$
$$+ b_5 * \ln\left(\Omega_{jt}\right) + b_6 * \ln\left(P_{it}\right) + e_{ijt} \tag{4}$$

where Ω_j is the "market potential" of the exporter (Baldwin and Taglioni 2006, 4) and P_i is the price of trading with the exporter.

The alternative methods discussed below are easier to understand if we regroup the MTR elements thus:

$$\ln\left(D_{ijt}\right) - \ln\left(P_{it}\right) - \ln\left(\Omega_{jt}\right) + \ln\left(G_t\right) \tag{5}$$

Because both P_{it} and Ω_{jt} are constants within a country-year, we can estimate them with country-year fixed effects, as Baldwin and Taglioni (2006) argue, but this causes G_t to drop.[9]

There are benefits and limitations to including country-year dummies. Because we are controlling for unobserved monadic factors that influence trade, we get better estimates of the effects of trade institutions.[10] Because many models limit the monadic variables to GDP, the effects of other monadic variables, such as tariff and nontariff barriers and shipping costs, are consigned to the error term. If countries that join the GATT or PTAs have lower trading costs, then the institution's effects will be overestimated, even relative to one-in trade. Because the country-year fixed effects control for all these unobservable monadic factors, we can derive more accurate estimates of the effects of institutions, obviating the need to collect tariff and nontariff barrier data.

A second benefit is that the sample of countries is less restricted than is the case with only dyadic and year fixed effects; specifically, we can use observations that lack GDP data. Because tariffs were an important source of government revenue for many countries before World War II, detailed sources of bilateral trade are available for the interwar period and earlier. Gross domestic product, on the other hand, was not calculated before World War II, and pre-1939 estimates of GDP are based on estimated growth rates, limiting country coverage. Country-year fixed effects allow us to bypass these and other limitations and use all of the available trade data.

On the other hand, the questions we can ask about trade differ because the variables we can include are limited and the coefficients are interpreted differently. When country-year fixed effects are included, we cannot include control variables such as GDP, population, or exchange rate variability (Magee 2008). The model controls for these variables and other unobserved monadic level factors. If a dummy variable approach is used, the coefficients for these variables may be estimated, but the coefficient will be for an excluded country-year dummy variable rather than the GDP or population effect. This point cannot be stressed enough. Depending on which time-varying country effects are dropped from the model, the coefficient on GDP may fluctuate widely and should not be interpreted.

Similarly, we cannot simultaneously include variables for both-in and one-in for an institution, as together they will be collinear with the country-year fixed effects. The coefficients in a model with country-year and dyadic fixed effects show the change in trade when both countries are in the institution compared to the change in trade when only one country in the dyad is in the institution. (If both countries are in an institution, then it cannot be the case that neither is an institution for the year.) The one-in effect is picked up by the country-year coefficients; the coefficients on the both-in institutions are picking up the change in trade relative to this excluded group.

We cannot tell if an institution is trade-creating or trade-diverting, and we cannot determine whether the institution led to an increase in trade compared to preinstitution trade; because the trade institution coefficient shows the change in trade relative to one-in trade, it could be positive for two reasons. First, one-in and both-in trade could both increase, but both-in trade by more than one-in trade. Alternatively, both could decrease, but both-in trade by less than one-in trade. In either case, both-in trade increases relative to one-in trade, and its coefficient will be positive with country-year and dyadic fixed effects. This shows the importance of knowing which questions we are asking. It would be incorrect to interpret the coefficient on trade institutions as showing that it increased trade compared to preinstitution trade.

The biggest limitation with the dummy variable approach to country-year fixed effects is that the number of variables needed to account for the country-year fixed effects grows quickly as the number of trading partners and years in the data increases and may exceed the computing power of many statistical packages. Stata, for example, allows a maximum of 11,000 variables on the right-hand side. With 60 years of trade data and an average of about 150 importers and 150 exporters per year, the variable limit is quickly reached. While we can condition out or absorb the dyadic fixed effects, we may have to account for the importer-year and exporter-year fixed effects with dummy variables. With large data sets, this just may not be possible.

The study of interwar trade by Gowa and Hicks (2013) is one of the few political science papers that empirically controls for country-year effects using dummy variables. Because their sample covers only about sixty countries over twenty years, the number of importer-year and exporter-year fixed effects is manageable. They find that the currency and trade blocs had little effect on trade. Insofar as any of the blocs did affect trade, they decreased trade relative to trade with nonbloc members. The only exceptions were the trade blocs centered around the United Kingdom and Germany, which did see an increase in hub-spoke trade relative to their trade with other countries.

Alternative Methods

For other studies, especially those examining trade after World War II, the number of dummy variables needed to account for importer-year and exporter-year fixed effects is too large to include. In order to resolve the computing issues, economists have advocated a number of alternative methods to approximate multilateral trade resistance. I discuss a few of these methods here.

Tetrad approach Head, Mayer, and Ries (2010) utilize the "tetrad" approach, which involves eliminating the monadic effects through the ratio of each variable with a common importer (k) and exporter (l).[11] Essentially, we take the value of a variable between country 1 and country 2 (D_{ijt}) relative to country 1's value with the common importer (P_{ikt}) and then take the ratio of that quantity with country 2's value with a common exporter (Ω_{jlt}) relative to the value between the common importer and exporter (G_{klt}).[12] The values of P_{ikt} and Ω_{jlt} are constant within importer-year and exporter-years and G_{klt} constant within a year. After transforming the variables, the dyadic values are demeaned to remove the dyadic fixed effects. Finally, the standard errors are corrected to account for the clustered nature.

The coefficients should then be similar as when including country-year and dyadic fixed effects. So rather than including dummy variables for the time-varying country fixed effects, we remove their effect. As with the inclusion of country-year dummy variables, variables such as GDP and GDP per capita should not be included in the model. The major shortcoming with the tetrad approach, as Head, Mayer, and Ries admit, is that the results will depend on the reference importer and exporter chosen (2010, 3). Specifically, if a country does not trade with either reference country in a year, the ratio of ratios cannot be constructed, and the observations for that country-year will be dropped.

Bonus vetus Unlike the tetrad method, Baier and Bergstrand (2009, 2010) estimate MTR terms for each variable. As discussed above, MTR is based on the bilateral costs of trade ($\Omega_{jt}-P_{it}$) compared to the average costs that each faces with all trading partners (G_t; Anderson and Van Wincoop 2003). Baier and Bergstrand discuss both an unweighted method (2010) and a weighted method (2009) to estimate MTR. The unweighted method adds in MTR as the average of the importer costs and the average of the exporter costs minus the world costs for each variable.[13] The weighted method weights the value by the partner country's share of world income and then sums the weighted values by country. Again, the average for the world, this time weighted, is subtracted from each observation.

In both the weighted and unweighted versions, the logged trade value is normalized by subtracting the logged GDP for both the importer and the exporter. After these transformations, standard OLS can be used on the new variables. Thus, Baier and Bergstrand are able to control for MTR rather than adding in dummy variables for each country or country-year. In their two articles, Baier and Bergstrand examine cross-sectional data. In the comparison below, I add a year component to the transformations to account for the panel structure of the data.[14]

Reg3hdfe The most promising innovation is a user-written Stata command called *reg3hdfe*, which stands for regression with three high dimension fixed effects (Guimaraes 2010; Carneiro, Guimaraes, and Portugal 2012).[15] Similar to the tetrad approach, the command conditions out three levels of fixed effects instead of including dummy variables. Rather than calculating a coefficient for each of the separate fixed effects, we calculate a new variable for each set of fixed effects.

The estimation process involves iterating over regressions, changing the values of the fixed effects observations after each iteration, until no further improvement in model fit can be made. The first step involves running a normal OLS with the values of the fixed effects set to 0. The residuals for the model are computed. Each fixed effect is then calculated as the mean of the residual plus the fixed effect coefficient multiplied by the value of the fixed effect. These values are then included in the next iteration of the regression. Iterations continue until the difference between the residual sum of squares in the new and previous model is below a certain threshold or tolerance. At that point, the coefficient on the fixed effects variable will be equal to 1. The *value* of each fixed effects observation will be equal to the coefficient on the fixed effects if each had been entered as a dummy variable.[16]

With two fixed effects, we would solve a system of three equations in a similar manner. Because the system of equations becomes more computationally intensive as the number of fixed effects increases, we can condition out one of the fixed effects by demeaning the data first. We again iterate over estimations until the desired tolerance is reached.

A comparison of the results of Gowa and Hicks (2013) that include dyadic fixed effects and dummy variables for the county-year fixed effects to their results using the reg3hdfe method shows the benefit of the method. As shown in Table 5.1, the coefficients are the same to the fourth or fifth decimal place. More important, there is a vast improvement in the computation time, as shown in the last row of the table. The dummy variable approach took almost seven minutes to run (409 seconds), while reg3hdfe took just under a minute and a half (84 seconds) with the tolerance set to .001. The coefficients for a couple of the variables differ very slightly at the fourth decimal place. As shown in model 3, the similarity of the coefficients can be improved by decreasing the tolerance level, though at the cost of increased computational time.[17]

Moreover, because the reg3hdfe command does not fall victim to the variable limitation that has plagued the application of multilateral trade resistance to the post–World War II analysis of trade, we can use the method as a baseline with which to compare dyadic and year fixed effects models and the alternative methods.[18] First, though, I briefly discuss the data used for the comparison of methods.

Table 5.1 Comparison of Methods: Interwar Period

	(1) Dummy Variable b/se	(2) Reg3hdfe Tolerance = .001 b/se	(3) Reg3hdfe Tolerance = .0001 b/se
Gold bloc	0.03979	0.03988	0.03976
	(0.09191)	(0.09193)	(0.09191)
IPS	−0.03758	−0.03759	−0.03760
	(0.24971)	(0.24973)	(0.24969)
Reichsmark bloc	−0.31964	−0.31969	−0.31963
	(0.19908)	(0.19900)	(0.19909)
Exchange controls	−0.72973***	−0.72967***	−0.72972***
	(0.12707)	(0.12705)	(0.12706)
Sterling	−0.10207	−0.10211	−0.10208
	(0.09925)	(0.09923)	(0.09924)
Alliance	−0.17840**	−0.17841**	−0.17840**
	(0.06968)	(0.06966)	(0.06967)
Joint democracy	0.15609*	0.15609*	0.15609*
	(0.08108)	(0.08108)	(0.08108)
N	35199	35199	35199
Time to run	411.437	83.820	122.211

Note: Model 1 uses Stata's areg with dyadic fixed effects absorbed and dummy variables for importer-year and exporter-years. Models 2 and 3 use reg3hdfe with dyadic, importer-year, and exporter-year fixed effects.

TRADE AND THE GATT

Only relatively recently have scholars examined whether the GATT/WTO increases trade among its members, finding different effects of the GATT.[19] These discrepancies are due partly to the different methods employed. Most of Rose's specifications include only year fixed effects with standard gravity model controls for both dyadic and monadic factors. Other authors use both year and dyadic fixed effects. All of them ignore the unobservable monadic components of trade, assuming that GDP and population will be sufficient to capture them.

Another limitation of the existing studies is that they focus only on whether both-in trade increased compared to its pre-GATT trade. That is, they do not examine whether a GATT member's trade with other GATT members increased more than its trade with non-GATT members. While Rose (2004) and Goldstein, Rivers, and Tomz (2007) both include a one-in GATT variable in their articles, neither compares its effect to the effect when both dyad members participate in the GATT. There is no attempt to measure the relative trade-creation and trade-diversion effects. Since the both-in and one-in GATT coefficients are both positive, this will reduce the GATT's overall effect.

Data To compare the estimation techniques, I use data from Goldstein, Rivers, and Tomz (2007). They have the most comprehensive list of GATT/WTO members, having gone back to the GATT archives to code formal members and nonmember participants. Their models include dichotomous variables indicating whether both countries are GATT members and whether only one participates, as well as dichotomous variables for the presence of a reciprocal PTA, a nonreciprocal PTA, and a currency union. There are also variables indicating whether the generalized system of preferences (GSP) exists in the dyad and whether the countries are in the same colonial orbit—that is, whether both countries are existing colonies of the same metropole or the dyad includes the metropole and a colony. Finally, they include the logged product of GDP of the countries in the dyad. The dependent variable is the log of imports in 1967 US dollars.

With dyadic fixed effects, we need at least one year in each dyad where one of the dichotomous variables, such as GATT participation, is equal to 0. To accommodate this, Goldstein, Rivers, and Tomz collected trade for 1946 and 1947 to supplement the IMF data, which begin in 1948, the same year the GATT began. While the extra data are sufficient to estimate a GATT effect, it is questionable how robust the estimate is, as I discuss below.

Comparison of Methods

Table 5.2 shows the results of the different analyses. Model 1 replicates the model using dyadic and year fixed effects from Table 2 of Goldstein, Rivers, and Tomz (2007). The coefficient of 0.35 for GATT participation represents an increase in dyadic trade of about 42 percent. This probably overestimates the impact of the GATT. Trade between one GATT country and one non-GATT country also increased by 24 percent during this period. The difference between the two coefficients is still highly significant, so the GATT still had a significant impact on trade, but the effect is smaller than as reported by Goldstein, Rivers, and Tomz (~18 percent).

Model 2 shows the results of including importer-year and exporter-year fixed effects with dyadic fixed effects (using reg3hdfe). Because of collinearity issues, the GATT one-in variable cannot be included in the regression; neither can the GDP variable. Any year-to-year factors that impact all partner countries equally will be picked up by the country-year fixed effects. The coefficient on the GATT both-in variable picks up change in trade in the year relative to the base group of trade; that is, relative to its change in trade with a non-GATT country. There is a much smaller, though still significant, effect of GATT membership. Compared to a GATT member's trade with non-GATT

Table 5.2 Comparison of Methods: Post–World War II

	(1) Dyad + Year b/se	(2) Country-year + Dyad b/se	(3) Tetrad: US–UK b/se	(4) Tetrad: US–Japan b/se	(5) Country + Year b/se	(6) Bonus Vetus (unwt) b/se	(7) Bonus Vetus (wt) b/se
GATT: Both-in	0.354*** (0.034)	0.064** (0.033)	0.177*** (0.055)	0.064 (0.062)	0.383*** (0.042)	0.150*** (0.055)	0.424*** (0.051)
GATT: One-in	0.200*** (0.029)						
Reciprocal PTA	0.343*** (0.022)	0.290*** (0.022)	0.500*** (0.029)	0.370*** (0.034)	0.301*** (0.027)	0.238*** (0.035)	0.250*** (0.031)
Nonreciprocal PTA	-0.053* (0.032)	0.113*** (0.032)	0.146*** (0.035)	0.045 (0.042)	0.087** (0.037)	0.111** (0.046)	0.275*** (0.039)
GSP	-0.099*** (0.019)	-0.122*** (0.020)	-0.072*** (0.023)	-0.096*** (0.021)	-0.104*** (0.023)	-0.184*** (0.029)	-0.402*** (0.022)
Currency union	0.492*** (0.088)	0.287*** (0.078)	0.537*** (0.065)	0.146 (0.098)	1.079*** (0.089)	1.146*** (0.099)	1.326*** (0.103)
Same colonial orbit	0.836*** (0.081)	0.631*** (0.087)	0.381*** (0.092)	1.103*** (0.125)	1.611*** (0.127)	1.612*** (0.154)	1.610*** (0.166)
GDP log product	0.661*** (0.011)						
Log of distance					-1.016*** (0.014)	-1.042*** (0.020)	-0.955*** (0.015)
N	381656	381656	346366	338073	381656	381656	381656

members, trade with other GATT members increases by about 7 percent. As Baldwin and Taglioni (2006) argue, if the unobserved monadic factors are positively correlated with greater trade, then the coefficients will overestimate the effect. Since countries that join the GATT are more likely to trade more, the unobserved monadic factors should be positively correlated with trade.

Interestingly, compared to model 1, the coefficient for nonreciprocal PTAs in model 2 switches signs. Nonreciprocal PTAs have a positive impact on trade when dyad and country-year fixed effects are included. This difference probably reflects the fact that at least one member of each nonreciprocal PTA dyad is a GATT member. There is thus complete overlap between both-in GATT, one-in GATT, and nonreciprocal PTAs. In model 1, the nonreciprocal variable is similar to an interaction, showing trade in nonreciprocal PTAs decreased compared to both-in or one-in GATT trade. But the coefficient is showing the average difference from both-in and from one-in. Goldstein, Rivers, and Tomz examine the relationship between nonreciprocal PTAs and GATT membership more closely, finding that nonreciprocal PTAs do have a positive effect in the one-in GATT dyads (2007, 60–61).

This is confirmed by the dyadic and country-year fixed effects results. Since these compare the nonreciprocal PTA coefficient to the excluded group, they show that nonreciprocal PTAs increase trade, relative to non-GATT trade. All the countries that give nonreciprocal benefits are in the GATT, but not all recipients are. For the providers of nonreciprocal benefits, the nonreciprocal PTA variable removes the beneficiaries from the base group. For the non-GATT beneficiaries, the nonreciprocal PTA coefficient shows the change in trade relative to the base group. All of this suggests that nonreciprocal PTAs do have some trade benefits, though the benefits are not as large as when both countries belong to the GATT.

There is not much change in the coefficients for the other variables—the effects of PTAs and the GSP are very similar. The coefficients on GSP suggest that not only does trade decrease when the GSP is introduced, but trade with other countries is not affected. The similarity of the coefficients on reciprocal PTAs suggests that they do increase trade within a dyad, and that there may not be that much trade-diversion going on.[20] Currency unions and colonial orbit both continue to have very strong effects on trade, though the effect weakens somewhat with the country-year fixed effects.

In models 3 and 4 I present two models using the tetrad approach. As Head, Mayer, and Ries caution, the results can change depending on the countries used as the reference categories. In model 3, the United States is used as the reference importer and the United Kingdom as the reference exporter; in model 4, the United States is again used as the reference importer and Japan as the reference exporter.

The first thing to notice is that the sample size changes, both compared to models 1 and 2 and also across tetrad models. Data cannot be used in years where a country did not trade with the reference importer or the reference exporter. Thus, it is important when using the tetrad command to choose reference countries with many trading partners.

Second, changing the reference countries has a very large impact on the estimated coefficients.[21] (As with the country-year fixed effects models, we cannot include variables for both-in and one-in the GATT in the same model.) The sizes of all of the coefficients except GSP change drastically, and the coefficients in neither tetrad model are particularly close to those estimated using country-year fixed effects. In model 3 the coefficients on both-in GATT, PTAs, nonreciprocal PTAs, and currency unions are all bigger than those in model 2.

The fifth model shows results with importer-year and exporter-year fixed effects, including the log of distance as a time-invariant dyadic variable. With cross-section data, including importer and exporter fixed effects is equivalent to controlling for multilateral resistance. Adding the time element accommodates for the panel aspect of the data. There are no dyadic fixed effects in this model; instead dyad factors are accounted for with the distance variable. Again, the effect of reciprocal PTAs and the GSP is very similar to that in the other models. Nonreciprocal PTAs again have a positive coefficient. The effects of GATT both-in, currency unions, and colonial orbit are much bigger than in the other models, probably reflecting unobserved dyadic factors.

Model 6 shows the results using the unweighted *bonus vetus* method. With the exception of the GATT both-in and the GSP coefficients, the coefficients are very similar to those in model 5. While the coefficient on both-in GATT is more similar to the other models, the GSP coefficient is smaller. The effects of currency unions and colonial orbit are again larger than in the other models.

Finally, the results using Baier and Bergstrand's weighted version of MTR are different than the other results. Both-in GATT and nonreciprocal PTAs have much larger positive effects and GSPs a much larger negative effect on trade.

4.1 Discussion While there is some overlap among the different methods, the results are not as similar as in Monte Carlo simulations done by the methods' advocates or by Head and Mayer (2013), all of which show a remarkable similarity in results. One difference is that most of the simulations are done with a cross-sectional structure. Probably the more important reason is that real-world data are messy. Countries break apart and unify, so dyads will enter and leave the data set. Political systems change and alter trading patterns. Both will prevent data from having a nice rectangular structure. Indeed, Head and Mayer (2013) show that as the number of missing observations increases in simulations, the alternatives to the dummy variable approach perform more poorly. We should not be surprised, then, that they do not do so well with real-world data.

Nevertheless, the comparison of the methods is enlightening both because of the differences in coefficients and their similarities. The effects of reciprocal PTAs and the GSP do not vary much—across the methods, the coefficient on reciprocal PTAs is around 0.3, while the coefficient on GSP is around –0.10. Both of these variables have lots of preinstitution and institution observations, and neither has much of an effect on one-in trade.

The coefficients on the other variables, especially currency unions, colonial orbit, and GATT participation, vary tremendously across methods. The largest effects for currency unions and colonial orbits are in the models that do not explicitly incorporate dyadic factors, except for distance. This suggests that, as with Baier and Bergstrand's argument about PTAs, both are endogenous to trade.

Finally, why does the GATT effect vary so much? While it is significant in most of the models, only sometimes does it exert a large impact on trade. The most important reason may simply be the lack of pre-GATT data. The effect of a dichotomous variable will be more consistent when there are a larger number of control and treatment observations. For the founding members of the GATT, there are only two years of pre-GATT data available, 1946 and 1947, and the world was experiencing a lot of changes then.

One solution may be to collect trade data before 1946. While such data do exist, the years before 1946 saw, first, the Great Depression, which lasted from 1930 to about 1938, and then World War II from 1939 to 1945, both of which had their own effects on trading patterns. This will present its own set of issues. If either the Depression or World War II changed trading patterns, then adding in the extra years without accounting for the change will not improve our estimates of the GATT effect. Imagine, for example, that countries that were allies during World War II were more likely to trade with one another during the war and were more likely to be founding GATT members. Including the World War II years may attenuate the GATT effect, because average dyadic trade before the GATT is larger.

A second limitation is, as discussed above, the fact that some countries such as the United States extended their GATT tariff cuts to all countries with which they had MFN status. Non-GATT trading partners of the United States benefited from the GATT even as nonmembers. That is, in the absence of the GATT, it is doubtful that the United States would have reduced trade barriers as much as it did under the GATT. The coefficient on one-in GATT, then, will pick up some of the GATT reforms, perhaps causing us to underestimate its effects. Thus, it may be difficult to obtain a true estimate of the GATT's effects given the historical peculiarities of its formation.

CONCLUSION

Recent advances in trade theory advocate controlling for multilateral resistance. Including country-year fixed effects accomplishes this task. They also control for any unobservable monadic factor that might affect trade. There is still a dyadic component to trade, which should be accommodated for with the inclusion of dyadic fixed effects.

Ignoring multilateral trade resistance and including only dyad and year fixed effects will lead to biased estimates, because any monadic unobservable variables are omitted, but the bias will depend on the relationship between the unobserved factors and trade. If there is a positive correlation, the effects of institutions such as the GATT will be overestimated. It seems likely that countries that trade more are also more likely to join the GATT/WTO, so we would expect dyadic and year fixed effect models to overestimate the GATT effect.

Economists have devised a few methods to control for MTR. Overall, the methods do a good job when the data are cross-sectional or a rectangular panel. The more missing trade values in the data and the more that new dyads enter the data and old ones leave, the worse these methods perform in comparison to the country-year and dyadic fixed effects approach (see also Head and Mayer 2013). Because the reg3hdfe command does produce the same results as including dyadic and country-year fixed effects, there is no excuse for not running models with time-varying country factors. The drawback of country-year fixed effects is that they cannot tell us whether the GATT increased trade; they only tell us whether GATT membership increased trade relative to trade with non-GATT members.

To conclude, I offer some recommendations for using the gravity model.

Recommendations

1. *When using fixed effects, be aware of the potential for collinearity.*

This applies not just to gravity models, but to any analysis using fixed effects, especially ones that use a dummy variable approach. For example, when GDP is included in a model with dummy variables for time-varying country effects, many statistical packages will drop one of the time-varying country dummies in order to calculate a coefficient for GDP. The GDP coefficient should not be interpreted as the effect of GDP on trade. If the fixed effects are conditioned out of the data, the collinear coefficients will simply drop.

2. *Estimating the effects of institutions when using fixed effects requires a sizeable number of observations when countries are in and not in an institution.*

As discussed above, one of the reasons that the GATT coefficient varies across methods is that there are only two years of pre-GATT trade data. The coefficients on reciprocal PTAs and GSPs, for which there is much more data both before and after the institutions form, are much more consistent across methods.

3. *Use the method that most closely fits the question asked.*

While this may be obvious, the different ways to estimate gravity models do affect the questions that can be answered. Models that include dyadic and year fixed effects are most flexible. They can answer whether institutions were trade-creating and trade-diverting as well as the relative effects of trade-creation and trade-diversion. But the effects will probably be overestimated.

In contrast, models that include dyadic and country-year dummies can only answer whether trade between GATT members increased more than their trade with non-GATT members. The coefficients show the change in trade when both countries are in the institution compared to the change in trade when only one country in the dyad is in the institution. The country-year fixed effects are picking up the change in trade of the excluded category. This also means that if we were to swap the both-in variable with a one-in GATT variable, the coefficient on the one-in variable would be half the size of the both-in coefficient and of the opposite sign. If trade between two GATT members increases relative to the trade of each with a non-GATT member, then trade of the latter has to decrease relative to the former.

The best strategy, then, is to report results using dyadic and year fixed effects as well as country-year and dyadic fixed effects. We can use the dyadic and year fixed effects to determine the direction and approximate size of trade-creation and trade-diversion, and the country-year fixed effects results will give us more precise estimates of the relative effects of the two. While we may never conclusively determine the true effects of the GATT, using models with dyadic and year fixed effects and country-year and dyadic fixed effects does give us a more precise picture of trade and the effects of trade institutions.

NOTES

1. Tinbergen was one of the first to apply the gravity model to trade, in 1962.
2. In the economics literature, Anderson (2011) provides a useful overview of the foundations of the gravity model; Head and Mayer (2013) discuss the microfoundations of the gravity model, but are also interested in different methods to estimate multilateral resistance. Finally, Shepherd (2012) provides a more general discussion.
3. Distance is not only geographic distance, but also includes cultural closeness, such as colonial linkages or a common language.
4. With no other right-hand side variables in the model, the coefficient would equal the difference between the average trade under the institution and the average trade before the countries joined the institution.
5. Without dyadic fixed effects, the interpretation of the both-in coefficient changes when the one-in variable is added. It is no longer in comparison to all excluded dyads, but to dyads where neither member is in the institution.
6. This may be the case if countries in an institution apply the institution's rules to both members and nonmembers. The United States, for example, extended tariff cuts made under the GATT to all countries with which it had most-favored nation (MFN) status. Similarly, European Economic Community countries extended tariff cuts made in their move toward a customs union to the countries with which they had MFN status. As discussed more below, this complicates estimates of the GATT/WTO effect.
7. The coefficients on the year variables will obviously differ in the two models.
8. The value for MTR will be a constant for each region. Thus, we can include fixed effects for each region as importer and for each region as exporter to approximate MTR, as Anderson and Van Wincoop admit (2003, 180). Indeed, many cross-section analyses of trade have done this.
9. Note that if we include country-year and dyadic fixed effects, Y_{it}, Y_{jt}, D_{ijt}, and G_t will all drop from the model. We can still estimate the effect of variables that are not constant within a country-year, such as trade institutions (or democracy and alliances).

10. Because trade costs vary over time, it is not sufficient to include time-invariant dummy variables for importers and exporters. They will also be collinear with the dyadic fixed effects and will drop out of the model.

11. There is a Stata version of the tetrad command available on Keith Head's web page: http://strategy.sauder.ubc.ca/head/sup/.

12. Head, Mayer, and Ries (2010) use exports as the dependent variable. Country 1 would be the exporter and country 2 the importer in their setup.

13. Recall that $\ln(A/B)$ is equal to $\ln(A)-\ln(B)$. Thus, $\ln((\Omega_j*P_i)/G)$ is equal to $\ln(\Omega_j)+\ln(P_i)-\ln(G)$. Since we are removing this effect from each variable, we get $(-\ln(\Omega_j)-\ln(P_i)+\ln(G))$.

14. Baier and Bergstrand suggest that "[i]ncluding GDP-share-weighted multilateral trade costs could create an endogeneity bias" and prefer the unweighted trade costs (2010, 104).

15. The command is available at http://www.aeaweb.org/articles.php?doi=10.1257/mac.4.2.133.

16. Technically, the value is equal to the difference between the dummy variable coefficient and the constant term.

17. The default tolerance level is much smaller (1.192e-07), and it takes more iterations for the transformation of each variable to converge. The model in Table 5.1 took about five minutes to run (297 seconds) at the default tolerance, still faster than the dummy variable approach.

18. Head and Mayer (2013) do a similar comparison of techniques, with two notable exceptions. First, they run a Monte Carlo simulation, based on a value of 1 for distance and 0.5 for reciprocal PTAs. Second, they use a cross-section approach. In contrast, this chapter uses real-world panel data (from Goldstein, Rivers, and Tomz 2007).

19. See Gowa's chapter in this volume for a review of the studies. There are also large literatures that focus on the effects of preferential trade agreements on trade (Rose 2004; Baier and Bergstrand 2007; Goldstein, Rivers, and Tomz 2007; Magee 2008) and the formation of trade agreements (Baccini and Dür 2010; Baier and Bergstrand 2004; Baldwin and Jaimovich 2010; Egger and Larch 2008; Magee 2003; Mansfield, Milner, and Rosendorff 2002; Mansfield, Milner, and Pevehouse 2007; Mansfield and Milner 2012).

20. Indeed, if we construct a one-in PTA variable that takes on the value of 1 if either the importer or the exporter has a reciprocal PTA in the year, but not with one another, and include it in the model from Table 5.2, model 1, the coefficient is insignificant, with a value of about 0.003.

21. I ran the results for a variety of combinations and found similar variation in coefficients.

REFERENCES

Anderson, John. 2011. The Gravity Model. *Annual Review of Economics* 3: 133–160.

Anderson, James, and Eric van Wincoop. 2003. Gravity with Gravitas: A Solution to the Border Puzzle. *American Economic Review* 93(1): 170–192.

Baccini, Leonardo, and Andreas Dür. 2010. Investment Discrimination and the Proliferation of Preferential Trade Agreements. Paper Presented at the Annual Meeting of the International Political Economy Society, Cambridge, MA, November 12–13.

Baier, Scott, and Jeffrey Bergstrand. 2010. Approximating General Equilibrium Impacts of Trade Liberalizations Using the Gravity Equation. In *The Gravity Model in International Trade*, edited by Peter van Bergeijk and Steven Brakman, 88–134. Cambridge, UK: Cambridge University Press.

Baier, Scott, and Jeffrey Bergstrand. 2009. *Bonus Vetus* OLS: A Simple Method for Approximating International Trade-Cost Effects Using the Gravity Equation. *Journal of International Economics* 77 (1): 77–85.

Baier, Scott, and Jeffrey Bergstrand. 2007. Do Free Trade Agreements Actually Increase Members' International Trade? *Journal of International Economics* 71, 1: 72–95.

Baier, Scott, and Jeffrey Bergstrand. 2004. Economic Determinants of Free Trade Agreements. *Journal of International Economics* 64: 29–63.

Baldwin, Richard, and Dany Jaimovich 2010. Are Free Trade Agreements Contagious? NBER Working Paper No. 16084.

Baldwin, Richard, and Daria Taglioni. 2006. Gravity for Dummies and Dummies for Gravity Equations. NBER Working Paper No. 12516.

Carneiro, Anabela, Paulo Guimaraes, and Pedro Portugal. 2012. Real Wages and the Business Cycle: Accounting for Worker, Firm, and Job Title Heterogeneity. *American Economic Journal: Macroeconomics* 4 (2): 133–152.

Egger, Peter, and Mario Larch. 2008. Interdependent Preferential Trade Agreement Memberships: An Empirical Analysis. *Journal of International Economics* 76: 384–399.

Ghosh, Sucharita and Steven Yamarik. 2004. "Are Regional Trading Arrangements Trade Creating?: An application of extreme bounds analysis." *Journal of International Economics* 63(2): 369–395.

Goldstein, Judith, Douglas Rivers, and Michael Tomz. 2007. Institutions in International Relations: Understanding the Effects of the GATT and the WTO on World Trade. *International Organization* 61 (1): 37–67.

Gowa, Joanne, and Raymond Hicks. 2013. Politics, Institutions, and Trade: Lessons of the Interwar Era. *International Organization* 67 (3): 439–468.

Gray, Julia. 2013. The Company States Keep: International Economic Organizations and Investor Perceptions. New York: Cambridge University Press.

Guimaraes, Paulo. 2010. Estimation of High-Dimensional Models. Presentation to the Portuguese Stata Users Group, September 17, Braga, University of Minho.

Head, Keith, and Thierry Mayer. 2013. Gravity Equations: Workhorse, Toolkit, and Cookbook. Sciences Po Economics Discussion Papers No. 2013–02.

Head, Keith, Thierry Mayer, and John Ries. 2010. The Erosion of Colonial Trade Linkages after Independence. *Journal of International Economics* 81 (1): 1–14.

Magee, Christopher. 2003. Endogenous Preferential Trade Agreements. *Contributions to Economic Analysis & Policy* 2 (1): 1–17.

Magee, Christopher. 2008. New Measures of Trade Creation and Trade Diversion. *Journal of International Economics* 75: 349–362.

Mansfield, Edward, Helen Milner, and B. Peter Rosendorff. 2002. Why Democracies Cooperate More: Electoral Control and International Trade Agreements. *International Organization* 56 (3): 477–513.

Mansfield, Edward, and Helen Milner. 2012. *International Trade and Cooperation: The Domestic and International Politics of Preferential Trade Agreements*. Princeton, NJ: Princeton University Press.

Mansfield, Edward, Helen Milner, and Jon Pevehouse. 2007. Vetoing Co-operation: The Impact of Veto Players on Preferential Trade Agreements. *British Journal of Political Science* 37 (3): 403–432.

Mansfield, Edward, Helen Milner, and Jon Pevehouse 2008. "Democracy, Veto Players, and the Depth of Regional Integration." *The World Economy* 31(1): 67–96.

Mathy, Gabriel, and Christopher Meissner. 2011. Trade, Exchange Rate Regimes and Output Co-movement. NBER Working Paper No. 16925.

McCallum, John. 1995. National Borders Matter: Canada-U.S. Regional Trade Patterns. *American Economic Review* 85 (3): 615–623.

Rose, Andrew. 2004. Do We Really Know That the WTO Increases Trade? *American Economic Review* 94 (1): 98–114.

Santos Silva, J. M. C., and Silvana Tenreyro. 2006. The Log of Gravity. *Review of Economics and Statistics* 88 (4): 641–658.

Shepherd, Ben. 2012. *The Gravity Model of International Trade.* ARTNeT Gravity Modeling Initiative. Bangkok: United Nations.

Tinbergen, Jan. 1962. *Shaping the World Economy.* New York: Twentieth Century Fund.

Viner, Jacob. 1950. *The Customs Union Issue.* New York: Carnegie Endowment for International Peace.

PART II

DOMESTIC SOCIETY

CHAPTER 6

....

INDIVIDUAL ATTITUDES

....

JASON KUO AND MEGUMI NAOI

INTRODUCTION

....

STUDIES on individual attitudes toward trade have flourished over the past two decades. These studies sought to understand how ordinary citizens form positions on trade policy and how voter attitudes can influence trade-policy outcomes. This research question differs from the dominant approaches to trade policy, which have focused on the roles of political and business elites (e.g., Schattscheider 1935; Bauer, de Sola Poole, and Dexter 1963; Milner 1989; Grossman and Helpman 1994; Goodhart, this volume; Plouffe, this volume; Hatch, Bair and Heiduk this volume) and domestic political institutions in making trade policy (e.g., Lohmann and O'Halloran 1994; Gilligan 1997; Mansfield, Milner, and Rosendorff 2000; Mukherjee, this volume; Rickard, this volume; Kono, this volume; Chase, this volume).

Three factors have contributed to the emergence of individual-level studies on trade policy. First, technological advancements in survey research (such as use of the Internet, randomized experiments, and computer-assisted enumeration) have vastly reduced the costs and time required for public opinion research. Second, formal, political economy models of trade-policy making, such as endogenous trade-policy theory developed since the 1980s (Magee, Block, and Young 1989; Mayer 1994; Grossman and Helpman 1994), explicitly address how legislators weigh votes and interest group contributions. Yet the development of this research program has been lopsided; that is, formal models with little empirical understanding of how voters view and influence trade policy have accumulated. The literature on individual attitudes has sought to fill this gulf. Finally, the previous elite-level analyses have failed to address emerging empirical puzzles. Examples of such puzzles are why we see more free-trade policies when elite-level theories have predicted a prevalence of protectionism (Grossman and Helpman 1994; Gawande, Krishna, and Olarreaga 2009) and why consumers, who are assumed to be free-trading in economic studies, are often protectionist (Coughlin 2002; Naoi and Kume 2011).

This chapter argues that although these motivations have substantially advanced this research program, the research has suffered from two major issues. The first is the missing link between individual attitudes and behaviors. Because the majority of work has analyzed citizens' stated preferences via public opinion surveys, the validity of the results comes into question, since it is unclear that costlessly expressed preferences can actually inform more costly behaviors, such as citizens' voting behaviors in elections or consumption decisions.

The second is the missing link between individual attitudes and group behaviors, through collective action and aggregation via social, political, and economic institutions. While the elite-centered approach has addressed how organized groups influence trade policy through collective actions (e.g., Olson 1965), the individual attitudes literature has largely ignored the question of interest aggregation and collective action, thus leaving much to be explained. Relatedly, research linking elite behaviors and attitudes with those of citizens has rarely gone beyond correlational studies using a one-shot public opinion survey. This begs the question of whether elites mold citizens' minds or respond to and represent citizens' trade-policy preferences. The remainder of this chapter critically discusses the development of this research program, the remaining questions to be solved, and some promising lines for future research.

Economic Origins of Trade Preferences

Earlier empirical research on individual attitudes toward trade was largely aimed at solving the theoretical disagreement over whether class (i.e., factor of production à la the Stolper-Samuelson theorem) or industry of employment (i.e., exporting or importing sectors à la the Ricardo-Viner model) determines individual positions on trade.[1]

Kenneth Scheve and Mathew Slaughter (2001b) offered the first empirical test of the two competing claims using nationally representative public opinion data from the American National Electoral Study (ANES). They showed that in the United States, respondents' factor profile, which was measured by years of education, better explained the trade preferences of citizens than their industry of employment. Consistent with the Stolper-Samuelson theorem, respondents with higher levels of education were more likely to support free trade than were those with less education.

The factor-based trade theorem finds empirical support beyond the US case. Using public opinion data obtained from twenty-four countries surveyed in the 1995 International Social Survey Program (ISSP), O'Rourke and Sinnott (2001) provided one of the first proper cross-national tests of the Stolper-Samuelson theorem, by controlling for country-level factor endowment, measured by GDP per capita. They demonstrate that in advanced industrialized countries, high-skilled respondents (measured by years of education) are more likely to support free trade, but this pattern is reversed in developing economies. Mayda and Rodrik (2005) obtained similar results, using the same ISSP 1995 data as well as the 1995–1997 World Value Survey (WVS) covering forty-seven countries. These findings were consistent with the factor-based trade theorem rather than the industry-based models of trade.

Despite the fact that the original Stolper-Samuelson theorem formulates both producer and consumer benefits of free trade (Baker 2005; Helpman 2011), empirical tests of these models using public opinion surveys have been limited to a focus on job-related attributes, such as respondents' skill levels, income and sector of employment (Naoi and Kume 2015). Andy Baker (2005) shifted the focus from production profiles of respondents to consumer profiles; that is, what bundle of goods citizens consume. He relaxed the assumption that consumers consume the same bundle of goods and hypothesized that consumers of exported goods would be more likely to prefer protection to free trade, as the expansion of exports raises the price of those particular goods. On the flip side, consumers of imported goods would be more likely to support free trade, as the expansion of imports lowers the prices on these goods. The 1995–1997 WVS data covering both developed and developing countries lends support to this hypothesis, although the survey does not directly measure the consumption bundle. The question thus remains whether we can use respondents' income level as a proxy for differences in their consumption bundles, as done by Baker (2005).

These early studies also found several deviations from what trade models have predicted. For instance, Scheve and Slaughter (2001b) showed that homeowners in depressed regions were more protectionist than non-homeowners, controlling for their factor profiles and sectors of employment. The authors interpreted from the results that homeowners in regions that are adversely affected by trade are more likely to worry about declining asset prices in a region. Hence, the housing market ties the income of homeowners to that of declining industries, regardless of the homeowners' sectors of employment.

These deviations, however, do not necessarily mean that we can no longer improve our understanding of the economic origins of individual trade-policy preferences. We see several promising lines for future research. First, these early studies took factor mobility in the national economy and individual skill specificity (to the extent that individual work skills are useable in other industries) as given when testing the rival theories of international trade, despite the fact that they are two of the key conditions under which class or sectoral conflicts arise in trade (Magee, Block, and Young 1989; Hiscox 2002). National-level measures of factor mobility over time, such as wage differentials across industries discussed in Hiscox (2002), would be a useful addition to future cross-national analysis of individual attitudes. Likewise, new measures of the individual-level skill specificity, like the one calculated by Torben Iversen for several waves of ISSP data (see Cusack, Iversen, and Rehm 2006; Iversen and Soskice 2001), could be a useful addition.

Second, scholars have pitched two competing trade models as rival theories by controlling for possible covariates. This mode of causal inference, however, is based on a strong statistical assumption that one theory trumps the other for the entire set of observations analyzed. The assumption does not allow scholars to specify an empirical scope under which one theory does better than the others. To address this problem, Imai and

Tingley (2012) developed the finite mixture modeling approach, which allowed some observations to be better explained by one theory and the others by its rival. Adopting this statistical method could help improve our understanding of the empirical scope of cases in which one theory does better than the other.

Third, economic self-interest hypotheses have not been fully tested, for two reasons. The first reason is that this research program needs a better measure of respondents' economic interests in trade. The early studies, for instance, used years of respondents' education as a proxy for their skill levels (i.e., factor profile), yet education could highly correlate with other things that determine trade attitudes, such as ideology, gender, and openness to foreign culture and new products (i.e., "cosmopolitanism"). Likewise, as Melitz's (2003) model of heterogeneous firms suggests, even individuals working for the same industry can have diverging economic interests in trade. Workers in highly productive firms can support free trade, and workers in low productive firms can oppose it (see Naoi and Urata 2013).

The second reason is that while the menu of trade policy options that governments can adopt is complex in reality, the majority of survey instruments used have asked for respondents' opinions about "placing new limits on imports" or "increasing trade" (see Table 6.1). While these questions might allow scholars to solicit citizens' gut-based, general reactions to trade, these survey instruments often diverge from the day-to-day context in which citizens think about trade policy.

We note three points in particular. First, political debates surrounding trade are most often about the increase in exports from a particular country (e.g., China or the United States) or the signing of free trade agreements with particular countries. Yet only a handful of studies have examined individual attitudes toward trade with particular countries (Baldwin and Magee 2000 on North America Free Trade Agreement, NAFTA; Hicks, Miller, and Tingley 2014 on Central America Free Trade Agreement, CAFTA; Chiang, Liu, and Wen 2013 on Economic Cooperation Framework Agreement, ECFA; Naoi and Urata 2013 on Trans-Pacific Partnership Agreements, TPP).[2] Moreover, survey instruments on trade policy rarely incorporate institutional designs of international trade agreements negotiated between or among states (e.g., Koremenos, Lipson, and Snidal 2001; Johns and Peritz, this volume; Kim, this volume; Davis and Wilf, this volume; Busch and Pelc, this volume). Survey conducted by the Program on International Policy Attitudes (PIPA) showed that public support for lowering trade barriers seemed contingent upon the principle of reciprocity (see Table 6.1 or Scheve and Slaughter 2001a, 16). Exploring effects of "rational design" of international trade institutions on trade preferences is a promising line of future research.

The second point is that the majority of the remaining trade barriers today are nontariff barriers, comprising regulatory and nonregulatory differences among states. Although existing survey instrument phrasing such as "placing new limits on imports" can include nontariff barriers, asking citizens more pointed questions about raising or lowering the standards of regulation, such as the safety and quality of products, would offer much needed insight. Similarly, because liberalization of service trade is the key

Table 6.1   A Variety of Survey Instruments for Trade Policy Preferences

Data sources	Question wording	Examples of works
ANES 1992 & 1996	Do you favor or oppose placing new limits on imports, or haven't you thought much about this?'	Scheve & Slaughter (2001b); Hainmueller & Hiscox (2006)
ISSP & GSS 1995	How much do you agree or disagree with the following statement? (*respondent's country*) should limit the import of foreign products in order to protect its national economy.	O'Rourke & Sinnott (2001); Mayda & Rodrik (2005); Daniels & von der Ruhr (2005); Hainmuller & Hiscox (2006)
WVS 1995-1997	Do you think it is better if (1) Goods made in other countries can be imported and sold here if people want to buy them; or that (2) There should be stricter limits on selling foreign goods here, to protect the jobs of people in this country.	Mayda & Rodrik (2005); Baker (2005); Kaltenthaler et al. (2004)
TESS 2004	Do you favor or oppose increasing trade with other nations?	Hiscox (2006)
PIPA 1999	Tell me which one you most agree with: A: The U.S. should lower barriers even if other countries do not, because . . . B: The U.S. should only lower its barriers if other countries do, because . . .	Scheve & Slaughter (2001a, 16)
Original (Japan) & CCES 2012	Do you support or oppose the Japanese (or U.S.) government's participation in the Trans-Pacific Partnership agreement?	Naoi & Urata (2013)

agenda of trade negotiations today, soliciting citizens' attitudes toward service trade liberalization would be an interesting line of inquiry.

Finally, citizens' opinions about trade could be industry specific. Scheve and Slaughter (2001a, 24–25) reviewed the battery of surveys done in the United States on public support for protecting specific industries, such as steel, textiles, and footwear. Naoi and Kume (2011) found that Japanese citizens' support for protectionism is low for general imports, yet their support for protectionism more than doubles for agriculture, especially among workers with low job security. Lu, Scheve, and Slaughter (2012) also found that both American and Chinese citizens show higher support for protecting low-skill industries than high-skill industries; they attribute this pattern to citizens' inequity aversion and redistributive concerns. Asking citizens' opinions about placing limits on particular industries, as done by Rho and Tomz (2013), is a promising line of future research.

Beyond Economic Self-Interests

The second wave of research has challenged these economic, self-interested explanations by identifying alternative sources of individual trade-policy attitudes, such as ideology and social identity.

Ideational Factors

Scholars have documented the effect of ideational factors beyond economic self-interests, such as economic ideology, openness to outsiders, and religious beliefs, on individual attitudes toward trade.

To the extent that trade is viewed as causing an increase in inequality, citizens' economic ideology, especially their normative views on the role of government in income redistribution, should affect their attitudes toward trade. Those who hold left-leaning ideology (i.e., supporting a larger role of government in income redistribution and regulation) should oppose free trade, while those who hold right-leaning ideology (i.e., supporting small government and an environment in which the market determines winners and losers) should support it. Indeed, studies on US legislators found that the ideology of legislators affected their positions on trade (Milner and Tingley 2011). Kaltenthaler, Gelleny, and Ceccoli (2004), however, found no evidence of the effect of ideology among the masses, using the 1995–1997 WVS data.

Another series of studies has shown that citizens might see international trade as cultural exchanges (i.e., benefits or threats) rather than economic exchanges. As a result, citizens' open-mindedness toward "outsiders" shapes their support for free trade. Kaltenthaler, Gelleny, and Ceccoli (2004), for instance, using the same WVS data, show that citizens' degree of "cosmopolitanism," a belief system viewing international trade as "an opportunity to try new products and interact with the broader world," impacts their relative support for free trade.

Mansfield and Mutz (2009) have also shown that citizens who have anxieties about being involved with "outer-groups" (immigrants, foreign culture, etc.) are more likely to oppose free trade, and that low educational attainment is a good proxy for this "outer-group" anxiety among American citizens. Consistent with these findings, Margalit (2012) has shown cross-nationally and experimentally in the United States that when individual citizens view international trade as a cultural threat rather than an economic opportunity, citizens' opposition to free trade increases.

Finally, citizens' religious beliefs might shape their attitudes toward trade through their predisposition against "outsiders." Daniels and von der Ruhr (2005) demonstrated that American voters who were pre–Vatican II Catholic or members of a fundamentalist Protestant denomination were more likely to prefer protection than those who were post-Vatican II Catholic or members of liberal or moderate Protestant denominations. Evidence drawn from the 1995 ISSP and General Social Survey (GSS) supported their claim.

These ideational findings are also consistent with earlier findings that protectionist trade attitudes were associated with nationalist sentiments or psychological attachments to regions, communities or nations, (O'Rourke and Sinnott 2001; Mayda and Rodrik 2005).

Socialization Through Group Membership

Individuals might form their trade attitudes by socializing and interacting with others through group membership. Goldstein, Margalit, and Rivers (2008) showed that married individuals are more protectionist than single or divorced people, controlling for other factors. They interpret this result as a consequence of married individuals having concern for the labor market prospects of the spouse, where even individuals who are themselves beneficiaries of free trade take more protectionist positions in concordance with their spouse's position. Whether the mechanism of marital convergence is through self-selection into the legal arrangement, socialization, or income maximization (or the minimization of income losses) for the household unit still remains a question.

Similarly, Ahlquist, Clayton, and Levi (2014) showed that workers who belong to anti-trade unions are more protectionist than workers in the same sector who do not belong to the union. The original survey of dockworkers on the US West Coast from 2007 to 2011 lends support to this argument.

Finally, Mansfield and Mutz (2009) have shown that citizens are more likely to form their attitudes toward trade based on its perceived effects on the national economy, rather than on their own jobs and income. They call this mechanism "socio-tropic" formation of attitudes. Investigating more directly what contributes to this "socio-tropic" formation—for example, whether it is driven by media coverage of economic news or strong national identities—is a promising line of future research.

Gender

The most robust empirical finding that emerged from the first two waves of research is that women were more likely to support trade protection than men, controlling for the other factors. Disagreements exist over why. Burgoon and Hiscox (2006) showed that neither the distributional effects of trade nor gender differences in skills and job characteristics account for female protectionism in the United States. They alluded to the role of the gender gap in what people learned during college—that is, women take fewer neoclassical economics courses than men—building on Hainmueller and Hiscox's findings (2006).

Analyzing cross-national survey data from the 1995 and 2003 ISSP, Beaulieu and Napier (2008) showed that the gender gap in support of free trade could not be explained by measurable characteristics such as education, labor market participation, and country location. They thus concluded that the robust gender gap in trade-policy stances could only be explained by differences in unobservable attributes of men and women, such as biology.

Using a survey experiment in Japan, Naoi and Kume (2015) identified two distinct sources of female protectionism, one on the labor market condition and another on consumption. They found that women are more protectionist when a rigid and gender-segregated labor market makes their job security lower than men's (Estevez-Abe 2006), and they are also more protectionist consumers because they care more about the safety and quality of food than men do. Indeed, marketing studies on organic food consumption have shown that women are more likely than men to purchase organic and natural food, which could lead to their opposition to cheap, imported food. Further disentangling the sources of female protectionism is thus a promising line of future research.

Risk Orientation

Finally, building on findings from behavioral economics, studies have found that individual dispositions toward risk can account for individual attitudes toward trade. Mayda, O'Rourke, and Sinnott (2007), using the Asia-Europe Survey (ASES) covering eighteen countries in Europe and Asia, reported that risk aversion was associated with anti-trade attitudes. Ehrlich and Maestas (2010) further showed that the college educated were more likely to support free trade if they were more risk-accepting to begin with; by contrast, the non-college educated were less likely to support free trade if they were risk-averse.

Although these studies challenge the economic self-interests approach in a fundamental way, there are several issues that need to be addressed. First, there is a chicken and egg problem regarding the relationship between ideational factors and trade attitudes. With single-shot survey data, we cannot trace which precedes the other (i.e., whether social identity shapes trade attitudes or trade attitudes lead to particular social identities). Thus, these studies cannot rule out well-known problems of simultaneity bias and reverse causality. Fordham and Klienberg (2012) therefore called for a more careful look at the process of socio-tropic formation of individual attitudes.

Similarly, most of the time citizens' decisions to join any particular group are by no means random. This leads to a self-selection issue between group membership and policy attitudes. It is thus important to be more mindful about identification strategies, such as establishing in the first stage that group membership is orthogonal to trade attitudes or identifying group membership that is highly path dependent. Alternatively, propensity score matching or lab and survey experiments might help, though none of these techniques fully addresses the problem of self-selection into groups that occurs in reality.

Beyond identification strategies, a promising line of future research is to examine the process and medium of information transmission from groups to individuals and among individuals and groups. For example, asking citizens directly about how they learn about trade policy and its distributional effects in surveys, as done by Bauer, de Sola Poole, and Dexter (1963), would be an easy step forward.

POLITICAL ORIGINS OF TRADE PREFERENCES

The studies discussed above have examined how the economic and social attributes of individuals are associated with their attitudes toward trade. By contrast, a series of studies have shown how institutions and the national political economy that individuals are embedded in, such as electoral systems, partisan competition, and the variety of capitalism defining their economic environment, can shape citizens' attitudes toward trade. In particular, studies have shown that these political economy institutions influence citizens' attitudes through two distinct channels: income and information.

First, emerging empirical studies have verified the micro-foundation of what Ruggie (1982) has termed "embedded liberalism," that government policies to shield citizens from income shocks of trade liberalization, through welfare and job-training programs, can mobilize support for free trade among citizens. These studies show that as long as citizens' assessments of trade depend on its effects on income, their attitudes toward trade are mutable with such government programs.

Using cross-national data on government spending and individual-level opinion data on trade attitudes among OECD countries, Hays, Ehrlich, and Peinhardt (2005) have shown that individual support for trade is higher in countries where governments provide generous welfare programs for labor and retirees. Ehrlich and Hearn (2013) further support this finding using a survey experiment in the United States. Respondent groups that were provided with facts about the Trade Adjustment Assistance (TAA) program were more likely to support free trade than the control group without the information about the TAA, and this increase was especially large among low-income respondents. Walter (2010) further disentangles the causal chains with the use of public opinion data from Switzerland and demonstrates that welfare expansion occurs through increased support for the Left among trade losers.

Political and economic institutions can also shape citizens' trade attitudes through controlling consumer price. Through cross-national observational studies, Rogowski and Kayser (2002) have shown that majoritarian electoral systems have lower consumer prices because they raise legislators' responsiveness to consumer interests over producer interests. Building on this logic, Naoi and Kume (2015) have shown, using ISSP

2003 data, that citizens' support for free trade is actually higher in majoritarian systems than in proportional representation systems when they are asked about trade's benefits for their consumer welfare. This finding is contrary to the conventional wisdom about majoritarian electoral systems leading to lower support for free trade due to citizens' concerns about lower job security (Hays, Ehrlich, and Peinhardt 2005).

An informational effect of institutions on citizens' trade attitudes comes through political persuasion and issue linkage in partisan competition. While the empirical evidence is mixed at best on whether trade continues to be a partisan issue (Milner and Judkins 2004; Naoi and Urata 2013), recent studies have shown that issue framing and political persuasion during elections and referendums can powerfully shape individual attitudes toward trade. Using district-level referendum results on CAFTA in Costa Rica, Hicks, Milner, and Tingley (2014) have shown that the left-leaning party was successful at persuading voters to oppose signing a free trade agreement with the United States. Likewise, Naoi and Urata (2013) show that anti-trade campaigns organized by agricultural cooperatives and the opposition Liberal Democratic Party mobilized much broader mass opposition to Japan's participation in the Trans-Pacific Partnership Agreement than could have been predicted from trade theorems.

Partisan orientations can also shape how consumers make consumption choices regarding domestically produced versus imported goods. Ehrlich (2010a) has shown that fair trade concerns (i.e., concerns about the labor conditions in developing economies) can mobilize protectionist sentiments among highly educated and wealthy liberals in the United States. Exploring how trade issues are linked to partisan debates and ideologies in citizens' minds is thus a promising line of future research.

The third informational effect of institutions on citizens' trade attitudes is through the structure of the media market in a given country. Because citizens learn the distributional effects of forthcoming trade policy mostly through media, who owns and finances media can have profound effects on citizen attitudes. No study exists, to our knowledge, of how citizens' views on trade can be influenced by what the media report in authoritarian systems with government-controlled or censored media. In democratic contexts, media ownership and marketing can also influence what trade-related news is reported. Using the case of the TPP, a comprehensive trade agreement currently under negotiation among twelve Asia-Pacific countries, Kuno and Naoi (2013) found that local news outlets, such as prefectural-level newspapers and geographically targeted television programs, are more likely to report negative estimates on the effect of the TPP on the local economy than are the national media in Japan. A promising line of future research is to study how citizens learn about the distributional effects of trade policies through media and interactions with elites.

International Politics: Trade as Foreign Policy

As much as domestic politics and concerns for redistribution influence how citizens view trade, international politics can also affect citizens' attitudes toward trade. Indeed, cross-national studies have shown that military allies are more likely than nonallies to sign free trade agreements, as trade generates security externalities to any third party in the international anarchy (Gowa and Mansfield 1993; Gowa 1994; Gowa, this volume). Also, democratic pairs of countries are four times as likely to sign preferential trade agreements as autocratic pairs, because to secure reelection, leaders in democracies need to signal voters that they are working hard to grow the economy and lower the price of goods (Mansfield, Milner and Rosendorff 2000).

Although studies linking trade and security alliances abound, most of these studies have focused on the role of elites in maximizing national welfare or seeking reelection. Few studies directly examine how voters view the effects of forming trade agreements on their economic and security welfare. Public opinion studies, however, have shown that anti-American or anti-Chinese sentiments among citizens, generated by the historical experience of conflicts, occupation, or the existence of military bases, can increase citizens' opposition to signing trade agreements with the United States or China (Kim 2011 on South Korea; Chiang, Liu, and Wen 2013 on Taiwan; Kume and Kohno 2011 on Japan). These findings direct us to study how voters perceive the benefits and costs of forming trade agreements with particular countries, such as security allies versus nonallies and democracies versus autocracies.

In sum, in spite of substantial progress in understanding the economic origins of individual trade attitudes, more research is called for on the political origins of trade attitudes, rooted in domestic politics and international politics.

EXPERIMENTAL APPROACHES

The third wave of research on individual attitudes toward trade has used experimental approaches, such as randomized survey experiments. Two considerations have spurred this approach. The first is a lack of faith in the efficacy of using public opinion surveys as proxies for citizens' attitudes toward trade. Experimental studies have demonstrated an instability and volatility in respondents' positions on trade depending on how questions are framed. Another concern is more empirical and aims to disentangle various sources of endogeneity that caused stagnation in the progress in research on individual attitudes toward trade. We review both of these literatures below.

Challenging the Validity of Survey Responses: Framing Experiments

While their study was not experimental, Scheve and Slaughter (2001a) were among the first to systematically document that the American public's support for free trade differs dramatically depending on the framing of the survey questions (see especially Chapter 2). For instance, American respondents were more likely to opt for protectionism if the wording of the question justified protectionism as "protecting American industries and jobs" as opposed to when the wording justified free trade as "permitting the widest choice and lowest prices for American consumers" (23). Moreover, they show that public support for free trade is much stronger when trade is described in broad and general terms (e.g., "how positive or negative you think the growth of international trade is"), rather than with specific reference to the US economy (e.g., "trade with other countries … good or bad for the U.S. economy?"; 33–34). American citizens' support for forming "trade agreements" in general seems high, if there is no specific reference to the United States or other countries (34–35). They interpret this gap as showing that the reference to the US economy provokes respondents' mercantilist sentiments.

To what extent is this instability in respondents' attitudes due to different issue framing and the wording of the instruments (e.g., telling respondents trade is good or bad) or to different trade policies having diverging distributional effects? This is an important distinction. For instance, "increasing trade" or "trade agreement" questions might make respondents consider both imports and exports (both losing and winning sides in a Ricardo-Viner sense), while a "limits on imports" question might make respondents only think about imports (i.e., the losing side in the R-V model). These two questions suggest different distributional implications of trade, and that this difference goes beyond the wording and framing of issues.

Hiscox (2006) provides one of the first survey experiments on the trade policy preferences of individuals with a nationally representative sample in the United States. He found that American citizens were very sensitive to job-threat framing—that is, trade being a threat to American jobs—but that they were not sensitive to consumer-benefits framing. He further found that less educated respondents were generally more sensitive to issue framing, and in particular, to the job-threat framing.

The experiment spurred interest in understanding which citizens are more likely to be framed by what type of information. In particular, there remains a question regarding whether the large effect of "job threat" framing for less educated respondents is due to their predisposition that trade is harmful to their job security (due to their low skill levels) or to their sensitivity to the framing in general (due to their lack of sophistication with political discourse).

Ardanaz, Murillo, and Pinto (2013) addressed this question directly by replicating the Hiscox experiment in Argentina, where there is a reversal of factor endowment from that of the United States (scarce high-skilled labor, and an abundance of low-skilled labor). This allowed them to separate out the effects of educational attainment and job security on respondents' sensitivity to framing. They found that respondents' material interests did shape their sensitivity to framing. The framing was effective among those whose economic interests were ambiguous, such as service sector workers, regardless of their levels of educational attainment or skills.[3] When respondents had clearly defined economic interests in trade, such as employment in import-competing manufacturing sectors, their trade positions were stable and resistant to various types of framing.

Disentangling Endogeneity and Collinearity: Priming Experiments

The second wave of experimental studies has sought to address common endogeneity and collinearity issues that have hampered the progress on individual attitudes toward trade.

For instance, Margalit (2012) documents with cross-national survey data the finding that citizens who see trade as a cultural threat are more likely to oppose free trade. Yet respondents who see the expansion of trade as a cultural threat tend to be those with low educational attainment, making it harder to identify the causal role of "cultural threat perception" that is orthogonal to respondents' standing in the labor market. To address this collinearity issue, Margalit (2012) also conducted a survey experiment in the United States, which primed respondents to think about cultural threats versus economic opportunity and proceeded to ask about their support for free trade. The results suggest that, among respondents with low educational attainment, those who were primed by "cultural threat" treatment showed higher opposition to free trade than those who received no priming. How much of this priming effect is due to less educated respondents' strong prior attitudes about trade's negative economic effects, and how much can be attributed to their lack of sophistication with political discourse, remains a task for future research.

Another group of studies has shown that citizens' concern for others in the country or community ("other-regarding preferences"), rather than self-interests, could dictate their trade attitudes. This line of inquiry sees trade policy as a government's decision to redistribute income across society.

Naoi and Kume (2011) sought to explain why there is high public support for agricultural protectionism in advanced industrialized nations, despite the fact that it financially burdens consumers. The difficulty in getting at this question, they argue, is that citizens can oppose agricultural liberalization as income-earners (e.g., they feel sympathetic to low-wage/low-skill farmers), or, as consumers (e.g., they care about the quality and safety of food). To solve this "duality of interests" problem, they conducted a survey experiment in Japan, which randomly assigned visual images that prime respondents to think about their jobs or about consumption and proceeded to solicit their support for agricultural protectionism. The results suggest that the main source of opposition to agricultural imports is labor market concerns, especially among the respondents with low job security, raising the support for protection out of their own concerns for job security (Naoi and Kume dub this "the projection" mechanism).

Lu, Scheve, and Slaughter (2012) have sought to solve the puzzle of why both developed and developing countries protect low-skilled workers more heavily than high-skilled workers. To do so, they conducted coordinated, nationally representative survey experiments in the United States (where low-skilled workers should be trade losers) and China (where low-skilled workers should be trade winners). They found that redistributive concerns, not self-interests, dictate citizens' attitudes toward protecting the low-skilled (proxied by their wage levels) workers regardless of low-skill workers' position in the international economy, which they call "altruism," and citizens oppose protecting high-skilled (high-wage) workers in developing economies due to "envy" toward the rich.

A promising line of future research is to ask whether these inequality aversions are innate, psychological traits of individuals or byproduct of politics and policy programs (e.g., profarmer discourse in Japan; small welfare programs in the United States and China).

Conclusion: Research Frontiers

Research on individual attitudes toward trade has progressed substantially thanks to newly available data, computational advancement, and the introduction of experimental methods to the field of international political economy. Yet the research program has large room for improvement, such as measuring respondents' economic self-interests more carefully and paying more attention to how individual preferences are rooted in the national political economy and international politics.

To conclude, we discuss two lines of the future research frontier. Both address the "so what" criticisms that are commonly levied on the literature covering individual trade attitudes discussed thus far. The first big critique is that opinions expressed through surveys are a relatively costless form of stated preferences and have little bearing on the actual behavior of individuals—such as voting and lobbying. In the survey, moreover, respondents are often forced to take positions on trade issues among multiple choice answers, despite their general low political salience.[4] Indeed, Guisinger (2009) found that trade is a low salience issue in the United States and that American voters rarely cast their votes based on party or legislators' positions on trade policy.[5]

Frontiers (1): Linking Attitudes to Behaviors

There have been three lines of inquiry to rebut this concern. One is to abandon public opinion survey methods altogether and instead use behavioral data such as voting on referendums on trade agreements or on an incumbent party. For instance, Irwin (1994) has shown that in the 1906 British general election, where trade was the defining issue for voters, voters in import-competing sectors opposed free trade, and those employed in exporting or nontraded goods sectors supported it. This is one of the first empirical studies that used district-level voting data to study constituents' interests in trade. The results lend strong support to the sector-based, Ricardo-Viner model.

Margalit (2011) has shown that trade-related job losses, measured by the number of applications for the TAA program in US counties, led to vote losses for the incumbent

Republican Party in the 2004 presidential election. Likewise, Hicks, Milner and Tingley (2014) examined district-level referendum data on the CAFTA trade agreement in Costa Rica and found that districts with a higher proportion of low-skilled labor opposed the agreement, contrary to the Stolper-Samuelson prediction. Using the same case of the CAFTA referendum in Costa Rica, Urbatsch (2013) showed that districts with a high proportion of pensioners were more likely to support the agreement, while districts with more Left party supporters opposed it.

While these studies explicitly address the "so what" question with voting data, there is an ecological inference problem (King 1997). The theory to be tested is at the individual level, yet empirical analyses use aggregate data from electoral districts or localities. Another common issue in using the voting data on general elections (not referendums on specific trade policies) is a potential omitted variable bias that trade is only one among multiple issues determining citizens' votes.

Second, to address these ecological inference problems and omitted variable biases, an emerging group of studies involves survey respondents' making optional, costly behaviors that can be easily monitored by scholars, such as sending e-mails to legislators regarding a policy issue (Betchel, Hainmueller, and Margalit 2014). Finally, scholars have devised field experiments in retail stores to estimate consumers' price premiums for ethical products compared to nonethical alternatives, such as goods produced with high labor standards in developing countries (Hiscox and Smyth 2011) and fair trade coffee (Hainmueller, Hiscox, and Sequeira 2011).

Frontiers (2): Linking Attitudes to Policy Outcomes

The second line of criticisms of the survey-based research concerns how individual opinions are aggregated into trade-policy outcomes. Indeed, although economists have formally shown how voting rules in democracies affect trade-policy outcomes (Baldwin 1976; Mayer 1994), this line of inquiry has been lopsided, with more formal models than empirical tests. When empirical tests are conducted, scholars tend to bypass the individual-level attitudinal data and estimate the effect of national-level institutions on trade-policy outcomes (e.g., Rogowski and Kayser 2002; one exception is Kono 2008).

Aggregation of individual attitudes can occur through group membership, such as labor union or partisanship. It can also occur through more elite-driven processes that are not rooted in socioeconomic organizations, such as media framing and political campaigns. A promising line of future research is examining how citizens form their attitudes through group membership (and nonmembership), with careful identification strategies for observational data (see Ahlquist, Clayton, and Levi 2014) or subgroup analyses of experimental data (Naoi and Kume 2013a).

Another solution to the missing link between mass attitudes and policy is to study the concordance between public attitudes and elites' position taking on trade. Although district-level studies on how constituents influence legislators' position taking are abundant, they have used district-level industry profiles and factor endowments as proxy measures of voters' interests. As a result, individual-level data are rarely incorporated into these studies. It would be worthwhile to examine direct legislative responsiveness to policy-specific public opinion, such as done by Lax and Phillips (2009) in the United States.

In sum, an exciting direction for future research is to link individual trade attitudes with costly behaviors of individuals, collective actions of groups, or policy responsiveness of legislators to address "so what" criticisms.

NOTES

1. Rodrik (1995) first called for more research on individual preferences over trade policy to better understand voters' positions on trade. Milner (2002) similarly advocated for more studies on trade policy preferences of individual voters to better explain the societal demand for trade policy.
2. There is an abundance of survey data, conducted by the media and public opinion research organizations, on citizen's opinions about trade agreements (general and specific), but scholarly works using these has been scant. See Scheve and Slaughter (2001a, Chap 2) for the detailed reviews.
3. They used a separate measure for skill-levels called "occupational scores", which is an index of how many subordinates employees respondents have. The higher this score, more "white-collar" management jobs respondents have.
4. Many existing surveys have given respondents options to choose "don't know" or neutral responses, such as "can't say one way or the other". Yet, the empirical analyses using these data often treat them as missing (in the case of "don't know") or as a baseline (in the case of neutral responses), rather than the outcome to be examined.
5. One could argue, though, that low salience of trade is expected from the low tariff rates and low ratio of export and import in the U.S. economy—the U.S. is thus a deviant case among OECD countries. Pelc (2013) provides the evidence to the contrary by using google's search volume data to examine ordinary people's "information-seeking" activities. He demonstrated that U.S. citizens were concerned with WTO dispute-related information involving the U.S. case.

REFERENCES

Ahlquist, John S., Amanda B. Clayton, and Margaret Levi. 2014. Provoking Preferences: Unionization, Trade Policy, and the ILWU Puzzle. *International Organization* 68 (1): 33–75.

Ardanaz, Martin, M. Victoria Murillo, and Pablo Pinto. 2013. Sensitivity to Issue Framing on Trade Policy Preferences: Evidence from a Survey Experiment. *International Organization* 67 (2): 411–437.

Baker, Andy. 2005. Who Wants to Globalize? Consumer Tastes and Labor Markets in a Theory of Trade Policy Belief. *American Journal of Political Science* 49 (4): 924–938.

Baldwin, Robert. 1976. The Political Economy of Postwar U.S. Trade Policy. *The Bulletin.* New York University Graduate School of Business Administration.

Baldwin, Robert, and Christopher S. Magee. 2000. Is Trade Policy for Sale? Congressional Voting on Recent Trade Bills. *Public Choice*, 105 (1-2): 79–101.

Bauer, Raymond, Ithiel de Sola Poole, and Lewis Dexter. 1963. *American Business and Public Policy*. New York: Atherton Press.

Beaulieu, Eugene, and Michael Napier. 2008. Why Are Women More Protectionist Than Men? Working Paper. Department of Economics, The University of Calgary.

Betchel, Michael, Jens Hainmueller, and Yotam Margalit. 2014. "Preferences for International Redistribution: The Divide Over the Eurozone Bailouts. *American Journal of Political Science* 58 (4): 835-856.

Burgoon, Brian, and Michael J. Hiscox. 2006. The Mysterious Case of Female Protectionism: Gender Bias in Attitudes Toward International Trade. Working Paper. Harvard University Weatherhead Center for International Affairs.

Chiang, Chun-Fang, Jin-Tan Liu, and Tsai-Wei Wen. 2013. Individual Preferences for Trade Partners in Taiwan. *Economists and Politics* 25 (1): 91–109.

Coughlin, Cletus C. 2002. The Controversy Over Free Trade: The Gap between Economists and the General Public. *Review, Federal Reserve Bank of St. Louis* 84 (1): 1–22.

Cusack, Thomas, Torben Iversen, and Philip Rehm. 2006. Risks at Work: The Demand and Supply Sides of Government Redistribution. *Oxford Review of Economic Policy* 22 (3): 365–389.

Daniels, Joseph P., and Marc von der Ruhr. 2005. Gold and the Global Economy: Religion and Attitudes toward Trade and Immigration in the United States. *Socio-Economic Review* 3 (3): 467–487.

Ehrlich, Sean. 2010a. The Fair Trade Challenge to Embedded Liberalism. *International Studies Quarterly* 54 (4): 1013–1033.

Ehrlich, Sean. 2010b. Who Supports Compensation? Individual Preferences for Trade-Related Unemployment Insurance. *Business and Politics* 12 (1): Article 3.

Ehrlich, Sean, and Eddie Hearn. 2013. Does Compensating Those Harmed Increase Support for Trade? An Experimental Test of the Embedded Liberalism Thesis. *Foreign Policy Analysis* 9 (1): 1–16.

Ehrlich, Sean D., and Cherie Maestas. 2010. Risk Orientation, Risk Exposure, and Policy Opinions: The Case of Free Trade." *Political Psychology* 31 (5): 657–684.

Estevez-Abe, Margarita. 2006. Gendering the Varieties of Capitalism: A Study of Occupational Segregation by Sex in Advanced Industrial Societies. *World Politics* 59 (1): 142–175.

Fordham, Benjamin, and Katja Kleinberg. 2012. How Can Economic Interests Support for Free Trade? *International Organization* 66 (2): 311–328.

Gawande, Kishore, Pravin Krishna, and Marcelo Olarreaga. 2009. What Governments Maximize and Why: The View from Trade. *International Organization* 63 (3): 491–532.

Gilligan, Michael. 1997. *Empowering Exporters: Reciprocity, Delegation, and Collective Action in American Trade Policy*. Ann Arbor: University of Michigan Press.

Goldstein, Judith, Yotam Margalit, and Dougalas Rivers. 2008. Producer, Consumer, Family Member: The Relationship between Trade Attitudes and Family Status. Paper presented at the Conference on Domestic Preferences and Foreign Economic Policy, Working Paper, Stanford University.

Gowa, Joanne. 1994. *Allies, Adversaries, and International Trade*. Princeton, NJ: Princeton University Press.

Gowa, Joanne, and Edward D. Mansfield. 1993. Power Politics and International Trade. *American Political Science Review* 87 (2): 408–420.

Grossman, Gene M., and Elhanan Helpman. 1994. Protection for Sale. *American Economic Review* 84 (4): 833–850.

Guisinger, Alexandra. 2009. Determining Trade Policy: Do Voters Hold Politicians Accountable? *International Organization* 63 (3): 533–557.

Hainmueller, Jens, and Michael J. Hiscox. 2006. Learning to Love Globalization: Education and Individual Attitudes toward International Trade. *International Organization* 60 (2): 469–498.

Hainmuller, Jens, Michael J. Hiscox, and Sandra Sequeira. 2011. Consumer Demand for the Fair Trade Label: Evidence from a Field Experiment. Review of Economics and Statistics. (Forthcoming 2015).

Hays, Jude C., Sean Ehrlich, and Clint Peinhardt. 2005. Government Spending and Public Support for Trade in the OECD: An Empirical Test of the Embedded Liberalism Thesis. *International Organization* 59 (2): 473–494.

Helpman, Elhanan. 2011. *Understanding Global Trade.* Cambridge, MA: Harvard University Press.

Hicks, Raymond, Helen Milner, and Dustin Tingley. 2014. Trade Policy, Economic Interests and Party Politics in a Developing Country: The Political Economy of CAFTA-DR. *International Studies Quarterly* 58 (1): 106–117.

Hiscox, Michael J. 2002. *International Trade and Political Conflict: Commerce, Coalitions, and Mobility.* Princeton, NJ: Princeton University Press.

Hiscox, Michael J. 2006. Through a Glass and Darkly: Attitudes Toward International Trade and the Curious Effects of Issue Framing. *International Organization* 60 (4): 755–780.

Hiscox, Michael J., and Nicholas Smyth. 2011. Is There Consumer Demand for Fair Labor Standards? Evidence from a Field Experiment. SSRN. http://papers.ssrn.com/sol3/papers.cfm?abstract_id=1820642 (accessed November 15, 2013).

Imai, Kosuke, and Dustin Tingley. 2012. A Statistical Model for Empirical Testing of Competing Theories. *American Journal of Political Science* 56 (1): 218–236.

Irwin, Douglas. 1994. The Political Economy of Free Trade: Voting in the British General Election of 1906. *Journal of Law and Economics* 37 (1): 75–108.

Iversen, Torben, and David Soskice. 2001. An Asset Theory of Social Policy Preferences. *American Political Science Review* 95 (4): 875–893.

Kaltenthaler, Karl, Ronald D. Gelleny, and Stephen J. Ceccoli. 2004. Explaining Citizen Support for Trade Liberalization. *International Studies Quarterly* 48 (4): 829–851.

King, Gary. 1997. *A Solution to Ecological Inference Problem: Reconstructing Individual Behaviors from Aggregate Data.* Princeton, NJ: Princeton University Press.

Kim, Mi-kyung. 2011. Foreign Economic Policy and Social Conflicts in South Korea: Preferences, Policy Paradigms, and the Formation of Political Coalitions. *Korean Political Science Review* 45 (5): 147–173.

Koremenos, Barbara, Charles Lipson, and Duncan Snidal. 2001. The Rational Design of International Institutions. *International Organization* 55 (4): 761–799.

Kono, Daniel Y. 2008. Does Public Opinion Affect Trade Policy? *Business and Politics* 10 (2): Article 2.

Kume, Ikuo, and Masaru Kohno. 2011. Political Conflicts over TPP Reflect the Public Divide over Dipolomacy. *Nikkei Shimbun*, Keizai Kyositsu Series, December 22.

Kuno, Arata, and Megumi Naoi. 2013. Framing Business Interests: How Campaigns Affect Firms' Positions on Preferential Trade Agreements. Working Paper, Kyorin University and UCSD.

Lax, Jeffery R., and Justin H. Phillips. 2009. Gay Rights in the States: Public Opinion and Policy Responsiveness. *American Political Science Review* 103 (3): 367–386.

Lohmann, Susanne, and Sharyn O'Halloran. 1994. Divided Government and U.S. Trade Policy: Theory and Evidence. *International Organization* 48 (4): 595–632.

Lu, Xiaobo, Kenneth Scheve, and Matthew J. Slaughter. 2012. Inequity Aversion and the International Distribution of Trade Protection. *American Journal of Political Science* 56(3): 638-654.

Magee, Stephen P., William A. Block, and Leslie Young. 1989. *Black Hole Tariffs and Endogenous Policy Theory*. Cambridge, UK: Cambridge University Press.

Mansfield, Edward D., Helen V. Milner, and B. Peter Rosendorff. 2000. Free to Trade: Democracies, Autocracies, and International Trade. *American Political Science Review* 94 (2): 305–321.

Mansfield, Edward, and Diana Mutz. 2009. Support for Free Trade: Self-Interest, Sociotropic Politics, and Out-group Anxiety. *International Organization* 63 (3): 425–457.

Margalit, Yotam. 2011. Costly Jobs: Trade-related Layoffs, Government Compensation, and Voting in U.S. Elections. *American Political Science Review* 105 (1): 169–188.

Margalit, Yotam. 2012. Lost in Globalization: International Economic Integration and the Sources of Popular Discontent. *International Studies Quarterly* 56 (3): 484–500.

Mayda, Anna Maria, and Dani Rodrik. 2005. Why Are Some People (and Countries) More Protectionist Than Others. *European Economic Review* 49 (6): 1393–1430.

Mayda, Anna Maria, Kevin H. O'Rourke, and Richard Sinnott. 2007. Risk, Government and Globalization: International Survey Evidence. Working Paper No. 13037. National Bureau of Economic Research.

Mayer, Wolfgang. 1994. Endogenous Tariff Formation. *American Economic Review* 74: 970–985.

Melitz, Marc J. 2003. The Impact of Trade on Intra-Industry Reallocations and Aggregate Industry Productivity. *Econmetrica* 71 (6): 1695–1725.

Milner, Helen, and Dustin Tingley. 2011. Who Supports Global Economic Engagement? The Sources of Preferences in American Foreign Economic Policy. *International Organization* 65 (1): 37–68.

Milner, Helen V. 2002. International Trade. In *Handbook of International Relations*, edited by Walter Carlsnaes, Thomas Risse, and Beth Simmons, 448–461. New York: Sage.

Milner, Helen V. 1989. *Resisting Protectionism: Global Industries and the Politics of International Trade*. Princeton, NJ: Princeton University Press.

Naoi, Megumi, and Ikuo Kume. 2013a. Coalition of Losers: Why Agricultural Protectionism Has Survived During the Great Recession. In *Politics in the New Hard Times*, edited by Miles Kahler and David Lake, 190–211. Ithaca, NY: Cornell University Press.

Naoi, Megumi, and Ikuo Kume. 2011. Explaining Mass Support for Agricultural Protectionism: Evidence from a Survey Experiment during the Global Recession. *International Organization* 65 (4): 771–795.

Naoi, Megumi, and Ikuo Kume. Forthcoming. Workers or Consumers? A Survey Experiment on the Duality of Citizens' Interests in the Politics of Trade. *Comparative Political Studies*.

Naoi, Megumi, and Shujiro Urata. 2013. Free Trade Agreements and Domestic Politics: The Case of TPP. *Asian Economic Policy Review* 2 (2): 326–349.

Olson, Mancur. 1965. *The Logic of Collective Action*. Cambridge, MA: Harvard University Press.

O'Rourke, Kevin H., and Richard Sinnott. 2001. The Determinants of Individual Trade-Policy Preferences: International Survey Evidence. *Brookings Trade Forum*: 157–196.

Pelc, Krzysztof J. 2013. Googling the WTO: What Search-Engine Data Tell US About the Political Economy of Institutions. *International Organization* 67 (3): 629–655.

Rho, Sungmin, and Michael Tomz. 2013. Industry, Self-Interest, and Individual Preferences over Trade Policy. Working Paper prepared for the 2013 International Political Economy Colloquium, Goa, India.

Rodrik, Dani. 1995. Political Economy of Trade Policy. In *Handbook of International Economics*, edited by Gene M. Grossman and Kenneth Rogoff, 3: 1457–1494. Amsterdam, Netherlands: Elsevier Science Press.

Rogowski, Ronald. 1987. Trade and the Variety of Democratic Institutions. *International Organization* 41 (2): 203–223.

Rogowski, Ronald, and Mark Kayser. 2002. Majoritarian Electoral Systems and Consumer Power: Price-level Evidence from the OECD Countries. *American Journal of Political Science* 46 (3): 526–539.

Ruggie, John G. 1982. International Regimes, Transactions, and Change: Embedded Liberalism in the Postwar Economic System. *International Organization* 36 (2): 379–415.

Schattschneider, Elmer E. 1935. *Politics, Pressures, and the Tariff: A Study of Free Private Enterprise in Pressure Politics, as Shown in the 1929–1930 Revision of the Tariff.* Prentice-Hall.

Scheve, Kenneth F., and Matthew J. Slaughter. 2001a. *Globalization and the Perceptions of American Workers.* Washington, DC: Institute for International Economics.

Scheve, Kenneth F., and Matthew J. Slaughter. 2001b. What Determines Individual Trade Policy Preferences. *Journal of International Economics* 54 (3): 267–292.

Urbatsch, Robert. 2013. A Referendum on Trade Policy: Voting on Free Trade in Costa Rica. *International Organization* 67 (1): 197–214.

Walter, Stefanie. 2010. Globalization and the Welfare State: Testing the Micro-foundation of the Compensation Hypothesis. *International Studies Quarterly* 54 (2): 403–426.

CHAPTER 7

....

LABOR AND PROTECTIONIST
SENTIMENT

....

ERICA OWEN

THE distributional consequences of trade in labor markets are one of the primary channels through which globalization affects the economic well-being of the public. This chapter focuses on the demand for protection by labor interests, which may correspond to producer demands more generally or put the interests of labor and capital at odds. Two questions are of particular importance: (1) What are the underlying cleavages or latent shared interests of labor? (2) When are protectionist interests likely to be reflected in policy outcomes? Failure by governments to include labor interests in their policies today will likely set the stage for unrest and protectionist backlash in the future.

Individual-level studies find mixed evidence regarding the role of economic theory in shaping preferences about trade. However, Fordham and Kleinberg (2012) suggest that it would be premature to dismiss self-interest as a determinant of trade preferences, and argue that groups (organized or not) play an important role in shaping attitudes toward trade. They suggest that people need not know clearly how trade will affect them for economic factors to shape trade preferences. Studies of mass public opinion show evidence of systematic preferences, eliminating noise in individual survey responses and reiterating the importance of latent shared interests.

Trade protection is the subject of large literatures in both political science and economics. This chapter reviews primarily the literature in political science, while drawing attention to work in economics that can shed light on lingering questions in political science. In particular, our thinking about protectionist demands and ways to satisfy these interests must evolve to keep pace with the changing nature of globalization. Recent advances in economic trade theory, in particular the heterogeneous firms theory, have important implications for the politics of protection (see Plouffe, this volume). In the first section I briefly review the various cleavages among labor predicted by trade theories prominent in political science. In the second section I discuss how the influence of labor interests on policy has been examined empirically. The third section covers policy alternatives to tariffs and nontariff barriers that may be used to satisfy protectionist demands, specifically temporary trade barriers and compensation. In the fourth section, I examine the implications of heterogeneous firms theory for protectionist demands. The fifth section presents directions for future research, followed by a section of conclusions.

DISTRIBUTIONAL CONSEQUENCES
AND DEMANDS FOR PROTECTION

This section only briefly reviews the canonical models of trade theory that shape preferences regarding trade, as they have been extensively reviewed elsewhere (e.g., Rogowski 2006), before discussing other sources of protectionist sentiment. Our understanding of how trade affects domestic factors of production, and subsequent preferences about trade policy, are primarily drawn from two underlying trade models.

The first, and arguably most widely used, is the factor endowments model. The Heckscher-Ohlin theory suggests that countries will have a comparative advantage in those factors that they have in abundance and a comparative disadvantage in those that are relatively scarce. The Stolper-Samuelson (HOS) theorem suggests that trade will increase returns to abundant factors and decrease returns to scarce factors through specialization and exchange (Stolper and Samuelson 1941). This insight is the foundation of a large body of work in political science because of the implied cleavages that will form. In his seminal work *Commerce and Coalitions*, Rogowski (1989) argues that protection (liberalization) will benefit owners of scarce (abundant) factors; thus cleavages will divide interests with respect to trade along factor lines. Owners of a given factor of production will have shared interests. This leads to the well-known hypothesis that labor will be protectionist in developed countries, because unskilled labor constitutes a majority of the workforce yet is relatively scarce; conversely, labor will be pro-trade in developing countries. In one test of this hypothesis, Baker (2005) calculates a country-level measure of support for free trade and finds that countries with greater skill abundance have lower aggregate support for free trade.

The Ricardo-Viner, also known as specific factors, model is the second primary theory of the distributional consequences of trade. Industries of comparative advantage use the abundant factor relatively intensively, while industries of comparative disadvantage use the scarce factor intensively. Unlike in the HOS model, factors are not fully mobile domestically. This means that owners of the same factor may have heterogeneous preferences; thus coalitions tend to form around industry rather than along class lines.

The key difference between the factor endowments and specific factors models is the level of domestic factor mobility. Hiscox (2002) suggests that cleavages will form along industry or factor lines depending on the level of inter-industry factor mobility. When asset mobility is high, cleavages are likely to form along factor lines; when mobility is low, industry cleavages form, because it is more difficult to move from one industry to another.

The assumption about the degree of factor mobility has implications for the types of coalitions that form, as well as the ease of collective action (Alt and Gilligan 1994). Conventional wisdom suggests that collective action is likely to be more successful when factors organize along industry lines, due to the lower costs of organizing a smaller number of actors.

Along with factor mobility, designation of the factors of production shapes the nature of protectionist demands. Traditionally, labor is treated as a homogenous factor of production. However, Chase suggests that scholars have emphasized the "antagonism between labor and capital in the United States" at the expense of examining cleavages within labor (2008, 658). The distinction between skilled and unskilled labor is particularly important for the distributional consequences of trade in developed countries because trade, in combination with other aspects of economic integration and technological change, has affected skilled and unskilled labor differently.

Empirical inconsistencies in the neoclassical (HOS and specific factors) models led to the development of new trade theory. In short, trade on the basis of comparative advantage predicts inter-industry trade between countries with dissimilar factor endowments. However, much international trade is between countries with similar factor endowments and occurs within the same industry. New trade theory accounts for this by introducing imperfect competition and differentiated goods. Standard distributional pressures are mitigated in this case because goods are differentiated and thus are not perfect substitutes. Therefore, intra-industry trade between countries with similar endowments should spur fewer demands for protection (Krugman 1981).

Macroeconomic factors like unemployment and the real exchange rate are also important sources of protectionist sentiment. Mansfield and Busch (1995) review the intuition guiding this theory. Recessions, and high unemployment in particular, are likely to lead to more demands for protection (Corden 1993). Workers who lose their jobs are likely to have a harder time finding new employment and may be forced to accept a lower wage. Cassing, McKeown, and Ochs (1986) suggest that politically effective demands for protection by import-competing sectors will be higher during periods of unemployment. Similarly, rising current account imbalances, or an appreciated exchange rate more generally, may lead to increasing protectionist sentiment, due in part to competitive pressures and perhaps perceptions of unfair practices. In the United States, anti-Japanese sentiment in the 1980 and anti-Chinese sentiment in the 2000 are excellent examples of this. Such conditions are likely to give rise to economic nationalism. Indeed, Baker (2005) finds that as aggregate nationalist sentiment increases, overall mean support for free trade decreases.

INFLUENCE OF LABOR ON TRADE POLICY

Rogowski (1989) and Hiscox (2002) are exemplary accounts of the coalitions that form around trade, but given a set of preferences, the next step is to examine how and under what conditions labor interests influence trade policy. Therefore, we must examine how the preferences generated by distributional consequences are translated into effective political demands and the incentives of politicians to place weight on competing interests. This literature largely follows the open economy politics (OEP) framework.[1] Theories of preference aggregation can generally be divided into two camps: those that emphasize the incentives created by institutions for politicians to cater to different constituencies and those that emphasize the collective action problem and political activity by organized interest groups.

Because it is difficult to observe lobbying behavior by groups with latent shared interests, we frequently rely on the incentives of politicians to cater to the interests of one group over another. Certain domestic institutional arrangements are thought to privilege narrow or broad coalitions and often correspond to factoral or sectoral cleavages. Institutional accounts thus emphasize the incentives of politicians to supply protection, given a set of preferences held by labor, rather than political activity by labor interests demanding protection. For example, democracies tend to place more weight on the preferences of citizens, who are primarily owners of labor (rather than capital).[2] Therefore, democracies are more likely to implement policies that benefit labor than are nondemocracies (e.g., Milner and Kubota 2005), although the effect of democracy on openness will depend on relative factor endowments (e.g., Tavares 2008; Milner and Mukherjee n.d.).

Government partisanship also affects the political influence of labor. Like regime type, arguments about partisanship tend to assume HOS cleavages. Parties have broad constituencies, and the Left, as a representative of labor, is more likely to promote the interests of labor with respect to trade, whereas the Right is more likely to represent the interests of capital. Thus we should see more protection under Left governments in developed countries and more openness under Left governments in developing countries. Indeed, in a study of twenty-five developed countries, Milner and Judkins (2004) find that Right governments are more likely to take pro-trade positions than Left governments, while Dutt and Mitra (2005) find that the reverse is true in countries with abundant labor. However, as labor interests become more heterogeneous, the constituency of Left parties is not obvious. For example, in a study of welfare spending, Rueda (2007) finds that the Left represents the interests of labor market insiders at the expense of outsiders. Similar pressures are likely to occur with trade as well.

Industry cleavages typically appear in the endogenous protection literature, which emphasizes the lobbying process and the ease of collective action. The protection-for-sale (PFS) model is the most prominent theory of endogenous trade protection. Grossman and Helpman's (1994) seminal PFS model emphasizes that in the policy-making process, governments face a trade-off between satisfying special interests that provide political contributions and increasing aggregate social welfare to appeal to voters. Traditionally, PFS models do not attempt to model collective action and assume protectionist interests are better able to overcome the collective action problem than are the winners from trade, which includes diffuse groups like consumers, and also exporters (as an exception, see Milner 1988). Busch and Reinhardt (2000) introduce geographic concentration as one factor that captures the ease of collective action and likelihood of mobilization, while Gawande and Magee (2012) introduce free riding into the model to address the empirical finding that governments appear to care almost solely about aggregate welfare. Labor does not often play an explicit role in PFS models, which largely lump protectionist interests together and in which societal welfare is based on consumer interests.

The norm has been to posit either factor—or industry—cleavages. However, in addition to Hiscox's work documenting changes in the type of cleavages, other scholars have sought to explicitly measure the level of factor mobility (especially of labor) and incorporate it into theories of protection. The level of factor mobility is an important determinant of the adjustment costs faced by labor and thus of demands for protection and, as discussed below, compensation. Mukherjee, Li, and Smith (2009) incorporate factor mobility, measured as a continuous variable, into a test of the PFS model, thereby allowing for either HOS or Ricardo-Viner cleavages to emerge. In a panel of majoritarian countries, they find that governments raise tariffs when factor mobility decreases, consistent with the notion that collective action becomes easier as the size of coalitions decreases.

As an alternative to trade on the basis of endowment-driven comparative advantage, new trade theory, which includes imperfect competition and intra-industry trade, has also been used to explain the politics of trade protection, though labor does not play a prominent role in these accounts. Milner (1988) suggests that internationally oriented firms tend to be less protectionist than domestically oriented ones. She further argues that these pro-trade preferences can act as a counterweight to protectionist ones, thus explaining why trade barriers do not increase significantly during periods of high import competition. Similarly, Hathaway (1998) suggests that openness dampens protectionist sentiment in industries hurt by imports, because larger firms are able to increase capital intensity or move labor-intensive activities abroad, while others are more likely to exit the industry. See also Chase (2003).

Protectionist sentiment is also associated with larger macroeconomic trends.[3] During bad economic times, governments often must respond to increased demands for protection. Seminal work by Goldstein (1986) and Milner (1988) suggests that the level of protection in the United States was lower than expected during the economic decline of the 1970s. Milner suggests that this was so because anti-protectionist interests limit the supply of protection, while Goldstein suggests that institutions and ideas biased toward free trade persist in the United States. On the other hand, Takacs (1981) finds that bad economic conditions increased petitions for safeguards in the United States between 1949 and 1979. In an analysis of US industry-level tariffs during the 1980s, Bradford (2006) finds that an industry's level of trade protection increases with the number of unemployed workers and decreases with the job turnover rate.

Protectionist pressures in the face of bad macroeconomic outcomes are one component of a society's pluralist interests, and thus institutions play an important role in shaping when those interests are reflected in policy. Mansfield and Busch (1995) examine the effect of the real exchange rate and unemployment on nontariff barriers (NTBs), conditional on variation in democratic institutions. Similarly, Henisz and Mansfield

(2006) examine the effects of unemployment on trade openness, conditional on the number of institutional constraints. They find that trade openness decreases as unemployment rises in democracies, though this effect is attenuated as the number of veto players increases. Together this research suggests that democratic governments are responsive to domestic protectionist pressures, though the degree of responsiveness varies in systematic ways.

Political activity and lobbying by labor is the subject of a much smaller literature. Due to the common assumption that protectionists are more likely to overcome collective action, labor interests are typically incorporated into the political economy of trade through institutional mechanisms or are assumed to align with producer interests. However, organized labor in particular shapes politicians' incentives to weigh the interests of labor interests more heavily. Matschke and Sherlund (2006) propose a labor-augmented Grossman-Helpman model that allows for lobbying by trade unions. They find that active lobbying and other labor market variables are important determinants of trade policy in a study of NTBs in US industries. Bradford (2006) also finds a positive effect of the level of unionization on the level of protection. Similarly, scholars have found that campaign contributions by labor groups affect legislative votes. For example, Steagall and Jennings (1996) demonstrate that House representatives who depended on labor political action committee (PAC) contributions were more likely to vote against the North American Free Trade Agreement (NAFTA). Similarly, Baldwin and Magee (2000) find that campaign contributions by labor unions increase the likelihood that US members of Congress will vote against trade liberalization bills.

The preceding discussion emphasizes protectionist demands by labor in developed countries because neoclassical models of trade suggest that capital (and skilled labor) is the source of protectionist sentiment in labor-abundant developing countries. In the section "Heterogeneous Firms and Labor Market Outcomes," I discuss new research in economics, which implies that skilled labor in developing countries also benefits from globalization relatively more than does unskilled labor.

STATE OF THE LITERATURE: PROTECTION AND REDISTRIBUTION

New research in international political economy (IPE) builds on earlier work by introducing additional distributional consequences and extending the analysis of protection to include other tools politicians can use to satisfy protectionist sentiments (aside from tariffs and NTBs). The development of global supply chains and the trade in intermediate goods and services has changed the shape of international trade. Other facets of openness, including the activity of multinational firms and immigration, may also fuel protectionist sentiments (e.g., Rogowski 2006). Politicians must find a way to respond to this new protectionism and do so in a world trading system that is much more institutionalized. "The WTO mediates the relationship between the domestic political processes that generate government policy preferences and the tariff rates that one observes" (Oatley 2011, 320). Because politicians are more constrained in their ability to use traditional protection measures (even if they should want to for domestic political reasons), we must consider alternative trade barriers like safeguards, as well as other tools like compensation.

Alternative Forms of Protection

Governments face a menu of options when responding to protectionist demands. For example, Naoi (2009) suggests that when governments choose to provide protection, they can choose unilateral instruments like subsidies, bilateral tools like voluntary export restraints, or measures compliant with the General Agreement on Tariffs and Trade (GATT)/World Trade Organization (WTO), such as escape clauses and antidumping. This is a fruitful area of further research, especially empirical research. Increasing legalization has limited the ability of governments to use tariffs and NTBs. However, flexibility built into international institutions, including countervailing duties (CVD) and antidumping (AD) and other escape clauses, provides governments with the means of responding to domestic protectionist pressures.[4]

Though AD and CVD are not new inventions, they are increasingly important as policy tools used to supply protection.[5] The United States established variants of these laws in the 1930s to deal with unfair trade practices or cheating by trade partners (Goldstein 1986). Though the largest users of AD laws traditionally were the United States, the European Union, Canada, and Australia, developing countries have adopted and are using AD laws at a higher rate in the WTO period (Bown 2011). These administered protection measures are sanctioned by the WTO, and of these, AD tools are the most widely used. Although the Great Recession of the late 2000s did not lead to large tariff increases, it did lead to an increase in the use of these temporary trade barriers (Bown 2011).

Hansen (1990) finds that political factors determine the supply of protection by the International Trade Commission (ITC) in the United States, while Drope and Hansen (2004) find that PAC spending in favor of protection has a positive effect on the likelihood of a favorable decision by the ITC. Temporary trade barriers can also be used to smooth over the costs of adjustment for workers in industries that experience shocks to terms of trade, an important component of the welfare consequences of trade (Davidson and Matusz 2004).

Finally, labor and environmental standards in free trade agreements (FTAs) may level the playing field and constitute another form of protection from the adjustment costs of trade. However, these standards are often criticized as being unenforceable. After NAFTA came into effect, US unions felt that labor standards were not enforced; thus there has been increasing opposition to more recent FTAs. On the other hand, Ehrlich (2010) argues that fair trade differs from general protectionism, suggesting that such side agreements are not protectionism in disguise. His findings suggest that labor and environmental side agreements, when enforced, may be a way to mitigate some protectionist demands that cannot be met by increasing barriers to trade or providing compensation.

Compensation in Lieu of Protection

Politicians can use compensation, as an alternative to trade protection, to address labor demands for protection, while simultaneously maintaining the current level of openness. Although labor as an actor in its own right does not play a central role in much of the IPE literature, it is central in studies of welfare outcomes. Compensation is a key component of the embedded liberalism hypothesis, which states that governments can "compensate" citizens for rising insecurity associated with international economic integration, in exchange for continued support for openness (Ruggie 1982). Boix (2006) highlights trade policy and redistribution as alternative policy choices that can be used to achieve a given domestic political goal.[6] Thus, protection and compensation can both be used to satisfy the demands of protectionists.

Compensation generates or maintains support for openness and may take the form of job retraining programs, unemployment benefits, or other general welfare programs. Survey data from the United States and elsewhere suggest that individuals have reservations about the effects of trade on jobs and job security and are more likely to support free trade when it is accompanied by policies to help those workers hurt by trade. Walter (2010) finds that globalization generates increased feelings of job insecurity, which in turn leads to increased preferences for welfare compensation among those hurt by globalization. Similarly, Rehm (2011) argues that preferences about redistribution are a function of income and income prospects. In a study of aggregate public opinion, Owen and Quinn (forthcoming) demonstrate that rising imports increase demands for larger government, and that the effect of aggregate public opinion on spending is conditional on the level of imports. In summary, compensation is likely to be demanded by those who experience or anticipate an increase in job insecurity or decline in income.

Whether the compensation mechanism successfully reduces anti-trade sentiment is the subject of a growing literature. Hays, Ehrlich, and Peinhardt (2005) find that compensation is an effective means to garner support for free trade. At the individual level, they find that higher levels of active labor market spending lead to higher levels of support for free trade. See also Hays (2009). In a different approach, Margalit (2011) examines the effect of trade adjustment assistance (TAA) on President George W. Bush's vote share in the 2004 election and finds that higher levels of TAA decreased the loss in vote share associated with negative trade outcomes. Thus constraints on the ability of governments to provide compensation increase the risk of protectionist backlash.[7]

This raises the question of when governments will choose different tools to appease protectionist interests. Hwang and Lee (2013) suggest that the form of redistribution depends on factor mobility and find that welfare politics are more likely when mobility is high, while targeted subsidies are more likely when mobility is low, conditional on government partisanship. Fewer studies have explored choices about protection and compensation simultaneously. In a theoretical paper, Dixit and Londregan suggest that protection is more politically manageable, though less efficient economically, than compensation, which encourages resource reallocation to more productive sectors. Ehrlich

(2010) suggests that true fair trade attitudes may limit the effectiveness of compensation as a means of addressing protectionist concerns, and that governments may need to use multiple policy tools to address anti-trade sentiments, including through the design of international agreements.

HETEROGENEOUS FIRMS AND LABOR MARKET OUTCOMES

Recent advances in economics, namely heterogeneous firms theory, introduce new distributional consequences for labor that are likely to increase protectionist sentiment, even in developing countries. In new new trade theory (NNTT), firms are heterogeneous in terms of size, export status, and productivity. In a seminal article, Melitz (2003) argues that firms have different levels of productivity; below a certain cutoff, firms are no longer active in the market. There is a second cutoff, and only firms with productivity levels above this threshold are able to engage in export behavior. Exporting firms expand through trade, while import-competing firms are likely to fail or change industries, and their plants are more likely to close and have lower employment and wage growth (Bernard, Jensen, and Schott 2006). Exceptions to this are firms that have reallocated production abroad and are engaged in importing back into their home countries.

Trade therefore changes the composition of firms in the economy, increasing the productivity level of an industry. This has important labor market implications, because firms with different productivity levels have systematically different demand schedules for labor, including demand for skilled relative to unskilled labor, wages paid, and the elasticity of demand. As suggested by Scheve and Slaughter, the distributional consequences (labor market outcomes) of globalization include "the level of real and relative wages, and insecurity in terms of the volatility of wages and employment" (2006, 225).

The consideration of foreign direct investment (FDI) and trade together is crucial and flows naturally from NNTT.[8] Protectionism leads not only to demands for compensation or trade protection, but also, for example, to new restrictions on cross-border mergers and acquisitions. Heterogeneous firms theory offers new, in some cases conflicting, distributional consequences relative to those generated by neoclassical theories, and which have important implications for political economy of protection.

Trade and Unemployment

Traditional trade theory assumes full employment; as a result, standard political economy stories tend to emphasize the wage effects of trade and do not account for the possibility of equilibrium unemployment, even in the presence of rising corporate profits. Economists have proposed several mechanisms, including fair wages and labor market frictions, to explain how trade increases unemployment. For example, Egger and Kreickemeier introduce firm-specific wages where "the wage considered to be fair depends inter alia on the productivity level (and thus the economic success) of the employer" (2009, 188). In this model, wages for identical workers are higher at more productive firms. Owners of highly productive firms are unwilling to reduce wages to clear the labor market, as is the case in traditional trade theory, leading to unemployment in equilibrium. Changes in overall productivity also affect the level of employment. Although output increases from trade and raises demand for labor, increasing overall industry productivity decreases labor demand, which may make some of the workforce redundant. Alternatively, Helpman and Itskhoki (2009) suggest that greater labor market frictions lead to higher unemployment, which can account for the different labor market outcomes in the United States (higher inequality) and Western Europe (persistent unemployment).

Moreover, those who lose their jobs because of import competition are unlikely to be hired by exporting firms, because these workers are likely to have lower skill levels than those demanded by exporters. Trade changes the composition of firms in the economy, thus inducing job creation, destruction, and dislocation. Workers displaced by import competition are likely to face reduced wages and perhaps jobs in the service sector (Kletzer 2001).

The number of jobs is also affected by offshoring and foreign direct investment. In a model proposed by Mitra and Ranjan (2010), offshoring can decrease unemployment if there is perfect factor mobility, but in the presence of labor market frictions, offshoring increases unemployment in the offshoring sector and decreases it in the non-offshoring sector. Empirical testing of these implications of NNTT is in the early stages. However, this finding that trade increases unemployment calls into question the conclusion that trade increases aggregate welfare.

Trade and Inequality

The introduction of heterogeneous firms also provides two insights into the relationship between trade and inequality.[9] First, the channels through which trade leads to higher inequality are more numerous than suggested by traditional trade theory. In particular, trade increases inequality even within industries of comparative advantage (e.g., Lawrence and Slaughter 1993). Moreover, this effect is not limited to inter-industry trade as predicted by the Stolper-Samuelson theorem. Intra-industry trade between countries with similar factor endowments (i.e., two developed countries) also increases inequality, because trade raises the skill premium as more productive firms increase their market share and less productive firms exit. While traditional trade theory predicts inequality will rise in labor scarce countries, and the empirical evidence bears this out, the findings here suggest that it may increase more than expected.

Second, NNTT predicts that trade will increase inequality in developing countries, in stark contrast to Stolper-Samuelson. Exporters in developing countries are again more skill intensive, and as they increase market share through trade, the skill premium, and by extension inequality, increase as well. Even without reference to the skill premium, Egger and Kreickemeier (2009) demonstrate that trade increases inequality among identical workers as more productive firms, which pay higher wages, increase their employment share. Intuitively, the positive effect of trade on inequality only strengthens in the presence of unemployment.

These effects are magnified by the offshoring of production activities and services, which contributes to rising inequality in both developed and developing countries. Feenstra and Hanson (1996) propose a model of offshoring in which firms can reallocate tasks to workers in another country based on skill intensity of the task and factor endowments, increasing inequality in both home and host. In political science, Chase (2008) emphasizes the importance of outsourcing as a source of cleavages between skilled and unskilled workers. He finds that inequality is correlated with offshoring, and that collective action in favor of countervailing duty petitions splits along skill level in the motion picture industry. The heterogeneous firms model of offshoring predicts a similar effect on inequality (Harrison et al. 2011).

DIRECTIONS FOR THE FUTURE

This section addresses three directions for future research. First, I argue that offshoring in services introduces new cleavages over trade and has the potential to increase the salience of trade in developed countries. Second, I discuss the implications of global production for the political influence of labor. Finally, I discuss the implications of heterogeneous firms theory for the politics of trade in developing countries.

Services Offshoring and New Trade Cleavages

Offshoring is the sourcing of inputs (goods and services) from foreign countries, through the migration of jobs from one country to another, regardless of whether activity remains wholly within the firm. Offshoring in manufacturing is not a new phenomenon and is the subject of a large literature (see, e.g., Feenstra and Hanson 1996). The development of global supply chains has increased the kinds of manufacturing activities that can be offshored, including the production of intermediate goods. Offshoring in manufacturing follows traditional patterns of comparative advantage; therefore, the production activities exported abroad from developed countries tend to be those that utilize unskilled labor.

However, declining transportation and telecommunications costs have generated not only trade in intermediate goods, but also trade in services. In the 1990s offshoring included more skill-intensive tasks, from a broader range of sectors, including services. Services, which were previously considered nontradable, are a large part of the economy in developed countries, and thus a sizable segment of the labor force may be exposed to international competition for the first time. Though there is some debate about how to measure the number of jobs that may be offshored, in general the literature agrees that the main characteristic of such jobs is that they may be provided from a distance; that is, over a wire. Blinder (2007) has generated an index of offshoreability, which emphasizes whether services are personal (requiring face-to-face interaction; e.g., child-care workers or surgeons), or impersonal (e.g., call center operators and software developers). Only the latter are potentially offshoreable, or vulnerable to offshoring. Though not all offshoreable jobs will be offshored, the scope for trade in services is increasing as telecommunications costs continue to fall (Blinder 2007).

In addition to exposing a large segment of the public to international competition for the first time, competitive pressures from services offshoring differ in important ways from those of manufacturing. This is likely to generate new cleavages over trade, not along factor or industry lines as in traditional trade theory, but rather along occupational lines. This suggests that within skill levels, industries, and even firms, workers may have heterogeneous preferences about trade. Empirical findings suggest that workers displaced due to offshoring sustained longer and more persistent earnings losses than those displaced for other reasons, and the effect is more pronounced for unskilled workers. Blinder (2007), for instance, finds that workers in offshoreable jobs experience lower wages, and that vulnerability to offshoring is not correlated with education. Across skill levels, some occupations will be exposed to offshoring, while others, especially high-skill jobs requiring creativity, will benefit from increasing exports of services. These fractionalized labor interests may make collective action by labor more difficult.

Offshoring is particularly politically salient. For example, Mankiw and Swagel (2006) discuss and document the political climate surrounding the offshore/outsourcing debate during the 2004 US election. They point to more than a thousand references to the issue of outsourcing in four major newspapers during that year (compared to fewer than three hundred in the preceding years). Margalit (2011) finds that voters are sensitive to offshoring-related job loss. Owen (n.d.-a) examines floor speeches on House debate over four FTAs between 2003 and 2004 and finds both that the issue of offshoring is raised frequently and that greater vulnerability to offshoring among constituents reduces the likelihood that House members will vote in favor of FTAs. As technological innovation and the economic integration of countries like China and India continue, offshoring is likely to become a salient political issue in developed countries, especially given that attitudes toward offshoring appear to be shaped by noneconomic factors such as nationalism and out-group attitudes, as suggested by Mansfield and Mutz (2013).

Elasticity of Demand and the Influence of Labor

Economic outcomes influence political ones, per Rogowski (1989), and thus the labor market outcomes of international trade have important implications for the ability of labor to influence trade and redistributive policy. Not only do trade and offshoring affect the composition and number of jobs in the economy, they also increase the elasticity of demand for labor and heterogeneity of labor interests. Together these affect the political power of protectionist labor interests, because they limit the bargaining power of unions, as well as the ease of collective action and nature of cleavages regarding trade.

In addition to generating feelings of job insecurity, the elasticity of demand is an important determinant of the bargaining power of labor. Fabbri, Haskel, and Slaughter (2003) find that outward FDI from the United States increased elasticity of demand for production and nonproduction workers. Multiple studies suggest that multinationals are more likely to close plants in response to wage shocks (e.g., Doms and Jensen 1998), suggesting the threat to exit is credible. The well-known article by Scheve and Slaughter (2004) suggests that workers are aware of this, because inward FDI is positively associated with feelings of job insecurity.

This weakens the economic position of labor, particularly in developed countries. Scholars have begun to examine the ways in which globalization hurts the bargaining power of unions over wages (e.g., Dumont, Rayp and Willeme 2006). Even the threat of relocation of production is enough to force unions to accept wage cuts. For example, trade unions in Belgium agreed to an increase in the workweek from thirty-five to thirty-eight hours, without additional pay, when Volkswagen threatened to close a plant in Brussels that was home to three thousand jobs.[10]

Globalization also is likely to impose constraints on the political influence of labor. Rogowski (1989) proposes a simple political model in which an increase (decrease) in wealth is associated with an increase (decrease) in political power and likely policy influence. For organized labor, it is a challenge to represent heterogeneous interests; thus the organization of unions becomes an important determinant of the political influence of labor. In other words, union density (rate of unionization) alone is not a sufficient measure of the strength of organized labor. It is an open question as to whether encompassing unions (i.e., those that are concentrated) are better able to navigate these internal divisions (Garrett 1998), or whether internal cleavages limit their effectiveness, as suggested by Chase (2008) in his concluding remarks. Unions in the past have been effective at influencing what comes into a country (e.g., imports and inward FDI) under certain conditions. For example, Owen (n.d.-b) finds that greater unionization leads to more barriers to inward FDI only when unions are highly concentrated. However, they have been less effective in shaping the behavior of domestically based firms that engage in outward FDI or offshoring.

Further research should examine how globalization interacts with labor market characteristics to shape the influence of labor interests on other policy outcomes, including compensation and redistribution. These trends are not limited solely to organized labor interests nor exclusively to developed countries. For example, Rudra (2008) argues that the bargaining power of labor is a function of the amount of surplus labor. She finds that certain aspects of globalization increase surplus labor, such that labor does not benefit much from openness even in labor-abundant countries.

New Challenges of Globalization in Developing Countries

Traditionally, the politics of trade were thought to be very different in developed and developing countries. However, the above NNTT suggests that openness tends to benefit skilled labor relatively more than unskilled labor, even in labor-abundant countries. This is consistent with survey findings from developing countries, in which more-educated respondents are more likely to favor openness than those who are less educated (Ardanaz, Murillo, and Pinto 2013). Thus, globalization is likely to generate political and social tension. Relative gains, even in the presence of absolute gains, have the potential to generate dissatisfaction, and inequality may be the source of demands for trade protection (e.g., Lu, Scheve, and Slaughter 2012). Similarly, Robertson and Teitelbaum (2011) argue that inward FDI is likely to increase social dislocations and lead to rising expectations and find that inward FDI leads to a higher incidence of strikes in low- and middle-income countries (especially in nondemocracies).

NNTT makes clear predictions that inequality in developing countries will increase. Though the empirical research on the relationship between inequality and globalization is vast, using a variety of measures and types of data (cross-national, subnational, etc.), recent work suggests that globalization does contribute to rising inequality. For example, Goldberg and Pavcnik (2007) find that the skill premium is rising in countries like Brazil, China, and Mexico. Regional differences in the level of development are exacerbated by differing levels of engagement with global economic forces, which contributes to rising within-country inequality.

As large developing countries like India and China become more integrated into the world economy, problems regarding the distribution of income will have to be addressed to mitigate social tension. Income inequality is a potential source of social instability, as suggested by Robertson and Teitelbaum, and something governments in developing countries appear to be taking seriously through a variety of policy measures. For example, the Chinese government has implemented a series of prorural policies, including the abolition of school fees in rural areas, though research suggests the inequality of opportunity may be just as important as, or even more important than, real income inequality (Lu 2013). Similarly, the Brazilian government has implemented incentives for foreign investors to locate in less-developed regions in the Northeast and Amazon regions. Brazil and other Latin American countries have also introduced policies like cash transfer programs targeted to the poor to address inequality.

The recent experiences of developing countries suggest that governments cannot continue to privilege economic growth without consideration of the distributional consequences. Moreover, they further suggest that globalization can lead to many of the same political issues for both developed and developed countries. Indeed, the potential for backlash may be greater given tighter constraints on countercyclical spending in developing and emerging markets.

CONCLUSIONS

As international trading relations evolve and become more open, the costs of adjustment facing labor will become increasingly important to navigate, particularly in light of the effects of trade on unemployment and inequality suggested by NNTT. In democracies in particular, failure to do so may lead to a protectionist backlash. Going forward, IPE scholars should reexamine how policies regarding trade and redistribution serve as substitutes or complements, and the influence of labor interests on both policy areas.

Continued openness has implications for the political influence of labor as well. Not only does the presence of mobile capital limit the ability to demand trade protection, but governments must be aware of a growing gap between labor and corporate income share as openness limits the ability to demand wage increases.

NOTES

1. See Lake (2009) for a summary of the OEP literature and Oatley (2011) for a critique.
2. Voters are consumers as well as workers. Baker (2005) concludes that even after considering the consumer interest, a HOS model seems to do well in explaining variation in individual level preferences.
3. See Milner (2002) for a summary of the debate over whether bad economic times allow politicians to push through necessary reforms like trade liberalization or makes them more likely to supply protection, as in the Great Depression.
4. On increasing legalization, see Goldstein and Martin (2000). On flexibility, see Rosendorff and Milner (2001) for an example emphasizing the role of institutional design, including flexibility and escape clauses, in the ability to promote cooperation.
5. See Bown (this volume) for more detailed discussion.
6. Industry subsidies are a different mechanism of redistribution. I focus on compensation because it is targeted toward workers.
7. The ability of governments to provide compensation is the subject of a large literature, which I do not address here. See Hays (2009) and Rickard (2012) as recent examples and reviews of existing literature.
8. Though they are not synonymous, I use FDI and offshoring interchangeably here.
9. See Harrison et al (2011) for a more extensive discussion and review of the empirical literature.
10. European Foundation for the Improvement of Living and Working Conditions (2008, 20).

REFERENCES

Alt, James, and Michael Gilligan. 1994. The Political Economy of Trading States: Factor Specificity, Collective Action Problems and Domestic Political Institutions. *Journal of Political Philosophy* 1 (2): 165–192.

Ardanaz, Martin, M. Victoria Murillo, and Pablo M. Pinto. 2013. Sensitivity to Issue Framing on Trade Policy Preferences: Evidence from a Survey Experiment. *International Organization* 67 (2): 411–437.

Baker, Andy. 2005. Who Wants to Globalize? Consumer Tastes and Labor Markets in a Theory of Trade Policy Beliefs. *American Journal of Political Science* 49 (4): 924–938.

Baldwin, Robert, and Christopher Magee. 2000. Is Free Trade for Sale? *Public Choice*: 105 (1/2): 79–101.

Bernard, Andrew B., J. Bradford Jensen, and Peter K. Schott (2006). Survival of the Best Fit: Exposure to Low-wage Countries and the (Uneven) Growth of U.S. Manufacturing Plants. *Journal of International Economics* 68: 219–237.

Blinder, Alan. 2007. How Many U.S. Jobs Might be Offshorable? CEPS Working Paper No. 142 (March).

Boix, Carles. 2006. Between Redistribution and Trade: The Political Economy of Protectionism and Domestic Compensation. In, *Globalization and Egalitarian Distribution*, edited by Samuel Bowles, Pranab Bardan, and Michael Wallerstein, 192–216, Princeton, NJ: Princeton University Press.

Bown, Chad. 2011. Taking Stock of Anti-dumping, Safeguards and Countervailing Duties, 1990–2009. *World Economy* 34(12): 1955–1998.

Bradford, Scott. 2006. Protection and Unemployment. *Journal of International Economics* 69 (2): 257–271.

Busch, Marc, and Eric Reinhardt. 2000. Geography, International Trade, and Political Mobilization in U.S. Industries. *American Journal of Political Science* 44 (4): 703–719.

Cassing, James, Timothy McKeown, and Jack Ochs. 1986. The Political Economy of the Tariff Cycle. *American Political Science Review* 80 (3): 843–862.

Chase, Kerry. 2003. Economic Interests and Regional Trading Agreements: The Case of NAFTA. *International Organization* 57 (1): 137–174.

Chase, Kerry. 2008. Moving Hollywood Abroad: Divided Labor Markets and the New Politics of Trade in Services. *International Organization* 62 (4): 653–687.

Corden, Max W. 1993. The Revival of Protectionism in Developed Countries. In *Protectionism and World Welfare*, edited by Dominick Salvatore, 54–79, New York: Cambridge University Press.

Davidson, Carl, and Steven Matusz. 2004. An Overlapping-generations Model of Escape Clause Protection. *Review of International Economics* 12 (5): 749–768.

Dixit, Avinash, and John Londregan. 1995. Redistributive Politics and Economic Efficiency. *American Political Science Review* 89 (4): 856–866.

Doms, Mark, and J. Bradford Jensen. 1998. Comparing Wages, Skills, and Productivity Between Domestically and Foreign-owned Manufacturing Establishments in the United States. In *Geography and Ownership as Bases for Economic Accounting*, edited by Robert Baldwin, Robert Lipsey, and J. David Richardson, 235–255, Chicago: University of Chicago Press.

Drope, Jeffrey, and Wendy Hansen. 2004. Purchasing Protection? The Effect of Political Spending on U.S. Trade Policy. *Political Research Quarterly* 57 (1): 27–37.

Dumont, Michael, Glenn Rayp, and Peter Willeme. 2006. Does Internationalization Affect Union Bargaining Power? An Empirical Study for Five EU Countries. *Oxford Economic Papers* 58: 77–102.

Dutt, Pusha, and Devashish Mitra. 2005. Political Ideology and Endogenous Trade Policy: An Empirical Investigation. *Review of Economics and Statistics* 87 (1): 59–72.

Egger, Hartmut, and Udo Kreickemeier. 2009. Firm Heterogeneity and the Labor Market Effects of Trade Liberalization. *International Economic Review* 50 (1): 187–216.

Ehrlich, Sean. 2010. The Fair Trade Challenge to Embedded Liberalism. *International Studies Quarterly* 54: 1013–1033.

European Foundation for the Improvement of Living and Working Conditions. 2008. Perceptions of Globalisation: Attitudes and Responses in the EU. http://www.eurofound.europa.eu/pubdocs/2008/07/en/1/ef0807en.pdf.

Fabbri, Francesca, Jonathan Haskel, and Matthew Slaughter. 2003. Does Nationality of Ownership Matter for Labor Demands? *Journal of the European Economic Association* 1 (2–3): 698–707.

Feenstra, Robert, and Gordon Hanson. 1996. Foreign Investment, Outsourcing, and Relative Wages. In *Political Economy of Trade Policy: Essays in Honor of Jagdish Bhagwati*, edited by Robert Feenstra and Gene Grossman, 89–128. Cambridge, MA: MIT Press.

Fordham, Benjamin, and Katja Kleinberg. 2012. How Can Economic Interests Influence Support for Free Trade? *International Organization* 66 (2): 311–328.

Garrett, Geoffrey. 1998. *Partisan Politics in the Global Economy*. New York: Cambridge University Press.

Gawande, Kishore, and Christopher Magee. 2012. Free Riding and Protection for Sale. *International Studies Quarterly* 56 (4): 1–13.

Goldberg, Pinelopi Koujianou, and Nina Pavcnik. 2007. Distributional Effects of Globalization in Developing Countries. *Journal of Economic Literature* 45 (1): 39–82.

Goldstein, Judith. 1986. The Political Economy of Trade: Institutions of Protection. *American Political Science Review* 80 (1): 161–184.

Goldstein, Judith, and Lisa Martin. 2000. Legalization, Trade Liberalization, and Domestic Politics: A Cautionary Note. *International Organization* 54 (3): 603–632.

Grossman, Gene, and Elhanan Helpman. 1994. Protection for Sale. *American Economic Review* 84 (4): 833–850.

Hansen, Wendy. 1990. The International Trade Commission and the Politics of Protectionism. *American Political Science Review* 84 (1): 21–46.

Harrison, Ann, John McLaren, and Margaret McMillan. 2011. Recent Perspectives on Trade and Inequality. World Bank Policy Research Working Paper 5754.

Hathaway, Oona. 1998. Positive Feedback: The Impact of Trade Liberalization on Industry Demands for Protection. *International Organization* 52 (30): 575–612.

Hays, Jude. 2009. *Globalization and the New Politics of Embedded Liberalism*. New York: Oxford University Press.

Hays, Jude, Sean Ehrlich, and Clint Peinhardt. 2005. Government Spending and Public Support for Trade in the OECD: An Empirical Test of the Embedded Liberalism Thesis. *International Organization* 59 (2): 473–494.

Helpman, Elhanan, and Oleg Itskhoki. 2009. Labor Market Rigidities, Trade and Unemployment. Centre for Economic Policy Research Working Paper 7502.

Henisz, Witold, and Edward Mansfied. 2006. Votes and Vetoes: The Political Determinants of Commercial Openness. *International Studies Quarterly* 50 (1): 189–211.

Hiscox, Michael. 2002. *International Trade and Political Conflict: Commerce, Coalitions and Mobility*. Princeton, NJ: Princeton University Press.

Hwang, Wonjae, and Hoon Lee. 2013. Globalization, Factor Mobility, Partisanship, and Compensation Policies. *International Studies Quarterly* 58(1): 1–14.

Kletzer, Lori. 2001. *Job Loss from Imports: Measuring the Costs*. Washington, DC: Institute for International Economics.

Krugman, Paul. 1981. International Trade and Income Distribution: A Reconsideration. NBER Working Paper No. 356.

Lake, David. 2009. Open Economy Politics: A Critical Review. *Review of International Organization* 4: 219–244.

Lawrence, Robert, and Matthew Slaughter. 1993. Trade and U.S. Wages: Giant Sucking Sound or Small Hiccup? *BPEA, Microeconomics* 2: 161–210.

Lu, Xiaobo. 2013. Equality of Education Opportunity and Attitudes Toward Income Inequality: Evidence from China. *Quarterly Journal of Political Science* 8 (3): 271–303.

Lu, Xiaobo, Kenneth Scheve, and Matthew Slaughter. 2012. Inequity Aversion and the International Distribution of Trade Protection. *American Journal of Political Science* 56 (3): 638–654.

Mankiw, N. Gregory, and Phillip Swagel. 2006. The Politics and Economics of Offshore Outsourcing. *Journal of Monetary Economics* 53 (5): 1027–1056.

Mansfield, Edward, and Marc Busch. 1995. The Political Economy of Non-tariff Barriers: A Cross-National Analysis. *International Organization* 49 (4): 723–749.

Mansfield, Edward, and Diana Mutz. 2013. Us vs. Them: Mass Attitudes toward Offshore Outsourcing. *World Politics* 65 (4): 571–608.

Margalit, Yotam. 2011. Costly Jobs: Trade-related Layoffs, Government Compensation, and Voting in U.S. Elections. *American Political Science Review* 105 (1): 166–188.

Matschke, Xenia, and Shane Sherlund. 2006. Do Labor Issues Matter in the Determination of U.S. Trade Policy. *American Economic Review* 96 (1): 405–421.

Melitz, Marc. 2003. The Impact of Intra-industry Reallocations and Aggregate Industry Productivity. *Econometrica* 71 (6): 1695–1725.

Milner, Helen. 2002. International Trade. In *The Handbook of International Relations*, edited by Walter Carlsnaes, Thomas Risse, and Beth Simmons, 448–461. London: Sage Publications.

Milner, Helen. 1988. *Resisting Protectionism*. Princeton, NJ: Princeton University Press.

Milner, Helen, and Bumba Mukherjee. N.d. Democracy and the Skill-Bias in Trade Policy in Developing Countries. Unpublished manuscript.

Milner, Helen, and Benjamin Judkins. 2004. Partisanship, Trade Policy, and Globalization: Is There a Left-Right Divide on Trade Policy? *International Studies Quarterly* 48: 95–119.

Milner, Helen, and Keiko Kubota. 2005. Why the Move to Free Trade? Democracy and Trade Policy in Developing Countries. *International Organization* 59 (1): 107–143.

Mitra, Devashish, and Priya Ranjan. 2010. Offshoring and Unemployment: The Role of Search Frictions Labor Mobility. *Journal of International Economics* 81 (2): 219–229.

Mukherjee, Bumba, Dale Smith, and Quan Li. 2009. Labor (Im)mobility and the Politics of Trade Protection in Majoritarian Democracies. *Journal of Politics* 71 (1): 291–308.

Naoi, Megumi. 2009. Shopping for Protection: The Politics of Choosing Trade Instruments in a Partially Legalized World. *International Studies Quarterly* 53: 421–444.

Oatley, Thomas. 2011. The Reductionist Gamble: Open Economy Politics in the Global Economy. *International Organization* 65: 311–341.

Owen, Erica. N.d.-a. Labor, Offshoring, and the Political Economy of Trade Liberalization. Paper presented at the meeting of the International Political Economy Society, Pomona, CA.

Owen, Erica. N.d.-b. The Strength of Organized Labor and the Politics of Foreign Direct Investment: The Impact of Union Membership and Concentration on Barriers to Inward

FDI in Developed Democracies. Paper presented at the meeting of the International Studies Association, San Francisco, CA.

Owen, Erica, and Dennis Quinn. Forthcoming. Does Economic Globalization Influence the U.S. Policy Mood? A Study of U.S. Public Sentiment, 1956–2011. *British Journal of Political Science.*

Rehm, Philipp. 2011. Risk Inequality and the Polarized American Electorate. *British Journal of Political Science* 41: 363–387.

Rickard, Stephanie. 2012. Welfare versus Subsidies: Governmental Spending Decisions in an Era of Globalization. *Journal of Politics* 74 (4): 1171–1183.

Robertson, Graeme, and Emmanuel Teitelbaum. 2011. Foreign Direct Investment, Regime Type, and Labor Protest in Developing Countries. *American Journal of Political Science* 55 (3): 665–667.

Rogowski, Ronald. 1989. *Commerce and Coalitions.* Princeton, NJ: Princeton University Press.

Rogowski, Ronald. 2006. Trade, Immigration, and Cross-Border Investment. In *The Oxford Handbook of Political Economy,* edited by. Barry Weingast and Donald Wittman, 814–830, Oxford: Oxford University Press.

Rosendorff, Peter, and Helen Milner. 2001. The Optimal Design of International Trade Institutions: Uncertainty and Escape. *International Organization* 55 (4): 829–857.

Rudra, Nita. 2008. *Globalization and the Race to the Bottom in Developing Countries: Who Really Gets Hurt?* Cambridge, UK: Cambridge University Press.

Rueda, David. 2007. *Social Democracy Inside Out: Partisanship and Labor Market Policy in Industrialized Democracies.* Oxford: Oxford University Press.

Ruggie, John. 1982. International Regimes, Transactions, and Change: Embedded Liberalism in the Postwar Economic Order. *International Organization* 36 (2): 203–223.

Scheve, Kenneth, and Matthew J. Slaughter. 2004. Economic Insecurity and the Globalization of Production. *American Journal of Political Science* 48 (4): 662–674.

Scheve, Kenneth, and Matthew Slaughter. 2006. Public Opinion, International Economic Integration, and the Welfare State. In *Globalization and Egalitarian Distribution,* edited by Samuel Bowles, Pranab Bardan, and Michael Wallerstein, 217–260, Princeton, NJ: Princeton University Press.

Stolper, Wolfgang, and Paul Samuelson. 1941. Protection and Real Wages. *Review of Economic Studies* 9 (1): 58–73.

Steagall, Jeffrey, and Ken Jennings. 1996. Unions, PAC Contributions, and the NAFTA Vote. *Journal of Labor Research* 17 (3): 515–521.

Takacs, Wendy. 1981. Pressures for Protectionism: An Empirical Analysis. *Economic Inquiry* 19: 687–693.

Tavares, Jose. 2008. Trade, Factor Proportions, and Political Rights. *Review of Economics and Statistics* 90 (1): 163–168.

Walter, Stephanie. 2010. Globalization and the Welfare State: Testing the Microfoundations of the Compensation Hypothesis. *International Studies Quarterly* 54 (2): 403–426.

CHAPTER 8

··

DOMESTIC POLITICS AND
INTERNATIONAL DISPUTES

··

B. PETER ROSENDORFF

INTERNATIONAL trade in goods and services occurs within a complex international legal framework, constituted by both negotiated treaties and customary international law.* The General Agreement on Tariffs and Trade (GATT), which is still operative under the structure of the World Trade Organization (WTO), subject to the modifications of 1994, forms the backbone of international trade law. Together with regional or preferential trade agreements (PTAs), it is designed to lower trade barriers and increase the flows and benefits of trade among member states.

States that accede to these international regulatory environments in general intend to comply with their obligations (Downs, Rocke, and Barsoom, 1996; Chayes and Chayes, 1993). Occasionally political pressures to protect certain industries, sectors, or interests may be difficult to avoid, even if the international agreements restrict such action (Rosendorff and Milner, 2001; Rosendorff, 2005). States therefore must balance the need to comply with their international obligations with the domestic political need to protect political supporters from international competition. Domestic politics matters for understanding the pattern of compliance with international obligations. Policy makers deviate from WTO and PTA obligations in search of enhanced electoral returns (Simmons 1998; Naoi 2009).

Responding to the needs of politically influential groups or voters at large, policy makers enter the gray area between compliance with and abrogation of their international commitments. Subsidies (usually implicit) in favor of export interests, for example, are rationalized as a legal response to unfair protection abroad; it is often argued that tariffs at home are reasonable and legal responses to foreign dumping or to provide temporary protection while an industry retools, or necessary to protect the health and safety of domestic consumers. Such trade policy choices may or may not be legal under the WTO or the PTAs to which a state is a signatory. Aware of this ambiguity, states have developed and refined dispute settlement mechanisms to more effectively adjudicate these disputes, to clarify obligations, to offer avenues for escape, and to enhance flexibility within the world trading system.

Domestic politics (actors and institutions) affects the decision to include a dispute settlement procedure (DSP) in an international trade agreement in the first place. Politics also affects the design of, and the rules that govern the practice of, the DSP and the choice to use the mechanism once in place. This chapter explores how domestic actors and institutions influence the presence or absence of dispute settlement mechanisms and how they influence the use and outcome of the adjudicatory procedure. The chapter closes with a recognition of a feedback effect: that the dispute settlement process and the disputes themselves in turn have an effect on the domestic politics (and economics) of the signatory states, an effect not unanticipated by the authors and designers of these international agreements and the drafters of international law.

Domestic Politics and Design

The procedures specified in the Dispute Settlement Understanding (DSU) adopted during the Uruguay Round of negotiations at the WTO permit a contracting party to file a complaint with the WTO regarding a perceived violation of the treaty on the part of another member. If formal, bilateral consultations are unproductive (an attempt at a negotiated resolution), the complainant may request that a panel of independent experts investigate the matter and make a recommendation. If the panel finds that the offending action is "inconsistent," the offending party is obliged to terminate the violating measure and bring its practice back into conformity with its obligations or compensate the complainant for damages.[1] Ultimately, if a measure is not rescinded and compensation is not paid, retaliation can be authorized. The finding by the panel can also be appealed to the Standing Appellate Body.

Across the realm of PTAs, there is significant variation in dispute settlement procedures, ranging from "weaker," nonbinding, informal opportunities for consultation and negotiation (a more diplomatic route); to "stronger," formal, binding, standing, third-party courts, the decisions of which have the force of international law, with appeals processes; to even stronger measures, including the possibility of sanctions for violation (more "legalistic" design). Scholars have developed a variety of measures of the degree of legalism, including Hofmann and Kim (2013a) and Haftel (2013).

The DESTA (Dür, Baccini, and Elsig 2013) data set is probably the most comprehensive and compelling compilation of facts regarding PTAs. Dür, Baccini, and Elsig studied 587 agreements for more than 100 measures, including details on embodied dispute settlement mechanisms. They find that 87 percent of agreements include some type of dispute settlement provision, and 6 percent create a standing legal body to adjudicate cases. Figure 8.1 offers a summary of the variation in the characteristics of DSPs identified in the DESTA data set.

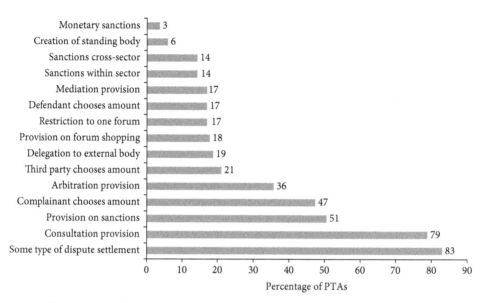

FIG. 8.1 Variation in DSP Design across PTAs.

Source: Dür, Baccini, and Elsig (2013). Percentages of the 587 PTAs coded that have the feature specified.

Political Uncertainty, Dispute Settlement, and Flexibility

Once an international agreement is in place, leaders experience uncertainty about the costs of compliance. Industries occasionally experience unanticipated surges of imports or technological shifts abroad that lower competitiveness of local sectors or particular skill sets held by local professions. These groups, if they are organized, will influence trade policy makers to provide protection. This has been described as a "time-consistency" problem, in which a treaty design that is optimal in expectation ex ante may not be so ex post.

Of course at the time these international trade agreements are negotiated, the member states are aware of these potential contingencies and are unlikely to build institutions and agreements they know they will have difficulty complying with. Leaders build flexibility into the agreements to manage this time-consistency problem, of which DSPs are a central flexibility-enhancing mechanism.

Some argue that the signatories use an instrument of international law to prevent them from succumbing to the particularistic demands of special interests to the benefit of social welfare. This "tying-of-the-hands" interpretation of trade agreements (e.g., Maggi and Rodriguez-Clare 1998) suggests that the stronger the agreement is in preventing violations, the more leaders can withstand domestic political pressure and the greater is the degree of international cooperation.

States interested in maximizing the gains from trade might then be expected to design very rigid agreements, with deep concessions and few (if any) opportunities for abrogation. This would especially be true of democratic states. If democracies are more responsive to political pressure to protect affected industries (at least on average), we might be inclined to predict that democracies will build agreements that bind very tightly.

In fact the agreements regulating international trade (and for that matter international investment, environmental, and other issue area agreements) to varying degrees embody a variety of flexibility-enhancing devices designed to reduce the rigidity of the agreements and to manage these periods of intense, unexpected political pressure to protect a sector, interest, or industry.[2] A "flexibility provision" is "any provision of an international agreement that allows a country to suspend the concessions it previously negotiated without violating or abrogating the terms of the agreement" (Rosendorff and Milner 2001).[3]

The WTO articles, for instance, explicitly allow signatories to renege on their commitments under certain circumstances. Article XIX allows a country, for a limited time, to suspend its obligations when increased imports "cause or threaten serious injury to domestic producers" of import-competing goods.[4] Article VI of the GATT, the anti-dumping (AD) and countervailing duties (CVD) codes, allow member states to apply duties when imports are "dumped" or when the foreign competitor is being subsidized. Balance of payments exceptions (Articles XVII and XII), infant industry protection (XVIII), and tariff renegotiation (XXVII) are also opportunities for WTO-legal application of trade barriers. Kim (2010) offers a historical account of how this need for flexibility resulted in these provisions in the original GATT texts. She finds, for example, that "uncertainty regarding domestic political support for free trade and trade liberalization in the United States . . . was a significant factor leading to flexibility in the design of the General Agreement" (2010, 41).

A state experiencing a set of circumstances that results in clamoring by a group or sector for a policy of protection may, in an exercise of policy discretion, choose to oblige the special interest. This runs the risk, of course, of opening up that state to complaints from its trading partners. A provision that provides protection for a domestic industry by definition reduces access to the market by the member's trading partners. The trading partners' complaints may eventually take the form of formal trade disputes under either the auspices of the WTO or the mechanisms of the applicable PTAs.[5]

If there are opportunities for signatories to escape their obligations (at least temporarily, until the unexpected political pressure passes and a more "normal" state of affairs prevails), an affected country may subject itself to the discipline of a DSP under the WTO or a PTA. The use of a DSP therefore allows a contracting partner to violate the (spirit, if not the letter of, the) agreement, yet remain within the community of cooperating nations and not be immediately punished or banished for its actions. Trading partners acquiesce, for they may be in need of similar tolerance sometime in the not too distant future. The dispute settlement processes built into the international trading regime add flexibility to an otherwise rigid system.

These opportunities for "tolerated defection" (Rosendorff 2005) (or "'forbearance" [Bowen 2010], "efficient breach" [Sykes 1991; Dunoff and Trachtman 1999], or

"involuntary defection" [Putnam 1988]) all suggest that states that are more susceptible to political pressure are less likely to sign onto agreements that lack these flexibility
provisions. Before being willing to sign agreements, political leaders need to know that
when their political survival is on the line, those agreements will permit them to take
ameliorative action. Compliance is a political decision; so is the decision to accede to a
compliance regime.

The evidence suggests that democratic polities are *more* likely to join PTAs
(Mansfield, Milner, and Pevehouse 2007), to trade more freely (Mansfield, Milner, and
Rosendorff 2000; Rosendorff 2006), and to join agreements that embody stronger dispute settlement procedures (Pevehouse, Hafner-Burton, and Zierler 2002; Pevehouse
and Buhr 2013).

Further evidence that flexibility provisions make accession to trade agreements
more likely comes from Kucik and Reinhardt (2008), who show that states that
are able to take advantage of a domestic antidumping mechanism (a key flexibility
device) are significantly more likely to join the WTO, agree to more tightly binding
tariff commitments, and implement lower applied tariffs. That is, flexibility makes
accession at deeper levels more likely. Kucik and Reinhardt take seriously the problem
of endogeneity when understanding the effect of a flexibility provision on the willingness to join an agreement. They correctly remark that "several different endogenous
variables are co-determined: specifically, 1) the existence of flexibility provisions in an
agreement; 2) a state's decision to enter into the agreement; and 3) the level of concessions" of the depth of the agreement (2008, 479). Johns (2013) establishes that once we
control for the benefits of trade liberalization, deep agreements will be more flexible,
while shallow agreements will be more rigid. Only if a leader knows that she or he has
the flexibility to violate a trade agreement when times are tough will she or he commit
to deeper tariff concessions, initially at the time of trade agreement negotiations.

Variation in Dispute Settlement Design across PTAs

Hofmann and Kim (2013a) identify a set of hypotheses in the literature that explain the
degree of delegation and obligation (terms defined by Goldstein et al. 2000), proxies
for the depth of legalized agreements. Pevehouse and Buhr (2013) and Smith (2000)
suggest that the depth of commercial integration in terms of trade volumes predicts
DSP legalism; depth in terms of specific assets susceptible to capture and holdup such
as foreign direct investment also predict a stronger DSP (Büthe and Milner 2008).
Haftel (2013) shows that strength of the negotiated DSP is correlated with the depth of
implementation of the agreement. Colonial history among the members makes stronger DSPs less likely, but democracy makes stronger DSPs more likely (Hofmann and
Kim 2013a).

There is significant cross-country spillover when it comes to PTA and DSP design.
More legalistic approaches to PTA formation appear to diffuse across borders. Within

the set of fifty-seven PTAs in the Asia-Pacific, Hofmann and Kim (2013a) find that despite the "ASEAN way" of Asian countries not engaging in open conflict with each other, more legalistic dispute settlement mechanisms are diffusing across agreements: the more legalistic the agreements are that the members have already joined, the more likely it is that a new PTA between them will be more legalistic. Like much of the literature on diffusion (Simmons and Elkins 2004), little explanation is offered for what is driving this diffusion: Is it learning, competition, emulation, or some other process?

These studies exploring the domestic and international sources of variation in the degree of "legalism" generally suffer from the problem of endogeneity. The strength of the dispute settlement procedure is codetermined with other dimensions of the treaty design: the depth, scope, and the scale of its membership (Johns 2013). Hence to isolate one dimension and look for independent causal variables, perhaps taking the other dimensions as given and exogenous, generates substantial misspecification bias.[6]

FUNCTIONING AND OUTCOMES OF DSPs

Once a mechanism is in place for dealing with the uncertainty associated with domestic politics and the pressure for protection, it follows that domestic politics will influence the incidence of disputes, or the relative frequency with which the various dispute settlement mechanisms are appealed to. Similarly, if political uncertainties are driving the design of DSPs and the frequency with which they are appealed to, they will necessarily influence the outcome of the dispute settlement process—in particular, how often cases are settled before trial and the circumstances under which cases actually make it to trial.

On the Incidence of Disputes: Who Files?

Democracy and Development

Within the context of the WTO, substantial modifications were made in the DSP in the shift from GATT to WTO in 1994. The diplomatic nature of the GATT made the hearing of a dispute rare and somewhat weak and ineffective. The WTO now entrenches a complainant's right to a panel, providing for the automatic adoption of panel reports (except in the case of "negative consensus," in which all member states, including the complainant and defendant, agree to void the report) and making appellate review available. The DSP in addition has jurisdiction over all disputes arising under the various GATT agreements that were rolled into the WTO.

Busch (2000) argues that the democratic dyads are more likely to escalate their disputes to the panel stage than are other dyads. Reinhardt (2000), using data on dispute initiation within all GATT/WTO directed dyads from 1948 through 1998, finds that democracies participate in more, not fewer, GATT/WTO disputes, and they resolve those disputes less cooperatively as well. Rosendorff and Smith (2013) find that the most democratic nations are between 6.5 and 51 times more likely to initiate a WTO dispute than the most autocratic nations. Dyads that have had recent disputes (defined as a dispute within the dyad in either of the two previous years) are far more likely to have future disputes than dyads without a recent history of disputes.[7] The rate of WTO dispute onset is less than 6 per 10,000 dyad years without a recent history of disputes. When there is a prior history of disputes, then the rate of dispute onset jumps to about 39 per 10,000 dyad years.

WTO disputes occur between large economically powerful nations. Rosendorff and Smith (2013) estimate that the predicted probability for a country at the 75th percentile of GDP and population of initiating a dispute is a mere 0.00007, less than one dispute per 10,000 dyad years. In larger nations (GDP and population at the 95th percentile) the rate of dispute onset is substantially higher: approximately 20 disputes per 10,000 dyad years.[8]

"Who Files?" Is Endogenous to "Who Violates?"

This literature ignores to a substantial degree the selection effect—not all violations end up as formal disputes. Some are settled via a negotiation process and are not even reported to the WTO. Davis reports that the United States National Trade Estimate Report (which monitors the trade barriers of US trade partners) listed 126 trade barriers by Japan between 1995 and 2004, of which only 6 were addressed in WTO dispute settlement (2012, 9). There is therefore an outstanding question: What determines the set of cases that are in fact adjudicated (from the set of actual violations)?

First, it could be the tough cases, in which there is genuinely an issue of interpretation or clarification of obligations required and not simply a matter of opportunistic protectionism taking place. Second, cases that are more likely to result in compliance once decided are perhaps more likely to be brought. Rulings are more likely to be limited to those that can be implemented cheaply rather than those that are (politically) expensive for the defendant. Hence bringing a case for which the expected ruling is unlikely to be complied with may potentially bring the court's legitimacy into question, an outcome a potential plaintiff state may not prefer to initiate.[9] If expected rulings are a function of the member state's and the court's concern for the legitimacy of the court, this will affect which cases are brought from the set of actual violations.[10]

Davis (2012) suggests that the checks and balances that characterize democracies bias dispute settlement toward public lawsuits (filings) and away from informal settlements (negotiations). Davis argues that leaders, to enhance their domestic political prospects, must be seen by their legislatures and politically influential sectors and industries to be enforcing international trade obligations abroad. Filing a lawsuit is a public signal of their commitment to redistributing in favor of that industry; negotiation as an alternative strategy may solve the problem, but it is done behind closed doors and prevents a credible signal of the leader's commitment to that industry from being sent. There is therefore a political demand for what Davis calls "adjudication," and this demand is heightened in polities in which leaders are more accountable, notably democracies.

The decision to file therefore is indeed a political one; we have argued that the decision to violate (or at least to appeal to the flexibility-enhancing devices as a basis for the violation) is also a political one. Most of the literature, however, treats the sample of filings as given. Davis and Shirato (2007) and Davis (2012) do consider the political determinants of the decision to file, given a set of observed violations. But the decision to violate depends crucially on whether the potential violator expects to be filed against. Hence taking the set of violations as somehow exogenous from domestic politics in both the domestic and foreign countries is probably a flawed approach.[11] The answer to the question "Who files?" is determined simultaneously with the answer to the question "Who violates?" Current work doesn't manage to address this endogeneity.

Leader Turnover

Leaders rely on a coalition of supporters to remain in office. Government changes, especially those associated with changes in the underlying coalition of supporters, generate a shift in the profile of trade policy. Leadership changes, especially those associated with shifts in the underlying support coalition, lead therefore to changes in a nation's tariff and subsidy profile. When a trade policy profile—a set of policies across industries or sectors—changes, it is likely that some outstanding disputes will now be settled, and other sectors will see new disputes initiated. Sectors that see their protection decline are associated with settlement of preexisting disputes; sectors receiving enhanced protection may be associated with new disputes initiated against their government.

Leader change, therefore, and especially those changes in leadership associated with changes in the underlying support coalition, are associated with changes in the pattern of dispute settlements and filings at the WTO. Bobick and Smith (2013) find that leader change leads to more new disputes and more settlements of disputes. Rosendorff and Smith (2013) show that this effect is accentuated when the leader turnover is associated with a change in the underlying support coalitions, compared to situations of either no leader change or leader change without a change in the underlying support coalition.

These findings are conditioned by regime type. The effect of leader change on dispute initiation is much larger in nondemocracies than in democracies. Elections in democracies that bring new leaders to office have a relatively small effect on new dispute initiation; leader changes in autocracies, especially those associated with changes in support coalition, have a much larger effect on dispute initiation.[12] Simulation of the size of the substantive effect suggests leader change in an autocracy increases the risk of dispute onset about eightfold when compared with a democracy (Rosendorff and Smith 2013).

A democracy requires a larger supporting coalition; protection is likely to cover a wider set of industries. However, protection for more sectors comes at a greater cost to the individual consumers and voters by way of higher prices for goods. In contrast, autocracies have smaller winning coalitions and little regard for consumers in general;

protection is likely to be deeper for a smaller set of industries. Since protection benefits industries (and workers in those industries), but harms consumers in general, protection will be wider but shallower in democracies than in autocracies that provide deep but narrow protections.

Since protection for any specific sector is shallower in democracies, the likelihood that the state will become a defendant in a WTO dispute filing in that sector is lower. The deep protection offered by an autocracy makes the likelihood of WTO dispute initiation much greater. Hence leader change in an autocracy is likely to be associated with more new dispute initiation than leader change in a democracy.

Politics and Outcomes: Adjudication or Settlement?

Disputes (once filed) can be concluded in one of three ways. The case can simply be "dropped"—35 percent of all cases that are filed fail to report any formal settlement with the WTO, and no panel is established, although many of these may actually have been settled but the settlement was simply not reported (Chaudoin, Kucik, and Pelc 2013). Settled cases (those that reach a mutually agreed solution) and those that go to rulings via litigation and a panel report (about 50 percent of all cases) make up the rest.

Busch (2000) establishes that cases are more likely to be paneled when the disputants are democracies. He also finds that those cases paneled by democratic dyads are more likely to end with concessions by the defendant states. Democracies are also more likely to be named in petitions filed by the United States in antidumping cases (Busch, Raciborski, and Reinhardt 2008). Democracies are more willing to participate in the adjudicatory mechanisms of the WTO and comply with its findings.

"Early settlement" offers the greatest chance of obtaining greater concessions from a defendant at the GATT/WTO. Developing countries, however, have been more likely to have disputes proceed to the panel stage against developed countries (Busch 2000). As a result, they have fared less well in extracting concessions from defendants. The newer, stronger DSP system reinforces this outcome, given both the incentives to litigate as well as developing countries' lack of capacity to push for early settlement (Busch and Reinhardt 2003).

The designers of the WTO's DSP clearly intended for member states to solve their differences via negotiation and settlement. Even when dispute reaches the panel stage, a ruling often takes the form of an interpretation of the text in the context of the dispute, rather than a finding of explicit violation. The WTO's various provisions require a (re-) negotiated solution whenever possible. Johns and her coauthors (Johns and Pelc 2014; Johns 2013; Gilligan, Johns, and Rosendorff 2010; Gilligan and Johns 2012) describe this as "post-adjudicative bargaining." Stronger courts—with higher levels of enforcement and jurisdiction—may come with hidden costs: if a plaintiff has private information about the value of a legal claim, as international courts grow stronger, legal claims matter more, and the asymmetrical information becomes more important. This lessens the likelihood of an early settlement to the dispute and increases the likelihood of costly litigation, exacerbating conflicts between states.

CLOSING THE LOOP: THE EFFECTS OF DSPs ON TRADE, TRADE POLICY, AND DOMESTIC POLITICS

Domestic politics has been shown to matter for the design of these mechanisms for settling international disputes. It influences the frequency with which violations occur, the decision to file a dispute, and the outcomes of the DSP. Domestic politics affects the design, form, and function of international institutions.

There is also a feedback effect. A dispute and the dispute settlement institution can influence domestic politics. It is of course a central question, of both international political economy scholars and those in international law, to ascertain the conditions under which international economic law can affect state behavior (Martin and Simmons 1998). State behavior, in turn, is the product of domestic political bargaining and conflict.

Disputes are "fire alarms" that sound when states violate their obligations (McCubbins and Schwartz 1987). They can activate domestic actors to punish their government politically for offering distortionary protection to industries (McGillivray and Smith 2000, 2004). If the public cannot observe the policy choices of their executives directly, these fire alarms may improve the quality of the information that the public can use to infer their government's behavior. An election in adverse conditions could result in the "unfair eviction" of the executive: eviction because the voters suspect the executive has been extractive; unfair because bad aggregate economic conditions rather than extractive behavior could have generated the adverse economic environment. To insure themselves against this unfair eviction, executives sign PTAs, especially those with DSPs, so that their nonextractive behavior can be more easily observed by the public. Democratically accountable executives are particularly sensitive to this logic and hence are more likely to trade away extractive opportunities in return for holding onto office during economic downturns by signing PTAs. Autocratic executives, less sensitive to the will of the voters, sign PTAs less frequently or are less concerned about embodying an effective DSP. As a result democracies are more likely to sign PTAs, especially those with DSPs, than are autocracies (Mansfield, Milner, and Rosendorff 2000, 2002; Rosendorff 2006). Democracies are also likely to cooperate more on trade issues due to other mechanisms. Mansfield, Milner, and Rosendorff (2000) argue, for instance, that the separation of powers characteristic of democracies leads to more cooperative behavior than in unitary states.

This feedback implies that there are both economic and political effects of trade disputes.

Economic: DSPs and Trade Policy

Domestic politics appears to condition the effect of DSPs on trade volumes. A recent flurry of papers (Chaudoin, Kucik, and Pelc 2013; Hofmann and Kim 2013b; Bechtel and Sattler 2011; Bown 2001) explore whether disputes increase trade. After all, a dispute is initiated if a measure adopted by a signatory state has restricted market access by another member state. Once the dispute is finalized—via either settlement or ruling—and the offending measure is removed or an equivalent concession is offered, one might expect trade volumes to resume to levels that existed prior to the implementation of the offending measure.

Bown (2001) and Chaudoin, Kucik, and Pelc (2013) find almost no effect of disputes on trade volumes; Bechtel and Sattler (2011) find a positive effect of dispute settlement on trade volumes—exports from a complainant country in a WTO dispute rise significantly in the three years after a panel ruling, and similar effects are evident in the exports of pro-complainant third parties. Furthermore, procomplainant third parties experience more exports than neutral or prodefendant third parties. Hofmann and Kim (2013b) find that settled cases end with more trade. However, among cases that end and then return to the WTO's DSP for compliance hearings—indicating that compliance is in dispute—trade falls. Furthermore, consistent with what Bhagwati (1988) has called the "law of constant protection," new barriers appear to rise when compliance is in dispute.

This confusing picture is probably the result of a misperception of the role of the DSP in the international trading system. The question that should be put is not, *Does trade increase after a dispute?* but rather, *Is there more trade in a world trading system with a DSP compared to a world trading system without one?*

There is a temptation to think of panel findings as ordering the removal of a policy that is ruled as a violation. There is no question that panels clarify obligations, demand that the parties return to the bargaining table, and renegotiate given the clarifications of the obligations that the panel has made. The panels, of course, have no enforcement power. The effect, as we have argued above, is to permit tolerated defection or forbearance and to add flexibility and enhance stability of the system. Panel rulings encourage further ("postadjudicative") negotiation and may actually facilitate collusion. Consequently, the DSP is not a mechanism to ensure that trade increases on average; it is instead a mechanism to manage tolerated defection.

A system with a DSP therefore better manages defections than a system without one. Defections are tolerated without the system collapsing into retaliatory trade wars. This enhanced stability of the system comes at some cost, however. There is less per period cooperation relative to a system without a DSP, but such a system is more prone to collapse when severe political shocks hit one or more of the member states. A DSP permits the member states to reap the long-term benefits of a more stable trading regime, even at the cost of some short-term defection.

The extra flexibility a DSP offers within a trading system also makes countries who are otherwise less likely to want to sign such an agreement more willing to do so. Leaders, concerned that the caps on the levels of permitted protection will prevent them from offering policies in favor of an industry in their supporting coalition when adverse shocks hit, will find that a DSP permits a government the flexibility to do what it needs to in times of enhanced political pressure. Such a system therefore is more inclusive and permits a greater number and variety of states to join it (Rosendorff 2005).

The benefits of a DSP therefore are not associated with more trade after a dispute is concluded; they are increased stability of the system and a larger membership within a more liberalized world trading system.

Political: DSPs, Information, and Leader Survival

The previous section suggested that the extra flexibility a trading system with a DSP offers reduces the likelihood of breakdown and increases membership. Presumably these features improve the political prospects of the leaders who join these agreements. Clearly the ability to protect an influential sector in times of political crisis has benefits for leaders concerned with their political survival. But the leaders are committing themselves to systems in which the levels of protection are capped, the procedures by which trade policy can be changed are restricted and limited, and heightened transparency over trade policy is required. They make these commitments because their (re-)electoral prospects are heightened by doing so.

Mansfield, Milner, and Rosendorff (2002) argue that the information generated by the DSP plays a crucial role in enhancing the electoral survival of leaders in democracies. The DSP, in its role as a clearinghouse for information regarding trade conflicts, clarifies whether a violation has occurred and when it has been resolved to the satisfaction of both sides. Protection for an industry acts like a tax on consumers and voters at large, but if voters are poorly informed about the trade policy choices of their leaders, it may be difficult for them to identify how much their current economic distress is the result of poor policy choices by their leaders and how much is due to unfavorable economic conditions. A trade agreement with a well-functioning DSP helps the voters disentangle these two effects. The information provided by the DSP helps the voters discern whether the bad current conditions are indeed the result of reallocation of income via trade policy or a consequence of circumstances beyond the leader's control.

Where the will of the voters matters for leader survival—say in democracies—leaders will be more likely to sign agreements with DSPs to insure themselves from being evicted from office in bad times. Leaders in autocracies, who are insulated from popular concerns, will find the information generated by a DSP less helpful and perhaps even a nuisance. Information plays a key role in the explanation here, and DSPs are providers of information voters use to discipline their leaders and keep them from being excessively extractive. The DSP, in addition to adding flexibility to the world trading system, adds transparency to the policy-making process domestically, which facilitates monitoring by voters, at least in democracies.

Mansfield, Milner, and Rosendorff (2002) don't actually test this informational mechanism. They offer a reduced-form empirical specification, linking democracies to trade. While consistent with the theoretical story, it is not quite a complete test. In an even more direct test of the mechanism—that voters use information generated by the international organization to make political decisions—Pelc (2012) investigates Google searches as a measure of the information flows from the WTO to voters. Using this innovative measure, he finds that US citizens are concerned about their country being branded a violator of international law, even when they have no direct material stake in the case at hand. He finds little evidence, however, that material interests magnify the reaction to US filings against trade partners.[13]

Hollyer and Rosendorff (2012) revisit this question and test two aspects of this problem more closely. First, presumably leaders who sign PTAs survive in office longer—on the basis of the political gains from signing discussed above. Second, this is more true of democratic leaders than of autocratic leaders.

PTAs codify and clarify the permitted policy choices by member states, and reduce the volatility of trade policy, and limit the trade-policy uncertainty experienced by domestic actors. When policy making becomes more predictable, domestic economic agents make better and more efficient investment and resource allocation decisions. Reduced uncertainty improves economic performance, strengthening the sitting government's hold on office, especially for governments responding to the will of the broader electorate. The effect of signing a PTA is accentuated by the degree to which the leadership is accountable to the electorate—the degree of democracy.

Hollyer and Rosendorff (2012) build a formal model in which PTAs reduce the volatility of noisy signals about the economy. A risk-averse voter hears these signals and chooses an action that most closely matches the true state of the economy. After learning the true state of the economy, the voter decides whether to reelect the government. PTAs provide an electoral benefit: less volatility increases the voter's expected utility, which in turn increases the likelihood that the voter will reelect the government. However, PTAs are costly for the government because they limit discretion over trade policy. When the government decides how many PTAs to sign, it balances the electoral benefits against the policy discretion costs. Hollyer and Rosendorff also provide convincing evidence that PTAs increase the likelihood that a government will survive in office, and this effect is heightened in democracies.

PTA accession increases leader survival, especially in democracies by virtue of reducing uncertainty. DSPs are a mechanism by which information is generated within a PTA: filings, panels, and rulings all produce information relevant to inferring the actions of policy makers and leaders. Less uncertainty and more transparency leads to improved resource allocation decisions and higher expected welfare of the voters at large—hence the enhanced effect within democratic polities.

CONCLUSION

The WTO's Dispute Settlement Understanding (DSU) plays an increasingly central role in the "legalized" realm of world trade (Goldstein and Martin 2000), especially in a period when the diplomatic or negotiating track of the multilateral system seems to be stalled and the gains from the Uruguay Round incomplete.

The WTO and the "spaghetti bowl"[14] of PTAs all attempt to manage a fundamental trade-off: deeper concessions in the form of lower tariff bindings increase the gains from freer trade, but countries are reluctant to join an institution that binds too tightly. If they do join, tighter bindings may lead to increased violations. The rules that govern international trade can't be too onerous, or states won't cooperate; treaties can't be too lax either, or they won't change behavior in any significant way and will have little effect in bolstering a freer trading regime.

Member states search for the line between permitted policy responses to domestic political pressure and violations of their international obligations. Policy choices, especially those that tack closely to the fine line between legal and not, are motivated by the political benefits that accrue to the government and the policy makers. When the legality of those policies is disputed by a trading partner, the dispute itself becomes subject to and explained by domestic political concerns.

Domestic political institutions—regime type, electoral rule, sectoral political influence—affect the presence and the form of DSPs in the agreements that regulate international trade. These political determinants are influential in understanding both the set of violations, as well as the set of disputed cases. Moreover, once a case is filed, whether it proceeds to adjudication or is settled via negotiation is a political question. Domestic politics affects the design and functioning of the international trade dispute settlement process.

It is essential to remember, however, that these agreements and the broader international trade law regime did not emerge independently of the leaders (and the policy choices they make) who find themselves subject to that law. That is, they choose a legal architecture via a negotiated process with an eye to its effects on their political survival. Hence there is a need to balance the benefits of freer trade with the flexibility associated with opportunities to protect politically influential industries in times of distress. Leaders design these instruments fully anticipating the effects of these institutional choices on the domestic politics they currently face (and might face in the future).

The inclusion of a DSP and its use are designed therefore to enhance political survival of the leaders who negotiate them in the first place. The presence and/or functioning of a DSP feeds back and affects domestic politics.

Consequently, this simultaneity of international design and domestic politics makes the identification of causal arguments difficult. This is especially true when one of the causal processes is via "information"—where information generated by the DSP affects a domestic political conflict—that is difficult to measure and observe.

This simultaneity makes one of the central questions of international relations scholarship more difficult to answer. What is the effect of international organizations on states' policies and behavior? Identifying the causal effects is all the more difficult because the international organizations are themselves the product of a political process. An emergent research agenda will take this simultaneity more seriously and develop theory and evidence consistent with this feedback process.

NOTES

    * Many thanks to Brett Allen Casper, Emine Deniz, and Pedro Silva for excellent research assistance on this chapter.

    1. Article 3.5 of the DSU requires that "all solutions . . . be consistent with [the WTO] agreements." Even bilateral deals reached in private consultations must, under the terms of the treaty, extend any trade concessions to all WTO members. Also, third parties may join a dispute's proceedings and observe and contribute to proceedings at every stage.

    2. Just a few non-trade examples: Hafner-Burton, Helfer, and Fariss (2011) view the opportunity for states to "derogate" from human rights treaties as a form of tolerated escape/flexibility necessary during emergencies; flexibility provisions have been studied in climate change treaties (von Stein 2008; Thompson 2010) and regional trade agreements (Baccini 2010), among others.

    3. Pelc (2009) suggests that "escape clauses, or 'pressure valves,' allow members of an agreement to temporarily suspend their obligations under that agreement following an exogenous shock, while assuring other state members a return to compliance in the following period."

    4. Sykes (1991) suggests that the purpose of Article XIX safeguards is to permit policy makers to respond to the political pressures of materially injured sectors.

    5. See Busch (2007) on forum shopping.

    6. Johns and Peritz (this volume) comprehensively catalog the important elements along which international trade institutions vary. In addition to depth, scope, and membership, they identify rigidity and institutionalization as being interdependent design elements that in combination affect state behavior.

    7. Davis and Bermeo (2009) make a similar finding: past experience in trade adjudication, as either a complainant or a defendant, increases the likelihood that a developing country will initiate disputes. States that frequently file GATT/WTO complaints are, however, less likely to be targeted in US antidumping decisions (Blonigen and Bown 2003; Bown 2001).

    8. Simmons and Guzman (2005) find evidence that poorer countries file fewer cases because they lack the resources to do so, but not that they fear retaliation from more powerful trading partners. In contrast, Sattler and Bernauer (2011) suggest that power does play a role in preventing cases from making it to the WTO, which are perhaps instead dealt with outside the WTO.

    9. Courts are usually treated as nonstrategic actors in this literature. Courts, however, concerned about their own legitimacy and anticipating increased compliance, might be willing to rule more severely (drawing from the same set of cases). Or if the court is concerned about having its rulings ignored—and undermining its legitimacy—it may rule less severely.

   10. Busch and Pelc (this volume) offer an innovative suggestion for dealing with this long-standing problem of selection. They suggest that there are now new data on *specific trade concerns* (STCs), reported to the committees on technical barriers to trade and sanitary and phytosanitary measures at the WTO. The key here is that not all of these STCs escalate into dispute settlement cases, giving the scholar a sense of the universe from which disputes may be drawn and insight into the dogs that didn't bark, the cases that didn't get filed.

   11. Rickard (2010) goes some way to explore the decision to violate—governments elected via majoritarian electoral rules and/or single-member districts are more likely to violate

GATT/WTO agreements than those elected via proportional electoral rules and/or multimember districts—but does so independent of the effect of the violation on the potential
dispute that might follow.

12. This work makes use of two new data sets, one collected by Bobick and Smith (2013), which
is an extension of the data collected by Busch and Reinhardt (2003) on the list of cases filed
at the WTO, and the second (the CHISOLS data set) on leader and coalition change, collected by Leeds and Mattes (2013).

13. In contrast to Davis (2012), who argues that countries file disputes to credibly convey to
industries that they are serving their interests. Filing, in Davis' view (partly), is pandering
to exporters.

14. A term credited to Bhagwati (1988).

References

Baccini, Leonardo. 2010. Explaining Formation and Design of EU Trade Agreements: The Role
of Transparency and Flexibility. *European Union Politics* 11 (2): 195–217.

Bechtel, M., and Thomas Sattler. 2013. What Is Litigation in the World Trade Organization
Worth? International Organization, forthcoming.

Bhagwati, Jagdish. 1988. *Protectionism*. Cambridge, MA: MIT Press.

Blonigen, Bruce, and Chad P. Bown. 2003. Antidumping and Retaliation Threats. *Journal of
International Economics* 60: 249–273.

Bobick, Talya, and Alastair Smith. 2013. The Impact of Leader Turnover on the Onset and the
Resolution of WTO Disputes. *Review of International Organizations* 8(4): 423–445.

Bowen, T. Renee. 2013. Forbearance in Optimal Multilateral Trade Agreements Stanford
University Working Paper.

Bown, Chad P. 2001. On the Economic Success of GATT/WTO Dispute Settlement. Review of
Economics and Statistics 86(3)811-823

Busch, Marc L. 2000. Democracy, Consultation, and the Paneling of Disputes under GATT.
Journal of Conflict Resolution 44 (4): 425–446.

Busch, Marc L. 2007. Overlapping Institutions, Forum Shopping, and Dispute Settlement in
International Trade. *International Organization* 61 (04): 735–761.

Busch, Marc L, Rafal Raciborski, and Eric Reinhardt. 2008. Does the Rule of Law Matter? The
WTO and US Antidumping Investigations. Working Paper, Georgetown University.

Busch, Marc L., and Eric Reinhardt. 2003. Developing Countries and GATT/WTO Dispute
Settlement. *Journal of World Trade* 37 (4): 719–735.

Büthe, Tim, and Helen V. Milner. 2008. The Politics of Foreign Direct Investment into
Developing Countries: Increasing FDI through International Trade Agreements? *American
Journal of Political Science* 52 (4): 741–762.

Chaudoin, Stephen, Jeffrey Kucik, and K Pelc. 2013. Do WTO Disputes Actually Increase
Trade? SSRN 2299651.

Chayes, Abram, and Antonia Handler Chayes. 1993. On Compliance. *International Organization* 47 (2): 175–205.

Davis, Christina. 2012. *Why Adjudicate? Enforcing Trade Rules in the WTO*. Princeton, NJ:
Princeton University Press.

Davis, Christina L., and Sarah Blodgett Bermeo. 2009. Who Files? Developing Country
Participation in GATT/WTO Adjudication. *Journal of Politics* 71 (03): 1033–1049.

Davis, Christina L, and Yuki Shirato. 2007. Firms, Governments, and WTO Adjudication: Japan's Selection of WTO Disputes. *World Politics* 59 (2): 274–313.

Downs, George W., D. M. Rocke, and P. B. Barsoom. 1996. Is the Good News About Compliance Good News About Cooperation? *International Organization* 50(3): 379–406.

Dunoff, Jeffrey L., and Joel P. Trachtman. 1999. Economic Analysis of International Law. *Yale Journal of International Law* 24 (1): 1–59.

Dür, Andreas, Leonardo Baccini, and Manfred Elsig. 2014. The Design of International Trade Agreements: Introducing a New Dataset. *Review of International Organizations.* 9(3):353–375.

Gilligan, Michael J., and Leslie Johns. 2012. Formal Models of International Institutions. *Annual Review of Political Science* 15: 221–243.

Gilligan, Michael J., Leslie Johns, and B. Peter Rosendorff. 2010. Strengthening International Courts and the Early Settlement of Disputes. *Journal of Conflict Resolution* 54 (1): 5–38.

Goldstein, Judith, Miles Kahler, Robert Keohane, and Anne-Marie Slaughter. 2000. Introduction: Legalization and World Politics. *International Organization* 54 (3): 385–400.

Goldstein, Judith, and Lisa L. Martin. 2000. Legalization, Trade Liberalization, and Domestic Politics: A Cautionary Note. *International Organization* 54 (3): 603–632.

Hafner-Burton, Emilie Marie, Laurence R. Helfer, and Christopher J. Fariss. 2011. Emergency and Escape: Explaining Derogation from Human Rights Treaties. *International Organization* 65 (4):673–707.

Haftel, Yoram Z. 2013. Commerce and Institutions: Trade, Scope, and the Design of Regional Economic Organizations. *Review of International Organizations* 8 (3): 389–414.

Hofmann, Tobias, and Soo Yeon Kim. 2013a. Designing Credible Commitment: The Political Economy of Dispute Settlement Design in PTAs. Unpublished manuscript, 1–40.

Hofmann, Tobias, and Soo Yeon Kim. 2013b. Does Trade Comply? The Economic Effect(iveness) of WTO Dispute Settlement. Unpublished manuscript.

Hollyer, James R., and B. Peter Rosendorff. 2012. Leadership Survival, Regime Type, Policy Uncertainty and PTA Accession. *International Studies Quarterly* 56 (4): 748–764.

Johns, Leslie. 2014. Depth versus Rigidity in the Design of International Trade Agreements. *Journal of Theoretical Politics*, 26 (3): 468–495.

Johns, Leslie, and Krzysztof J. Pelc. 2014. Who Gets to Be in the Room? Manipulating Participation in WTO Disputes. *International Organization* 68 (3): 663–699.

Kim, Soo Yeon. 2010. *Power and the Governance of Global Trade: From the GATT to the WTO.* Ithaca, NY: Cornell University Press.

Kucik, Jeffrey, and Eric Reinhardt. 2008. Does Flexibility Promote Cooperation? An Application to the Global Trade Regime. *International Organization* 62 (3): 477–505.

Leeds, Brett Ashley, and Michaela Mattes. 2013. Change in Source of Leader Support (CHISOLS) Dataset: Coding Rules. Unpublished manuscript.

Maggi, Giovanni, and Andres Rodriguez-Clare. 1998. The Value of Trade Agreements in the Presence of Political Pressures. *Journal of Political Economy* 106: 574–601.

Mansfield, Edward D., Helen V. Milner, and Jon C. Pevehouse. 2007. Vetoing Cooperation: The Impact of Veto Players on Preferential Trading Arrangements. *British Journal of Political Science* 37 (03): 403.

Mansfield, Edward D., Helen V. Milner, and B. Peter Rosendorff. 2000. Free to Trade: Democracies, Autocracies and International Trade. *American Political Science Review* 94 (2): 305–322.

Mansfield, Edward D., Helen V. Milner, and B. Peter Rosendorff. 2002. Why Democracies Cooperate More: Electoral Control and International Trade Agreements. *International Organization* 56 (3): 477–514.

Martin, Lisa L., and Beth Simmons. 1998. Theories and Empirical Studies of International Institutions. *International Organization* 52 (4): 729–757.

McCubbins, Matthew D., and T. Schwartz. 1987. Congressional Oversight Overlooked: Police Patrols verus Fire Alarms. In *Congress: Structure and Policy*, edited by Matthew D. McCubbins and Terry Sullivan, 426–440. New York: Cambridge University Press.

McGillivray, Fiona, and Alastair Smith. 2004. The Impact of Leadership Turnover on Trading Relations Between States. *International Organization* 58: 567–600.

McGillivray, Fiona, and Alastair Smith. 2000. Trust and Cooperation Through Agent-specific Punishments. *International Organization* 54 (4): 809–824.

Naoi, M. 2009. Shopping for Protection: The Politics of Choosing Trade Instruments in a Partially Legalized World. *International Studies Quarterly* 53(2): 421–444.

Pelc, Krzysztof J. 2012. Googling the WTO: What Search Engine Data Tell Us About the Political Economy of Institutions. *International Organization* 67 (3): 629–655.

Pelc, Krzysztof J. 2009. Seeking Escape: The Use of Escape Clauses in International Trade Agreements. *International Studies Quarterly* 752: 349–368.

Pevehouse, Jon C., and Renee Buhr. 2013. Democracy, Legalism, and the Design of Preferential Trade Agreements. Unpublished manuscript, University of Wisconsin.

Pevehouse, Jon C., Emilie Hafner-Burton, and Matthew Zierler. 2002. Regional Trade and Institutional Design: Long After Hegemony? Paper presented at the 2002 Midwest Political Science Association Meetings.

Putnam, Robert D. 1988. Diplomacy and Domestic Politics: The Logic of Two-Level Games. *International Organization* 42 (3): 427–460.

Reinhardt, Eric. 2000. Aggressive Multilateralism: The Determinants of GATT / WTO Dispute Initiation, 1948–1998. Working Paper, Emory University.

Rickard, S. J. 2010. Democratic Differences: Electoral Institutions and Compliance with GATT/ WTO Agreements. *European Journal of International Relations* 16 (4): 711–729.

Rosendorff, B. Peter. 2006. Do Democracies Trade More Freely? In *Democratic Foreign Policy Making: Problems of Divided Government and International Cooperation*, 83–106, edited by Robert Pahre. London: Palgrave.

Rosendorff, B. Peter. 2005. Stability and Rigidity: Politics and the Design of the WTO's Dispute Resolution Procedure. *American Political Science Review* 99 (3): 389–400.

Rosendorff, B. Peter, and Helen V. Milner. 2001. The Optimal Design of International Trade Institutions: Uncertainty and Escape. *International Organization* 55 (4): 829–857.

Rosendorff, B. Peter, and Alastair Smith. 2013. Domestic Political Determinants of the Onset of WTO Disputes. Working Paper, New York University.

Sattler, Thomas, and Thomas Bermauer. 2011. Gravitation or Discrimination? Determinants of Litigation in the World Trade Organisation. *European Journal of Political Research* 50 (2): 143–167.

Simmons, B. A. 1998. Compliance with International Agreements. *Annual Review of Political Science* 1: 75–93.

Simmons, Beth A., and Zachary Elkins. 2004. The Globalization of LIberalization: Policy Diffusions in the International Political Economy. *American Political Science Review* 98 (1): 171–189.

Simmons, Beth A., and Andrew Guzman. 2005. Power Plays & Capacity Constraints: the Selection of Defendants in WTO Disputes. *Journal of Legal Studies* 34: 557–598.

Smith, James McCall. 2000. The Politics of Dispute Settlement Design: Explaining Legalism in Regional Trade Pacts. *International Organization* 54 (1): 137–180.

Sykes, Alan. 1991. Protectionism as a Safeguard. *University of Chicago Law Review* 58: 255–305.

Thompson, Alexander. 2010. Rational Design in Motion: Uncertainty and Flexibility in the Global Climate Regime. *European Journal of International Relations* 16 (2): 269–296.

von Stein, Jana. 2008. The International Law and Politics of Climate Change: Ratification of the United Nations Framework Convention and the Kyoto Protocol. *Journal of Conflict Resolution* 52: 243–268.

PART III

INDUSTRY-LEVEL PROTECTION

CHAPTER 9

....

INDUSTRY-LEVEL
PROTECTION

....

LUCY M. GOODHART

EMPIRICAL studies abound with descriptions of the industries that are the classic targets of protective measures, highlighting the loyalty that they inspire within regional strongholds (McGillivray 2004). Similarly, followers of American football will recognize that an industry often becomes a local emblem and source of identity, with the Steelers and Packers both named for industries that were once the mainstay of local prosperity. It would not be odd if we wondered, as scholars, whether their many connections to local welfare and consciousness also assist those industries in gaining protection.

While we wish to avoid explanations that amount to "just so stories," tailored to individual industries, the distribution of trade barriers across industries is a key starting point for theory-building. One test of theory is that it must be able to explain the cross-sectional variation that we actually observe. Moreover, our capacity to both build and test theory is growing as disaggregated data on protection by industry become more available.[1]

Yet the study of industry-level protection contains a central conundrum. The cross-sectional, industry-level patterns of protection are well-established from existing empirical analysis (with some recent updating for developing countries). Further, these patterns appear stable. Many industries, once established as the recipients of trade protection, see consistent protection over time, even given changes in institutional regime that imply dramatic shifts in the mechanisms used to protect them (Goldstein and Gulotty 2014; Bown and Tovar 2011). The stylized facts of industry-level protection, in other words, are clear and persistent. We would be blind not to recognize that steel and sugar in the United States have been protected by governments of the left and right, that the auto industry has counted on government support in many European countries, and that this has continued despite the leadership of these countries in negotiating multilateral agreements for free trade.

And yet, while these empirical patterns are well understood, we can find little evidence that being employed in a given industry affects an individual's attitudes to trade.[2]

The striking evidence of industry effects in protection, therefore, cannot be linked quickly and easily to a causal mechanism that involves individuals in either lobbying or voting. Indeed, we face clear difficulties in connecting the empirical record of protection across industries to the available conceptual frameworks. Even the most widely respected and frequently invoked model of trade protection, the "protection for sale" model (discussed later in this chapter and elsewhere in this volume), offers little in the way of explanation for some of the key findings on industry-level protection.

In this chapter, and as part of efforts to achieve greater resolution of theory and data, I do four things. First I summarize the key findings on the industry-level pattern of protection, advancing beyond existing reviews where possible, to include accounts of protection in the developing world and the agricultural sector. Next I turn to the related work on individual attitudes showing the disjuncture between trade-policy outcomes and preferences. Third, I relate industry-level protection to models of endogenous protection based on *lobbying* and indicate where the empirical findings are at odds with the "protection for sale" model. Finally, I introduce and discuss more contemporary work that uses the conundrum as a launching pad for research that extends or departs from that last model in key ways. This work acknowledges particular features of industries that enable them to overcome the collective action issues of lobbying but also considers alternative explanations that neither depend on lobbying nor assume an a priori interest in compensating workers whose jobs are threatened by international trade. This new analysis goes far beyond the simple treatment of industry as a fixed effect and enters into the political dynamics that help to generate trade protection for particular categories of industry. As such, this exploration of industry-level protection plays a key role in extending our understanding of the political economy of protection more generally.

EMPIRICAL FINDINGS

Canonical reviews of the literature on the political economy of trade policy are available from Rodrik (1995) and Alt and colleagues (1996). Gawande and Krishna (2003) update the earlier reviews and offer a more synthesized discussion of the relationship between theory and empirical analysis.

The broad outlines of the findings on industry-level protection, however, have not altered since these reviews and indeed are generally consistent with earlier findings for the United States and other industrialized nations (Ray and Marvel 1984; Marvel and Ray 1983; Ray 1991). That earlier work has examined trade protection measured by nominal and effective tariffs, the coverage of nontariff barriers (NTBs), and exemptions from multilateral agreements on trade liberalization. The key findings can be summarized as follows. An industry is more likely to receive protection if it

- is labor intensive and/or employs low-skill or low-wage workers,
- has high or increasing import penetration or has been in decline,

- produces consumer goods rather than intermediate products, and
- is not mainly engaged in intra-industry trade.[3]

It is worth considering in greater detail the results of two relatively recent studies, by Trefler (1993) and Lee and Swagel (1997), both of which look at the coverage ratio of NTBs by industry. Trefler (1993) analyzes NTB coverage ratios by industry for the United States in 1983, while Lee and Swagel (1997) look at NTB coverage ratios by industry for forty-one countries in 1988, incorporating both industry and country fixed effects. These two studies are highlighted because both take into account the endogeneity of regressors to the dependent variable, so that import penetration (for example) is responsive to the level of protection. Thus, and in response, both papers estimate the determinants of NTBs in a simultaneous equation model in which NTBs and trade flows are jointly estimated.

Both of these papers find a large and significant effect of import penetration on protection (although Trefler finds that it is the change in import penetration that is significant and substantively important). The result for import penetration was significant across nearly all specifications estimated by Lee and Swagel (1997) and was substantively large in the one equation in which it could not be precisely estimated. The finding that industries are more likely to be protected when they see more competition from imports, then, bears up when the sample set is expanded beyond the United States, and the specification takes account of endogeneity.

Results on the responsiveness of trade protection to low wages (or the intensive use of low-skilled workers) are less clear-cut. Lee and Swagel (1997) show that NTBs are higher in low-wage industries (a finding that echoes that of Baldwin 1985 for the United States) but that this result does not hold once country fixed effects are introduced. For his part, Trefler (1993) finds that protection is actually higher in industries in which higher-skill occupations (including scientists and engineers) are well-represented. Thus, there are indications that protection might go to low-skill and low-wage industries, but this is not a consistent finding.[4]

To summarize, and in two studies that set a high standard for the methodological treatment of data on trade protection, we see the following results. First, and using the terminology employed by Gawande and Krishna (2003), there is strong support for a "status quo" tendency in trade policy.[5] Protection seems to be responsive to deviations from status quo industry conditions, as if trade policy protects workers and capital owners from adjustment costs, and with protection advancing as import penetration and industry unemployment rise (see Corden 1974 for a classic statement of this approach).[6] In addition, we see some support, albeit mixed, for a "social justice" tendency in which policy makers use trade policy to address issues of inequality, directing the benefits of trade policy to workers with lower pay.

The studies of protection by industry cited above are mostly based on analysis of the industrialized economies and some emerging economies. Our potential to expand upon these analyses has been expanded with the availability of data on trade restrictiveness for a much greater number of countries (see Nicita and Olarreaga 2007) and the compilation of data on temporary trade barriers such as antidumping and counter-vailing duties for developed and developing countries (see Bown 2005). Initial analysis of those data suggests that while developing countries have seen significant liberaliza-tion over time, trade barriers are still higher in countries where gross domestic product (GDP) per capita is lower, but that developing countries also encounter higher barriers to their exports (Milner and Kubota 2005; Looi Kee, Nicita, and Olarreaga 2009). While there has been less attention directed to the inter-industry patterns of protection in developing countries, Milner and Mukherjee (2009) find that developing countries that are also democratic are marked by a skill-bias whereby high-skill sectors have seen more protection than low-skill sectors.[7] They connect this finding to the additional respon-siveness of democratic policy makers to both electoral competition and campaign con-tributions. Where labor is the abundant factor, a reduction in trade barriers to low-skill goods is a boon for the low-skill median voter if it can be paired with access to foreign markets through reciprocal liberalization. Trade liberalization may then reap electoral gains. By contrast, democratic leaders in developing countries might offer selective pro-tection to the high-skill, relatively scarce factor in return for campaign contributions. This pattern suggests that the "social justice" tendency seen by Baldwin (1985) might be reversed in developing countries, and that the use of trade policy to benefit particular skill groups could be related to electoral strength.

The findings above come, obviously, from the study of manufacturing. This does not exhaust the potential for protection, however, with trade distortions pervasive in the market for agricultural commodities, and with trade policy for services now being incorporated into the World Trade Organization (WTO) structure (see Barton et al 2006). Francois and Hoekman (2010) provide a review of the emerging work on ser-vices. They conclude that the General Agreement on Trade in Services (GATS) of 1994 has been ineffectual in promoting broad liberalization. When it has been accomplished, services liberalization has been part of the negotiation of bilateral investment treaties or the investment chapters of preferential trade agreements (see Manger 2008).

The literature on agricultural protection is far more extensive (see Swinnen 2010).[8] As canonical work by both Lindert (1991) and Anderson (1986) highlights, agricultural protection is higher in wealthier economies; "anti-trade" in that protection is higher (or taxation lower) in economies in which agricultural commodities are mainly imported, whereas export taxes are often applied where agricultural commodities are exported; and "anticomparative advantage" in that protection rises as a country's comparative advantage in the production of a given commodity falls. As such, agricultural protection in the developed world may be thought of as exhibiting the same "status quo" tendency as trade policy in manufactured goods, which is biased against trade and toward declin-ing industries. The key difference is that agricultural price distortions, and protection to domestic producers, have been consistently higher than those seen for manufacturing goods.[9]

To help explain the observed features of agricultural protection, Thies and Porche (2007) test what they describe as "mid-range" theories of agricultural protection, noting the greater ability of farmers (vis-à-vis consumers) to organize as their numbers decrease and the lower electoral salience of agricultural protection as the percent of expenditure devoted to food falls with greater wealth. Their conclusion is that agricultural protection, although an "inefficient curiosity" for economists, can be readily explained by acknowledging and modeling the role of interest groups organized as lobbies (see also Anderson, Rausser, and Swinnen 2013). The political consequence of higher food imports and a shrinking domestic agricultural sector is that a smaller nucleus of remaining farmers is easier to organize. However, this statement of the literature serves to highlight the central issue in studying the political economy of industry-level protection. We lack a unifying framework that would explain why it is that certain interest groups become politicized around trade and effective as lobbies, while others do not. I turn next to the role of individual preferences regarding trade policy as possible drivers of political action, including lobbying.

ATTITUDES TO TRADE AND INDUSTRY-LEVEL PROTECTION

As the preceding discussion implies, political economy theories relate trade policy outcomes to preferences, with preferences regarding trade policy generally related to the distributive consequences for the factors (i.e., different types of labor and capital) involved in the production of a particular type of good.[10] Thus, and in explaining why it is that protection, for industrial goods, so often goes to industries that use low-skilled labor intensively (at least in advanced, industrialized economies) and that have high or increasing import penetration, we might first look to attitudes toward trade among individuals who are employed in low-skill or import-competing industries. Owners of capital might also lobby, and might be very effective, but many political economy accounts focus explicitly on the role of labor in lobbying.[11]

Thus, and before proceeding to the formal models of trade protection and their implications for the distribution of trade barriers across industries, it is worth mentioning the empirical findings on attitudes toward trade. In addition, it is important to connect those attitudes to our understanding of labor as a mobile or specific factor. If labor is a mobile factor, as in the standard Heskscher-Ohlin model of trade, then employees move easily among different industries, wage rates equalize across sector, and trade interests are broad. In other words, the attitude of labor (and most individuals) toward trade policy will depend on whether greater protection helps or hurts the interests of labor (or different skill groups within labor), and this in turn will depend on whether the imported good uses labor intensively.

On the other hand, and if labor is a fixed or specific factor (at least in the short term), as implied by the Ricardo-Viner model, then individuals cannot move seamlessly across industries and will face a drop in wages if they do so. In this case, trade interests will be narrow, in that the welfare of workers will depend on how trade policy helps or hurts their specific industry. As an implication, and once again if attitudes influence policy, trade-policy outcomes will then be very differentiated by industry.

While most accounts of trade policy assume that labor and other factors have limited mobility, we do not have to accept this constraint on modeling. Mayer (1984) develops a model in which labor is mobile, the median voter is everywhere reliant on labor income only, and trade policy follows from the interest of the median voter given the country's endowments (so that we should see import tariffs in richer countries in which labor is relatively scarce and import subsidies elsewhere). As Gawande and Krishna (2003) note, however, empirical evidence is stacked against this model in that trade policy is protectionist everywhere, even where labor is the relatively abundant factor.[12]

More important is that the distribution of protection across goods is also inconsistent with an account of trade policy that assumes mobile factors. Rather than legislating and maintaining a broad set of trade barriers that act similarly for all goods produced by the relatively scarce factor or factors, most countries administer a relatively small set of tariffs or NTBs, with large variance in protection across goods, even within industries, and noticeable tariff "peaks" amid striking dispersion in protection levels (Hoekman 2001). In many countries, tariff and nontariff measures are distinct to the eight- or even ten-digit level of commodity codes, using the harmonized system of codes operated by the World Customs Organization. Trade policy, in other words, is granular.

One of the challenges, then, for political economy analysis of protection is to connect policy outcomes to preferences. To start on that challenge, scholars have first examined how trade policy preferences are manifested in individual attitudes. Recent work has examined this issue in detail, looking directly at stated preferences on trade policy. Scheve and Slaughter (2001), for example, examine responses of individuals in the United States, while Mayda and Rodrik (2005) analyze data from individuals in twenty-three countries included in the World Values Survey (WVS) or the International Social Survey Programme (ISSP).

The two studies consider the broad array of factors that might affect preferences, but both also take care to include controls for the economic implications of trade policy for individual welfare. If factors are relatively mobile, under the "factor endowments" model that assumes a Stolper-Samuelson result and follows from Heckscher-Ohlin, then interests should be associated with an individual's membership in broad categories of labor defined by skill level and will vary with the country's labor endowments. If factors are relatively immobile, as in the "specific factors" or Ricardo-Viner model, then preferences will be far more closely tied to individual industries or sectors, since it is the fate of that industry that will affect returns to labor. The different authors investigate this by including controls for skill level (proxied by years of education or the average wage for the respondent's occupation as a measure of skill) and for the exposure of the respondent's industry or sector to international trade (generally measured from net exports from or imports into the industry). Both studies offer strong support for the factor endowments model and at best lukewarm support for a model of the world in which individual preferences are linked to their specific industry of employment and its competitiveness.[13]

If these results do not give us pause, then perhaps they should. Most political economy models of trade policy have assumed a specific-factors model, with small, cohesive interest groups formed from capital and labor, and this has been so standard that Beaulieu (2002b) calls it the "maintained assumption." By contrast, analysis of survey data indicates that individual preferences are more consistent with interests linked to broad factor type. Indeed, Scheve and Slaughter (2001, 288) suggest that canonical models of trade policy be reworked to follow a Hechscher-Ohlin, mobile factors account of economic interests over trade policy. Yet the variation in the ultimate dependent variable, trade protection, is hardly consistent with a model in which the preferences of broad factor coalitions are enacted after an electoral and legislative struggle. While accounts of major historical shifts in trade regime have been couched in these terms, the current pattern of trade protection is quite different (see Rogowski 1989 for a discussion of broad coalitions motivated by trade in the nineteenth century). In the advanced, industrialized countries, trade protection is industry-specific, highly differentiated, often implemented through the imposition of temporary trade barriers, and (in between the negotiation of major trade liberalization agreements) carried out through technocratic and administrative politics (Kono 2006; Caddel 2014). It does not, in short, conform to a view of politics in which the distributive effects of trade mobilize popular coalitions for systematic liberalization or protection across a range of goods associated with a given factor.[14]

So why might popular preferences regarding trade policy indicate a strong role for broad interests related to skill endowments when actual outcomes seem more consistent with highly differentiated interests? One answer might be that public preferences are relatively disconnected from outcomes because trade policy has not, generally, been a salient issue in electoral politics and mass mobilization.[15] When it has been so, as in the 1988 Canadian federal election, votes have followed economic interests based on factor endowments (Beaulieu 2002a). Further, when a particular industry becomes more important to residents, industry interests also become more meaningful. Scheve and Slaughter (2001), for instance, find that respondents who own a home in a county in which import-competing industries are concentrated, and who are therefore exposed to the broader effects of industry decline, are more likely to oppose trade. Relatedly, Busch and Reinhardt (2000) show that there is far greater political action around trade-exposed industries that are also geographically concentrated (see also Busch and Reinhardt 2005).

Individual preferences, in other words, are mutable and can be activated as trade becomes more salient. In general, however, voters' inferred concerns about the distributive effects of trade do not appear to be directly instantiated into political outcomes. Where such effects do not operate, we might expect that trade politics reflect the preferences of a narrower group of actors, who are not well-represented in mass public surveys. If this is so, however, we need to understand how an interest group account of trade policy could help us explain the industry-level patterns of protection described in the first section of this chapter. What are the main precepts of the core, specific-factors, political economy models of protection, those that are centered on lobbying behavior, and what are their implications?

PROTECTION FOR SALE AND
INDUSTRY-LEVEL PROTECTION

In this section I offer a condensed description of the core political economy models of protection based on lobbying by the owners of specific factors.[16] I then describe the predictions of these models for industry-level protection and assess how well they explain the stylized facts presented earlier.

The most recent contribution, the "protection for sale" model developed by Grossman and Helpman (1994), is the preeminent existing theoretical account, but built off precursors that tapped some of the same dynamics. The first of those earlier works was the tariff formation function of Findlay and Wellisz (1982), in which tariffs are the result of competition between two lobbies that represent individuals as consumers and producers. The rewards to lobbying come from trade policy that increases the domestic price of the protected good and raises the returns to the owners of the specific factor involved in its production, with losses to consumers as prices rise. The government is represented only as a "tariff formation function," which assigns a particular tariff to each combination of lobbying dollars from the two groups and assumes a marginal rate of substitution between the dollars spent by each group (so that government favors one lobby over another). This model captured the dynamics of competition between groups but does not assign any objectives to government, beyond the maximization of dollars received from lobbies.

In turn, the political support function, developed by Hillman (1982), assumes that the government has a political interest in maintaining the welfare of a particular specific factor and thus protects the good it produces as world prices fall, but also cares about the effects on consumer welfare.[17] In determining the trade policy for each industry, therefore, the government trades off benefits to the producer group and the welfare costs to consumers from protection. As Rodrik (1995) notes, this model is far more explicit about government objectives, but is in turn opaque on the strategic behavior of potential interest groups and how much they will lobby.

In addition, and as Gawande and Krishna (2003) highlight, these models are untestable because they incorporate unknown quantities.[18] The protection for sale ((PFS) model from Grossman and Helpman (1994) overcomes these issues by assuming that the government trades off welfare and contributions from the different lobbies in a linear fashion (and this linear rate of substitution can be estimated from the model). Further, lobbies act to maximize the joint welfare of members given the expected contributions from other lobbies and the anticipated decision rule of government. This decision rule is modeled as a menu auction (due to Bernheim and Whinston 1986). Each lobby (for any industry that is organized as a lobby) presents a "menu" of offers to the government of the different contributions that it will deliver in return for a given schedule of trade policy measures that raise the domestic price of the good produced by lobby members. The technical assuredness of the model, its comprehensive depiction of groups and

government, and its relative tractability have put the PFS model front and center in discussions of the political economy of protection. Moreover, a signal virtue of the PFS
model is that it serves as a focal point for empirical analysis, identifying the factors that
are assumed to affect outcomes if the model holds true and providing a framework for
more precise testing of assumptions (Gawande and Krishna 2003).

While the derivation of the model is more complicated, its central prediction, indicating the factors that will affect the industry-level pattern of protection, is relatively simple
and is shown below:

$$\frac{t_i}{1+t_i} = \frac{I_i - \alpha_L}{a + \alpha_L}\left(\frac{z_i}{e_i}\right), \quad i = 1, ..., \tag{1}$$

Here, $t_i = (p_i - p)/p$ is the ad valorem tariff or subsidy on good I where p_i is the
domestic price and p is the world price of the good, I_i is an indicator variable that
takes the value 1 if the industry is organized and 0 otherwise, and α_L is the proportion
of industries that are organized into lobbies (not all industries are organized so that
$\alpha_L < 1$).[19] Further, a is the weight that the government places on consumer welfare relative to lobbying dollars, z_i is the inverse import penetration ratio (or more formally, it
is domestic output of good i over imports), and e_i is the price elasticity of demand for
the good.

To clarify the implications of the model, I indicate what Equation 1 would predict for
industries that produce an imported good. In this case, and if the industry is organized,
then the expected tariff is positive, because $(I_i - \alpha_L) > 0$, and tariffs are higher if less of
the productive sector is organized (because sectors do not waste money bidding against
each other). If, however, the sector is not organized, then the expected outcome is that
the government offers a subsidy on the imported good, reducing its price. Why does it
do so? The government can offer benefits to organized groups at a lower welfare cost if
it recompenses consumers for part of the consumer surplus they lose with subsidies on
the goods produced by groups that are not organized.

In addition, and whatever the fraction of industries that are organized, α_L, tariffs (and
other trade barriers) are expected to be *lower* for industries with higher import penetration (and thus lower z_i).[20] Why is this so? If imports into a sector are very high, then the
benefits to producers of a tariff are relatively small in relation to welfare costs borne by
consumers, simply because there are relatively few of those producers. Tariffs also fall as
the price elasticity of demand rises, for the reasons associated with the Ramsey rule; any
price distortion will have larger welfare costs when demand is elastic.

The PFS model has been empirically tested with results from Gawande and
Bandyopadhyay (2000) and Goldberg and Maggi (1999). That analysis essentially tests
the marginal effects that flow from PFS; that protection should rise as z_i rises (and
import penetration falls) for organized industries with the reverse effect for industries
that are not organized and for which a higher z_i (and lower import penetration) is associated with lower subsidies to imports.[21] These marginal effects are confirmed by the
empirical analysis. Yet in other ways the PFS model is markedly inconsistent with what

we know about protection. For example, and while the model predicts that sectors that are not organized will see import subsidies, these trade measures are almost unknown in practice.[22] Perhaps more disturbing is that one of the main and consistent empirical findings on trade protection is that industries facing high or rising import penetration are more likely to receive protection and to exhibit higher trade barriers. Yet, and within PFS, it is precisely the industries that are most exposed to trade that should see the smallest trade distortions and those that are the least involved in trade that are predicted to have the largest. How then can we explain the pattern of protection that we actually observe in the world?

Bridging Theory and Empirical Results on Industry-Level Protection

The research that has developed since the publication of the PFS model, and which has sought to resolve the disjuncture between theory and broad findings, has proceeded in two directions. The first has been to extend the PFS framework, especially by discarding the assumption of a given α_L, or proportion of industries that are organized, and developing a more explicit framework to explain which industries will be able to lobby and how the selection into lobbying will affect outcomes. The second direction has been to articulate a political theory of protection that neither depends on campaign contributions nor assumes an a priori objective of assisting declining industries.

Under the first heading, and endogenizing the formation of lobbies, authors have built upon intuitions first modeled by Olson (1965). Lobbying is a form of collective action; those firms that do not lobby cannot be excluded from policy benefits; and so individual firms may shirk from joining lobbies, reducing the overall amount of lobbying activity we see. If lobbying is comparatively easy for declining industries, then we will see more effort from these groups and more protection provided to them. This is precisely the logic that Baldwin and Robert-Nicoud (2007) set out in a theoretical contribution. Lobbies create rents for any firm producing the protected good. In their model, Baldwin and Robert-Nicoud (2007) show that firm entry will tend to erode the rents that go to existing industry "incumbents." Thus, it is only in declining industries, in which the future prospects are sufficiently dim that new firms do not enter, that firms have an incentive to lobby. Baldwin and Robert-Nicoud therefore have a simple explanation for the "status quo" tendency within protection that supports declining firms; "It is not that government policy picks losers, it is that losers pick public policy" (2007, 1064).

The empirical work on lobbying has not directly tested the predictions of the Baldwin and Robert-Nicoud (2007) model to determine whether "losing" firms and industries lobby more. Rather, Baldwin and Robert-Nicoud have built in additional assumptions on lobbying cohesion and effectiveness in order to see whether this improves the predictive power of the PFS model and, particularly, to check whether this can account for anomalous findings in the original tests. For example, the relatively low incidence of actual protection implies that policy makers place an extremely large weight on welfare, relative to contributions. Equally, contributions appear very low when compared to the gains from existing protection. More contemporary research has thus sought to explain which industries can lobby and whether modeling the lobbying decision more closely can improve model fit.

Bombardini (2008), for example, notes that larger firms (relative to the size of the industry) internalize more of the benefits from lobbying, so that industries with a small number of relatively large firms are likely to be able to lobby more effectively. She then uses the dispersion of firm size within an industry to proxy for the sectors that should be able to overcome the collective action issues of lobbying. Estimating a model that includes the control for size dispersion adds predictive power over the original PFS model in explaining the distribution of protection across sectors. Similarly, Gawande and Magee (2012) add a category of "partially organized" indus- tries to the existing dichotomy of organized or not to account for free-riding behav- ior and find that this extended modeling of lobbying types helps to explain variation across sectors and yields more realistic estimates of the weight placed on welfare. Finally, and in the same vein, Gawande, Krishna, and Olarreaga (2012) allow for com- petitive lobbying between upstream and downstream producers and find similar results.

The research referenced above makes advances on the standard PFS model. It brings greater detail and realism into the depiction of lobbying behavior. It is not clear, how- ever, whether this research brings us closer to understanding the mechanism that might be contributing to the "status quo" tendency in the observed pattern of industry-level protection and the benefits extended to declining industries. Is it that only losers lobby? If not, what can explain the anti-trade bias seen in trade policy and the relationship between protection and import competition?

In attempting to confront this conceptual issue more directly, some authors have re-emphasized risk or loss aversion on the part of both the public and policy makers. These motivations help to explain why governments are more likely to protect indus- tries that are losing market share to imports. Tovar (2009), for instance, shows that if loss aversion among the public is sufficiently strong, protection will go to industries that are declining due to trade pressures and there will be an anti-trade bias. Freund and Ozden (2008) develop an augmented PFS model with loss aversion and show that if loss aversion is sufficiently deep, there will be compensating protection in the face of price declines.

This work returns to a classic theme of the political economy literature on protec- tion (Corden 1974; Hillman 1982) and makes important contributions to our under- standing of how trade policy is often depicted and perceived (see also Lü, Scheve, and Slaughter 2012). It too, however, confronts questions that derive from the stylized facts. First, and if public preferences on loss aversion have an impact on implemented policy, why is that policy more consistent with a specific factor's account than with the broad interests related to factor endowments that are evident in mass preferences? Second, and if the public cares about loss, why haven't we seen more broad protective measures in response to dramatic declines in manufacturing output across the developed world? Last, and as argued forcefully by Rodrik (1995), given the tremendous inefficiencies and social costs inherent in compensating for risk via trade policy, why is it that policy makers use this mechanism to do so? As Mayda and Rodrik (2005) point out, trade policy is one of the few policy areas in which all expert advisors agree. Trade distortions are bad for welfare. And yet, with other options available, policy makers still use this one. Can we explain this outcome without simple reliance on exogenous loss aversion preferences among policy makers?

Goodhart (2014) develops a model that contains a separate, political economy mechanism by which policy makers choose trade protection. In her account, policy makers wish to target benefits to particular districts within a multi-district electoral system (consistent with a majoritarian electoral system or limited proportionality). However, and in the presence of legal prohibitions against direct cash transfers to potential voters, politicians use trade policy to target benefits to districts. The reason for protecting the declining industries that have lost ground to imports is similar to the rationale set out by Baldwin and Robert-Nicoud (2007). In expanding industries, the increase in domestic prices that is generated by protection would likely trigger investment in new firms, meaning that the additional output and jobs associated with protection will take place at facilities whose location is uncertain when the government sets policy. As such, protecting expanding industries is not an efficient mechanism for targeting transfers. Declining industries, however, solve the problem of targeting benefits to particular places. The spare capacity created by decline enables politicians to generate additional rents in specific locations using trade barriers that divert production to underutilized facilities at existing firms.[23]

Further, the industries with the highest start-up costs of capital are also those in which firms are slowest to leave, and these industries offer the greatest potential for targeting benefits, because they will have high levels of excess capacity during a downturn. Using data on temporary trade barriers in the United States, Goodhart (2014) finds that the predictions of the model are borne out. Decline is associated with protection, but only in industries in which the start-up capital costs of production are large, and this result holds even when controlling for campaign contributions.

This work could be further formalized, but it offers a meaningful alternative to the PFS model and allows testing for related predictions that focus on electoral laws and the rewards to targeting swing districts. Moreover, it provides a theory that is consistent with the "status quo" tendency apparent in industry-level protection and the highly differentiated pattern of protection across sectors. Industries like steel, chemicals, and autos have been frequent recipients of trade barriers, while others, like footwear and telecommunications apparatus, have undergone wrenching contractions with little support via trade policy. Last, but not least, it can explain why, as others have noted, we see "political" effects on trade policy even after we control explicitly for the campaign contributions that are the central explanatory variable in the PFS model (Ludema, Mayda, and Mishra 2010; Conconi, Facchini, and Zanardi 2011).

CONCLUSION

It is a sobering undertaking to re-read Rodrik (1995) and Alt and colleagues (1996) as summaries of the available literature on the political economy of protection that were available nearly twenty years ago. It is sobering because so many of the conceptual challenges laid down by Rodrik (1995), in particular, are still relevant, and the disjuncture between theory and findings on the inter-industry pattern of protection still holds. A major question for the field, then, is what we have gained in understanding industry-level protection during that time.

There has been some progress. First, a number of new data sets have been developed that enable much more direct testing of new theory. Second, the development of the PFS model has focused empirical analysis either on this model as the maintained assumption or on alternative mechanisms and has put paid to generalized empirical analysis that is consistent with a number of different theories. Third, we have seen an emerging interest in patterns of protection in developing countries and emerging economics. This can only be to the good, in part because of the difference in factor endowments from the advanced, industrialized world that allow us to test predictions related to the factor endowments model. Last, but not least, we have seen progress even on the thorny issue of connecting theory to findings more closely in the developed economy cases that are best known. Moreover, that work offers tantalizing opportunities for new research to both economists and political scientists, both because of its focus on the industrial organization of lobbying and because of the development of models that allow for political, and electoral, influences on protection independent of campaign contributions.

NOTES

1. This chapter focuses on barriers to trade, including tariff and nontariff barriers, at the industry level. As Rodrik (1995) highlights, our focus on observed trade measures often reproduces the anti-trade bias that is endemic to trade policy, with little use seen of import subsidies, export subsidies, or export taxes. A full and richer account of trade policy would explain both the observed trade restrictions and the absence of subsidies to trade.

2. See the chapter by Kuo and Naoi in this volume for a comprehensive discussion of individual attitudes to trade.

3. See the chapter by Thies in this volume for a discussion of intra-industry trade and that by Plouffe on heterogeneous firms. The emergence of "new new" trade theory from Melitz (2003) has highlighted the role of firm productivity in determining participation in trade and preferences regarding trade liberalization. Work inspired by this literature has stressed

the potential for variation in preferences across firms, within a given sector or industry, similarly to the work on intra-industry trade. Both point to the role of heterogeneity in countering the lobbying efforts of protectionist forces. For recent work on this topic see Kim (2013) and Osgood (2013).

4. See Lü, Scheve, and Slaughter (2012), who report a negative correlation between tariffs and wages by industry for a large cross-section of countries, and Milner and Mukherjee (2009) for an apparent reversal of this pattern among developing countries that are also democracies.

5. This terminology is originally from Baldwin (1985).

6. This is related to the finding that trade policy is "counter-cyclical," with protection rising as the macro-economy declines (Bown and Crowley 2013).

7. See also the chapter in this volume by Mukherjee on trade protection in new democracies.

8. Empirical work on agricultural protection has been enriched in recent years by the compilation of new data sets, notably the World Bank's database of Distortions to Agricultural Incentives; see Anderson and Valenzuela (2008).

9. Anderson, Rausser, and Swinnen (2013, 2) offer a particularly good statement of the higher relative costs of agricultural protection: "In 2004, existing agricultural and trade policies [on agricultural and food products] accounted for an estimated 70 percent of the global welfare cost of all merchandise trade distortions, even though the agricultural sector contributed only six percent of global trade and three percent of global GDP."

10. This does not, however, exhaust the potential explanations for individual attitudes toward trade. For an analysis of the role of *consumer* interests, see Baker (2003, 2006), and for a consideration of cosmopolitan interests over globalization, see Hainmueller and Hiscox (2006). Last, Mansfield and Mutz (2009) explore the role that sociotropic concerns over the impact of trade on the economy as a whole play in determining attitudes.

11. Magee, Brock, and Young (1989), for instance, argue that lobbying from declining industries will increase as the industry wage falls, reducing the opportunity cost of lobbying for labor.

12. However, Dutt and Mitra (2002) test a related proposition, given the evidence of consistent protectionism, that the degree of protectionism will depend on the degree of inequality, with higher inequality conditioning the level of protection because it further separates the interest of the median voter from that of capital. Thus, higher inequality should be associated with greater protection in capital rich countries and lower protection in poor, capital-scarce countries, a finding that holds in the data.

13. O'Rourke et al. (2001) similarly find evidence for preferences that are consistent with mobile factors and the Heckscher-Ohlin model of trade effects on welfare, while Beaulieu (2002b) finds an important role for skill in determining preferences around the 1988 federal election in Canada (seen as a referendum on the Canada-US Free Trade Agreement), with some role for industry of employment.

14. The literature on whether factor or industry effects operate in campaign contributions and congressional votes is also lively (see Ladewig 2006; Beaulieu 2002b). Milner and Mukherjee (2009) find that it is when labor is relatively immobile (so that industry concerns might be operative) that majoritarian democracies raise trade barriers.

15. This also, of course, raises the issue of why trade is not, in the current era, a salient electoral issue (Hiscox 2002).

16. This review is primarily based on Rodrik (1995) and Gawande and Krishna (2003).

17. Hillman (1982) assumes that the government is motivated to offset losses to workers in the import-competing industry and spreads the costs of support to that industry across consumers via trade policy.

18. In Findlay and Wellisz (1982) the unknown parameter is the marginal rate of substitution between the dollars from different lobbying groups, and in Hillman (1982) it is the trade-off between the income of the affected interest group and consumer welfare.

19. If all sectors are organized, their lobbying efforts cancel each other out, and there are no deviations from the free trade equilibrium.

20. Sectors with a lower z_i that do not organize will have lower import subsidies imposed on them.

21. Industries are categorized as organized if they contribute more or if their contributions vary more with trade flows.

22. To be fair, few if any of the existing political economy models can explain why we do not observe the full range of potential trade-policy instruments, including import subsidies.

23. Margalit (2011) highlights the local, electoral gains from compensating workers for job losses associated with foreign trade if trade policy is not used to maintain employment.

REFERENCES

Alt, James E., Jeffry Frieden, Michael J. Gilligan, Dani Rodrik, and Ronald Rogowski. 1996. The Political Economy of International Trade: Enduring Puzzles and an Agenda for Inquiry. *Comparative Political Studies* 29 (6): 689–717.

Anderson, Kym, Yujiro Hayami, and Aurelia George. 1986. *The Political Economy of Agricultural Protection: East Asia in Comparative Perspective.* Sydney and Boston: Allen and Unwin.

Anderson, Kym, Gordon Rausser, and Johan Swinnen. 2013. Political Economy of Public Policies: Insights from Distortions to Agricultural and Food Markets. *Journal of Economic Literature* 51 (2): 423–477.

Anderson, Kym, and Ernesto Valenzuela. 2008. *Estimates of Global Distortions to Agricultural Incentives, 1955–2007.* Washington, DC: World Bank.

Baker, Andy. 2006. Who Wants to Globalize? Consumer Tastes and Labor Markets in a Theory of Trade Policy Beliefs. *American Journal of Political Science* 49 (4): 925–939.

Baker, Andy. 2003. Why Is Trade Reform So Popular in Latin America? A Consumption-Based Theory of Trade Policy Preferences. *World Politics* 55: 423–455.

Baldwin, Robert E. 1985. *The Political Economy of US Import Policy.* Cambridge, MA: MIT Press.

Baldwin, Richard E., and Frédéric Robert-Nicoud. 2007. "Entry and Asymmetric Lobbying: Why Governments Pick Losers." *Journal of the European Economic Association* 5 (5): 1064–1093.

Barton, John H., Judith L. Goldstein, Timothy E. Josling, and Richard H. Steinberg. 2006. *The Evoluation of the Trade Regime: The Politics, Law and Economics of the GATT and WTO.* Princeton, NJ: Princeton University Press.

Beaulieu, Eugene. 2002a. Factor or Industry Cleavages in Trade Policy? An Empirical Analysis of the Stolper–Samuelson Theorem. *Economics & Politics* 14 (2): 99–131.

Beaulieu, Eugene. 2002b. The Stolper–Samuelson Theorem Faces Congress. *Review of International Economics* 10 (2): 343–360.

Bernheim, B. Douglas, and Michael D Whinston. 1986. Menu Auctions, Resource Allocation, and Economic Influence. *Quarterly Journal of Economics 101* (1): 1–31.

Bombardini, Matilde. 2008. Firm Heterogeneity and Lobby Participation. *Journal of International Economics 75* (2): 329–348.

Bown, Chad P. 2005. Global Antidumping Database Version 1.0. World Bank Policy Research Working Paper.

Bown, Chad P., and Meredith A. Crowley. 2013. Import Protection, Business Cycles, and Exchange Rates: Evidence from the Great Recession. *Journal of International Economics* 90(1): 50–64.

Bown, Chad P., and Patricia Tovar. 2011. Trade Liberalization, Antidumping, and Safeguards: Evidence from India's Tariff Reform. *Journal of Development Economics 96* (1): 115–125.

Busch, Marc L., and Eric Reinhardt. 2000. Geography, International Trade, and Political Mobilization in US Industries. *American Journal of Political Science 44*(4): 703–719.

Busch, Marc L., and Eric Reinhardt. 2005. Industrial Location and Voter Participation in Europe. *British Journal of Political Science 35* (4): 713–730.

Caddel, Jeremy. 2014. "Domestic Competititon over Trade Barriers in the International Trade Commission." *International Studies Quarterly 58* (2): 260-268.

Conconi, Paola, Giovanni Facchini, and Maurizio Zanardi. 2011. Policymakers' Horizon and Trade Reforms. Discussion Paper Series, Center for Economic Policy Research, London, UK.

Corden, W. Max. 1974. *Trade Policy and Economic Welfare.* Oxford: Clarendon Press.

Dutt, Pushan, and Devashish Mitra. 2002. Endogenous Trade Policy Through Majority Voting: An Empirical Investigation. *Journal of International Economics 58* (1): 107–133.

Findlay, Ronald, and Stanislaw Wellisz. 1982. Endogenous Tariffs, the Political Economy of Trade Restrictions, and Welfare." In *Import Competition and Response*, edited by Jagdish Bhagwati, 223–244. Chicago: University of Chicago Press.

Francois, Joseph, and Bernard Hoekman. 2010. Services Trade and Policy. *Journal of Economic Literature 48* (3): 642–692.

Freund, Caroline, and Caglar Ozden. 2008. Trade Policy and Loss Aversion. *American Economic Review 98* (4): 1675–1691.

Gawande, Kishore, and Christopher Magee. 2012. Free Riding and Protection for Sale *International Studies Quarterly 56* (4): 735–747.

Gawande, Kishore, Pravin Krishna, and Marcelo Olarreaga. 2012. Lobying Competition over Trade Policy. *International Economic Review 53* (1): 115–132.

Gawande, Kishore, and Usree Bandyopadhyay. 2000. Is Protection for Sale? Evidence on the Grossman-Helpman Theory of Endogenous Protection. *Review of Economics and Statistics 82* (1): 139–152.

Gawande, Kishore, and Pravin Krishna. 2003. The Political Economy of Trade Policy: Empirical Approaches In *Handbook of International Trade*, edited by E. Kwan Choi and James Harrigan, 139–152. Oxford: Blackwell.

Goldberg, Pinelopi Koujianou, and Giovanni Maggi. 1999. Protection for Sale: An Empirical Investigation. *American Economic Review 89* (5): 1135–1155.

Goldstein, Judith, and Robert Gulotty. 2014. America and Trade Liberalization: The Limits of Institutional Reform. *International Organization 68*(2): 263–295.

Goodhart, Lucy M. 2014. "Protection as Targeting: Why Governments Protect Declining Industries." Paper presented at the Annual Meetings of the Midwest Political Science Association, Chicago IL.

Grossman, Gene, and Elhanan Helpman. 1994. Protection for Sale. *American Economic Review* 84 (4): 833–850.

Hainmueller, Jens, and Michael J. Hiscox. 2006. Learning to Love Globalization: Education and Individual Attitudes Toward International Trade. *International Organization* 60 (02): 469–498.

Hillman, Arye. 1982. Declining Industries and Political Support Protectionist Motives. *American Economic Review* 72 (5): 1180–1187.

Hiscox, Michael J. 2002. *International Trade and Political Conflict: Commerce, Coalitions, and Mobility*. Princeton, NJ: Princeton University Press.

Hoekman, Bernard, Francis Ng, and Marcelo Olarreaga. 2001. *Tariff Peaks in the Quad and Least Developed Country Exports*. Washington, DC: World Bank.

Kim, In Song. 2013. "Political Cleavages within Industry: Firm-level Lobbying for Trade Liberalization." Paper presented at the Annual Meeting of the American Political Science Association, Chicago, IL.

Kono, Daniel Y. 2006. Optimal Obfuscation: Democracy and Trade Policy Transparency. *American Political Science Review* 100 (3): 369–384.

Ladewig, Jeffrey W. 2006. Domestic Influences on International Trade Policy: Factor Mobility in the United States, 1963 to 1992. *International Organization* 60 (1): 69–103.

Lee, Jong-Wha, and Phillip Swagel. 1997. Trade Barriers and Trade Flows across Countries and Industries. *Review of Economics and Statistics* 79 (3): 372–382.

Lindert, Peter H. 1991. Historical Patterns of Agricultural Policy. In *Agriculture and the State: Growth, Employment, and Poverty in Developing Countries*, edited by C. Peter Timmer, 29–83. Ithaca, NY: Cornell University Press.

Looi Kee, Hiau, Alessandro Nicita, and Marcelo Olarreaga. 2009. Estimating Trade Restrictiveness Indices. *Economic Journal* 119 (534): 172–199.

Lü, Xiaobo, Kenneth Scheve, and Matthew J. Slaughter. 2012. Inequity Aversion and the International Distribution of Trade Protection. *American Journal of Political Science* 56 (3): 638–654.

Ludema, Rodney D., Anna Maria Mayda, and Prachi Mishra. 2010. Protection for Free? The Political Economy of US Tariff Suspensions. Discussion Paper Series, Centre for Economic Policy Research, London, UK.

Magee, Stephen P., William A. Brock, and Leslie Young. 1989. *Black Hole Tariffs and Endogenous Policy Theory: Political Economy in General Equilibrium*. New York: Cambridge University Press.

Manger, Mark. 2008. International Investment Agreements and Services Markets: Locking in Market Failure? *World Development* 36 (11): 2456–2469.

Mansfield, Edward D., and Diana C. Mutz. 2009. Support for Free Trade: Self-Interest, Sociotropic Politics, and Out-Group Anxiety. *International Organization* 63(3): 425–457.

Margalit, Yotam. 2011. Costly Jobs: Trade-related Layoffs, Government Compensation, and Voting in U.S. Elections. *American Political Science Review* 105 (1): 166–188.

Marvel, Howard P., and Edward J. Ray. 1983. The Kennedy Round: Evidence on the Regulation of International Trade in the United States. *American Economic Review* 73 (1): 190–197.

Mayda, Anna Maria, and Dani Rodrik. 2005. Why Are Some People (and Countries) More Protectionist Than Others? *European Economic Review* 49 (6): 1393–1430.

Mayer, Wolfgang. 1984. Endogenous Tariff Formation. *American Economic Review* 74 (5): 970–985.

McGillivray, Fiona. 2004. *Privileging Industry: The Comparative Politics of Trade and Industrial Policy*. Princeton, NJ: Princeton University Press.

Melitz, Marc J. 2003. The Impact of Trade on Intra-industry Reallocations and Aggregate Industry Productivity. *Econometrica* 71 (6): 1695–1725.

Milner, Helen V., and Keiko Kubota. 2005. Why the Move to Free Trade? Democracy and Trade Policy in the Developing Countries. *International Organization* 59 (01): 107–143.

Milner, Helen V., and Bumba Mukherjee. 2009. "Democracy and the Skill-Bias in Trade Policy in Developing Countries." Unpublished manuscript, Princeton University.

Nicita, Alessandro, and Marcelo Olarreaga. 2007. Trade, Production, and Protection Database, 1976–2004. *World Bank Economic Review* 21 (1): 165–171.

O'Rourke, Kevin H., Richard Sinnott, J. David Richardson, and Dani Rodrik. 2001. The Determinants of Individual Trade Policy Preferences: International Survey Evidence [with Comments and Discussion]. *Brookings Trade Forum* (January): 157–206.

Olson, Mancur. 1965. *The Logic of Collective Action: Public Goods and the Theory of Groups*. Cambridge, MA: Harvard University Press.

Osgood, Iain. 2013. "Resistance at Home and Allies Abroad: Firms, Industry Associations and Support for Trade." Paper presented at the Annual Meeting of the American Political Science Association, Chicago, IL.

Ray, Edward J. 1991. Protection of Manufactures in the United States. In *Global Protectionism: Is the U.S. Playing on a Level Field?*, edited by David Greenaway, 12–36. London: Macmillan.

Ray, Edward J., and Howard P. Marvel. 1984. The Pattern of Protection in the Industralized World. *Review of Economics and Statistics* 66 (3): 452–458.

Rodrik, Dani. 1995. Political Economy of Trade Policy. *Handbook of International Economics* 3: 1457–1494.

Rogowski, Ronald. 1989. *Commerce and Coalitions*. Princeton, NJ: Princeton University Press.

Scheve, Kenneth F., and Matthew J. Slaughter. 2001. What Determines Individual Trade-Policy Preferences? *Journal of International Economics* 54 (2): 267–292.

Swinnen, Johan F. M. 2010. Political Economy of Agricultural Distortions: The Literature to Date. In *The Political Economy of Agricultural Price Distortions*, edited by Kym Anderson, 81–104. Cambridge, UK: Cambridge University Press.

Thies, Cameron G., and Schuyler Porche. 2007. The Political Economy of Agricultural Protection. *Journal of Politics* 69 (1): 116–127.

Tovar, Patricia. 2009. The Effects of Loss Aversion on Trade Policy: Theory and Evidence. *Journal of International Economics* 78 (1): 154–167.

Trefler, Daniel. 1993. Trade Liberalization and the Theory of Endogenous Protection: An Econometric Study of U.S. Import Policy. *Journal of Political Economy* 101 (1): 138–160.

....

CHAPTER 10

INTRA-INDUSTRY TRADE
AND POLICY OUTCOMES

....

TIMOTHY M. PETERSON
AND CAMERON G. THIES

Introduction

There is little dispute that international trade influences domestic politics and has consequences for a wide variety of international interactions. How the *composition* of trade conditions these relationships is less understood. Trade has evolved over time such that traditional patterns in distinct commodities—aka, inter-industry trade—has diminished, while the two-way exchange of similar, yet differentiated, commodities—aka, intra-industry trade—has grown. Given that classical theories of trade explain only the existence of inter-industry trade, economists have devoted considerable attention to the economic determinants of intra-industry trade. Scholars of international political economy (IPE) have also examined the consequences of intra-industry trade for lobbying, trade policy, and economic integration. Less research has explored other international political outcomes of intra-industry trade.

The central argument of this chapter is that there is considerable opportunity to synthesize theories of intra-industry trade with those linking trade more broadly to a wide variety of international interactions. These include topics of perennial interest to IPE scholars, such as the formation and subsequent performance of preferential trade agreements (PTAs), the design of international economic institutions, and the relative use of the dispute resolution mechanism within the World Trade Organization (WTO). If we broaden traditional IPE to include conflict studies, then we might also consider how intra-industry trade conditions militarized conflict between states and the formation of alliances or rivalries. Implicit in contributions to these topics would be an increased understanding of the domestic distributional consequences associated with increases in intra-industry trade and how such changes affect the supply and demand of protectionism. In essence, we suggest that carefully considering the composition of trade may cause us to rethink many of our well-worn arguments in the IPE literature.

In the next section we review the evolution of the literature on intra-industry trade, noting that its consequences for politics have been explored primarily in studies of lobbying and trade policy. In the subsequent section we summarize three questions on the conceptualization and operationalization that political scientists might consider when designing studies linking intra-industry trade to international politics. Then we explore some ways in which bilateral intra-industry trade could influence political affinity, as well as the occurrence of militarized conflict. We conclude with a summary of the opportunities to explore broader political consequences of intra-industry trade.

Gains from Comparative Advantage versus Gains from Scale

David Ricardo (1817) laid the foundations for an understanding of international trade that has endured hundreds of years. His theory holds that by specializing in production of commodities wherein a state has a comparative advantage and trading for other commodities, the state can reap efficiency gains that would be impossible under autarky. Ricardo provides a simple illustration of his theory using two countries (England and Portugal) and two commodities (textiles and wine). England can produce textiles more efficiently, while Portugal can produce wine more efficiently.[1] Accordingly, Ricardo argues that English production of wine and Portuguese production of textiles would be (relatively) wasteful. England and Portugal could increase their welfare if England exports textiles to Portugal, while Portugal exports wine to England, each state foregoing production of the other good. The Heckscher-Ohlin (HO) model (e.g., Ohlin 1933), which has become the dominant model of inter-industry trade, extends Ricardo's basic argument to incorporate three factors of production. Until the twentieth century, essentially all international trade could be explained in terms of trading states' relative endowments of land, labor, and capital.

Although the theory of comparative advantage and the HO model remain relevant and useful today, scholars have noted that an increasing proportion of international trade no longer fits the expectations of these models. Since the end of World War II there has been an increasing proportion of trade within, rather than between, industries—often among states with very similar factor endowments. A large body of research in economics has followed from this observation that the composition of trade did not mirror theoretical expectations. To explain the two-way exchange of similar commodities, scholars have noted that states might seek to capture gains from scale rather than gains from specialization, and from the satisfaction of varied consumer tastes (e.g., Krugman 1979). Accordingly, whereas inter-industry trade consists of relatively homogenous commodities, intra-industry trade is characterized by the exchange of varied products (e.g., Grubel and Lloyd 1975).

INTRA-INDUSTRY TRADE, DOMESTIC POLITICS, AND TRADE POLICY

Early economists did not ignore the potential political consequences of trade; however, research in this vein focused on its consequences for lobbying and trade policy. Following from classical models of inter-industry trade, Stolper and Samuelson (1941) extended the Heckscher-Ohlin model to predict how returns to holders of scarce and abundant factors would respond to liberalization of trade. Expanding on this research, others (e.g., Rogowski 1987) demonstrate that support or opposition to trade openness can be explained by the factor of production that a given group utilizes. Using similar logic, Viner (1950) predicts that increasing economic integration in Europe following World War II could lead to heightened political resistance by groups harmed by foreign competition.

Yet protectionist backlash against European integration was minimal. Scholars noted that resistance to liberalization in Europe might be lessened because of the intra-industry nature of European trade in the post-World War II period (e.g., Balassa 1961). Observing the two-way trade of similar commodities, scholars reasoned that adjustment costs could be lower when trade did not reflect comparative advantage stemming from distinct factor endowments. This follows because intra-industry trade does not lead to the elimination of relatively unproductive industries; although a given industry in a given state could be less productive, the unique variety of commodities produced therein remains marketable for export. Accordingly, given the presence of internal economies of scale, the industry is less likely to mobilize for protectionism when it is exposed to imports of other varieties of the same commodity. As a result, resistance to liberalization should also be lower in the presence of two-way trade.

However, a study by Gilligan (1997) suggests that intra-industry trade could increase lobbying by firms; it is associated with greater ease of overcoming collective action problems, because the presence of differentiated commodities suggests that the benefits of lobbying will not be distributed across the entire industry. Kono (2009) extends this work, noting that the nature of domestic political institutions will condition the influence of intra-industry trade on lobbying—whether for or against protectionism. Specifically, when institutions reward narrow interests, lobbying will increase when firms engage in intra-industry trade. Conversely, in the presence of intra-industry trade, lobbying will decrease when political institutions foster wider competition, such as along geographic or party lines. Recent work by Madeira (2013) suggests that intra-industry trade will cause shifts in the nature of political coalitions, reducing incentives to form industry-level associations and increasing firm-level lobbying. While an unproductive industry engaging in intra-industry trade is not likely to exit due to foreign competition, less productive firms *within* an industry will face pressure to exit. Taken together, these studies suggest that we could see a qualitative shift in the makeup of lobbying entities rather than a mere decrease in overall lobbying.

While political scientists have begun to explore the relationship between intra-industry trade and political competition, work has emphasized preferences regarding liberalization, ability to organize for collective action, and trade-policy outcomes. Wider, international political determinants and consequences of intra-industry trade have received far less consideration. Yet the studies conducted thus far suggest that there could be important links between the structure of trade and international politics. For example, Gowa and Mansfield (2004) argue that alliances should have a greater trade-facilitating impact in the presence of scale economies and similar factor endowments, such that increasing trade is more likely to flow within industries. One study has examined the connection between intra-industry trade and conflict-propensity among trade partners, noting that intra-industry trade should be robustly pacifying, while inter-industry trade has more ambiguous effects (Peterson and Thies 2012a). This follows because, at the state level, inter-industry trade can provoke asymmetrical dependence more easily than intra-industry trade. Specifically, inter-industry trade could lead one state to rely on its trade partner for its supply of vital commodities like fuel, metals, or food. While the trade partner also benefits from such exchange, it could perceive potential to make a demand of the dependent state, using its advantageous position as leverage (e.g., Hirschman [1945] 1980). Conversely, with intra-industry trade, neither state imports commodities that it does not also produce domestically. Furthermore, at the subnational level, a higher proportion of intra-industry trade suggests the presence of fewer interests opposed to trade exposure, who might otherwise lobby for protectionism and who could prefer militarized conflict to protect their bottom line. Finally, there could be consequences for the Kantian mechanism of increased cultural understanding for trade in branded commodities, which lead to greater consumer awareness and deeper understanding of trade partners.

CONTROVERSIES AND REFINEMENTS IN OUR UNDERSTANDING OF INTRA-INDUSTRY TRADE

While theoretically there should be little controversy surrounding the notion that intra- and inter-industry trade may have different effects on policy outcomes, empirically demonstrating that this is the case poses some particular challenges. In the following discussion we review some of the basic controversies surrounding the measurement of intra-industry trade, including our own views on what seems most appropriate for the kind of research typically carried out by political scientists. We argue that there are three critical concepts to consider when designing studies linking intra-industry trade to international politics. First, what level of product-level aggregation is appropriate? Second, is it appropriate to separate horizontal and vertical intra-industry trade? Third, is it better to examine intra-industry trade at the state or dyad level? As we show below, each of these decisions carries implications for empirical analysis. We explore how a researcher's theoretical orientation suggests answers to each of these three questions.

Product-level Aggregation (What Is an Industry?)

Measures of intra-industry trade can vary when using different levels of aggregation (Grimwade 1989, 101–106). Early research into intra-industry trade often disaggregated trade to the Standard International Trade Classification three-digit (SITC-3) level. However, some argued that intra-industry trade was a statistical artifact of this aggregation; the resulting "industries" were arguably broad enough to obscure whether exchange consisted truly of similar commodities or internationalization of production led to the exchange of related but distinct commodities (e.g., Finger 1975). We argue that it is vital for the measure of intra-industry trade to be consistent with the theoretical expectations of the study. For example, in Peterson and Thies (2012a) we are most concerned with a measure that captures consumer substitutability of commodities. This leads us to use the following conceptual and empirical approach.

Specifically, given our theoretical focus on the benefits of intra-industry trade in part following from satisfying consumer demand for variety, we define an "industry" as a group of trade goods that can generally be considered substitutes by consumers (a group in which we include firms as well as individuals). This distinction is useful because some trade that appears to flow within industries could in fact follow from the internationalization of production. Specifically, a case in which a commodity is imported, experiences further production, and then is re-exported while retaining the same commodity code would likely be recorded as vertical intra-industry trade.[2] However, this scenario suggests that the value added to the traded commodity by each trade partner does not follow from intra-industry specialization, but rather from differing factor endowments. Indeed, this form of trade is most similar to classic HO trade.[3] Accordingly, consumers will not benefit from a variety of similar goods. To operationalize intra-industry trade that reflects consumer tastes, disaggregated enough that substitute commodities are coded the same while internationally produced commodities are distinct, we use data recording commodity flows from exporter to importer at the Standard International Trade Classification four-digit level (Peterson and Thies 2012a).

Table 10.1, created using data available from the US Census Bureau, presents a few examples of aggregation at the SITC three-, four-, and five-digit levels. It demonstrates that the three-digit level aggregates commodities that consumers would not view as substitutes. For example, all motorcars intended to carry individuals (other than public transportation), including passenger vehicles and racing vehicles, are aggregated into one commodity code. Similarly, all motorcycles and nonmotorized bicycles are aggregated to the same commodity code. Conversely, the SITC five-digit level in many cases either offers no additional disaggregation from the four-digit level or disaggregates commodities too much with respect to the goal of capturing consumer substitutes. For example, cars intended for passenger transportation are already disaggregated fully at

Table 10.1 Aggregation by SITC Commodity Codes

SITC 3-, 4-, and 5-Digit	Description
781	**MOTOR CARS AND OTHER MOTOR VEHICLES PRINCIPALLY DESIGNED FOR THE TRANSPORT OF PERSONS (NOT PUBLIC TRANSPORT), INCLUDING STATION WAGONS AND RACING CARS**
7811	*VEHICLES SPECIALLY DESIGNED FOR TRAVEL ON SNOW; GOLF CARTS AND SIMILAR VEHICLES*
78110	VEHICLES SPECIALLY DESIGNED FOR TRAVEL ON SNOW; GOLF CARTS AND SIMILAR VEHICLES
7812	*MOTOR VEHICLES FOR THE TRANSPORT OF PERSONS (OTHER THAN PUBLIC TRANSPORT), NOT ELSEWHERE SPECIFIED (N.E.S.)*
78120	MOTOR VEHICLES FOR THE TRANSPORT OF PERSONS (OTHER THAN PUBLIC TRANSPORT), N.E.S.
782	**MOTOR VEHICLES FOR THE TRANSPORT OF GOODS AND SPECIAL PURPOSE MOTOR VEHICLES**
7821	*MOTOR VEHICLES FOR THE TRANSPORT OF GOODS*
78211	DUMPERS DESIGNED FOR OFF-HIGHWAY USE
78219	MOTOR VEHICLES FOR THE TRANSPORT OF GOODS, N.E.S.
785	**MOTORCYCLES (INCLUDING MOPEDS) AND CYCLES, MOTORIZED AND NOT MOTORIZED; INVALID CARRIAGES**
7851	*MOTORCYCLES (INCLUDING MOPEDS) AND CYCLES FITTED WITH AN AUXILIARY MOTOR, WITH OR WITHOUT SIDE-CARS; SIDE-CARS*
78511	MOTORCYCLES WITH RECIPROCATING INTERNAL COMBUSTION PISTON ENGINE OF A CYLINDER CAPACITY NOT EXCEEDING 50 CC
78513	MOTORCYCLES WITH RECIPROCATING INTERNAL COMBUSTION PISTON ENGINE OF A CYLINDER CAPACITY EXCEEDING 50 CC BUT NOT 250 CC
78515	MOTORCYCLES WITH RECIPROCATING INTERNAL COMBUSTION PISTON ENGINE OF A CYLINDER CAPACITY EXCEEDING 250 CC BUT NOT 500 CC
78516	MOTORCYCLES WITH RECIPROCATING INTERNAL COMBUSTION PISTON ENGINE OF A CYLINDER CAPACITY EXCEEDING 500 CC BUT NOT 800 CC
78517	MOTORCYCLES WITH RECIPROCATING INTERNAL COMBUSTION PISTON ENGINE OF A CYLINDER CAPACITY EXCEEDING 800 CC
78519	MOTORCYCLES (INCLUDING MOPEDS) AND CYCLES FITTED WITH AN AUXILIARY MOTOR, WITH OR WITHOUT SIDE-CARS, N.E.S.

Note: Bold text denotes 3-digit level. Italics denote 4-digit level. Plain text denotes 5-digit level.

the four-digit level. On the other hand, motorcycles are grouped into a single four-digit product code, whereas at the five-digit level they are disaggregated into six different categories based on relatively minor variations in engine size. This latter disaggregation arguably fails to group together motorcycles of varying engine power that consumers might consider purchasing.

Practically, this level of product aggregation is useful because the UN Comtrade system records data at the SITC-4 level (revision 1) for the period spanning 1962 to the present. In addition, these Comtrade data include records for unit value, which allows for the disaggregation of vertical and horizontal intra-industry trade using price thresholds. However, the SITC four-digit level is not used universally. For example, Kono (2009) advocates the Harmonized System (HS) six-digit level of aggregation. Notably, however, the SITC four-digit level is quite similar to the HS six-digit level, with close to a one-to-one correspondence. Yet dyadic SITC-4 level data are more widely available on a yearly basis,[4] while dyad-year HS-6 level data are more difficult to obtain.

Horizontal and Vertical Intra-industry Trade

Disaggregation of trade to the commodity rather than industry level has facilitated improvement in the measurement of intra-industry trade. For example, an examination of commodities has led to the distinction between horizontal and vertical variants of trade within industries (e.g., Falvey 1981). Horizontal intra-industry trade is the exchange of commodities that perform essentially the same function but are differentiated by variety. It occurs primarily among states with similar factor endowments and in the presence of monopolistic competition and is determined primarily by consumer tastes for variety and the presence of increasing returns to scale for firms in each trade partner (Krugman 1979). Horizontal intra-industry trade as a share of total trade appears larger between states that have higher income per capita and have similar income levels (Fontagné, Freudenberg, and Péridy 1998). Conversely, vertical intra-industry trade is an exchange of commodities that fulfill the same function but are distinguished by quality. In some ways, vertical intra-industry trade is more like inter-industry trade than to horizontal intra-industry trade (Blanes and Martin 2000). Specifically, vertical intra-industry trade can arise due to comparative advantage among states with differing factor endowments under the condition of perfect competition (Falvey 1981). According to the findings of Fontagné, Freudenberg, and Péridy (1998), vertical intra-industry trade composes a larger share of dyadic trade when trade partners have differing incomes, as does inter-industry trade.

The distinction between horizontal and vertical intra-industry trade could have implications for international politics. Horizontal intra-industry trade suggests the presence of similar factor endowments (and most likely similar development levels as well). Accordingly, coalitions within each state are more likely to have complementary interests. Critically, participating firms in neither state have unilateral incentives to lobby for protectionism. With vertical intra-industry trade, distributional considerations could spark resistance in one or both participating states. However, this consequence is less certain than when trade follows primarily from inter-industry specialization.

Whereas horizontal and vertical intra-industry trade could vary somewhat in their influence on producers, we contend that the influences of both on consumer preferences, as well as on the structure of trade dependence, are similar. Accordingly, from our consumer-oriented, product substitutability perspective, horizontal and vertical intra-industry trade are nearly identical in their influence on a number of international political relationships.[5] Notably, if researchers wish to focus on the role of producers in lobbying for protection, then isolating vertical intra-industry trade could be important, because exposure to it might involve relatively greater distributional consequences. However, from the Kantian perspective, as well as from a focus on dependence and vulnerability, quality distinctions are probably no more meaningful than horizontal variations.

The (Sub)state and Dyad Levels of Analysis

An understanding of how intra-industry trade affects international politics depends in part on whether we examine the phenomenon at the state or the dyad level. At the state level, intra-industry trade exists when a given state imports and exports similar commodities in a given industry. As discussed above, such patterns of trade have implications for the productivity of firms and therefore influence incentives to lobby for trade policy, as well as resulting levels of protectionism. However, there is no guarantee that country-level indicators of imports and exports within a given industry imply the existence of bilateral intra-industry trade. When two countries engage in bilateral intra-industry trade, there is potential for additional political consequences. All else being equal, it is more likely that coalitions favoring the continuance of amicable bilateral trade relations will exist in both states. An examination of bilateral intra-industry trade is also important to consider given that economic and political agreements between states could be intended to create an advantage relative to third parties. We discuss this more fully below. For example, a firm might lobby for PTAs with trade partners with which it engages in intra-industry trade, while seeking protection against other states that could also export similar commodities, but with which existing intra-industry trade levels are low. Bilateral intra-industry trade suggests a *complementarity* of interests in the two participating states. As Peterson and Thies (2012a) note, bilateral intra-industry trade also suggests that trade gains are high *and* symmetrical. Dyads engaging in intra-industry trade should therefore be less likely to experience asymmetrical vulnerability, which could lead to coercion attempts and conflict.

Operationalizing Intra-industry Trade for Use in Models of International Politics

Taking the three considerations above into account, we suggest that a bilateral version of Grubel and Lloyd's intra-industry trade measure, using data disaggregated to the SITC-4 (or HS-6) level, incorporating horizontal and vertical variants, is useful for many studies of international politics. Specifically, at the commodity level,

$$G_{ij}^k = 1 - \left[\frac{X_{ij}^k - X_{ij}^k}{X_{ij}^k + X_{ij}^k} \right]$$

where X_{ij}^k is the value of exports from country i to country j (or, conversely, imports of j from i) of commodity k, and X_{ij}^k is the value of exports from country j to country i (or imports of i from j) of commodity k. To create a single measure for a given dyad-year, we take the weighted average of each commodity-level measure with respect to the proportion of dyadic trade comprised by the given commodity, as follows:

$$G_{ij} = \sum_{j=1}^{N} G_{ij}^k - \frac{X_{ij}^k + X_{ij}^k}{X_{ij}^k + X_{ij}^k}$$

where X_{ij} is the value of exports from i to j across all commodities and X_{ji} is the value of exports from j to i across all commodities. Our final measure varies from 0 to 1, where 0 represents no intra-industry trade and 1 signifies that *all* trade within the dyad, in a given year, flows within industries.[6]

Notably, this measure might be less useful if one's theoretical aim is to explain firm lobbying for a state's multilateral trade policy. To explain firm- and industry-level preferences within a single state, researchers might prefer a measure of intra-industry trade that uses the combined total of imports from all other states to state i, rather than the dyadic measure we propose above. Looking within one state, researchers can use the industry or commodity as the unit of analysis. Doing so reduces possible aggregation bias inherent in the dyadic measure. Specifically, because the dyadic measure is a weighted average of intra-industry trade across all industries, an indicator of 0.5 obscures whether 50 percent of trade is two-way in every industry or some industries are characterized entirely by two-way trade while others are characterized entirely by one-way trade. Lobbying for protection at the industry level likely depends primarily on the proportion of two-way trade specifically in that industry.[7]

POTENTIAL ADVANCES IN THE STUDY
OF INTERNATIONAL POLITICAL ECONOMY

Given that intra-industry trade follows from economies of scale, participating firms in both countries face similar incentives to promote openness—although this favorability could be limited to specific trade partners benefiting from bilateral intra-industry trade. Conventional wisdom has long asserted a causal connection between the simultaneous increase in intra-industry trade and reduced protectionism in the post–World War II period. As noted above, lessened distributional consequences associated with reducing trade barriers render liberalization—whether multilateral or preferential—associated with intra-industry trade politically more feasible (e.g., Balassa 1961, 1966; Aquino 1978). However, recent research challenges this conventional wisdom (e.g., Gilligan 1997; Kono 2009), leaving open a number of new research questions. We explore a few of these below.

Bilateral Intra-industry Trade and PTA Formation

Most of the research in IPE on PTA formation focuses on the domestic institutional constraints on moving from a state of protectionism to one of preferentially liberalized trade. A variety of approaches to understanding how to change this domestic status quo have focused on the role of regime type (e.g., Mansfield, Milner, and Rosendorff 2002; Baccini 2012), bureaucratic interests (Elsig and Dupont 2012), electoral concerns (Hollyer and Rosendorff 2011), the use of trade institutions as a means of locking in domestic commitment (Maggi and Rodriquez-Clare 2007), interest groups (e.g., Grossman and Helpman, 2002), and veto players (Henisz and Mansfield 2006; Mansfield, Milner, and Pevehouse 2007, 2008). Most large-N statistical research has tended to use veto players as a useful surrogate for domestic-level political activity, since this concept represents an easily comparable measure of such activity across nations and time. While having higher numbers of veto players leads to decreased likelihood of PTA formation, the determinants of domestic support for PTAs are largely left unexamined in this stream of research.

In most cases there is likely to be considerable variation in domestic support for PTAs. All else being equal, this variation should affect the likelihood that states enter into trade agreements. When there is considerable support for PTA formation (e.g., when firms want export markets or foreign products), we should expect greater lobbying on behalf of the agreements. Conversely, we expect more lobbying against PTAs as detractors (primarily import competitors) proliferate. Our own research suggests that the aforementioned intra-industry trade index is a useful way to gauge this balance of supporters and opponents of PTA formation and preferential liberalization. The higher the proportion of a dyad's trade that is intra-industry, the more likely is the support for PTA formation.

We contend that higher intra-industry trade within a dyad will encourage firms in each dyad member to lobby for preferential trade agreements in order to facilitate gains from increased trade without risking the potential loss that might accrue if trade barriers were reduced for all states. PTAs result in expanded markets, which allow firms engaging in intra-industry trade to benefit further from economies of scale (e.g., Chase 2003, 2005).[8] However, whereas Chase examines industry-level determinants of lobbying in favor of a PTA, we consider the dyad-level likelihood of PTA formation. At the firm level, the existence of economies of scale alone is sufficient to encourage lobbying in favor of a PTA. Yet if firms in one state enjoy productivity advantages over their counterparts in a potential PTA partner, resistance to the agreement by their potential competitors could thwart their own support for PTA formation, regardless of how many resources they invest in lobbying in favor of the agreement. Yet when intra-industry trade already exists, it suggests the presence of economies of scale and a mutual benefit thereof for firms in each state. Accordingly, there is mutual willingness to form a PTA across state borders. One might argue that, logically, the increased competition from firms in partner states would cancel out the benefit associated with a larger market. While ambiguous gain is perhaps true regarding multilateral liberalization, the net gain associated with PTA formation becomes evident once one considers the third-party effects of these trade agreements as discussed by Baldwin (1995). Our argument in this regard rests in part on the role of third parties.

Bilateral Intra-industry Trade and Third Parties

Previous research shows that intra-industry trade is associated with industry-level productivity gains because exposure to international competition will drive the least productive firms to exit, while the more productive firms benefit from increased sales (e.g., Melitz 2003). While it has been noted that this added efficiency adds to the gains provided by intra-industry trade, scholars have paid less attention to the fact that these more productive industries in trading states A and B could represent a threat to competing industries in third-party state C. An increase in productivity of a given firm in state A or B would have an effect similar to a lowered tariff in that industry in state C. Accordingly, import competitors in C could lobby to increase protectionism in response to this shock. If intra-industry trade leads states A and B to form a preferential trade agreement, then state C might seek some other state D with which to form a competing agreement.

The indirect implications of intra-industry trade between two states on each of these states' political relationship with third parties is worth further examination. For example, PTA formation would result in productivity gains for member-state firms that engaged in intra-industry trade due to the enlargement of markets (Baldwin 1995; Melitz 2003; Melitz and Ottaviano 2008); as such, competing firms in nonmember states are rendered relatively less efficient and therefore less competitive. Alternatively, if third-party firms are considerably more efficient than those in states contemplating a PTA, its formation is attractive because it would lead to expansion of markets with similarly unproductive firms, while trade barriers could be maintained or even raised against nonmembers (see Levy 1997). This potential for PTAs to be "trade diverting" has been suggested repeatedly in extant literature (e.g., Viner 1950; Bhagwati 1991). While trade diversion is typically viewed in negative terms, rational firms should pursue it when it protects them from more efficient competitors. As such, there should be considerable domestic lobbying for entrance into PTAs on behalf of sectors and industries engaged in intra-industry trade.

Importantly, because intra-industry trade signifies that trade partners do not specialize (as they do under conditions of inter-industry trade), it is less likely that firms (or entire industries) will be driven out of business because a trade partner has the comparative advantage in producing a given traded good. As such, there will be fewer losers due to expanded trade, and therefore there will be fewer actors lobbying against entrance into PTAs, relative to cases in which there is a high degree of inter-industry trade. It is important to note that, counter to conventional wisdom, this aspect of intra-industry trade would not be sufficient for PTA formation if not for the third-party competitive element discussed above. Yet the combination of substantial gains for exporters in both potential PTA members (relative to third parties) and relatively little loss for importers meets Grossman and Helpman's (1995) necessary conditions for the formation of a PTA.

In our own work, we empirically test these arguments about the importance of intra-industry trade to PTA formation (Peterson and Thies 2011; Thies and Peterson forthcoming). We find that intra-industry trade is associated with a higher likelihood of PTA formation, regardless of how PTAs are conceived. Substantively, we find that moving from one standard deviation below to one standard deviation above mean intra-industry trade produces an average 25 percent increase in the probability of entrance into a PTA. We find that PTA formation is also more likely when there are third-party PTAs in force. In addition to these central findings, we also reconfirm the negative effects of veto players on PTA formation found in the existing literature as well as the effects of the standard control variables in this literature.

WTO Dispute Resolution

The WTO dispute settlement procedure (DSP) represents a legalization of international trade disputes that serves to increase transparency and foster credible commitments of WTO members to abide by WTO rules (e.g., Goldstein and Martin 2000). By "binding" states to the cause of liberalization, the DSP provides insulation for national governments against potentially powerful domestic interests that favor protectionism (e.g., Goldstein and Martin 2000; Rosendorff 2005). However, previous research has shown that the DSP does not necessarily foster decreased trade competition between states, and that democracies, because they are more responsive to domestic interests, are more likely to initiate trade disputes (Reinhardt 1999).

We suggest that bilateral intra-industry trade could serve as an indicator of decreased willingness to initiate a trade dispute against a given trade partner via the DSP. This logic follows because a higher proportion of intra-industry trade suggests that fewer industries face harm due to trade exposure. Furthermore, given the tendency of states to initiate countersuits (Reinhardt 1999), firms engaging in intra-industry trade should be especially resistant to the use of the DSP, because they are exporters as well as importers. Initial results from Thies and Peterson (forthcoming) confirm the expectation that higher proportions of intra-industry trade within a trading relationship reduce the likelihood of either party making use of the DSP.

INTRA-INDUSTRY TRADE AND THE
TRADE-CONFLICT LITERATURE

A large literature examines the link between trade policy and international political relations, with a focus on the potentially pacifying impact of liberalized trade (e.g., McDonald 2004; McDonald and Sweeney 2007; Gartzke and Zhang, this volume). A synthesis of these theories with those linking intra-industry trade to liberalization suggests at least an indirect link between a higher proportion of intra-industry trade and a lower propensity for conflict. Specifically, to the extent that resistance to liberalization is lower in the presence of more intra-industry trade, exposure to this two-way trade could lead to the reduction—or at least the maintenance—of preexisting trade barriers. Accordingly, all else being equal, a given value of trade could imply lower trade barriers, and therefore have a stronger pacifying impact, when the trade is intra-industry in nature.

Although theories of trade and conflict advanced in recent years tend to focus on the role of domestic politics, the period from the end of World War II through the end of the Cold War saw numerous state-level theories focusing with realist origins. These theories emphasized vulnerability from trade, noting that gains from trade were also potential losses to be leveraged by trade partners. From the perspective of interdependence theory, a higher proportion of intra-industry trade could imply a lower likelihood of asymmetrical dependence. We have argued in previous work that the resulting symmetry of trade gains (and therefore opportunity costs) maximizes the pacifying impact of trade (Peterson and Thies 2012a). We find that higher levels of intra-industry trade are associated with lower levels of dyadic militarized conflict. Overall trade interaction typically has no effect on the likelihood of dyadic conflict when controlling for intra-industry trade. This finding stands in contradiction to much of the peace-through-trade literature. Finally, development has no effect on the likelihood of dyadic conflict in the absence of intra-industry trade. These findings have helped to define some of the boundary conditions for the commercial peace thesis.

Bilateral Intra-industry Trade, Preference Similarity, and Allied/Rival Relationships

Most of the existing literature has focused on the effects of alliances and political similarity on trade, with little explicit work on how rivalry might affect trade and no explicit consideration of the effects that the composition of trade might have on alliances, political similarity, or rivalry. For example, Gowa (1989) argues that free trade agreements are more likely to occur within alliances than outside them and more likely to occur in a bipolar than a multipolar system. These arguments are replicated in Gowa and Mansfield (1993), who provide statistical analysis demonstrating that alliances significantly increase trade, in particular during periods of bipolarity. Morrow, Siverson, and Tabares (1998) provide analyses that support the idea that similarity of political relations and democratic dyads increase trade flows. Alliances increase trade under multipolarity, but decrease it under bipolarity (or in many cases have no significant effect in the models). Subsequent work also tends to confirm a positive relationship between alliances and trade under varying conditions (e.g., Long 2003; Long and Leeds 2006).

Long (2008) is one of the few empirical pieces that includes explicit consideration of rivalry, which is conceived of as a measure of the "shadow of conflict." The argument is that firms engaged in trade are risk-averse and look for indications that armed conflict may disrupt their normal trading relationship (Li and Sacko 2002). If such indications look likely, as in the case of a rivalry, then trade should be lower. Long's empirical analyses demonstrate a negative relationship between rivalry and trade.

Gowa and Mansfield (2004) is the only article in the literature on alliances and trade that began to investigate the distinction between intra-industry and inter-industry trade, supporting our belief that this is an important avenue of investigation. They note that increasingly in the post–World War II era, trade between developed states has taken on a different form than in the preceding century. As they note, "*Ex ante*, a firm has a wide array of alternative investment and production opportunities available to it. *Ex post*, however, the firm locks itself into a bilateral monopoly whenever its investment is to some degree 'specific to an export destination'" (2004, 780). The sunk costs associated with intra-industry trade make exporting firms especially vulnerable with regard to ex post attempts to renegotiate, thus weakening their incentive to export. While firms themselves may create mechanisms to deter opportunism on the part of other states, alliances between governments are argued to be especially desirable in this regard. Alliances reduce the risks associated with sunk costs in export production, since the income of both the exporting and importing states depends on the relationship. Government and firms have an interest in maintaining stability and peace under conditions of intra-industry trade. Gowa and Mansfield (2004) thus argue that alliances will promote trade overall, but that due to this time inconsistency problem, they will foster intra-industry trade to an even greater extent than inter-industry trade. They find statistical support for their argument.

Rather than focus exclusively on the effects of alliances, rivalry, and preference similarity on trade, we suggest that the composition of trade may condition the likelihood of alliance and rivalry formation as well as preference similarity between states. In essence, the causal arrow may have been pointed in the wrong direction by scholarship heavily shaped by the overlay of the Cold War. We draw inspiration from Rogowski (1987), who focuses on the effects that trade may have on shaping democratic institutions within the state, to consider how different forms of trade may shape political relationships between states. If trade can generate changes within domestic political structures through the reshaping of societal preferences, and if those preferences are also related to decisions about restriction or expansion of trade, then we believe it stands to reason that decisions about the characterization of states' larger political relationships with each other are also at stake. Preference similarity, and even formal alliances and rivalries, may be born of many expedient factors, but underlying societal views about other states must also figure into this decision. Those views are shaped by the cultural information conveyed by different forms of trade. Trading relationships should therefore be an important structural consideration for policy makers when forging larger political relationships between states. Those decisions could then influence future trade between states, as an allied relationship casts a very different light on intersocietal relations than a rival relationship does.

We have begun to test some of these relationships in our own work (Peterson and Thies 2012b; Thies and Peterson forthcoming). Accordingly, we argue that intra-industry trade promotes the emergence of similar foreign policy preferences among trade partners. However, we contend that the reverse case does not follow: more similar states do not necessarily engage in more intra-industry trade because restrictions on trade in strategic commodities are lower against friendly states. Specifically, security-conscious states might not wish to rely on foreign imports of fuels, minerals such as iron, or food, which could then be used as leverage for coercion (e.g., Hirschman [1945] 1980). However, when a state is confident that its trade partner will remain friendly, perhaps due to naturally harmonious preferences or the presence of a common enemy, the incentive to prevent such dependence could give way to the incentive to maximize gains from trade. Simultaneous equations models and error correction models spanning 1962 to 2000 confirm that intra-industry trade promotes political similarity among trade partners. We also find some evidence that intra-industry trade is associated with a lower likelihood that states will become rivals while, simultaneously, rivalry is associated with relatively more intra-industry trade.

CONCLUSION

If our arguments and evidence are correct, then future work on intra-industry trade and political outcomes holds the possibility of overturning the predominant views held by scholars of IPE about the role that trade plays in shaping global institutions and the balance of peace and conflict between states. The importance of trade and war, as well as the relationship between these two processes, is well known to scholars of systemic leadership, those in the interdependence and conflict literature, and those studying the formation of institutional arrangements. Yet we believe that often these scholars are relying on outdated theoretical arguments about trade, as well as inappropriate measures of the kind of trade that matters most for political outcomes. Our work suggests that the time has come to completely rethink the relationship between trade and politics in our global political economy, because while the composition of trade has changed dramatically in the twenty-first century, our thinking remains rooted in nineteenth-century understandings of trade and its political effects.

The study of intra-industry trade is not without its conceptual and operational difficulties, as we have noted above. We expect that further refinements at the conceptual level may be possible as considerations of trade composition are synthesized into theories of cooperation and conflict. Conceptual refinements will then lead to more accurate operational measures dependent on the context of the study in question. We have suggested a number of future directions for research in various substantive literatures, including PTA formation, WTO dispute initiation, conflict outcomes, and preference similarity. These literatures are enriched by the incorporation of intra-industry trade concepts and measures. We believe that future work will build on this agenda to generate a more nuanced understanding of the relationship between trade and politics for the twenty-first century.

NOTES

1. In this case, each state holds an absolute as well as comparative advantage. However, the same logic would hold if, for example, England were more efficient producing both textiles and wine. It would still hold a comparative advantage in textiles if its relative efficiency with respect to Portugal were greater for textiles than for wine.
2. Its classification as vertical is probable because price differentials would likely exceed the 15 percent or 25 percent threshold used to distinguish vertical from horizontal intra-industry trade.
3. However, the fact that production is internationalized could imply the existence of intra-firm trade across states. This form of trade could also have implications for international politics, although we leave examination of these effects to future researchers.
4. In addition to those data hosted by the UN, Feenstra et al. (2005) have made available SITC4-level data.
5. Again, we except trade following from what appears to be vertical intra-industry specialization, but which actually follows from production sharing, from our conceptualization and operationalization of intra-industry trade.
6. In Peterson and Thies (2012a), we used a version of this measure that adjusts for multilateral trade imbalances as suggested by Aquino (1978) in order to avoid under-representing intra-industry trade. For example, if, for example, a country has a severe trade deficit, then even if all of its imports and exports were within a single industry (and hence the measure should equal 1), the simple measure would report a smaller proportion of intra-industry trade because exports minus imports cannot equal zero. However, all results are essentially identical using the simpler Grubel and Lloyd (1975) measure (at the dyad-year level). Furthermore, given criticism of the trade-balance weights (e.g., Greenaway and Milner 1981), we now prefer using the simpler measure.

    Because total imports and exports are at the country-year level, we generally avoid problems of divi3sion by zero, as there are no examples of years in which countries do not import or export at all. However, to ensure that we do not lose observations at the commodity level, we add.01 to all commodity-level trade flows.
7. In theory, researchers could use the dyad-industry level of analysis. However, this would require a large number of observations, potentially straining computer resources, particularly if the analysis spans multiple years.
8. Economies of scale refer to advantages obtained due to increased size or scale of operation. The cost per unit generally declines with increased scale as the fixed costs associated with production are spread over more units. These increasing returns from economies of scale are one of the mechanisms that generates the gains from intra-industry trade.

REFERENCES

Aquino, Antonio. 1978. Intra-industry Trade and Inter-industry Specialization as Concurrent Sources of International Trade in Manufactures. *Review of World Economics* 114 (2): 275–296.

Baccini, Leonardo. 2012. Democratization and Trade Policy: An Empirical Analysis of Developing Countries. *European Journal of International Relations* 18 (3): 455–479. doi: 10.1177/1354066110391307

Balassa, Bela. 1961. Towards a Theory of Economic Integration. *Kyklos* 14 (1): 1-17.

Balassa, Bela. 1966. Tariff reductions and trade in manufactures among industrial countries. *American Economic Review* 56: 466-73.

Baldwin, Richard. 1993. A Domino Theory of Regionalism. NBER working paper #4465.

Bhagwati, Jagdish. 1991. *The World Trading System at Risk*. Princeton, NJ: Princeton University Press.

Blanes, José V., and Carmela Martín. 2000. The Nature and Causes of Intra-industry Trade: Back to the Comparative Advantage Explanation? The Case of Spain. *Review of World Economics* 136: 423–441.

Chase, Kerry A. 2003. Economic Interests and Regional Trading Arrangements: The Case of NAFTA. *International Organization* 57: 137–174.

Chase, Kerry A. 2005. *Trading Blocs: States, Firms, and Regions in the World Economy*. Studies in International Political Economy, University of Michigan Press.

Elsig, Manfred, and Cedric Dupont. 2012. European Union Meets South Korea: Bureaucratic Interests, Exporter Discrimination and the Negotiations of Trade Agreements. *Journal of Common Market Studies* 50 (3): 492-507.

Falvey, R. E. 1981. Commercial Policy and Intra-industry Trade. *Journal of International Economics* 11 (4): 495–511.

Feenstra, Robert, Robert E. Lipseym, Haiyan Deng, Alyson C. Ma, and Hengyong Mo. 2005. World Trade Flows: 1962–2000. NBER Working Paper 11040. http://www.nber.org/papers/w11040.

Finger, J. M. 1975. Trade overlap and intra-industry trade. *Economic Inquiry* 13: 581-589.

Fontagné, L., Freudenberg M. and N. Péridy. 1998. Intra-industry Trade and the Single Market: Quality Matters. CEPR Discussion Paper, #1959.

Gilligan, Michael J. 1997. Lobbying as a Private Good with Intra-Industry Trade. *International Studies Quarterly* 41 (3): 455–474.

Goldstein, Judith, and Lisa L. Martin. 2000. Legalization, Trade Liberalization, and Domestic Politics: A Cautionary Note. *International Organization* 54: 603–632.

Gowa, Joanne. 1989. Bipolarity, Multipolarity, and Free Trade. *American Political Science Review* 83 (4): 1245–1256.

Gowa, Joanne, and Edward Mansfield. 2004. Alliances, Imperfect Markets, and Major Power Trade. *International Organization* 58 (4): 775–805.

Gowa, Joanne, and Edward Mansfield. 1993. Power Politics and International Trade. *American Political Science Review* 87 (2): 408–420.

Greenaway, David, and Chris Milner. 1981. Trade Imbalance Effects in the Measurement of Intra-Industry Trade. *Weltwirtschaftliches Archiv* 117 (4): 756–762.

Grimwade, Nigel. 1989. *International Trade: New Patterns of Trade, Production, and Investment*. London and New York: Routledge.

Grossman, Gene M., and Elhanan Helpman. 2002. *Interest Groups and Trade Policy*. Princeton, NJ: Princeton University Press.

Grossman, Gene M., and Elhanan Helpman. 1995. The Politics of Free-Trade Agreements. *American Economic Review* 85: 667–690.

Grubel, H. G., and D. J. Lloyd. 1975. *Intra-industry Trade, The Theory and Measurement of International Trade in Differentiated Products.* London: Macmillan.

Henisz, Witold J., and Edward D. Mansfield. 2006. Votes and Vetoes: The Political Determinants of Commercial Openness. *International Studies Quarterly* 50 (1): 189–212.

Hirschman, Albert O. [1945] 1980. *National Power and the Structure of Foreign Trade.* Berkeley: University of California Press.

Hollyer, James, and Peter Rosendorff. 2011. Leadership Survival, Regime Type, Policy Uncertainty and PTA Accession. Unpublished manuscript.

Intra-industry Trade: Cooperation and Conflict in the Global Political Economy

Kono, Daniel Y. 2009. Market Structure, Electoral Institutions, and Trade Policy. *International Studies Quarterly* 53: 885–906.

Krugman, Paul R. 1979. Increasing Returns, Monopolistic Competition, and International Trade. *Journal of International Economics* 9: 469–479.

Levy, Philip I. 1997. A Political-Economic Analysis of Free-Trade Agreements. *American Economic Review* 87 (4): 506–519.

Long, Andrew G. 2008. Bilateral Trade in the Shadow of Armed Conflict. *International Studies Quarterly* 52 (1): 81–101.

Long, Andrew G. 2003. Defense Pacts and International Trade. *Journal of Peace Research* 40 (5): 537–552.

Long, Andrew G., and Brett Ashley Leeds. 2006. Trading for Security: Military Alliances and Economic Agreements. *Journal of Peace Research* 43 (4): 433–451.

Madeira, Mary Anne. 2013. The New Politics of the New Trade: The Political Economy of Intra-Industry Trade. PhD diss., University of Washington.

Maggi, Giovanni, and Andres Rodriquez-Clare. 2007. A Political Economy Theory of Trade Agreements. *American Economic Review* 97 (4): 1374–1406.

Mansfield, Edward D., Helen V. Milner, and Jon C. Pevehouse. 2008. Democracy, Veto Players and the Depth of Regional Integration. *World Economy* 31 (1): 67–96.

Mansfield, Edward D., Helen V. Milner, and Jon C. Pevehouse. 2007. Vetoing Co-operation: The Impact of Veto Players on Preferential Trading Arrangements. *British Journal of Political Science* 37: 403–432.

Mansfield, Edward D., Helen V. Milner, and Peter Rosendorff. 2002. Why Democracies Cooperate More: Electoral Control and International Trade Agreements. *International Organization* 56: 477–514.

McDonald, Patrick J. 2004. Peace through Trade or Free Trade? *Journal of Conflict Resolution* 48: 547–572.

Melitz, Marc J. 2003. The Impact of Trade on Intra-Industry Reallocations and Aggregate Industry Productivity. *Econometrica* 71: 1695–1725.

Melitz, Marc J., and Giancarlo I. Ottaviano. 2008. Market Size, Trade, and Productivity. *Review of Economic Studies* 75: 295–316.

Morrow, James D., Randolph M. Siverson, and Tressa E. Tabares. 1998. The Political Determinants of International Trade: The Major Powers, 1907–90. *American Political Science Review* 92 (3): 649–661.

Ohlin, Bertil. 1933. *Interregional and International Trade* (Cambridge: Harvard University.

Peterson, Timothy M., and Cameron G. Thies. 2012a. Beyond Ricardo: The Link between Intra-Industry Trade and Peace. *British Journal of Political Science* 42 (04): 747–767. http://dx.doi.org/10.1017/S0007123412000129.

Peterson, Timothy M., and Cameron G. Thies. 2011. Intra-industry Trade, Veto Players, and the Formation of Preferential Trade Agreements. Paper presented at the International Political Economy Society, University of Wisconsin, Madison, WI, November 11-12.

Peterson, Timothy M., and Cameron G. Thies. 2012b. Trade and the Variety of International Relationships: How Intra- and Inter-Industry Trade Conditions Alliances and Rivalries. Paper presented at the American Political Science Association, New Orleans, LA, August 30–September 2.

Reinhardt, Eric. 1999. Aggressive Multilateralism: The Determinants of GATT/WTO Dispute Initiation, 1948–1998. Paper presented at International Studies Association Meetings, Washington, DC.

Ricardo, David. [1817] 1981. *The Principles of Political Economy and Taxation*. Cambridge: Cambridge University Press.

Rogowski, Ronald. 1987. Trade and the Variety of Democratic Institutions. *International Organization* 41 (2): 203–223.

Rosendorff, B. Peter. 2005. Stability and Rigidity: Politics and Design of the WTO's Dispute Settlement Procedure. *American Political Science Review* 99 (3): 389–400.

Stolper, Wolfgang, and Paul Samuelson. 1941. Protection and Real Wages. *Review of Economic Studies* 9 (1): 58-73.

Thies, Cameron G., and Timothy M. Peterson. Forthcoming. *Intra-industry Trade: Cooperation and Conflict in the Global Political Economy*. Palo Alto, CA: Stanford University Press.

Viner, Jacob. 1950. *The Customs Union Issue*. New York: Carnegie Endowment for International Peace.

CHAPTER 11

··

HETEROGENEOUS FIRMS AND POLICY PREFERENCES

··

MICHAEL PLOUFFE

THE redistributional effects of international trade create clear winners and losers, and a large body of research in international political economy has been devoted to identifying them and the ways in which they might impact potential trade-policy outcomes. Scholarship on the sources of demand for trade policy has primarily fallen into two broad categories. One body of work concentrates on aggregated groups of actors, whether industries or owners of various factors of production. The second research program examines characteristics of voters at the individual level to ascertain the sources of preferences regarding trade policy.[1] However, a third strand of research, relying on recent advances in modern trade theory, has brought about an increased focus on firms as key actors in the formation of trade policy. Like factor owners, industries, and individuals, firms may be positively or negatively impacted by a change in trade policy, and these potentially significant shifts of fortune lead to divergences in policy preferences.

Trade engagement within industries is exceedingly dependent on firm-level characteristics. Highly productive firms can afford to overcome the significant costs associated with lucrative foreign trading, while low-productivity firms cannot. In the face of liberalization, high-productivity producers favor reducing these costs or gain access to foreign markets, while low-productivity firms seek protection from relatively cheap foreign imports. Helen Milner's work on the efforts of multinational corporations (MNCs) to further trade liberalization was very prescient in this regard.[2] However, MNCs are not alone among producers seeking to reduce trade barriers. In the global economy, a small but significant portion of producers engages foreign markets through trade or investment, while many more firms benefit from these links indirectly.

In this chapter I briefly overview some of the influential international political economy research on firms and trade policy that predates the firm heterogeneity revolution. I then outline the impact of firm heterogeneity on the economics of trade and the supporting empirical findings. I extend the model to its political implications and discuss the importance of firms' policy preferences.

PRODUCERS AND TRADE POLITICS

The study of the role of producers in trade politics has a rich history that long predates the firm heterogeneity revolution in economics. Bauer, Pool, and Dexter[3] provide an early effort to open up the black box of decision-making processes within the firm, focusing on trade-policy engagement. A number of their findings have become common starting points for subsequent research on trade-policy preferences. While the individual decision-makers at any firm may hold a number of distinct sources of preferences over trade policy stemming from sociological or economic concerns,[4] when they need to request policy-based support for their firms, these people frequently make requests in response to specific problems that go against their own personal trade-policy preferences. Different sources of preferences may be activated through different sorts of stimuli (framing), but the stability of firm-based preferences has formed a starting point for a significant and growing body of research.

Perhaps the seminal approach to the firm in trade politics is found in Helen Milner's[5] work, which disaggregates the trade-policy interests of MNCs and exporters from those of domestic producers. Exporting firms and MNCs depend on access to markets abroad, leading to policy positions that diverge from those of other producers. While domestic producers would seek protection from foreign-produced goods, MNCs seek access to these markets. This leads to a clear delineation of producers based on their activities. While the predictions of this model match nicely with some of those made by current firm heterogeneity models, there are some key differences, detailed later in this chapter. Woll (2008) extends Milner's argument to address MNC-government relations in service industries.

Whereas Milner's work anticipated the preference heterogeneity among producers that is a consequence of firm heterogeneity, the dominant approach linking producers to trade politics, the "protection for sale" paradigm,[6] ignores this, largely relying on a Ricardo-Viner industry-based framework with homogenous industry-level preferences. In the usual formulation of models in this vein, industries organize to lobby politicians through campaign contributions for import protection. Subsequent advancements have introduced producer heterogeneity, but retained industry-based preferences.[7] While the incorporation of heterogeneous firms has contributed to a model that better explains observed patterns of political engagement, the directionality of political activities has largely remained constant: firms are assumed to pursue protectionist policies. Recent extensions to these models have incorporated aspects of preference heterogeneity, but they have remained largely overlooked, perhaps because of the increased demands they require of data.[8]

REVOLUTION IN THE ECONOMICS OF TRADE

The trade models currently utilized by international political economists are largely based on variants of the Hecksher-Ohlin model, which focused on an economy's endowments in factors of production as a way to explain patterns in cross-national trade flows. These models were replaced in the economics profession in the 1980s by new trade theory,[9] which took advantage of the relatively late formalization of monopolistic competition by Avinash Dixit and Joseph Stiglitz (1977) to create more parsimonious models, incorporating increasing returns to scale and product differentiation. The new trade theory allowed for improved understanding of trade flows, providing an accounting of intra-industry trade as well as inter-industry trade; however, its shortcomings became apparent with the advent of new firm-level data sets in the early 1990s. Despite its ability to describe and predict macro-level patterns of trade, new trade theory could not explain patterns in the internationalization of production (such as intra-firm trade), nor could it link firm-level characteristics to patterns of international economic engagement.

In response to these shortcomings, a growing literature has focused on firm heterogeneity in what has been inelegantly referred to as "new new trade theory." Theoretical frameworks to explain these behaviors arose in models by Melitz[10] and Bernard, Eaton, Jensen, and Kortum,[11] with the Melitz model becoming a workhorse for many recent innovations in trade theory.[12] This new generation of trade models accounts for the incorporation of intra-firm trade and also reflects the reality of the rarity of trade engagement among firms. In addition, because trade varies significantly across industries, theories have been developed to integrate the Melitz model into the Heckscher-Ohlin framework,[13] to account for variations in product differentiation across industries.[14] These theoretical innovations have provided a solid framework for elucidating patterns revealed in the growing body of empirical work on trade.

The Empirics of Heterogeneous Firms

As more sources of firm-level data have become available, a number of empirical regularities have emerged and become accepted as stylized facts. Exporters differ from firms that only serve the domestic market. Compared to nonexporters, they are more productive, larger in terms of both shipments and employment, are more skill and capital intensive, and pay higher wages.[15] Even prior to entry into the export market, prospective exporters are larger and more productive than other producers. This indicates that high-productivity firms select into exporting; less-productive firms cannot afford to pay the high fixed (and sunk) costs of export-market entry.[16]

Given that exporters are both large and highly productive, one might expect the productivity between them and nonexporters to be merely evidence of exploitation of economies of scale. Controlling for firm size, Bernard et al. (2007, 5) show that American exporters remain significantly more productive than nonexporters, so exporters possess some intrinsic characteristics that enhance their productivity, in addition to their economies of scale. This combination of inputs is described as total factor productivity (TFP). Although not all firms with high levels of TFP engage in trade, all traders have relatively high levels of TFP. This relationship is characteristic of firms worldwide.[17]

The relative skill- and capital-intensive nature of exporters holds across economies at all levels of development, in contrast with expectations based on a standard factor-based trade model. In a developed (capital or skilled-labor abundant) economy, this is to be expected, but in a developing economy (land or unskilled-labor abundant), comparative advantage would seem to dictate that exporters would utilize production processes that intensively use the abundant factors of production (land or unskilled labor). However, this is not the case; exporters remain relatively skilled-labor or capital intensive, even within comparative advantage industries.[18] Thus, both sector- and factor-based models face significant difficulties in explaining these behaviors.

The Melitz Model and Other Approaches to Heterogeneous Firms

The Melitz model (first presented in Melitz 2003) is the starting point for most theoretical approaches to trade that incorporate heterogeneous firms. Like Krugman (1980), who introduced product differentiation to a single industry, Melitz models intra-industry dynamics in a monopolistic competition framework. Unlike previous models, Melitz's model accounts for empirically observed asymmetries in firm productivity and size, rather than dismissing them by assumption. These dissimilarities in firms' characteristics drive variations in their market behaviors.

The Melitz model introduced "new new trade theory," which deals explicitly with these intra-industry features by incorporating heterogeneous firms into a trade model based on monopolistic competition. According to Melitz's model and others like it, firm heterogeneity occurs because, prior to entering the domestic production market, firms face uncertainty over both their immediate and future levels of productivity. Immediate productivity is only revealed if the firm chooses to pay the fixed (then sunk) cost of entry to enter the market.

At this point, if productivity is revealed to be at the low end of the distribution, a firm may never realize any profits and will choose to exit without producing anything, in order to avoid incurring further costs (this point is often referred to as the zero-profit productivity cutoff). Where production is profitable, firms do not exit the market, and they incur variable costs of production. In the face of increased exposure to trade, an industry becomes more productive on average. This happens as inter-firm reallocations lead to the most productive firms gaining in market share and factors of production, while the least productive firms exit.

Firm heterogeneity also provides an explanation for variations in firms' export behaviors. Engaging a foreign market requires payment of a high fixed cost of entry, much like the initial domestic market entry decision, and the variable costs associated with producing goods sold abroad are higher (and in iceberg form—more than one unit must be exported for one unit to be sold abroad) than for those sold domestically. Similarly, export sales are lucrative relative to domestic sales. Consequently, only an industry's most productive firms can afford to enter export markets, leaving a large portion of producers engaging the domestic market alone.

Firm Heterogeneity Beyond Exporting

While much of the firm heterogeneity literature has focused on exporting, productivity also segments other forms of internationalization by firms. For example, many exporting firms also engage in importing, sourcing intermediate goods from abroad.[19] Importers share many characteristics with exporters. They are rare, they are more productive, and they are larger; in addition, they spend more on intermediate goods than do nonimporters.[20] They also employ more workers and pay them higher wages and are more skill- and capital-intensive than nontraders.[21] Firms that only import, while more productive than nonimporters, are slower growing and less innovative than two-way traders and firms that only export.[22] This could be due to the fact that importers, when grouped by behaviors, are a relatively diverse lot: some firms import intermediate inputs, while others import final products for domestic distribution. Even the economic implications of these activities are understudied, possibly due to a lack of availability of sufficiently disaggregated and detailed data.

Similarly, firms that engage directly in trade can be differentiated from those that trade through intermediaries, employing the distribution networks of other firms to either source inputs or final products abroad or sell portions of their own production in foreign markets. This rapidly growing body of research focuses on explaining variation in firms' export behaviors,[23] and much of it deals with characteristics of the intermediaries themselves, rather than the firms employing them. The use of an intermediary firm is driven primarily by country-specific fixed costs, meaning a firm that directly exports to one country may use an intermediary to reach another market.[24] Intermediaries themselves tend to be smaller than direct traders in terms of employment, but this differential decreases when total sales are compared.

An early extension of the Melitz model incorporated the firm-level decision to engage in foreign direct investment (FDI). A very small subset of the most productive firms may choose to invest directly in a foreign market to avoid transportation costs associated with exporting finished goods (horizontal FDI); similar to exporting, FDI is lucrative compared to domestic sales. However, compared to export sales, FDI entails higher sunk costs, but potentially higher profits over time.[25] Relative to exporters, firms investing in plants abroad are more productive. Similarly, firms that outsource portions of their production processes overseas are more productive than their counterparts.[26]

While theoretical approaches to these behaviors have explored the boundaries of the firm, they have not yet incorporated trading activities. Ultimately, firms have a large menu for accessing international markets; heterogeneity in their characteristics, especially productivity, leads to significant diversity in their actual engagement activities. These patterns of engagement can provide valuable insight for political economists attempting to understand and explain firms' political positions and behaviors in a global economy.

In addition, a number of researchers have extended the Melitz model to study the implications of heterogeneous firms for other economic phenomena. For example, Bernard, Redding, and Schott (2007) follow Helpman and Krugman (1985) in working new theoretical innovations into the existing Heckscher-Ohlin framework. Nesting the Melitz model into a two-sector integrated equilibrium structure allows for the examination of cross-industry adjustments to trade, in addition to the intra-industry adjustments revealed in the Melitz model. While postliberalization asset and market-share reallocations benefit high-productivity firms in both industries, they also benefit the comparative advantage industry over the comparative disadvantage industry. In short, the comparative-advantage industry grows, while its counterpart shrinks.

The New Political Economy of Trade: Incorporating Firm Heterogeneity

Plouffe (2011b)[27] was the first to extend a model of heterogeneous firms to include their political interests and behaviors. As in other heterogeneous firm models, producers within an industry are differentiated by their levels of TFP, which determines firms' ability to produce, as well as their ability to engage foreign markets through trade, investment, or other means. Policy preferences then follow from these economic abilities.

The production market in this model follows that of Melitz. The behaviors firms engage in can be stylized as occurring sequentially within a period of time. These periods can then be treated as repeating infinitely, with industry structure evolving dynamically over time. Industry dynamics reflect adjustments to trade and trade-policy reform; business cycles are omitted from the model.

Firms are differentiated by TFP, but a firm's TFP draw is unobserved prior to domestic market entry. Payment of the fixed (and then sunk) cost of domestic market entry allows new firms to observe their initial productivity draws. If a firm's TFP draw is sufficiently high for it to produce profitably, meaning it will have relatively low variable costs of production, it will begin to produce for the domestic market; if the TFP draw would lead to unprofitable production, the firm will exit the market without producing. For firms that entered the market in a previous period, the analogous decision that must be made is whether to continue operating (which does not require a repayment of the sunk costs of entry) or to exit the market. Firms that incurred losses in the previous period will exit, whereas those that either broke even or realized a profit will choose to continue.

After firms make the market entry/continuation decision, they choose whether to export a portion of their production or pursue political action (these actions are not mutually exclusive). Decisions about exporting tend to be linked with certain investment and research decisions[28] and to be implemented in conjunction with each other. The same can be expected for political decisions, which are discussed in the following section.

Firms pursue export sales, as they are more profitable than domestic-market sales; however, export-market entry is limited to firms with sufficiently high productivity to overcome the significant fixed costs of entry and higher variable costs—this point is referred to as the exporting cutoff. Likewise, other forms of internationalization—FDI, offshore outsourcing, and importing—can be lucrative activities, provided firms can overcome the significant fixed costs of entry for these activities.

In general, the claim can be made that firms in the upper portion of the productivity distribution—those with TFP such that engaging foreign markets is a potentially profitable prospect—can expect to gain from trade liberalization. It follows that these firms, as well as the factors of production they employ, both prefer and seek trade liberalization, so they will have incentives to enter the political market to gain access to foreign markets and goods. However, less-productive firms cannot surmount the high costs of export-market entry. Assuming reciprocity, they face reduced margins from liberalized trade, with the least productive firms forced out of the market. While these unproductive firms may favor protection, they lack the necessary resources to enter the political market.

Finally, firms produce, incurring variable costs and realizing profits or losses based on their TFP draw and production decision. At this point, the model transitions to the next period, repeating these steps with a new mass of firms.

Policy Preferences with Heterogeneous Firms

Perhaps unsurprisingly, models of the political economy of trade with heterogeneous firms point unequivocally to intra-industry cleavages over trade policy. In most cases, highly productive firms favor increased access to foreign markets through liberalization, while unproductive producers favor protection from competition that may be intensified by heightened exposure to imports.

Likewise, the configuration of preferences matters for the incorporation of trade-policy interests into policy. High-productivity firms are likely to pursue their interests through lobbying activities, while their unproductive counterparts do not. Plouffe accounts for this disparity in activities by focusing on the high costs of political engagement. As in other markets, highly productive firms benefit from participation, while unproductive firms cannot afford entry.

In this model, the political market resembles a miniature version of the production market. Evidence suggests that the market for lobbying is structured in the same manner as a production market: firms face a significant fixed (and sunk) cost of entry and incur relatively low variable costs of continuation, should they choose to remain politically active.[29] Regardless of the manner of political engagement, entry costs may be associated with gaining an understanding with relevant political institutions, actors, policies, and regulations, or may be linked directly to searching for a good lobbyist and gaining access to key players. Costs of continuation may not be insignificant, but familiarity with the components of the political system should make them relatively low relative to the fixed costs.

Firms that choose to engage in political activities—or reveal their preferences—are assumed to make truthful contributions, meaning they seek the trade-policy outcome that enhances their business activities. Thus, highly productive firms that lobby are likely to pursue liberalization, while unproductive firms, if they can afford to enter the political market, will seek protection.[30]

Both Kim (2013) and Osgood (2013) frame these observed patterns as the result of the level of product differentiation within an industry. In Kim's model, the protection for sale logic is flipped on its head: in highly differentiated industries, exporting interests are concentrated among a small number of firms that seek profit-improving export sales, while potentially protectionist interests are diffuse. Those pursuing liberalization can more easily overcome any collective-action problem over trade policy, while import-competing firms are relatively unthreatened by imported varieties.

For within-industry preferences, Osgood largely ignores collective action, instead focusing on the theoretical differences between a shift from autarky to liberalization and from postliberalization to increased liberalization. In the first instance, firms are cleanly divided: exporters favor liberalization, while domestic-focused producers prefer autarky. In the second, a shift from a postliberalization environment to one with even freer trade, the producers that would favor further liberalization are exporters of middling productivity, as these firms stand to gain the most in terms of the percentage gain in their exporting profits. Consequently, the most productive firms, like those solely competing with imports, oppose liberalization, as the potential reductions to their costs would be countered by increased competition, both at home and abroad.

Plouffe (2012) similarly omits collective action, arguing that highly productive firms—both exporters and nonexporters—are more likely to favor liberalization than unproductive firms. However, as productivity increases above the exporting cutoff, trade liberalization is less likely to be a salient issue, as the marginal gains for a firm with extremely low variable production costs are smaller than for one with relatively high variable costs. Thus, the firms that are most likely to hold strong liberalizing preferences are those with TFP draws nearest to, but greater than, the exporting cutoff.

Finally, these preference expectations are shaped by status quo barriers to trade. High tariffs and nontariff barriers should lead to a relatively large mass of high-productivity firms seeking liberalization; consequently, low-productivity firms will be less likely to seek increased protection. Likewise, relatively low tariffs and nontariff barriers should be associated with fewer high-productivity firms pursuing further liberalization and a greater portion of low-productivity firms seeking protection.

Evidence of Heterogeneous Preferences

The evaluation of firms' heterogeneous policy preferences is often a data-intensive task. While the firm-level financial data that provide the inputs for TFP estimation are generally readily available, international trade and investment data are less rigorously collected and distributed at the firm level. Cross-nationally, the availability of information on firms' political activities varies widely. Under the Lobbying Disclosure Act of 1995, the United States requires lobbyists to report data on clients, expenditures, and issues. Other countries do not have similar transparency requirements.

Following a number of broad-based studies of business lobbying,[31] some efforts have been made to assess the variations in trade-policy lobbying activities among American firms.[32] Both Plouffe (2012) and Kim (2013) find a positive relationship between productivity and the likelihood of lobbying. In the same manner as market activities, lobbying is a costly endeavor. The high fixed costs of lobby-market entry and variable continuation costs preclude participation by less-productive producers, while highly productive producers may not seek to incur lobbying's additional costs. Lobbying among the most productive firms is more likely when products are highly differentiated or highly substitutable, while lobbying is less likely among firms in industries with middling levels of product differentiation.[33] These highly productive firms, across all industries, are very likely to be lobbying for liberalization, relative to less-productive firms, and this productivity-lobbying relationship persists across both exporting firms and domestic producers.[34]

While lobbying-based studies capture producers' political activities or revealed preferences, they do not capture the variation of latent preferences along the productivity distribution of firms. Plouffe (2011b) uses a survey-based design to capture latent preferences among Japanese manufacturers, finding that highly productive manufacturers are more likely to favor liberalization than are less-productive firms. Furthermore, the relationship between productivity and pro-trade preferences persists when controlling for actual trading behaviors.

The data-intensive nature of firm-level empirical studies makes it difficult to explore the historical nature of these theories using the same approach that can be applied to contemporary examinations, but a surprisingly rich wealth of data exists for use in historical case studies. For example, Plouffe (2013) examines the impact of productivity heterogeneity on producer cleavages over the Smoot-Hawley Tariff of 1930, relying on firm size (a common proxy for TFP among economists), geographically induced differences in TFP distributions, and mechanization rates to find evidence of intra-industry cleavages over the Tariff. Similar studies could utilize these techniques to reinvestigate other watershed events, such as the formation of the Coalition of Iron and Rye or the coalitions behind the passage of the Reciprocal Trade Agreements Act of 1934.

Comparative Advantage and Heterogeneous Firms

In addition to predicting variations in trade-policy preferences within industries, heterogeneous firm theories can explain differences in how preferences are distributed across industries. In keeping with a rich literature emphasizing the impact of factor endowments on trade flows,[35] Plouffe (2011a, 2012) identifies variations in political interests between comparative-advantage and comparative-disadvantage industries. Because production in comparative-advantage industries is relatively cheap when compared to same-industry production abroad, a relatively large mass of firms can expect to benefit from trade liberalization. Likewise, because production is relatively dear in comparative-disadvantage industries, a fairly small portion of highly productive producers gains from liberalization.

Following a liberalizing reform to trade policy, both output and the employment of the factors of production shift from comparative-disadvantage industries to comparative-advantage industries. At the same time, both of these shares also shift from unproductive firms, especially those that are forced out of the production market, to highly productive producers. The shifts in the employment of factors of production lead to an adjustment in the composition of their demand. Recall that across all industries (and at all levels of economic development), highly productive firms are more skill- and capital-intensive than their counterparts. Thus, following liberalization, the prices of these factors increase as market share and means of production are reallocated to these high-productivity firms.

However, while the aggregate postliberalization trends follow the Ricardian predictions of production specialization according to comparative advantage, reliance on a classical trade model generates the overprediction of specialization, as well as painting an inaccurate portrait of the micro-level implications of liberalization. Incorporating heterogeneous firms into a comparative-advantage framework generates predictions for developing economies that markedly contradict the conventional wisdom. Factor owners employed by highly productive firms gain from trade liberalization, while those employed by unproductive firms lose. Similarly, across different levels of development, skill and capital owners face better postliberalization prospects than labor owners. As market share is reallocated to the firms that benefit from trade, demand for capital and skills increases, drawing from the pool of these factors freed from the unproductive firms forced to exit the market. Because the producers that gain from trade do not require labor as intensely as their counterparts who ceased production, labor loses from liberalization. The reduction in demand may lead to decreases in nominal returns, even as the growth in trade brings about welfare growth in real terms.

Ultimately, while factor abundance in classical models leads to variation in the distributional consequences from liberalization at different levels of economic development in classical models, this is not the case in models with heterogeneous firms. Rather, across all levels of development, owners of skills and capital are predicted to benefit the most from trade, while owners of unskilled labor face reduced demand for employment.

Product Differentiation Across Industries

Kim (2013) and Osgood (2013) focus on intra-industry product differentiation as a means of distinguishing industry-level variations.[36] High levels of product differentiation reduce the impact of import liberalization on the margins of existing products within an industry relative to the impact in an industry with low levels of product differentiation, as individual products are less readily substitutable. Thus, in industries with low levels of product differentiation, where even a small shift in competitors' prices can have large consequences for competitiveness, even highly productive firms may favor protection, seeking to maintain their domestic margins.[37]

While neither model explicitly incorporates the dynamics of adjustment to a liberalizing reform, the adjustment dynamics would likely resemble those discussed in the previous section. In a skill- or capital-abundant economy, output and factor employment shift to both highly productive firms and industries with high levels of product differentiation, and away from unproductive firms and industries with relatively undifferentiated products. In an economy abundant in unskilled labor, employment and output would shift to highly productive firms in industries with low levels of differentiated products, with these producers competing in foreign markets based primarily on price advantages. As an economy develops, it experiences increasing product differentiation in skill- and capital-intensive sectors.

Regardless of whether industries are divided based on product differentiation of comparative-advantage lines, models of trade policy with heterogeneous firms generate political cleavages that differ from those of models based on the Ricardo-Viner and Stolper-Samuelson frameworks. Rather than political cleavages forming along factor or sector lines, they are dictated by firm-level productivity.

The Policy Implications of Firm Heterogeneity

Just as the distributional and political predictions of heterogeneous firm models differ from those of classical models, so do the policy implications deviate from the conventional wisdom. Where the workhorse theories in international political economy predict political victories as accrued by those seeking protection, heterogeneous firm models primarily predict the opposite outcome: liberalization results from the political activities of pro-trade firms. This outcome is the consequence of two features of political engagement by producers. First, only highly productive firms possess the capacity to engage in political behavior, as such activities divert resources from production. These businesses are more likely than others to favor liberalization, biasing policy outcomes toward liberalization rather than protection. Second, because the productivity distribution of firms within a given industry is typically shaped such that the majority firms are relatively unproductive, with a small highly productive portion, collective action can be expected to be less problematic for these politically active firms than for the many firms that do not stand to benefit from liberalization. Thus, in contrast with the ubiquitous protection for sale paradigm, we should generally expect to see political activities that incentivize policy makers to implement liberalizing reforms.

However, there are important theoretical and empirical exceptions, arising especially from Osgood's prediction of highly productive firms opposing further liberalization in a postliberalization environment. Here it is instructive to differentiate between tariffs and nontariff barriers (NTBs). The highest productivity firms never favor increased tariffs. However, they do prefer increases in NTBs, as long as trade can be maintained. A unilateral increase in NTBs shifts the distribution of export profits away from the least productive exporters to the most productive exporters.[38] This effect is discussed in greater detail in the following section.

Firms and Nontariff Measures

Nontariff measures/barriers (NTM/Bs) include both behind-the-border and at-the-border restrictions on trade and form an important, if difficult to study, component of trade policy. The extent to which these regulations supplement or complement tariffs is beyond the scope of this chapter, but characteristics of the demand for them runs somewhat counter to the conventional wisdom that MNCs promote liberalization because of their heavy investment in foreign markets.[39] Under certain conditions in Osgood's model, the most productive firms in an industry seek the implementation of protection through NTBs.

Where tariffs impact a trading firm's variable costs on top of its productivity draw, NTBs increase the fixed cost of market entry. This serves to restrict market access to potential entrants, preventing the less productive ones from engaging the market, regardless of the intent behind the NTB. Thus, multinationals might support the implementation of NTBs to restrict the foreign market expansion of their competitors, reducing competition in those markets. Gulotty (2013) illustrates this using the case of a 2007 reform of European Union chemical legislation. The reform, which required the registration and testing of chemical products, was initially strongly opposed by American industry members, but both Dow Chemical and BASF vocally supported its implementation. Further investigation provides evidence that highly productive MNCs support the implementation of NTBs, providing an explanation for the persistence and progression of NTBs while tariffs have steadily decreased.

Looking Forward

The body of research incorporating heterogeneous firms into the study of the international political economy of trade is very much in its infancy, but these theories have the potential to induce a sea change in the study of the subject. The focus of much of the literature on factors and industries lacks both solid micro-foundations and mechanisms for translating preferences into policy. Heterogeneous firm approaches provide both.

The implications of these theories range beyond the topic of trade politics. Similar productivity-based breakdowns can be identified for other foreign economic behaviors, like FDI, importing, behaving as an intermediating trade, or engaging in intermediated trade.[40] For each of these activities, despite differing entry cutoffs, highly productive firms can expect to benefit from participation, while unproductive firms cannot afford to participate. These activities are not mutually exclusive, so a single producer may engage in some combination of any or all of them (in addition to exporting) to reach different target markets.

Similarly, productivity impacts firm-level preferences over tasks trade. The most productive firms engaging in tasks trade offshore various functions, while less productive task traders will onshore, outsourcing production to another domestic firm.[41] Like other markets, participation entails a fixed entry cost, precluding the participation of the least productive. Firms that can obtain benefits from reducing the costs to offshoring will favor this, as it resembles a factor-specific increase in productivity.[42] Firms that cannot afford to offshore face two effects: the factor that is offshored becomes cheaper as a result of its increased productivity, while competition from offshoring firms potentially becomes more intense as the unit price of their output is adjusted for their new variable costs. Firms that cannot offshore are likely to oppose the liberalization of offshoring, as the availability of the cheaper factor is likely to lag behind the competition effects, although this depends on the extent of product differentiation within the industry. Although the effects of offshoring break down in a similar manner to those of trade, the effect of increasing the dispersion of an industry's TFP distribution leads to political battles that are often highly pitched relative to those over trade policy, as shifts in employment across international borders exacerbate domestic tensions between producers based on offshoring capabilities as well as among factor owners fearing their own future employment prospects.

In addition to improving political economy understandings of economic flows, heterogeneous firm studies can enhance research in other related fields. For example, while much progress has been made in determining the factors that lead firms to lobby on trade policy in the United States, little work has been done to expand these findings to other political activities and institutional arrangements. Similarly, there is much room for research exploring the configurations of producer interests within domestic and international institutions. Producer associations vary significantly in membership, organizational structure, and issue scope. Firm-focused studies of the nature of those discussed in this chapter should provide a stepping stone for building an improved producer-association literature through an increased appreciation of the variations in members' political interests.

While research on the implications of heterogeneous firms for the international political economy of trade is still in its youth, it challenges the conventional wisdom of the structure of demand for trade policy. Furthermore, firms are thrust into a central role in the policy-making process, refocusing the emphasis on policy mechanisms from voting to lobbying. These models provide explanations for the general postwar reductions in barriers to trade, as well as the more recent turn to NTBs. By further assessing the varied nature of producer interests, based on firm-level heterogeneity, political economists will be able to build on existing understanding of the interactions between political interests and policy makers to improve descriptions, explanations, and predictions of policy outcomes and their consequences.

NOTES

1. In economics, "preference" is typically used to refer to individual-level attitudes. However, the convention in international political economy, followed here, aggregates the use of "preference" to also refer to the collective position taken on an issue by an interest group.
2. Milner (1988); Milner and Yoffie (1989).
3. Bauer, Pool, and Dexter (1972).
4. Megumi Naoi discusses the sources of individual trade-policy preferences in Chapter Six.
5. Milner (1988); Milner and Yoffie (1989).
6. Grossman and Helpman (1994). Lucy Goodhart discusses this body of research in much greater detail in Chapter 9.
7. Bombardini (2008).
8. Chang and Willmann (2006); Abel-Koch (2010).
9. Krugman (1980); Helpman and Krugman (1985).
10. Melitz (2003).
11. Bernard et al. (2003).
12. Redding (2011) provides an overview of the developments of these and related models.
13. Bernard, Redding, and Schott (2007).
14. Melitz and Ottaviano (2008).
15. Bernard et al. (2011).
16. Roberts and Tybout (1997); Bernard and Jensen (1999); De Loecker (2007).
17. Bernard et al. (2007); Helpman (2006); and Bernard et al. (2011) provide more in-depth surveys.
18. Alvarez and Lopez (2005); Bernard, Redding, and Schott (2007).
19. Bernard et al. (2007); Helpman (2006).
20. Kasahara and Lapham (2013); Gibson and Graciano (2011).
21. Bernard et al. 2007.
22. Seker 2011; Plouffe 2011a.
23. Ahn et al. 2011; Antràs and Costinot 2011; Bernard et al. 2010.
24. Bernard et al. 2010.
25. Helpman, Melitz, and Yeaple (2004); Head and Ries (2003).

26. Antràs 2003; Antràs and Helpman 2004.
27. Kim (2013) and Osgood (2013) provide alternative formal specifications.
28. See Costantini and Melitz (2008) for a look at linkages between investment and export decisions.
29. Kerr, Lincoln, and Mishra (2011).
30. Osgood (2013) and Gulotty (2013) provide an important counterpoint to this logic, discussed later in this chapter.
31. See, for example, Hansen and Mitchell (2000); Hansen, Mitchell, and Drope (2005); Richter, Samphantharak, and Timmons (2009).
32. Plouffe (2012); Kim (2013).
33. Kim (2013, 26).
34. Plouffe (2012).
35. Helpman and Krugman (1985); Bernard, Redding, and Schott (2007).
36. Kim (2013); Osgood (2013).
37. It is interesting to note that in developed economies, comparative-advantage sectors tend to have high levels of product differentiation, whereas comparative-disadvantage sectors tend to have low levels of product differentiation.
38. Osgood (2013, 25).
39. Milner (1988).
40. For more on intermediated trade, see Bernard, Grazzo, and Tomasi (2010) and Plouffe (2011a).
41. Antràs and Helpman (2004).
42. Grossman and Rossi-Hansberg (2008).

References

Abel-Koch, Jennifer. 2010. "Endogenous Trade Policy with Heterogeneous Firms." Unpublished manuscript.

Ahn, JaeBin, Amit K. Khandelwal, and Shang-Jin Wei. 2011. "The Role of Intermediaries in Facilitating Trade." *Journal of International Economics* 84 (1): 73–85.

Alvarez, Roberto and Ricardo A Lopez. 2005. "Exporting and Performance: Evidence from Chilean Plants." *Canadian Journal of Economics* 38 (4): 1384–1400.

Antràs, Pol. 2003. "Firms, Contracts, and Trade Structure." National Bureau of Economic Research, Working Paper No. w9740.

Antràs, Pol, and Elhanan Helpman. 2004. Global Sourcing. *Journal of Political Economy* 112: 552–580.

Antràs, Pol, and Arnaud Costinot. 2011 "Intermediated Trade." *The Quarterly Journal of Economics* 126 (3): 1319–1374.

Bauer, Raymond A., Ithiel de Sola Pool, and Lewis Anthony Dexter. 1972. *American Business and Public Policy: The Politics of Foreign Trade*. Chicago: Aldine-Atherton, Inc.

Bernard, Andrew B., and J. Bradford Jensen. 1999. "Exceptional Exporter Performance: Cause, Effect, or Both?" *Journal of International Economics* 47 (1): 1–25.

Bernard, Andrew B., Jonathan Eaton, J. Bradford Jensen, and Samuel S. Kortum. 2003. Plants and Productivity in International Trade. *American Economic Review* 93 (4): 1268–1290.

Bernard, Andrew B., Marco Grazzi, and Chiara Tomasi. 2010. Intermediaries in International Trade: Direct vs. Indirect Modes of Export. National Bank of Belgium Working Paper Series no. 199.

Bernard, Andrew B., J. Bradford Jensen, Stephen J. Redding, and Peter K. Schott. 2011. The Empirics of Firm Heterogeneity and International Trade. NBER Working Paper No. w17627.

Bernard, Andrew B., J. Bradford Jensen, Stephen J. Redding, and Peter K. Schott. 2007. Firms in International Trade. *Journal of Economic Perspectives* 21 (3): 105–130.

Bernard, Andrew B., Stephen J. Redding, and Peter K. Schott. 2007. Comparative Advantage and Heterogeneous Firms. *Review of Economic Studies* 74: 31–66.

Bombardini, Matilde. 2008. "Firm Heterogeneity and Lobby Participation." *Journal of International Economics* 75 (2): 329–348.

Chang, Pao-Li and Gerald Willmann. 2006. "Protection for Sale with Heterogeneous Interests within Industries." Unpublished manuscript.

Costantini, James and Marc Melitz. 2008. "The Dynamics of Firm-Level Adjustment to Trade Liberalization." In *The Organization of Firms in a Global Economy*, edited by Elhanan Helpman, Dalia Marin and Thierry Verdier. Cambridge: Harvard University Press. 107–141.

De Loecker, Jan. 2007. "Do Exports Generate Higher Productivity? Evidence from Slovenia." *Journal of International Economics* 73 (1): 69–98.

Dixit, Avinash K., and Joseph E. Stiglitz. 1977. "Monopolistic Competition and Optimum Product Diversity." *The American Economic Review*: 297–308.

Gibson, Mark J., and Tim A. Graciano. 2011. Trade Models with Heterogeneous Firms: What about Importing? Unpublished manuscript.

Grossman, Gene M., and Elhanan Helpman. 1994. "Protection for Sale." *American Economic Review* 84 (4): 833–850.

Grossman, Gene M., and Esteban Rossi-Hansberg. 2008. Trading Tasks: A Simple Theory of Offshoring. *American Economic Review* 98 (5): 1978–1997.

Gulotty, Robert. 2013. Regulatory Protectionism, MNC Profits, and the Limits of International Cooperation. Unpublished manuscript.

Hansen, Wendy L., and Neil J. Mitchell. 2000. Disaggregating and Explaining Corporate Political Activity: Domestic and Foreign Corporations in National Politics. *American Political Science Review* 94 (4): 891–903.

Hansen, Wendy L., Neil J. Mitchell, and Jeffrey M. Drope. 2005. The Logic of Private and Collective Action. *American Journal of Political Science* 49 (1): 150–167.

Head, Keith and John Ries. 2003. "Heterogeneity and the FDI versus Export Decision of Japanese Manufacturers." *Journal of Japanese and International Economies* 17 (4): 448–467.

Helpman, Elhanan. 2006. Trade, FDI, and the Organization of Firms. *Journal of Economic Literature* XLIV: 589–630.

Helpman, Elhanan, and Paul Krugman. 1985. *Market Structure and Foreign Trade*. Cambridge, MA: The MIT Press.

Helpman, Elhanan, Marc Melitz, and Stephen Yeaple. 2004. Export Versus FDI with Heterogeneous Firms. *American Economic Review* 94 (1): 300–316.

Kasahara, Hiroyuki, and Beverly Lapham. 2013. "Productivity and the Decision to Import and Export: Theory and Evidence." *Journal of International Economics* 89 (2): 297–316.

Kerr, William R., William F. Lincoln, and Prachi Mishra. 2011. The Dynamics of Firm Lobbying. NBER Working Paper No. 17577.

Kim, In Song. 2013. Political Cleavages within Industry: Firm-level Lobbying for Trade Liberalization. Unpublished manuscript, Princeton University.

Krugman, Paul. 1980. Scale Economies, Product Differentiation, and the Pattern of Trade. *American Economic Review* 70: 950–959.

Melitz, Marc. 2003. The Impact of Trade on Intra-Industry Reallocations and Aggregate Industry Productivity. *Econometrica* 71 (6): 1695–1725.

Melitz, M. J., and G. I. P. Ottaviano. 2008. Market Size, Trade, and Productivity. *Review of Economic Studies* 75 (1): 295–316.

Milner, Helen. 1988. *Resisting Protectionism: Global Industries and the Politics of International Trade*. Princeton, NJ: Princeton University Press.

Milner, Helen V., and David B Yoffie. 1989. Between Free Trade and Protectionism: Strategic Trade Policy and a Theory of Corporate Trade Demands. *International Organization* 43 (2): 239–272.

Osgood, Iain. 2013. Differentiated Products, Divided Industries: Firms and the Politics of Intra-Industry Trade. PhD diss., Harvard University. ProQuest/UMI 10982.

Plouffe, Michael. 2011a. Firms and Foreign Market Engagement: Internationalization Activities among Japanese Firms. Paper presented at the meeting of the Japan Society of International Economics, Tokyo, 23 October 2011.

Plouffe, Michael. 2011b. The New Political Economy of Trade: Heterogeneous Firms and Trade-Policy Positions. Paper presented at the meeting of the International Political Economy Society, Madison, WI, 11 November 2011.

Plouffe, Michael. 2012. Liberalization for Sale: Heterogeneous Firms and Lobbying over FTAs. Paper prepared for the meeting of the American Political Science Association, New Orleans, Louisiana, 30 August 2012.

Plouffe, Michael. 2013. The New Political Economy of Trade: Heterogeneous Firms and Trade Policy. PhD diss., University of California, San Diego.

Redding, Stephen. 2011. Theories of Heterogeneous Firms and Trade. *Annual Review of Economics* 3: 77–105.

Richter, Brian Kelleher, Krislert Samphantharak, and Jeffrey F. Timmons. 2009. Lobbying and Taxes. *American Journal of Political Science* 53, (4): 893–909.

Roberts, Mark J., and James R. Tybout. 1997. "The Decision to Export in Colombia: An Empirical Model of Entry with Sunk Costs." *The American Economic Review*: 545–564.

Seker, Murat. 2011. "Importing, Exporting, and Innovation in Developing Countries." Unpublished manuscript.

Woll, Cornelia. 2008. *Firm Interests: How Governments Shape business Lobbying on Global Trade*. Ithaca, NY: Cornell University Press.

......

CHAPTER 12

THE POLITICS OF MARKET COMPETITION

Trade and Antitrust in a Global Economy

......

TIM BÜTHE

THE TRADE-ANTITRUST LINKAGE

......

ANTITRUST law and enforcement—known as "competition policy" outside the United States—is one of the most powerful tools that states have at their disposal to shape the structure and operation of markets (e.g., Baron 2010, 265–310; Fligstein 1990). Competition law authorizes and regulates government intervention against anticompetitive behavior, such as price-fixing or bid-rigging, and the concentration of economic power, for instance through mergers and acquisitions. When it succeeds in safeguarding or increasing market competition such that both buyers and sellers are generally price-takers, it brings widely recognized economic benefits, boosting economic efficiency, growth, and innovation, increasing both consumer and aggregate welfare (e.g., Gellhorn, Kovacic, and Calkins 2004; Rey 1997; Weiss 1989). In various countries and at various times, competition policy has also had a number of other legitimate objectives—many of them quite familiar to scholars of trade politics and policy—ranging from industrial policy and economic development goals to economic freedom.[1] But even when it only seeks to enhance economic welfare, effective competition policy is inherently deeply political, since it entails the use of political power to constrain or even redistribute economic power.

Ever since the adoption of the first modern antitrust statutes in Canada and the United States at the end of the nineteenth century, competition policy has been closely intertwined with trade policy.[2] To be sure, a diverse coalition of interests came together in passing these first national competition laws (e.g., Baggaley 1991; Letwin 1965, esp. 53–99), but a central motivation was clearly an understanding of antitrust as a substitute for trade openness. Senator John Sherman (for whom the first US federal antitrust statute, the Sherman Act of 1890, is named) sought antitrust enforcement in large part to counterbalance the protectionist tariff for then-nascent northern industries. As a Republican senator from Ohio, he was a proponent of the controversial protectionist measures that subsequently came to be known as the McKinley tariff, but he also recognized that such protection would threaten the effective operation of still emerging and often oligopolistic markets for many of those industries' products. Like many of his contemporaries, Sherman thought that vigorously enforced laws against anticompetitive practices, especially the abuse of market power, would make a protectionist foreign economic policy compatible with an efficient market economy domestically (DiLorenzo 1985, esp. 82f.; Hazlett 1992).

The contemporary belief that antitrust could substitute for free trade is even more important for understanding the politics of the original Canadian competition legislation, the Act for the Prevention and Suppression of Combinations Formed in Restraint of Trade of 1889. "Combines" (known as "trusts" in the United States)—groups of companies cooperating to "manage" production and prices and keep competitors at bay—were still rather rare and commercially unimportant in the Canadian economy. Consequently, populist hostility to the power of ever larger corporations, an important source of political support for the US antitrust legislation, was much weaker in Canada (e.g., Cohen 1938, 453f.; Bliss 1974, 33–54; though cf. Benidickson 1993). Why then did the Canadian legislature pass the first modern, national competition law fourteen months before the US Congress? Archival research and a close reading of the Canadian legislative record suggest that the parliamentary majority's enthusiasm for the law was mostly about trade policy—"a calculated manoeuvre" by N. Clarke Wallace of the governing Conservative Party, the champion of the 1889 Act, "to deflect criticism from the combine-creating effects of the protective tariff" that his Conservative majority had put in place (Bliss 1973, 182f., 185, 188). And the opposition Liberals in the Canadian House of Commons accordingly portrayed the Act as a cynical distraction from the ill effects of tariff protection (Bliss 1973, 182). Some went so far as to call it a legislative or political "fraud" (Halladay 2012, 158; Trebilcock 1991).

The view of trade openness and antitrust enforcement as substitutes, which informed Sherman and his contemporaries, can ultimately be traced back to the work of the classical political economists. Adam Smith, who warned against anticompetitive behavior in numerous passages of the *Wealth of Nations* and other works, saw such private restrictions on market competition as equally as damaging as governmental measures such as royal grants of monopolies. David Ricardo, best known to trade scholars for having shown that the principles of comparative advantage can (under classical assumptions) ensure that every country is better off under free trade than autarky, formalized some of Smith's key insights in his theory of rents (a key element of Ricardo's *Principles of Political Economy and Taxation*).[3] From these sources, the substitutability of trade openness and competition policy became the traditional view in trade economics, discussed more fully in the next section.

Starting in the 1990s, however, this traditional approach faced a major empirical anomaly when the rapid, institutionalized spread of trade openness (evidenced in particular by the shift from the General Agreement on Tariffs and Trade to the World Trade Organization and the explosive growth in the number of preferential trade agreements) coincided with a similarly explosive diffusion of antitrust legal norms. During the first century after the US Congress passed the Sherman Act, between 1890 and 1990, the number of countries with competition laws on the books increased from 2 to 37. During the next twenty years, between 1990 and 2010, the number of countries with competition laws more than tripled, to about 120, even though the sustained, institutionalized increase in international market integration during the same period of time should have made the adoption of such laws ever more superfluous if trade openness were a substitute for competition policy.

This observation prompted scholars of the law and economics of competition policy to rethink the relationship between trade and competition policies. Newer theoretical models tend to emphasize the possibility that competition law might—through selective, discriminatory enforcement—be abused as a trade barrier. These models differ regarding the level of aggregation at which they operate, the attribution of causality, and their implicit or explicit causal mechanisms. Yet, they have in common that they view competition policy as a substitute for protectionism rather than as a substitute for free trade. These new theoretical perspectives have been very influential in policy circles and have informed sometimes heated debates over the question of whether antitrust law and enforcement need to be brought under the umbrella of the WTO.[4]

The remainder of this chapter examines these different theoretical approaches to thinking about the relationship between trade openness and competition policy, focusing in the second section on how compelling they are deductively and in the third section on how useful they are for understanding key aspects of antitrust in open economies. I argue that both perspectives suffer from truncated or missing models of politics, which undermines their explanatory leverage. In the fourth section, I provide a sketch of ongoing research that seeks to address these weaknesses of the existing theoretical approaches and aims to provide a sounder empirical basis for understanding the international dimension of antitrust enforcement.

THEORETICAL APPROACHES: THE LAW, ECONOMICS, AND POLITICS OF MARKET COMPETITION

Free Trade as a Substitute for Competition Policy—and Vice Versa

Trade economists have traditionally viewed trade openness as a substitute for competition policy, because they see barriers to entry as the key economic rationale for competition policy. In any standard neoclassical model with profit-maximizing, self-interested economic agents, barriers to entry are a prerequisite for maintaining cartels and other forms of anticompetitive behavior through which some economic actors benefit at everyone else's expense. Competition policy seeks to constrain anticompetitive behavior *directly* by prohibiting such behavior and identifying and punishing those who engage in it. Such a policy lowers barriers to market entry insofar as competition regulators target anticompetitive behavior that creates or raises such barriers or industries in which barriers to entry are high for other reasons, e.g., industries with high start-up costs. Free trade promises to constrain anticompetitive behavior *indirectly* by opening national markets to foreign producers. Free trade thus allows foreign producers to enter and seize market share whenever domestic anticompetitive behavior keeps prices at supra-competitive levels. And sustaining the expectation that foreign producers will indeed do so requires us only to assume that competitive foreign producers for the product in question exist and are materially self-interested, which should lead them to offer their goods at lower prices, up to the point where those prices approximate the foreign producers' marginal costs.

In sum, trade liberalization checks market power, reducing the need for regulatory intervention to safeguard competition. As Blackhurst puts it: "Trade Policy is Competition Policy" (1991). In fact, from the point of view of economic efficiency under the conventional assumption of trade economics, free trade is superior to competition policy because it achieves the same ends without the need to create and maintain a sizable bureaucracy and without the potential for abuse. Trebilcock (1991) hence refers to competition policy as a "second best" approach to safeguarding market competition.

The logic of the argument that economic openness increases competition is impeccable, given its assumptions, which are common and conventional in the trade literature. In more recent decades, it has found support not just in formal models but also some support from empirical analyses. As summarized by Irwin, "there is . . . overwhelming [empirical] evidence that free trade improves economic performance by increasing competition in the domestic market" (2009, 43).[5] Note, however, that it does not necessarily follow that trade liberalization goes sufficiently far to constitute a real substitute for regulatory enforcement of competition law—nor that economic openness is equally effective in checking market power and safeguarding against anticompetitive behavior in internationally integrated industries.

Three concerns motivate my skepticism about viewing free trade as a substitute for competition policy. First, as Dixit (1984) pointed out thirty years ago, much international trade occurs in industries whose structure more closely approximates oligopoly than perfect competition. Second, competition policy may have important objectives beyond maximizing consumer welfare or generally enhancing economic efficiency. Ordo-liberals, for instance, attribute to competition policy an essential role in safeguarding economic (and therefore inherently also political) freedom, because high concentrations of economic power can be readily leveraged into political influence.[6] The debate about "too-big-to-fail" industrial and financial firms in the last few years suggests that concerns about economic power remain timely. It is unclear, however, how trade openness would address them. Third, and maybe most importantly, the theoretical logic underpinning the argument that free trade is a substitute for competition policy rests on the assumption that firms are simply reactive to the constraints that public policy might place on them, so that those constraints can be theoretically treated as exogenous. But a large literature on the domestic *politics* of trade policy shows that, even though genuine liberalization is possible (Gawande, Krishna, and Olarreaga 2009; Milner 1987; Rogowski 1989), it is difficult and politically costly to use trade policy to force foreign competition on a previously well-protected industry. Such long-protected industries are likely—not least thanks to the rents afforded by being protected from foreign competitors—to have material resources, strong incentives, and concentrated interests (including often an organizational structure for overcoming collective action problems) to simply replace one kind of protection with another (e.g., Grieco 1990; Limão and Tovar 2009; Kono 2006; Naoi 2009; WTO 2012). In sum, once the politics of trade policy are taken seriously, the theoretical case for viewing a generally liberal foreign economic policy as a substitute for domestic competition policy becomes deductively much less compelling.

When we look at the theoretical argument the other way (competition policy as a substitute for free trade), it is similarly built on shaky foundations. As a theory of antitrust enforcement, this approach assumes that competition regulators—and the politicians who are in a position to influence them through statutory changes, resource allocation, or other means—are disinterested guardians of market efficiency.[7] Such heroic assumptions about policy makers' objectives might not be surprising given that this approach is devoid of politics. But competition law enforcement is inherently deeply political in that it entails the use of public authority to constrain private actors' exercise of market power. Once we take politics seriously, the theoretical case for viewing competition policy as a substitute for free trade becomes much weaker.

Competition Policy as a Substitute for Protectionism

A second perspective on the relationship between trade openness and competition policy exhibits a greater (though still truncated) awareness of the politics of both trade and competition policy. It posits competition policy as a substitute for trade restrictions rather than trade openness, based on the assumption that competition law can be selectively enforced to the benefit of domestic stakeholders and the detriment of their foreign counterparts, including the foreign competitors of domestic firms. It is theoretically useful to distinguish two variants of this antitrust-as-protectionism approach.

What may be called the aggregate national welfare variant, with strong affinities to statist theories of International Relations, treats governments as unitary actors and assumes that each government seeks to maximize the country's aggregate welfare. Under this assumption, (net) imports create an incentive for overly stringent enforcement, because such an "oversupply" of antitrust enforcement creates benefits for domestic consumers, whereas the costs are borne disproportionately by foreign producers. By contrast, (net) exports create an incentive for overly lax enforcement, because the gains from uncorrected anticompetitive behavior are disproportionately enjoyed by domestic producers, whereas the costs are disproportionately borne by foreign consumers (e.g., Horn and Levinsohn 2001; Williams and Rodriguez 1995). Such selective enforcement is clearly attractive (and hence expected) for economically large countries, because it should yield a gain in aggregate economic welfare for them: for countries with sufficiently large markets, changes in their production or consumption induced by such selective antitrust enforcement affect the world price and hence improve the country's terms of trade (Guzman 1998, 2004).

The other variant, which may be called the domestic political economy variant of the "antitrust-as-protectionism" perspective, has strong affinities to the public choice critique of regulation, with its assumption that the state and any specific manifestations of public authority tend to get captured by special, usually private interests. This approach takes firms more seriously as (potential) political actors than trade economists traditionally have done. Specifically, scholars in this tradition assume that domestic firms, when faced with trade liberalization that threatens to expose them to increased foreign competition, will turn to the government or state agencies to achieve a similar level of protection through other (ab)uses of public authority. And firms' "actions aimed at effectively locking competing imports or foreign investors out of their domestic market" (Trebilcock and Howse 2005, 591) can include the "use of antitrust to subvert competition" (Baumol and Ordover 1985, 247). The argument still lacks an explicit theory of politics or policy making, but typically assumes a pluralistic responsiveness of policy makers—including competition regulators—to political lobbying (e.g., Shughart, Silverman, and Tollison 1995). Consequently, it yields observable implications similar to those noted for the aggregate national welfare variant but for all countries (rather than just economically large countries), because there is no assumption that policy makers seek to maximize aggregate welfare and therefore will only engage in selective enforcement that is "efficient" for the national economy.

While both variants of this theoretical approach address certain weaknesses of the traditional trade economics approach, they also both suffer from theoretical weaknesses of their own. The logical structure of the argument underpinning the aggregate national welfare variant, for instance, is essentially the same as for optimal tariff theory (e.g., Krugman 1986), so that the well-known critiques of optimal tariff theory should equally apply here. For example, critics of optimal tariff theory have long pointed out that a country's attempts to achieve welfare gains at the expense of its trading partners (here through selective enforcement) invite retaliation by some of those trading partners, since no country is economically large in all industries. Such retaliation turns the hypothetically possible tactical welfare gain for the one side into a welfare loss for both. And since the loss is predictable, we have no reason to expect that we will empirically observe the selective enforcement that was the original cause of concern.

Moreover, both variants, while more attentive to the politics of antitrust than the traditional trade economics perspective, still rely on an overly truncated model of politics. Even in the domestic political economy variant of the antitrust-as-protectionism perspective, firms are recognized as political actors only domestically, where they lobby regulators and the politicians who oversee them. They are denied *transnational* political agency, even though substantial research shows firms to be increasingly important transnational political actors (e.g., Baron 2001; Büthe 2010; Büthe and Mattli 2011; Cutler, Haufler, and Porter 1999). A similar problem affects the conceptualization of governments: Although they are recognized as pertinent political actors across borders, they are conceptualized only as unitary actors. Much research about the politics of international economic relations and global governance, however, emphasizes the increasing importance of transnational politics and transgovernmental networks (e.g., Keohane and Nye 1989; Newman and Posner 2011; Slaughter 2004).

In sum, if we take both firms and regulators seriously as transnational political actors, then there is no reason to expect firms to have a preference for public over private protection, which motivates the exclusive focus on the [ab]use of public power in the domestic political economy model. Nor need we assume that regulatory practices and actions are shaped only by the domestic political environment in which the regulators operate.[8] Once we relax those assumptions, there is no compelling reason to expect that the increasing international integration of product markets would result in the (ab)use of competition policy for protectionist purposes.

Empirical Analyses

Putting aside, for the moment, the above critiques of the deductive logic of the existing theoretical approaches, I now turn to a brief assessment of their explanatory leverage for understanding key aspects of competition policy in open economies. I undertake this assessment with the caveat that few of the existing empirical studies were set up to test the theoretical approaches presented in the preceding section vis-à-vis each other. Moreover, many gaps remain, even in the basic descriptive information available about antitrust law and enforcement across countries and over time. Yet, the theoretical approaches discussed above yield a number of clearly distinct observable implications concerning various aspects of competition policy (King, Keohane, and Verba 1994). Specifically, we should want these approaches to provide insights into whether and, if so how, international economic integration and in particular trade openness affect

- countries' decisions about whether and when to adopt competition legislation, allowing for the possibility of network effects;
- variation in the substantive focus or stringency of antitrust laws across countries and over time;
- variation in antitrust enforcement across countries and over time;
- the broader pattern of international diffusion of antitrust law and enforcement;
- patterns of competition and anticompetitive behavior; and
- international conflict and cooperation over antitrust law and enforcement.

Overall, with regard to these six sets of *explananda*, many and maybe most of the implications of the different theoretical approaches remain untested. A few clear findings nonetheless emerge, and identifying the gaps in our knowledge also helps specify avenues for future research.

Adoption of national antitrust law and its content or stringency: Here the trade economics approach suggests that there should be a *negative* relationship between a country's *trade openness* and the likelihood that the country adopts a competition law or increases its stringency. By contrast, the antitrust-as-protectionism approach implies that there should be a *positive* relationship between the likelihood that a country adopts or strengthen its competition law and the country's level of net *imports*.

Strikingly, there is, as noted by Gutmann and Voigt, "no established dataset based on one consistent definition of what constitutes a competition law" (2014, 6) and no comprehensive database of countries' competition laws, which would allow easy access to even such basic information as the year when a country adopted a competition law for the first time.[9] There is consequently very little large-N, comparative empirical work on the adoption of national competition legislation. In joint work with Anu Bradford, I am currently building a comprehensive panel data set of national antitrust laws, based on a detailed coding of their substantive provisions and secondary legislation/implementing regulations. That database, however, is still a work in progress. To provide a preliminary sense of the explosive spread of competition laws over the 125 years since 1889, I have included in Figure 12.1 information from the gap- and error-prone antitrust-worldwiki (see also Hylton and Deng 2007), complemented by data from Kronthaler (2010), Petersen (2013), Voigt (2009), and Waked (2010), each of whom has collected

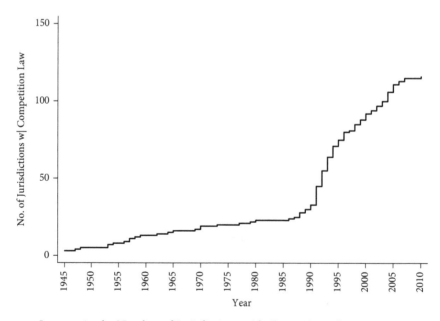

FIG. 12.1   Increase in the Number of Jurisdictions with Competition Laws, 1945–2010.

more specific information for different subsets of countries. The figure shows the striking pattern of the number of countries with a competition law that at least prohibits cartels, from 1945, when only Canada and the United States had such a law on the books, to 2010.

Given that trade openness has generally increased over the course of the sixty-five years captured in the graph and especially during the two decades after the WTO replaced GATT, the overall pattern in Figure 12.1 seems clearly inconsistent with a view of trade openness and competition policy as substitutes. The graph does not, however, provide us with insights into what motivated the adoption of antitrust laws across these countries, especially whether an increase in net imports might have driven their adoption, as suggested by the antitrust-as-protectionism perspective. In the absence of a well-established empirical model, Table 12.1 takes a first cut at this question by reporting the trade patterns in the years prior to a country's first adoption of an antitrust law for the ninety-three countries that enacted their first competition law between 1980 and 2010 (subject to data availability).

To be sure, bivariate correlations with no consideration of possible confounding factors cannot yield conclusive results. That said, the empirical findings in Table 12.1 offer no support for the trade economics approach, which suggests that the probability of adopting antitrust legislation increases during periods of unusual low trade openness. Table 12.1 instead show slightly higher average levels of trade openness in the 1–3 years immediately preceding the adoption of a first antitrust law, thought the difference is not statistically significant. Moreover, net imports are on average *lower* in the years preceding the adoption of a first antitrust law, and significantly so for the year t-1. This preliminary empirical finding directly runs counter to the expectation of the antitrust-as-protectionism approach.

Table 12.1 Trade Patterns Before the Enactment of a Country's First Antitrust Law, 1980–2010

	1 year before first AT Law	All other years and countries	3 years before first AT law avg. (t-1, t-2, t-3)	All other years and countries
trade openness	84.2%	83.9%	84.6%	83.9%
	(4.70)	(0.731)	(3.06)	(0.739)
net imports	3.69%	6.90%	5.68%	6.88%
	(1.32)	(0.252)	(0.940)	(0.253)
N	84	4839	222	4797
Countries	84	187	74	187

Note: Mean levels of trade (X + M) and net imports, as a percentage of GDP; standard errors in parentheses. Trade data from *World Development Indicators* (Nov. 2011). Analysis of trade patterns 1 year before the adoption of the country's first antitrust law omits, due to missing trade data, 9 jurisdictions with an antitrust law (first enacted since 1980): Argentina, Channel Islands, Faroe Islands, Greenland, Kazakhstan, Liechtenstein, Montenegro, Poland, and Taiwan. Missing data cause the loss of another ten countries with AT laws in the analysis of trade flows during the 3 years prior to the adoption of the first antitrust law: Belarus, the Czech Republic, Estonia, Lithuania, Latvia, Moldova, Russia, Slovenia, Ukraine, and Uzbekistan.

Enforcement: Analyses of legal provisions must be supplemented by analyses that consider their enforcement in order to avoid falling into the trap of the old institutionalist literature of mistaking formal rules for practice.[10] Information about enforcement also requires careful interpretation: A highly effective antitrust enforcement agency, in equilibrium, needs to undertake little or no enforcement actions, because it successfully deters all violations.

Unfortunately, internationally comparable enforcement data are even scarcer than data about national laws, and as Petersen notes, "there is no [agreed] perfect way to measure the existence of an *effective* antitrust regime" (2013, 606, emphasis added). Consequently, very few comparative analyses have been conducted—with mixed results.[11] In an unpublished paper based on field research in Africa and Asia, Waked (2010) finds a negative empirical relationship between trade openness and input measures of antitrust enforcement (budget and staff), which might be interpreted as support for the view that trade is a substitute for antitrust law and enforcement. The estimated coefficients for her measures of enforcement, however, are statistically significant in only seven of her twelve models, and her analysis is limited to twenty-eight to thirty developing countries, with five observations over time on average. Moreover, some other empirical analyses reach opposite findings. Consistent with earlier anecdotal evidence that "the one action taken" under the 1910 Canadian Combines Investigation Act "was against a foreign corporation" (McFall 1922, 182), Shughart, Silverman, and Tollison (1995) find significant support for the antitrust-as-protectionism approach in their analysis of the antitrust enforcement budgets for the US Department of Justice's Antitrust Division and for the Federal Trade Commission. However, their work is limited to a single country, ends in 1981, and does not address concerns about multicollinearity and spurious correlation, which inevitably arise when regressing a trending time series on several other time series (see Büthe and Morgan with Bradford 2014 for a critique). More robust analyses of the effect of economic openness on antitrust enforcement would include a more diverse set of countries, more comprehensive measures of the stringency of antitrust enforcement, and/or longer time series.

Patterns of competition and anticompetitive behavior: Patterns of competition are merely an indirect but substantively important implication of the theoretical approaches discussed above. Analyses of patterns of competition and anticompetitive behavior moreover provide information about the suitability of key assumptions of the different models (see Coase 1994). A number of studies have found that increases in trade openness increase the level of competition within a country, confirming one of the key assumptions of the trade economics approach. Other studies find that the stringency and/or independence of antitrust enforcement increases market competition in a country (e.g., Voigt 2009). Without assessing the effect of trade openness and competition policy simultaneously, however, these studies do not speak to the question of whether free trade and antitrust work as substitutes or in some other relationship with each other. Including both factors in multicountry, industry-level analyses is one of the key contributions of Kee and Hoekman (2007). And while they confirm that free trade increases competition, they also find—contrary to what we should expect based on the trade economics model—that competition policy significantly further increases the level of competition, at least indirectly.

AN ALTERNATIVE APPROACH: FREE TRADE AND COMPETITION POLICY AS GENUINE COMPLEMENTS

To address the theoretical weaknesses of the analytical approaches discussed in the second section and provide a better understanding of the law and politics of antitrust in a global economy I have, initially in joint work with Anu Bradford, developed an alternative approach, which views trade openness and competition policy as genuine complements (see, e.g., Büthe and Bradford 2012). I briefly sketch this approach here. It departs from the previous approaches in two main ways.

First, I take firms seriously as (potential) political as well as economic actors—and not just vis-à-vis their domestic governments but also transnationally. Conceptualized in this way, firms can not only turn to their government when they seek protection but also pursue "private protection,"[12] for instance by colluding with other firms. And trade liberalization, by putting firms that previously did not meaningfully compete into competition with each other, creates new opportunities to gain from transnational collusion, at the same time that it lowers the risk of detection because monitoring global markets is more difficult and costly than monitoring purely domestic markets, and because evidence of transnational collusion can more easily be kept out of reach of enforcement agencies that operate at the national level.[13]

Second, this approach takes governments and regulatory agencies seriously as political actors at both the national and inter/transnational levels. Specifically, it assumes that governments (and competition regulators) understand that free trade creates opportunities and incentives for private protection. While recognizing that regulatory agencies and elected officials *can* be captured by special interests, this approach does not elevate the possibility to a general assumption.[14] To the contrary, it assumes that competition regulators see safeguarding market competition as their primary objective unless institutional features (such as the lack of agency independence) provide specific reasons to expect otherwise.

What are the empirical implications of this new approach to thinking about the relationship between economic openness and competition policy? The first point above implies that we should see an increase in transnational anticompetitive behavior as a function of the institutionalization of product market integration—that is, as governments' options for providing public protection decline and firms' opportunities and incentives for transnational collusion increase. Transnational anticompetitive behavior is therefore expected to increase even while we might see a decrease in purely domestic anticompetitive behavior in industries that have been opened to foreign competition. It is naturally difficult to establish comprehensive patterns of anticompetitive business behavior, because what is in most jurisdictions now illegal behavior will surely not be fully detected. But a striking number of multinational cartels have been discovered in recent years (e.g., Bond 2005; Connor 2007; Kovacic et al. 2007; Levenstein and Suslow 2008). And the often near-global reach, complexity, and persistence of many of these cartels show that anticompetitive behavior does not stop at borders, as the traditional approaches assume, and that cartels are not nearly as unstable as most economics textbooks would have us believe.

Interviews with competition regulators suggest that the increase in the detection of such cartels has been at least in part a function of increased enforcement efforts, including increased monitoring of international rather than just domestic markets and increased transgovernmental enforcement cooperation (discussed below). Importantly, the transnational collusion appears to have begun, for most of the major transnational cartels that have been detected, only after the relevant markets experienced a substantial increase in international openness.

The second point above implies that competition regulators will recognize the increased probability of transnational anticompetitive behavior, and that they will seek to counteract it.[15] Empirically, this implies a *positive* relationship between trade openness and the probability of adopting a competition law, as in fact shown in Table 12.1, which yielded anomalous findings for the other theoretical approaches. It implies further that we should expect to see greater trade openness (across countries and over time) result in more resources being devoted to monitoring international rather than just domestic markets. There is strong anecdotal evidence that this has occurred, at least in the United States, several European countries, and the European Union, though research completed to date does not allow a full assessment of this observable implication.

Relatedly, we should expect to see trade openness result in increased efforts to establish and institutionalize transgovernmental antitrust enforcement collaboration. Preliminary empirical findings provide substantial support for this hypothesis. The long-existing but loose and entirely informal transgovernmental network of competition regulators, now known as the International Competition Network, has over the last twenty years become increasingly institutionalized; it also has grown tremendously (Aydin 2010; Djelic and Kleiner 2006; Svetiev 2010). It has been complemented by efforts to foster international and transgovernmental collaboration on antitrust enforcement through the Organisation for Economic Co-operation and Development and the UN Conference on Trade and Development.

There also is growing evidence of increased bilateral (and occasionally minilateral) enforcement cooperation among competition regulators. In a detailed analysis of antitrust provisions in a random sample of 182 preferential trade agreements (PTAs), Bradford and Büthe (2015) find that competition provisions generally were rare and usually minimalist through the early 1990s, but since the mid-1990s have become a common and prominent feature of PTAs. This increase in the frequency and detail of antitrust provision in PTAs has coincided with the qualitative shift toward a much more institutionalized multilateral trade regime under the WTO (and with a general increase in specificity and scope of PTAs, i.e., the increase in the institutionalization of minilateral trade agreements). Importantly, Bradford and Büthe find that provisions for information exchange and mutual assistance in antitrust enforcement are strikingly common, suggesting a real interest in facilitating transgovernmental cooperation. By contrast, provisions that seek to exempt a country's firms from the other country's domestic competition regime or in other ways signal concern about the other side's abuse of competition policy for protectionist purposes are relatively rare (Bradford and Büthe 2015).

This institutionalization of enforcement cooperation in trade agreements is supplemented by a nearly simultaneous growth in dedicated antitrust enforcement cooperation agreements over the same time period, shown in Figure 12.2, as well as a similar increase in antitrust provisions in international agreements from broad cooperation and friendship agreements and general (non-PTA) economic agreements to bilateral law enforcement agreements. These findings provide further support for the hypothesis that governments do indeed see effective competition policy as a complement to trade openness (Büthe and Bradford 2012).

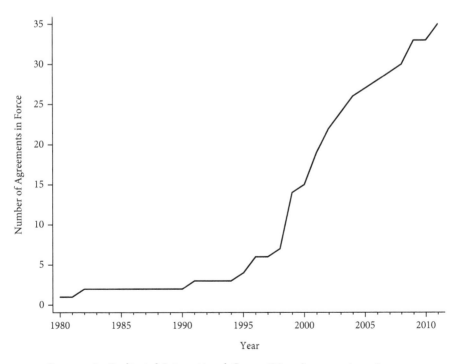

FIG. 12.2   Increase in Dedicated International Competition Agreements, 1980–2010.

CONCLUSION

Political economists since Adam Smith and David Ricardo have recognized increased market competition as an important benefit of a free trade policy. Antitrust law and its enforcement is supposed to achieve the same end by intervening directly against price-fixing, bid-rigging, and other forms of anticompetitive behavior and increases or abuses of market power. And indeed, trade policy and competition policy have been deeply intertwined since the very beginning of modern competition law in late nineteenth-century North America.

Yet, the major schools of thought that have shaped antitrust law and its enforcement—structuralism, ordo-liberalism, the Chicago school, and even the new industrial organization approach—have largely failed to recognize and address this trade-competition policy nexus: They generally assume, at least implicitly, that the boundaries of the market coincide with the boundaries of the antitrust jurisdiction. The question of how economic openness affects competition policy has therefore become the focus in a distinct set of theoretical approaches.

This chapter has provided an overview of different ways of thinking theoretically about the relationship between the international integration of product markets on the one hand and competition law and enforcement on the other. Based on both a theoretical and an empirical assessment, I argued that the dominant approaches in economics and law (the disciplines that have dominated the existing literature on the trade-competition policy nexus) suffer from either being devoid of politics or relying on a model of politics that deprives both firms and competition regulators of transnational and transgovernmental agency, respectively.

I have sketched a more overtly political approach, based on recent and forthcoming joint work (e.g., Büthe and Bradford 2012; Bradford and Büthe 2015). It takes firms seriously as sophisticated transnational actors, not just able to lobby their domestic governments for public protection but alternatively capable of setting up systems of private protection in an increasingly global economy. At the same time, it takes government regulators seriously as political actors with often considerable independence and hence a capacity to pursue their own, distinct interests, including in a transgovernmental network of competition regulators, in which they are embedded.

The empirical analysis of the international and comparative dimension of competition policy is still in its infancy. Preliminary results suggest, however, that a theoretical model that allows for transnational as well as transgovernmental politics can explain the simultaneous spread of competition law and trade openness in the last two decades and more generally yields an understanding of trade and antitrust in the global economy that is at least equally as plausible as the traditional model of trade economics and models that posit antitrust as a substitute for protectionism. This finding should not come as a surprise: antitrust enforcement inherently entails the use of public authority to constrain private actors' concentration and exercise of market power. Hence, if we want to understand competition policy in a global economy, we need not just legal and economic but also political analysis.

AUTHOR'S NOTE

For helpful comments, I thank Anu Bradford, Cindy Cheng, Lisa Martin, and members of the audience at presentations at the World Trade Institute, Bern, and at Yale University (Leitner Seminar). Research for this chapter has been supported in part by grants from the Law and Social Sciences program of the National Science Foundation (grant no. 1228483) and from the Josiah Charles Trent Memorial Foundation (grant 12-06).

NOTES

1. See, e.g., Böhm (1961); Crane and Hovenkamp (2013); Eucken (2001); Fox (2011); Gerber (2010); Lande (1982). Even within economics, multiple distinct notions of competition are common (Stigler 1957; Martin 2012, esp. 5–11) and in fact have persisted for a long time; see De Roover (1951) and McNulty (1968).
2. Federal antitrust legislation in the United States was preceded by state-level antitrust statutes in more than twenty states, though in most cases only by a few years or even just months. Previously, English common law had been seen as providing a sufficient safeguard through its prohibitions against anticompetitive behavior since at least the 1700s, but its competition law elements had successively weakened since the 1840s, eventually prompting the adoption of statutory competition law in Canada and the United States (see, e.g., Bliss 1973, 178f.; Letwin 1965, esp. 19–52).
3. For excerpts of key passages from Smith and Ricardo's works, see Crane and Hovenkamp (2013, 5-40).
4. As Iacobucci (1997, 5f.) points out, the ultimately abandoned 1947/1948 Havana Charter for an International Trade Organization already included rules concerning anticompetitive business practices. Proposals for a supranational competition regime in the context of the global trade regime in fact have often sought to increase the aggregate welfare gains from competition policy rather than "just" to constrain national competition regulators in order to forestall abuse (e.g., Anderson and Holmes 2002; Fox 2003; Guzman 2004; Marsden 2003; Zäch and Correa 1999). For key critiques of a WTO-based competition regime, see Bradford (2007) and McGinnis (2004). From a trade policy perspective, arguably the greatest benefit of a formal international competition policy regime linked to the WTO and the international trade regime might be that it would provide an opportunity to reign in the abuses of antidumping, since allegations of dumping would be antitrust violations if it were not for the foreign nationality of the allegedly dumping producer.
5. Moreover, anecdotal evidence suggests some substitutability insofar as (detected) antitrust violations in Canada during the early decades appeared to be disproportionately concentrated in industries "protected from foreign competition by substantial tariffs or other barriers to trade" (Trebilcock et al. 2002, 642).

6. Ordo-liberalism is a philosophical school of thought that is liberal in rejecting government intervention when it seeks to direct economic activity but sees the state as having a necessary "ordering" function in the economy to safeguard individuals against any concentration of political *and economic* power that would threaten their freedom and equality of opportunity. From the 1950s through at least the 1990s, it shaped the European (EU-level) approach to competition policy.

7. These assumptions are usually entirely implicit, but I submit that they are necessary and in effect drive the models' conclusions.

8. "Private protection" refers to economic actors protecting themselves against the consequences of increased exposure to competitors through collusion or other anticompetitive measures. It is discussed in greater detail below.

9. The challenge is illustrated by the history of Austria's competition laws. The country adopted its first "cartel legislation" in 1951. That legislation, however, primarily required cartel agreements to be notified to a state agency in order to be enforceable as contracts. It subjected cartel agreements to certain disciplines and created a quasi-judicial procedure allowing the Austrian federal government to prohibit a cartel agreement if it had detrimental consequences for the Austrian economy, but it made clear that agreements on production quotas, prices, etc., would not per se be considered as having detrimental consequences. Amendments in 1956, 1957, 1958, 1962, and 1968 and a new version of the law in 1972 provided for more elaborate administrative and judicial review processes and increasingly restricted the permissiveness of cartels that sought to raise prices or keep them from falling, but a general prohibition of cartels was not included in the law until 1988. Which year should count as the first year for Austria's competition legislation?

10. Some of the most comprehensive, stringent antitrust laws are found in countries with generally very limited state/administrative capacity and a weak rule-of-law tradition.

11. An alternative approach is to conduct time series analysis within a single country with a long history of antitrust enforcement, such as the United States. Existing longitudinal data sets of US enforcement, however, lack information on the nationality of the parties against which enforcement actions have been directed, as well as detailed information about the industries involved (for disaggregated analyses of the relationship between trade patterns and enforcement). Büthe and Bradford are developing a new data set for US Department of Justice enforcement actions, 1960–2010, including such information.

12. See Ludema (2001); Trebilcock (1996); and Williams and Rodriguez (1995).

13. Furthermore, insofar as *institutionalized* trade liberalization succeeds in constraining governments' urge to protect domestic firms, it creates further incentives for firms to turn to private protection.

14. This assumption is consistent with the finding that capture is much less common than often assumed (Carpenter and Moss 2014).

15. Put another way, governments (or at least those within the "state" who see it as their objective to guard competition) should see trade openness and the *need for* vigorous competition policy as complements.

REFERENCES

Anderson, Robert D., and Peter Holmes. 2002. Competition Policy and the Future of the Multilateral Trading System. *Journal of International Economic Law* 5 (2): 531–563.

Aydin, Umut. 2010. The International Competition Network: Cooperation and Convergence in Competition Laws. *Rekabet Derisi* [Competition Journal] 11 (3): 51–78.

Baggaley, Carman. 1991. Tariffs, Combines and Politics: The Beginning of Canadian Competition Policy, 1880–1900. In *Historical Perspectives on Canadian Competition Policy*, edited by R. S. Khemani and W. T. Standbury, 1–51. Halifax, NS: Institute for Research on Public Policy.

Baron, David P. 2001. Private Politics, Corporate Social Responsibility, and Integrated Strategy. *Journal of Economics & Management Strategy* 10 (1): 7–45.

Baron, David P. 2010. *Business and Its Environment.* 6th ed. Upper Saddle River, NJ: Prentice Hall.

Baumol, William J., and Janusz A. Ordover. 1985. Use of Antitrust to Subvert Competition. *Journal of Law and Economics* 28 (2): 247–265.

Benidickson, Jamie. 1993. The Combines Problem in Canadian Legal Thought, 1867–1920. *University of Toronto Law Journal* 43 (4): 799–850.

Blackhurst, Richard. 1991. Trade Policy Is Competition Policy. In *Competition and Economic Development*, 253–258. Paris: OECD.

Bliss, Michael. 1973. Another Anti-Trust Tradition: Canadian Anti-Combines Policy, 1889–1910. *Business History Review* 47 (2): 177–188.

Bliss, Michael. 1974. *A Living Profit: Studies in the Social History of Canadian Business, 1883–1911.* Toronto: McClelland and Stewart Ltd.

Böhm, Franz. 1961. Democracy and Economic Power. In *Cartel and Monopoly in Modern Law: Reports on Supranational and National European and American Law, Presented to the International Conference on Restraints of Competition at Frankfurt am Main, June 1960*, edited by the Institut für ausländisches und internationales Wirtschaftsrecht and der Johann-Wolfgang-Goethe-Universität, Frankfurt am Main, in cooperation with the Institute for International and Foreign Trade Law of the Georgetown University Law Center, Washington D.C. 25–45. Karlsruhe: Verlag C. F. Müller.

Bond, Eric W. 2005. Antitrust Policy in Open Economies: Price Fixing and International Cartels. In *Handbook of International Trade: Economic and Legal Analyses of Trade Policy and Institutions*, edited by E. Kwan Choi and James C. Hartigan, 333–357. Malden, MA: Blackwell Publishing.

Bradford, Anu. 2007. International Antitrust Negotiations and the False Hope of the WTO. *Harvard International Law Journal* 48 (2): 383–440.

Bradford, Anu, and Tim Büthe. 2015. "The Politics of Competition Policy and Free Trade: Antitrust Provisions in PTAs." In *Trade Cooperation: The Purpose, Design and Effects of Preferential Trade Agreements*, edited by Andreas Dür and Manfred Elsig, 246–274. Cambridge, UK: Cambridge University Press.

Büthe, Tim. 2010. Private Regulation in the Global Economy: A (P)Review. *Business and Politics* 12 (3): 1–38.

Büthe, Tim, and Anu Bradford. 2012. Wettbewerbspolitik und internationaler Handel—Macht und Politik in Offenen Märkten: A Research Agenda and Some Preliminary Results. Paper presented at the 25th Biennial Convention of the German Political Science Association (DVPW), Tübingen, September 25.

Büthe, Tim and Stephen Morgan with Anu Bradford. 2014. Antitrust Enforcement and Foreign Competition: Special Interest Theory Reconsidered. Paper presented at the Conference on Empirical Legal Studies, University of California, Berkeley, November 8.

Büthe, Tim, and Walter Mattli. 2011. *The New Global Rulers: The Privatization of Regulation in the World Economy.* Princeton, NJ: Princeton University Press.

Carpenter, Daniel P., and David A. Moss, eds. 2014. *Preventing Regulatory Capture: Special Interest Influence and How to Limit It*. New York: Cambridge University Press.

Coase, Ronald H. 1994. How Should Economists Choose? First delivered as the 1981 G. Warren Nutter Lecture in Political Economy. In *Essays on Economics and Economists*, 15–33. Chicago: University of Chicago Press.

Cohen, Maxwell. 1938. The Canadian Anti-Trust Laws: Doctrinal and Legislative Beginnings. *Canadian Bar Review* 16 (6): 438–465.

Connor, John M. 2007. *Global Price Fixing*. 2nd ed. Berlin/New York: Springer.

Crane, Daniel A., and Herbert Hovenkamp, eds. 2013. *The Making of Competition Policy: Legal and Economic Sources*. Oxford: Oxford University Press.

Cutler, A. Claire, Virginia Haufler, and Tony Porter, eds. 1999. *Private Authority and International Affairs*. Albany: State University of New York Press.

De Roover, Raymond. 1951. Monopoly Theory Prior to Adam Smith: A Revision. *Quarterly Journal of Economics* 65 (4): 492–524.

DiLorenzo, Thomas J. 1985. The Origins of Antitrust: An Interest-Group Perspective. *International Review of Law and Economics* 5 (1): 73–90.

Dixit, Avinash. 1984. International Trade Policy for Oligopolistic Industries. *Economic Journal* 94 (supp.): 1–16.

Djelic, Marie-Laure, and Thibaut Kleiner. 2006. The International Competition Network: Moving Towards Transnational Governance. In *Transnational Governance: Institutional Dynamics of Regulation*, edited by Marie-Laure Djelic and Kerstin Sahlin-Andersson, 287–307. New York: Cambridge University Press.

Eucken, Walter. 2001. *Wirtschaftsmacht und Wirtschaftsordnung: Londoner Vorträge zur Wirtschaftspolitik und zwei Beiträge zur Antimonopolpolitik*. Münster: LIT Verlag für das Walter-Eucken-Archiv.

Fligstein, Neil. 1990. *The Transformation of Corporate Control*. Cambridge, MA: Harvard University Press.

Fox, Eleanor M. 2003. International Antitrust and the Doha Dome. *Virginia Journal of International Law* 43: 911–932.

Fox, Eleanor M. 2011. Competition, Development, and Regional Integration: In Search of a Competition Law Fit for Developing Countries. In *Competition Policy and Regional Integration in Developing Countries*, edited by Josef Drexl et al., 273–290. Cheltenham, UK: Edward Elgar.

Gawande, Kishore, Pravin Krishna, and Marcelo Olarreaga. 2009. What Governments Maximize and Why: The View from Trade. *International Organization* 63 (3): 491–532.

Gellhorn, Ernest, William E. Kovacic, and Stephen Calkins. 2004. *Antitrust Law and Economics in a Nutshell*. 5th ed. St. Paul, MN: West Publishing.

Gerber, David J. 2010. *Global Competition: Law, Markets, and Globalization*. New York: Oxford University Press.

Grieco, Joseph M. 1990. *Cooperation Among Nations: Europe, America, and Non-Tariff Barriers to Trade*. Ithaca, NY: Cornell University Press.

Gutmann, Jerg, and Stefan Voigt. 2014. Lending a Hand to the Invisible Hand? Assessing the Effects of Newly Enacted Competition Laws. Unpublished manuscript, University of Hamburg, February.

Guzman, Andrew T. 1998. Is International Antitrust Possible? *New York University Law Review* 73 (5): 1501–1548.

Guzman, Andrew T. 2004. The Case for International Antitrust. *Berkeley Journal of International Law* 22 (3): 355–374.

Halladay, Casey W. 2012. The Origins of Canada's Cartel Laws. *Canadian Competition Law Review* 25 (1): 157–163.

Hazlett, Thomas W. 1992. The Legislative History of the Sherman Act Re-Examined. *Economic Inquiry* 30 (2): 263–276.

Horn, Henrik, and James Levinsohn. 2001. Merger Policies and Trade Liberalisation. *Economic Journal* 111 (470): 244–276.

Hylton, Keith N., and Fei Deng. 2007. Antitrust Around the World: An Empirical Analysis of the Scope of Competition Laws and Their Effects. *Antitrust Law Journal* 74 (2): 271–341.

Iacobucci, Edward M. 1997. The Interdependence of Trade and Competition Policies. *World Competition* 21 (2): 5–33.

Irwin, Douglas A. 2009. *Free Trade Under Fire*. 3rd ed. Princeton, NJ: Princeton University Press. First published 2002.

Kee, Hiau Looi, and Bernard Hoekman. 2007. Imports, Entry, and Competition Law as Market Disciplines. *European Economic Review* 51 (4): 831–858.

Keohane, Robert O., and Joseph S. Nye. 1989. *Power and Interdependence*. 2nd ed. New York: HarperCollins. First published 1977.

King, Gary, Robert O. Keohane, and Sidney Verba. 1994. *Designing Social Inquiry: Scientific Inference in Qualitative Research*. Princeton, NJ: Princeton University Press.

Kono, Daniel Y. 2006. Optimal Obfuscation: Democracy and Trade Policy Transparency. *American Political Science Review* 100 (3): 369–384.

Kovacic, William E., et al. 2007. Lessons for Competition Policy from the Vitamins Cartel. In *The Political Economy of Antitrust*, edited by Vivek Ghoshal and Johan Stennek, 149–176. Amsterdam/Boston: Elsevier.

Kronthaler, Franz. 2010. Factors Influencing the Implementation of Recently Enacted Competition Laws: An Empirical Analysis. *International Research Journal of Finance and Economics*, no. 51, 71–87.

Krugman, Paul R., ed. 1986. *Strategic Trade Policy and the New International Economics*. Cambridge, MA: MIT Press.

Lande, Robert H. 1982. Wealth Transfer as the Original and Primary Concern of Antitrust: The Efficiency Interpretation Challenged. *Hastings Law Journal* 34 (1): 65–151.

Letwin, William. 1965. *Law and Economic Policy in America: The Evolution of the Sherman Antitrust Act*. New York: Random House.

Levenstein, Margaret C., and Valerie Y. Suslow. 2008. International Cartels. *Issues in Competition Law and Policy* 2: 1107–1126.

Limão, Nuno, and Patricia Tovar. 2009. Policy Choice: Theory and Evidence. NBER Working Paper No. 14655.

Ludema, Rodney D. 2001. Market Collusion and the Politics of Protection. *European Journal of Political Economy* 17 (4): 817–833.

Marsden, Philip. 2003. *Competition Policy for the WTO*. London: Cameron May.

Martin, Stephen. 2012. Globalization and the Natural Limits of Competition. In *The International Handbook of Competition*, edited by Manfred Neumann and Jürgen Veigand, 4–56. Cheltenham, UK/Northampton, MA: Edward Elgar.

McFall, Robert James. 1922. Regulations of Business in Canada. *Political Science Quarterly* 37 (2): 177–210.

McGinnis, John O. 2004. The Political Economy of International Antitrust Harmonization. In *Competition Laws in Conflict: Antitrust Jurisdiction in the Global Economy*, edited by Richard A. Epstein and Michael S. Greve, 136–151. Washington, DC: American Enterprise Institute.

McNulty, Paul J. 1968. Economic Theory and the Meaning of Competition. *Quarterly Journal of Economics* 82 (4): 639–656.

Milner, Helen V. 1987. Resisting the Protectionist Temptation: Industry and the Making of Trade Policy in France and the United States During the 1970s. *International Organization* 41 (4): 639–666.

Naoi, Megumi. 2009. Shopping for Protection: The Politics of Choosing Trade Instruments in a Partially Legalized World. *International Studies Quarterly* 53 (2): 421–444.

Newman, Abraham L., and Elliot Posner. 2011. International Interdependence and Regulatory Power: Authority, Mobility, and Markets. *European Journal of International Relations* 17 (4): 589–610.

Petersen, Niels. 2013. Antitrust Law and the Promotion of Democracy and Economic Growth. *Journal of Competition Law & Economics* 9 (3): 593–636.

Rey, Patrick. 1997. Competition Policy and Economic Growth. Mimeograph, Unversité de Toulouse (IDEI), September.

Rogowski, Ronald. 1989. *Commerce and Coalitions: How Trade Affects Domestic Political Alignments.* Princeton, NJ: Princeton University Press.

Shughart, William F., Jon D. Silverman, and Robert D. Tollison. 1995. Antitrust Enforcement and Foreign Competition. In *The Causes and Consequences of Antitrust: The Public Choice Perspective*, edited by Fred S. McChesney and Willam F. Shughart II, 179–187. Chicago: University of Chicago Press.

Slaughter, Anne-Marie. 2004. *A New World Order.* Princeton, NJ: Princeton University Press.

Stigler, George J. 1957. Perfect Competition, Historically Contemplated. *Journal of Political Economy* 65 (1): 1–17.

Svetiev, Yane. 2010. Partial Formalization of the Regulatory Network. Unpublished manuscript, Brooklyn Law School. Online at http://ssrn.com/abstract=1564890

Trebilcock, Michael J. 1996. Competition Policy and Trade Policy: Mediating the Interface. *Journal of World Trade* 30 (4): 71–106.

Trebilcock, Michael J. 1991. Competition Policy, Trade Policy, and the Problem of Second Best. In *Canadian Competition Law and Policy at the Centenary*, edited by R. S. Khemani and W. T. Stanbury, 29–44. Halifax, NS: Institute of Research on Public Policy.

Trebilcock, Michael J., and Robert Howse. 2005. *The Regulation of International Trade.* 3rd ed. New York: Routledge.

Trebilcock, Michael J., et al. 2002. *The Law and Economics of Canadian Competition Policy.* Toronto: University of Toronto Press.

Voigt, Stefan. 2009. The Effects of Competition Policy on Development: Cross-Country Evidence Using Four New Indicators. *Journal of Development Studies* 45 (8): 1225–1248.

Waked, Dina I. 2010. Antitrust Enforcement in Developing Countries: Reasons for Enforcement & Non-Enforcement Using Resource-Based Evidence. Mimeograph, Harvard Law School, July, http://ssrn.com/abstract=1638874).

Weiss, Leonhard W., ed. 1989. *Concentration and Price.* Cambridge, MA: MIT Press.

Williams, Mark D., and A. E. Rodriguez. 1995. Antitrust and Liberalization in Developing Countries. *International Trade Journal* 9 (4): 495–518.

World Trade Organization (WTO). 2012. *World Trade Report 2012: Trade and Public Policies—A Closer Look at Non-Tariff Measures in the 21st Century.* Geneva: World Trade Organization.

Zäch, Roger, and Carlos M. Correa, eds. 1999. *Towards WTO Competition Rules: Key Issues and Comments on the WTO Report (1998) on Trade and Competition.* Berne: Stämpfli and The Hagues: Kluwer Law International.

CHAPTER 13

......

CONNECTED CHANNELS

MNCs and production networks in global trade

......

WALTER HATCH, JENNIFER BAIR,
AND GÜNTER HEIDUK

INTRODUCTION

FORMAL and informal business groups are now associated with a large and perhaps increasing share of international trade. Lanz and Miroudot (2011, 12) estimate that intrafirm shipments account for one-third of the world's commodity exports, while Borga and Zeile (2004, 2) estimate that "vertical trade"—by which intermediate goods produced in one country move through other countries, where value is added via fabrication, processing, or assembly—accounts for roughly one-quarter of global exports.

We face two major questions. The first has to do with the fact that, although there is widespread recognition of the scale of this activity, there is only limited agreement on how to explain it. Some, whom we might call liberals, tend to view it as the sum of economic flows moving through largely disembodied or neutral entities. They use equilibrium models to measure relative factor intensities of processes and relative factor endowments of locations, giving only scant attention to the organizational context in which transnational production is embedded. Others, whom we might call structuralists, prefer to view it as a coordinated activity. Instead of corporate vessels seeking efficiencies, the business groups engaged in this transnational activity are political and social agents striving to control assets and exercise influence.

A related question is this: How should we characterize these groups? The traditional approach focuses narrowly on multinational corporations (MNCs), which are held together by equity or ownership ties. A new approach, however, insists on the increasingly important role of global production networks (GPNs), which are more loosely affiliated. The latter is a broad category that includes, but is not limited to, the former.

Let us address the second question first. Scholars have long been fascinated with MNCs, far-flung conglomerates such as GE, Procter & Gamble, Nestlé, Monsanto, and BP that engage in foreign direct investment (FDI), operating factories, stores, and hotels or providing services such as legal advice and logistics through affiliated companies or subsidiaries in another country. Dunning (1977), who developed the complex model upon which much analysis of FDI is now based, suggests that MNCs seek to exploit ownership, location, and internalization (OLI) advantages as they move overseas. Ownership has to do with a firm's legal title to particular assets, such as technical and managerial know-how. Location has to do with the distinctive endowment of resources and factors in a particular place that determines its comparative advantage for specialized production and exporting. And internalization has to do with a conglomerated firm's ability to reduce transaction costs by establishing intrafirm channels rather than relying on the external market.

More recently, however, scholars have looked beyond MNCs to analyze GPNs, which have been described variously as "international fragmentation" (Jones and Kierzkowski 1990), "the slicing up of the value chain" (Krugman 1995), "the international disintegration of production" (Feenstra 1998), "global production sharing" (Yeats 2001), and "international outsourcing" (Milberg 2004). Unlike MNCs, they do not necessarily consist of equity ties; instead, these networks tend to be held together informally by close and durable business relationships between, for example, a machine assembler and different parts suppliers. Like some MNCs in manufacturing, however, they rely on a geographic dispersion of production activities that yields "vertical trade" and is guided by both economic and political calculations. The former includes the technological capacity of, and wage levels in, different business environments, while the latter includes tax rates, export incentives, and many other policies in the home and host countries.

Global production networks may be more obscure simply because they tend to resist measurement by our standard empirical tools for studying transnational activity. For example, FDI data can tell us about the countries and industries in which parent firms invest (or disinvest) each year, but they are not able to capture transactions such as offshore outsourcing that take place outside both established hierarchies and atomized markets (Williamson 1975). However, some sociologists have suggested that, to measure the level of fragmentation or networking in a particular sector, we can use the ratio of global trade to global value-added in that sector. Mahutga (2012, 12), building on an insight from Feenstra (1998, 34), describes the ratio this way: "As the number of countries involved in the production of a good increases, the extent to which value added in manufacturing is double counted in trade will also increase for the industry in which the good is classified."

This empirical discussion brings us back to the first, and perhaps meatier, theoretical question in the literature on MNCs and GPNs: How do they operate? Do they function according to liberal logic as neutral entities for mostly market-driven economic flows, or in line with structuralist logic, as political and social organizations that seek control and influence?

There is division even among economists. Mundell (1957), perhaps the pioneer in this field and clearly a liberal, uses neoclassical analysis to portray FDI as the global movement of physical capital in search of higher returns. But Hymer (1976), inspired by

Marxist theory, counters that MNC behavior is strategic and conforms better to models of industrial organization than to traditional trade theories such as comparative advantage. He argues that these transnational entities seek to monopolistically control their assets as they invest abroad.

It should come as no surprise that sociologists have tended to view these transnational business groups as social and strategic actors, not as disembodied vessels. A valuable contribution has come from Gereffi (1994, 1995) and others (see Bair 2009), who focus on global commodity chains (GCCs) and global value chains (GVCs).[1] These scholars distinguish between producer- and buyer-driven chains. The former tend to be characterized by higher levels of vertical integration and are orchestrated by major manufacturers, such as Matsushita or Siemens, that use a far-flung division of labor, sourcing raw materials and intermediate goods from certain countries, assembling final goods in another country, and then distributing those products to markets around the world. The latter, by contrast, are led by firms that organize both supplier and consumer markets for brand-name goods produced by independent contractors to the precise specifications provided by those organizers. Initially, buyer-driven commodity or value chains were associated with labor-intensive consumer goods such as apparel, footwear, and toys, and were dominated by retailers such as Walmart or merchandisers such as Nike. More recently, however, higher-technology goods such as computers, video game consoles, and cell phones are being produced via similar arrangements. Apple is perhaps the best-known "manufacturer without a factory," contracting with original design manufacturers (ODMs) such as Foxconn Technology Group of Taiwan to produce its popular iPads and iPhones.[2]

As Sturgeon (2009, 128–130) notes, the GCC/GVC approach draws our attention to the governance of transnational production. Lead firms are able to coordinate the chain's activities, choosing and replacing suppliers, but also directing them to reduce costs, adopt specific business strategies, and even invest in particular locations. Other scholars have focused on different aspects of power, especially the technological capability of a firm or coalition of firms to move an entire industry in its favored direction. Gawer and Cusumano (2002) have referred to this as "platform leadership," while Kim and Hart (2002) coined a more descriptive term, "Wintelism," to describe the way in which the coalition of Microsoft (producer of Windows) and Intel set the standard for many years in the personal computer industry. Some contend that these forms of power depend on a relatively high level of asset specificity, based on brands or technology.

Political scientists used to write extensively about the influence of transnational business organizations, especially as they set up shop in "Third World" countries. For example, Moran (1974) analyzed the relationship between MNCs and host states, outlining a model of bargaining power that evolves over time. Gilpin (1973), by contrast, presented MNCs as tools of powerful states in the global political economy. But with notable exceptions such as Mosley (2011), political scientists today adopt a liberal line, tending to treat MNCs and GPNs as disembodied vessels for capital flows rather than as organized actors. Li and Resnick (2003) document the different ways in which democratic institutions in the host country can promote or retard FDI, while Jensen (2006) shows how federal systems empower local elites and thereby may attract flows of investment.

For some geographers and culturally minded political economists, this treatment of MNCs and GPNs is troubling. Because they view transnational business groups as spatially differentiated actors that shape, and are shaped by, the locations in which they operate, these scholars are aligned squarely with the structuralists. Henderson and colleagues (2002) note that these transnational business groups are more or less embedded in specific places, whether they be nations or regions, and thus reflect and influence the social dynamics (norms and institutions) of those places. A US MNC (e.g., General Motors) operates differently from a Japanese MNC in the same industry (e.g., Toyota), even when they invest in the same foreign market (e.g., Mexico). Likewise, transnational business organizations may have different developmental consequences, depending on how they are embedded in host environments. For example, a highly flexible network of footloose manufacturers may not allow local actors—economic or political—to capture many of the gains generated by that cross-border activity. Among other effects, wages may remain relatively flat in this sector of the host economy. Katzenstein (2005) has extended this analysis to regions, suggesting that government and business actors in East Asia, for example, are motivated by distinctive values, compared to their counterparts in Europe. Both, however, are subject to a common, globalizing force he calls "the American Imperium."

Liberals, meanwhile, suggest that mobile capital always poses an opportunity and challenge for states and citizens, regardless of its organizational shape. States, they argue, may attract FDI by creating export-processing zones and conversely by adopting trade policies that are protectionist, which allow foreign manufacturers to jump trade barriers and enjoy rents on domestic-oriented production. But the structure of investment should not matter. Likewise, citizens will prosper or suffer from investment flows, but not based on the organization of transnational investors. For example, Rudra (2008) offers an analysis of the impact of FDI on the economic standing of different social classes in host countries, ignoring the structure of investing business groups. Freed from this taxonomical condition, capital flow becomes a more easily measured variable.

This chapter looks at three regions of the world—East Asia, Latin (especially North) America, and Europe—and summarizes the research on MNCs and GPNs in each. For the sake of comparison, the discussion is limited to transnational automobile and electronics operations in these three regions. The chapter concludes with some general observations based on this comparative analysis.

MNCs and Production Networks in East Asia

East Asia today enjoys perhaps the world's thickest web of interconnected transnational business organizations.[3] Although scholars writing about this region have highlighted the activities of both MNCs and GPNs, they increasingly tend to emphasize the latter. Liberals note that economies in East Asia differ dramatically in their factor endowments and add that states there tend to pursue relatively open trade policies—a set of conditions that conspires to attract heavy flows of export-oriented FDI. Structuralists focus instead on the strategies used by dominant firms to stitch those economies together, turning this region into the "factory to the world" that manufactures a rich blend of electronics, automobiles, machine tools, and other goods. Those products tend to be assembled in Asian locations filled with cheap labor, using designs and sophisticated inputs from Asian countries with high-tech capabilities and less sophisticated inputs from Asian countries with more modest capabilities. Over time, the vertical division of labor established and led by Japanese MNCs in the 1980s has turned into a more horizontal and open model. Developing economies in the region, such as Indonesia and Vietnam, have benefited as they have become more deeply incorporated into the thick web of business ties.

History

Until the 1980s, Japanese industry had been reluctant to invest heavily overseas. Managers of manufacturing firms, in particular, preferred to exploit social networks in the domestic political economy, networks that included close personal relationships with government officials; bankers, parts suppliers, and distributors; and long-term employees. That reluctance crumbled after 1985, when the governments of Japan, the United States, France, West Germany, and the United Kingdom agreed to a significant appreciation of nondollar currencies, especially the yen. Export-oriented firms in Japan, often supported by low-interest loans from their own government, increasingly shifted production to South Korea, Taiwan, Thailand, Malaysia, Indonesia, and the Philippines. Over time, and especially after Deng Xiaoping's more aggressive economic reforms began to take effect, manufacturing FDI flowed even more heavily from Japan to coastal China.

Observers described an emerging "yen bloc" in East Asia as Japanese machine assemblers, followed by their long-standing parts suppliers, general trading companies, and main banks, set up operations in the region. Even government agencies, especially JETRO (Japan External Trade Organization) and JICA (Japan International Cooperation Agency), jumped into the networking business, advising both Japanese manufacturers investing in East Asia and host country officials striving to turn their economies into nodes in the evolving web of networks. In the automobile industry these production networks manufactured parts for all of Southeast Asia and finished vehicles for the domestic market in this subregion. Toyota, for example, set up large assembly plants in Thailand, Malaysia, Indonesia, and the Philippines. But it also helped set up specialized supply operations in different locations: Thailand became the base for pressed parts, diesel engines, and electronics; Malaysia for steering gears and electronics; Indonesia for pressed parts and gasoline engines; and the Philippines for transmissions. Toyota sourced different parts from these specialized bases throughout the region, as well as from suppliers in Japan, then sold finished vehicles in the same market in which they were assembled.[4] By contrast, in the electronics industry Japanese production networks often relied on a triangular pattern of trade, importing components from Japan or Japanese suppliers in the region, assembling them at affiliates in East Asia, and exporting finished goods to consumers in the United States and Europe. As of 1992, for example, Sony's Penang affiliate purchased half of its computer drive inputs from the parent firm in Japan and another 40 percent from suppliers in Malaysia, Singapore, and Thailand. But 95 percent of these "Southeast Asian" suppliers were Japanese affiliates operating in the region. Sony exported all of the drives it assembled in Penang, and most shipments went to the United States or Europe.[5]

In the 1990s Hatch and Yamamura (1996), as well as scholars at the Berkeley Roundtable on the International Economy (BRIE), conducted empirical research on East Asian production networks in the electronics industry. Ernst (1994, 1997) noted, for example, that large parent firms based in Japan tended to control manufacturing affiliates in the region, requiring them to use Japanese expatriates as managers and technicians, and to acquire inputs from long-standing domestic suppliers or their Asian affiliates. This, he argued, made Japanese production networks less flexible and less open than networks directed by MNCs based in other countries. Borrus (1997) extended this finding, arguing that a primary reason for the revival of the US electronics industry in the 1990s was the ability of American MNCs to tap into the relatively flexible and open supply base of what he called the "China circle," consisting of ethnic Chinese manufacturers on the mainland, in Taiwan, and throughout Southeast Asia. Thanks to their access to this dynamic supply base, he contended, US producers gained a competitive edge over their stodgier rivals from Japan.

At the same time, scholars noted that despite efforts by Japan to maintain its technological edge and avoid "industrial hollowing," less advanced economies in East Asia were steadily catching up. The region's network-based macro-economy was developing in a "flying geese pattern," with industries in Japan, the lead goose, adopting successively more sophisticated technologies and shedding others, which second-tier economies then acquired, adapted, and eventually shed to third-tier economies. It quickly became apparent that "Little Tigers" or "New Dragons" were chasing Japan and building impressive, high-tech industries of their own.[6]

Scholars using the GCC or GVC approach (see, e.g., Feenstra and Hamilton 2006) heralded the rise of what they called "demand-responsive economies" in Asia, especially South Korea and Taiwan. These economies boasted a large number of manufacturers that initially gained technical expertise by capitalizing on backward linkages, producing household appliances, footwear, and other simple goods for big retailers and merchandisers in the United States, Europe, and Japan. Eventually, however, many of these suppliers and OEM producers became MNCs, with their own production networks churning out relatively sophisticated products. In South Korea, *chaebol* owners met the demands of buyer-driven value chains primarily via internalization. They used their well-greased connections to secure internal financing for expanded production in existing firms or new members of the corporate group. In Taiwan, by contrast, the smaller suppliers satisfied demand by subcontracting with other, even nimbler, firms, many in Southeast Asia.

With the dawn of a new millennium, some of these Korean and Taiwanese manufacturers emerged as technological rivals to the Japanese MNCs that had spun the very first web of East Asian production networks. In semiconductors, for example, Samsung of Korea acquired its own brand reputation, becoming nearly as well-regarded as Hitachi. And in computers, for example, Acer of Taiwan closed some of the gap with Toshiba.

But many scholars note that smaller companies in other, less developed parts of Asia also have tapped into the region's sprawling web of production networks, helping their economies grow without large "national champions." Baldwin (2012) notes that heavily populated developing economies like China and India may enjoy success in squeezing technology from MNCs, but less populous developing economies might do better to emulate Thailand, where dozens of suppliers now earn profits producing and exporting automobile parts for Japanese, Korean, American, and European assemblers. Thailand, he writes, is benefiting from an economic policy that encourages its manufacturers to join a GVC rather than build one of their own: its "success in becoming the Detroit of Southeast Asia shows supply-chain industrialization can work even without muscular technology transfer policies" (34).

Gone, then, is the traditional model of vertically organized networks dominated by Japanese MNCs. Scholars tend to agree that Asia today is home to a complex, criss-crossing pattern of production networks that are at once more global and more regional than before. They are more global in the sense that they increasingly include production of intermediate goods for European and American MNCs, not just for Japanese and Korean MNCs. But they also are more regional in the sense that the finished goods produced by these networks increasingly are consumed in Asia. As a result of successful supply-chain industrialization, consumers in the region are now wealthy enough to purchase a larger and larger share of the fruits of network labor. Urban Chinese families, in particular, have developed a strong appetite for high-technology goods. This means that triangular trade is giving way to greater intraregional (or intra-Asian) trade.

The Impact of MNCs and Production Networks on East Asia

By spinning the first of what has become a dynamic web of regional production networks, Japanese MNCs and Japanese state agencies, collectively and individually, enjoyed tremendous political clout in Asia, especially in Southeast Asia, from the mid-1980s until roughly the end of the twentieth century. On the public side, agencies such as MITI (Ministry of International Trade and Industry) dispatched officials to Bangkok, Jakarta, Kuala Lumpur, and Manila, advising their counterparts on such things as how to build supporting industries for automobile and electronics manufacturing. Concessionary yen loans helped finance "hard infrastructure" such as roads, power lines, and new industrial estates, while Japanese government grants helped finance "soft infrastructure" such as new Japanese-style organizations reflecting coop-eration between the state and industry.[7] On the private side, Japanese MNCs became leading suppliers of jobs, exports, and (to a more limited extent) new technology in countries throughout Southeast Asia. It is safe to say that those developing coun-tries came to depend increasingly on Japan, and that dependence manifested itself in government policy and industry practice. In 1985, for example, Malaysia turned to Mitsubishi for help in developing its first "national automobile," the Proton Saga. And in 1991, when Chrysler was trying to introduce the Jeep Cherokee into Thailand, the Thai government treated the four-by-four SUV as a luxury car, which called for a hefty excise tax, even though it had tagged Mitsubishi's rival four-by-four as a pickup truck, which qualified it for a far lower excise tax. American and European automo-bile manufacturers also complained routinely that they could not persuade Japanese parts producers, who dominated the supply base in Southeast Asia, to sign contracts with them; they chose instead to deal exclusively with Japanese assemblers like Toyota or Nissan.[8]

Before long, however, host governments cooled on Japan and its MNCs in the region. They were especially frustrated by exclusionary behavior (hiring only Japanese man-agers, using predominantly Japanese suppliers) that seemed to limit technology trans-fer. The Thai Board of Investment, in a brochure designed to encourage non-Japanese MNCs to invest in Thailand's automotive and auto parts industries, expressed it this way: "The Japanese have never been keen on transferring design and engineering exper-tise to their Thai counterparts."[9]

But the auto industry was unique. In other industries, alternative production net-works emerged, attracting the interest of host governments and suppliers in Asia. Nearly every economy in the region is now part of networks created by not only Japanese but also Korean, Taiwanese, European, and American MNCs, capitalizing on complementary labor skills and technology levels and creating a remarkable num-ber of backward and forward linkages within and across industries. In the production of electronic machinery, Hayakawa, Ji, and Obashi (2009, 9) find that the scale of an industry in one country is positively correlated with that industry's scale in neighbor-ing countries. This suggests that Asian countries, by participating in regional networks that break the manufacturing process into different pieces, are enjoying simultane-ous expansion of output. Wang, Powers, and Wei (2009) demonstrate that developing economies in Asia, led by China, have become far more integrated into the region's web of networks, especially in electronics. "In contrast, automobile production still mainly involved Japan and Korea in 2000, with developing Asia just starting to show up in the value chain" (32–33).

It is rather obvious today that the web of production networks in East Asia has dra-matically reshaped host economies, from Dalian to Jakarta, while also influencing the regional and global economies. These networks have dramatically expanded trade, raising both levels of employment and income in areas most integrated into the web through their different advantages in labor costs or technological capacity. A joint study carried out by IDE-JETRO (Japan) and the WTO (2011, 68) suggests that cross-border trade generated new employment opportunities for all of the ten Asian countries it studied, but that China, which has emerged as the new hub of the region's networks, benefited the most—by far. In 2000 intraregional trade generated fifty-six million new job opportunities for China; in 2005 that number was eighty-nine million. What studies like this often fail to note, however, is that the effects of trade generated by FDI and production networks vary wildly within individual countries. For example, cities and towns along China's Pacific coast, compared to more rural and inland areas, have benefited disproportionately from this paradoxical process of manufacturing fragmentation and trade integration. The process has contributed to the widening income gap in various Asian countries, but especially China.

The Impact of Public Policy on MNCs and Production Networks in East Asia

Governments have influenced the behavior and organization of MNCs and production networks in Asia. As Hatch (2004) notes, this is perhaps most obvious through a quick comparison of the region's automobile and electronics industries. Most host governments have maintained relatively high tariff walls around auto assemblers. This allowed Japanese automotive MNCs to hang onto market share in the region, but also caused them to sell heavily in domestic rather than foreign markets. Baldwin (2012, 17–19) notes that Malaysia also used an import substitution policy to build its own automobile network, but fell short because its car manufacturers proved to be inefficient. By contrast, host governments eliminated tariffs on electronics, making that industry highly competitive. Japanese computer and semiconductor MNCs, for example, lost their dominant position in the region's markets, which became relatively efficient and export-oriented.

Kimura and Obashi (2011, 13–14) argue that although countries in the region, especially members of the Association of Southeast Asian Nations (ASEAN), have tried to liberalize trade both unilaterally and through bilateral and regional agreements, much more could be done. MNCs and their production networks have prospered despite limited progress in reducing tariffs. They note that some countries in the region have emerged as major nodes in production networks by investing in shipping terminals and other transportation infrastructure. Singapore is the region's leading entrepot.

Summary

Although scholars offer competing explanations, they tend to agree that East Asia has emerged as the world's leading center of transnational business networks for export-oriented manufacturing. Some attribute this outcome to local conditions, such as an abundant supply of cheap labor and different levels of technological capacity; others emphasize the organizational strategies used by firms enjoying market power.

MNCs and Production Networks
in Latin America

The Americas have long been at the center of debates regarding the costs and benefits of economic globalization, including the role of MNCs and production networks in the development process. North America in particular is unique because it is home to neighboring countries with starkly different levels of development and diverse resource endowments. Today the region's developing economies are scrambling not just to attract foreign investment, but also to cultivate the manufacturing capabilities necessary to upgrade beyond their traditional comparative advantage in lower-wage labor. This section recounts the history of FDI in Latin America and examines the developmental implications of the region's role in transnational production coordinated by foreign lead firms.

History

During the nineteenth and early twentieth centuries, European investors played an important role in Latin America (Grosse 1989). Key sectors included railroads and utilities, but foreign ownership was also significant in mining and oil in Mexico and South America, and in agricultural commodities such as bananas and sugar in Central America and the Caribbean (Chapman 2007; Ayala 1999). The political clout of foreign capital was amply demonstrated during the opening decades of the twentieth century, with multiple interventions by the US military in what came to be known as "banana republics."

Through the middle decades of the twentieth century, international investors repositioned themselves within changing political economies. Mexico is a case in point. In 1938 President Lazaro Cardenas nationalized the country's oil industry in what was one of the region's earliest and most significant expropriations. By 1946 FDI from the United States had plunged 50 percent (Gereffi and Evans 1981). When investment resumed, much of it flowed into the manufacturing sector—a pattern that was repeated elsewhere, as the adoption of import-substituting industrialization (ISI) strategies stimulated market-seeking FDI into the region's largest economies. Latin American governments encouraged foreign investment in manufacturing because they believed that multinationals could play an important role in developing the domestic industrial base prized by the ISI model. Companies in strategic sectors such as autos were invited to establish subsidiaries from which they could serve a growing (and protected) national market. In return, they were expected to comply with policies, such as local content rules and joint ownership requirements, designed to ensure technology transfer and other positive spillovers. By 1967 two-thirds of US FDI in Mexico and Brazil was in manufacturing, with foreign firms generating between 30 and 40 percent of total industrial output in these economies (Bulmer-Thomas 1994).

The debt crisis and the subsequent "lost decade" witnessed a sharp contraction of FDI in Latin America, which fell from $7.5 billion in 1981—the year before Mexico's default—to $2.8 billion in 1986. Within a few years the region's position as the leading destination for foreign investment had eroded. In 1980 almost 70 percent of all FDI flows to developing countries went to Latin America; by 1986, this percentage fell to less than 20 percent (Paus 1989).

In the aftermath of the debt crisis, countries throughout the region implemented reforms to liberalize trade and restore macroeconomic stability. Governments eliminated restrictions that prohibited foreign investment in certain sectors or required joint ventures with national firms. Privatization of state-owned assets created new ownership opportunities for multinational corporations. Tariff barriers were reduced, bringing to an end the import protection that foreign and domestic enterprises had enjoyed. Many of the policies designed to promote linkages between multinationals and local firms were eliminated. The far-reaching process of economic restructuring and liberalization carried out during the 1980s and early 1990s replaced the earlier emphasis on domestic industrialization with an outward-looking strategy of global economic integration and export promotion. This shift in development strategy, from an import-substitution to an export-led model, corresponded to a shift in the nature of FDI, from "horizontal"/domestic market to "vertical"/foreign market, as subsidiaries that had been established to serve domestic markets were reconfigured as links in international value chains (Dunning and Narula 2004).

The Impact of Reform and Regional Integration on MNCs and GPNs in North America

Following the economic reforms of the late 1980s, governments in North America turned their attention to the promotion of preferential trade agreements to stimulate investment and intraregional trade flows. The initial impetus for the North American Free Trade Agreement (NAFTA) originated with Mexican President Carlos Salinas de Gortari, who hoped that a free trade agreement with its northern neighbors would assure foreign investors of Mexico's commitment to reform. Signed by the leaders of Canada, the United States, and Mexico in 1993, NAFTA went into effect on January 1 of the following year. The agreement proved successful in stimulating increased investment in Mexico; between 1994 and 2002, an annual average of $13 billion in FDI flowed into Mexico, as compared with average yearly inflows of $4.5 billion in the eight years prior to the agreement.

Fueled by increased FDI, Mexico's manufactured exports soared in the immediate post-NAFTA period. Growth in clothing exports, in particular, caused significant concern among the countries of Central America and the Caribbean, whose less-diversified industrial sectors depend heavily on the garment trade (Heron 2003). These nations lobbied the US government for an agreement giving them "NAFTA parity"; their efforts resulted in the passage of the Caribbean Basin Trade Partnership Act in 2000 and in

2004 the signing of the Central American Free Trade Agreement (CAFTA) among the United States, the Dominican Republic, El Salvador, Guatemala, Honduras, and Nicaragua (Bair and Peters 2006).

Implications of MNCs and GPNs in North America

The passage of NAFTA and then CAFTA triggered a new round of debate about the degree to which the increased investment and trade stimulated by these agreements would yield more enduring benefits than those associated with the export-processing model typified by Mexico's maquiladoras. Unlike in East Asia, where numerous economies managed to parlay "triangular trade" into sustained growth and industrial upgrading during the post–World War II period, cross-border production networks between US firms and assembly plants in Mexico and the Caribbean had produced mostly disappointing results through the 1980s (Sklair 1993). However, there is some evidence that this is changing since the establishment of NAFTA, at least in Mexico's two largest manufacturing sectors: autos and electronics.

As the global auto industry has become organized into regional production blocs, Mexico has emerged as a central manufacturing hub for the North American market. In 1994 the country hosted eight auto assembly plants and produced fewer than one million vehicles per year. By 2010 the number of plants had more than doubled, to twenty-two, and output reached 2.2 million units. More important, domestic suppliers are playing a growing, if still relatively small, role in these production networks (Contreras and Carrillo 2012). The evolution of the electronics industry has been more uneven. After a sharp contraction in the early 2000s, Mexico's electronics sector upgraded to more sophisticated, higher value-added manufacturing, including larger products (such as flat-screen TVs) for which proximity to the US confers particular advantage. Yet in Mexico's most dynamic electronics cluster, located near Guadalajara, upgrading has not been accompanied by expanded employment, and national companies have a minimal presence (Sturgeon and Kawakami 2010).

The effect of FDI on productivity in Mexico has been found to be positive (Waldkirch 2010), though at least one study showed that including reverse FDI flows (i.e., repatriated profits and dividends) in the net FDI capital variable attenuated the effect (Ramirez 2006). Aitken, Harrison, and Lipsey (1996) concluded that FDI had a positive effect on wages in Mexico, but Waldkirch (2010), using data from the post-NAFTA period, found no positive effect on overall wages and a marginal negative effect on the wages of unskilled workers. Beyond research on FDI, scholars are asking how the incorporation of subcontractors and suppliers into nonequity production networks is affecting the region's developing economies. Some have expressed concern that insofar as countries are hosting narrower "slices" of a disaggregated value chain, they may find opportunities for positive spillover and learning effects minimized, especially if these "slivers of specialized activity" are of the low value-added sort (Buckley and Ghauri 2004).

Although MNCs based in the global North continue to play the pivotal role in most of the GPNs crisscrossing Latin America, intraregional investment is growing as a percentage of all FDI flows. In 2012, 14 percent of all FDI in Latin America originated from another Latin American country. This trend reflects the emergence of indigenous multinational firms within the region, referred to as "multilatinas" (Santiso 2008) or "trans-Latinas" (ECLAC 2012). Mexico is home to the largest number of domestic MNCs, while Brazil has the largest FDI stock abroad. Latin America's largest multinationals have emerged from a diverse set of sectors, including construction, mining, telecommunications, and food and beverages.

Summary

The manufacturing sector absorbs about half of the FDI flowing into the economies of Mexico, Central America, and the Caribbean. In contrast to South America, which receives significant investment from European countries in primary sectors, the developing economies of the northern subregion continue to depend heavily on the United States, both as a source of manufacturing FDI and as a market for their exports. Given the role that these countries play in production networks coordinated by foreign lead firms, competition with Asian exporters in global industries is increasingly seen as a prerequisite for successful development.

MNCs and Production
Networks in Europe

The fall of the Iron Curtain in late 1989 has resurrected Europe's prewar economic landscape, consisting of western, central, and eastern European countries. The fast-emerging east-west integration built on centuries-old cultural proximity gained momentum from the economic underdevelopment of countries in Central and Eastern Europe (CEE) due to their isolation from growing markets in the west. Unlike in East Asia and Latin America, the debate over MNCs and GPNs in this region appears to revolve around their role in deepening the European Union (EU). Scholars have carefully analyzed the transformational and integrative impact of production networks in Central and Eastern Europe. Before 1989, the industrialized CEE differed from Asia and Latin America in that it did not offer a large low-skilled, cheap labor force that could be used to absorb low-end production processes Today, however, this area not only offers opportunities for MNCs to establish production networks, but also motivates small and medium enterprises (SMEs) to cooperate with suppliers in CEE. The common cultural tradition and the intensive and deep prewar ties create a welcoming environment that clearly differs from the tensions that US and Japanese MNCs often face in their regions.

From a theoretical point of view, the focus of the literature is on trade and FDI as integrative vehicles. The major concerns about Asia and Latin America—the difference between horizontal and vertical intra-industry trade (IIT), efficiency-seeking or strategic FDI, and the political clout of MNCs—do not appear to dominate the debate over Europe.

History

Enlargement of the EU in 2004 and 2007 propelled western European manufacturing companies to allocate production of parts and components to the new member states in CEE because they hoped to exploit comparative advantages. Although MNCs did not prune production networks in peripheral economies along the Mediterranean Sea, FDI flowed even more heavily to CEE countries. Only Greece failed to attract higher levels of FDI. According to Kokkinou and Psycharis (2004), this was a result of disincentives associated with the Greek government, especially its complicated tax system and its relatively corrupt bureaucracy.

The 1989 miracle offered western European companies new opportunities to invest and produce in a large and diversified region. In 1997, well ahead of eastern enlargement, the EU signaled clearly in its "Agenda 2000" that it would follow through on the pre-accession strategy by negotiating and implementing accession agreements with the applicant countries in CEE.

From the middle of the 1990s, progress in transition ("transition factor"), along with the advantages of pre-accession agreements with the EU ("EU factor"), combined to induce western companies to explore local capabilities and/or to use CEE as a regional supply base. There is evidence that MNCs predominantly create intrafirm production networks via FDI and extend them by subcontracting with local companies. SMEs on the German-Polish and German-Czech border have established contract-based regional production networks that are often embedded in the institutional concept of Euroregions. Grix and Knowles (2002) stress the importance of the "networks of reciprocal trust" as a basis for cross-border businesses. Due to the strong prewar ties Germany had with countries on its eastern border, it is unsurprising that German companies are the largest investors in CEE.

A number of studies (e.g., Damijan et al. 2013) confirm that FDI promoted the industrial restructuring and export growth of CEE economies. At the end of the 1990s around 80 percent of Hungary's exports and 40 percent of Poland's exports to the EU originated from foreign firms (Kaminski 2001, 33). Evidence suggests that foreign firms increasingly integrated local CEE producers into their regional production networks.

In addition to the "transition factor" and the "EU factor," scholars have identified gravity determinants, especially proximity to Germany, as the major forces driving FDI in and manufacturing-related trade with CEE in the 1990s (see, e.g., Kaminski 2001). Mode of privatization, changes in the institutional environment, macroeconomic stability, success in reducing sovereign debt, and speed of opening-up seem to be the major factors explaining the differences in FDI inflows to the new members. Multinationals engaged in manufacturing were attracted to CEE by the large pool of skilled workers, low unit labor costs, and existing foundation of capital-intensive production.

Resmini's (2000) analysis of FDI flows to this subregion shows a pattern that varies according to industry. Market-driven FDI dominates in traditional sectors; transition success, as well as proximity to Western Europe, attracts FDI in science-based and capital-intensive sectors; and wage differentials affect FDI in scale-intensive sectors. Overall, Güngör and Binatli (2010, 26) conclude that efficiency-seeking motives prevail across the region rather than market-seeking and resource-seeking motives. Approaches that go beyond the advantage- and gravity-based explanation of production networks improve the explanatory value of western European companies' engagement in CEE. According to Altomonte (1998), institutional climate and economic uncertainty are factors that significantly influence the decision to reach out to transition countries as well as the location, mode of entry, scope, and type of relocated activities.

The Impact of New West-East Production Networks on CEE Countries

Studies by Mateev and Tsekov (2013), as well as others, reveal the following about MNCs' FDI in CEE. Germany is the leading source of FDI, Hungary the leading destination, and the automotive industry the leading investor. FDI stock, as of 2010, had reached more than 50 percent of GDP (Pojar, 2012, 23). Last but not least, FDI positively contributed to export restructuring via MNCs' production networks (see, e.g., Damijan et al. 2013). Spillover effects to domestic firms are not generally confirmed.

Despite limits on measuring cross-border production networks, the considerable west-east FDI flows, accompanied by a significant increase in IIT in intermediate and equipment goods, especially in machinery, electrical, and automotive industries, suggest a vertical specialization pattern (Damijan et al. 2013). Production networks allow MNCs to improve their market competitiveness by exploiting CEE countries' production competitiveness.

A simplified view of intra-EU west-east trade generates the following conclusions. First, in the early 1990s low-tech industries shifted labor-intensive production to CEE countries, mostly for assembling. Second, at the end of the 1990s those CEE countries became net exporters of parts in capital- and skill-intensive industries. Third, the quality of their exports has increased markedly, reaching the level of western EU industries in recent years. Fourth, since the mid-1990s FDI has been an important driver of the trade specialization pattern in CEE. Ambroziak's (2012, 20) empirical test (which excludes Bulgaria and Romania) confirms that the estimated impact of FDI on all types of IIT was positive and highly significant. Likewise, Kutan and Vuksic (2007) argue that FDI has increased production capacity in CEE countries, resulting in increasing export supply capacity.

Kravtsova and Radosevic (2012) suggest that FDI in CEE countries has generated positive spillovers for domestic firms, helping them increase their competitiveness.

Negative effects would occur if foreign firms "steal the market" of domestic firms. Kosová (2010), using data from the Czech Republic, shows evidence of both possible outcomes.

The effect of FDI on employment in CEE countries seems ambiguous. Due to the rapid evolution from low-tech to medium- and high-tech FDI, the originally large demand for low-skilled workers was replaced by a relatively small demand for high-skilled workers. Empirical studies suggest that the effects of FDI on employment in CEE generally have been modest. FDI inflows in manufacturing may have a negative effect, indirectly, on local suppliers, but this may be outweighed by the positive effect of direct employment by MNCs (Hunya and Geishecker 2005). Studies on the "feedback" effect of this FDI on labor markets in western Europe do not show a general pattern; in fact, results differ among countries, industries, and the skill level of workers (see, e.g., Castellani et al. 2008). Empirical studies on the effects of FDI and trade on wages in CEE countries show different results depending on the country, industry, type of FDI, and trade, as well as on the relation between imports and exports (Egger and Stehrer 2001; Stehrer and Wörz 2006).

EU's Multilevel Governance and Its Impact on European MNCs

It is difficult to evaluate the impact of European MNCs on the policy-making process in the European Union, just as it is difficult to evaluate the impact of EU policy making on MNC practice. In both cases one has access to only limited evidence and must resort to speculation.

European production networks are affected most critically by two sets of policies: external trade policy, which is laid out and enforced entirely at the level of the EU, and single market policies, which are largely determined by the Council of the EU and the European Commission but implemented by member states. The power of the Commission is enhanced by its administrative expertise, while the power of the Council is weakened by the constraints of the complex system of qualified majority voting and the resulting need to secure compromise. In highly specialized cases (e.g., antidumping policy or technical regulations), the Commission turns to industry for advice. It is well known that the Commission would like to adopt industrial policies designed to increase the competitiveness of core industries. This likely would strengthen the power of national and European trade associations. In addition, fifty of Europe's top corporate executives pool their individual knowledge and company-backed power in the European Round Table of Industrialists (ERT), lobbying policy makers on everything from antitrust to intellectual property rights. The ERT may represent a distinctively EU style of lobbying, which Woll (2012, 194) calls informational, constructive, and consensus-oriented, compared to the aggressive advocacy approach used in the United States. MNCs with headquarters in large member states and production networks that are spread over many smaller/medium-sized member states may benefit from the Council's voting system when lobbying for their interests (Coen 2007). The higher the number of involved national governments, the higher the potential power of these MNCs. But even in the case of common interests, large member states are often forced to logroll and package deals. The existing literature does not clarify whether trade associations and business groups drive the Commission into a more protectionist or more open direction, which enhances competition (Vassalos 2012).

Summary

The thick west-east production networks in Europe emerged from the political change in 1989 and the following integration of CEE countries into the EU. This allows western European MNCs to make full use of CEE's cost and proximity advantages. The deep vertical specialization is documented by high shares of intermediate and equipment goods in the EU's west-east IIT. Due to the EU's multilevel governance system and its complex decision-making processes, MNCs' power to shape external trade policy as well as common market policies is difficult to evaluate and needs further industry-specific research.

CONCLUSION

Although they agree that a large and perhaps increasing share of global trade occurs inside corporate channels, scholars are divided on how to explain this phenomenon. Some attribute it to economic flows that are pushed and pulled by market forces; others credit corporate strategies. At the same time, scholars differ over how to characterize the business groups engaged in this cross-border activity. For manufacturing investment, the traditional approach has described them as MNCs that either circumvent trade barriers by establishing offshore but domestic market-oriented operations or capitalize on host country incentives by assembling parts in foreign enclaves and shipping finished goods back home. More recently, students of FDI have highlighted a new model: the GPN that slices up the manufacturing process into separate pieces located in different countries based on the presumed technological capacity of host economies.

This chapter has shown that relatively complex networks are emerging in the three leading regions of the global economy, reshaping trade patterns and development prospects in Asia, Latin (especially North) America, and Europe. These networks tend to be dominated by Japanese or Korean, US, and German firms, either manufacturers or retailers, which have established close and long-standing ties with suppliers and contractors in neighboring countries. Lead firms promote and exploit government policies, especially preferential trade regimes at the regional level, while also using novel business practices that allow them to capture the gains of specialization via segmentation. For example, automobile assemblers—whether they are headquartered in Nagoya, Detroit, or Stuttgart—are outsourcing more and more production to nominally independent but often foreign affiliates in regional hubs like Poland, Mexico, and Thailand. But our case studies also revealed differences in the nature and depth of networking in these three regions.

Asia is home to the most extensive production networks in the world today. Japanese multinationals initiated this trend in the 1980s, but Korean and Taiwanese producers soon got into the act. China then emerged as a low-cost production and export base for MNCs from around the world. Other economies in the region—including India, Bangladesh, and Vietnam—are now becoming alternative sites for low-cost manufacturing. Even though formal-legal institutions in Asia, especially Northeast Asia, are relatively weak, GPNs are well-established here and are characterized by massive spatial and technological differentiation. This suggests that transnational firms, rather than states, are driving the process of integration in Asia.

In Latin America, US producers have established low-cost bases in Mexico and different parts of Central America, often manufacturing "reverse imports" for the US market. NAFTA and CAFTA have contributed to the US-led process of production sharing, though the advantages these regimes provide may not be sufficient to offset pressures from Asian competitors. Further south and east, in places like Brazil and Argentina, US producers are less dominant; European and Latin American investors are more active here, especially in this subregion's primary industries.

The eastward expansion of the European Union has, by contrast, created a far-flung single market that capitalizes on the lower costs, especially lower wages, in the new members' economies. Intermediate and equipment goods account for a significant share of the EU's west-east IIT, indicating the progress of vertical specialization.

NOTES

1. In the 1990s, "value" upstaged "commodity" as the unit of analysis for many scholars in this school. They argued that it covered a broader range of transnational business activity.
2. ODMs used to be referred to as OEMs (original equipment manufacturers).
3. See Aminian, Fung, and Ng (2009) for a comparison of East Asia and Latin America. See Kimura, Takahashi and Hayakawa (2007) for a comparison of East Asia and Europe.
4. See Hatch and Yamamura (1996, 26).
5. See Hatch and Yamamura (1996, 160).
6. This discussion relies heavily on Hatch (2010).
7. See Hatch and Yamamura (1996, 130–145).
8. See Yamamura and Hatch (1997).
9. Thai Board of Investment, Investment Opportunities Study: Automotive and Autoparts Industries in Thailand, 1995.

REFERENCES

Aitken, B., A. Harrison, and R. Lipsey. 1996. Wages and Foreign Ownership: A Comparative Study of Mexico, Venezuela, and the United States. *Journal of International Economics* 40 (3–4): 345–371.

Altomonte, Carlo. 1998. FDI in the CEECs and the Theory of Real Options: An Empirical Assessment. LICOS Discussion Paper, 76/1998, KU Leuwen.

Ambroziak, Lukasz. 2012. FDI and Intra-Industry Trade: Theory and Empirical Evidence from the Visegrad Countries. *International Journal of Economics and Business Research* 4 (1–2): 180–198.

Aminian, Nathalie, K. Fung, and Francis Ng. 2009. A Comparative Analysis of Trade and Economic Integration in East Asia and Latin America. *Economic Change and Restructuring* 42 (1): 105–137.

Ayala, C. 1999. *American Sugar Kingdom: The Plantation Economy of the Spanish Caribbean, 1898–1934*. Chapel Hill: University of North Carolina Press.

Bair, J., and E. D. Peters. 2006. Commodity Chains and Endogenous Growth: Export Dynamism and Development in Mexico and Honduras. *World Development* 34 (2): 203–221.

Bair, Jennifer, ed. 2009. *Frontiers of Commodity Chain Research*. Stanford, CA: Stanford University Press.

Baldwin, Robert. 2012. Trade and Industrialization after Globalization's 2nd Unbundling: How Building and Joining a Supply Chain Are Different and Why It Matters. NBER Working Paper No. 17716. http://siteresources.worldbank.org/INTRANETTRADE/Resources/Baldwin_NBER_Working_Paper_17716.pdf.

Borga, Maria, and William J. Zeile. 2004. International Fragmentation of Production and the Intrafirm Trade of U.S. Multinational Companies. Bureau of Economic Analysis, Commerce Department, Working Paper No. 2004-02.

Borrus, Michael. 1997. Left for Dead: Asian Production Networks and the Revival of U.S. Electronics. BRIE Working Paper No. 100. http://brie.berkeley.edu/publications/WP100.pdf.

Buckley, P., and P. Ghauri. 2004. Globalisation, Economic Geography and the Strategy of Multinational Enterprises. *Journal of International Business Studies* 35 (2): 81–98.

Bulmer-Thomas, V. 1994. *The Economic History of Latin America since Independence*. New York: Cambridge University Press.

Castellani, Davide, Ilaria Mariotti, and Lucia Piscitello. 2008. The Impact of Outward Investment on Parent Company's Employment and Skill Composition. Evidence from the Italian Case. *Structural Change and Economic Dynamics* 19: 81–94.

Chapman, P. 2007. *Bananas: How the United Fruit Company Shaped the World*. New York: Cannongate.

Coen, David. 2007. Lobbying in the European Union. Paper requested by the European Parliament's Committee on Constitutional Affairs, European Parliament, PE 393.266, Brussels, Belgium.

Contreras, O., and J. Carrillo. 2012. Local Entrepreneurship within Global Value Chains: A Case Study in the Mexican Automotive Industry. *World Development* 40 (5): 1013–1023.

Damijan, Joze, Crt Kostevc, and Matija Rojek. 2013. Global Supply Chains at Work in Central and Eastern European Countries: Impact of FDI on Export Restructuring and Productivity Growth. Vives Discussion Paper No. 37, KU Leuwen.

Dunning, J., and R. Narula. 2004. *Multinationals and Competitiveness: A New Agenda*. Cheltenham, UK: Edward Elgar.

Dunning, John H. 1977. Trade, Location of Economic Activity and the MNE: A Search for an Eclectic Approach. In *The International Allocation of Economic Activity*, edited by Bertil Ohlin, Per-Ove Hesselborn, and Per Magnus Wijkman, pp. 395-418. London: Macmillan.

Economic Commission for Latin America and the Caribbean (ECLAC). 2012. *Foreign Direct Investment in Latin America and the Caribbean*. Santiago, Chile: Economic Commission for Latin America and the Caribbean.

Egger, Peter, and Robert Stehrer. 2001. International Outsourcing and the Skill-specific Wage Bill in Easter Europe. The Vienna Institute for International Economic Studies, Research Reports No. 17.

Ernst, Dieter. 1994. Carriers of Regionalization: The East Asian Production Networks of Japanese Electronics Firms. BRIE Working Paper No. 73. http://brie.berkeley.edu/publications/wp%2073.pdf.

Ernst, Dieter. 1997. Partners for the China Circle? The Asian Production Networks of Japanese Electronics Firms. BRIE Working Paper No. 91. http://brie.berkeley.edu/publications/wp%2091.pdf.

Feenstra, Robert C. 1998. Integration of Trade and Disintegration of Production in the Global Economy. *Journal of Economic Perspectives* 12 (4): 31–50.

Feenstra, Robert C., and Gary Hamilton. 2006. *Emergent Economies, Divergent Paths: Economic Organization and International Trade in South Korea and Taiwan*. Cambridge, UK: Cambridge University Press.

Gawer, Annabell, and Michael A. Cusumano. 2002. *Platform Leadership: How Intel, Microsoft and Cisco Drive Industry Innovation*. Cambridge, MA: Harvard Business School Press.

Gereffi, Gary. 1995. Global Production Systems and Third World Development. In *Global Change, Regional Response: The New International Context of Development*, edited by Barbara Stallings, 100–142. Cambridge, UK: Cambridge University Press.

Gereffi, Gary. 1994. The Organization of Buyer-Driven Global Commodity Chains: How US. Retailers Shape Overseas Production Networks. In *Commodity Chains and Global Capitalism*, by Gary Gereffi and Miguel Korzeniewicz, 95–122. Westport, CT: Praeger.

Gereffi, G., and P. Evans. 1981. Transnational Corporations, Dependent Development, and State Policy in the Semiperiphery: A Comparison of Brazil and Mexico. *Latin American Research Review* 16 (3): 31–64.

Gilpin, Robert. 1973. *US Power and the Multinational Corporation: The Political Economy of Foreign Direct Investment*. New York: Basic Books.

Grix, Jonathan, and Vanda Knowles. 2002. The Euroregion as a Social Capital Maximizer: the German-Polish Euroregion Pro-Europa Viandrina. *Regional and Federal Studies* 12 (4): 154–176.

Grosse, R. 1989. *Multinationals in Latin America*. London: Routledge.

Güngör, Hakan, and Ayla O. Binatli. 2010. The Effect of European Accession Prospects on Foreign Direct Investment Flows. Izmir University of Economics, Izmir, Working Papers on Economics No. 10/06.

Hatch, Walter F. 2010. *Asia's Flying Geese: How Regionalization Shapes Japan*. Ithaca, NY: Cornell University Press.

Hatch, Walter. 2004. When Strong Ties Fail: US-Japan Manufacturing Rivalry in Asia. In *Beyond Bilateralism: US-Japan Relations in the New Asia-Pacific*, edited by Ellis Krauss and T. J. Pempel, pp. 154-175, Stanford, CA: Stanford University Press.

Hatch, Walter, and Kozo Yamamura. 1996. *Asia in Japan's Embrace: Building a Regional Production Alliance*. Cambridge, UK: Cambridge University Press.

Hayakawa, Kazunobu, Zheng Ji, and Ayako Obashi. 2009. Agglomeration versus Fragmentation: A Comparison of East Asia and Europe. IDE Discussion Paper No. 212.

Henderson, Jeffrey, Peter Dicken, Martin Hess, Neil Coe, and Henry Wai-Chung Yeung. 2002. Global Production Networks and the Analysis of Economic Development. *Review of International Political Economy* 9 (3): 436–464.

Heron, T. 2003. The U.S.-Caribbean Apparel Connection and the Politics of NAFTA Parity. *Third World Quarterly* 23 (4): 753–767.

Hunya, Gabor, and Ingo Geishecker. 2005. Employment Effects of Foreign Direct Investment in Central and Eastern Europe. The Vienna Institute for International Economic Studies, Research Reports No. 321.

Hymer, Stephen H. 1976. *The International Operations of National Firms: A Study of Direct Foreign Investment*. Cambridge, MA: MIT Press. (1960 PhD diss. published posthumously.)

IDE-JETRO and WTO. 2011. *Trade Patterns and Global Value Chains in East Asia: From Trade in Goods to Trade in Tasks*. Geneva: World Trade Organization Centre.

Katzenstein, Peter J. 2005. *A World of Regions: Asia and Europe in the American Imperium*. Ithaca, NY: Cornell University Press.

Kim, Sangbae, and Jeffrey A. Hart. 2002. The Global Political Economy of Wintelism: A New Mode of Power and Governance in the Global Computer Industry. In *Information Technologies and Global Politics: The Changing Scope of Power and Governance*. edited by James N. Rosenau and J. P. Singh, 143–168. Albany: State University of New York Press.

Kimura, Fukunari, and Ayako Obashi. 2011. Production Networks in East Asia: What We Know So Far. ADBI Working Paper 320. Tokyo: Asian Development Bank Institute. http://www.adbi.org/working-paper/2011/11/11/4792.production.networks.east.asia/.

Kimura, Fukunari, Yuya Takahashi, and Kazunobu Hayakawa. 2007. Fragmentation and Parts and Components Trade: Comparison between East Asia and Europe. *North American Journal of Economics and Finance* 18 (1): 23–40.

Krugman, Paul R. 1995. Growing World Trade. Brookings Papers on Economic Activity No. 1.

Jensen, Nathan M. 2006. *Nation-States and the Multinational Corporation: The Political Economy of Foreign Direct Investment*. Princeton, NJ: Princeton University Press.

Jones, Ronald W., and Henryk Kierzkowski. 1990. The Role of Services in Production and International Trade: A Theoretical Framework. In *The Political Economy of International Trade: Essays in Honor of Robert E. Baldwin*, edited by Ronald Jones and Anne Krueger, pp. 31–48. Oxford: Basil Blackwell.

Kaminski, Bartlomiej. 2001. How Accession to the European Union Has Affected External Trade and Foreign Direct Investment in Central European Economies. World Bank Working Papers 2578. Washington, DC.

Kokkinou, Aikaterini, and Psycharis, Ioannis. 2004. Foreign Direct Investment, Regional Incentives and Regional Attractiveness in Greece. Department of Planning and Regional Development, School of Engineering, University of Thessaly, Volos, Greece, Discussion Paper Series No. 10(11). http://www.prd.uth.gr/uploads/discussion_papers/2004/uth-prd-dp-2004-11_en.pdf.

Kosová, Renáta. 2010. Do Foreign Firms Crowd Out Domestic Firms? Evidence from the Czech Republic. *Review of Economics and Statistics* 92 (4): 861–881.

Kravtsova, Victoria, and Slavo Radosevic. 2012. Are Systems of Innovation in Eastern Europe Efficient? *Economic Systems* 36 (1): 109–126.

Kutan, Ali M., and Goran Vuksic. 2007. Foreign Direct Investment and Export Performance: Empirical Evidence. *Comparative Economic Studies* 49: 430–445.

Lanz, R., and S. Miroudot. 2011. Intra-Firm Trade: Patterns, Determinants and Policy Implications. OECD Trade Policy Papers No. 114. OECD Publishing.

Li, Quan, and Adam Resnick. 2003. Reversal of Fortunes: Democratic Institutions and Foreign Direct Investment to Developing Countries. *International Organization* 57 (1): 175–211.

Mahutga, Matthew C. 2012. When Do Value Chains Go Global? A Theory of the Spatialization of Global Value Chains. *Global Networks* 12 (1): 1–21.

Mateev, Miroslav, and Ilya Tsekov. 2013. Do Central and Eastern European Countries Possess FDI Advantages to More Developed Western Countries? Paper presented at the Annual Meeting of the Midwest Finance Association, Chicago, March 13–16. http://bmabg.s801. sureserver.com/assets/var/docs/papers/do-cee-FDI.pdf.

Milberg, William S. 2004. The Changing Structure of Trade Linked to Global Production Systems: What are the Policy Implications? *International Labour Review* 143 (1–2): 45–90.

Moran, Theodore H. 1974. *Multinational Corporations and the Politics of Dependence: Copper in Chile*. Princeton, NJ: Princeton University Press.

Mosley, Layna. 2011. *Labor Rights and Multinational Production*. New York: Cambridge University Press.

Mundell, Robert. 1957. International Trade and Factor Mobility. *American Economic Review* 47 (3): 321–335.

Paus, E. 1989. Direct Foreign Investment and Economic Development in Latin America: Perspectives for the Future. *Journal of Latin American Studies* 21 (2): 221–239.

Pojar, Simona-Valeria. 2012. The Influence of Foreign Direct Investment on Firms' Performance in Central and Easter in European Countries. Master's thesis, Aarhus University. http://pure. au.dk/portal-asb-student/files/44523221/Master_Thesis.pdf.

Ramirez, M. 2006. Is Foreign Direct Investment Beneficial for Mexico? *World Development* 34 (5): 802–817.

Resmini, Laura. 2000. The Determinants of Foreign Direct Investment in the CEECs—New Evidence from Sectoral Patterns. *Economics of Transition* 8 (3): 665–689.

Rudra, Nita. 2008. *Globalization and the Race to the Bottom in Developing Countries: Who Really Gets Hurt?* New York: Cambridge University Press.

Santiso, J. 2008. The Emergence of Latin Multinationals. *CEPAL Review* 95: 7–30.

Sklair, L. 1993. *Assembling for Development: The Maquila Industry in Mexico and the United States*. San Diego, CA: Center for U.S.-Mexican Studies.

Stehrer, Robert, and Julia Wörtz. 2006. Attract FDI!—A Universal Global Rule? Empirical Evidence for Europe and Asia. Paper presented at the 3rd Conference on RTN "Trade, Industrialization and Development," Universita degli Studi di Milano. http://dev3.cepr.org/ meets/wkcn/2/2360/papers/Woerz.pdf.

Sturgeon, T., and M. Kawakami. 2010. Global Value Chains in the Electronics Industry: Was the Crisis a Window of Opportunity for Developing Countries? The World Bank Policy Research Working Paper No. 5417.

Sturgeon, Timothy J. 2009. From Commodity Chains to Value Chains: Interdisciplinary Theory Building in an Age of Globalization. In *Frontiers of Commodity Chain Research*, edited by Jennifer Bair, 110–135. Stanford, CA: Stanford University Press.

Vassalos. 2012. Who's Driving the Agenda at DG Enterprise and Industry? Alliance for Lobbying Transparency and Ethics Regulation—ALTER-EU, Brussels. http://www.alter-eu. org/sites/default/files/documents/DGENTR-driving_0.pdf.

Waldkirch, A. 2010. The Effects of Foreign Direct Investment in Mexico since NAFTA. *World Economy* 35 (5): 710–745.

Wang, Zhi, William Powers, and Shang-jin Wei. 2009. Value Chains in East Asian Production Networks: An International Input-Output Model Based Analysis. U.S. International Trade Commission, Office of Economics Working Paper No. 2009-10-C.

Williamson, Oliver. 1975. *Markets and Hierarchies*. New York: Free Press.

Woll, Cornelia. 2012. The Brash and the Soft-Spoken: Lobbying Styles in a Transatlantic Comparison. *Interest Groups & Advocacy* 1 (2): 193–214.

Yamamura, Kozo, and Walter Hatch. 1997. A Looming Entry Barrier? Japan's Production Networks in Asia. *NBR Analysis* 8 (1). http://nbar.org/publications/analysis/pdf/vol8no1.pdf.

Yeats, Alexander J. 2001. Just How Big Is Global Production Sharing. In *Fragmentation: New Production Patterns in the World Economy*, edited by Sven Arndt and Henryk Kierzkowski, 108–143. Oxford: Oxford University Press.

PART IV

....

DOMESTIC
INSTITUTIONS

....

CHAPTER 14

....

NEW DEMOCRACIES

....

BUMBA MUKHERJEE

WHAT is the impact of democratization on trade protection in developing states? Are governments in newly democratized developing countries more likely to adopt trade reforms? Political scientists and economists have invested substantial effort in addressing these two questions (e.g., Frye and Mansfield 2004; Giavazzi and Tabellini 2005; Milner and Kubota 2005; Rudra 2005; Eichengreen and Leblang 2008; López-Córdova and Meissner 2008; Tavares 2008; Milner and Mukherjee 2009a). While debates persist over how democratization increases the likelihood of trade liberalization, scholars generally converge on the view that governments in newly democratized developing states have *political* incentives to reduce trade barriers (Giavazzi and Tabellini 2005; Milner and Kubota 2005; Eichengreen and Leblang 2008; Milner and Mukherjee 2009a). Mutual agreement among students of political economy about the impact of domestic political institutions (in this case, the transition to democracy) on economic outcomes such as trade policy is rare.

Indeed, the widely accepted view that democratization fosters trade reforms stands in sharp contrast to debates about the impact of *established* democracies on trade protection. Some scholars suggest, for instance, that democracy is mutually compatible with free trade (Mansfield, Milner, and Rosendorff 2000; Guisinger 2001; Eichengreen and Leblang 2008). Others claim that democracy promotes free trade only under certain electoral systems[1] or economic conditions (Tavares 2008). Furthermore, some researchers find that democratic governments employ nontraditional means such as nontariff barriers (NTBs) to protect their economies (Kono 2006). Although claims about the effects of established democratic institutions on trade policy are far from settled, it is clear from the preceding summary of the relevant literature that students of international political economy (IPE) are far more confident that the transition to democracy leads to trade liberalization in developing states. Is this confidence justified?

A close look at some cases suggests that the link between democratization and trade reforms in developing countries is more complex than suggested in extant studies. For example, during the initial post-transition years between(i) 1986 and 1989, the Sarney administration in Brazil's newly democratized state and (ii) 1987 and 1990, the Corazon

Aquino–led government in Philippines' new democracy sharply reduced trade restrictions (Weyland 2002; UNCTAD 2005). After Bangladesh and Ghana experienced a transition to democracy in 1991 and 1996, respectively, the first post-transition government in each of these two countries increased tariffs to protect domestic industries from import competition (UNCTAD 2005). These examples suggest that extant research on trade politics in developing states has arguably painted the link between democratization and trade reforms with a broad brush.

This should not be taken to mean that insights provided by current studies on democratic transitions and trade policy are inadequate. These studies provide an excellent foundation for conducting further research on *when*—rather than just *why*—democratization is likely to engender trade liberalization in developing countries. Conducting further research on how the emergence of democracy influences trade protection is substantively important, as it may help us to address the variation in trade policy in the post-transition years across "new democracies." Developing nuanced insights about the conditions under which leaders in newly democratized states adopt trade reforms also allows us to understand whether (and when) democratic transitions promote economic growth, if we believe that more trade openness fosters growth.

Given the importance of understanding the link between democratic transitions and trade policy, the objective of this chapter is thus twofold. The first objective is to consider the state of the literature on democracy (including democratization) and trade policy. One cannot provide an exhaustive analysis of all the relevant literature in this issue area. That said, key insights from this literature are highlighted in this review. The second objective is to address the following three questions:

- What do the data tell us about trade reforms during the immediate post-transition years in newly democratized regimes in the developing world? Are some post-transition governments more likely to liberalize trade policies than others?
- Is there variation in industry-level tariffs in new democracies during the initial years after the transition to democracy? If so, what is the nature of this variation, and what does it tell us about democratization and trade politics?
- Does trade liberalization positively influence the likelihood of democratization? Is there statistical evidence for an endogenous relationship between democracy and trade reforms?

The next section of this chapter begins with a discussion of the existing literature on the impact of democratic transitions as well as established democracies on trade policy. In the third section I analyze some data that reveal both variation in import duties and trade protection of skill-intensive versus low-skilled industries in newly democratized states. This is followed by a concise discussion of various arguments that may account for the variation in trade barriers mentioned above. The fourth section explores both the data and the literature that evaluate the impact of trade openness on the likelihood of democratization. I conclude with a discussion of key research issues that need to be addressed in the study of democratization and trade policy.

STUDIES ON DEMOCRACY AND TRADE

Economists generally agree that trade protection generates deadweight losses.[2] Yet it is common knowledge that governments in both developed and developing countries protect domestic industries from import competition through the use of tariffs and NTBs. Why do governments protect their domestic industries from import competition? The literature that addresses this question is vast, and there is no space to discuss this literature in detail in this chapter. Stated briefly, however, academic research on the political economy of trade protection can be broadly divided into two categories: "demand-side" and "supply-side" explanations for trade policy. Demand-side explanations largely employ the Stolper-Samuelson theorem and the Ricardo-Viner model to account for the trade-policy preferences of individuals. Demand-side studies of trade policy primarily explain how trade-policy preferences of individuals or firms may influence the prospects for trade liberalization (Rogowski 1989; Busch and Reinhardt 1999, 2000; Scheve and Slaughter 2001; Hiscox 2002; Baker 2005; Mayda and Rodrik 2005; Mansfield and Mutz 2009).

According to these "demand-side" studies, the trade policy preferences of individuals, including voters, are determined by their degree of occupational specificity, education, or income; their beliefs about whether or not trade openness is beneficial for them; and their sociotropic perceptions of trade's influence on the national economy. Theories about trade-policy preferences held by individuals have been extensively tested by using survey-response data sets.[3] In contrast to the focus on individual preferences, other demand-side explanations examine how campaign contributions and lobbying pressure from "special interests" affect trade politics (Baldwin and Magee 2000; Grossman and Helpman 2006). Empirical tests of the effects of industry-based campaign contributions provided by industries on trade policy outcomes are rare, however, given the paucity of publicly available data about contributions provided by industries.

Unlike the demand-side approach, supply-side explanations about trade policy analyze the impact of political institutions on international trade. Some of these studies have explored the effects of international institutions such as the General Agreement on Tariffs and Trade/World Trade Organization (GATT/WTO) on international trade flows or the settlement of inter-state trade disputes (Gowa and Kim 2005; Tomz, Goldstein, and Rivers 2007; Davis and Bermeo 2009). Other supply-side studies theorize and find empirically that democratic regimes—including newly democratized states and established democracies—are more likely to liberalize their trade policies (Frye and Mansfield 2004; Milner and Kubota 2005; Eichengreen and Leblang 2008; Milner and Mukherjee 2009a). Several studies also statistically evaluate and find robust support for the influence of specific democratic institutions on trade policy (Nielsen 2003; Hankla 2006; Henisz and Mansfield 2006). These institutions include electoral systems, the number of veto players, electoral particularism, political partisanship, and the numbers of effective parties in democracies. Notwithstanding these demand-side and supply-side explanations for the determinants of trade protection, there is little ambiguity in the fact that trade barriers have decreased sharply across developing states during the past three decades. This is corroborated by a substantial body of statistical evidence showing that trade barriers have declined significantly across several developing countries since 1980 (Harrison and Hanson 1999; Goldberg and Pavcnik 2004; Milner and Kubota 2005).

Preceding and concurrent with the move to free trade in the developing world, there has been a global movement toward democracy. For instance, in their careful and detailed empirical study of democratic transitions and economic growth, Papaionnou and Siourounis (2004) identify as many as fifty-nine episodes of "full" democratization and twenty-four episodes of "partial" democratization between 1970 and 2002.[4] This is further confirmed by Milner and Kubota (2005, 158–159), who point out that the number of democracies in the developing world grew at least threefold between 1975 and 2002. It is precisely this "dual transition" phenomenon, characterized by simultaneous democratization and trade liberalization in the developing world (since the early 1980s), that has encouraged researchers to claim that the transition to democracy leads to trade liberalization. Scholars have also employed a variety of statistical models to evaluate whether the emergence of democracy leads to a decline in trade protection. These studies show that democratization indeed exerts a positive and statistically significant effect on trade liberalization or, in other words, leads to a significant decline in aggregate country-year trade protection measures such as import duties (Giavazzi and Tabellini 2005; Milner and Kubota 2005; Eichengreen and Leblang 2008).

In addition to the empirical research alluded to above, a fairly rich literature examines why democratization engenders trade liberalization (Stokes 2001; Weyland 2002; Milner and Kubota 2005). The most comprehensive theoretical analysis of democratization on trade liberalization to date is by Milner and Kubota (2005). They argue that since democratization expands the "selectorate" in a polity, it empowers whole groups in society that were formally excluded from the political process. In the context of developing countries, this implies that democratization empowers and enfranchises particularly labor in the rural and urban informal sectors, who, given the Stolper-Samuelson theorem, favor trade openness, as they are the abundant factors that gain from trade in developing countries. As a result, governments in new democracies have political incentives to respond positively to the preferences of labor by lowering trade barriers.

Unlike Milner and Kubota (2005), Weyland (2002, 60) suggests in his work that democratization weakened the political power of vested interests that favored protectionism in Latin American states. This facilitated the adoption of trade reforms by political leaders in various newly democratized Latin American states such as Argentina and Brazil (Weyland 2002, 60–61). An important difference between Weyland (2002) and Milner and Kubota's (2005) theoretical analysis is that the latter set of scholars identify *which* social classes are more likely to benefit from trade reforms. Milner and Kubota (2005) also develop a logically consistent causal mechanism that links democratization specifically to trade liberalization, while Weyland's (2002) book focuses more broadly on a larger set of economic reform (including trade reform) policies.

Other scholars (mainly comparativists) have also suggested either implicitly or explicitly that democratization generally promotes economic reform and more specifically trade liberalization. For instance, early research on the topic of political regimes and economic reform questioned the presumption that authoritarian governments have an inherent advantage with respect to implementing trade reform (Geddes 1995; Remmer 1998). Geddes (1995) and Remmer (1998) instead suggest that democratizing states are quite capable of implementing reform policies, including trade liberalization. Stokes (2001) argues in her book that if trade reforms provide benefits to large sections of society in developing countries, then democratization will foster trade liberalization in these states. This is because leaders in new democracies will be subject to electoral punishment if they resist trade liberalization. In addition, since governments in newly democratized states anticipate political rewards from liberalization ex post, they have political incentives ex ante to liberalize trade policies (Stokes 2001).

The discussion in the preceding paragraphs indicates that extant studies on democratic transitions and trade policy primarily focus on *why* democratization leads to trade reforms. While numerous studies emphasize that both democratization and higher levels of democracy are negatively correlated with trade protection, not all researchers agree with the claim that democracy helps to reduce trade barriers. For example, Kono (2006) finds that democracies have a negative effect on tariffs but a positive impact on NTBs. Garrett (2000, 973) posits that even though "on the one hand, democracy" helps with respect to "promoting trade liberalization. . . . On the other hand, democracy also empowers distributional coalitions with intense interests, making higher levels of protectionism more likely."

The possibility that democracy may not always promote free trade, as suggested by Garrett (2000), has motivated scholars to focus on variation in trade barriers across democracies. Some studies find, for instance, that left-leaning parties espouse more protectionist policies than their right-leaning counterparts in developed countries but are more pro free-trade in developing countries (Milner and Judkins 2004; Dutt and Mitra 2006). Nielson (2003) argues that trade protection is lower in presidential systems across developing countries, while Henisz and Mansfield (2006) show that the conditional effect of veto players matters for trade policy. Rogowski (1989) argued that closed-list proportional representation (PR) systems are more likely to have lower trade barriers. Building on this, Mansfield and Busch (1995) suggested more broadly that PR systems tend to have lower levels of NTBs. Finally, Grossman and Helpman (2005) claim that in majoritarian systems, parties cannot prevent individual legislators from pursuing protectionist policies for the interests of their own constituencies.

It is important to note here that extant research on variation in trade barriers across democratic states focuses on trade policies in established and "consolidated" democracies across the developed and developing world.[5] Less attention has, however, been paid to the possibility that the degree of trade protection (and thus the prospects for trade reform) may also *vary substantially* during the initial post-transition years in newly democratized developing states. Indeed, as discussed earlier, anecdotal evidence reveals that although post-transition governments in Brazil and the Philippines sharply reduced trade barriers, other newly democratized states like Ghana and Bangladesh increased trade restrictions during the initial post-transition years. Moreover, as shown below, variation in trade barriers during the immediate post-transition period is also prevalent in a larger pooled sample of "new democracies."

DEMOCRATIZATION AND TRADE BARRIERS: THE DATA

The possibility that trade protection varies substantially across newly democratized states during the immediate postdemocratic transition years is supported in a data set on trade barriers for the years following a democratic transition across several developing countries. Consider figure 14.1, which plots the moving-average of the import duty coverage ratio (a widely accepted measure of tariff barriers)[6] during the first five years *after* a democratic transition across a comprehensive list of fifty-six developing countries that have experienced a transition to democracy in the previous three decades. These countries and the year in which each made a transition to democracy (as identified in the Polity V and the Przeworski, Alvarez, Cheibub, and Limongi 2000 data sets) are listed in table 14.1.[7]

Figure 14.1 shows that although import duties decreased in the first five post-transition years for 62 percent of these "new democracies," it increased or maintained the status quo in the remaining 38 percent of the developing countries that also successfully made a transition to democracy. This figure therefore reveals that trade liberalization (i.e., a decrease in import duties) in the initial post-transition years occurred in a certain share of but not all newly democratized developing states.

It is worth emphasizing here that it is not merely an aggregate country-year measure of trade barriers across several industries—for example the import duties measure employed to extract figure 14.1—that varies across newly democratized states in the post-transition period. If, for instance, one makes a distinction between trade protection on high skilled goods produced by skill-intensive industries (e.g., the petrochemical industry) and low skilled goods (e.g., agriculture) in developing states, one finds that the relationship between democratization and trade protection in the developing world is more complex.[8] Consider figure 14.2, which illustrates the mean of output-weighted (average) tariffs for several high skilled goods and low skilled goods at the three-digit International Standard of Industrial Classification[9] (ISIC) level (i) for a sample of *established* developing country democracies[10] between 1980 and 2006 and (ii) during the first five postdemocratic transition years for the fifty-six developing countries listed in table 14.1.[11] Before discussing the pattern of industry-level tariffs in this figure, it is important to explain the three-step procedure

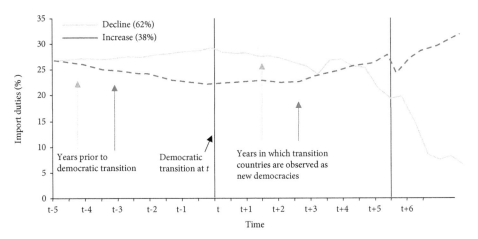

FIG. 14.1   New Democratic Regimes and Import Duties.

Note: Data sources used to compute the moving average of import duties are listed in the text.

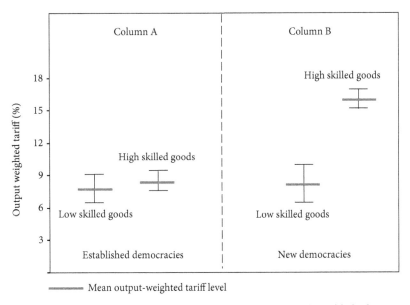

FIG. 14.2   Tariffs for High Skilled and Low Skilled Goods in New and Established Democracies.

that I employed to operationalize the output-weighted average tariff level for low skilled goods (labeled *low skilled tariff*) and high skilled goods (*skilled tariff*) illustrated in figure 14.2. First I collected ad valorem tariff country-year data for thirty industries—including the agricultural sector—that are disaggregated and classified at the three-digit ISIC level (Revision 2) for each established developing democracy and newly democratized state. Tariff data at the disaggregated three-digit ISIC level for developing countries are only available for these thirty industries.[12] These

Table 14.1 New Democracies in the Developing World

Country	Democratic Transition Year	First 5 Post-Transition Years (includes transition year)	Country	Democratic Transition Year	First 5 Post-Transition Years (includes transition year)
Albania	1992	1992–1996	Lithuania	1991	1991–1995
Argentina	1983	1983–1987	Madagascar	1993	1993–1997
Bangladesh	1991	1991–1995	Malawi	1994	1994–1998
Benin	1991	1991–1995	Mali	1992	1992–1996
Bolivia	1982	1982–1986	Mexico	1997	1997–2001
Brazil	1985	1985–1989	Mongolia	1992	1992–1996
Bulgaria	1990	1990–1994	Mozambique	1994	1994–1998
Cape Verde	1991	1995–1999	Nepal	1991	1991–1995
Central African Republic	1993	1993–1997	Nicaragua	1990	1990–1994
Chile	1990	1990–1994	Nigeria	1999	1999–2003
Comoros	1990	1990–1994	Pakistan	1988	1988–1992
Croatia	2000	2000–2004	Panama	1994	1994–1998
Czech Republic	1993	1993–1997	Peru	1980	1980–1984
Dominican Republic	1978	1978–1982	Philippines	1987	1987–1991
Ecuador	1979	1979–1983	Poland	1990	1990–1994
El Salvador	1994	1994–1998	Slovak Republic	1993	1993–1997
Estonia	1991	1991–1995	Slovenia	1992	1992–1997
Ethiopia	1995	1995–1999	South Africa	1994	1994–1998
Ghana	1996	1996–2000	Thailand	1992	1992–1996
Guatemala	1996	1996–2000	Uruguay	1985	1985–1989
Guyana	1992	1992–1996	Paraguay	1993	1993–1997
Haiti	1994	1994–1998	Russia	1993	1993–1997
Honduras	1982	1982–1986	Senegal	2000	2000–2004
Hungary	1990	1990–1994	Suriname	1991	1991–1995
Indonesia	1999	1999–2003	Tanzania	1995	1995–1999
Korea, Republic of	1988	1988–1992	Turkey	1983	1983–1987
Latvia	1991	1991–1995	Ukraine	1991	1991–1995
Lesotho	1993	1993–1997	Zambia	1991	1991–1995

Table 14.2   Three–Digit ISIC Industries

ISIC #	Description	S/L Ratio	ISIC #	Description	S/L Ratio
331	Wood products except furniture	0.109	342	Printing and publishing	0.397
323	Leather products	0.091	354	Miscellaneous petroleum & coal products	0.414
311	Food products	0.164	355	Rubber products	0.396
111	Agriculture & agric. raw materials	0.047	356	Plastic products	0.358
313	Beverages	0.126	361	Pottery, china & earthenware	0.140
314	Tobacco	0.075	362	Glass and glass products	0.216
322	Wearing apparel except footwear	0.193	372	Nonferrous metal basic industries	0.392
331	Wood products except furniture	0.138	381	Fabricated metal products	0.404
332	Furniture except metal	0.125	382	Machinery except electrical	0.426
324	Footwear except rubber or plastic	0.216	383	Electrical machinery	0.611
312	Textiles	0.112	390	Other manufactured products	0.587
371	Iron and steel	0.283	353	Petroleum refineries	0.630
369	Other nonmetallic mineral products	0.205	351	Industrial chemicals	0.592
372	Nonferrous metals	0.176	384	Transport equipment	0.465
341	Paper products	0.391	385	Professional goods & scientific equipment	0.726

industries and the goods that they produce are listed in table 14.2. The goods listed there range from low skilled goods such as wood products and goods produced in the agricultural sector to relatively high skilled goods that include, for example, scientific equipment.

Second, after collecting country-year tariff data for the thirty industries, I classified them and therefore the goods that they produce into two broad categories: low and high skilled goods, as follows. First, following existing studies, I calculated the S/L ratio, that is, the ratio of skilled workers S (workers with greater than or equal to twelve years of schooling) to low-skilled workers L (workers with fewer than twelve years of schooling) employed in each industry to rank-order the goods produced in the industry according to their skill-intensity of production (Nunn and Trefler 2006).[13] As suggested by Nunn and Trefler (2006), if the ratio of skilled to low skilled workers employed in an industry listed in table 14.2 is $S/L \geq 0.39$, then the good produced by the industry is classified as high skilled; if $S/L < 0.39$ for an industry, then the good produced by that industry is classified as low skilled.

Using the S/L ratio of 0.39 as a threshold to classify the thirty industries and the goods that they produce into low or high skilled, I obtained seventeen low skilled goods that are produced in low skilled industries and thirteen high skilled goods produced in skill-intensive industries. The mean low skilled and skilled tariff levels illustrated in figure 14.2 do not change when I use any value in the $S/L \in [0.36, 0.42]$ range as the threshold for the S/L ratio to categorize the goods produced in the thirty industries as low or high skilled. Third, following extant studies on trade protection at the three-digit ISIC industry level,[14] I used the tariff data for each low and high skilled good to compute the output-weighted average tariff for the seventeen low skilled goods (*low skilled tariff*) and thirteen high skilled goods (*skilled tariff*) for each country in the group of (i) established developing democracies and (ii) newly democratized states.[15] I then calculated the within-group mean of *low skilled tariff* and *skilled tariff* for each of the two groups mentioned above to extract figure 14.2.

Figure 14.2 shows the group mean of these two measures between established developing democracies and newly democratized states. Column B and a simple difference-of-means test show that the mean of *skilled tariff* is substantially and significantly (in the statistical sense) higher than the mean of *low skilled tariff* in the immediate post-transition years for newly democratized states. In contrast, column A reveals that there is little or no difference between the mean of *skilled tariff* and *low skilled tariff* in the set of established developing country democracies. Figure 14.2 also shows that the mean of *skilled tariff* in newly democratized developing states is much higher than the mean of this measure for established democracies across the developing world. But the difference in the mean level of *low skilled tariff* between newly democratized states and established developing democracies is marginal. Hence, we learn from this figure that there is a "skill bias" in trade protection during the initial post-transition years in new democracies, in that trade barriers on high skilled goods are much higher than those for low skilled goods in the post-transition years for these states.

Figures 14.1 and 14.2 therefore unambiguously reveal that there is no simple inverse relationship between the emergence of new democracies and trade restrictions in the developing world. Instead, these figures show that both aggregate measures of trade barriers (e.g., import duties) as well as industry-level tariffs—conceptualized here as the distinction in tariffs on goods produced by low skilled industries versus those produced by skill-intensive industries—varies significantly across new democracies in the developing world. They also suggest that some but not all newly democratized states enthusiastically embraced trade reforms during the initial post-transition years. These two figures also raise the following questions: Why do import duties decrease in the immediate years following a democratic transition in some new democratic regimes across the developing world but not others? Why are tariffs on goods produced by skill-intensive industries significantly higher than tariffs placed on low skilled goods in the initial post-transition years in new democracies? Answering these questions is critical to understanding the link between new democratic regimes and trade protection. This is substantively vital, given that the variation illustrated in figures 14.1 and 14.2 has not to the best of my knowledge been carefully studied by scholars. Addressing these questions is also important given that trade policy has critical economic consequences in developing countries. The next section thus provides some brief answers to the two questions posited above.

WHY TRADE PROTECTION VARIES ACROSS NEW DEMOCRACIES

Various arguments can be put forth to address the first question, which focuses on why some but not all newly democratized states adopt trade reforms. One approach that can be used to answer this question is to explore how the trade-policy preferences of the empowered electoral majority in new democracies, namely workers, influence the trade-policy responses of political parties in these states. To see this in more detail, consider a situation in which political parties "strategically interact" in a Downsian setting with workers (i.e., labor)—a key productive group in society (who, as mentioned above, are also an electoral majority)—during the immediate post-transition period in a new democracy. Suppose that the trade-policy preferences of workers in the new democracy are determined by their degree of inter-industry occupational mobility. As shown in some "demand-side" theories of trade policy, occupationally mobile workers tend to support trade liberalization, as they gain monetarily from higher levels of trade openness (Wacziarg and Wallack 2004; Mukherjee, Smith and Li 2009). Conversely, occupationally specific workers typically favor higher levels of trade protection, because they are more likely to suffer from unemployment when import competition increases (Mukherjee, Smith, and Li, 2009).

Building on these "demand-side" claims in the literature, suppose further that the inter-industry occupational mobility of workers in the newly democratized state's economy is sufficiently high. If this is the case, then it follows that the distribution of the workers' occupational mobility in the economy will be positively skewed. In this positively skewed distribution, the median voter (who is also a worker) is more occupationally mobile than the mean voter. In other words, the median voter in this case will be a "mobile-type" individual characterized by a relatively high degree of occupational mobility across industries. This is important, because when the median voter is indeed occupationally mobile between industries in the new democratic state, he or she is more likely to gain from more trade openness and will thus be receptive toward trade liberalization.

Note that in the Downsian equilibrium, the political parties in the newly democratized state will observe that the median voter's level of inter-industry occupational mobility is sufficiently high and will thus recognize that the median voter favors trade reforms. Since the parties in the new democracy are interested in winning the election, they have political incentives to appeal to the "occupationally mobile" median voter by reducing tariff barriers in equilibrium. The main hypothesis that emerges from this simple story is that policy makers in new democracies will reduce tariffs (i.e., adopt trade reforms) during the initial post-transition years if the inter-industry occupational mobility of workers in the economy is sufficiently high. Is this hypothesis empirically valid? I briefly assess this hypothesis by broadly evaluating the impact of a recently developed measure of inter-industry occupational mobility of labor (in short, inter-industry labor mobility) on import duties for the first five post-transition years across the fifty-six newly democratized developing states listed in table 14.1. This measure of inter-industry occupational mobility of labor (labeled here *labor mobility*) has been developed by Wacziarg and Wallack (2004) and Hiscox and Rickard (2005). The *labor mobility* measure is computed for each country-year in my sample by isolating the fraction of jobs that move from one industry to another independent of overall employment gains or losses. Let $E_{j,i}^{t}$ denote employment in industry j in country i at time t. Hence

$$labor\ mobility = \frac{\sum_{j=1}^{N}\left|E_{j,i}^{t} - E_{j,i}^{t-\delta}\right| - \left|\sum_{j=1}^{N}E_{j,i}^{t} - \sum_{j=1}^{N}E_{j,i}^{t-\delta}\right|}{\frac{1}{2}\sum_{j=1}^{N}(E_{j,i}^{t} + E_{j,i}^{t-\delta})} \tag{1}$$

where the summation ($\sum_{j=1}^{N}$) is over all $N = 30$ industries at the three-digit ISIC level listed in table 14.2.

The difference between the expression $\left|E_{j,i}^{t} - E_{j,i}^{t-\delta}\right|$ on the left and the expression $\sum_{j=1}^{N}E_{j,i}^{t} - \sum_{j=1}^{N}$ on the right in the numerator in equation 1 gives the employment changes that result from the pure shifts of jobs across different industries.[16] The denominator in *labor mobility* computes the average of total employment for the industries in consideration between t and $t - \delta$. I set $\delta = 1$ year given that I am interested in examining the impact of the labor mobility measure on import duties on for each of the five initial post-transition years across the fifty-six new democracies. The *labor mobility* measure is a continuous variable that ranges from low to high inter-industry occupational mobility.

The scatterplot in figure 14.3 shows that higher levels of *labor mobility* indeed have a strong negative effect on import duties during the initial five post-democratic transition years. This indicates that higher levels of inter-industry labor mobility encourage policy makers in newly democratized developing states to embrace trade liberalization during the immediate post-transition period. Figure 14.3 also shows that import duties tend to be much higher in new democracies when labor mobility is low or, in other words, workers are characterized by a high level of occupational specificity. This is perhaps not surprising, as a high level of occupational specificity in the labor force will ensure that the median voter is occupationally specific and will hence favor higher trade protection. This in turn will drive Downsian parties to raise trade barriers in the post-transition period. The simple scatterplot shown in figure 14.3 therefore provides an intuitive account of why there is variation in trade barriers across new democracies. That said, it needs to be studied in far more depth.

The results discussed above are interesting, but they merely tell us something about the correlation between labor mobility (or lack thereof) and trade protection in new developing country democracies. They do not explain causality per se between democratic transitions and trade liberalization in developing countries. Furthermore, it may be possible that it is not the level of inter-industry labor mobility in new democracies but other alternative arguments that may account for why policy makers in some newly democratized states embrace trade liberalization immediately after the transition to democracy. For instance, there are sound reasons to suspect that in some new democracies "geographically concentrated" export-oriented industries—which are less susceptible to collective action problems owing to their geographic concentration—may have extensively lobbied their respective governments to reduce trade barriers. Examples from the post-transition years in newly democratized states such as Brazil and Indonesia suggest that geographically concentrated export-oriented industries indeed put pressure on policy makers in these countries to slash tariffs.[17] Others have suggested that new democracies in especially Central and Eastern Europe acquiesced to pressure from international institutions like the International Monetary Fund and the World Bank to reduce trade restrictions (Shafaeddin 2006). Such pressure may have induced policy makers in these states to adopt trade reforms in the initial post-transition years. In short, the claims posited above, as well as these alternative causal claims, suggest that studies on trade politics need to develop parsimonious yet lucid causal theories to

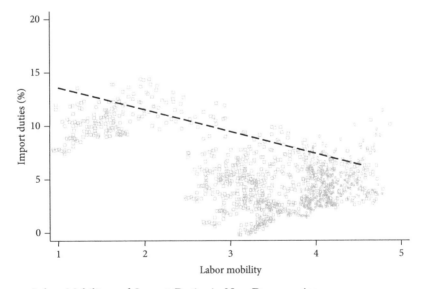

FIG. 14.3 Labor Mobility and Import Duties in New Democracies.

Notes: Scatterplot of *import duties* against the index offender-industry *labor mobility* for the first five post-transition years for the 56 new democracies in table 14.1. Each point represents one postdemocratic transition country-year for which both variables are observed. The scatterplot is overlaid with a dashed line, which is the pooled OLS best fit line that accounts for the within-country correlation of *import duties* across time.

account for the variation in trade protection across "new democracies" that is illustrated in figure 14.1.

Let us next briefly explore the second question posited above: Why are tariffs on goods produced by skill-intensive industries significantly higher than tariffs placed on low skilled goods in the initial post-transition years in new democracies? A variety of explanations can arguably answer this question. Recent studies by some economists that examine industry-level tariffs at the six-digit ISIC level in developed and developing democracies suggest that leaders in majoritarian democracies adopt higher trade barriers on goods produced by skill-intensive industries but reduce trade restrictions on low skilled goods such as agricultural products (Ardelean and Evans 2013). This claim is intuitive. Yet a cursory examination of my data on *skilled tariff* and *low skilled tariff* for new democracies shows that this claim does *not* hold for newly democratized states.

Specifically, the vast majority (73 percent) of the fifty-six new democracies in table 14.1 adopted the PR electoral system or variants of it immediately after the transition to democracy. The mean of *skilled tariff* during the initial post-transition years in these new democracies that adopted the PR system is higher than the mean of *low skilled tariff* in these countries. It is also higher than the mean of both *skilled* and *low skilled* tariff in new democracies that adopted the majoritarian system. This suggests that focusing on the distinction between electoral systems may not be fruitful in accounting for why trade restrictions on goods produced by skill-intensive industries are high during the post-transition period in new democracies. Instead, it might be worthwhile to pay more attention to how certain domestic industry-level characteristics within new democracies may shape the economic and political relationship between governments and industries in these states. This relationship in turn may potentially account for different patterns of trade protection that we observe at the industry level in new democracies.

DOES TRADE OPENNESS INFLUENCE DEMOCRATIZATION?

Understanding the impact of democratization on trade policy is undoubtedly a central area of research for students of IPE. Yet scholars have suggested that there is theoretically a potential for reverse causality between democratic transitions and trade reforms; that is, higher levels of trade openness that result from trade liberalization may increase the likelihood of democratization in developing countries (Lipset 1959; Boix 2003; Acemoglu and Robinson 2006). The theoretical literature on the impact of trade openness on democratization is indeed quite rich. For instance, Lipset (1959) suggested almost five decades ago that trade can spark development and create a larger middle class, which in turn might foster the emergence of democracy.

Acemoglu and Robinson (2006) build on their well-known models of the link between inequality and democratization to explore how trade openness influences the prospects of democratic transition in developing states. They incorporate a Stolper-Samuelson model of international trade, which assumes perfect labor mobility, and essentially argue that higher levels of trade openness decreases income inequality in developing countries, which consequently increases the probability of democratization in these states. This is because if one assumes that developing countries are abundant in labor, then one would expect increased trade openness to increase real returns for labor (the relatively abundant factor) and reduce real returns for owners of capital (the relatively scarce factor) under the Stolper-Samuelson theorem. This in turn reduces income inequality in these countries. Lower inequality then reduces the costs of tolerating democracy for elites in authoritarian developing countries, as tax redistributions are less severe for elites when income inequality is low. In short, because greater trade openness reduces income inequality in labor-abundant developing authoritarian states and lower inequality reduces the costs that elites may incur from a democratic transition, political elites in these states have incentives to adopt democracy.

In contrast to Acemoglu and Robinson (2006), Boix (2003) suggests that the effect of trade openness on democracy is contingent on the distribution of factors within a particular economy. When skilled workers are the abundant factor, trade openness increases income inequality within society by driving up the wages of skilled workers and deflating the wages of already poorer low skilled or unskilled workers. Growing income inequality in turn discourages democratization. Adsera and Boix (2002) argue that greater trade openness actually endangers democratic institutions in emerging democracies. They emphasize that in countries in which democratic institutions are less well established, interest groups that benefit from more trade openness might try to void democratic institutions and impose openness through a dictatorship.

A careful examination of the relevant empirical literature indicates that statistical support for the theoretical claim that trade openness positively influences democratization is either weak or at best conditioned by other domestic factors. Some studies, for example, find that trade openness does not have a significant effect on the likelihood that democracy may occur (Bussmann 2002). Li and Reuveny (2003) find that trade openness is negatively associated with democratic institutions. Rudra (2005) suggests that the effect of trade openness on democratization is conditional on the bargaining power of labor in developing countries. The one exception is Lopez-Cordova and Meissner (2008), who find that trade openness positively influences democratization.

The studies cited in the previous paragraph employ samples that include developed and developing countries for their statistical tests, as well as (in some cases) using a long temporal domain that typically includes observations from the late nineteenth century (Lopez-Cordova and Meissner 2008; Eichengreen and Leblang 2008). While including developed and developing countries in the sample and using a longer temporal sample range increases the generalizability of the reported results, it also raises the following question: Is there statistical support for the theoretical prediction that trade openness has increased the probability of democratization in developing countries in the previous three to four decades?

To address this question, I briefly conducted a simple empirical exercise to check whether trade openness (the sum of exports and imports as a share of gross domestic product) has a statistically positive effect on the likelihood of democratization in a sample of 128 developing countries from 1972 to 2008. To this end, I estimated a dynamic probit model with random effects to assess the statistical effect of trade openness on the dummy dependent variable *democracy*. This dummy variable is set equal to 1 for democratic countries that satisfy Przeworski and colleagues' (2000) criteria for a democracy.[18] Standard control variables such as *log GDP per capita, ethno-linguistic fractionalization, log population,* and *the number of past transitions to authoritarianism* are also included in the dynamic probit specification, as these variables are known to influence the probability of democratization (for this see Przeworski et al. 2000). Estimates from the dynamic probit model, which are not reported here to save space, reveal that the effect of *trade openness* on the dummy dependent variable *democracy* is positive but statistically insignificant. This result requires more research. But it does confirm extant findings that cast doubt on the claim that trade openness positively influences democratic transitions.[19]

Researchers should not conclude from the consistent lack of robust statistical support for the effect of trade openness on the likelihood of democratization that this issue area is not worth assessing in more depth. I believe that future research on democratic transitions and trade policy may potentially benefit more by rigorously evaluating *when*—rather than whether—trade openness may positively influence the probability of democratization in developing states. Doing so may help to empirically clarify the potential link between trade openness and democratization. This is substantively necessary considering that proponents of the view that trade openness leads to democratization arguably accept this causal relationship far too easily. Alternatively, skeptics tend to be excessively dismissive a priori about the potential effects that trade liberalization may have on the prospects for democratic transition in developing states.

Conclusion: Future Research

The third wave of democratization across the developing world, combined with the sharp decline in trade barriers in these states, has produced a rich literature that explores the impact of democracy on trade policy. While much progress has been made with respect to unpacking the link between democracy and trade policy, less attention has been paid to understanding the political dynamics of trade reforms during the initial post-transition years in newly democratized developing states. That said, some studies have theorized extensively about why the emergence of democracy fosters trade reforms. However, the most significant advance made in the study of democracy and trade (as discussed in the previous sections) is empirical.

Despite the empirical progress made so far, it would be far-fetched to claim that scholars have developed a thorough and comprehensive understanding of the design of trade policy in both newly democratized developing states. Instead, in this section

I briefly discuss three main areas for future research that may help to move the research agenda on democracy and trade forward. First and foremost, this chapter has analyzed variation in tariff barriers such as import duties and output-weighted industry-level tariffs during the immediate postdemocratic transition period. Yet an important area of research on trade politics has shown that established democracies tend to use NTBs rather than tariffs for protectionist purposes (Mansfield and Busch 1995; Kono 2006). This suggests that it may not be sufficient to simply explore easily observable tariff barriers in newly democratized states, given that developing country democracies may use NTBs as a nontransparent tool for protectionist purposes. Instead, it may be worth exploring whether democratization in developing countries discourages or encourages the use of nontariff instruments for trade protection. Doing so will be challenging given the paucity of reliable data on NTBs in the developing world. But given the importance of NTBs, it makes sense to at least broadly understand the relationship between democratization and the use of NTBs as an instrument for trade protection.

Second, I emphasized earlier that political scientists often use aggregate country-year measures such as import duties to assess the political economy of trade protection in developed as well as developing countries (e.g. Milner and Kubota 2005; Henisz and Mansfield 2006; Eichengreen and Leblang 2008). These measures are limited, as they are not designed to capture substantial variation in industry-level tariff barriers across both new and established democracies in the developing world. This is unfortunate, because as I showed in a previous section of this chapter, even a cursory examination of industry-level tariffs reveals that governments in newly democratized states tend to protect domestic skill-intensive industries from import competition. In contrast, policy makers in new democracies tend to reduce trade restrictions on low skilled goods.

I presented some brief arguments that may explain why we observe the variation in industry-level tariffs posited above. Yet these arguments are at best conjecture. It is difficult to provide a thorough answer here to the issue of variation in industry-level tariffs across new democracies, given space constraints. But the illustration in figure 14.2 certainly needs to be explored in greater empirical and theoretical detail. The intriguing relationship between the emergence of democracy and variation in industry-based tariffs also suggests that researchers should continue to develop trade-policy measures that account for both cross-sectional and temporal variation in industry tariffs across developing countries rather than relying on standard aggregate tariff measures.

Third, some scholars debate whether or not capital account openness and trade liberalization are substitutes or complements for developing country governments (McKinnon 1991; Giavazzi and Tabellini 2005). A key lesson that one learns from this debate is that governments in newly democratized developing states may account for the extent to which their country's capital account is open when deciding to adopt trade reforms. It is beyond the scope of this essay to explore the link between capital account openness and trade liberalization. But it might be worthwhile for scholars to explore (i) if capital account policies matter for trade reforms in newly democratized states and (ii) how domestic politics may potentially influence the simultaneous choice of capital account and trade reforms during the initial post-transition period.

NOTES

1. Grossman and Helpman (2005) argue that majoritarian democracies are associated with higher trade barriers. Rogowski (1989) and McGillivray (2004) claim that trade restrictions are likely to be lower in democracies that employ the closed-list PR electoral system.
2. For the claim that trade protection engenders deadweight losses in developed and developing countries, see, for example, Harrison and Hanson (1999).
3. For studies that employ survey-response data sets or conduct survey experiments to assess trade-policy preferences, see, for example, Scheve and Slaughter (2001); Mayda and Rodrik (2005); Baker (2005); and Mansfield and Mutz (2009).
4. Papaioannou and Siourounis (2004, 8) define full democratization as "where both the Polity and the Freedom House indicators have reached an almost perfect score like Spain, Portugal, or Argentina." They define "partial democratization" as including countries that have abandoned autocratic rule, but in which civil rights protection has not reached Western world levels (like Nigeria, Guatemala, or Albania).
5. The term "consolidated" democracies, as used here, refers to new democratic regimes that did not relapse back into autocratic rule within three years after these countries made a formal transition to a full-fledged democracy.
6. The import duty coverage ratio, labeled *import duties*, is defined as the total value of a country's import duties divided by the total value of its imports in a given year and is expressed as a percentage. Data for this variable are drawn from World Bank (2011).
7. The democratic-transition year for each country in table 14.1 is identified using the Polity indicator of the year of democratic transition in the Polity V database. The Polity V database identifies a total of sixty-five democratic transition episodes across all developing states from 1976 to 2005. Since data on import duties are available for fifty-six developing countries out of the total of sixty-five (sixty-one) developing states that experienced a democratic transition, Figure 18.1 is derived based on the available import duties data for these fifty-six "new democracies" listed in table 14.1.
8. Scholars are increasingly focusing on industry-level tariffs, including tariffs on goods produced by skill-intensive industries versus those produced by low skilled industries (see, e.g., Milner and Mukherjee 2009b; Lu, Scheve, and Slaughter 2012).
9. The low and high skilled goods for which 1 collected output-weighted industry-level tariff data at the three-digit ISIC level and which are included in Figure 14.2 are listed in table 14.2.
10. This sample includes a total of fifty-one established developing-county democracies such as Brazil, India, Costa Rica, and other developing democracies (i) where democracy has lasted for more than fifteen years and (ii) that have not relapsed back into an authoritarian regime.
11. The criterion that I employ to classify produced goods into either low or high skilled is drawn from economists such as Nunn and Trefler (2006); it is described below.
12. The data for *skilled* and *low skilled* tariff are drawn from Milner and Mukherjee (2009b). The primary and secondary sources employed to operationalize *skilled* and *low skilled* tariff are listed in detail in Milner and Mukherjee (2009b). These sources are not listed here to save space.
13. The data to calculate the *S/L* ratio are taken from Milner and Mukherjee (2009b); the sources employed to compute the S/L ratio are also listed in detail in Milner and Mukherjee (2009b).
14. See, e.g., Nunn and Trefler (2006). Output-weighted tariffs are used because they accurately capture the relative weight (and thus importance) in the economy of each industry that produces tradable goods.

15. Data on output to calculate output-weights for goods produced by each industry at the three-digit ISIC level listed in table 14.2 are drawn from Milner and Mukherjee (2009b).

16. The expression $\left|E_{j,i}^{t} - E_{j,i}^{t-\delta}\right|$ on the left of *labor mobility* refers to the number of job changes between t and $t - \delta$ while the expression $\Sigma_{j=1}^{N} E_{j,i}^{t} - \Sigma_{j=1}^{N} E_{j,i}^{t-\delta}$ on its left refers to the number of job losses or gains not offset by a gain or loss in other sectors.

17. For Brazil and Indonesia, see UNCTAD (2005).

18. Their criteria for a democracy are that (i) the chief executive and legislature must be directly elected, (ii) there must be more than one party in the legislature, and (iii) incumbents must allow a lawful alternation of office if defeated in elections.

19. See, e.g., Milner and Mukherjee (2009a).

References

Acemoglu, D., and J. A. Robinson. 2006. *Economic Origins of Dictatorship and Democracy.* New York: Cambridge University Press.

Adsera, A., and C. Boix. 2002. Trade, Democracy, and the Size of the Public Sector: The Political Underpinnings of Openness. *International Organization* 56 (2): 229–262.

Ardelean, A., and C. L. Evans. 2013. Electoral Systems and protectionism: An Industry-Level Analysis. *Canadian Journal of Economics* 46 (2): 725–764.

Baker, A. 2005. Who Wants to Globalize: Consumer Tastes and Labor Markets in a Theory of Trade Policy Beliefs. *American Journal of Political Science* 49 (4): 924–938.

Baldwin R., and C. Magee. 2000. Is Trade Policy for Sale? Congressional Voting on Recent Trade Bills, *Public Choice* 105 (1-2): 79–101.

Boix, Carles. 2003. *Democracy and Redistribution.* New York: Cambridge University Press.

Busch, M. L., and E. Reinhardt. 2000. Geography, International Trade, and Political Mobilization in US Industries. *American Journal of Political Science* 44: 703–719.

Busch, M. L., and E. Reinhardt. 1999. Industrial Location and Protection: The Political and Economic Geography of U.S. Nontariff Barriers. *American Journal of Political Science* 43 (4): 1028–1050.

Bussmann, Margit. 2002. Examining Causality Among Conflict, Democracy, Openness, and Economic Growth. University of Alabama Working Paper.

Davis, C. L., and S. B. Bermeo. 2009. Who Files? Developing Country Participation in GATT/ WTO Adjudication. *Journal of Politics* 71 (3):1033–1049.

Dutt, P., and D. Mitra. 2006. Labor versus Capital in Trade Policy: The Role of Ideology and Inequality *Journal of International Economics* 69 (2): 310–320.

Eichengreen, B., and D. Leblang. 2008. Democracy and Globalization. *Economics and Politics* 20 (3): 289–334.

Frye, T., and E. D. Mansfield. 2004. Timing Is Everything: Elections and Trade Liberalization in the Post-Communist World, *Comparative Political Studies* 37 (May): 371–398.

Garrett, G. 2000. The Causes of Globalization. *Comparative Political Studies* 33: 941–991.

Geddes, B. 1995. The Politics of Economic Liberalization. *Latin American Research Review* 30 (2): 195–214.

Giavazzi, F., and G. Tabellini. 2005. Economic and Political Liberalization. NBER Working Paper No. 10657.

Goldberg, P., and N. Pavcnik. 2004. Trade, Inequality, and Poverty: What Do We Know? Evidence from Recent Trade Liberalization Episodes in Developing Countries. NBER Working Paper No. 10593.

Gowa, J., and S. Y. Kim. 2005. An Exclusive Country Club: The Effects of the GATT on Trade, 1950–1994. *World Politics* 57 (July): 453–478.

Grossman, G. M., and E. Helpman. 2006. *Interest Groups and Trade Policy*. Princeton, NJ: Princeton University Press.

Grossman, G. M., and E. Helpman. 2005. Protectionist Bias in Majoritarian Politics. *Quarterly Journal of Economics* 120 (4): 1239–1282.

Guisinger, A. 2001. The Determinants of Trade Tax Liberalization. Unpublished manuscript, Yale University.

Hankla, C. 2006. Party Strength and International Trade: A Cross National Analysis. *Comparative Political Studies* 39 (9): 1133–1156.

Harrison, A., and G. Hanson. 1999. Who Gains from Trade Reform? Some Remaining Puzzles. *Journal of Development Economics* 59 (June): 125–154.

Henisz, W. J., and E. D. Mansfield. 2006. Votes and Vetoes: The Political. Determinants of Commercial Openness. *International Studies Quarterly* 50 (1): 189–211.

Hiscox, M. J. 2002. *International Trade and Political Conflict: Commerce, Coalitions, and Mobility*. Princeton, NJ: Princeton University Press.

Hiscox, M. J., and S. Rickard. 2005. Birds of a Different Feather? Varieties of Capitalism, Factor Specificity, and Inter-industry Labor Movements. Unpublished manuscript, London School of Economics.

Kono, D. Y. 2006. Optimal Obfuscation: Democracy and Trade Policy Transparency. *American Political Science Review* 100: 369–384.

Li, Q., and R. Reuveny. 2003. Economic Globalization and Democracy: An Empirical Analysis. *British Journal of Political Science* 33 (1): 29–54.

Lipset, S. M. 1959. Some Social Requisites of Democracy: Economic Development and Political Development. *American Political Science Review* 53: 69–105.

Lu, X., K. Scheve, and M. J. Slaughter. 2012. Inequity Aversion and the International Distribution of Trade Protection. *American Journal of Political Science* 56 (3): 638–654.

Lopez-Cordova, E., and C. Meissner. 2008. The Globalization of Trade and Democracy: A Long-run Perspective. *World Politics* 60 (4): 539–575.

Mansfield, E. D., and M. Busch. 1995. The Political Economy of Nontariff Barriers: A Cross-National Analysis *International Organization* 49: 723–749.

Mansfield, E. D., H. V. Milner, and B. P. Rosendorff. 2000. Free to Trade: Democracies, Autocracies, and International Trade. *American Political Science Review* 94 (2): 305–321.

Mansfield, E. D., and D. Mutz. 2009. Support for Free Trade: Self-Interest, Sociotropic Politics, and Out Group Anxiety. *International Organization* 63 (3):425–457.

Mayda A. M., and D. Rodrik. 2005. Why Are Some People (and Countries) More Protectionist Than Others? *European Economic Review* 49 (6):1393–1430.

McGillivray, F. 2004. *Privileging Industry: The Comparative Politics of Trade and Industrial Policy*. Princeton, NJ: Princeton University Press.

McKinnon, R. 1991. *The Order of Economic Liberalization: Financial Control in the Transition to a Market Economy*. Baltimore, MD: John Hopkins University Press.

Milner, H. V., and B. Judkins. 2004. Partisanship, Trade Policy, and Globalization: Is there a Left–Right Divide on Trade Policy? *International Studies Quarterly* 48 (1): 95–119.

Milner, H. V., and K. Kubota. 2005. Why the Move to Free Trade? Democracy and Trade Policy in the Developing Countries. *International Organization* 59: 107–143.

Milner, H. V., and B. Mukherjee. 2009a. Democratization and Economic Globalization. *Annual Review of Political Science* 12: 163–181.

Milner, H. V., and B. Mukherjee. 2009b. Democracy and Skill-Bias in Trade Protection in Developing Countries. Princeton University, Department of Politics Working Paper.

Mukherjee, B., D. L. Smith, and Q. Li. 2009. Labor (Im)mobility and the Politics of Trade Protection in Majoritarian Democracies. *Journal of Politics* 71 (1): 1–18.

Nielson, D. 2003. Supplying Trade Reform: Political Institutions and Trade Policy in Middle-Income Democracies. *American Journal of Political Science* 47: 470–491.

Nunn, N., and D. Trefler. 2006. Putting the Lid on Lobbying: Tariff Structure and Long-Term Growth When Protection Is for Sale. NBER Working Paper No. 12164.

Papaioannou, E., and G. Siourounis. 2004. Democratization and Growth. Unpublished manuscript, London Business School.

Przeworski, A., M. E. Alvarez, J. A. Cheibub, and F. Limongi. 2000. *Democracy and Development: Political Institutions and Well-being in the World, 1950–90.* New York: Cambridge University Press.

Remmer, K. 1998. The Politics of Neoliberal Economic Reform in South America, 1980–1994. *Studies in Comparative International Development* 33 (2): 3–29.

Rogowski, R. 1989. *Commerce and Coalitions: How Trade Affects Domestic Political Alignments.* Princeton, NJ: Princeton University Press.

Rudra, N. 2005. Globalization and the Strengthening of Democracy in the Developing World. *American Journal of Political Science* 49: 704–730.

Scheve, K., and M. Slaughter. 2001. What Determines Trade Policy Preferences? *Journal Of International Economics* 54 (2): 267–292.

Shafaeddin, M. 2006. Does Trade Openness Favor or Hinder Industrialization and Development? Working Paper., Kuala Lumpur, Malaysia: TWN Trade and Development Series.

Stokes, S. 2001. *Mandates and Democracy: Neoliberalism by Surprise in Latin America.* New York: Cambridge University Press.

Tavares, J. 2008. Trade, Factor Proportions, and Political Rights. *Review of Economics and Statistics* 90 (1): 163–168.

Tomz, M., J. L. Goldstein, and D. Rivers. 2007. Do We Really Know That the WTO Increases Trade? Comment. *American Economic Review* 97 (5): 2005–2018.

UNCTAD. 2005. *Trade and Development Report.* New York and Geneva: United Nations.

Wacziarg, R. and J. Wallack. 2004. Trade liberalization and intersectoral labor movements, Journal of International Economics 64(2): 411–439.

Weyland, Kurt. 2002. *The Politics of Market Reform in Fragile Democracies: Argentina, Brazil, Peru, and Venezuela.* Princeton, NJ: Princeton University Press.

World Bank. 2011. *World Development Indicators.* Washington, DC: World Bank.

CHAPTER 15

··

ELECTORAL SYSTEMS
AND TRADE

··

STEPHANIE J. RICKARD

IN democracies, politicians compete to win votes, and subsequently office, in free and fair elections. Elected representatives should therefore be responsive to citizens' demands. Yet leaders in some democracies are more reactive to pressures for trade protection than are leaders in other countries. The varied responsiveness of elected officials to protectionist demands may result from the dissimilar rules that govern democratic elections around the world.

A growing body of scholarship examines the relationship between electoral rules and trade policy. Despite increased attention to electoral institutions, no consensus exists about which system makes politicians most responsive to protectionist demands. Some argue that majoritarian systems provide legislators with the greatest incentives to cater to demands for trade barriers (e.g., Rogowski 1987; Grossman and Helpman 2005). Others contend that proportional electoral systems lead politicians to be most responsive to protectionists (e.g. Mansfield and Busch 1995; Rogowski and Kayser 2002; Hays 2009). The debate continues unresolved as both arguments find credible empirical support.

Conflicting conclusions about the effects of electoral systems are surprising given that these institutions lie at the heart of democratic politics. Elections, and accordingly electoral rules, are a defining feature of democracy. Electoral systems connect voters to policy makers; thus, it is reasonable to expect different rules to produce different policy outcomes. Why then have scholars reached inconsistent inferences about the effects of electoral systems on trade policy? This question is the central focus of this chapter. Understanding why scholars have reached this stalemate is important if future research is to progress beyond it. Failure to resolve the impasse may result in the premature demise of this research agenda.

The following section outlines the contours of the debate. Potential reasons for the disagreement about the relationship between electoral systems and trade policy are discussed. The concluding section suggests possible ways forward.

DEFINING ELECTORAL SYSTEMS

An electoral system is a set of laws and regulations that govern electoral competition between candidates or parties or both (Cox 1997, 38). These procedures comprise a multitude of items, such as the electoral formula, the ballot structure, and district magnitude. Of these items, the electoral formula has received the most attention from trade scholars. Electoral formulas refer to the method by which vote totals translate into claims upon legislative seats (Cox 1990). Two main categories of electoral formulas exist: majoritarian and proportional. Together they govern 80 percent of elections held across the world (Clark, Golder, and Golder 2012; Inter-Parliamentary Union 2013).

Majoritarian rules stipulate that the candidates or parties who receive the most votes win. Votes are cast for individual candidates, and the top k vote-recipients win seats, where k is the magnitude of the district (Cox 1990, 906). The most commonly used majoritarian formula is the single-member district plurality system (SMDP). In an SMDP system, citizens cast one vote for a candidate in a single-member district, and the candidate with the most votes is elected. This system is used, for example, in the United States. Forty-five percent of countries use some type of majoritarian electoral formula (Clark, Golder, and Golder 2012, 590).

Majoritarian electoral formulas typically help the largest party obtain a legislative majority. For example, in the post-World War II period, governments in Great Britain received 45 percent of the popular vote on average, but 54 percent of the legislative seats (Norris 1997). In contrast, proportional electoral rules (PR) are intended to produce proportional outcomes (Cox 1997). In a fully proportional system, a party that won 45 percent of the vote would win 45 percent of the legislative seats. In order to achieve proportional outcomes, PR systems employ multimember districts and a quota- or divisor-based electoral formula that determines the number of votes that a candidate or party needs to win a seat (Clark, Golder, and Golder 2012, 564). Thirty-seven percent of countries use some type of proportional electoral formula.

While most countries employ either a majoritarian or a proportional electoral formula, nearly one-fifth of countries employ a mixed system. Mixed systems combine majoritarian and proportional formulas in the same election. In such elections, voters select representatives through two different electoral formulas that run alongside each other.

THE PROTECTIONIST BIAS
IN MAJORITARIAN SYSTEMS

The idea that trade openness is systematically related to countries' electoral systems has a long intellectual history. Early studies by Ronald Rogowski (1987) and Peter Katzenstein (1985) suggested a natural affinity exists between trade openness and proportional electoral rules. More recently, Grossman and Helpman (2005) developed a theoretical model that envisages a protectionist bias in majoritarian systems. In this seminal model, two parties compete in legislative elections, and each party has an equal chance of winning a given seat in a given district. There are three electoral districts; each contains one-third of the population and elects one legislator. Legislators represent districts with interests tied to district-specific industries. Upon forming the government, the delegation from the majority party seeks to maximize the welfare of its constituents. If the party in power represents all three districts, then the legislature will work to maximize the welfare of the entire country by setting tariffs at zero. In contrast, if the governing party represents only two of the three districts, it will set a positive tariff rate. A nonzero tariff emerges because trade policy is chosen by the majority delegation, and legislators in the minority have limited means to influence policy decisions. Legislators in the majority use tariffs to redistribute income to industries in their own districts, rather than maximizing national welfare by setting an optimal tariff of zero. In majoritarian systems, the governing party is unlikely to represent all three districts, whereas in proportional systems it is more likely to represent all three. Consequently, the prediction emerges that tariffs will be lower in PR systems than in majoritarian systems.

Several studies provide empirical support for the predicted "protectionist bias" in majoritarian systems. In a sample of 147 countries from 1981 to 2004, Evans (2009) finds that majoritarian systems have higher average tariffs than countries with proportional electoral systems, all else being equal. Similarly, Ardelean and Evans (2013) demonstrate that tariffs are higher on average in majoritarian systems than in proportional systems using product-level tariff rates for a cross-section of developed and developing countries between 1988 and 2007. These results suggest that a protectionist bias exists in majoritarian systems with regard to tariffs, but leave unanswered the question of whether or not this bias extends to other forms of trade protection.

Governments increasingly use nontariff barriers (NTBs), rather than tariffs, to protect domestic producers. Studies that examine only tariffs, such as Evans (2009), leave open the possibility that electoral rules have an ambiguous effect on total trade protection. Governments in majoritarian systems may provide no more (or less) protection than those in proportional systems; instead, majoritarian governments may simply use tariffs more often than other forms of trade protection.

Different types of governments may prefer different forms of trade barriers because they entail different cost-benefit analyses. Tariffs are a relatively blunt policy tool; they typically cover a specific product and thereby affect all firms producing that product. Although tariffs are blunt and thus potentially inefficient, they generate revenue for governments. In contrast, subsidies cost governments money.[1] While subsidies are expensive, they can be targeted narrowly. For example, a subsidy can be provided to a single firm rather than to an entire industry. Different governments may prefer different types of trade barriers given their varied policy goals and budget constraints. An important but unanswered question therefore exists; does the protectionist bias in majoritarian politics extend beyond tariffs to other forms of trade protection?

A recent study suggests that the protectionist bias in majoritarian politics extends to subsidies, which are an increasingly common NTB (Ford and Suyker 1990; OECD 1998; Rickard 2012c). Rickard (2012b) reports that the share of total government expenditures allocated to subsidies is higher in countries with majoritarian electoral rules than in those with proportional electoral rules, holding all else equal. On average, governments in majoritarian systems spend 2.5 percentage points more on subsidies than governments in PR systems (Rickard 2012b). This evidence suggests that the protectionist bias in majoritarian politics does, in fact, extend beyond tariffs to subsidies.

The majoritarian protectionist bias appears to extend even further, to "illegal" forms of trade protection. Democracies with majoritarian electoral rules are named as defendants in disputes litigated via the World Trade Organization (WTO) more often than those with proportional electoral rules (Rickard 2010; Davis 2012). One interpretation of this finding is that majoritarian democracies simply have more barriers to trade than do PR democracies. Another possibility is that majoritarian democracies have relatively more non-WTO-compliant trade barriers. The electoral incentives to provide protection may be so compelling in majoritarian systems that legislators are willing to supply trade barriers even when doing so violates international rules. In contrast, legislators may choose to provide only WTO-compliant protection in countries where electoral systems are proportional (Naoi 2009).

In sum, convincing empirical evidence suggests a protectionist bias exists in majoritarian systems. This bias appears to extend beyond tariffs to subsidies and other trade barriers proscribed by WTO rules.

TRADE PROTECTION IN PROPORTIONAL RULE SYSTEMS

Although convincing evidence exists of a protectionist bias in majoritarian systems, some scholars argue that proportional electoral rules generate higher barriers to trade. A model developed by Rogowski and Kayser (2002), although not exclusively a model of trade protection, implies that trade barriers will be higher in PR democracies than in majoritarian systems. In the Rogowski and Kayser model, the key distinction between electoral systems is the seat-vote elasticity. Majoritarian systems have greater seat-vote elasticities than PR systems; as a result, a loss of votes translates into a greater loss of legislative seats for parties competing in majoritarian systems. In proportional systems, politicians are able to cater to narrow interests without having to be overly concerned with any election losses they might incur for doing so. In contrast, politicians in plurality systems cannot stray far from the preferences of the median voter, because a small change in vote share can produce a large change in seat share. Rogowski and Kayser posited that politicians in proportional rule systems will therefore be relatively more responsive to narrow interests, such as industry-specific demands for trade protection.

A theoretical model developed by De Mesquita and Smith (2005) also implies that trade barriers will be higher in PR systems than in majoritarian systems. Their model examines the political consequences of a winning coalition's size. A winning coalition is a subset of the selectorate large enough to allow it to endow leadership with political power to negate the influence of the remainder of the selectorate and the disenfranchised members of the society (De Mesquita and Smith 2005, 51). The winning coalition is larger in majoritarian systems than in PR systems, according to De Mesquita and Smith (2005).[2] As the size of the winning coalition grows, the cost of private goods, such as trade barriers, increases. According to their logic, trade protection should be lower in majoritarian systems than in PR systems.

Some evidence exists to suggest that proportional electoral rules incentivize relatively higher trade barriers. Nontariff barriers are higher, on average, in PR democracies than in majoritarian systems (Mansfield and Busch 1995). Proportional rule systems are also associated with higher consumer prices (Rogowski and Kayser 2002; Chang, Kayser, and Rogowski 2008; Chang et al. 2010). Higher consumer prices arguably reflect governmental policies that privilege producer groups at the expense of consumers. One such policy is trade protection. Legislatively imposed barriers to trade raise the prices of consumer goods. The presence of larger trade barriers in PR countries may explain why consumer prices are higher in PR systems than in majoritarian systems.

In sum, it remains unclear which electoral formula generates higher levels of trade protection. Possible reasons for this impasse are explored in the following section. Understanding why scholars have reached this stalemate is important for future research to progress beyond it and advance understanding of how a fundamental democratic institution impacts trade policy.

Resolving the Debate

One explanation for the mixed empirical results may be that electoral rules have varied effects on different types of trade barriers. Existing studies employ diverse measures of trade protection; Evans (2009) uses tariffs; Rickard (2012b) uses subsidies; and Mansfield and Busch (1995) use nonsubsidy, nontariff barriers, such as quotas and restrictive import licensing requirements. The varied conclusions reached by these investigations may simply reflect the dissimilar measures of trade protection examined.

Electoral rules might have different effects on different types of trade barriers because they shape the incentives of parties and politicians to target benefits more or less narrowly (Milesi-Ferretti, Perotti, and Rostagno 2002; Persson and Tabellini 2003; Rickard 2009). In majoritarian systems, electoral incentives exist to narrowly target economic benefits. With majoritarian rules and single-member districts, a party need only receive a plurality of votes in half the districts plus one to win an election and form a government. Politicians need to win only a plurality of votes in their geographically defined electoral districts. Therefore, politicians' optimal reelection strategy in majoritarian rule systems is to supply benefits narrowly to only those voters in their districts (Milesi-Ferretti, Perotti, and Rostagno 2002; Persson and Tabellini 2003).

In PR systems, politicians and parties have fewer incentives to target benefits narrowly (Lizzeri and Persico 2001; Persson and Tabellini 2003; Rogowski 1987). Parties competing under PR electoral rules do not win elections district by district. In fact, no single district is critical to the electoral success of a party (McGillivray 2004). Instead, parties work to maximize their aggregate vote share, because this determines the number of legislative seats a party will control. By targeting policies to a broad segment of the electorate, parties are able to buy the support of a wide range of voters. Thus, leaders in proportional systems have greater incentives to supply broadly beneficial policies.

If some forms of trade protection are inherently "narrower" than others (i.e., easier to target to select constituencies), then electoral rules may have varied effects on different types of trade protection. Narrow trade barriers should be more prevalent in majoritarian systems than in proportional systems. In contrast, broad trade barriers should be more widespread in proportional systems. Two key questions arise from this discussion: Are some forms of trade protection inherently "narrower" than others (i.e., easier to target to select constituencies). If so, which ones? These questions remain largely unexplored.[3] Nonetheless, it is easy to imagine that some forms of trade protection may be more targetable than others. Subsidies, for example, can be provided to a single firm. In contrast, restrictive import licenses often apply to products that typically benefit more than just one firm. In this example, subsidies should be higher in majoritarian systems, while import licenses should be more restrictive in PR systems. Findings reported by Rickard (2012b) and Mansfield and Busch (1995) provide preliminary support for these expectations.

The idea that electoral rules may have varied effects on different types of trade barriers has several implications. First, it suggests a straightforward explanation of why existing studies have come to conflicting conclusions about the empirical relationship between electoral rules and trade protection: it depends on which type of trade barrier they examine. Second, this idea offers a possible explanation of why governments choose a particular policy instrument from their vast arsenal of policy tools. Why, for example, do some governments choose to use discriminatory procurement practices rather than tariffs to privilege domestic producers?[4] Choice of policy instrument remains an important research agenda, because even today no form of trade protection is trivial: tariffs still account for approximately 30 percent of global protection, while NTBs and subsidies account for the remaining 70 percent (Kono 2009).

The idea that electoral rules may have varied effects on different types of trade protection implies that the challenge of relating electoral rules to policy outcomes might be unique to trade because of the myriad tools governments can use to protect domestic producers from competition with low-cost foreign imports. However, research in other areas is plagued by similar ambiguity. For example, it remains unclear which electoral formula generates better outcomes in terms of inflation, economic growth, or budget deficits (Taagepera and Qvortrup 2011, Table 1). The mixed effects of electoral rules across a multitude of policy areas suggest that the problem may reside on the right-hand side of the equation rather than the left.

VARIATION WITHIN ELECTORAL SYSTEMS

The simple distinction between majoritarian and proportional electoral rules may be too blunt to explain the cross-national variation in trade protection. Most investigations of trade policy use a rudimentary measure of electoral rules; that is, a dichotomous variable that takes PR (and majoritarian) electoral systems to be a monolithic phenomenon. Yet what trade scholars typically characterize as being one uniform phenomenon in fact contains multiple structures each with different dynamics and political implications. For example, among systems classified as being majoritarian, eight different electoral formulas are used to translate votes into seats (Clark, Golder, and Golder 2012, 543).

Similar diversity exists among PR systems-even though most can be characterized as list systems.[5] In a list PR system, each party presents a list of candidates for a multimember district, and parties receive seats in proportion to their overall share of the votes. Despite sharing this common feature, list PR systems vary significantly. Seven distinct electoral formulas are used to allocate seats to parties in list PR systems. List PR systems also differ in their district magnitude, the use of higher electoral tiers, the use of electoral thresholds, and the type of party list employed (Gallagher, Laver, and Mair 2006, 354). These dissimilar proportional systems are often grouped together in a single category labeled "PR".

Mixed electoral systems introduce even more variance. Mixed electoral systems combine majoritarian and proportional electoral formulas in the same election. Many scholars simply include mixed systems together with "pure" systems for convenience.[6] Germany, for example, is classified as being a mixed-proportional system because the total number of legislative seats received by a party is proportional to its list-tier results (Shugart and Wattenberg 2001; Thames and Edwards 2006). Germany is therefore grouped together with pure PR systems in many empirical studies (e.g., Rickard 2012a). Because of this common practice, the dichotomous "PR versus majoritarian" variable includes even greater diversity than suggested by the already significant variation in proportional (or majoritarian) systems alone.

This diversity raises questions about the usefulness of the blunt distinction between PR and majoritarian systems. Taagepera and Qvortrup (2011) warn that only non-specialists can persuade themselves that all electoral systems can be characterized by a single dichotomous indicator. They call the majoritarian/proportional distinction a "procrustean bed" (Taagepera and Qvortrup 2011, 255) and warn researchers to "forget about such coarse dichotomy" (Taagepera and Qvortrup 2011, 253). Scholars of trade politics should heed this warning and take seriously the variation that exists within majoritarian and proportional electoral systems. Doing so may help to clarify the precise relationship between electoral systems and trade policy. For example, some types of majoritarian systems may generate higher levels of trade protection than some types of proportional systems. Such within-system variance could explain the mixed empirical results reported to date and help to clarify the precise mechanism through which electoral institutions influence trade policy. If some majoritarian systems generate higher levels of trade protection than others, a common feature may characterize these particular majoritarian systems, and it may be this shared attribute that influences trade policy, rather than the electoral formula itself. Several such possible traits are explored in the following section.

Identifying Causal Mechanisms

The causal mechanism linking electoral formulas to trade policy remains unclear. Few theories articulate how the translation of votes into seats affects trade policy.[7] Instead, scholars typically refer to other features of a country's electoral system that tend to covary with electoral formula, such as district size. Rogowski (1987), for example, argues that the large electoral districts that typify proportional systems insulate politicians from protectionist demands. The implication is that the electoral formula itself may not matter much for trade policy; instead, other features of countries' electoral systems that tend to go together with electoral formulas, such as district size, are important.

District Size

District size may help to explain the apparent protectionist bias in majoritarian countries. A district's size is the number of people living in an average electoral district. District size is assumed to increase with district magnitude (i.e., number of representatives elected in a district). The single-member districts that characterize majoritarian systems are presumed to be smaller than the multimember districts used in PR systems.[8] Smaller districts are understood to produce higher levels of trade protection, because they give protectionists greater influence over elected representatives (e.g., Alt and Gilligan 1994; Mansfield and Busch 1995; McGillivray 2004). McGillivray (2004, 28) provides the following illustrative example. An industry with 100 employees represents 10 percent of the electorate in a district with 1,000 voters. The same industry represents only 0.1 percent of the electorate in a district of 100,000 voters. In the larger district, refusing to protect the industry is unlikely to affect the politician's reelection chances, because the industry is only 0.1 percent of the representative's electorate. Given this, politicians elected from smaller districts are more likely to supply trade protection than politicians elected from larger districts.

Few empirical studies test this claim. One of the only cross-national measures of district size is provided by Hankla (2006). He divides the total number of seats in a country's lower legislative chamber by mean district magnitude and divides that number into the country's total population to estimate the number of people living in each electoral district. This variable most closely measures the concept of district size articulated by McGillivray (2004) and Rogowski (1987). Hankla reports a negative correlation between this measure and import duty coverage ratios: "District size can explain decreases in import duty coverage ratios of more than 3.5 percent" (2006, 1149). In other words, larger districts correspond with lower levels of trade protection, as expected. Similarly, Rogowski (1987) reports a negative correlation between the number of parliamentary constituencies and trade openness. He asserts that the number of electoral districts is "an inverse measure of average constituency size." Rogowski's evidence also suggests that larger districts are associated with lower trade barriers.

A series of studies makes use of the differences in constituency size that occur within the United States. Using tariff votes from the US Senate in the late nineteenth and early twentieth centuries, Hauk (2011) finds that industries concentrated in smaller constituencies receive more trade protection than those located in larger constituencies. In contrast, Karol (2007) finds no correlation between constituency size and protectionism in the United States in recent decades. He concludes that constituency size does not account for the differences in preferences among the House, Senate, and presidency on trade issues.

Although most arguments relate district size to trade protection, it is possible that district magnitude, that is, the number of representatives elected per district, influences trade policy. Single-member districts allow voters to assign credit (or blame) for trade barriers. In multimember districts, however, voters observe the total amount of protection provided to the district but not the amount produced by individual legislators. As a result, voters do not know which of their representatives to credit for providing trade protection (Ashworth and Bueno de Mesquita 2006). Thus, the electoral benefits of providing protection are relatively lower in multimember districts. If many legislators can claim responsibility for a trade policy with local ramifications, each individual's incentives to provide such policies decrease (Lancaster 1986). Politicians in multimember districts may thus provide less trade protection than politicians in single-member districts (Magee, Brock, and Young 1989).

As anticipated by this logic, democracies with single-member districts appear to have more "illegal" trade barriers than those with multimember districts, holding all else constant (Rickard 2010). The number of WTO disputes filed against democracies with single-member districts is 186 percent higher, on average, than against democracies with multimember districts, all else being equal (Rickard 2010). Moving from a multimember district system with seven seats on average to a single-member district system increases the probability of being named as a defendant in a GATT/WTO dispute by more than 6 percentage points in a given year (Rickard 2010). This evidence suggests that district magnitude has a direct effect on trade policy.

District magnitude may also have an indirect effect on trade policy by mediating the influence of electoral formulas. The effects of a proportional electoral formula may depend on the district magnitude (Carey and Shugart 1995; Carey and Hix 2011). When district magnitude is high, electoral systems are relatively more proportional, because smaller parties are more likely to win seats (Cox 1997; Rae 1967; Taagepera and Shugart 1989). A party would need to win more than 25 percent of the vote to guarantee a seat in a three-seat district, but it would need to win only a little more than 10 percent of the vote to guarantee winning a seat in a nine-seat district. The electoral system is likely to be disproportional whenever the district magnitude is small, irrespective of the particular formula used to translate votes into seats. For example, when PR is used in very small districts, as in Australia or Ireland, its effects become similar to those of plurality elections. For this reason, many political scientists, such as Duverger (1964), argue that district magnitude is the single most important dimension by which electoral systems differ.

The Nature of Electoral Competition

District magnitude cannot, however, explain the nature of electoral competition, which has been shown to influence trade policy (Nielson 2003). Electoral competition is characterized as being either candidate centered or party centered (Carey and Shugart 1995). Party-centered competition encourages voters to emphasize their party preference over that for specific candidates. In contrast, candidate-centered competition encourages the voter to see the basic unit of representation as the candidate rather than the party (Shugart 1999, 70).

Candidate-centered electoral competition can emerge from either single-member or multimember districts. In multimember districts with open party lists, voters are able to indicate their preferred party and also their favored candidate within that party. As a result, candidates have incentives to appeal directly to voters. Candidates may go against the interests of their party to curry favor with constituents in their districts. Similar incentives exist in single-member districts, like those in the United States, where candidates are rewarded by voters for bringing pork-barrel projects home to their districts.

In candidate-centered systems, the optimal reelection strategy is to cultivate a personal vote (Shugart 1995). A personal vote occurs when an individual votes based on the characteristics of a particular candidate rather than the characteristics of the party to which the candidate belongs (Carey and Shugart 1995). To develop a personal vote, representatives can provide private or local public goods and services to their geographically defined constituents. Subsidies and other trade barriers are expedient means by which to achieve this goal. As such, trade protection may rise as politicians' incentives to cultivate personal votes increase (Nielson 2003).

Few incentives exist for politicians to cultivate a personal vote in party-centered systems, because voters emphasize their party preferences over those for specific candidates. Closed-list PR systems, for example, engender party-centered competition because voters are not able to express a preference for a particular candidate. Ballot papers in closed-list systems often do not even contain the names of individual candidates. Voters select a party and parties then receive seats in proportion to the number of votes that they obtain. These seats are filled by the party using a predetermined list of candidates. On this list, candidates are rank-ordered by party leaders. Candidates closer to the top of the list are more likely to get a seat in the legislature. Therefore, candidates' best electoral strategy is to work to promote the party's national popularity. Doing so maximizes the party's vote share and candidates' own positions on the party list. Because politicians have few incentives to cultivate personal votes, tariffs will tend to be lower in party-centered systems than in candidate-centered systems (Nielson 2003).

In a sample of eighteen middle-income presidential democracies, Nielson (2003) finds that both collected tariffs and official tariff rates are higher in candidate-centered systems than in party-centered systems. This evidence suggests that the nature of electoral competition influences trade policy. The distinction between candidate- and party-centered systems may prove to be more useful for understanding trade policy outcomes than the PR/majoritarian dichotomy.

Party Strength

The nature of electoral competition is often conflated with party strength.[9] However, these two concepts are distinct. Party strength typically refers to party discipline, which is defined as the ability of a political party to get its legislators to support the policies of the party's leadership. Party discipline is a legislative phenomenon; party-centered competition is an electoral arena phenomenon. Cox (1987) argues in support of the coevolution of these two concepts, but other scholarship shows only a weak relationship between electoral competition and the party-centered nature of the legislature (Martin 2014). Candidate-centered electoral competition exists, for example, in systems with high party discipline, as is the case in Ireland. It is also possible to have low levels of party discipline in party-centered electoral systems (e.g., in South Korea). Scholars must be careful not to conflate party-centered electoral competition with party strength when theorizing about their potential effects on trade policy. Conflating these two concepts adds further confusion to an already muddled field of inquiry.

Party discipline has been proposed as an explanation for the relatively low levels of trade protection in proportional electoral systems (e.g., Rogowski 1987). Such arguments typically assume that PR systems produce disciplined parties that insulate politicians from protectionist interests. However, the origins of party discipline are unclear. While electoral systems may have some effect on party discipline, many other factors also matter, including, for example, regime type, party organization structures, and the allocation of power inside legislatures. In short, proportional electoral rules are neither necessary nor sufficient to engender high levels of party discipline.[10]

Arguments that identify party discipline as a key causal mechanism therefore cannot be tested using measures of proportionality. Instead, it is necessary to develop cross-country indicators of party discipline. Such measures can then be included in empirical models along with measures of countries' electoral formula, subjecting them to various statistical horse races. Empirical tests have been conducted on limited Organisation for Economic Co-operation and Development (OECD) data. Ehrlich

(2007), for example, initially finds that proportional electoral rules have a robust nega-tive effect on tariffs.[11] Specifically, he reports that PR is associated with 7.3 percent lower tariffs in the long run in a sample of twenty-one OECD countries, from 1948 to 1994 (Ehrlich 2007, 595). However, after controlling for party strength (and the number of electoral districts), Ehrlich finds that electoral rules no longer have a robust long-run effect on tariffs. Failing to control for party strength may lead to inaccurate conclusions about the role of electoral rules in trade policy making.

INTERESTS AND INSTITUTIONS

A concluding explanation for the mixed results found to date is that electoral institutions alone cannot explain why some countries are more open to trade than others. Instead, the impact of electoral rules on trade policy may depend on the nature of the electorate, or what Rae called "the surrounding envelope of societal forces" (1971, 167) (Rogowski 1987, 210). Electoral institutions aggregate citizens' interests. Therefore, to fully under-stand the effects of electoral rules on trade policy, it may be necessary to understand voters' economic interests. Although a growing body of literature examines individuals' preferences about trade,[12] such individual-level analyses have not yet been integrated into research on electoral institutions. However, two recent studies link economic inter-ests, electoral rules, and trade policy.

Rickard (2009) argues that the electoral benefits of providing trade protection are jointly determined by a country's electoral rules and voters' preferences regarding trade policy. Voters' preferences about trade are shaped by their mobility. Voters who find it prohibitively costly to move to a new job prefer policies that target protection only to their current industry of employment. In contrast, voters able to move easily between industries are less interested in narrowly targeted protection. Politicians' responsiveness to these demands is a function of a country's electoral system.

Examining the prevalence of countervailing duties and narrow trade barriers alleged to violate WTO rules, Rickard (2009) finds that policy makers in PR systems are more responsive to increases in demand for narrow trade barriers. The implication is that under certain conditions, trade protection will be higher in PR countries than in majori-tarian countries. Specifically, when voter demand for narrow trade barriers is high, pro-tection will be greater in PR countries than in majoritarian countries. When demand for trade protection is low, majoritarian systems will tend to have greater trade protection than PR systems. This study demonstrates how voters' economic interests can help to resolve the debate over which electoral system is most prone to protectionism.

In a subsequent study, Rickard (2012a) argues that the geographic concentration of protectionist interests mediates the impact of electoral rules on trade policy. When pro-tectionists are geographically diffuse, politicians in PR systems will be more responsive to their demands than politicians in majoritarian countries. Governmental spend-ing patterns in fourteen countries over a twenty-year period provide support for this conditional argument. When voters with a shared economic interest in industrial subsidies are geographically diffuse, spending on subsidies constitutes a larger share of government expenditures in PR systems than in majoritarian systems. In contrast, spending on subsidies constitutes a larger share of government expenditures in majoritarian systems when voters with an interest in subsidies are geographically concentrated.[13] In short, the geographic dispersion of protectionist interests provides a potential bridge between two prominent, rival arguments about the effects of electoral systems on trade policy and specifies the conditions under which one is more appropriate than the other. Together, these studies point to the value of considering voters' economic interests and geographic location along with electoral institutions to understand trade policy outcomes.

Going Forward

No consensus exists about which electoral system makes politicians most responsive to protectionist demands. Explanations for the conflicting conclusions reached to date are put forward in this chapter. By means of this discussion, several suggestions emerge for future research. First, trade scholars must take seriously the variation that exists within proportional and majoritarian electoral systems. To this end, an expedient first step would be to move away from using the dichotomous PR/majoritarian variable to "measure" countries' electoral institutions. Credible alternative measures exist (e.g. Gallagher 1991; Johnson and Wallack 2012). However, before adopting an off-the-shelf-measure, researchers should think carefully about precisely what aspect of a country's electoral system matters for trade policy outcomes. The widespread use of the dichotomous PR/majoritarian variable has allowed scholars to obfuscate the exact mechanism linking electoral institutions and trade policy. To advance this research agenda and move beyond the current impasse, scholars need to think carefully about precisely how electoral institutions influence trade policy.

Rather than trying to connect trade policy outputs to broad labels such as "proportional representation," scholars should investigate the connection of policy outputs to theoretically motivated and potentially intervening variables, such as district magnitude. One way to achieve greater clarity empirically would be to specify unique implications of each causal mechanism beyond a simple correlation between electoral rules and trade barriers—for example, by explaining which type of barrier politicians will prefer under different electoral institutions. Alternatively, it would be useful to find cross-country indicators that capture one causal claim or another and use them as independent variables in equations estimating trade protection levels, subjecting them to various statistical horse races.[14]

One way to shed new empirical light on potential causal mechanisms is to isolate the effects of specific institutions, as suggested above. Investigating institutions individually helps identify which dimensions of institutions matter for which outcomes. This type of knowledge will enable better theories of institutions to be developed and practical policy recommendations to emerge (Taagepera and Qvortrup 2011, 654–655). The strategy of "unbundling institutions"—that is, understanding the role of specific components of the broad bundle of laws and regulations that make up a country's electoral system—may be critically important.

An alternative approach is to consider the combined effect of "institutional bundles" in an effort to build a general theory that can incorporate multiple institutional differences within a single dimension. Several such general theories exist, such as veto players (Tsebelis 2011) and access points (Ehrlich 2007). These theories incorporate the effects not only of electoral institutions but of other institutional features as well, such as the executive-legislative relationship and the policy-making bureaucracy. For scholars interested specifically in the effect of electoral institutions on policy outcomes, additional work is needed. Future research may make progress by specifying how various features of a country's electoral system work together to influence legislators' electoral incentives and subsequent policy decisions.

Finally, studies of electoral institutions must not neglect the importance of interests. Electoral institutions aggregate interests; therefore, to fully understand the effects of institutions, such as electoral rules, one must understand citizens' economic interests. Important advances have been made in understanding voters' preferences about trade policy.[15] Building on these developments may help engender an improved understanding of the interactive effects of interests and institutions on trade policy.

CONCLUSION

Research on trade and electoral systems has come full circle. Initial arguments linking electoral systems and foreign trade proposed a causal connection that ran from countries' dependence on international trade to leaders' choice of electoral institutions. More recent work assumes that the choice of electoral systems is exogenous to trade. Once instituted, electoral systems are believed to generate incentives for leaders to be more or less responsive to protectionist demands. While these two arguments are not mutually exclusive, they highlight the causal complexities that plague research on this topic.

A requisite question is whether a robust correlation exists between electoral systems and trade policy. No consensus has yet emerged on this issue. However, a second, even more challenging, question exists. Is it possible to assess whether electoral rules "cause" distinct trade policy outcomes, given the myriad unobservable factors that drive the selection of electoral systems and trade policies? Ultimately, to know this we would need to answer the counterfactual question: If we picked a country at random and went back in history to change its electoral rules, how would this alter its current trade policies? The problem, of course, is that we cannot observe the relevant counterfactual.

These difficulties should not lead scholars to abandon research on electoral systems and trade. Understanding how a fundamental democratic institution influences policy outcomes is an important and valuable research agenda. Besides, there is still much to be learned from observational data, as demonstrated by the suggestions for future research offered in this chapter. Although observational data do not typically identify causal effects, they can uncover interesting patterns and robust relationships, which can then be used as valuable inputs into theory building. Armed with better theories about precisely how and why electoral systems might affect trade policy, scholars can then work to empirically identify causal effects, using, for example, within-country changes in electoral institutions.

Notes

1. See Rickard (2012c) for a discussion of how these fiscal effects matter for governments facing tight budget constraints.
2. However, Persson and Tabellini (2003) make the opposite claim.
3. However, trade barriers in GATT/WTO disputes are coded as being either narrow or broad based on a set of criteria in Rickard (2010).
4. On this point, see Kono and Rickard (2014).
5. Some proportional systems do not employ any type of party list. In single transferable vote systems, candidates' names appear on the ballot, often in alphabetical order, and voters rank at least one candidate in order of their own preferences. Candidates who surpass a specified quota of first-preference votes are immediately elected. In successive counts, votes from eliminated candidates and surplus votes from elected candidates are reallocated to the remaining candidates until all the seats are filled (Clark, Golder, and Golder 2012, 578).
6. See, for example, Rickard (2012b). However, Davis (2012) cautions against such as a strategy, as some of her findings are sensitive to the way in which mixed systems are coded.
7. The notable exception is Rogowski and Kayser (2002).
8. Although all PR systems employ multimember districts, the magnitude of these districts varies significantly from one country to another. In the Netherlands, for example, all 150 of the legislators in the lower chamber are elected from a single, national district. In contrast, Chile elects its legislators in 60 relatively small, two-seat districts. Even allowing for the cross-national variation in the size of multimember districts, single-member districts are on average smaller than multimember districts (Powell and Vanberg, 2000).
9. For example, party discipline is often estimated using variables that capture the distinction between candidate-centered and party-centered competition (e.g., Ehrlich 2007).
10. The strength of parties also varies within majoritarian systems (McGillivray 1997, 2004). For example, national parties in Canada and Great Britain are generally stronger than parties in the United States.
11. McGillivray (1997) finds evidence that strong parties in majoritarian systems provide trade policies favorable to voters in marginal districts.
12. See Kuo and Naoi (current volume) for an excellent review of this literature.
13. In a study of two majoritarian countries, McGillivray (1997) finds that electorally concentrated industries receive higher levels of protection than electorally decentralized industries (602–603).

14. See, for example, Ehrlich (2007). His results suggest that the impact of electoral rules on trade protection is attenuated when party strength and district magnitude are added to the statistical model.
15. As illustrated clearly by Kuo and Naoi's discussion in this volume.

REFERENCES

Alt, James E., and Michael Gilligan. 1994. The Political Economy of Trading States: Factor Specificity, Collective Action Problems and Domestic Political Institutions. *Journal of Political Philosophy* 2 (2): 165–192.

Ardelean, Adina, and Carolyn L. Evans. 2013. Electoral Systems and Protectionism: An Industry-Level Analysis. *Canadian Journal of Economics* 46 (2): 725–764.

Ashworth, Scott, and Ethan Bueno de Mesquita. 2006. Delivering the Goods: Legislative Particularism in Different Electoral and Institutional Settings. *Journal of Politics* 68 (1): 168–179.

Carey, John M., and Simon Hix. 2011. The Electoral Sweet Spot: Low-Magnitude Proportional Electoral Systems. *American Journal of Political Science* 55 (2): 383–397.

Carey, John M., and Matthew Soberg Shugart. 1995. Incentives to Cultivate a Personal Vote: A Rank Ordering of Electoral Formulas. *Electoral Studies* 14 (4): 417–439.

Chang, Eric C. C., Mark Andreas Kayser, and Ronald Rogowski. 2008. Electoral Systems and Real Prices: Panel Evidence for the OECD Countries. *British Journal of Political Science* 38: 739–751.

Chang, Eric C. C., Mark Andreas Kayser, Drew A. Linzer, and Ronald Rogowski. 2010. *Electoral Systems and the Balance of Consumer-Producer Power*. Cambridge, UK: Cambridge University Press.

Clark, William Roberts, Matt Golder, and Sona N. Golder. 2012. *Principles of Comparative Politics*. Washington DC: Sage CQ Press.

Cox, Gary W. 1990. Centripetal and Centrifugal Incentives in Electoral Systems. *American Journal of Political Science* 34: 903–935.

Cox, Gary W. 1987. Electoral Equilibrium under Alternative Voting Institutions. *American Journal of Political Science* 31(1): 82–108.

Cox, Gary W. 1997. *Making Votes Count: Strategic Coordination in the World's Electoral Systems*. Cambridge, UK: Cambridge University Press.

Davis, Christina. 2012. *Why Adjudicate? Enforcing Trade Rules*. Princeton, NJ: Princeton University Press.

De Mesquita, Bruce Bueno, and Alastair Smith. 2005. *The Logic of Political Survival*. Cambridge, MA: MIT Press.

Duverger, Maurice. 1964. *Political Parties: Their Organization and Activity in the Modern State*. Taylor & Francis.

Ehrlich, Sean D. 2007. Access to Protection: Domestic Institutions and Trade Policy in Democracies. *International Organization* 61(3): 571–605.

Evans, Carolyn L. 2009. A Protectionist Bias in Majoritarian Politics. *Economics & Politics* 21: 278–307.

Ford, Robert, and Win Suyker. 1990. Industrial Subsidies in the OECD Economies. OECD Department of Economics and Statistics Working Papers No. 74. Paris: OECD Publications.

Gallagher, Michael. 1991. "Proportionality, Disproportionality and Electoral Systems." *Electoral Studies* 10(1): 33–51.

Gallagher, Michael, Michael Laver, and Peter Mair. 2006. *Representative Government in Modern Europe*. Berkshire: McGraw-Hill.

Grossman, Gene M., and Elhanan Helpman. 2005. A Protectionist Bias in Majoritarian Politics. *Quarterly Journal of Economics* 120: 1239–1282.

Hankla, Charles R. 2006. Party Strength and International Trade A Cross-National Analysis. *Comparative Political Studies* 39 (9): 1133–1156.

Hauk, William R. 2011. Protection with Many Sellers: An Application to Legislatures with Malapportionment. *Economics & Politics* 23 (3): 313–344.

Hays, Jude C. 2009. *Globalization and the New Politics of Embedded Liberalism*. Oxford: Oxford University Press.

Inter-Parliamentary Union. 2013. PARLINE Database. http://www.ipu.org/parline/parline-search.asp

Johnson, Joel W. and Jessica S. Wallack. 2012. "Electoral Systems and the Personal Vote", http://hdl.handle.net/1902.1/17901 V1 [Version]

Karol, David. 2007. Does Constituency Size Affect Elected Officials' Trade Policy Preferences? *Journal of Politics* 69 (2): 483–494.

Katzenstein, Peter J. 1985. *Small States in World Markets: Industrial policy in Europe*. Ithaca, NY: Cornell University Press.

Kono, Daniel Yuichi. 2009. Market Structure, Electoral Institutions, and Trade Policy. *International Studies Quarterly* 53: 885–906.

Kono, Daniel Yuichi, and Stephanie J. Rickard. 2014. Buying National: Democracy and Public Procurement. *International Interactions* 40 (5): 657-682.

Lancaster, Thomas D. 1986. Electoral Structures and Pork Barrel Politics. *International Political Science Review* 7 (1): 67–81.

Lizzeri, Alessandro, and Nicola Persico. 2001. The Provision of Public Goods under Alternative Electoral Incentives. *American Economic Review* 91: 225–239.

Magee, Stephen P., William A. Brock, and Leslie Young. 1989. *Black Hole Tariffs and Endogenous Policy Theory: Political Economy in General Equilibrium*. Cambridge, UK: Cambridge University Press.

Mansfield, Edward, and Marc Busch. 1995. The Political Economy of Nontariff Barriers: A Cross National Analysis. *International Organization* 49: 723–749.

Martin, Shane. 2014. Why Electoral Systems Don't Always Matter: The Impact of "Mega-seats" on Legislative Behavior in Ireland. *Party Politics* 20(3): 467–479.

McGillivray, Fiona. 1997. Party Discipline as a Determinant of the Endogenous Formation of Tariffs. *American Journal of Political Science* 41(2): 584–607.

McGillivray, Fiona. 2004. *Privileging Industry: The Comparative Politics of Trade and Industrial Policy*. Princeton, NJ: Princeton University Press.

Milesi-Ferretti, Gian Maria, Roberto Perotti, and Massimo Rostagno. 2002. Electoral Systems and Public Spending. *Quarterly Journal of Economics* 117: 609–665.

Naoi, Megumi. 2009. Shopping for Protection: The Politics of Choosing Trade Instruments in a Partially Legalized World. *International Studies Quarterly* 53 (2): 421–444.

Nielson, Daniel L. 2003. Supplying Trade Reform: Political Institutions and Liberalization in Middle-Income Presidential Democracies. *American Journal of Political Science* 47 (3): 470–491.

Norris, Pippa. 1997. Choosing Electoral Systems: Proportional, Majoritarian and Mixed Systems. *International Political Science Review* 18 (3): 297–312.

OECD. 1998. *Improving the Environment through Reducing Subsidies*. Paris: OECD.

Persson, Torsten, and Guido Tabellini. 2003. *The Economic Effects of Constitutions.* Cambridge, MA: MIT Press.

Powell, G. Bingham, and Georg S. Vanberg. 2000. Election Laws, Disproportionality and Median Correspondence: Implications for Two Visions of Democracy. *British Journal of Political Science* 30 (3): 383–412.

Rae, Douglas. 1967. *The Political Consequences of Electoral Laws.* New Haven, CT: Yale University Press.

Rickard, Stephanie J. 2010. Democratic Differences: Electoral Institutions and Compliance with GATT/WTO Agreements. *European Journal of International Relations* 16 (4): 711–729.

Rickard, Stephanie J. 2012a. Electoral Systems, Voters' Interests and Geographic Dispersion. *British Journal of Political Science* 42 (4): 855–877.

Rickard, Stephanie J. 2012b. A Non-Tariff Protectionist Bias in Majoritarian Politics: Government Subsidies and Electoral Institutions. *International Studies Quarterly* 56 (4): 777–785.

Rickard, Stephanie J. 2012c. Welfare versus Subsidies: Governmental Spending Decisions in an Era of Globalization. *Journal of Politics* 74 (4): 1171–1183.

Rickard, Stephanie J. 2009. Strategic Targeting the Effect of Institutions and Interests on Distributive Transfers. *Comparative Political Studies* 42 (5): 670–695.

Rogowski, Ronald. 1987. Trade and the Variety of Democratic Institutions. *International Organization* 41: 203–223.

Rogowski, Ronald, and Mark A. Kayser. 2002. Majoritarian Electoral Systems and Consumer Power: Price-level Evidence from the OECD Countries. *American Journal of Political Science* 46: 526–539.

Shugart, Matthew Soberg. 1999. Presidentialism, Parliamentarism, and the Provision of Collective Goods in Less-Developed Countries. *Constitutional Political Economy* 10 (1): 53–88.

Shugart, Matthew, and Martin Wattenberg. 2001. Mixed-Member Electoral Systems: A Definition and Topology. In *Mixed-Member Electoral Systems: The Best of Both Worlds?*, edited by Matthew Shugart and Martin Wattenberg, 9–24. Oxford: Oxford University Press.

Taagepera, Rein, and Matt Qvortrup. 2011. Who Gets What, When, How—Through Which Electoral System. *European Political Science* 11 (2): 244–258.

Taagepera, Rein, and Matthew Soberg Shugart. 1989. *Seats and Votes: The Effects and Determinants of Electoral Systems.* New Haven, CT: Yale University Press.

Thames, Frank C., and Martin S. Edwards. 2006. Differentiating Mixed-Member Electoral Systems Mixed-Member Majoritarian and Mixed-Member Proportional Systems and Government Expenditures. *Comparative Political Studies* 39 (7): 905–927.

Tsebelis, George. 2011. *Veto Players: How Political Institutions Work.* Princeton, NJ: Princeton University Press.

CHAPTER 16

....

AUTHORITARIAN REGIMES

....

DANIEL YUICHI KONO

ALTHOUGH democracy is on the rise, autocracies remain a major part of the global political economy. According to one popular measure, 39 percent of countries were autocratic as of 2008,[1] and major trading powers such as China remain under autocratic rule. Moreover, when it comes to trade policy, these autocracies are remarkably diverse. Some, such as Botswana and Namibia, have overall tariff equivalents of less than 1 percent.[2] Others, such as Sudan and Tanzania, have overall rates of protectionism in excess of 50 percent. Trade policies in the rest of the world's autocracies vary continuously across this range. As these figures make clear, autocratic trade policies vary tremendously. Acquiring a full understanding of the global economy thus requires us to ask why autocracies choose to participate (or not) in international trade.

Extant research provides surprisingly few answers to this question. The voluminous literature on regime type and trade shows that autocracies have different trade policies than democracies (e.g., Frye and Mansfield 2004; Kono 2006, 2008; Milner and Kubota 2005; Mansfield, Milner, and Rosendorff 2000, 2002; Tavares 2008; Verdier 1998).[3] Research on electoral institutions and trade shows that democracies themselves differ in important ways (Hankla 2006; Kono 2009; Mansfield and Busch 1995; Nielson 2003; Rogowski 1987).[4] However, neither body of research asks whether or why some autocracies are more open to trade than others. Instead, to the extent that autocracies are considered at all, they are treated as an implicitly homogeneous reference category against which democracies are compared.

This inattention to autocratic trade policy is perhaps less surprising than it seems, as it reflects a more general neglect of politics in authoritarian regimes. As Geddes (1999) notes, the study of autocracies has lagged behind that of democracies, perhaps because the former are less institutionalized and transparent. Whatever the reason, "this focus has left [us]... with few shoulders of giants on which to stand as we try to understand political change in less democratic and less institutionalized settings" (Geddes 1999, 1). Likewise, those studying trade policy in autocracies have few well-developed models on which to build.

This chapter surveys the small but growing literature on trade policy in autocracies. Following Alvarez and colleagues (1996), I define autocracies as regimes that do *not* choose their chief executives and legislatures through regular, contested elections. This is admittedly a residual definition—autocracies are not democracies—but it does highlight what is common to all autocracies while allowing for their diversity. My central question is: Why are some nonelected governments open to international trade, while others are not?

Because I seek to explain variation among autocracies, I largely avoid work that is generic with respect to regime type (e.g., Grossman and Helpman 1994), as well as the extensive literature on regime type and trade (e.g., Frye and Mansfield 2004; Kono 2006, 2008; Milner and Kubota 2005; Mansfield, Milner, and Rosendorff 2000, 2002; Tavares 2008; Verdier 1998), which emphasizes variation across regime types. I say "largely" because this work provides a natural starting point for thinking about autocratic trade policy. I thus begin by considering extensions of this work to autocracies, before moving on to research that focuses on autocracies alone.

Specifically, I consider four sets of factors that may influence autocratic trade policy: economic structure, coalition size, time horizons, and the leader's mode of entry into power. My central conclusion is that while all four factors help explain autocratic trade policy, research on this topic remains largely an extension of earlier work on democracies and regime type. This is not meant as a criticism: research on this topic has barely begun,[5] and scholars have understandably built on well-established and familiar models. Nonetheless, scholars have yet to develop trade policy models that are uniquely tailored to autocracies. Doing so will require trade policy scholars to build on more basic research on authoritarian politics (e.g., Gandhi and Przeworski 2006; Geddes 1999; Magaloni 2006; Svolik 2009; Weeks 2008; Wright 2008a), just as research on democratic trade policy built on earlier work on comparative electoral institutions. This process has only begun, but seems likely to accelerate as trade policy scholars become increasingly familiar with comparative work on authoritarian regimes.

ECONOMIC STRUCTURE

When trying to explain policy outcomes, political scientists are naturally inclined to look to political institutions. If such institutions do not matter, then this chapter's focus on autocracies—an institutional distinction—makes little sense. For precisely this reason, however, it is worth asking whether autocracies really are different. Do autocratic institutions really matter, or are trade policies driven by more fundamental, noninstitutional forces? Much work on the political economy of trade points to the importance of economic structure: factor endowments (e.g., Rogowski 1989), sectoral characteristics (e.g., Grossman and Helpman 1994), and so forth. If trade policy is largely determined by such factors, then there is little need to refer to political institutions or to study autocracies as a distinct group.

In support of this "structural" approach, I note that all political leaders face the same fundamental problem of gaining and maintaining power (Bueno de Mesquita et al. 2003). This requires all leaders to respond to societal demands of various kinds. Political institutions arguably matter because different institutions may subject leaders to different societal pressures. Yet scholars from Marx onward have argued that some pressures are too fundamental for any politicians to ignore. As Alesina and Rodrik (1994, 466) note, "Even a dictator cannot completely ignore social demands, for fear of being overthrown. Thus, even in a dictatorship, distributional issues affecting the majority of the population will influence policy decisions." For example, the Chinese leadership allegedly sets high growth targets to deter popular unrest. More generally, societal pressures may have similar effects in all political systems, if they are sufficiently powerful. If so, then models based on these pressures may explain trade policy in autocracies as well as democracies.

The dominant model in the trade policy literature, Grossman and Helpman's (1994) "protection for sale" model, implies that trade policy variation—specifically, variation across sectors—can be explained by a small number of sectoral characteristics. Protectionism should fall with the elasticity of import demand, rise with the output-import ratio in organized sectors, and fall with the output-import ratio in unorganized sectors. The cross-sector structure of protectionism can thus be explained with very few variables—demand elasticities, output-import ratios, and sectoral organization—all of which are arguably exogenous to political institutions.[6] Tests of the model's predictions find strong empirical support (Gawande and Bandyopadhyay 2000; Goldberg and Maggi 1999).

At first glance the Grossman-Helpman (1994) model appears to describe trade politics in democracies: the frequent references to lobbying and campaign contributions suggest a democratic political process. In fact, however, the model is quite general. The government's objective function is very simple: it maximizes a weighted sum of financial contributions and aggregate welfare. It seems likely that all governments care about these things, and hence that the Grossman-Helpman model is broadly applicable.

Empirical research supports this point. Although initial tests of the model's predictions focused on US trade policy (Gawande and Bandyopadhyay 2000; Goldberg and Maggi 1999), subsequent tests have examined autocracies as well. For example, Mitra, Thomakos, and Ulubasoglu (2002) have tested the model's predictions using Turkish data, both before and after Turkey became a democracy. Their tests support these predictions in both democratic and nondemocratic periods. This suggests that the Grossman-Helpman (1994) model is useful for explaining trade policy in autocracies as well as in democracies.

Another canonical trade policy model, that of Mayer (1984), also points to the importance of economic structure. In this model trade policy is determined by the median voter, whose preferences are in turn determined by her factor ownership and national factor endowments. If the median voter's capital-labor ratio is lower than the national mean, the median voter will seek protectionism for labor-intensive imports but an import subsidy for capital-intensive imports. If the median voter's capital-labor ratio is above the national mean, she will have the opposite preferences.

It may seem odd to refer to Mayer's model (1984) as "structural," since its reliance on the median voter suggests an important role for political institutions. Indeed, Mayer (1984) provides the foundation for several arguments about regime type and trade (Kono 2008; O'Rourke and Taylor 2007; Tavares 2008), a point I return to below. Nonetheless, Mayer specifies precisely how economic variables should affect trade policy, and some research shows that these variables have similar effects across regime types. For example, Dutt and Mitra (2002) extend Mayer to predict that inequality affects trade policy. Since higher inequality increases the distance between the (invariably capital-poor) median voter and the national mean, higher inequality also intensifies the median voter's trade policy preferences. Higher inequality thus leads to higher protectionism in capital-abundant countries but to lower protectionism in capital-scarce countries. Dutt and Mitra (2002) find strong empirical support for this hypothesis. Interestingly, they also find that the inequality-trade policy relationship is much the same in democracies and autocracies. This implies that regime type does not alter the identity of the median "voter"—that is, the person whose political support is crucial to maintaining power[7]—and hence that cross-country variation in trade policy is largely driven by economic factors.

In a study focused on autocracies, Wu (2014) explores this relationship in greater depth. Building on Acemoglu and Robinson (2005) and Boix (2003), Wu notes that rising inequality generates rising demands for redistribution—and possibly for democratization—in dictatorships. Dictators seeking to prolong their rule must respond to these demands in some way, through either increased repression or income redistribution. Assuming Stolper-Samuelson (1941) effects, trade liberalization provides one means for autocrats in labor-abundant countries to redistribute income toward unskilled workers. Empirically, Wu (2014) finds that increases in inequality lead to lower trade openness in labor-scarce autocracies but to higher trade openness in labor-abundant autocracies. He also finds that higher trade openness reduces inequality in autocracies, even after controlling for the former's endogeneity to the latter. This suggests that autocrats indeed liberalize trade in response to popular pressures for income redistribution.

These studies suggest that at least some economic-structural variables affect trade policy similarly in democracies and autocracies.[8] Scholars may thus be able to employ a common set of models to understand trade policy under both regime types. This is worth remembering, as there is much to be said for parsimonious explanations that do not require us to reinvent the wheel. That said, it also seems unlikely that we can fully understand autocratic trade policies without delving into the institutional structure of authoritarian regimes.

First, the large literature on regime type and trade (e.g., Frye and Mansfield 2004; Kono 2006, 2008; Milner and Kubota 2005; Mansfield, Milner, and Rosendorff 2000, 2002; O'Rourke and Taylor 2007; Tavares 2008; Verdier 1998) demonstrates that autocracies have different trade policies than democracies. This alone points to the importance of autocratic political institutions. Second, even the abovementioned work on economic structure indicates important differences across regimes. For example, Mitra,

Thomakos, and Ulubasoglu (2002) find that the Turkish government attached a higher weight to general welfare—that is, adopted lower trade barriers—after Turkey democratized. Hence, while the Grossman-Helpman (1994) sectoral variables explained the cross-industry pattern of protectionism in both autocratic and democratic periods, average protectionism tended to be lower during the latter. This suggests that the weight attached to general welfare—exogenous in the Grossman-Helpman model—is endogenous to political institutions.

Finally, there is evidence that the impact of economic structure itself varies across regime types. Mayer (1984) noted that the identity of the median voter depends on political institutions: she is the median member of society given universal suffrage and complete voter turnout, but the median member of a small elite when the franchise is restricted. Given the nature of real-world income distributions, scholars have taken this to mean that the median voter is capital-poor in democracies but capital-rich in autocracies (Kono 2008; Milner and Kubota 2005; O'Rourke and Taylor 2007; Tavares 2008). If so, then factor endowments should affect trade policy differently under the two regime types: an increase in an economy's capital-labor ratio should lead to higher trade barriers in democracies but to lower trade barriers in autocracies.

As this example suggests, the impact of economic-structural variables may depend on political institutions. This limits our ability to explain autocratic trade policy with economic variables alone. A more complete explanation must take autocracies' institutional structures into account.

COALITION SIZE

Political institutions vary in many ways. Perhaps the most central concept in the vast literature on such institutions is *constituency size*. Put simply, every politician must satisfy some constituency to stay in power. The US president needs the support of half the voting public. Members of Congress require majorities within their electoral districts. Legislators in closed-list proportional representation systems are beholden to party leaders, who in turn must capture the largest possible share of the electorate. Although constituencies are most clearly defined in democracies, autocratic leaders must satisfy constituencies as well, whether the latter are military elites, party members, nobles, or some other group. A key insight from the literature on political institutions is that the size of a leader's constituency affects her policy choices.

One prominent model based on constituency size is Bueno de Mesquita and colleagues (2003) "selectorate model." In this model, leaders seek the support of a "winning coalition," defined as the set of individuals whose support is needed to gain and maintain power. The winning coalition can be small—for example, nobles in a monarchy, military elites in a military dictatorship, party officials in a single-party regime—or large, for example, half the electorate in a democracy. As these examples suggest, democracies tend to have larger winning coalitions than autocracies. According to Bueno de

Mesquita and colleagues, larger winning coalitions induce leaders to provide more public goods, which benefit large groups of people at minimal cost, and fewer private goods, which benefit only a small elite. Democracies should thus provide more public goods than autocracies. Bueno de Mesquita and colleagues employ this logic to explain, inter alia, why democracies are more open to international trade.

Milner and Kubota (2005) apply the concepts—though not the strict logic—of the selectorate model to explain the relationship between regime type and trade policy in developing countries. Following Bueno de Mesquita and colleagues (2003), they note that democracies have larger winning coalitions than autocracies. However, Milner and Kubota's (2005) argument rests more on the income effects of trade policy than on the distinction between public and private goods. As the winning coalition grows larger, it is more and more likely to include unskilled workers, who, in labor-abundant developing countries, should benefit from freer trade (Stolper and Samuelson 1941). Democratization thus induces politicians to adopt the liberal trade policies that benefit unskilled workers.

As the Milner and Kubota (2005) example suggests, constituency-size arguments are often used to explain differences between democracies and autocracies. However, research on electoral institutions demonstrates that constituency size varies within as well as across regime types. Some electoral institutions cause politicians to represent larger constituencies than others: for example, some legislators may represent larger and more heterogeneous electoral districts than others, and popularly elected presidents represent larger districts than individual legislators. Research shows that such variation in constituency size matters for trade policy. As Rogowski (1987) notes, small electoral districts create incentives to protect industries within those districts, since the costs of such protectionism largely fall elsewhere. In contrast, large electoral districts internalize more of the costs of protectionism, thus creating countervailing pressures for liberalization. Lohmann and O'Halloran (1994) formalize this logic, showing that presidents should be more liberal than legislatures because the former represent larger constituencies that bear the costs as well as the benefits of protectionism. Similarly, Nielson (2003) and Hankla (2006)—building on Carey and Shugart (1995)—show that strong party discipline, which induces legislators to cater to larger (party-wide) constituencies, leads to more liberal trade policies.

The works discussed above show, from a variety of perspectives, that constituency size affects trade policy: larger constituencies generally encourage freer trade. They also show that constituency size can vary within as well as across regime types. Therefore it is not surprising that initial attempts to understand autocratic trade policies have rested heavily on the concept of constituency size. In this sense, the early work on trade policy in autocracies is a natural extension of that on democracies.

Such an extension requires an understanding of autocratic institutions: how they vary, and how such variation affects constituency size. Although various scholars have conceptualized autocratic institutions in different ways, studies of autocratic trade policy have relied heavily on Geddes's (1999, 2003) typology of such institutions.[9] I thus preface my discussion of these studies by briefly reviewing this typology.

Geddes (1999, 2003) divides autocracies into three broad subtypes: military, single-party, and personalist. She summarizes these regime subtypes as follows (2003, 51):

> In military regimes, a group of officers decides who will rule and exercises some influence on policy. In single-party regimes, one party dominates access to political office and control over policy, though other parties may exist and compete as minor players in elections.[10] Personalist regimes differ from both military and single-party in that access to office and the fruits of office depend much more on the discretion of an individual leader. The leader may be an officer and may have created a party to support himself, but neither the military nor the party exercises independent decision-making power insulated from the whims of the ruler.

As the last point makes clear, the crucial distinction between personalist regimes and the other two subtypes is one of institutional autonomy. In institutionalized military regimes—for example, Brazil from 1964 to 1985 or Argentina from 1976 to 1983—"senior officers have agreed upon some formula for sharing or rotating power, and consultation is somewhat routinized (Geddes 2003, 52). Likewise, in institutionalized single-party regimes—for example, the Institutional Revolutionary Party in Mexico or Communist parties in Eastern Europe—the party organization "exercises some power over the leader at least part of the time, controls the selection of officials, organizes the distribution of benefits to supporters, and mobilizes citizens to vote and show support for party leaders" (Geddes 2003, 52). In contrast, personalist military rulers (e.g., Rafael Trujillo in the Dominican Republic; Idi Amin in Uganda) have concentrated power in their own hands and are relatively unconstrained by their militaries, just as personalist party leaders (e.g., Manuel Odria in Peru; Etienne Eyadema in Togo) have effectively monopolized control over their parties. Militaries and parties in personalist regimes are thus subservient to their leaders rather than checking the latter's power.

A fourth regime subtype, not considered by Geddes (1999, 2003), is monarchies, defined by Hadenius and Teorell (2007, 146) as "regimes in which a person of royal descent has inherited the position of head of state in accordance with accepted practice or the constitution." Examples include Saudi Arabia and other "dynastic" Gulf monarchies, "where successors are chosen by a consensus of the royal family" (Hadenius and Teorell 2007, 146). To be a monarchy, dynastic succession must be institutionalized in norms or the constitution: hence, for example, Hadenius and Teorell do not consider North Korea a monarchy, as the father-to-son transitions are not institutionalized but ad hoc. Institutionally, monarchies share aspects of all of Geddes's (1999, 2003) regime subtypes. Like personalist regimes, they often concentrate power in the hands of a single ruler. However, like military and single-party regimes, they transfer power in an orderly manner that requires the support of a well-defined group.

This brief discussion suggests that autocratic regime subtype may influence winning coalition size. Military and single-party leaders are accountable to a wider group of officers or party members, respectively. They should thus have larger winning coalitions than personalist leaders, who are accountable only to themselves. Military and single-party leaders probably also have larger coalitions than monarchs, since the latter require support from only a small group of nobles. Milner and Kubota (2005) and Hankla and Kuthy (2013) build on this insight in their research on autocratic trade policy.

Although Milner and Kubota (2005) focus mainly on the democracy-autocracy distinction, they note that their argument also predicts trade policy differences among autocratic subtypes. Building on Geddes (1999), they argue that single-party dictatorships have the largest winning coalitions, followed by military dictatorships and then by personalist regimes. Given their general argument about coalition size, this implies that single-party regimes should be most responsive to unskilled workers and hence the most liberal. Empirically, they find that single-party autocracies have significantly lower tariffs than personalist regimes, suggesting that coalition size affects trade policy within autocracies as well as within democracies and across regime types.

Hankla and Kuthy (2013) build on this insight, focusing exclusively and in greater depth on variation among autocracies. They argue that more institutionalized autocracies, such as single-party and multiparty regimes, should be more liberal than less institutionalized ones such as monarchies and personalist regimes. Like Milner and Kubota (2005), Hankla and Kuthy (2013) stress the importance of constituency size, arguing that more institutionalized autocracies have larger winning coalitions. Unlike Milner and Kubota (2005), Hankla and Kuthy (2013) distance themselves from Stolper-Samuelson (1941) or any particular model of trade; instead, they argue that protectionism generally provides private goods to concentrated interests, while free trade provides a public good to the economy as a whole, and hence to a majority of people. In this sense, Hankla and Kuthy's argument is both more faithful to the selectorate model and potentially more generalizable to capital-abundant as well as labor-abundant autocracies. Hankla and Kuthy perform a wide range of empirical tests and find that single-party and multiparty regimes are generally more liberal than other autocratic regime types.

Frye and Mansfield (2003) advance a similar argument. Focusing on postcommunist countries, they argue that fragmentation of power in autocracies encourages trade liberalization. Fragmentation of power is "the extent to which a national government includes competing partisan and institutional actors whose agreement is necessary to make policy. These actors include rival branches of government, as well as legislative and executive coalitions involving different political parties" (2003, 639). As Frye and Mansfield note, the degree of fragmentation varies greatly even among nondemocratic regimes.

Fragmentation matters for trade policy because highly concentrated power facilitates protectionist rent seeking by a small elite. In contrast, the fragmentation of power increases the likelihood that policy will also be influenced by groups that gain from liberalization. Although Frye and Mansfield (2003) do not employ the language of constituency size, their argument is essentially the same as that of Rogowski (1987) and Lohmann and O'Halloran (1994): as the government's support coalition grows, it is more and more likely to include groups that are hurt by trade protectionism. Frye and Mansfield (2003) find strong support for this argument, showing that autocracies are more likely to liberalize trade when their power is fragmented than when it is concentrated.

Wu (2013) provides a different perspective on the effects of constituency size in autocracies. Like Milner and Kubota (2005) and Hankla and Kuthy (2013), Wu (2013) starts from the premise that single-party autocracies have larger winning coalitions than other autocratic regime subtypes. However, in contrast to the former scholars, Wu emphasizes the impact of coalition size on the structure rather than the level of trade protectionism. Building on Ehrlich (2007, 2011), Wu (2013) argues that larger coalitions provide more "access points" for interest groups that benefit from protectionism. Large-coalition dictators may thus face pressures for trade liberalization, but they also have incentives to tailor trade policies specifically to those groups that have access. The result is a wedge between tariffs for coalition insiders and outsiders: the former receive high tariff protection, while the latter do not. Hence, while large-coalition dictatorships may have lower average tariff levels, they should also have higher tariff dispersions. Empirically, Wu finds that single-party autocracies in fact have more dispersed tariffs. This suggests that Ehrlich's (2007, 2011) access point theory can help us understand trade policy in autocracies as well as democracies.

These studies point to the potential importance of coalition size for autocratic trade policies. This is encouraging, as it suggests that the central concept in the study of democracies and regime type also helps explain trade policy in autocracies. However, these studies also raise questions about the causal mechanisms at work. First, because autocracies' winning coalitions are often not explicitly defined, regime subtypes are proxies for coalition size—and, like most proxies, probably exhibit measurement error. Perhaps for this reason, the studies that use these proxies generate empirical anomalies. For example, Milner and Kubota (2005) find that military regimes are (insignificantly) more protectionist than personalist regimes, while Hankla and Kuthy (2013) find that monarchies are as liberal as multiparty regimes and that military and single-party regimes do not differ significantly from each other. In all of these cases, the authors' coalition-size argument predicted a different result. While these anomalies do not undermine the authors' central results, they do raise questions about the mapping between regime subtypes and coalition size, and perhaps about the importance of coalition size itself.

Second, regime subtypes possess other characteristics that covary with coalition size. As discussed below, Hankla and Kuthy (2013) argue that large-coalition regimes also have longer time horizons, which may also encourage trade liberalization. Although this correlation between coalition size and time horizons strengthens the theoretical case for Hankla and Kuthy's predictions, it also raises questions about which features of autocratic subtypes actually drive differences in trade policy.

Despite these caveats, the studies discussed above constitute an important first step toward understanding trade policy in autocracies. The evidence strongly suggests that coalition size affects such policies. More conclusive tests, however, will require scholars to disentangle the effects of coalition size from those of other factors that vary across regime subtypes, such as the time horizons of autocratic leaders.

TIME HORIZONS

Another dimension along which autocratic leaders vary is their time horizons: that is, how long they expect to stay in power. Some autocratic regimes are highly stable, while others exhibit frequent leadership turnover. Scholars have long argued that time horizons affect policy choice in democracies; for example, the proximity of elections may influence macroeconomic policies (Franzese 2002). We might thus expect time horizons to affect autocratic policies as well.

Much work on autocratic time horizons builds on Clague and colleagues (1996) argument about time horizons and property rights. They argue that leaders have short-term incentives to violate property rights by seizing property they can enjoy now. However, they also have long-term incentives to respect property rights, since secure property rights encourage long-run economic growth and higher tax revenues. It follows that leaders' respect for property rights should depend on their time horizons. Short-sighted leaders, who expect to lose power soon, should violate property rights because they will not be around to enjoy the long-term revenue gains from respecting them. In contrast, far-sighted leaders who expect to stay in power should respect property rights to maximize these long-term gains.

Although Clague and colleagues (1996) focus on property rights, their argument should apply more generally to any policies that have different short-run and long-run effects. For example, Wright (2008b) builds on this argument to explore the effects of foreign aid on economic growth. He argues that leaders with short time horizons are likely to spend resources—including foreign aid—in unproductive ways. Not only might they keep this money for themselves, but they also have strong incentives to use it to prolong their rule by repressing or buying off threats to the regime. In contrast, leaders with long time horizons have more freedom and incentive to spend resources in growth-enhancing ways. Wright (2008b) thus hypothesizes, and finds empirically, that foreign aid is more likely to promote growth when given to leaders with long time horizons.

These arguments have implications for trade policy, because the costs and benefits of trade policy are also unevenly distributed over time: the costs are immediate, as trade liberalization causes politically unpopular adjustment costs (Porto and Hoekman 2010), but the benefits are deferred, in the form of longer-term growth and higher potential tax revenues (Edwards 1998; Frankel and Romer 1999; Sachs and Warner 1995). The incentives to liberalize trade should thus depend on leaders' time horizons. Politically insecure leaders should fear the short-term costs of liberalization while discounting the long-term benefits; politically secure leaders should be willing to bear the short-term costs for the sake of long-term gains. Longer time horizons should thus encourage trade liberalization.

Hankla and Kuthy (2013) employ this logic in their study of autocratic subtypes and trade policy. They argue that more institutionalized autocracies, such as single-party and multiparty regimes, are more stable and have longer time horizons than less institutionalized autocracies such as monarchies and personalist regimes. More institutionalized autocracies should thus have more liberal trade policies. Hankla and Kuthy find empirical support for this hypothesis, although their test is indirect: regime subtypes serve as proxies for time horizons. This seems reasonable, as Wright (2008b) finds that single-party regimes are indeed less likely to fail than military, personalist, or monarchical regimes. However, because regime subtypes also have different winning coalitions, it is difficult to say whether Hankla and Kuthy's (2013) results point to the importance of time horizons, coalition size, or both.

Kono and Montinola (forthcoming) test the time-horizons hypothesis more directly, using Wright's (2008b) measure of time horizons. In brief, this measure is based on an analysis of authoritarian regime failure: higher failure probabilities correspond to shorter time horizons. Using various measures of trade policy, Kono and Montinola (forthcoming) find that longer time horizons lead to more liberal trade policies. They also find, however, that foreign aid attenuates this relationship. Because foreign aid helps unstable governments survive, it effectively lengthens their time horizons, thus weakening the relationship between Wright's (2008b) time horizons measure and trade policy. This nonetheless tends to support the posited link between time horizons and trade policy, as foreign aid can be seen as operating primarily through a time-horizons channel.

Like the work on coalition size, research on autocratic time horizons has its roots in earlier work on democracies. The literature on political business cycles has long maintained that short time horizons—induced by the proximity of elections—induce short-sighted macroeconomic policies in democracies (Franzese 2002). Although the factors that influence time horizons in autocracies are different—as are the time horizons themselves—the central intuition is the same.

Where the democratic and autocratic literatures differ is in their degree of theoretical and empirical development. In the literature on democracies, there is widespread agreement that elections are the main determinant of time horizons. This theoretical consensus has allowed scholars to narrow their focus and specify more precisely both the conditions under which elections should matter and how to measure their effects empirically. The political business cycle literature has consequently generated ever more nuanced and context-contingent results (Franzese 2002). In contrast, there is still little consensus about what determines autocratic time horizons. And, while measures like Wright's (2008b) have the advantage of being multidimensional, they also leave us wondering exactly what political circumstances induce short-sighted or far-sighted behavior. It would be useful, in future research, to explore these circumstances in greater depth.

It would be particularly useful to know what causes autocratic time horizons to vary over time. Perhaps the main contribution of the political business cycle literature is that it sheds light on why democratic policies fluctuate. To date, there is no analog in the literature on autocratic trade policy. Hankla and Kuthy (2013) identify regime subtype as a main determinant of time horizons. However, since these subtypes are quite

stable, they cannot explain why autocratic trade policies vary over time. This is important, since autocratic trade policies are in fact quite volatile: for example, the Democratic
Republic of Congo's average tariff fell from 25 percent in 1990 to only 4 percent in 1992,
then jumped back to 34 percent in 1994.[11] Explaining such variation will require more
attention to less stable features of autocratic regimes.

MODE OF ENTRY

Economic structure, coalition size, and time horizons are features of all polities and may
have similar effects across regime types. This conceptual continuity between work on
democracies and autocracies is useful, but it also begs the question of whether and how
autocracies are unique. Svolik (2009, 479) notes at least one way in which autocracies
differ qualitatively from democracies: "[P]olitical power in dictatorships, even when
nominally exercised through political institutions, must be ultimately backed by a credible threat of violence." This is not the case in democracies, where the central political
actors generally obey constitutional rules without being implicitly or explicitly coerced.
Moreover, the threat of violence is not a constant, but varies considerably across space
and time (Svolik 2009). Given this, it is worth asking whether threats of violence affect
trade politics in authoritarian regimes.

Chow and Kono (2014) explore this possibility, developing a model of trade politics in
which coup threats play a central role. They begin by noting that autocratic leaders enter
power in different ways: some enter in "a *regular manner*, according to the prevailing
rules, provisions, conventions and norms of the country," while others enter in "an *irreg-
ular manner*, such as a coup" (Goemans, Gleditsch, and Chiozza 2009, 272–273). Chow
and Kono (2014) refer to the first mode of entry as "legal" and to the second as "extralegal." Both modes of entry are common in autocracies, with extralegal entries accounting
for about 40 percent of autocratic power transitions (Goemans, Gleditsch, and Chiozza
2009). This clearly distinguishes autocracies from democracies, in which essentially all
power transitions are legal.[12]

Why might the mode of entry matter for trade policy? Chow and Kono (2014) argue
that it affects the new leader's vulnerability to coups. All autocrats must fear coup
attempts by other ruling elites. However, the magnitude of this threat depends on the
ruler's ability to identify and neutralize coup plotters through co-optation or repression. This can be difficult to do because, as Svolik (2009, 480) notes, autocratic regimes
are particularly prone to "secrecy and back-channel politics." In other words, autocratic
leaders often do not know who is up to what. In such an environment, knowledge is the
key to survival. Chow and Kono (2014) argue that legal leaders are more knowledgeable
than extralegal ones and hence less vulnerable to coups.

New legal leaders are generally regime "insiders": they emerge from the officer corps
in military regimes, the party leadership in single-party regimes, the royal family in
monarchies, and so forth. They are thus familiar with other ruling elites: who is allied

with whom, who wants what, who can be bought, who must be incarcerated, and so forth. This knowledge helps new legal leaders identify and neutralize coup plotters. In contrast, new extralegal leaders are typically regime "outsiders": they enter power extralegally precisely because they cannot do so under the established regime. Compared with new legal leaders, new extralegal leaders are thus less familiar with the political landscape, less able to neutralize coup plotters, and more vulnerable to attempted coups.

Vulnerability to coups heightens the incentives to placate mass publics, since public unrest increases both the likelihood of coup attempts and the chances that they will succeed (Galetovic and Sanhueza 2000; Powell 2012; Thyne 2010). Extralegal leaders who feel threatened by coups thus have strong incentives to adopt policies—such as trade liberalization—that benefit mass publics. Politicians have understood since Roman times that high prices can lead to protests and riots, and that providing cheap "bread" is one solution to such problems. When high commodity prices in 2007–2008 led to food riots around the globe,[13] many leaders responded to this unrest by using trade policy to reduce prices (World Bank 2008). Chow and Kono (2014) argue, more generally, that leaders worried about coups should discourage public unrest by liberalizing trade.

For these reasons, a leader's mode of entry affects trade policy. Legal leaders who are relatively unthreatened by coups adopt high tariffs to maximize rents. In contrast, extralegal leaders who are vulnerable to coups reduce tariffs, forgoing rents to reduce public unrest and hence to improve their chances of survival. This difference between legal and extralegal leaders is short-lived, however: over time, extralegal leaders accumulate knowledge about other ruling elites, eventually becoming regime insiders. As this happens, they become similar to legal leaders and adopt similar trade policies. Chow and Kono (2014) thus hypothesize that extralegal entries lead to short-term tariff reductions that are reversed as new leaders consolidate their rule. They support this hypothesis with data on average tariffs, the Sachs-Warner (1995) openness measure, and the leader's mode of entry. Their results point to the mode of entry as an important determinant of autocratic trade policy.

Chow and Kono's (2014) main contribution is to incorporate into the study of trade policy the threat of violence that is both central and largely unique to authoritarian regimes. This represents a clear departure from previous work on trade policy in democracies. In addition, because the mode of entry varies over time within regimes, Chow and Kono help explain longitudinal variation in autocratic trade policies. This is also a departure from previous work on autocratic trade policy (Hankla and Kuthy 2013; Milner and Kubota 2005), which focuses on institutions that rarely change over time. That said, Chow and Kono's (2014) model implies that the mode of entry cannot explain persistent cross-national differences among autocratic regimes. Because the effects of extralegal entries diminish rather quickly, countries governed by extralegal leaders are, in the long run, no less protectionist than countries governed by legal leaders.

THE ROAD AHEAD

This chapter has highlighted four sets of variables that may affect trade policy in autocracies: economic structure, coalition size, time horizons, and the autocrat's mode of entry. These factors collectively help explain the level, structure, and changes in protectionism in authoritarian regimes. In this sense, research on trade policy in autocracies is off to a good start. It is also clear, however, that theories of autocratic trade policy have barely begun to move beyond previous work on democracies and regime type. Economic-structural research on autocracies (Dutt and Mitra 2002; Mitra, Thomakos, and Ulubasoglu 2002) is a direct application of Grossman and Helpman (1994) and Mayer (1984). Similarly, research on autocratic coalition size (Hankla and Kuthy 2013; Milner and Kubota 2005; Wu 2013) builds closely on Bueno de Mesquita and colleagues (2003) and Ehrlich (2007, 2011), while work on autocratic time horizons (Hankla and Kuthy 2013; Kono and Montinola, forthcoming) has roots in the democratic political business cycle literature. Although theories about the mode of entry (Chow and Kono 2014) are *sui generis*, they are also at an early stage of development. It thus seems fair to say that scholars have barely begun to develop trade policy models that are uniquely tailored to autocracies.

This is not a criticism, but an acknowledgment of the current state of the field. The first article to focus exclusively on autocratic trade policy was Hankla and Kuthy (2013). This is thus a very new field of study, and one that, understandably, has begun by building on well-established and familiar models. At this point, however, it is possible to do more. Trade policy scholars can now draw on a growing body of "basic" research on autocratic politics. This research illuminates, for example, the factors that promote regime stability (Geddes 1999, 2003), elite power sharing (Svolik 2009), policy concessions and rent sharing between the leader and the opposition (Gandhi and Przeworski 2006), and audience costs (Weeks 2008). The implications of this research for trade policy are not yet clear. However, this was also initially the case for research on democratic institutions. For example, Downs's (1957) median voter theorem did not find its way into trade policy research until the work of Mayer (1984), just as Carey and Shugart's (1995) work on electoral particularism was not applied to trade policy until Nielson (2003) and Hankla (2006). There is always a lag between basic research on political institutions and its application to a specific topic such as trade policy. The task for trade policy scholars is now to give autocracies the same attention that they have historically given to democracies.

NOTES

1. Based on the dichotomous regime type measure developed by Alvarez et al. (1996) and extended by Cheibub, Gandhi and Vreeland (2010).
2. Based on Kee, Nicita, and Olarreaga's (2009) index of overall protection, measured as the ad valorem tariff equivalent of all trade barriers in 2009. Data are available at http://econ.

worldbank.org/WBSITE/EXTERNAL/EXTDEC/EXTRESEARCH/0,,contentMDK:2257
4446~pagePK:64214825~piPK:64214943~theSitePK:469382,00.html.

3. See also Mukherjee, this volume.

4. See also Rickard, this volume.

5. The first article to focus exclusively on autocratic trade policy is Hankla and Kuthy (2013).

6. I say "arguably" because one could also argue that these variables are influenced by political institutions: for example, perhaps a country's institutional structure affects the pattern of sectoral organization. Although such arguments are plausible, the Grossman-Helpman (1994) model itself treats these variables as exogenous to political institutions. For a more detailed discussion of this model, see Goodhart, this volume.

7. Dutt and Mitra (2002) emphasize that the median-voter language is not to be taken literally, but is a metaphor for any political process in which mass pressures are brought to bear.

8. However, in contrast to Dutt and Mitra (2002), Wu (2014) obtains different results for democracies and autocracies.

9. For extensions and refinements of this typology, see, for example, Hadenius and Teorell (2007) and Wright (2008a).

10. As the reference to minor parties suggests, Geddes (1999, 2003) classifies most multiparty autocracies as single-party regimes.

11. Based on World Bank tariff data, available at http://econ.worldbank.org/WBSITE/EXTERNAL/EXTDEC/EXTRESEARCH/0,,contentMDK:21051044~pagePK:64214825~piPK:64214943~theSitePK:469382,00.html (accessed August 28, 2012).

12. Over 98 percent, according to Goemans, Gleditsch, and Chiozza (2009).

13. "The New Face of Hunger," *The Economist,* April 17, 2008.

References

Acemoglu, Daron, and James A. Robinson. 2005. *Economic Origins of Dictatorship and Democracy.* New York: Cambridge University Press.

Alesina, Alberto, and Dani Rodrik. 1994. Distributive Politics and Economic Growth. *Quarterly Journal of Economics* 109 (2): 465–490.

Alvarez, Mike, José Antonio Cheibub, Fernando Limongi, and Adam Przeworski. 1996. Classifying Political Regimes. *Studies in Comparative International Development* 31 (2): 3–36.

Boix, Carles. 2003. *Democracy and Redistribution.* Cambridge, UK: Cambridge University Press.

Bueno de Mesquita Bruce, Alastair Smith, Randolph M. Siverson, and James D. Morrow. 2003. *The Logic of Political Survival.* Cambridge, MA: MIT Press.

Carey, John M., and Matthew S. Shugart. 1995. Incentives To Cultivate A Personal Vote: A Rank Ordering of Electoral Formulas. *Electoral Studies* 14 (4): 417–439.

Cheibub, José Antonio, Jennifer Gandhi, and James Raymond Vreeland. 2010. "Democracy and Dictatorship Revisited." *Public Choice* 143 (1–2): 67–101.

Chow, Wilfred M., and Daniel Yuichi Kono. 2014. Entry, Vulnerability, and Trade Policy: Why Some Autocrats Like International Trade. Working paper.

Clague, Christopher, Philip Keefer, Stephen Knack, and Mancur Olson. 1996. Property and Contract Rights in Autocracies and Democracies. *Journal of Economic Growth* 1: 243–276.

Downs, Anthony. 1957. *An Economic Theory of Democracy.* New York: Harper & Row.

Dutt, Pushan, and Devashish Mitra. 2002. Endogenous Trade Policy Through Majority Voting: An Empirical Investigation. *Journal of International Economics* 58: 107–133.

Edwards, Sebastian. 1998. Openness, Productivity and Growth: What Do We Really Know? *Economic Journal* 108: 383–398.

Ehrlich, Sean D. 2011. *Access Points: An Institutional Theory of Policy Bias and Policy Complexity.* New York: Oxford University Press.

Ehrlich, Sean D. 2007. Access to Protection: Domestic Institutions and Trade Policy in Democracies. *International Organization* 61 (3): 571–605.

Frankel, Jeffrey A., and David Romer. 1999. Does Trade Cause Growth? *American Economic Review* 89 (3): 379–399.

Franzese Robert J. 2002. Electoral and Partisan Cycles in Economic Policies and Outcomes. *Annual Review of Political Science* 5: 369–421.

Frye, Timothy, and Edward D. Mansfield. 2003. Fragmenting Protection: The Political Economy of Trade Policy in the Post-Communist World. *British Journal of Political Science* 33 (4): 635–657.

Frye, Timothy, and Edward D. Mansfield. 2004. Timing Is Everything: Elections and Trade Liberalization in the Postcommunist World. *Comparative Political Studies* 37 (4): 371–398.

Galetovic, Alexander, and Ricardo Sanhueza. 2000. Citizens, Autocrats, and Plotters: A Model and New Evidence on Coups d'Etat. *Economics & Politics* 12 (2): 183–204.

Gandhi, Jennifer and Adam Przeworski. 2006. "Cooperation, Cooptation, and Rebellion Under Dictatorships." *Economics & Politics* 18 (1): 1–26.

Gawande, Kishore, and Usree Bandyopadhyay. 2000. Is Protection for Sale? Evidence on the Grossman-Helpman Theory of Endogenous Protection. *Review of Economics and Statistics* 82 (1): 139–152.

Geddes, Barbara. 1999. Authoritarian Breakdown: Empirical Test of a Game Theoretic Argument. Paper presented at the annual meeting of the American Political Science Association, Atlanta, GA, September.

Geddes, Barbara. 2003. *Paradigms and Sand Castles: Theory Building and Research Design in Comparative Politics.* Ann Arbor: University of Michigan Press.

Goemans, H. E., Kristian Skrede Gleditsch, and Giacomo Chiozza. 2009. Introducing *Archigos*: A Data Set of Political Leaders. *Journal of Peace Research* 46 (2): 269–283.

Goldberg, Penelopi, and Giovanni Maggi. 1999. Protection for Sale: An Empirical Investigation. *American Economic Review* 89: 1135–1155.

Grossman, Gene M., and Elhanan Helpman. 1994. Protection for Sale. *American Economic Review* 84 (September): 833–850.

Hadenius, Axel, and Jan Teorell. 2007. Pathways from Authoritarianism. *Journal of Democracy* 18 (1): 143–157.

Hankla, Charles R. 2006. Party Strength and International Trade: A Cross-National Analysis. *Comparative Political Studies* 39 (9): 1133–1156.

Hankla, Charles R., and Daniel Kuthy. 2013. Economic Liberalism in Illiberal Regimes: Authoritarian Variation and the Political Economy of Trade. *International Studies Quarterly* 57 (3): 492–504.

Kee, Hiau Looi, Alessandro Nicita, and Marcelo Olarreaga. 2009. Estimating Trade Restrictiveness Indices. *Economic Journal* 119 (534): 172–199.

Kono, Daniel Yuichi. 2008. Democracy and Trade Discrimination. *Journal of Politics* 70 (4): 942–955.

Kono, Daniel Yuichi. 2009. Market Structure, Electoral Institutions, and Trade Policy. *International Studies Quarterly* 53 (4): 885–906.

Kono, Daniel Yuichi. 2006. Optimal Obfuscation: Democracy and Trade Policy Transparency. *American Political Science Review* 100 (3): 369–384.

Kono, Daniel Yuichi, and Gabriella R. Montinola. Forthcoming. Foreign Aid, Time Horizons, and Trade Policy. Forthcoming in *Comparative Political Studies*.

Lohmann, Susanne, and Sharyn O'Halloran. 1994. Divided Government and U.S. Trade Policy: Theory and Evidence. *International Organization* 48 (4): 595–632.

Magaloni, Beatriz. 2006. *Voting for Autocracy: Hegemonic Party Survival and Its Demise in Mexico.* New York: Cambridge University Press.

Mansfield, Edward D., and Marc L. Busch. 1995. The Political Economy of Nontariff Barriers: A Cross-National Analysis. *International Organization* 49 (4): 723–749.

Mansfield, Edward D., Helen V. Milner, and Peter Rosendorff. 2000. Free to Trade: Democracies, Autocracies, and International Trade. *American Political Science Review* 94 (2): 305–322.

Mansfield, Edward D., Helen V. Milner, and Peter Rosendorff. 2002. Why Democracies Cooperate More: Electoral Control and International Trade Agreements. *International Organization* 56 (3): 477–514.

Mayer, Wolfgang. 1984. Endogenous Tariff Formation. *American Economic Review* 74 (5): 970–985.

Milner, Helen V., and Keiko Kubota. 2005. Why the Move to Free Trade? Democracy and Trade Policy in the Developing Countries. *International Organization* 59 (1): 107–144.

Mitra, Devashish, Dimitrios D. Thomakos, and Mehmet A. Ulubasoglu. 2002. "Protection for Sale" in a Developing Country: Democracy vs. Dictatorship. *Review of Economics and Statistics* 84 (3): 497–508.

Nielson, Daniel L. 2003. Supplying Trade Reform: Political Institutions and Liberalization in Middle-Income Presidential Democracies. *American Journal of Political Science* 47 (3): 470–491.

O'Rourke, Kevin H., and Alan M. Taylor. 2007. Democracy and Protectionism. In *The New Comparative Economic History: Essays in Honor of Jeffrey G. Williamson*, edited by Timothy J. Hatton, Kevin H. O'Rourke, and Alan M. Taylor, 193–216. Cambridge, MA: MIT Press.

Porto, Guido, and Bernard M. Hoekman, eds. 2010. *Trade Adjustment Costs in Developing Countries: Impacts, Determinants and Policy Responses.* Washington, DC: World Bank.

Powell, Jonathan. 2012. Determinants of the Attempting and Outcome of Coups d'état. *Journal of Conflict Resolution* 56 (6): 1017-1040.

Rogowski, Ronald. 1989. *Commerce and Coalitions: How Trade Affects Domestic Political Alignments.* Princeton, NJ: Princeton University Press.

Rogowski, Ronald. 1987. "Trade and the Variety of Democratic Institutions." *International Organization* 41 (2): 203–223.

Sachs, Jeffrey D., and Andrew Warner. 1995. Economic Reform and the Process of Global Integration. *Brookings Papers on Economic Activity* 1: 1–118.

Stolper, Wolfgang F., and Paul A. Samuelson. 1941. Protection and Real Wages. *Review of Economic Studies* 9 (November): 58–73.

Svolik, Milan W. 2009. Power Sharing and Leadership Dynamics in Authoritarian Regimes. *American Journal of Political Science* 53 (2): 477–494.

Tavares, José. 2008. Trade, Factor Proportions and Politics. *Review of Economics and Statistics* 90 (1): 163–168.

Thyne, Clayton L. 2010. Supporter of Stability or Agent of Agitation? The Effect of US Foreign Policy on Coups in Latin America, 1960–99. *Journal of Peace Research* 47 (4): 449–461.

Verdier, Daniel. 1998. Democratic Convergence and Free Trade. *International Studies Quarterly* 42 (1): 1–24.

Weeks, Jessica L. 2008. Autocratic Audience Costs: Regime Type and Signaling Resolve. *International Organization* 62 (1): 35–64.

World Bank. 2008. Rising Food Prices: Policy Options and World Bank Response. Background Note for the Development Committee 43225 (http://www-wds.worldbank.org/external/default/WDSContentServer/WDSP/IB/2008/04/09/000334955_20080409041811/Rendered/PDF/43225oBRoSecM211081020080Box327353B.pdf).

Wright, Joseph. 2008a. Do Authoritarian Institutions Constrain? How Legislatures Affect Economic Growth and Investment. *American Journal of Political Science* 52 (2): 322–343.

Wright, Joseph. 2008b. To Invest or Insure? How Authoritarian Time Horizons Impact Foreign Aid Effectiveness. *Comparative Political Studies* 41 (7): 971–1000.

Wu, Wen-Chin. 2014. When Do Dictators Decide to Open Trade Regimes? Inequality and Trade Openness in Authoritarian Countries. *International Studies Quarterly*. doi: 10.1111/isqu.12149

Wu, Wen-Chin. 2013. Disguised Protectionism under Authoritarianism: Why Do Some Dictatorships Have Lower But More Dispersed Tariffs? Working paper.

CHAPTER 17

....

DOMESTIC GEOGRAPHY AND POLICY PRESSURES

....

KERRY A. CHASE

In the study of political economy, policy pressures figure prominently. Policy pressures arise because self-interested economic agents have preferences about policies (and correspondingly, policy-making institutions). Stakeholders act on their preferences by politicking on their own or in groups. Whenever government action has the potential to redistribute income, policy making tends to be politicized.

Analytical approaches to policy pressures work from three building blocks. The first is preferences, defined in terms of individual interests; the second is strategies for pursuing these preferences by way of lobbying and collective action; and the third is the aggregation of preferences into policy through the workings of political institutions (Frieden 1999; Lake 2009). Domestic geography can factor in at every step. If the material endowments that shape underlying interests are location specific in some way, geography may influence preference formation. Geography also affects collective action capabilities, helping or hindering efforts to pressure government. If elected office is organized territorially, geography can structure the representation of interests inside political systems.

Political economy research has analyzed the channels through which domestic geography conditions policy pressures and the ultimate effects on policy outputs. Many of these studies touch on geography without engaging it squarely. Only recently have place and space entered the literature more systematically. One author remarks that "the use of geography as an explanatory variable has been underutilized in theories of interest group politics" (Schiller 1999, 770). Fifteen years later progress is evident, yet this research agenda remains young.

Geography shows up in distinctive ways in different lines of research—thus it takes on different meanings. In one perspective, geography is the distribution of economic endowments, or of other locational advantages and disadvantages, across place. This literature carves national landscapes into zones to explain how geographically specialized production shapes policy preferences, forms cleavages, and creates distributional conflict. In a second perspective, geography is about concentration in space. The focus of this research is whether spatial proximity helps common interests exert pressure through collective action. In a third perspective, geography is defined by the electoral map: it is the location of policy pressures in relation to institutional sources of leverage in democratic political systems. These studies assess how the concentration or dispersion of organized interests across electoral units affects political responsiveness to policy pressures.

Because domestic geography is still new to political economy—and rigorous analysis of it is a large-scale data enterprise that demands good measures of underlying concepts, challenges that have held back scholarship—big puzzles persist, and conflicting answers abound. When and why is geography a primary line of cleavage, independent of industry? Is it better for organized interests to be concentrated or dispersed? If concentration is better, then where: in space or in high-leverage electoral districts?

While political economy research generally takes patterns of specialization as given, the study of economic geography provides theoretical and methodological underpinnings. Before turning to policy pressures, this survey begins with a brief synopsis of economic geography.

Economic Geography, Old and New

Geography matters to political economy because economic activities are not evenly distributed in space. Inside countries, as between them, areas differ in endowments, so they specialize in different industries. Natural advantages rooted in local endowments parcel out crop production according to land and climate suitability; mining clusters around resource deposits; logging flourishes in timberlands. To reduce transport costs and prevent spoilage, resource-using enterprises ordinarily bunch near sources of basic inputs—sugar processing near cane and beet fields; wineries alongside vineyards—while producers of many processed foods and beverages disperse for much the same reasons. Industries such as shipbuilding and petroleum refining are often hitched to coastal topography. These forms of natural advantage, dubbed "first-nature geography" because they reflect attributes of the physical environment independent of human activity, are easily understood in the traditional Heckscher-Ohlin trade model.

Stretching the limits of this "old" economic geography, the "new" economic geography, in spotlighting efficiency gains that flow from spatial relationships between economic agents, introduces "second-nature geography." Disciples of the new economic geography point out that economic activity is more concentrated than the neoclassical approach expects; this tendency to localize, they argue, must reflect advantages of proximity between or among firms, workers, and consumers. Without delving into the nuances, one set of approaches, pioneered by Krugman (1991), finds incentives for industries with increasing returns to scale to congregate near consumers to economize on transport costs; over time, these clusters may be self-reinforcing as inward labor migration further enlarges the local market, enhancing the temptation for firms to set up shop close by.[1] Another set of approaches formalizes the insights of Alfred Marshall (1920), who attributed agglomeration to externalities and spillovers from close economic interactions. These gains from proximity generally fall into three categories: advantages of specialized skilled labor pools, which reduce labor costs and deepen labor markets; synergies between downstream producers and upstream suppliers, which increase supply and cut prices for specialized inputs; and knowledge spillovers between firms that use similar technologies or that share common labor requirements.[2]

Empirical appraisals of formal models inspired by the new economic geography have lagged.[3] Studies have documented the unevenness of industrial location across the United States, Europe, and Japan (e.g., Ellison and Glaeser 1997; Brülhart 2001; Kalemli-Ozcan, Sørensen, and Yosha 2003). Others assess the relative importance of natural advantage, increasing returns to scale, and spillovers in variation across industries and time (e.g., Ellison and Glaeser 1999; Kim 1995, 1999). Most pertinent for political economy research is the difficulty of measuring location patterns. Concentration, Krugman (1991, 5) writes, "is the most striking feature of the geography of economic activity," but calculating it is no simple task. Following Krugman's example, many studies use a "location Gini," a Herfindahl index of an industry's regional and national employment shares. Standard concentration indices such as this—though straightforward to compute and relatively manageable in their data requirements—are problematic. These measures do not take account of industrial concentration; thus they cannot distinguish geographic agglomeration from production that is centralized in a few large firms at specific places. More significant for scholars interested in the political effects of industrial location, not its underlying economic causes, geographic areas (however they are defined territorially) differ in economic size, population, and other spatial features that introduce measurement bias.

To overcome these drawbacks, scholars have devised theoretically informed and highly sophisticated geographic concentration measures. The most widely cited, the "dartboard approach" developed by Ellison and Glaeser (1997), controls for variation in the size distribution of plants in an industry and in the size of geographic areas. This index finds that industrial location in US manufacturing looks more centralized than darts thrown aimlessly at a board: well over half of industries are at least somewhat concentrated, and more than a quarter are highly concentrated. Yet the measure presents problems of its own; like the simpler location Gini, it misses neighborhood effects in industry agglomerations that cross spatial aggregates (in the US context, states, counties, and zip codes). This "checkerboard problem" afflicts any measure that neglects proximity in the distribution of economic activities across areal units of analysis—on the figurative checkerboard, there is no way to distinguish congregation in adjacent spaces from opposite ends.

An alternative approach by Busch and Reinhardt (1999) solves the checkerboard problem, calculating concentration around a geographic central point as a negative exponential function of distance. (Their findings are reviewed later in the chapter.) Despite its advantages over other methods, the measure has not found its way into empirical work on economic geography. It has, however, established a new standard for political economy research on domestic geography and policy pressures.[4]

This brief review of economic geography has three important implications for the study of policy pressures. First, economic activity indeed tends to congregate in space; at the same time, the degree of concentration varies across different activities. If domestic geography affects the policy pressures that governments feel, the patterns should be visible in industry and country cross-sections. Second, though more speculatively, geographic concentration—in any theoretical framework—signals some sort of advantage, natural or created. Particularly where clustering reflects increasing returns to scale or location-specific externalities, economic agents are likely to be involved in foreign trade. Economic geography models in fact suggest that the concentration-trade relationship may be self-reinforcing: the more firms and workers congregate, the easier it is to trade; concentrated industries in turn possess unique advantages, which should facilitate exports. If the same economic processes drive both location decisions and trade exposure, then it is reasonable to expect concentrated and nonconcentrated industries to behave differently politically. Third, testing hypotheses about domestic geography and policy pressures requires good measures of the spatial distribution of economic activity. Core concepts such as concentration and dispersion, however, lack clear operational definition. Not only does effective measurement involve large data requirements, but the consideration of space also raises methodological obstacles that continue to complicate empirical studies of location patterns.

If geographic concentration poses methodological challenges for economic geography, it raises even more complications for political economy research, to which this chapter now turns.

GEOGRAPHY AND PREFERENCE FORMATION

The geographic sources of policy preferences are a recurrent theme of pressure group analyses. Gerschenkron (1966) famously spotlights the agricultural lands of Imperial German East Elbia, where the topography favored grain cultivation on big estates, as a champion of higher tariffs. Kindleberger's (1975) classic study of nineteenth-century European trade repeatedly identifies organized interests—not only Manchester textile merchants—by city as well as industry. Another landmark study, by Bauer, Pool, and Dexter (1963), dubbed the seat of the US automotive industry, Detroit, a "hotbed of free traders" for its civic activism on trade issues in the 1950s. Both Manchester and Detroit, like Germany's Junkers, eventually swung over to protectionism amid competitive decline. Yet the linkage of policy preferences with place has a long and rich history. Behind this association are the conjectures that geographic area is synonymous with a dominant industry, a connection drawn from factor endowments or other location-specific traits, and that spatial proximity nurtures common interests, even shared identity, on economic policy questions. In most accounts, the imputation of preferences from place functions as an interpretive scheme not intended for rigorous testing. Only lately have more careful and systematic investigations been undertaken of domestic geography as a source of policy preferences.

The study of sectionalism in the United States provides an example of place as a proxy for preferences. "Historically, preferences regarding the tariff have been geographically determined," O'Halloran (1994, 45) writes of nineteenth-century tariff debates. The notion that trade policy orientations sorted into "politically relevant regional groupings" (Lake and James 1989, 12) is characteristic of analyses of this period. A considerable literature interprets tariff swings in terms of the shifting positions of three geographic sections, the Northeast, South, and Midwest. In the early nineteenth century, northeastern shipping and mercantile interests joined southern planters in opposing tariffs, while midwestern areas favored protectionism. In midcentury these alignments reshuffled, the industrializing North turning to protectionism as the agrarian West allied with the pro-trade South, a union that Lake and James (1989) attribute to the boost in grain exports after Britain's repeal of the Corn Laws. From the Civil War to the 1920s, not only production structures but the party system also organized along sectional lines, creating partisan divisions on tariff issues. According to Hiscox (1999, 682), the interweaving of party and section reflected in protariff capitalists of the Republican Northeast and antitariff agrarians in the Democrats' Solid South "emerges as a consequence of the factoral-regional distinctiveness of party constituencies." Partisan and regional cleavages are likewise apparent in the making of the Smoot-Hawley tariff, though by this time both industry and agriculture were fracturing over tariffs (Eichengreen 1989). Only in the 1930s did partisan conflict—and by implication sectional division—begin to subside as production grew less regionally concentrated, causing regions to converge in their trade profiles, and as party constituencies became more diversified (O'Halloran 1994; Hiscox 1999, 2002).

Geography also features prominently in accounts of US foreign policy. Earlier works by Smuckler (1953) and Rieselbach (1966) consider the geographic insularity of the Great Plains and mountain West a source of political attachment to isolationism after the world wars. Recent research continues this line of thought. Politicians from the Northeast were more inclined to support, and those from the South and West to oppose, military action against Germany in World War I, a division that Fordham (2007) links to wartime changes in state-level exports. During the early Cold War, senators from the Midwest, mountain West, and South were less supportive than northerners of military buildup and overseas commitments, primarily because of regional differences in trade exposure and overseas investment (Fordham 1998). Over a longer time span, Trubowitz (1998, 4) accentuates "America's regional diversity as the most important source of tension and conflict over foreign policy." In his view foreign policy divisions in Congress reflect regional cleavages over the costs and benefits of international economic exchange and national defense programs. After 1890 these rifts split the Republican Northeast and Midwest from the Democratic South; in the 1930s, the pivot of conflict separated coastal areas from the interior; and in the 1960s, new fault lines formed between the traditional manufacturing belt and the Sunbelt. At each turn, sectional and often partisan division in foreign policy attitudes mounted (Trubowitz 1998).

While the historical US context is the focus of many sectional interpretations, this mode of analysis travels more widely. In a study of imperial German tariffs, for example, Schonhardt-Bailey (1998) posits that a regional split between Ruhr heavy industry and Saxon light industry fractured the party system and eventually the historic "marriage of iron and rye" with eastern plantation owners. Her empirical analysis confirms that the industrial regions voted for different parties, while their Reichstag deputies broke over agricultural tariffs after 1879.

All in all, the works referenced in the preceding paragraphs are strongly suggestive of connections between domestic geography and preference formation, even if geography is often incidental to the story. These studies also point to directions for future research. For one thing, policy pressures are rarely observed directly: it is difficult to systematically document collective behavior on the part of regional economic actors, so preferences are generally seen by proxy in political behavior at higher levels, such as legislative voting. More centrally for the relationship between place and preferences, a region—in many of these examples, groupings of ten or more US states, defined less by economic structures than by conventional classifications such as date of statehood or status in the Civil War—is too blunt an indicator for industry location. Not only are the exact boundaries of the three canonical US regions of the pre-1930 period arbitrary, but each was more economically diverse than simplified labels like industrial North or agrarian South can apprehend. Getting at the causal links between geography and policy preferences calls for more exact spatial measurement of economic activity—a demanding task for sure, but a potentially surmountable one with available census data. The cross-referencing of industry-level indicators and electoral districts in Schonhardt-Bailey (1998) is an exemplar in this regard.

One way around the problem of directly observing policy preferences in spatial context is to exploit election referendums and survey-generated data. For example, Irwin (1994) analyzes the British general elections of 1906, in effect a referendum on free trade. His models reveal that areas where export industries and traded goods occupations congregated went strongly for the antitariff party, the Liberals, who carried the election, perpetuating the free-trade policy. Urbatsch (2013) examines Costa Rica's 2007 referendum on the Central American Free Trade Agreement; one result was that districts with more manufacturing workers were more supportive of ratification, a surprise given the country's trade deficit in manufactured goods. Ardanaz, Murillo, and Pinto (2013) use survey responses to evaluate urban-rural cleavages over trade in postcrisis Argentina. They find that respondents from import-competing industrial areas, predominantly the major cities, are less favorable to trade than are respondents from the agricultural hinterlands, where import exposure is lower. This suggests that trade policy attitudes are specific to place as much as to industry, at least in contemporary Argentina, where urban workers in both tradable manufactures and nontradable services feel the effects in their food bills.

Other research indicates that geography factors into political backlash against job loss. In the United States, regional disparities are present in the incidence of trade-related layoffs in manufacturing, which have concentrated in the Northeast, Rust Belt, South, and Midwest but have largely bypassed the Great Plains. Higher layoffs, Margalit (2011) finds, reduced votes for the incumbent, George W. Bush, in the 2004 presidential race, but federal Trade Adjustment Assistance for hard-hit areas cushioned these losses at the ballot box. Compared to manufacturing, agglomeration is less common in services; however, geographically concentrated services are more tradable internationally, placing workers in these sectors at greater risk of offshoring. Using a locational Gini index, Jensen and Kletzer (2006) identify the sectors and occupations in which offshoring is easiest. An implication of their study is that job loss should be centralized in the urban areas where service agglomeration is most prevalent. In that case, political reactions—lobbying activity, petitions for administered remedies, or shifts in individual attitudes and voting behavior—may replicate these spatial lines of cleavage. Focusing on a single industry, motion pictures, one of the most heavily traded and densely localized services, Chase (2008) explains that an outmigration of filming from Hollywood set the area's labor groups at odds: low-skilled workers organized to demand policy measures against offshoring, but high-skilled occupations were less inclined to join this campaign.

Close analysis of specific sectors allows more nuanced empirical tests as a complement to the wider national and cross-national studies that dominate political economy scholarship. Sector-level approaches may be especially useful for deepening understanding of trade in services, an area of growing importance. While most services are scattered geographically to be near end markets, a few, such as motion pictures and investment banking, tend to cluster (Kolko 2010). Not only in Hollywood does motion picture production crowd in a central area; in other places too it is highly centralized, for example in France, where the industry bunches in and near the eighth arrondissement of Paris, and in England west of London (Scott 2000). Financial services likewise consolidate in financial centers, and some have persisted as "capitals of capital" for centuries (Kindleberger 1974). In both instances, geographic concentration signals the presence of location-specific externalities of the sort accentuated in the new economic geography. Both sectors are highly exposed to trade, as agglomeration models would expect.

These attributes point to some testable political implications. One is a close identity of interests, hence common preferences, among firms and workers in agglomerations of these sorts. Scott (2000, 4) notes of motion pictures that "producers' individual competitive destinies are all intertwined with one another, which implies . . . that they are also bound together in a sort of de facto political coalition." These coalitions may begin to fray, however, if agglomeration gives way to dispersion, as Chase (2008) intimates about labor-market divisions over offshoring. Another implication is that core-periphery cleavages are likely to be cut between producers housed inside and outside these industrial clusters, suggesting that geography can function as a primary line of cleavage within an industry. In this context, Verdier (1998) posits that the internationalization, amalgamation, and spatial centralization in banking under the gold standard divided money-center banks, which benefited from the concentration of capital, and financial institutions in the hinterlands, which lost out as deposits flowed to the center.[5] Though this hypothesis is not tested directly, it offers a compelling picture of the political rifts that are bound to arise when location differentiates how globalization affects a sector.

Future research could find theoretical footing in the new economic geography or in other theoretical models that give preference formation a spatial component. Most existing studies of place and policy preferences build off factor-based or sector-based trade models. Geography only enters these approaches ad hoc when certain advantages and disadvantages happen (or are believed) to be unevenly distributed in space. Rarely does theoretical work connect geography and preference formation directly. If economic assets are specific both to industry and to place, however, then there should be "a coincidence of spatial economic interests among a region's residents" (Cassing, McKeown, and Ochs 1986, 848). This raises the possibility of within-industry cleavages between producers in different regions, for example at points in the business cycle at which tariff rents are not evenly shared. Suggestive examples exist of regional realignment within US industry, such as the migration of textiles from New England to the Carolinas or of steel mini-mills to the Sunbelt as integrated steelworks suffered Rust Belt decline. Yet the trade preferences of "old" and "new" industrial regions have not been systematically analyzed.

Further theoretical groundwork is needed to add rigor to the study of geography and preference formation. Geography has loosely guided sectional accounts of broad national trends, especially in the history of US foreign economic policy, and impressionistic examples of place as a factor in preferences abound. But a fuller understanding of the locational determinants of policy preferences demands more spatially informed research designs.

GEOGRAPHY AND COLLECTIVE ACTION

Geography has an impact on collective action because the location of economic agents in space influences the capacity to organize in pursuit of common policy goals. The causal linkage between political mobilization and geography originates in Olson's (1971) *Logic of Collective Action*, though geography is nowhere in the study. Olson's insight was that shared interests do not guarantee successful organization; to exert political pressure as a group, individuals with common concerns must first overcome free riding. A favorable policy, in this setup—a tariff, in the canonical example—benefits all producers independent of how much each one contributes to obtaining it. Action on behalf of collective interests therefore resembles a public good, which tempts free riders to contribute less than their fair share in the hopes of partaking of the fruits of others' labor. Interests that cannot effectively monitor contributions and police shirking, Olson (1971, 165) concluded, are fated to be "forgotten groups," consigned to "suffer in silence."

While group size was Olson's focus, concentration dominates the empirical analysis of collective action. Concentrated interests, the thinking goes, have fewer numbers to manage than dispersed ones, aiding the assignment of costs, and each contributor captures a larger share of the gains, making the benefits of the effort easier for all to pocket.

In these ways, concentration aids collective action—a proposition widely accepted before Olson, perhaps most of all through Schattschneider's (1935) demonstration that concentrated producer interests dominated diffuse consumer interests in the making of the historic Smoot-Hawley tariff.

A persistent puzzle is that while concentration helps to mobilize group pressure, it ought to be detrimental to forming majoritarian coalitions in a democracy. Pincus's (1975) analysis of the 1824 Tariff Act in the United States was one of the first to bring geography into the study of collective action. On the one hand, Pincus reasoned, the communications of the time were poor, and interests spread over a wide expanse could not easily find one another; thus potential lobby partners needed to be in close proximity to exchange information, monitor effort, and punish slacking. On the other hand, the interests most favored organizationally would be too narrow to sway many votes. Leaving the apparent contradiction unresolved, geographically concentrated industries received higher tariff rates in the 1824 bill, but so did industries present in many states.

It is conceivable that concentration and dispersion could interact in supportive ways, with concentration helping to mobilize pressure and dispersion increasing the number of legislators who will plead a pressure group's case. An illustrative example is Britain's repeal of the Corn Laws (Schonhardt-Bailey 1991). The core export interest, textiles, was centered in Lancashire County, its bull's-eye the city of Manchester. This localization of textile production concentrated the gains from free trade and the resources to pursue it, spawning a free-trade lobby in the anti–Corn Law League, likewise centralized in Lancashire. But pressure from this one region was not enough to overturn agricultural duties, which required a parliamentary majority.[6] The key to the anti–Corn Law League's ultimate success, according to Schonhardt-Bailey, was the growing industrial diversification of British exports after 1830, hence the wider spread of export interests across parliamentary constituencies. Because of growing textile concentration, which provided financial and organizational backing, and the increased dispersion of other exporters, which turned out the votes on a national basis, "the league had the best of both worlds" (Schonhardt-Bailey 1991, 48).

The coincidence of concentration and dispersion helps to clarify Britain's move to free trade in the 1840s, raising the question of whether coalitions of concentrated and dispersed interests have formed in other settings to pool their political advantages. For any one industry, however, concentration comes at the expense of dispersion and vice versa; it is not possible to have both. At the industry level, the competing implications of concentration versus dispersion have been tested in statistical models of trade protection, but with inconclusive results. Studies focused on the United States find support for one or the other effect, or neither (e.g., Ray 1981; Lavergne 1983; Godek 1985; Gardner 1987; Trefler 1993). Analyses of other countries are equally mixed: geographically concentrated industries receive more trade protection in Australia (Conybeare 1978) and the United Kingdom (Greenaway and Milner 1994), but not in Canada (Caves 1976). In a study of thirty-two democracies, geographic concentration is a statistically significant correlate of trade protection in developed countries; it is not significant, however, for developing countries or in the full sample (Mukherjee, Smith, and Li 2009). In sum, results are sensitive to measurement and model specification, and conflicting findings abound.

Articles by Busch and Reinhardt (1999, 2000, 2005) significantly clarify the terms of the concentration-dispersion debate. The first of these contributions points out three major flaws in earlier research (Busch and Reinhardt 1999). First, authors tend to conflate geographic and political concentration without precisely identifying which effect is being measured and assessed. Geographic concentration in physical space is part of a demand-side explanation of group pressure exerted via collective action, while political concentration across electoral constituencies is a supply-side hypothesis about how political systems react to these pressures in policy outputs.[7] Second, commonly used measures of geographic concentration, by omitting distance, fall prey to the "checkerboard problem" described in the first section; thus they cannot discern whether concentrated interests live side by side. Third, earlier studies neglect conditional relationships between concentration and group size, which raises the possibility that too much political concentration harms a large group less than a small one, even if size, as Olson (1971) suggests, handicaps large groups in collective action.

Unraveling the expected effects of economic concentration and political concentration yields two alternative hypotheses about geography. One proposition, the "close-group" hypothesis, is about organizing costs: it expects close physical proximity among the members of a group to allow greater contact, aid information exchange, facilitate knowledge sharing, and increase the density of social networks, lowering organizational and monitoring costs for the lobbying effort. Geographically concentrated interests, in the close-group hypothesis, are more apt to effectively mobilize pressure, increasing the chances that policy demands translate into outcomes. The other proposition, the "dispersed-group" hypothesis, is about representation: it expects a presence in many constituencies to broaden representation, enhancing the prospects for legislative coalition-building, hence influence, in majoritarian systems. To test the independent effects of each, Busch and Reinhardt (1999) introduce measures to capture concentration on two maps, a spatial one in which distance matters, and an electoral one in which it does not.

The results of their analysis of nontariff barriers in the United States strongly favor the close-group hypothesis: geographically concentrated industries are more likely to obtain import relief than industries that are not concentrated in space. This effect trumps the benefits of political dispersion—as one might expect, given that Congress does not legislate trade remedies, instead delegating this authority to administrative judgment of industry petitions—though it is notable that a few very large, politically concentrated industries receive nontariff barriers as well (Busch and Reinhardt 1999). A follow-up study considers how geographic concentration affects individual-level behavior (Busch and Reinhardt 2000). Using survey data, this inquiry finds that workers in trade-exposed industries are more inclined to have an opinion about trade, contribute to political campaigns, and cast ballots at election time if their industry is geographically concentrated than if it is not. Moving beyond the United States to Europe, a third study shows that higher turnout rates at the polls by workers in geographically concentrated traded goods industries hold up across countries—even in the Netherlands, where the electorate votes as a national constituency rather than for local office (Busch and Reinhardt 2005). These results indicate that the advantages of geographic concentration in amplifying "voice" do not depend on how political systems represent interests; they translate to any electoral setting.

Taken together, these are the strongest conclusions the literature on geographic concentration has produced to date. Still, questions for future research persist. Above all, more direct observation would help to flesh out the causal pathways from proximity to pressure to policy. Convincing evidence tying spatial proximity to effective mobilization would document and explain some kind of behavior taking place at the group level. Existing studies of geography and collective action instead generally rely on policy outputs, such as tariffs or nontariff barriers, to proxy for the pressure that organized groups exert in politics. While this is a sensible way to pit clashing arguments about concentration and dispersion against one another, it assumes that all industries want government assistance, other things being equal, and that they want it in the form that the researcher chooses to study. A standard measure such as nontariff barriers, it is true, may well bias statistical tests against (not in favor of) finding an effect, since industries that do not ask for or obtain import relief count against one hypothesis or the other. Yet it is still worth knowing whether geographically concentrated interests are more inclined to file petitions for import relief, testify at hearings, initiate contacts with legislators, expend funds on lobbying efforts, or vote in blocks. While these variables may harbor their own biases, precise measures of pressure are lacking in this line of research. In the few instances where they have been tried (e.g., Bombardini and Trebbi 2012), the evidence is mixed.

Without direct observation, it is also hard to know whether technological progress affects the geography of collective action. Physical proximity, it stands to reason, was pivotal in the nineteenth century, when common interests had to collaborate to send petitions to the capital or refashion voter rolls nationwide, operations made difficult by poor communications (Pincus 1975; Schonhardt-Bailey 1991). But why should distance continue to inhibit collective action in today's information age? Busch and Reinhardt (2000, 2005) suggest that there remains no good substitute for direct social contact. But their outcomes of interest—opinion formation, campaign contributions, and voter turnout—are individual behaviors with tenuous connections to collective action. Other research concludes that geographically concentrated US industries do not in fact contribute more money to political campaigns, precisely because they have better ways to flex their political muscle, such as lobbying or direct appeals to voters (Grier, Munger, and Roberts 1994; Damania, Fredriksson, and Osang 2004). This raises doubts that individual behavior maps directly into group pressure, just as one might expect in light of Olson's famous theory of conflict between individual and group. Until research takes a closer look at collective action, the close-group hypothesis, though compelling, remains unproven.

GEOGRAPHY AND POLITICAL
REPRESENTATION

Geography has the potential to affect the representation of interests in politics because interests are not evenly scattered across electoral divisions. Whether geography matters for representation and exactly how it matters depends, however, on electoral rules (see Rickard, this volume). In political systems in which elected office is geographically assigned, the location of interests in electoral space is pivotal for office seekers, who must compete for power on a territorial basis. In situations where electoral rules allocate representation according to territory irrespective of population, such as the US Senate or Japan's erstwhile single-nontransferable vote, minority groups—namely farmers in lightly settled rural areas—are reputed to hold sway. On these grounds, Rogowski (2002, 204) adds to the criterion of a territorially defined electorate that "[o]nly in small-district electoral systems does the geographical concentration or dispersion of interests affect their institutional power." Under proportional representation, in contrast, politics are less responsive to geography: candidates for office compete nationally, not locally, and constituencies tend to be larger in size. It is therefore little surprise that research often focuses on the United States, where geographic representation in single-member districts forces members of Congress to pay close attention to the location of interests on the electoral map.

Arguments about geography and representation, like those emphasizing collective action by organized interests, place the "close-group" and "dispersed-group" hypotheses in opposition. In its simplest form, the dispersed-group hypothesis posits that the larger the number of electoral constituencies in which an interest resides, the wider its representation in politics. But clearly dispersion does not translate so easily into influence in politics—bakeries and milk distributors can be present in every district without commanding any one legislator's attention. Thus there is a tension between interests being a wide enough presence nationally for their voices to be heard by more than a few representatives and being a large enough presence in local electorates for representatives to do their bidding (Pincus 1975; Caves 1976; Salamon and Siegfried 1977). On the one hand, larger employment and production shares in a district (or state) give an industry its representative's ear, so Hollywood holds the attention of California's congressional delegation, and the stature of aircraft production in Seattle earned Senator Henry Jackson (D-WA) the memorable moniker "Senator from Boeing." On the other hand, centralization in a few places limits the number of legislators pleading an industry's case, necessitating coalition-building to secure patronage. Viewed in this way, the most successful interests must be large industries whose voting strength is geographically dispersed enough to command extensive concern in the legislature—turning on its head Olson's pronouncement about the advantages of small groups and concentration. An excellent example of this sort is the US steel industry.[8]

One resolution to the concentration versus dispersion trade-off is to split the difference. Moderately concentrated industries are dispersed enough to be present in many electoral districts and also concentrated enough to have clout with their elected representatives. Thus it pays to be concentrated, but not too concentrated. Rogowski (2002) measures employment concentration across congressional districts and finds that industries widely thought to be influential in politics, such as automobiles, sugar, and steel, are in fact moderately concentrated. He concludes that the increased geographic dispersion of US industry since 1960 may explain why trade has become more contested in Congress—protectionist pressures are gaining strength as they grow less centralized. Future research might test whether the nonlinear effect of concentration on protection stands up to scrutiny in a larger sample.

Other studies come down more strongly in favor of political dispersion over geographic concentration. In this line of thought, the central factor in political system responsiveness is not how much pressure organized groups can bring to bear; it is how much electoral gain politicians can expect from channeling rewards to certain interests rather than others. McGillivray (2004, 8–9) takes this tack, stating that "politicians do not automatically respond to the loudest demands. They listen to the industries that affect their chances of reelection." From this standpoint, concentrated interests may be able to mobilize pressure, as studies of geography and collective action suggest, but they will lack sufficient representation when electoral rules favor dispersed interests. If the influence effect of political dispersion in fact outweighs the mobilization effect of geographic concentration, then redistributive rewards by government should strongly correlate with the distribution of interests across electoral boundaries, irrespective of their centralization in physical space. McGillivray (2004) finds evidence for this: large, decentralized industries gain higher tariffs in the United States, as do electorally concentrated industries, which hold greater salience with their local representatives.[9]

Where industry is precisely located on the electoral map may matter even more than how dispersed it is. On this count, McGillivray (2004) posits that the effects of industrial location depend on the level of party discipline in the political system. In a strong-party system such as Britain's, parties have powerful incentives to grant assistance to groups concentrated in marginal electorates that are up for grabs in the next election. In a weak-party system such as the United States, alternatively, seniority and committee positions channel redistributive rents to safe seats because these politicians can more credibly promise future vote trades. The evidence confirms that in high-party-discipline Canada, marginal districts receive higher tariffs, whereas in the United States the opposite occurs: districts whose representatives hold greater seniority in office and powerful committee assignments instead receive more protection.[10] Having firms in the district of powerful committee members also increases the chances that an industry will win administered trade relief in the United States (Hansen 1990). Outside the US context, Hankla (2008) finds that increased party centralization in India shifted party patronage to battleground areas for upcoming elections, a pattern that did not emerge when the parties were decentralized. These analyses lend support to the expectation that strong party systems reward electoral marginality, while weak party systems favor proximity to institutional sources of power.

Partisan effects have received less attention. In the aggregate, one study finds, industries concentrated in districts held by the majority party in Congress secure higher tariffs (Fredriksson, Matschke, and Minier 2011). On its face this seems to be further evidence of agenda control, yet attribution is not so easily assigned. Rarely are industrial location and party constituencies both organized along the same geographic lines—at least not today; industry-party overlap may have been more extensive in the past, as the sectional approaches to US foreign economic policy reviewed earlier suppose—so most industries have incentives to cultivate and maintain support across the party spectrum. Yet a handful of US industries do show strong party associations, a byproduct of their centralization in areas with little party competition; examples include cotton and tobacco growers in the South and corn and dairy producers in the Midwest (Fordham and McKeown 2003, 535). In these instances, industry-party alliances may form. The consequences of these alliances, however, remain to be fleshed out more fully.

If geography shapes an industry's overall representation in politics and its access to well-placed politicians, then industries will have incentives to build coalitions that accentuate their political strengths and mitigate their shortcomings. How the geography of representation cycles back into lobbying strategies has not been extensively studied. An exception is Schiller (1999), who proposes that industrial location across US states shapes coalition-building. Industries concentrated in populous states, she posits, will be strong in the House through their presence in a number of electoral districts, but weak in the Senate; conversely, industries concentrated in less populous states will be strong in the Senate, where representation is population independent, but weak in the House. To improve the prospects for passing favorable legislation in both chambers, industries with different strengths ought to seek each other out as coalition partners.

Case study evidence lends cautious support to this assertion. In the 1980s the US textile industry, with strong champions in the Senate from the North and South Carolina delegations, joined forces with apparel producers, whose primary backers were northeastern House Democrats. This alliance pushed multiple import quota bills through Congress. However, a counter-coalition of apparel retail and farm exporters—one influential in the House, the other in the Senate—mobilized against quotas, assembling enough votes to block the override of successive presidential vetoes. Lobbying over textile quotas contrasts with the case of steel, whose "more balanced political geography" (Schiller 1999, 379) gave the industry leverage with both parties and in both chambers of Congress, enabling protectionists to "go solo," mobilizing on their own without having to barter compromises with coalition allies.

Even the redistributive policy instruments that governments choose may be an outcome of interactions between industrial geography and political representation. For example, electoral rules and party systems may predispose the use of one set of policy tools over another. In weak-party majoritarian systems, distributionally blunt policies such as tariffs and nontariff barriers make it possible to scatter industry rents nationwide, facilitating the construction of legislative coalitions. High party discipline, however, allows the parties to target constituencies in specific areas where the potential for electoral gain is greatest, for example by allocating subsidies on a regional basis (McGillivray 2004). In that case geographic cleavages are likely to form, not in response to differential demand for redistribution from producers in different areas (e.g., as in Cassing, McKeown, and Ochs 1986), but rather because areas where industry locates differ in their electoral value.

Conclusion

Domestic geography surely matters to the policy pressures that organized interests bring to bear. It matters because interests are unevenly distributed, both in physical space and on the electoral map, and this unevenness filters through multiple channels: preference formation, collective action, and political representation. When it comes to redistribution, we might say, all politics is spatial. Yet research on geography and policy pressures is still in its infancy, and long-standing puzzles persist. Researchers often define geography in different ways, hampering comparison of findings, and empirical work remains largely confined to the US context, where data are easier to obtain and geography is reputed to have its greatest effects.

These shortcomings aside, research on the geographic sources of policy pressures is gaining theoretical and empirical sophistication as better measures are formulated and spatially organized data are more fully exploited. The proliferation of information sources, such as geocoded census results and other geographically referenced indicators, and the enhancement of desktop applications to organize, integrate, and analyze these data augur future advancement in this research agenda. To date, political economy scholarship has not taken maximum advantage of geographic software systems, which hold enormous promise for overcoming challenges that have held back earlier work.[11] Better data and measurement allow for more rigorous empirical tests, resulting in more refined spatial hypotheses and stronger theorizing. With these advances, political economy is poised to develop substantial new knowledge about domestic geography and policy pressures in the years ahead.

Notes

1. For Krugman (1991), this helps to illuminate the historical persistence of the US "manufacturing belt" stretching from the mid-Atlantic coast to the Great Lakes region.
2. These three causes of agglomeration also appear in Krugman (1991). Surveys of the new economic geography include Krugman (1998); Ottaviano and Puga (1998); and Neary (2001).
3. There is nevertheless a large and growing empirical literature on industrial localization and its causes; this section singles out just a few of the highlights. For a survey, see Redding (2010).

4. Another issue is that extant measures of geographic concentration are sensitive to the scale of aggregation, known as the "modifiable areal unit problem," which originates in the arbitrary boundaries that spatial units of analysis impose. As a result, any one industry's geographic concentration relative to others is dependent on the level of aggregation. Some US industries, for example, are more concentrated at the state or county level than at smaller units such as zip codes or metropolitan statistical areas; for others, it is the reverse. See Kolko (2010). For a good portion (though not all) of political economy research, concentration matters only in relation to predefined political aggregates, such as electoral districts, making the modifiable areal unit problem a lesser concern.

5. This core-periphery division appears to characterize lobbying for a central bank in the United States, as the New York City financial elite pushed for the creation of the Federal Reserve while consumer banks in the interior showed little interest in financial reform (Broz 1997).

6. Employment in cotton textiles surpassed 1 percent of the voting population in only 5 percent of electoral districts, so the industry's clout was too limited in Parliament. McKeown (1989, 358–359).

7. This distinction is clear in Pincus (1975), but it was clouded in later empirical studies.

8. Steelworks historically were centralized in a few states with significant numbers of electoral votes (Pennsylvania, Ohio, Illinois, Michigan, and Indiana). This industrial geography earned the industry the backing of a bipartisan caucus in both chambers of Congress dedicated to its interests. Moore (1996) cites recent changes in this industrial geography as the central factor behind "the waning influence of big steel."

9. As noted in the last section, Busch and Reinhardt (1999) qualify this conclusion after testing both economic and political geography in the same model: only a few very large industries reap benefits from electoral dispersion in the setting of nontariff barriers.

10. These results are surprising in light of the heavy time dependence in US tariff rates (see Lavergne 1983). If the interindustry tariff structure persists over decades even as seat holders come and go, then district-level protection may be less responsive to legislator seniority and agenda-setting power than the evidence appears to indicate.

11. Cognate areas of research, particularly studies of elections, redistricting, and ethnic conflict, have used geographic software systems more extensively. These packages offer numerous possibilities, including the ability to geocode spatial data and to match information compiled at different spatial levels; enhanced visualization tools, such as maps overlain with symbols, shading, or coloring to identify spatial patterns; and statistical routines for multilevel modeling and geographically weighted regression analysis. See Tam Cho and Gimpel (2012).

REFERENCES

Ardanaz, M., M. V. Murillo, and P. M. Pinto. 2013. Sensitivity to Issue Framing on Trade Policy Preferences: Evidence from a Survey Experiment. *International Organization* 67: 411–437.

Bauer, R. A., I. De Sola Pool, and L. A. Dexter. 1963. *American Business and Public Policy: The Politics of Foreign Trade*. New York: Atherton Press.

Bombardini, M., and F. Trebbi. 2012. Competition and Political Organization: Together or Alone in Lobbying for Trade Policy? *Journal of International Economics* 87: 18–26.

Broz, J. L. 1997. *The International Origins of the Federal Reserve System* . Ithaca, NY: Cornell University Press.

Brülhart, M. 2001. Evolving Geographical Concentration of European Manufacturing Industries. *Weltwirtschaftliches Archiv* 137: 215–243.

Busch, M. L., and E. Reinhardt. 2000. Geography, International Trade, and Political Mobilization in US Industries. *American Journal of Political Science* 44: 703–719.

Busch, M. L., and E. Reinhardt. 1999. Industrial Location and Protection: The Political and Economic Geography of US Nontariff Barriers. *American Journal of Political Science* 43: 1028–1050.

Busch, M. L., and E. Reinhardt. 2005. Industrial Location and Voter Participation in Europe. *British Journal of Political Science* 35: 713–730.

Cassing, J., T. J. McKeown, and J. Ochs. 1986. The Political Economy of the Tariff Cycle. *American Political Science Review* 80: 843–862.

Caves, R. E. 1976. Economic Models of Political Choice: Canada's Tariff Structure. *Canadian Journal of Economics* 9: 278–300.

Chase, K. A. 2008. Moving Hollywood Abroad: Divided Labor Markets and the New Politics of Trade in Services. *International Organization* 62: 653–687.

Conybeare, J. 1978. Public Policy and the Australian Tariff Structure. *Australian Journal of Management* 3: 49–63.

Damania, R., P. G. Fredriksson, and T. Osang. 2004. Collusion, Collective Action and Protection: Theory and Evidence. *Public Choice* 121: 279–308.

Eichengreen, B. 1989. The Political Economy of the Smoot-Hawley Tariff. *Research in Economic History* 12: 1–43.

Ellison, G., and E. L. Glaeser. 1997. Geographic Concentration in US Manufacturing Industries: A Dartboard Approach. *Journal of Political Economy* 105: 889–927.

Ellison, G., and E. L. Glaeser. 1999. The Geographic Concentration of Industry: Does Natural Advantage Explain Agglomeration? *American Economic Review* 89: 311–316.

Fordham, B. O. 1998. *Building the Cold War Consensus: The Political Economy of US National Security Policy, 1949–51*. Ann Arbor: University of Michigan Press.

Fordham, B. O. 2007. Revisionism Reconsidered: Exports and American Intervention in World War I. *International Organization* 61: 277–310.

Fordham, B. O., and T. J. McKeown. 2003. Selection and Influence: Interest Groups and Congressional Voting on Trade Policy. *International Organization* 57: 519–549.

Fredriksson, P. G., X. Matschke, and J. Minier. 2011. Trade Policy in Majoritarian Systems: The Case of the US. *Canadian Journal of Economics* 44: 607–626.

Frieden, J. A. 1999. Actors and Preferences in International Relations. In *Strategic Choice and International Relations*, edited by D. A. Lake and R. Powell, 39–76. Princeton, NJ: Princeton University Press.

Gardner, B. L. 1987. Causes of US Farm Commodity Programs. *Journal of Political Economy* 95: 290–310.

Gerschenkron, A. 1966. *Bread and Democracy in Germany*. Berkeley: University of California Press.

Godek, P. E. 1985. Industry Structure and Redistribution through Trade Restrictions. *Journal of Law and Economics* 28: 687–703.

Greenaway, D., and C. Milner. 1994. Determinants of the Inter-industry Structure of Protection in the UK. *Oxford Bulletin of Economics and Statistics* 56: 399–419.

Grier, K. B., M. C. Munger, and B. E. Roberts. 1994. The Determinants of Industry Political Activity, 1978–1986. *American Political Science Review* 88: 911–926.

Hankla, C. R. 2008. Parties and Patronage: An Analysis of Trade and Industrial Policy in India. *Comparative Politics* 41: 41–60.

Hansen, W. L. 1990. The International Trade Commission and the Politics of Protectionism. *American Political Science Review* 84: 21–46.

Hiscox, M. J. 2002. *International Trade and Political Conflict: Commerce, Coalitions, and Mobility*. Princeton, NJ: Princeton University Press.

Hiscox, M. J. 1999. The Magic Bullet? The RTAA, Institutional Reform, and Trade Liberalization. *International Organization* 53: 669–698.

Irwin, D. A. 1994. The Political Economy of Free Trade: Voting in the British General Election of 1906. *Journal of Law and Economics* 37: 75–108.

Jensen, J. B., and L. G. Kletzer. 2006. Tradable Services: Understanding the Scope and Impact of Services Offshoring. In *Brookings Trade Forum 2005: Offshoring White-Collar Work*, edited by S. M. Collins and L. Brainard, 75–133. Washington, DC: Brookings Institution Press.

Kalemli-Ozcan, S., B. E. Sørensen, and O. Yosha. 2003. Risk Sharing and Industrial Specialization: Regional and International Evidence. *American Economic Review* 93: 903–918.

Kim, S. 1995. Expansion of Markets and the Geographic Distribution of Economic Activities: The Trends in U.S. Regional Manufacturing Structure, 1860–1987. *Quarterly Journal of Economics* 110: 881–908.

Kim, S. 1999. Regions, Resources and Economic Geography: The Sources of US Regional Comparative Advantage, 1880–1987. *Regional Science and Urban Economics* 29: 1–32.

Kindleberger, C. P. 1974. *The Formation of Financial Centers: A Study in Comparative Economic History*. Princeton Studies in International Finance no. 36. Princeton, NJ: International Finance Section, Department of Economics, Princeton University.

Kindleberger, C. P. 1975. The Rise of Free Trade in Western Europe, 1820–1875. *Journal of Economic History* 35: 20–55.

Kolko, J. 2010. Urbanization, Agglomeration, and Coagglomeration of Service Industries. In *Agglomeration Economics*, edited by E. L. Glaeser, 151–180. Chicago: University of Chicago Press.

Krugman, P. 1998. What's New about the New Economic Geography? *Oxford Review of Economic Policy* 14: 7–17.

Krugman, P. R. 1991. *Geography and Trade*. Cambridge, MA: MIT Press.

Lake, D., and S. James. 1989. The Second Face of Hegemony: Britain's Repeal of the Corn Laws and the American Walker Tariff of 1846. *International Organization* 43: 1–29.

Lake, D. A. 2009. Open Economy Politics: A Critical Review. *Review of International Organizations* 4: 219–244.

Lavergne, R. P. 1983. *The Political Economy of US Tariffs: An Empirical Analysis*. Toronto: Academic Press.

Margalit, Y. 2011. Costly Jobs: Trade-related Layoffs, Government Compensation, and Voting in US Elections. *American Political Science Review* 105: 166–188.

Marshall, A. 1920. *Principles of Economics*. London: Macmillan.

McGillivray, F. 2004. *Privileging Industry: The Comparative Politics of Trade and Industrial Policy*. Princeton, NJ: Princeton University Press.

McKeown, T. J. 1989. The Politics of Corn Law Repeal and Theories of Commercial Policy. *British Journal of Political Science* 19: 353–380.

Moore, M. O. 1996. Steel Protection in the 1980s: The Waning Influence of Big Steel? In *The Political Economy of American Trade Policy*, edited by A. O. Krueger, 73–132. Chicago: University of Chicago Press.

Mukherjee, B., D. L. Smith, and Q. Li. 2009. Labor (Im)mobility and the Politics of Trade Protection in Majoritarian Democracies. *Journal of Politics* 71: 291–308.

Neary, J. P. 2001. Of Hype and Hyperbolas: Introducing the New Economic Geography. *Journal of Economic Literature* 39: 535–561.

O'Halloran, S. 1994. *Politics, Process and American Trade Policy* . Ann Arbor: University of Michigan Press.

Olson, M. 1971. *The Logic of Collective Action: Public Goods and the Theory of Groups* . Cambridge, MA: Harvard University Press.

Ottaviano, G. I. P., and D. Puga. 1998. Agglomeration in the Global Economy: A Survey of the "New Economic Geography". *World Economy* 21: 707–731.

Pincus, J. J. 1975. Pressure Groups and the Pattern of Tariffs. *Journal of Political Economy* 83: 757–778.

Ray, E. J. 1981. The Determinants of Tariff and Nontariff Trade Restrictions in the United States. *Journal of Political Economy* 89: 105–121.

Redding, S. J. 2010. The Empirics of New Economic Geography. *Journal of Regional Science* 50: 297–311.

Rieselbach, L. N. 1966. *The Roots of Isolationism: Congressional Voting and Presidential Leadership in Foreign Policy* . Indianapolis, IN: Bobbs-Merrill.

Rogowski, R. 2002. Trade and Representation: How Diminishing Geographic Concentration Augments Protectionist Pressures in the US House of Representatives. In *Shaped by War and Trade: International Influences on American Political Development*, edited by I. Katznelson and M. Shefter, 181–210. Princeton, NJ: Princeton University Press.

Salamon, L. M., and J. J. Siegfried. 1977. Economic Power and Political Influence: The Impact of Industry Structure on Public Policy. *American Political Science Review* 71: 1026–1043.

Schattschneider, E. E. 1935. *Politics, Pressure, and the Tariff* . New York: Prentice-Hall.

Schiller, W. J. 1999. Trade Politics in the American Congress: A Study of the Interaction of Political Geography and Interest Group Behavior. *Political Geography* 18: 769–789.

Schonhardt-Bailey, C. 1991. Lessons in Lobbying for Free Trade in 19th-century Britain: To Concentrate or Not. *American Political Science Review* 85: 37–58.

Schonhardt-Bailey, C. 1998. Parties and Interests in the "Marriage of Iron and Rye". *British Journal of Political Science* 28: 291–332.

Scott, A. J. 2000. French Cinema: Economy, Policy and Place in the Making of a Cultural-products Industry. *Theory, Culture and Society* 17: 1–38.

Smuckler, R. H. 1953. The Region of Isolationism. *American Political Science Review* 47: 386–401.

Tam Cho, W. K., and J. G. Gimpel. 2012. Geographic Information Systems and the Spatial Dimensions of American Politics. *Annual Review of Political Science* 15: 443–460.

Trefler, D. 1993. Trade Liberalization and the Theory of Endogenous Protection: An Econometric Study of US Import Policy. *Journal of Political Economy* 101: 138–160.

Trubowitz, P. 1998. *Defining the National Interest: Conflict and Change in American Foreign Policy* . Chicago: University of Chicago Press.

Urbatsch, R. 2013. A Referendum on Trade Theory: Voting on Free Trade in Costa Rica. *International Organization* 67: 197–214.

Verdier, D. 1998. Domestic Responses to Capital Market Internationalization under the Gold Standard, 1870–1914. *International Organization* 52: 1–34.

PART V

INTERNATIONAL NEGOTIATIONS AND INSTITUTIONS

....

CHAPTER 18

THE DESIGN OF TRADE AGREEMENTS

....

LESLIE JOHNS AND LAUREN PERITZ

INTRODUCTION

IN recent decades there has been an explosion in the number and importance of preferential trade agreements. As of 2012, more than 250 of these agreements are in effect, and dozens more are under negotiation. Every country in the world has signed at least one, while some have signed more than thirty-five. This increase has prompted many economists and political scientists to analyze the design of trade agreements.

These agreements have a common objective—to promote international trade—and all operate independently of the multilateral trade regime. Yet they vary dramatically in their design. Some preferential trade agreements (PTAs) are bilateral, while others are regional. Some impose shallow trade obligations, whereas others impose deep obligations. Some exist only on paper; others have complex institutions. This variation suggests two questions. First, how does the design of a PTA affect the behavior of its members? Second, what designs are optimal for a given political-economic context?

Our primary objective in this chapter is to distill the existing research on PTA design. Most of this research focuses on the treaty level. That is, scholars have examined how the design of individual treaties shapes state behavior. Our secondary objective is to suggest that future research should consider the design of PTAs at the system level. In addition to studying agreements as isolated "observations" or data points, we should also ask how these agreements interact with one another and with the multilateral trade regime, previously manifested in the General Agreement on Tariffs and Trade (GATT) and now in the World Trade Organization (WTO).

A preferential trade agreement creates legal restrictions on its members' trade policies. Such agreements aim to promote economic integration among member countries by improving market access. For example, the North American Free Trade Agreement (NAFTA) creates a free trade area in which trade barriers are reduced or eliminated on products exchanged among Canada, Mexico, and the United States. In contrast, customs unions like the Andean Community eliminate internal trade barriers and set common tariffs for nonmember countries. Empirical scholars use the term "PTA" in slightly different ways. We use this term to denote any international agreement with limited membership that restricts the trade policies of its members. This inclusive definition covers bilateral and regional agreements, free trade areas, customs unions, common markets, and economic unions (Bhagwati 1993; Krueger 1999; Mansfield and Milner 2012). While these kinds of agreements differ in certain respects, all constrain trade policy in some way.

We adopt a strategic, game-theoretic perspective to examine how a PTA changes the incentives, and hence the behavior, of its members. This perspective allows us to consider the relationship between an institution's design and its effect. We focus on preferential trade agreements because these instruments collectively illustrate broad variation in institutional design. Different design features constrain members in particular ways; we leverage PTA variation to explain their potential effects on countries' behavior. This chapter builds on insights from the literature on the multilateral trade regime. Over time, new design features have been incorporated into the GATT and now the WTO. Scholars have shown how changes in these design elements—flexibility, dispute settlement procedures, scope, and so forth—can influence cooperation among WTO members (Rosendorff and Milner 2001; Rosendorff 2005; Barton et al. 2008; Kucik and Reinhardt 2008). We draw on these insights throughout this chapter, integrating our study of institutional *design* with a discussion of institutional *effects*.

Throughout this chapter we use data from several sources, drawing primarily on the WTO's *Regional Trade Agreements Database,* which includes all preferential trade agreements notified to the WTO between 1951 and 2012. These agreements are reciprocal, meaning that all members commit to granting market access to one another. Because the WTO records the date a PTA enters into force and whether it is active, we are able to approximate the number of agreements in effect at a given time.[1] We supplement this information with data from Mansfield and Milner (2012). In addition, the *Design of Preferential Trade Agreements* data set from Kucik (2012) provides information on many design features—flexibility, dispute settlement procedures, and so forth—for approximately 330 PTAs signed between 1960 and 2008. For a measure of the depth and scope of trade agreements, we refer to two additional data sets: *Reciprocal Trade Agreements in Asia* from Hicks and Kim (2012), which records the depth and pace of trade commitments in sixty-seven Asian trade agreements, and the *World Trade Report 2011,* which is an updated version of the data in Horn, Mavroidis, and Sapier (2010) that documents the scope of a sample of approximately one hundred PTAs.[2]

We begin by focusing on the treaty level. We describe the immense variation in the design of PTAs and examine how this variation shapes the behavior of members. We then step back and examine PTAs at the system level. We show that the proliferation of PTAs has created complex networks of overlapping treaties and ask how these networks might promote or hinder international trade cooperation.

Design Elements

The growing plethora of trade agreements has created immense variation in the design of PTAs. In this section we discuss five major PTA design elements: depth, scope, membership, rigidity, and institutionalization.

Depth

Preferential trade agreements vary in depth, the extent to which a PTA constrains state behavior. Deeper agreements place more significant limits on state behavior. Depth often refers to tariff bindings, which are the highest tariffs that a state can impose while still complying with the agreement. Lower tariff bindings require deeper cooperation because they grant a state less policy discretion.

Depth can also refer to nontariff barriers, including quantitative restrictions. When a state imposes a quantitative restriction, such as an import quota, it limits the quantity of an imported good to protect domestic producers. For example, the United States restricts sugar imports—especially from Mexico and Brazil—to protect US farmers. Many PTAs prohibit quantitative restrictions or limit the circumstances under which they can be used. Deeper agreements impose stricter limits on the use of these restrictions.

Preferential trade agreements also often address regulations that create barriers to trade, such as customs procedures, licensing rules, product standards, and government procurement rules. For example, states often require government entities to purchase goods and services from domestic firms. The American Recovery and Reinvestment Act of 2009 contained a "Buy American" clause that required fund recipients to purchase goods and services from US companies (Uchitelle 2009). Preferential trade agreements often limit government procurement rules like the "Buy American" clause to ensure that foreign firms can compete for government contracts. Nearly 40 percent of trade agreements address government procurement (*World Trade Report* 2011).

In short, deeper agreements have lower tariff bindings and make it more difficult for treaty members to impose nontariff barriers, such as quantitative restrictions and regulations that restrict trade.

Scope

Preferential trade agreements also vary in scope, the number of issue areas covered by the agreement. All PTAs regulate the trade of goods, but not all cover agricultural goods (Davis 2003). Nearly 73 percent of the PTAs in our sample address nontariff barriers on agricultural goods, but these provisions tend to differ significantly from one agreement to the next, reflecting members' domestic political concerns. In addition, roughly half of PTAs regulate the trade of services, such as accounting and telecommunications (*World Trade Report* 2011).

These agreements can also address nontrade issues. Approximately half of PTAs have intellectual property provisions (*World Trade Report* 2011), which typically require members to recognize and protect copyrights, patents, and trademarks. Similarly, many PTAs regulate competition policy (53 percent) by prohibiting monopolies and cartels and protect foreign investment (42 percent) by, for example, requiring expropriating countries to provide compensation to foreign investors. Trade agreements also increasingly address noneconomic issues, such as human rights and environmental protection (Hafner-Burton 2005; Steinberg 2002).[3]

On average, the scope of PTAs has increased over time. Whereas the average PTA in the 1970s regulated nine trade and nontrade issues, the average PTA in the 2000s covers fifteen issues (*World Trade Report* 2011). There is some ambiguity in the empirical literature about the difference (if any) between the depth and scope of a PTA (Horn, Mavroidis, and Sapier 2010; Baccini, Dür and Elsig 2012). From a theoretical perspective, agreements with a broader scope place more constraints on state behavior and therefore require deeper cooperation. We thus consider scope to be one specific form of depth.

Membership

Trade agreements vary in the size of their membership. The majority of PTAs are bilateral, but there are also many important multilateral trade agreements (Mansfield and Milner 2012). These vary dramatically in size. While NAFTA has only three members, the Global System of Trade Preferences among Developing Countries has forty-five. Most multilateral PTAs are regional—they include members from the same geographical area (Baccini and Dür 2012). This is not particularly surprising, because countries tend to trade most with their neighbors.

Some scholars argue that there is a fundamental trade-off between the depth of a treaty and the size of its membership. When an agreement has more members, they argue, it will demand less because the agreement must be acceptable to the state least willing to cooperate. Agreements with more members may thus be shallower than agreements with fewer members (Downs, Rocke, and Barsoom 1998; Gilligan and Johns 2012). Agreements like the Association of South-East Asian Nations (ASEAN) PTA—which has many members and is very shallow—support these arguments. However, many other trading agreements, like the European Union's single market program—which also has many members and is relatively deep—do not. There is thus mixed evidence about whether agreements with fewer members lead to deeper commitments.

The relationship between membership and depth is likely to be influenced by the design of treaty commitments. When a PTA requires all members to commit to a common policy, then more members may lead to shallower commitments following the logic stated above. However, when a PTA allows different members to commit to different policies, then treaties with many members can generate deep cooperation, because the states least willing to cooperate can accept shallow commitments without hindering those states that want to make deeper commitments (Gilligan 2004).

Rigidity

There is also tremendous variation in the rigidity of trade agreements. Flexible agreements sometimes allow states to violate their trading obligations without abrogating the treaty, while more rigid agreements allow few (if any) opportunities for temporary escape. For example, most PTAs contain safeguard rules that allow states to restrict trade if an import surge harms a domestic industry. Preferential trade agreements also often contain antidumping rules, which allow members to impose an additional tax—an antidumping duty—if a domestic industry is harmed by an import that is sold below its normal value. Similarly, roughly 28 percent of PTAs allow states to impose a countervailing duty if a subsidized import harms a domestic industry (Kucik 2012). All three of these mechanisms reduce the rigidity of a PTA.

Even among those treaties that do contain flexibility mechanisms, treaty rules vary dramatically in the criteria and procedures that states must use to restrict trade and in the limits on the duration and magnitude of these restrictions. In the case of safeguards, some treaties require consultations between the importer and exporter before safeguards can be used, whereas others allow states to take unilateral action. In addition, many (but not all) PTAs place strict constraints on the duration and magnitude of safeguard measures (29 percent and 66 percent, respectively). For example, the US-Australian PTA only allows safeguards for two years and limits the size of the safeguard on certain products. By contrast, the Pacific Island Countries Trade Agreement allows four-year renewable safeguard measures and does not limit the size of these safeguards.

Some PTAs—often called "fair trade" agreements—also give states the discretion to restrict trade to accommodate competing values. For example, many European PTAs allow trade restrictions that are "necessary to protect human, animal or plant life or health."[4] Similarly, some PTAs promote labor protection through rules on minimum wages, child labor, and occupational safety (Kim 2012). These provisions all give countries flexibility to balance trade liberalization with other social objectives.

Institutionalization

Finally, PTAs vary widely in their institutionalization. Some treaties simply articulate goals for cooperation, while others create complex bureaucracies and dispute settlement procedures (DSPs).

When PTAs have bureaucracies, members can delegate the authority to modify and create rules (Johns and Pelc 2014). Bureaucracies can also monitor compliance with the treaty. For example, the European Union (EU) is a highly institutionalized customs union with a bureaucratic entity—the European Commission—that monitors policy implementation. The commission publishes annual implementation reports and can file lawsuits against a state that violates its treaty obligations.

Most PTAs also contain DSPs, which are rules for trade disputes among members. These DSPs play a vital role in providing information about state behavior and coordinating informal enforcement of treaty rules (Johns and Rosendorff 2009; Johns 2012).[5] Few scholars have examined DSPs in a comparative context, so there is no standard method for measuring their institutionalization. Some DSPs are relatively informal and only require states to conduct good faith negotiations to resolve their trade disputes. Others allow members to refer disputes to the International Chamber of Commerce—which oversees international arbitration—or the International Court of Justice.

Approximately 70 percent of PTAs currently in force contain formal dispute settlement procedures (Kucik 2012). They usually allow an individual or panel to hear arguments from affected parties and then issue some form of opinion. The DSPs used vary in the selection of individuals or panels, as well as the legal status of the opinion. Some DSPs only allow the individual or panel to make nonbinding recommendations; others allow legally binding rulings. The latter sometimes have implementation procedures to ensure the disputants adopt the decision in a reasonable period of time.

Most scholars believe that more formal DSPs make a treaty more rigid, but they disagree about how the *existence* of DSPs affects rigidity. We believe that this confusion stems from differences in how scholars conceptualize dispute settlement in the absence of formal procedures. Some scholars believe that treaties without DSPs are sustained using grim-trigger punishment, which leads to the total collapse of a treaty if any state commits a single violation. For these scholars, the existence of DSPs reduces rigidity because it provides opportunities for states to violate their substantive treaty obligations without abrogating the agreement (Rosendorff 2005; Rosendorff and Milner 2001). Dispute settlement procedures are therefore more "forgiving" than anarchy. Other scholars assume (usually implicitly) that a treaty without DSPs continues to be in force even if a state violates it. For these scholars, the existence of DSPs increases rigidity because it allows for the punishment of treaty violations that would otherwise be ignored (Goldstein et al. 2000; Smith 2000; Guzman 2002). They believe that DSPs are therefore more "punishing" than anarchy.

IMPACT OF DESIGN ON STATE BEHAVIOR

Because the primary objective of trade agreements is to promote international trade, most trade scholars care inherently about the causal effect of PTAs: the extent to which trade agreements actually increase international trade. As Martin (2013, 605) notes, "[a] causal effect is stated as a counterfactual: how does state behavior in the presence of an institution differ from the behavior that would have occurred in the absence of the institution?" Because it is very difficult, if not impossible, to measure something that has not happened—for example, how much a PTA member would have traded if it were not a PTA member—we must rely on theoretical tools like game theory, which allows us to compare state behavior both with and without a PTA to understand the impact of PTA design on state behavior.

The design of a PTA determines the extent to which a treaty requires a state to change its behavior. Ceteris paribus, a PTA will be more effective when it imposes deep obligations for a broad scope of issues on many members. However, rules can only be effective if member states actually change their behavior. In the short term, PTAs will be more effective when members comply with treaty rules. In the long term, PTAs will be more effective when they create stable regimes that endure over time. In this section we provide a summary of previous research that examines the impact of treaty design on compliance and stability.[6]

Domestic Political Pressure

The study of trade agreements cannot be divorced from domestic politics (Goldstein and Martin 2000). While trade agreements can generate aggregate economic benefits for a society, they have a distributional impact: some domestic groups benefit from trade liberalization while others suffer. This distributional impact means that trade agreements have political implications. When governments negotiate treaties and choose trade policies, they must balance the competing interests of three domestic groups: import-competing industries, exporters, and consumers. Import-competing industries are harmed by trade liberalization because free trade increases market competition. They therefore want their government to impose high tariffs on imported goods. Exporters are not directly affected by their own government's tariffs, but they support trade liberalization if it leads to lower tariffs in other countries, because exporters want to compete in foreign markets. Finally, consumers care about the price of goods and services in their country. Consumers are not directly affected by the tariffs of other countries, but they benefit from the market competition that is created by free trade. Of course the real world is considerably more complex than this simple account, but this basic framework provides insight into the interests competing over trade policy.

The relative political power of these three groups will fluctuate over time. As discussed elsewhere in this volume by Rosendorff, economic factors, such as import surges and changes in foreign production technology, can increase pressure to protect an import-competing industry from foreign competition at the expense of consumers and exporters. Similarly, political factors, such as a closely contested election, can affect the willingness of a government to meet the demands of an import-competing industry. Finally, random and unexpected events—such as floods, droughts, and earthquakes—can also lead governments to temporarily protect domestic industries by imposing trade barriers.

These changes in domestic political pressure from import-competing industries, relative to consumers and exporters, ensure that a leader's incentive to cooperate fluctuates over time. When states negotiate trade agreements, they know that domestic political pressure from import-competing industries will fluctuate in the future. But states cannot perfectly anticipate the amount of future domestic political pressure; they will always be at least somewhat uncertain about the future difficulty of trade cooperation.

PTA Components

Trade agreements must therefore contain at least two elements. First, a treaty must create primary rules that specify appropriate behavior. Some examples of primary rules are tariff bindings, the maximum tariffs that are permissible under the treaty; the prohibition of quantitative restrictions; and government procurement rules. In the following discussion we focus on tariff bindings, but our arguments apply to any primary rule that constrains a government's trade policy. The deeper the treaty, the more it constrains its members. When treaty members follow these primary rules, there is first-order compliance with the treaty.

Second, a treaty must create secondary rules about how members will respond when a member violates its primary obligations. These secondary rules are usually created by dispute settlement procedures.[7] When secondary rules are relatively lax, the treaty is flexible. As secondary rules grow stricter, the treaty becomes more rigid. In the international system, states cannot be compelled to follow a treaty's secondary rules. For example, a state that violates a tariff binding can either abide by a regime's secondary rules or leave the treaty altogether. When treaty members follow these secondary rules, there is second-order compliance with the treaty.

In the following discussion we conceptualize DSPs as imposing a penalty for treaty violations. Penalties can come in many forms, including trade retaliation, equivalent concessions, technical assistance, reputational costs, and even the cost of negotiations and litigation. The specific design of a DSP will affect a state's expected cost of second-order compliance. Rather than modeling specific DSPs, scholars have focused on the underlying concept of rigidity; namely, more rigid treaties make it more costly for a state to violate first-order rules and remain a member of the regime. We therefore model the rigidity of a PTA by the size of the penalty that it imposes for first-order violations.

Equilibrium Behavior with and without a PTA

Absent a cooperative agreement, a leader's optimal action in each period is to choose the tariff that maximizes his or her own one-period utility. This "defection tariff" increases as the domestic political pressure to protect grows larger. Leaders have little incentive

to choose low tariffs, because these will harm their import-competing industries without benefiting their exporters. Consumers prefer low tariffs that reduce the domestic
price of goods and services, but they usually exert less influence than import-competing
industries, which can lobby the government for protection.

When states write trade agreements, they are implicitly "trading" benefits for exporters. When state A lowers its trade barriers, it helps exporters in another state, B, and
harms its own import-competing industries. State A is only willing to do this if, in
exchange, state B lowers its trade barriers, thus benefiting A's exporters. Cooperation
is therefore conditional: one country is only willing to make trade concessions if other
members do so as well. Members may want to allow treaty violations when a state faces
high pressure to protect, but a treaty must impose a penalty for a rule violation, or
members will dissemble about their true political pressure and the treaty will collapse
(Rosendorff and Milner 2001).[8] So a treaty member must make two decisions: (1) Will
it comply with the treaty? and (2) If it does not comply, will it accept the penalty to settle
the dispute or leave the treaty regime?

Many theoretical models generate the equilibrium behavior shown in Figure 18.1.[9]
The horizontal axis represents domestic political pressure to protect, and the vertical axis represents the tariff. The dotted horizontal line shows the tariff binding that is

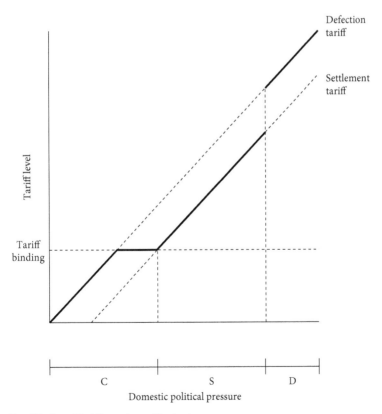

FIG. 18.1 Equilibrium Tariffs under a Trade Agreement.

mandated by the trade agreement. The "defection tariff" line shows the state's optimal tariffs when the PTA is not in effect. The "settlement tariff" line shows the optimal tariffs if a state violates a PTA but then accepts the penalty to settle the resulting dispute and remain a member of the PTA in future periods. The "settlement tariff" line is therefore the "defection tariff" line shifted downward by the penalty amount. The bold line denotes the tariffs that a leader will choose in equilibrium under the trade agreement.

Suppose that domestic political pressure is low. If a leader were to choose the optimal tariff without regard to the country's international obligations, then the tariff he or she would choose (the "defection tariff") is lower than the treaty binding. In such situations, a leader's trade policy is unconstrained by the treaty, and he or she complies. However, as domestic political pressure increases, the defection tariff breaks the binding. To comply with the treaty, the leader will need to choose the tariff binding, as shown by the flat portion of the bold line. The full compliance region is shown in the bottom portion of the figure by region C.

As domestic political pressure grows even larger, leaders are better off violating the binding and then settling under the treaty's dispute settlement procedures. The optimal tariff in these circumstances, the "settlement tariff," rises with the level of domestic political pressure. However, the settlement tariff is always less than the defection tariff, because the treaty's violation penalty tempers the magnitude of treaty violations. The more rigid a treaty is, the larger the violation penalty. The settlement interval is indicated by region S of Figure 18.1.

Finally, if domestic political pressure grows very large, leaders will no longer be willing to settle trade disputes to remain within the treaty regime. It is instead optimal to defect by reverting to the defection tariff and leaving the trade regime altogether. This occurs in region D of the figure.

To understand how depth and rigidity affect the likelihood of full compliance and stability, we must investigate how the design of the treaty affects regions C and D. As region C expands, the likelihood of full compliance increases, because leaders are more likely to choose tariffs at or below their binding. As region D expands, stability decreases because a treaty member is more likely to defect by violating the treaty terms and exiting the regime.

Impact of Depth on State Behavior

When a trade agreement grows deeper, it imposes stricter constraints on its members. For example, a deep tariff binding requires lower tariffs than a shallow binding. As a treaty grows deeper, it thus becomes more difficult for members to comply and, not surprisingly, the likelihood of compliance decreases. This is the primary reason we should not confound the concepts of compliance and effectiveness: if a treaty places few constraints on states, it is unlikely to change behavior, even if we observe

high compliance rates (Downs, Rocke, and Barsoom 1996). In addition, by requiring more from its members a deep treaty makes it more difficult for a state to temporarily violate its obligations and then settle the resulting dispute. If a state breaks
its binding, the magnitude of any violation—the difference between the chosen tariff and the binding—increases as a treaty grows deeper. This in turn makes it more
costly for a state to settle its dispute within the DSP. Accordingly, deeper treaties are
inherently less stable than shallower treaties, because states are more likely to exit
deep treaties.

Figure 18.2 shows the effect of lowering the tariff binding from a shallow to a deep
binding. This makes the agreement more demanding on the member states, because the
treaty requires deeper cooperation. The solid line denotes equilibrium tariffs under the
shallow binding, and the dashed line shows equilibrium tariffs under the deep binding.
As the bottom portion of Figure 18.2 indicates, when the tariff binding grows deeper, the
region of full compliance shrinks from C to $\bar{C}$ and the region of instability (defection)
grows from D to $\bar{D}$. A treaty regime is stable if there is either full compliance or settlement. Trade agreements that demand deeper cooperation thus lead to less compliance
(region C) and less stability (regions C and S combined).

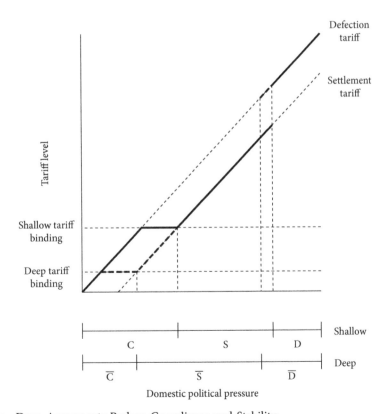

FIG. 18.2 Deep Agreements Reduce Compliance and Stability.

Impact of Rigidity on State Behavior

When a treaty is flexible, it is relatively permissive of occasional defections and imposes only small penalties on treaty violators. As a treaty grows more rigid, it becomes less permissive of these violations and imposes larger penalties on treaty violators. Increasing the rigidity of a treaty thus makes it more costly for a state to violate its binding and then settle the resulting dispute. When a leader faces relatively low domestic political pressure to protect, increasing rigidity makes full compliance more desirable relative to settlement. However, when a leader faces high domestic political pressure, rigidity makes defection more desirable relative to settlement. Rigidity—which makes it more difficult for a state to temporarily violate and then settle—thus increases the probability of full compliance and decreases the stability of the regime.

Figure 18.3 shows the impact of moving from a flexible to a rigid design. The solid line denotes equilibrium tariffs under a flexible agreement, and the dashed line shows equilibrium tariffs under a rigid agreement. The first thing to note is that states choose lower settlement tariffs under the rigid regime: if a state is going to be more severely penalized for a violation, then it will violate less by choosing a lower tariff. For the settlement (S) region of the figure, states do not fully comply with either treaty, but the magnitude of

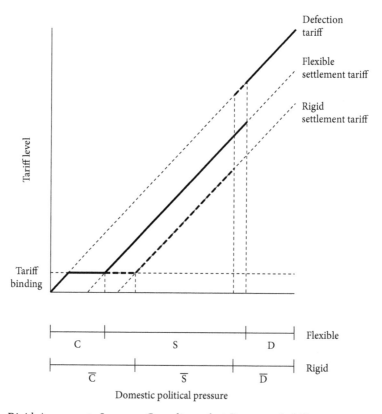

FIG. 18.3   Rigid Agreements Increase Compliance but Decrease Stability.

violations—how much the chosen tariff varies from the tariff binding—is larger under the more flexible treaty. In addition, as rigidity increases, the zones for both full compliance and instability increase (from C to $\overline{C}$ and D to $\overline{D}$, respectively), which demonstrates that rigidity increases the likelihood of full compliance (region C), but decreases stability (regions C and S combined).

The specific design of a trade agreement changes the way its members behave. The overall effectiveness of a treaty in reducing trade barriers is thus determined by the treaty's rules and how states respond to changes in domestic political pressure. This framework does not provide clear predictions about which specific designs will be optimal in promoting trade liberalization. However, it does suggest that the design of a trade agreement should be conditioned, at least in part, on the cost of leaving the treaty regime (Johns 2015).

When a state leaves a treaty, it can no longer expect to receive the benefits of cooperation. Yet some trade agreements are nested in political environments that increase the cost of exit even further. If treaty membership is linked to a multilateral organization, such as the WTO or the EU, exit should be more costly. In such situations treaty designers can worry less about the impact of the treaty design on stability and write trade agreements that are both deeper and more rigid. However, when trade agreements are not nested in such a political context, stability is a greater concern, and treaty designers should thus be more likely to write shallow and flexible treaties.

NETWORKS AND COMPLEXITY

In this section we move to a system-level analysis of trade agreements. As the number of PTAs has increased, an overlapping and complex network has emerged. We examine the interaction among PTAs and ask how this complex network of agreements affects trade liberalization.

PTA Proliferation and Expansion

Preferential trade agreements have proliferated over time. As shown in Figure 18.4, the first PTAs began to appear in the 1950s, and the number of PTAs in force grew at a steady pace until around 1990. After 1990 the number of PTAs exploded. Figure 18.4 also shows that the number of countries participating in at least one PTA has increased over time.[10] European countries have contributed significantly to the proliferation of PTAs, but as of this writing, almost every country is a member of at least one PTA.

Several factors drive the global proliferation of PTAs. These agreements reduce trade barriers and thereby lower the price of imports from member countries, which benefits both exporters and consumers at the expense of import-competing industries. However, PTAs can generate negative externalities for exporters in nonmember

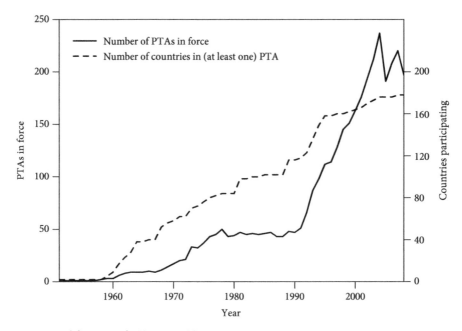

FIG. 18.4   Proliferation of PTAs over Time.

Source: Data from Kucik (2012) and the World Trade Organization
Regional Trade Agreements Database.

states (Chang and Winters 2002). All else being equal, a PTA lowers the profit of
nonmember exporters because they face higher tariffs than their competitors from
member states. Preferential trade agreements with deeper commitments or broader
scope magnify this effect. Economists have shown that such trade diversion—to
members and away from nonmembers—encourages PTA membership (Grossman
and Helpman 1995; Krishna 1996). Moreover, the tariffs applied by PTA members
against nonmembers may be even higher than they were in the absence of the PTA
(Panagariya and Findlay 1996). By granting benefits to members and generating
losses for nonmembers, countries have an incentive to either create new PTAs or join
existing ones.

Some scholars argue that when the membership of a PTA expands, incentives to
join intensify because larger PTAs magnify the trade diversion effect (Hoekman and
Kostecki 2009, 499). Remaining outside the regime becomes more costly. So each
time a country joins a PTA, the pressure on other countries to join increases, creating a "domino effect" (Baldwin 1995). The more countries are involved in a PTA and
the more effective that PTA is at generating in-group advantages, the more appealing it is for nonmembers to accede (Baldwin 2006). The EU exemplifies this "domino effect" of PTA expansion. Originally a trade agreement among six countries, the
European Economic Community went through successive enlargements. By 2007
there were twenty-seven members and several other countries undergoing the accession process.

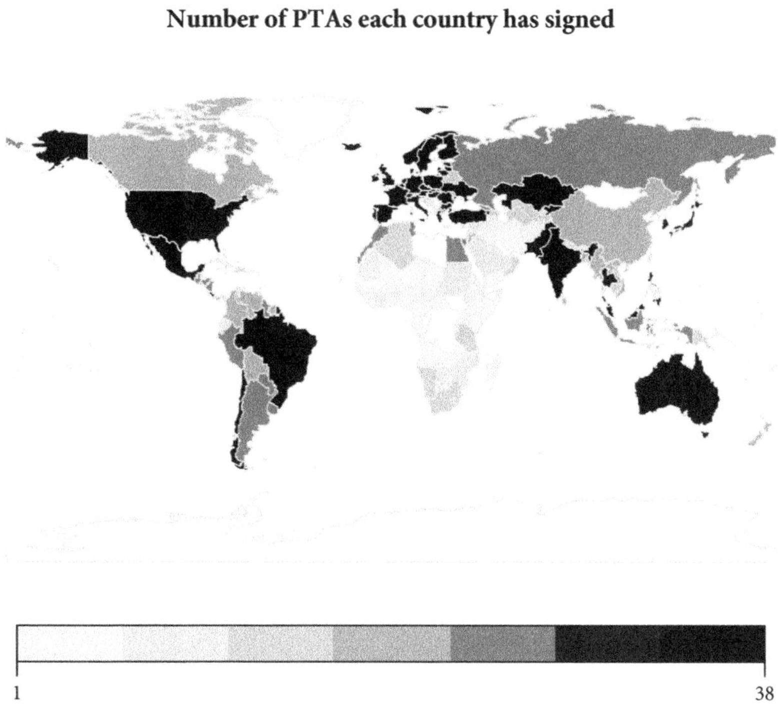

Number of PTAs each country has signed

FIG. 18.5   Density of PTA Membership.

Source: Data from Kucik (2012); image created with R package "rworldmaps."
We only show PTAs in force and notified to the WTO.

As PTAs proliferate and expand, nonmembers also encounter stronger incentives to form their own trade blocs. Some scholars argue that PTA members might limit accession of new members, prompting outsiders to create separate trade agreements (Panagariya 2000). By cooperating with one another, these other countries strengthen their multilateral bargaining position. For example, a primary objective of Mercado Común del Sur (MERCOSUR) was to improve the bargaining power of its members vis-à-vis NAFTA and the EU (Whalley 1998, 72; Bevilaqua, Catena and Talvi 2001, 153). Its members enjoy more bargaining leverage as a group than they would as individuals. Some empirical studies show that MERCOSUR is not a unique case; countries' decisions to form PTAs are highly interdependent (Egger and Larch 2008; Baccini and Dür 2012). Thus membership limits, an important design choice, can affect PTA proliferation.

Network Complexity

As PTAs have proliferated and expanded, a complex network has emerged. While some countries enter only one or two trade agreements, others join many. Figure 18.5 shows global PTA density by country. Darker colors indicate that a country has signed more

PTAs. The most active users of PTAs to date are the European countries, Singapore, India, and Chile.

Much of the recent growth in PTAs is through "hub and spoke" agreements, in which an established trade regime (the "hub") creates separate agreements with other countries outside the regime (the "spokes").[11] These agreements usually vary in the benefits and obligations created for the "spoke" members. For example, the EU functions as a "hub" of members that have committed to a common market. Over time the EU has signed many preferential trading agreements with non-EU countries, including Chile, Korea, and Mexico. These "spoke" arrangements vary widely in their depth, scope, and rigidity, but none impose the same terms as the "hub" agreement. In addition, PTAs sometimes bind together two existing "hub" regimes, like the 2008 agreement between the EU and CARIFORUM, a group of Caribbean countries that have committed to regional integration.

Because each country can be a member of multiple agreements, and some of these agreements are linked to other trade regimes, countries usually have complex and overlapping trade commitments. Figure 18.6 shows the PTA connections for four major ("focal") PTA signatories: the European Union, India, Japan, and the United States. Each of these four members has numerous trade agreements with other countries. For example, the United States has PTAs with Australia, Chile, Israel, and many others. In addition, many nonfocal countries have trade agreements with multiple focal countries. For example, Chile has PTAs with all four of the focal members shown in Figure 18.6. Individual countries often have overlapping treaties with multiple trade partners, and PTAs as a whole create a complex network of trading obligations.

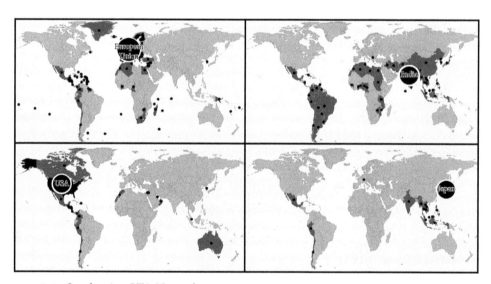

FIG. 18.6   Overlapping PTA Networks.

Note: Each panel shows the PTAs between the focal countries (labeled)
and their trade partners (black dots).
Source: World Trade Organization Regional Trade Agreements Database.

Perils of Complex Networks

While PTAs individually should increase trade cooperation, a network of overlapping PTAs can hinder trade cooperation by creating conflicting legal obligations. These conflicts can be most easily seen in the WTO, which has heard several cases over conflicting WTO and PTA rules.[12] For example, all WTO members are required to adhere to the most-favored nation (MFN) principle, which requires that if a member extends a benefit to another WTO member, it must extend the same benefit to *all* other WTO members. Yet Article XXIV of the GATT allows members to sign PTAs, which implies that benefits provided to PTA members do not have to be extended to all WTO members. There is thus a tension between a core tenet of the multilateral trade regime—the MFN principle—and the proliferation of PTAs. One WTO panel report noted that this relationship between the MFN principle and Article XXIV "has not always been harmonious" and has led to numerous trade disputes.[13]

For example, Turkey has signed multiple trade agreements with the European Communities (EC) since 1963 that gradually developed into a Turkey-EC customs union.[14] As part of this process, Turkey negotiated new agreements with its trading partners in the early 1990s so that its textile rules would match those of the EC. India, a major textile exporter, refused to participate in these negotiations, and Turkey imposed unilateral restrictions on textile imports from India in 1996. India quickly filed a WTO dispute against Turkey, arguing that Turkey had violated multiple WTO rules.[15] Turkey argued that it should be exempt from these rules under Article XXIV because it was changing its laws to form a Turkey-EC customs union. Both the WTO panel and Appellate Body ruled against Turkey, stating that "Article XXIV does not allow Turkey to adopt, upon the formation of a customs union with the European Communities, quantitative restrictions . . . which were found to be inconsistent with" WTO rules.[16] This created a legal quandary: Turkey violated WTO rules by changing its policies to match those of the EC, but Turkey would have violated its agreement with the EC if it had not changed its policies.

This example illustrates one of the perils of using PTAs to promote international trade: they create complex and often contradictory networks of legal obligations. The multilateral trade regime—first under the GATT, then under the WTO—has created detailed legal obligations for its members, which now include almost every state. The growth of PTAs has created complex sets of rules that overlap with the multilateral regime and even with other PTAs. Overlapping rules can create uncertainty about legal commitments and prompt trade disputes, which hinder international cooperation (Gilligan, Johns, and Rosendorff 2010). This complexity and uncertainty may be an inevitable, but acceptable, cost if PTAs promote aggregate international cooperation. However, if PTAs merely divert trade, rather than increase it, the cost of PTAs may outweigh their benefits. A network of overlapping bilateral and regional agreements may be less beneficial than shallower multilateral cooperation or even no agreements whatsoever.

Complexity may be an inevitable result of the growing PTA network, but the ill effects of conflicting and uncertain legal obligations can be mitigated through the design of PTA DSPs. While DSPs can clarify ambiguous or conflicting legal commitments, the proliferation of PTA-specific DSPs could be problematic if they adopt conflicting jurisprudence. Some recent PTAs allow members to choose which DSP they will use when a conflict arises, effectively "outsourcing" dispute settlement to another institution, most commonly the WTO.[17] We believe that this trend is promising because it increases the likelihood that trade disputes will be adjudicated under common legal principles and jurisprudence. If more PTAs were designed to share dispute settlement capacity, then conflicts over mismatched commitments might be more easily resolved. It may even be optimal for states to create a single dispute settlement mechanism with jurisdiction to hear all trade disputes involving the WTO and PTAs.

In addition, we suspect that more specialized PTAs could avert problems that arise from overlapping commitments by restricting their obligations to a narrow domain. For example, new PTAs could be designed with narrower scopes that focus more precisely on particular trade issues like agriculture, intellectual property, and technical barriers. Moreover, specialized PTAs could be designed to account for issue-specific cooperation problems, such as lenient safeguard measures for agriculture and greater institutionalization for technical issues like intellectual property. We find little evidence, however, of any such specialization; most recently signed PTAs have tended to be broader in scope than their earlier counterparts.

Steppingstones or Stumbling Blocks to Multilateralism?

As the network of PTAs becomes increasingly tangled, many scholars question whether these agreements promote or hinder multilateral trade cooperation.[18] We unfortunately lack a clear answer. Preferential trade agreements may foster multilateralism if their initial reciprocal tariff cuts allow export sectors to expand and thereby change the balance of political power between import-competing industries and exporters (Baldwin and Freund 2011). In addition, many policy experts believe that successful PTAs may persuade nonmembers to support deeper multilateral cooperation by demonstrating the benefits of international trade.[19]

On the other hand, PTAs may hinder multilateralism. Members can leverage their market power and increase their tariffs against the rest of the world, which makes multilateral cooperation less attractive (Saggi and Yildiz 2010). Some scholars argue that the economic context of a PTA determines whether it becomes a steppingstone or stumbling block for multilateral cooperation.[20] However, this scholarship reaches no clear conclusions, because its results are highly contingent on assumptions about the structure of the member economies. The impact of PTAs on multilateral cooperation is important but understudied. We hope that future scholarship, particularly in political science, will address this topic.

CONCLUSION

Existing research has provided many insights into PTA design variation and its impact on state behavior. This treaty-level analysis shows that PTAs must carefully balance their impact on compliance and stability. Agreements that are nested in political-economic contexts that make exit infeasible can impose deep and rigid constraints and create institutions with the authority to monitor behavior and enforce obligations. However, agreements that are nested in contexts that do not constrain exit must be more carefully calibrated to the trade-off between compliance and stability. Deeper concessions must be paired with less rigidity in order for these agreements to survive over time, and weaker institutions are best suited for promoting cooperation.

We know relatively less about the effects of PTAs at the system level. The proliferation and expansion of PTAs has created an increasingly complex network of overlapping legal obligations. These agreements must also operate in the shadow of the WTO. While it is reasonable to expect that more PTAs will lead to more cooperation, complexity comes with costs. Overlapping PTAs can create ambiguous and even contradictory legal obligations that provoke trade disputes. These disputes reduce the efficiency of the system as a whole and reduce stability. This suggests that PTAs with more members can have a multiplier effect on cooperation because they create more consistent—and hence more precise—rules than can be created by a network of overlapping bilateral and regional agreements. Multilateralism is more than just the sum of its parts.

NOTES

1. This is the most comprehensive current list of PTAs available, since almost all countries are members or observers of the WTO.
2. Most PTAs in the *World Trade Report 2011* data set involve the United States or European Union as a member and have a large volume of trade.
3. See also the chapters in this volume by Aaronson and Barkin.
4. Some of these PTAs include: EC-Mexico 2000, EC-CARIFORUM 2008, and EC-Eastern and Southern Africa 2012 Interim Agreement.
5. See also the chapters in this volume by Rosendorff (chapter 8) and Busch and Pelc (chapter 5).
6. These arguments come from Johns (2014), which builds on Rosendorff (2005) and Rosendorff and Milner (2001).
7. Like any institution, a trade agreement must create common beliefs about how members should respond to first-order noncompliance, even if the treaty does not contain formal DSPs (North 1990). The law of treaties, as articulated in the Vienna Convention on the Law of Treaties, creates secondary rules for those trade agreements that lack formal DSPs.
8. Pelc (2009) provides an alternative account in which states can violate a treaty without any penalty whatsoever. However, this account relies on the assumption that a treaty creates an adjudicative body that can perfectly observe each state's domestic pressure to protect and

impose punishments on states that cheat. This account is therefore more compelling for understanding a well-developed institution, like the WTO, than PTAs generally.

9. See Johns (2014, 2015). Rosendorff (2005) and Rosendorff and Milner (2001) present similar models, but do not allow settlement tariffs.

10. The occasional decrease in PTAs is due to EU enlargements in 2004 and 2007.

11. This term refers to any arrangement in which one partner has "a network of radial bilateral PTAs with some of these trading partners but these trading partners do not have PTAs with each other" (Baldwin and Freund 2011, 129).

12. For example, *Argentina—Poultry* (DS241) and *Mexico—Taxes on Soft Drinks* (DS308) both addressed jurisdictional conflicts for dispute settlement. In other cases, countries invoking safeguards excluded their PTA partners, contrary to WTO obligations: for example, *Argentina—Footwear* (DS121), *United States—Wheat Gluten* (DS166), and *United States—Line Pipe* (DS202).

13. See the panel report for *Turkey—Restrictions on Imports of Textile and Clothing Products*, DS34, para. 2.3. WTO Document WT/DS34/R.

14. This case summary is based on WTO records.

15. India invoked claims from both the GATT and the WTO Agreement on Textiles and Clothing.

16. See the Appellate Body report for *Turkey—Restrictions on Imports of Textile and Clothing Products*, DS34, para. 64. WTO Document WT/DS34/AB/R.

17. Those PTAs that allow members to use the WTO's dispute settlement body to resolve conflicts include NAFTA, the Australia-Chile PTA, the Israel-Mexico PTA, and the CARICOM-Costa Rica PTA. See also Busch (2007) on forum shopping in dispute settlement.

18. For example, see Bagwell and Staiger (1998); Baldwin and Freund (2011); Bhagwati (1991); Bhagwati and Panagariya (1999); Krueger (1999); Kono (2002); Limão (2006); and Limão (2007).

19. Remarks by Robert Zoellick, former US Trade Representative, at Princeton University on November 29, 2012.

20. For example, see Bagwell and Staiger (2001); Freund (2000); Goyal and Joshi (2006); and Saggi (2006).

References

Baccini, Leonardo, and Andreas Dür. 2012. The New Regionalism and Policy Interdependence. *British Journal of Political Science* 42: 57–79.

Baccini, Leonardo, Andreas Dür, and Mafred Elsig. 2012. The Politics of Trade Agreement Design: Depth, Scope and Flexibility. Paper presented at the Annual Conference on the Political Economy of International Organizations, Philadelphia, PA, January 26–28.

Bagwell, Kyle, and Robert W. Staiger. 2001. Reciprocity, Non-discrimination and Preferential Agreements in the Multilateral Trading System. *European Journal of Political Economy* 17: 281–325.

Bagwell, Kyle, and Robert W. Staiger. 1998. Will Preferential Agreements Undermine the Multilateral Trading System? *Economic Journal* 108: 1162–1182.

Baldwin, Richard. 1995. A Domino Theory of Regionalism. In *Expanding Membership of the European Union*, edited by R. Baldwin, P. Haaparanta, and J. Kiander, 25–53. Cambridge, UK: Cambridge University Press.

Baldwin, Richard. 2006. Multilateralising Regionalism: Spaghetti Bowls as Building Blocs on the Path to Global Free Trade. *World Economy* 29: 1451–1581.

Baldwin, Richard, and Caroline Freund. 2011. Preferential Trade Agreements and Multilateral Liberalization. In *Preferential Trade Agreement Policies for Development: A Handbook*, edited by Jean-Pierre Chauffour and Jean-Christophe Mau, 121–141. Washington, DC: The World Bank.

Barton, John H., Judith L. Goldstein, Timothy E. Josling, and Richard H. Steinberg. 2008. *The Evolution of the Trade Regime: Politics, Law, and Economics of the GATT and the WTO*. Princeton, NJ: Princeton University Press.

Bevilaqua, Alfonso S., Marcelo Catena, and Ernesto Talvi. 2001. Integration, Interdependence and Regional Goods: An Application to Mercosur. In *Economia*, edited by Andres Velasco, 153–207. Washington, DC: Brookings Institution Press.

Bhagwati, Jagdish. 1993. Regionalism and Multilateralism: An Overview. In *New Dimensions in Regional Integration*, edited by Jaime de Melo and Arvind Panagariya, 22–51. Cambridge, UK: Centre for Economic Policy Research.

Bhagwati, Jagdish. 1991. *The World Trading System at Risk*. Princeton, NJ: Princeton University Press.

Bhagwati, Jagdish, and Arvind Panagariya. 1999. Preferential Trading Areas and Multilateralism—Strangers, Friends, or Foes? In *Trading Blocs: Alternative Approaches to Analyzing Preferential Trade Agreements*, edited by Jagdish Bhagwati, Arvind Panagariya, and Pravin Krishna, 33–100. Cambridge, MA: MIT Press.

Busch, Marc L. 2007. Overlapping Institutions, Forum Shopping, and Dispute Settlement in International Trade. *International Organization* 61: 735–761.

Chang, W., and L. A. Winters. 2002. How Regional Blocs Affect Excluded Countries: The Price Effects of MERCOSUR. *American Economic Review* 92: 889–904.

Davis, Christina L. 2003. *Food Fights Over Free Trade: How International Institutions Promote Agricultural Trade Liberalization*. Princeton, NJ: Princeton University Press.

Downs, George W., David M. Rocke, and Peter N. Barsoom. 1996. Is the Good News about Compliance Good News about Cooperation? *International Organization* 50: 379–406.

Downs, George W., David M. Rocke, and Peter N. Barsoom. 1998. Managing the Evolution of Multilateralism. *International Organization* 52: 397–419.

Egger, Peter, and Mario Larch. 2008. Interdependent Preferential Trade Agreement Memberships: An Empirical Analysis. *Journal of International Economics* 76: 384–399.

Freund, Caroline. 2000. Different Paths to Free Trade: The Gains from Regionalism. *Quarterly Journal of Economics* 115: 1317–1341.

Gilligan, Michael J. 2004. Is There a Broader-Deeper Trade-off in International Multilateral Agreements? *International Organization* 58: 459–484.

Gilligan, Michael J., and Leslie Johns. 2012. Formal Models of International Institutions. *Annual Review of Political Science* 15: 221–243.

Gilligan, Michael J., Leslie Johns, and B. Peter Rosendorff. 2010. "Strengthening International Courts and the Early Settlement of Disputes." *Journal of Conflict Resolution* 54: 5–38.

Goldstein, Judith, Miles Kahler, Robert Keohane, and Anne-Marie Slaughter. 2000. Introduction: Legalization and World Politics. *International Organization* 54: 385–399.

Goldstein, Judith, and Lisa L. Martin. 2000. Legalization, Trade Liberalization, and Domestic Politics: A Cautionary Note. *International Organization* 54: 603–632.

Goyal, Sanjeev, and Sumit Joshi. 2006. Bilateralism and Free Trade. *International Economic Review* 47: 749–778.

Grossman, Gene, and Elhanan Helpman. 1995. The Politics of Free Trade Agreements. *American Economic Review* 85: 667–690.

Guzman, Andrew T. 2002. The Cost of Credibility: Explaining Resistance to Interstate Dispute Resolution Mechanisms. *Journal of Legal Studies* 31: 303–326.

Hafner-Burton, Emilie M. 2005. Trading Human Rights: How Preferential Trade Agreements Influence Government Repression. *International Organization* 59: 593–629.

Hicks, Raymond, and Soo Yeon Kim. 2012. Reciprocal Trade Agreements in Asia: Credible Commitment to Trade Liberalization or Paper Tigers? *Journal of East Asian Studies* 12: 1–29.

Hoekman, Bernard M., and Michel M. Kostecki. 2009. *The Political Economy of the World Trading System*. New York: Oxford University Press.

Horn, Henrik, Petros C. Mavroidis, and André Sapir. 2010. Beyond the WTO? An Anatomy of EU and US Preferential Trade Agreements. *The World Economy* 33: 1565–1588.

Johns, Leslie. 2012. Courts as Coordinators: Endogenous Enforcement and Jurisdiction in International Adjudication. *Journal of Conflict Resolution* 56: 257–289.

Johns, Leslie. 2014. Depth versus Rigidity in International Trade Agreements. *Journal of Theoretical Politics* 26: 468–295.

Johns, Leslie. 2015. *Strengthening International Courts: The Hidden Costs of Legalization*. Ann Arbor: University of Michigan Press.

Johns, Leslie, and Krzysztof J. Pelc. 2014. Who Gets to Be in the Room? Manipulating Participation in WTO Disputes. *International Organization* 68: 663–699.

Johns, Leslie, and B. Peter Rosendorff. 2009. Dispute Settlement, Compliance, and Domestic Politics. In *Trade Disputes and the Dispute Settlement Understanding of the WTO: An Interdisciplinary Assessment*, edited by James C. Hartigan, 139–163. San Diego, CA: Emerald Group Publishing.

Kim, Moonhawk. 2012. Ex Ante Due Diligence: Formation of PTAs and Protection of Labor Rights. *International Studies Quarterly* 56: 704–719.

Kono, Daniel Yuichi. 2002. Are Free Trade Areas Good for Multilateralism? Evidence from the European Free Trade Association. *International Studies Quarterly* 46: 507–527.

Krishna, Pravin. 1996. A Political Economy Analysis of Preferential Trading and Multilateralism. *Eastern Economic Journal* 22: 477–483.

Krueger, Anne O. 1999. Are Preferential Trading Arrangements Trade-Liberalizing or Protectionist? *Journal of Economic Perspectives* 13: 105–124.

Kucik, Jeffrey. 2012. The Domestic Politics of Trade Agreement Design: Producer Preferences over Trade Agreement Rules. *Economics & Politics* 24: 95–118.

Kucik, Jeffrey, and Eric Reinhardt. 2008. Does Flexibility Promote Cooperation? An Application to the Global Trade Regime. *International Organization* 62: 477–505.

Limão, Nuno. 2006. "Preferential Trade Agreements as Stumbling Blocks for Multilateral Trade Liberalization: Evidence for the U.S." *American Economic Review* 96: 896–914.

Limão, Nuno. 2007. Are Preferential Trade Agreements with Non-trade Objectives a Stumbling Block for Multilateral Liberalization? *Review of Economic Studies* 74: 821–855.

Mansfield, Edward D., and Helen V. Milner. 2012. *Votes, Vetoes, and the Political Economy of International Trade Agreements*. Princeton, NJ: Princeton University Press.

Martin, Lisa L. 2013. Against Compliance." In *Interdisciplinary Perspectives on International Law and International Relations: The State of the Art*, edited by Jeffrey L. Dunoff and Mark A. Pollack, 591–610. New York: Cambridge University Press.

North, Douglass C. 1990. *Institutions, Institutional Change and Economic Performance*. Cambridge, UK: Cambridge University Press.

Panagariya, Arvind. 2000. Preferential Trade Liberalization: The Traditional Theory and New Developments. *Journal of Economic Literature* 38: 287–331.

Panagariya, Arvind, and Ronald Findlay. 1996. "A Political Economy Analysis of Free Trade Areas and Customs Unions." In *The Political Economy of Trade Policy: Papers in Honor of Jagdish Bhagwati*, edited by Robert Feenstra, Gene Grossman, and Douglas Irwin, 265–288. Cambridge, MA: MIT Press.

Pelc, Krzysztof. 2009. Seeking Escape: Escape Clauses in International Trade Agreements. *International Studies Quarterly* 53: 349–368.

Regional Trade Agreements Database. Geneva: The World Trade Organization. http://rtais.wto.org/UI/PublicSearchByCr.aspx.

Rosendorff, B. Peter. 2005. Stability and Rigidity: Politics and the Design of the WTO's Dispute Resolution Procedure. *American Political Science Review* 99: 389–400.

Rosendorff, B. Peter, and Helen V. Milner. 2001. The Optimal Design of International Institutions: Uncertainty and Escape. *International Organization* 55: 829–857.

Saggi, Kamal. 2006. Preferential Trade Agreements and Multilateral Tariff Cooperation. *International Economic Review* 47: 29–57.

Saggi, Kamal, and Halis Murat Yildiz. 2010. Bilateralism, Multilateralism and the Quest for Global Free Trade. *Journal of International Economics* 81: 26–37.

Smith, James McCall. 2000. The Politics of Dispute Settlement Design: Explaining Legalism in Regional Trade Pacts. *International Organization* 54: 137–180.

Steinberg, Richard H. 2002. Understanding Trade and the Environment: A Conceptual Framework. In *The Greening of Trade Law: International Trade Organizations and Environmental Issues*, edited by Richard H. Steinberg, 1–20. New York: Rowman & Littlefield.

Uchitelle, Louis. 2009. "Buy America" in Stimulus (but Good Luck with That). *New York Times*, February 20. http://www.nytimes.com/2009/02/21/business/21buy.html (accessed May 31, 2013).

Whalley, John. 1998. Why Do Countries Seek Regional Trade Agreements? In *The Regionalization of the World Economy*, edited by Jeffrey A. Frankel, 63–90. Chicago: University of Chicago Press.

World Trade Report 2011—The WTO and Preferential Trade Agreements: From Coexistence to Coherence. 2011. Geneva: World Trade Organization.

CHAPTER 19

DEEP INTEGRATION AND REGIONAL TRADE AGREEMENTS

SOO YEON KIM

DEEP integration provisions in regional trade agreements (RTAs) seek to strengthen the contestability of markets for firms in partner economies. Such provisions have three main functions: protection of foreign firms and their interests; liberalization of "beyond-the-border" barriers to trade (i.e., domestic trade-related laws and regulations that go beyond traditional "barriers-at-the-border," such as tariffs and quotas); and harmonization of domestic trade rules to enhance the efficiency of international production. The road to deep integration has been paved by the demands of multinational firms, their production networks, and the increasing complexity of the international supply chain (Hatch, Bair, and Heiduk, this volume). Trade governance, which first focused under the General Agreement on Tariffs and Trade (GATT) on reducing border measures such as tariffs, quotas, and other quantitative restrictions, has moved toward constraining domestic policies such as technical regulations. The role of RTAs in fostering deep integration is also shaped by the failure of the Doha Round to reach a successful conclusion and the emergence of RTAs as the main institutional venue for forging new trade rules.

Deep integration is the hallmark of the modern RTA. Deep integration RTAs emerged in the late twentieth century as international production and trade became more complex, driven by extensive foreign direct investment and the internationalization of production. Prominent examples of deep integration RTAs are the US-Mexico part of the North American Free Trade Agreement (NAFTA); the European Union's RTAs; and more recently, Japan's push for economic partnership agreements (EPAs) that seek to incorporate an extensive array of issues, as well as the US-led Trans-Pacific Partnership (TPP) agreement currently under negotiation. Deep integration RTAs are not exclusive to the developed North or only between North and South countries. Many

South-South RTAs have also begun to feature deep integration commitments. The most advanced deep integration RTA is the customs union, in which member countries not only remove trade barriers but also adopt a common external tariff (CET) and pool their economic sovereignty in economic policy. The exemplar is the European Union (EU), which created a single market that not only provided for the free flow of the factors of production but also established piecemeal the institutional convergence of domestic policies.

This chapter examines the relationship between deep integration and RTAs and how commitments for achieving greater compatibilities in national regulatory systems are manifested in the provisions of trade agreements. The objective is to delineate the main lines of research that has been conducted in this area, emphasizing the questions that have been raised in the literature and the extensive data collection efforts that have attended scholarly interest in deep integration and in RTAs. The chapter is divided into four main parts. The first section discusses the properties, both conceptual and practical, of deep integration and their legal counterparts in RTAs. The second and third sections examine, respectively, why states make deep integration commitments in RTAs and the effects of such deep integration commitments, focusing on the prospects for convergence and competition of deep integration models at the systemic level. The chapter concludes with a discussion of avenues for further research.

WHAT IS DEEP INTEGRATION, AND HOW IS IT RELATED TO REGIONAL TRADE AGREEMENTS?

Deep integration refers to a process of economic integration that erodes differences in national economic policies and regulations and renders them more compatible for economic exchange. As a concept, deep integration is widely associated with Robert Z. Lawrence (1996), who defined it essentially as "behind-the-border" integration in a study that examined the tensions between RTAs and national autonomy. Deep integration is also synonymous with "positive integration," which is associated with the liberalization approach of the World Trade Organization (WTO) era. Positive integration involves the active establishment of domestic rules and regulations that render a country's trade regime more consistent with its obligations under the "single undertaking" that is the WTO. Positive integration, or deep integration, can also be contrasted with the "negative integration" or "shallow integration" approach of the GATT era. Under shallow integration, member states had the option to enroll in GATT agreements in an à la carte fashion. For example, only some countries chose to sign onto plurilateral agreements such as the Tokyo Round's Standards Code governing technical regulations, which precluded the use of the GATT's dispute set-tlement process by signatories against nonsignatories. More broadly, states' commit-ments during the GATT era extended only to the agreement not to raise "barriers at the border," such as raising their tariffs above the bound level, imposing quantitative restrictions, or implementing indirect taxes to protect domestic industries and dis-criminate against foreign firms.

The Role of Regional Trade Agreements

Deep integration and RTAs are not naturally related. Rather, they are currently con-nected due to the weakened legislative function of the WTO, which has been unable to conclude its first round of multilateral trade negotiations. With the Doha Round well past its first decade of negotiations and without an end in sight, RTAs have emerged as the most active institutional setting for governments to negotiate the lowering of "behind- the-border" barriers to trade, thus either superseding or continuing the work of the multilateral trade regime that began essentially with the Kennedy Round under the GATT (Hoekman and Kostecki 2009, 582).

In the context of regional trade agreements, deep integration refers to provisions that go to the heart of domestic policies that concern the contestability of the market. Deep integration commitments promote harmonization or at least mutual recognition of trade rules (Birdsall and Lawrence 1999), an idea that can be traced back as far as Tinbergen's (1954) work on economic integration. Deep integration facilitates the glo-balization of production and trade along the international supply chain. RTA provi-sions for deep integration have two defining features. First, the commitments focus on "behind-the-border" trade rules; that is, domestic laws, regulations, and administrative mechanisms that comprise a country's trade regime. Second, in addition to their focus on "behind-the- border barriers," deep integration provisions in RTAs are also wide in scope (Koremenos, Lipson, and Snidal 2001). They cover an extensive range of issues that are mostly trade related but in some cases fall outside the governance purview of existing WTO agreements.

Figure 19.1 is an example of a deep integration agreement that is, at the time of writing, under active negotiation. The TPP agreement, involving twelve coun-tries including the United States, is a twenty-first-century deep integration agree-ment that features "regulatory coherence" as a key objective.[1] Prospective members advance the TPP as a high-standard agreement among "like-minded" countries. It covers the key areas of deep integration, such as investment, services, competition, labor, and environment, as well as the traditional areas of market access in goods and trade remedies. Most relevant to this discussion of deep integration is that one important goal of the agreement is to make the regulatory systems of the members more compatible so that firms may operate more seamlessly and efficiently across the partner economies.

Areas of Negotiation

Market Access for Goods

Trade Remedies

Legal Issues/Dispute Settlement

Cross-Border Services

Financial Services

Telecommunications

Competition Policy

Government Procurement

Intellectual Property

Investment

Sanitary and Phytosanitary Standards (SPS)

Technical Barriers to Trade (TBT)

Temporary Entry

Rules of Origin

Textiles and Apparel/ROOs

Cooperation and Capacity Building

Customs

E-Commerce

Environment

Labor

FIG. 19.1 The Trans-Pacific Partnership (TPP) Agreement: A Deep Integration RTA for the 21st Century.

Properties of Deep Integration Provisions in RTAs: Protection, Liberalization, and Harmonization

Deep integration provisions in RTAs have three common properties: protection, liberalization, and harmonization. They concern adjustments in domestic laws, regulations, and administrative mechanisms that allow greater market contestation by foreign firms. Provisions for deep integration allow for the leveling of the playing field in national economies between domestic and foreign firms, overall decreasing the levels of discrimination against the latter. Protection involves the representation of the economic interests of foreign firms by enhancing their legal rights in the domestic arena and providing for mechanisms of redress in cases where their interests are harmed. Liberalization refers to the enhancement of market access for foreign firms by allowing greater participation in all stages of economic activities. Last but not least, harmonization entails consistency across countries of rules and policies that govern production for the purposes of trade.

In the existing scholarship, studies of deep integration commitments in RTAs vary in their relative emphasis on protection, liberalization, and harmonization depending on the particular issue area. The relative emphasis on these properties is determined by the cooperation problems inherent in the particular issue area under consideration. For RTA provisions on technical barriers to trade (TBTs), for example, the cooperation problems emanate from cross-national differences in standards and technical regulations. The motivation to reduce production costs by making standards and technical regulations more compatible across countries calls for commitments to mutual recognition of partner countries' standards, technical regulations, and conformity of assessment procedures, at a minimum.[2] The strongest provisions in TBTs expressly stipulate harmonization though the promotion of specific regional or international standards. Piermartini and Budetta's (2009) study of TBT provisions in RTAs reflects this emphasis on harmonization: beyond its reference to the TBT agreement of the WTO, their classification focuses on the approach to integration—mutual recognition or harmonization—in the areas of standards, technical regulations, and conformity assessment.

In another issue area, Kotschwar (2009) examines investment provisions in RTAs that emphasize the properties of protection and liberalization. The presence or absence of an investor-state dispute resolution mechanism, as well as provisions for expropriation, minimum standard of treatment, and treatment in case of strife, are common features in RTAs to protect investor firm interests and assets. In areas relevant to liberalization, Kotschwar's classification includes the approach to the scheduling of bindings under the most-favored nation (MFN) and national treatment principles. Scheduling refers to the specific listing of liberalization commitments, and it may take a positive-list or negative-list approach. A positive-list approach liberalizes only the sectors that are listed, while a negative-list approaches liberalizes all sectors for investment except those for which parties claim exemptions. Kotschwar's study also specifies the scope of coverage across the stages of investment: establishment, acquisition, postestablishment, and resale. In the area of competition, another key area of deep integration provisions, Teh (2009) classifies commitments that emphasize liberalization to enhance the contestability of national markets. Teh's study covers national regulations governing competition, including provisions by sector and improving upon earlier work by the Organisation for Economic Co-operation and Development (OECD) (Solano and Sennekamp 2006). The study examines nine areas of competition-related regulations, including commitments to cooperation; promotion of national competition and regulation of anticompetitive behavior; dispute settlement; institutional arrangements; and general and horizontal principles of nondiscrimination, procedural fairness, and transparency.

The above studies reflect the broader direction of the existing literature, which exhibits an overall trend toward mapping of RTA provisions, but are also relevant for the study of deep integration. Current RTA-mapping projects include the Design of Trade Agreements (DESTA) project (Dür et al. 2012), perhaps the largest-scale project, comprising more than 500 coded agreements; Estevadeordal, Suominen, and Teh's (2009) focused study of a sample of seventy-four agreements chosen for diversity in economic development, trade flows, and geography in their participants; and Chauffour and Maur's (2011) study of developing country strategies in negotiating RTAs, building on seminal works by De Melo and Panagariya (1996) and Schiff and Winters (2003) and the World Bank's *Trade Blocs* (2000). While they stand as independent RTA-mapping projects, each also demonstrates how the properties of deep integration—protection, liberalization, and harmonization—are written into specific commitments in RTAs.

Measuring Deep Integration

Though a voluminous literature exists on the impact of RTAs on trade flows, the literature on the effects specifically of deep integration commitments in RTAs is less well-developed. One reason has been the difficulty of measuring what exactly constitutes deep integration provisions in RTAs. The literature so far features several types of measures of deep integration, from qualitatively driven indexes based on the agreement's scope to statistically driven scores.

The widely known metric devised by Horn, Mavroidis, and Sapir (2009) is a qualitative measure to distinguish the RTAs of the United States and the EU. Though the study does not focus explicitly on deep integration commitments, the analysis does enumerate the kinds of issue areas that are relevant. Provisions in US and EU RTAs are classified as WTO-plus and WTO-X. WTO-plus provisions cover issue areas under the purview of WTO agreements but whose commitments go beyond current disciplines. WTO-X provisions cover policy areas that are not currently covered by WTO agreements. They include but are not limited to "competition policy, environmental laws, investment, IPRs, capital movements, consumer and data protection, cultural cooperation, education, energy, health, human rights, illegal immigration, illicit drugs, money laundering, R&D, SMEs, social matters, statistics, taxation, and visa and asylum policies" (pp. 12–15).

The WTO's annual *World Trade Report* (2011) extended the Horn, Mavroidis, and Sapir study and their assessment of deep integration provisions to ninety-seven more RTAs, in addition to the original thirty-three for the EU and eleven for the United States. The report found that RTAs increasingly include deep integration provisions that are legally enforceable. RTA provisions include not only WTO-plus commitments, but also more and more WTO-X areas. In particular, the report finds a striking pattern in particular issue areas that are included in RTAs: competition policy, movement of capital, intellectual property rights beyond TRIPS, and investment.

Existing scholarship has also proposed alternative methodologies to measure deep integration commitments in terms of the general "depth" of a trade agreement. Perhaps the most straightforward approach has been to construct an additive and usually unweighted index of all the provisions in a particular RTA that are geared toward liberalization, including not only border barriers such as tariffs but also behind-the-border deep integration provisions and enforcement mechanisms. Hicks and Kim (2012) and Baccini, Dür, and Elsig (2013) construct such indexes, though the latter explicitly label the measure as "depth." Kim (2012) also develops an additive index of deep integration commitments in RTAs based on TBTs and competition provisions and analyzes the impact of production network trade on the strength of commitments in these two issue areas. Orefice and Rocha (2011) also employ an additive index, but the index is constructed as an unweighted measure of the number of legally enforceable provisions in an agreement defined according to Horn, Mavroidis, and Sapir (2010). A more data-driven approach utilizes exploratory factor analysis or principal components analysis (Orefice and Rocha 2011; Baccini, Dür, and Elsig 2013) to generate an index that captures the overall (and latent) depth of an RTA. This approach yields a weighted index of deep integration in an RTA, and it is computed using all the provisions included in the agreement. The index constructed as a comprehensive measure of deep integration is essentially the factor score for each agreement, in which the index is weighted according to the factor loadings for each provision of the RTA.

There is no widely employed measure of "deep integration" commitments in RTAs. Rather, studies have operationalized deep integration using both substantively driven and data-driven measures. These measures were uniformly constructed to capture the "depth" of RTA commitments, whether in a comparison of EU and US trade agreements or a broader set of RTAs. The literature has so far not produced discrepant findings that highlight the strengths and drawbacks of different measurements of deep integration; however, the few studies that exist do form a critical mass of scholarship to draw major conclusions, and the measurement issue would benefit from additional and methodologically systematic investigation.

WHY DO STATES COMMIT TO DEEP INTEGRATION AGREEMENTS?

The most important factor pushing governments toward deep integration commitments in RTAs is the increasing fragmentation of international production and trade along the international supply chain. Declining transport costs, as well as advances in information, communications, and technology, have allowed for greater geographical fragmentation of the production process. In this connection, firms that rely on intermediate inputs, whether multinational or national, are especially likely to push for deep integration commitments in investment, services, and the protection of intellectual property rights in their countries' agreements with trade partners.

Production Networks and Deep Integration

An emerging empirical literature in economics has examined the links between production networks and deep integration RTAs. The studies consistently find that high levels of trade in parts and components—the favored proxy for measuring production network trade (Yeats 1998; Hummels, Ishii, and Yi 2001; Athukorala 2011)—is associated with strong deep integration commitments in RTAs.[3] The success of production networks in generating profits for firms relies on low(er) trade costs that derive from domestic-trade-related regulations and, equally important, stable expectations regarding these regulations. As barriers at the border such as tariffs and other quantitative restrictions have become lower through the successful rounds of GATT negotiations, trade and production costs generated by incompatibilities in trade-related domestic regulations across countries now figure more prominently in the strategies of multinational firms that rely heavily on the movement of intermediate goods. Their operations are affected by inadequate infrastructure and services, such as transportation and communications.

Baldwin (2011) calls this intensification and increasing complexity of the international supply chain the "second unbundling." It has created a trade-investment-services nexus in which the conventional links between factories and offices have been internationalized and dispersed across different countries. The expansion of production networks thus requires sufficient convergence in legal and regulatory systems, as well as economic institutions, in relevant areas such as product and production standards, intellectual property rights, and protection and liberalization of investment. Such initiatives toward harmonization are thus encoded into provisions in RTAs, and commitments in these areas are supported by a strong and highly legalized dispute settlement system. The literature also suggests that a two-way link exists between production networks and deep integration RTAs (Orefice and Rocha 2011; WTO 2011). Countries strongly embedded in the international supply chain and engaged in the fragmentation of production are more likely to sign on to deep integration RTAs so as to secure their position as providers of intermediate goods and services. Kim (2012) has found that high levels of production network trade are associated with stronger commitments in TBT provisions, but only weak effects in the area of competition policy. Moreover, there is a distinct pattern in US and EU RTAs, in which the US RTAs produce stronger commitments in TBTs, while the EU RTAs demonstrate stronger commitments to liberalization of competition policy.

It should be noted that deep integration commitments are practical only after states achieve a certain level of "shallow integration," as only when the more traditional trade policy measures such as tariff and quantitative restrictions have been lowered does the need arise to attend to differences in national regulatory systems. Thus deep integration

RTAs with strong commitments are most likely to be found for countries that have already achieved low levels of border protection, such as developed countries. For North-South RTAs and South-South RTAs, "shallow integration" or "negative integration" can still be expected to figure prominently in RTA provisions (see also Manger and Shadlen, this volume).

Multinational Firms and the Political Economy of Deep Integration

In the political economy of deep integration, the role of multinational firms comprises an important area of research. In earlier eras multinational firms supported trade liberalization (Milner 1988), but more recently the operational needs of international business and multinational firms have been instrumental in promoting regional trade arrangements. The EU initiative toward a single market was buttressed by European firms that sought economies of scale to boost international competitiveness. NAFTA was actively supported by US firms as well as Mexico's large industrial groups that formed regional production networks (Fishlow and Haggard 1992). In Asia, where levels of production network trade are among the highest in the world (Athukorala 2005, Athukorala, 2011), regional integration has been largely informal and led largely by private foreign and regional multinational firms.

The existing literature also identifies variability across sectors. Trade in goods, for example, is different from trade in services. Where production networks and deep integration are concerned, the political economy of trade in services is strongly related to foreign direct investment (FDI). Indeed, in the area of services, where export interests are weak relative to the manufacturing or agricultural sectors, it is the investors—the multinational firms—that function as "export" interests that drive trade negotiations. Kerry Chase has produced studies on the political economy of integration in different sectors, including investment (2004), rules of origin (2008a), and services (2008b). Though the studies largely focus on the United States, they are as a collection illustrative of the interests at play in each sector and also indicative of the kinds of cross-linkages between sectors that would complicate negotiations in a deep integration RTA.

Governments sign on to deep integration RTAs in an effort to facilitate the operations of production networks. Multinational firms are the key promoters of making national regulatory systems compatible, as this helps to reduce the cost of doing business abroad and generally improves the operation of the international supply chain. In the politics of production networks in the design of RTAs, firms that rely on trade along the international supply chain, whether they are multinational or national, are likely to figure as important political actors that have incentives to lobby governments for deep integration commitments.

The Effects of Deep Integration RTAs

The effects of deep integration RTAs may be assessed in terms of costs in two areas. On the one hand, the mix of developmental stages of agreement partners results in uneven costs and benefits for agreement partners. North-North, North-South, and South-South RTAs are affected by the level of asymmetry in market size. North-South agreements increase the prospects for the importation of the more developed country's regulatory regime by the less developed country, as the latter is likely to have an underdeveloped domestic trade regime in the first place. Disparities in levels of economic development will be reflected in institutional preferences as well, as the less-developed economy is likely to focus on industrial market access, while the more developed economy is likely to seek to export its regulatory regime. Second, the cost of deep integration will also depend on how non-members are likely to be affected by deeper integration between RTA members. Competing and largely incompatible models of trade governance written into these RTAs will increase discrimination against nonmembers and also lower the possibility that deep integration norms in RTAs can serve as a focal point for cooperation in the WTO or other multilateral forum.

Current scholarship on the effects of deep integration RTAs is limited (WTO 2011, 145), due largely to the problem of measuring deep integration, as noted above. Existing studies can be divided into those that examine economic effects, specifically the impact on production network trade, and those that examine the consequences for multilateral trade liberalization, largely along the lines of RTAs as "stumbling blocks" or "building blocks." Empirical studies of the trade effects of deep integration RTAs include Orefice and Rocha (2011), who found strong positive effects of deep integration RTAs on production network trade defined in terms of trade in parts and components. This effect is pronounced in trade in automobile parts and in intermediate products in information and technology. The WTO's (2011) report on trade agreements corroborates these results. Deep integration RTAs have a positive and statistically significant impact on trade in parts and components, and every additional deep integration provision adds to this positive effect. The WTO study finds further evidence that individually, commitments to harmonize standards (under TBT provisions) and to adopt competition laws also enhance production network trade among members.

Convergence or Competition?

Another area of the literature has extended the debate on RTAs as "stumbling blocks" or "building blocks" to multilateral trade liberalization (see also Johns and Peritz, this volume). This debate has focused on the degree to which the deep integration commitments in these agreements can be multilateralized to provide an alternative venue for the negotiation of multilateral trade rules—the convergence route for managing international trade. The other side of this debate privileges the role of power politics in producing "hubs of governance," or competing models of trade governance in which leading economies pursue particular models of deep integration that are essentially discriminatory to non-RTA members.

Multilateralization of deep integration commitments in RTAs, which would extend commitments beyond the agreement partners, is a significant prospect. Given that deep integration commitments reach into domestic laws, regulations, and administrative mechanisms, multilateralizaton may be easier to achieve, as reforming these laws may be equivalent to unilateral liberalization. The issue of convergence is not exclusive to RTAs, but rather is a broader issue of concern when it comes to the governance of globalization (Kahler and Lake 2003). In arguing for a convergence route to multilateral trade liberalization, Hoekman and Kostecki (2009, 509) point to regulatory convergence in the process of deep integration under the single market program of the EU. Across trade in goods and services, the European Commission and the European Court of Justice actively intervened to remove not only barriers-at-the border such as tariffs and quotas, but also regulatory limitations on the movement of goods and services. In the area of standards, a key component of deep integration, the European Commission and European Court of Justice provided for mutual recognition of standards across member countries, thus achieving regulatory convergence to facilitate the movement of goods and services.

Hubs of Governance

Another scenario in this debate privileges the role of power politics in which the web of RTAs that populate the global trading system diverge in a hub-and-spokes pattern, with each "hub of governance" centered on a leading economy. This form of "hegemonic liberalization" (Hoekman and Winters 2009) is one form of cooperation through RTAs on market regulation and domestic economic policies. It may result in the multilateralization of trade rules, but could just as likely lead to competition between models of governance. That is, leading economies may utilize their market power to negotiate deep integration provisions in RTAs. To the extent that partner economies accept and adopt these deep integration provisions, some degree of multilateralization of trade rules results. Moreover, where partner countries extend these same deep integration commitments in their subsequent RTAs, a higher-order effect is also achieved for the particular deep integration model of the RTA, such as the spread of RTAs between the United States and its regional neighbors across the Americas (Shadlen 2005, Shadlen, 2008).

However, the multilateralization scenario assumes that there is little divergence across the deep integration models pursued by the leading economies. This assumption is not tenable, as studies have shown that leading economies such as the United States and EU pursue different priorities in their deep integration RTAs. The United States, for example, utilizes a standard template for all partners in bilateral investment treaties (BITs) and also follows a consistent template for the protection of intellectual property rights in RTAs (World Bank 2005). The EU prioritizes reform and harmonization of competition policy and also seeks to maintain its system of geographical indications (GI), which denote the geographical origins of certain products (such as French wines and Swiss cheeses), in its RTAs (Schiff and Winters 2003). Horn, Mavroidis, and Sapir (2009), in their comparative study of US and EU FTAs, find that the United States pursues a "hard" legalization approach (Abbott et al. 2001; Abbott and Snidal 2000), while the EU pursues a "soft" legalization approach in its RTAs. The US RTAs contain more WTO-plus provisions that are highly legalized and enforceable. While US RTAs do not include as many WTO-X provisions, they do include them consistently in the areas of anticorruption (not found in EU RTAs), competition policy, environmental laws, investment, IPRs, labor market regulation, and capital movement. The EU is the "market leader" in WTO-X provisions; however, the majority of provisions lack any meaningful enforcement mechanisms. Even superficially, the "hard" legalization approach of the United States and the "soft" legalization approach of the EU reflect a broader divergence in the deep integration strategies and governance models of these two leading economies.

The different priorities that leading economies place on the wide range of issue areas that fall under deep integration produce different governance models for trade, and to the extent that they are supported by the accumulation of second-order RTAs created by RTA partners, are likely to obstruct efforts to harmonize or to adopt mutual recognition practices at the multilateral level. The problem of competition in governance models becomes more acute when we take into account the role of emerging markets—the BRICS countries including Brazil, Russia, India, China, and South Africa, and beyond (Mattoo and Subramanian 2009). In Asia, for example, where the importance of China as an economic power is most evident, Kim and Manger (2013) find striking differences in the services liberalization provisions in RTAs signed by the United States and by China.

More broadly, the idea of "hubs of governance" formed by RTAs with varying degrees of deep integration commitments is especially compelling given the recent trend toward forming "mega-FTAs." Agreements under negotiation—such as the Transatlantic Trade and Investment Partnership (TTIP) between the United States and EU, the TPP between the United States and Asian trade partners, and the Regional Comprehensive Economic Partnership Agreement (RCEP) between China and its trade partners—bring under one large-scale umbrella agreement countries that already have existing RTAs between them. These agreements not only offer competing models of trade liberalization and deep integration, but they also reflect how the world's leading economies are competing for influence in global trade relations.

AVENUES FOR FUTURE RESEARCH

The study of deep integration commitments in RTAs remains a highly promising area for fruitful research in trade agreements and trade governance more broadly. In an effort to promote more scholarship in this frontier in the study of trade governance, this section poses questions that would benefit from further study.

What is the Baseline?

Existing studies of deep integration in RTAs would benefit greatly from an assessment of "depth" with respect to some baseline in the regulatory status quo of signatories. Studies have emphasized the degree to which states make legally binding commitments in a range of governance areas that purportedly increase the contestability of markets in partner economies. However, this raises the question of the baseline that constitutes the basis for comparison: Do RTA commitments really promote reform to protect, to liberalize, and to harmonize, or are states simply formalizing and internationalizing their existing regulatory regimes? Downs, Rocke, and Barsoom (1996) advanced the widely acknowledged argument that the contributions of international institutions are greatly exaggerated, as they mostly provide for only modest commitments that do not depart significantly from what signatories would have undertaken in the absence of such institutional obligations. Hoekman and Winters (2009) similarly find little evidence that deep integration provisions actually promote regulatory reform. Rather, the study finds that in most cases, states pursue regulatory reform unilaterally.

The absence of a baseline that reflects the regulatory sophistication of a country also makes it difficult to determine causal direction: one cannot infer that the templates for reform provided by RTA provisions are promoting regulatory changes and improvements beyond what governments have already decided autonomously to pursue. Put differently, the lack of a baseline as the basis of comparison may also lead to selection effects (Von Stein 2005; Simmons and Hopkins 2005), in which an international institution simply reflects signatories' preferences rather than a commitment to change. An implication of this argument is that the net benefits of such RTAs would be marginal.

Many of the mapping projects in existence today rely on the coding and interpretation of legal text and do not base assessments of deep integration on existing multilateral or international commitments or on current levels of national legislation in the relevant issue areas. This baseline problem is exacerbated by the fact that RTA provisions themselves do not imply or explicate the extent to which signatory governments must change national laws or regulations. One approach for a comparative assessment would be to take commitments in existing multilateral and bilateral treaties as the baseline for comparison. One baseline that researchers have employed is the relevant WTO agreement itself, in an effort to assess the extent to which an RTA advances commitments beyond the status quo defined under the multilateral trade regime.

Teh (2009) and Teh, Prusa, and Budetta (2009) evaluate the strictness of trade remedy provisions of RTAs vis-à-vis current commitments on antidumping duties, countervailing duties, and bilateral and global safeguards under WTO rules. The study finds that RTAs on average do not exceed the strictness of current WTO rules. However, deep integration RTAs do stand out as agreements that place prohibitions on at least one type of trade remedies, such as exempting the partner country from any invocation of global safeguards. A study on services undertaken in Roy (2011) and expanding on Roy, Marchetti, and Lim (2009) and Marchetti and Roy (2008), assesses service commitments in RTAs for fifty-three countries across sixty-seven agreements.[4] For every RTA to which a country is a signatory, the RTA's commitments were evaluated against commitments in the General Agreement on Trade in Services (GATS) and against current Doha Round offers. This study explicitly avoids a "legal interpretation" of the agreements and provides only an assessment of the extent to which the selected countries have gone beyond current levels of GATS commitments and Doha Round offers. It nonetheless constitutes one of the few studies that provide a basis of comparison for RTA commitments. The data also cover only mode 1 (cross-border trade) and mode 3 (commercial presence), but these are the sectors in which most services trade is conducted.

While these studies take the WTO agreements as the baseline, and scholarship would certainly benefit from more detailed study of individual issue areas, this approach has two weaknesses. First, it cannot accommodate newer issues that are not governed by the WTO. In this connection, future work may look toward, for example, existing obligations in other multilateral treaties, such as multilateral environmental agreements for environmental standards, International Labour Organization (ILO) criteria for labor standards, and bilateral investment treaties for investment provisions.[5] Second and more important, this approach does not capture the domestic regulatory landscape of the members and therefore cannot gauge the extent to which an RTA actually represents a commitment beyond the regulatory status quo of its signatories. Assessment vis-à-vis WTO rules or any other international agreement is essentially a comparison between legal texts, and the current literature provides little insight into how these rules map onto the domestic regulatory landscape. Indeed, assessing not only the actual level of deep integration commitments but also the benefits that can be accrued from them hinges on whether the agreement requires actual regulatory reform on the part of signatories.

Regulatory Disarray in Trade Governance

The issue of whether the increasingly complex and growing network of RTAs is likely to lead to convergence or discrimination in international trade is closely related to the question of how states' memberships in numerous RTAs matters. At a time when the rule-making function of the multilateral trade regime is greatly impaired, the dramatic expansion of RTAs in the global economy advances the much-needed development of national trade regimes in areas either underdeveloped in the WTO or currently outside its governance purview. There is, however, a crucial drawback to this phenomenon: the possible emergence of a "spaghetti bowl" of rules from overlapping agreements, which can contribute to regulatory disarray.

The multitude of RTAs and the overlapping memberships of countries pose a challenge to the management of RTA obligations. According to Chaffour and Maur (2011, 1), countries in Africa belong, on average, to at least four RTAs. In Latin America, the average country has signed at least seven agreements. Modern deep integration RTAs are legally complex, and each agreement has its own tariff schedule, list of exclusions and implementation times, rule of origin, and customs procedures. Thus, in the aggregate, obligations across overlapping agreements are likely to diminish the efficiency of managing trade and its rules, as well as the transparency that a single multilateral trade regime would make possible. In the absence of efforts to multilateralize RTA obligations or toward open regionalism in which all trading partners may benefit, legal diversity and conflicts between rules are likely to have a negative impact on progress toward a more developed multilateral trading system (Bhagwati 2008).

Scholarship needs to move beyond the long-standing debate on trade-creation versus trade-diversion from RTAs (Viner 1950) to take account of the impact of deep integration commitments. In thus shifting the debate, Mansfield and Reinhardt (2008), for example, have found that membership in RTAs leads to less trade volatility among their members, as RTAs reduce uncertainty. The regulatory disorder that can result from overlapping RTAs may undermine not only WTO agreements but also other existing international institutions. In the case of environmental provisions, where there are treaties—multilateral environmental agreements (MEAs)—in force, RTAs can either conflict with the legal obligations in them or go beyond them to push the current boundaries of environmental standards in trade (Kernohan and De Cian 2007). The mapping projects discussed above are equipped with the basic materials to examine the broader issue of regulatory conflict.

Finally, the question of regulatory disorder beyond the contracting parties of the RTA also calls for more extensive research into nonviolation cases in WTO disputes. Nonviolation complaints fall under Article 26 of the WTO's Dispute Settlement Understanding (DSU). The DSU allows for the filing of cases involving a domestic policy measure that does not necessarily violate WTO obligations but has the effect of "nullification and impairment" of the benefits of an existing concession (Trebilcock and Howse 2005, 143).[6] Nonviolation complaints are especially suited for examining the impact of regulatory reform brought about by deep integration RTAs, given that the core provisions of deep integration RTAs concern protection, liberalization, and harmonization of trade-related domestic regulatory rules. Such rules, to the extent that they produce regulatory conflicts with the concessions already in effect under the WTO, are likely to bring an increase in nonviolation complaints under the WTO system and would be strongly indicative of regulatory disorder.

Conclusion

Deep integration is not a new phenomenon in the politics of international trade. Negotiations for the liberalization of domestic trade rules began with the Kennedy Round of the GATT as the negotiating rounds achieved success in reducing tariffs and quantitative restrictions. As tariff levels receded, national differences in domestic laws and regulations governing trade became more visible and thus a focal point for negotiating trade rules. GATT members proposed coordination of national policies and outright harmonization of regulatory systems. This trend continues in the Doha Round era through deep integration RTAs, incorporating not only competition policy and investment but also long-standing initiatives on labor and environmental standards.

Deep integration as encoded in the legal texts of RTAs, however, is indeed a recent development in the regulation and management of trade. Robert Lawrence's early study of deep integration (1996) focused on the tension between national autonomy in economic policy and the demands on domestic reform of regional trade agreements. Since this path-breaking study, the depth in deep integration RTAs has only intensified, as RTAs have increasingly widened the scope of issue areas they cover. This chapter has provided a survey of the existing scholarship on the defining features and functions of deep integration, the determinants of states' choices to enter into deep integration RTAs, and the consequences for international trade of these agreements. The discussion has also raised questions and avenues for future research.

Deep integration in RTAs emphasizes the reduction or dismantling of behind-the-border barriers, thus largely supporting the "positive integration" approach of the WTO in actively reforming national regulatory systems to be more WTO-consistent. Provisions for deep integration are wide in scope and increasing over time to include issue areas not under the purview of the WTO agreements. Deep integration commitments in various issue areas protect the interest of foreign firms, liberalize domestic trade rules to level the playing field for foreign firms, and harmonize regulatory systems to make them more compatible between RTA partners. Current scholarship provides measures of deep integration in individual issue areas as well as aggregate measures to gauge the overall depth of an agreement.

Governments enter into deep integration RTAs as a response to the internationalization and increasing geographic fragmentation of international production. The trade-investment-services nexus (Baldwin 2011) figures importantly in the strength of commitments in deep integration RTAs, as they facilitate the operation of production networks and reduce the cost of doing business. In the political economy of deep integration, multinational firms are key political actors that drive the negotiation of RTAs. Existing studies show that deep integration RTAs lead to higher levels of production network trade and vice versa. At the systemic level, the network of RTAs may lead to convergence in deep integration provisions and subsequently national regulatory systems within "hubs of governance," as well as to competition between these hubs and models of deep integration espoused by the leading economies.

Scholarship would benefit from research that provides a baseline for comparison of the actual regulatory change that would be required for RTA members. Whereas for less developed countries regulatory reform under a deep integration RTA may be far-reaching, developed countries with established and well-functioning domestic regulations may simply be formalizing their institutional status quo. In addition, there is a need for the debate on regionalism to move beyond trade-creation versus trade-diversion, to examine the possibility of regulatory disarray in international trade and inconsistencies between deep integration commitments in RTAs and obligations in relevant multilateral treaties, such as between provisions on environmental standards and legal obligations in multilateral environmental agreements. Finally, given that deep integration RTAs seek greater regulatory coherence among partners, research on nonviolation complaints in WTO dispute cases would lend insights into the impact of these agreements on existing commitments under the multilateral trade regime.

Notes

1. The current members of the agreement are Australia, Brunei Darussalam, Canada, Chile, Japan, Malaysia, Mexico, New Zealand, Peru, Singapore, the United States, and Vietnam. (http://www.ustr.gov).
2. Following the language of the WTO's Agreement on Technical Barriers to Trade (TBT Agreement), standards refer to voluntary standards for products, technical regulations are mandatory standards, and conformity assessment refers to the formal process by which products are certified as having met the standards and technical regulations of a particular country. The WTO's TBT Agreement covers the above three governance areas for products but not for production standards.
3. Athukorala's (2011) definition of parts and components trade is the most expansive of the three studies. In measuring parts and components, the study identifies six product categories in which network trade is heavily concentrated: SITC 75-SITC 78, including 1) office machines and automatic data processing machines, 2) telecommunications and sound recording equipment, 3) electrical machinery, 4) road vehicles; and 5) SITC 87-SITC 88, which include professional and scientific equipment and photographic apparatus. This measure differs from the OECD approach and from Yeats (1998) and Hummels, Ishii, and Yi (2001). Athukorala's study also provides a very useful survey and critique of existing measures of production network trade (67–69).
4. The coding scheme is based on Hoekman (1996), which evaluated GATS commitments of GATT members during the Uruguay Round.
5. For the case of investment provisions, Kotschwar (2009) has pointed out that RTAs go beyond many bilateral investment treaties in terms of protection, liberalization, and harmonization in investment provisions.
6. A well-known case of a nonviolation dispute is the Kodak-Fuji dispute between the United States and Japan (DS44), in which the former claimed that competition policies of the Japanese government regarding the distribution and domestic sale of imported film and paper constituted nonviolation nullification and impairment of benefits.

References

Abbott, Kenneth W., and Duncan Snidal. 2000. Hard and Soft Law in International Governance. *International Organization* 54: 421–456.

Abbott, Kenneth W., Robert O. Keohane, Andrew Moravcsik, Ann-Marie Slaughter, and Duncan Snidal. 2001. The Concept of Legalization. *International Organization* 54: 401–419.

Athukorala, Prema-chandra. 2005. Product Fragmentation and Trade Patterns in East Asia. *Asian Economic Papers* 4 (3): 1–27.

Athukorala, Prema-chandra. 2011. Production Networks and Trade Patterns in East Asia: Regionalization or Globalization? *Asian Economic Papers* 10 (1): 65–95.

Baccini, Leonardo, Andreas Dür, and Manfred Elsig. 2013. Depth, Flexibility, and International Cooperation: The Politics of Trade Agreement Design. Unpublished manuscript.

Baldwin, Richard. 2011. 21st Century Regionalism: Filling the Gap between 21st Century Trade and 20th Century Trade Rules. Centre for Economic Policy Research Policy Insight No. 56.

Bhagwati, Jagdish. 2008. *Termites in the Trading System: How Preferential Trade Agreements Undermine Free Trade*. Oxford: Oxford University Press.

Birdsall, Nancy, and Robert Z. Lawrence. 1999. Deep Integration and Trade Agreements. In *Global Public Goods: International Cooperation in the 21st Century*, edited by Inge Kaul, Isabelle Grunberg, and Marc A. Stern, 128–151. Oxford: Oxford University Press.

Chase, Kerry. 2004. From Protectionism to Regionalism: Multinational Firms and Trade-Related Investment Measures. *Business and Politics* 6 (2): 1–36.

Chase, Kerry. 2008a. Moving Hollywood Abroad: Divided Labor Markets and the New Politics of Trade in Services. *International Organization* 62 (4): 653–687.

Chase, Kerry. 2008b. Protecting Free Trade: The Political Economy of Rules of Origin, *International Organization* 62 (3): 507–530.

Chauffour, Jean-Pierre, and Jean Christophe Maur, eds. 2011. *Preferential Trade Agreement Policies for Development: A Handbook*. Washington, DC: International Bank for Reconstruction and Development/World Bank.

De Melo, J., and A. Panagariya, eds. 1996. *New Dimensions in Regional Integration*. Cambridge, UK: Cambridge University Press.

Downs, George W., David M. Rock, and Peter N. Barsoom. 1996. Is the Good News about Compliance Good News about Cooperation? *International Organization* 50 (3): 379–406.

Dür, Andreas, Leonardo Baccini, and Manfred Elsig, 2013. The Design of International Trade Agreements: Introducing a New Database. *Review of International Organizations*. DOI 10.1007/s11558-013-9179-8.

Estevadeordal, Antoni, Kati Suominen, and Robert Teh, eds. 2009. *Regional Rules in the Global Trading System*. Cambridge, UK: Cambridge University Press.

Fishlow, Albert, and Stephan Haggard. 1992. *The United States and the Regionalization of the World Economy*. Paris: OECD Development Centre.

Hicks, Raymond, and Soo Yeon Kim. 2012. Reciprocal Trade Agreements in Asia: Credible Commitment to Trade Liberalization or Paper Tigers? *Journal of East Asian Studies* 12 (1): 1–30.

Hoekman, Bernard. 1996. Assessing the General Agreement on Trade in Services. In *The Uruguay Round and Developing Countries*, edited by Will Martin and L. Alan Winters, 88–124. Cambridge, UK: Cambridge University Press.

Hoekman, Bernard, and Michel M. Kostecki. 2009. *The Political Economy of the World Trading System*. 3rd ed. Oxford: Oxford University Press.

Hoekman, Bernard, and L. Alan Winters. 2009. Multilateralizing Preferential Trade Agreements: A Developing Country Perspective. In *Multilateralizing Regionalism: Challenges for the Global Trading System*, edited by Richard Baldwin and Patrick Low, 636–680. Cambridge, UK: Cambridge University Press.

Horn, H., P. C. Mavroidis, and A. Sapir. 2010. Beyond the WTO? An Anatomy of EU and US Preferential Trade Agreements. *World Economy* 33 (1): 1565–1588.

Hummels, David, Jun Ishii, and Kei-Mu Yi. 2001. The Nature and Growth of Vertical Specialization in World Trade. *Journal of International Economics* 54: 75–96.

Kahler, Miles, and David Lake, eds. 2003. *Governance in a Global Economy: Political Authority in Transition*. Princeton, NJ: Princeton University Press.

Kernohan, David, and Enrica De Cian. 2007. Trade, the Environment and Climate Change: Multilateral versus Regional Agreements. In *Climate and Trade Policy: Bottom-up Approaches Towards Global Agreement*, edited by Carlo Carraro and Christian Egenhofer, 70–93. Cheltenham, UK: Edward Elgar.

Kim, Soo Yeon. 2012. Negotiating the Nexus: Production Networks and Behind-the-Border Commitments in Regional Trade Agreements. Unpublished manuscript.

Kim, Soo Yeon, and Mark Manger. 2013. Hubs of Governance: Path-Dependence and Higher-Order Effects of PTA Formation. Unpublished manuscript.

Koremenos, Barbara, Charles Lipson, and Duncan Snidal. 2001. The Rational Design of International Institutions. *International Organization* 55 (4): 761–799.

Kotschwar, Barbara. 2009. Mapping Investment Provisions in Regional Trade Agreements: Towards and International Investment Regime? In *Regional Rules in the Global Trading System*, edited by Antoni Estevadeordal, Kati Suominen, and Robert Teh, 365–417. Cambridge, UK: Cambridge University Press.

Lawrence, Robert Z. 1996. *Regionalism, Multilateralism, and Deeper Integration*. Washington, DC: The Brookings Institution.

Mansfield, Edward D., and Eric Reinhardt. 2008. International Institutions and the Volatility of International Trade. *International Organization* 62 (4): 621–652.

Marchetti, Juan A., and Martin Roy. 2008. Services Liberalization in the WTO and in RTAs. In *Opening Markets for Trade in Services; Countries and Sectors in Bilateral and WTO Negotiations*, edited by Juan A Marchetti and Martin Roy, 61–112. Cambridge, UK: Cambridge University Press and WTO.

Mattoo, Aaditya, and Arvind Subramanian. 2009. From Doha to the Next Bretton Woods: A New Multilateral Trade Agenda. *Foreign Affairs* 88 (1): 15.

Orefice, Gianluca, and Nadia Rocha. 2011. Deep Integration and Production Networks: An Empirical Analysis. World Trade Organization Staff Working Paper No. ERSD-2011-11.

Piermartini, Roberta, and Michele Budetta. 2009. A Mapping of Regional Rules on Technical Barriers to Trade. In *Regional Rules in the Global Trading System*, edited by Antoni Estevadordal, Kati Suominen, and Robert Teh, 250–315. Cambridge, UK: Cambridge University Press.

Roy, Martin. 2011. Services Commitments in Preferential Trade Agreements: An Expanded Dataset. World Trade Organization Staff Working Paper No. ERSD-2011-18.

Roy, Martin, Juan Marchetti, and Hoe Lim. 2009. Services Liberalization in the New Generation of Preferential Trade Agreements: How Much Further Than the GATS? In *Regional Rules in the Global Trading System*, edited by Antoni Estevadeordal, Kati Suominen, and Robert Teh, 316–364. Cambridge, UK: Cambridge University Press.

Schiff. M., and L. A. Winters 2003. *Regional Integration and Development*. Washington, DC: World Bank.

Shadlen, Kenneth C. 2005. Exchanging Development for Market Access? Deep Integration and Industrial Policy under Multilateral and Regional-Bilateral Trade Agreements. *Review of International Political Economy* 12 (5): 750–775.

Shadlen, Kenneth C. 2008. Globalisation, Power and Integration: The Political Economy of Regional and Bilateral Trade Agreements in the Americas. *Journal of Development Studies* 44 (1): 1–20.

Simmons, Beth A., and Daniel J. Hopkins. 2005. The Constraining Power of international Treaties: Theory and Methods. *American Political Science Review* 99 (4): 623–631.

Solano, Oliver, and Andreas Sennekamp. 2006. Competition Provisions in Regional Trade Agreements. OECD Trade Policy Working Papers No. 31. Paris: OECD.

Teh, Robert. 2009. Competition Provisions in Regional Trade Agreements. In *Regional Rules in the Global Trading System*. edited by Antoni Estevadordal, Kati Suominen, and Robert Teh, 418–491. Cambridge, UK: Cambridge University Press.

Teh, Robert, Thomas J. Prusa, and Michele Budetta. 2009. Trade Remedy Provisions in Regional Trade Agreements. In *Regional Rules in the Global Trading System*, edited by Antoni Estevadeordal, Kati Suominen, and Robert Teh, 166–249. Cambridge, UK: Cambridge University Press.

Tinbergen, J. 1954. *International Economic Integration*. Amsterdam: Elsevier.

Trebilcock, Michael J., and Robert Howse. 2005. *The Regulation of International Trade*. 3rd ed. London: Routledge.

Viner, J. 1950. *The Customs Union Issue*. New York: Carnegie Endowment for International Peace.

Von Stein, Jana. 2005. Do Treaties Constrain or Screen? Selection Bias and Treaty Compliance. *American Political Science Review* 99 (4): 611–622.

World Bank. 2005. *Global Economic Prospects: Trade, Regionalism, and Development*. Washington, DC: World Bank.

World Bank. 2000. *Trade Blocs*. Oxford: Oxford University Press.

World Trade Organization. 2011. *The WTO and Preferential Trade Agreements: From Co-existence to Coherence (World Trade Report 2011)*. Geneva: WTO.

Yeats, A. J. 1998. Just How Big Is Global Production Sharing? World Bank Policy Research Working Paper No. 1871. Washington, DC: World Bank.

CHAPTER 20

....

WTO MEMBERSHIP

....

CHRISTINA L. DAVIS AND MEREDITH WILF

INTRODUCTION

THOSE who created the post–World War II trade regime sought to establish rules that would prevent the kind of breakdown of the economic order that occurred in the 1930s. Secretary of State Cordell Hull of the United States led in the commitment to establish free trade as the basis for peaceful international relations. The General Agreement on Tariffs and Trade (GATT), adopted in 1947, emerged as the compromise outcome to reduce trade barriers and promote growth of world trade.[1] The refusal of the United Kingdom to end the imperial preference system and the reluctance of the US Congress to accept ambitious institutional commitments for the negotiated International Trade Organization resulted in the GATT serving as the core institution that would govern trade for the next forty-eight years. Despite its origin as a temporary arrangement, the GATT oversaw an era of rapidly expanding trade. It evolved as an institution by means of members negotiating more tariff reductions and new rules in trade rounds while using panels of diplomats in a form of dispute settlement process that helped avoid trade wars when disagreements arose among members. The creation of the World Trade Organization (WTO) in 1995 further broadened the scope of agreement and increased the strength of the existing, legalized enforcement process.

Whether the trade regime is responsible for the phenomenal postwar growth of trade is hotly debated, as world trade volume and trade as a percent of country's gross domestic product (GDP), a standard measure of a country's trade openness, has grown steadily among both members and nonmembers (see Figure 20.1). Nevertheless, the GATT/WTO is widely credited with helping states to expand trade. Members choose to resolve major trade disputes through the regime's adjudication process and have largely complied with its rulings. In line with the motivation of leaders at the founding of the institution, major world economic downturns have not led to rampant protectionism or to a breakdown of the rules.

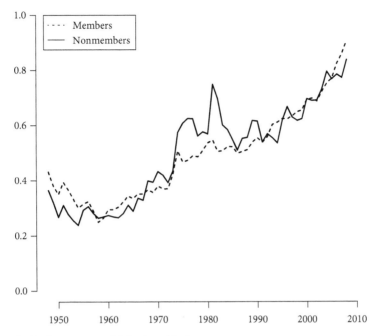

FIG. 20.1 Trade Openness and Membership.*

*Mean value of trade openness (imports plus exports as percent of GDP) for GATT/WTO members and all other countries. In any given year, members and nonmembers enjoy similar levels of trade openness.

As states manage incentives to pursue mercantilist policies against broader gains from free trade, power and interest underlie their support of the regime. But members' uncertainty about future preferences and economic circumstances has led them to adopt an institutional design with flexibility for escape from commitments, discretionary terms over new member accession, and decentralized enforcement. Far from high delegation to a supranational organization, the GATT/WTO remains a largely member-driven organization. Therefore it is critical to understand the conditions that explain membership. What are the gains from membership that lead countries to join? Membership in the regime has grown from 23 to 159, from 23 percent of all countries in 1948 to 80 percent of all countries in 2012 (see Figure 20.2). The Ministerial Conference in December 2013 approved the accession of Yemen to become the 160th member, and twenty-three other countries are currently in negotiations to join. Clearly, states view advantages from membership such that most seek entry to the organization. At the same time, this member expansion presents problems as the increasingly heterogeneous preferences of the broad membership prevent agreement, as seen in the latest trade negotiating round. Why were major powers willing to grant the expanded membership that brought forth this scenario?

This chapter begins with a brief overview of the literature on why states benefit from the trade regime. The theories about regime formation and empirical research

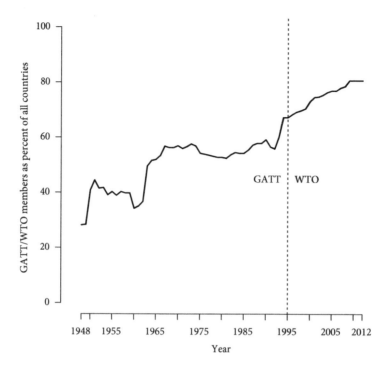

FIG. 20.2   GATT/WTO Membership Growth: Expanding Membership of the Trade Regime.*

*Growing share of countries that have become members. "Member" is defined as any state that has completed formal accession to GATT/WTO.

on the effects of membership provide insights into the motivation of states to join the trade regime. Next we examine the process of joining the regime and explain selection patterns that result from both the decisions of countries to apply and decisions of the membership to accept new members. The final section summarizes the discussion.

The Benefits of Regime Membership

Several explanations—each placing a different emphasis on the role of power, preferences, institutions, and social purpose—have been given for the establishment and evolution of the multilateral regime to support free trade. These theories also highlight competing reasons for states to join the regime. One view is that states simply join as an act that follows the lead of the dominant state. Alternatively, states join because they need the regime as a tool for coordinating behavior or share principled beliefs with other members.

Why Form a Multilateral Trade Regime?

When the state system is characterized by a highly asymmetrical distribution of power, the dominant hegemon will support free trade that will enhance its own income and power over other states (Krasner 1976). Hegemonic states build a framework of rules to maintain stable order. Kindleberger (1986) blamed the US failure to ascend to this role in the 1930s as the source of breakdown in the economic order. When the United States did rise to the leadership position and shape the postwar trading regime, it closely adapted the rules to its interests. For industries in which the United States sought exceptions to free trade—such as in agriculture—liberalization demands were lenient. Further, exceptions to free trade were crafted around US domestic laws. As the US economic structure shifted to become more service and technology based in the 1970s, it pushed to expand the regime's scope to include service trade and intellectual property rights, beginning in the Tokyo Round. Some see the WTO as an "American creation" (Gilpin 2001, 222). In his book on hierarchy in international relations, Lake (2009) emphasizes the contractual relationship of the United States with subordinate states and offers membership in the GATT/WTO as an example of how the United States exercises authority over other states without the costs of coercive enforcement of its interests. The mechanism by which the United States exerts this power is identified by Kim (2010) as the product-by-product bargaining protocol that gives advantage to market size. The informal trade round negotiation process has allowed the United States to shape rule making on an ongoing basis through ad hoc threats of exclusion or exit that would leave other states worse off if they lost access to the large US market (Steinberg 2002; Stone 2011). To the extent that the rules reflect US interests, delegation to a legal enforcement mechanism allows the United States to avoid the hostility provoked by unilateral market access demands.

While none deny the influential role of the United States as first among equals in the formation and evolution of the trade regime, others contend that US power alone is insufficient to drive the multilateral trade regime. Even as US economic dominance declined in the 1970s, the trade regime was sustained. This outcome arose from the "stickiness" of the trade rules within an institution—once created, the institution persisted—and also from the functional demand for the regime. From the perspective of institutional theories, the GATT acts as a central bargaining forum that promotes more efficient communication among states with repeated interactions. It supports linkage and punishment strategies to uphold commitments to free trade (Keohane 1982; Martin 1992; Morrow 1994). One prominent explanation of the trade regime contends that large states would be tempted to set unilateral, high tariffs in an effort to manipulate terms of trade to their own advantage. The costs of such protective measures are forced onto foreign exporters and consumers. Based on the core principles of reciprocity and nondiscrimination, multilateral agreement allows states to escape this "prisoner's dilemma" and to achieve greater welfare benefits through a low tariff equilibrium (Johnson 1953–1954; Bagwell and Staiger 1999). This logic extends beyond the largest states to also explain the behavior of a wide range of countries (Broda, Limao, and Weinstein 2008).

These theories present the WTO as a self-enforcing set of rules based on state interest. The implication is that all states will gain from regime membership.

Solving the prisoner's dilemma at the international level, however, does not eliminate domestic pressures for protection. Even as the supposed leader of the move to free trade, the United States resisted liberalization for many of the tariff lines that were politically too sensitive to cut (Goldstein and Gulotty 2014). Tariff reductions have generally occurred through slow reduction of rates over repeated rounds of negotiations, with exceptions leaving high barriers to protect sensitive sectors such as agriculture and textiles. Herein lies a second rationale for joining the regime. Leaders who see gains from free trade can use the trade rules to overcome domestic resistance. Governments face a time inconsistency problem whereby short-term lobbying and electoral pressures may induce protection that would harm long-term prospects for economic growth and for free trade that benefits diffuse consumers (Staiger and Tabellini 1999; Maggi and Rodriquez-Clare 1998). Issue linkage in the form of reciprocity, and package deals for broad trade reform, mobilize exporters who benefit from reciprocity and help to build domestic coalitions in support of liberalization (Gilligan 1997; Davis 2003). Through design of flexible rules, it is possible to lower tariffs without going beyond what is sustainable at home. Members address their uncertainties about preferences and future trade shocks through use of escape clauses and tolerance of limited noncompliance as defined by system rules (Rosendorff and Milner 2001; Rosendorff 2005).

Legal obligations also create constraints against protection. Jackson (1997) portrays the trade regime as changing the nature of the interaction among states from power politics toward the rule of law. The relatively high levels of precision in agreements and use of third-party dispute settlement make the trade regime stand out as having greater legalization than other institutions (Goldstein et al. 2000). This legitimacy has constrained even the most powerful states—including the United States—by making unilateral trade threats less effective (Schoppa 1997; Pelc 2010). Rule of law is upheld not only by the empowerment of specific configurations of domestic actors, but also by shared norms. The normative basis to the regime has allowed it to withstand many challenges and to evolve so that even as rules carved out exceptions to free trade—due to the kinds of political exigencies noted above—members' shared purpose to pursue liberal trade supported continuity of the regime (Ruggie 1982). The establishment of the WTO in 1995 was the next step of delegation by members toward a centralized trade regime with a more robust legal enforcement mechanism and a new trade-policy review process for peer monitoring.

Do Members Enjoy Higher Trade Levels?

Andrew Rose (2004) was the first to empirically test the proposition that the GATT facilitated postwar trade growth. Analyzing trade at the dyadic level and using a gravity model to control for factors that affect states' natural affinities to trade, he surprisingly found that pairs of states that are members of the GATT/WTO did not seem to enjoy higher trade than pairs of nonmember states.[2] He concluded that member states do not enjoy significant trade increases, with the implication that the trade regime may not actually fulfill its basic goal to increase trade for members.

Judith Goldstein, Douglas Rivers, and Michael Tomz (2007) highlight the importance of the GATT's de facto practice that granted most-favored nation (MFN) benefits to entire categories of nonmember states—specifically, colonies and former colonies—*as if* they were regime members. In contrast to Rose's focus on formal members, Goldstein, Rivers and Tomz argue that it is more appropriate to compare regime "participants"—*both* formal members *and* states that received MFN multilateral trade benefits—to "non-participants," states that were nonmembers without MFN benefits. Re-running Rose's analysis using participation (instead of formal membership) and focusing on a country's exports within a directed dyad (instead of nondirected, average dyadic trade), they found that regime participants *do* enjoy higher levels of trade than do nonparticipants. They attribute a causal mechanism—a state's access to export markets at MFN tariff rates—to tie membership to trade levels, moving beyond Rose's focus on the association between formal membership and trade levels.

Allee and Scalera (2012) posit an alternative causal mechanism—a state's own level of tariff liberalization—as the channel through which the GATT affects trade levels. States that significantly liberalize tariffs upon joining the regime—determined by their type of accession process—enjoy increased levels of trade compared to states that join the institution without significant trade-policy liberalization.

The many studies debating trade regime effects on trade use slightly different methods and units of analysis. Rose uses nondirected dyads (where the dependent variable is the average of *both* states' bilateral trade), but subsequent research has largely used directed dyads to model each state's individual bilateral trade level. Similarly, Rose uses year fixed effects, while other studies use year *and* dyad fixed effects. Subramanian and Wei (2007, 158) argue that dyadic fixed effects capture the multilateral resistance of each country—a key assumption of the gravity model—and therefore including dyadic fixed effects provides more accurate estimates. Imai and Kim (2013), who examine the debate with specific attention to fixed effects methodology, confirm that empirical results are highly model dependent. Their analysis finds that, as a result of greater across-country than across-year variation in membership, dyadic fixed effect specifications yield more volatile results of WTO membership effect than do year fixed effect specifications. That results are highly model dependent means that substantive researchers must use theory to justify the assumptions underlying their chosen specification.

There is some consensus that the effects of membership and participation on trade are greatest for developed countries and for trade in manufactured products. Subramanian and Wei (2007) decompose the effects on imports versus exports, level of country development, and country trade profile; they find that significant trade benefits accrue to industrial countries. Dutt, Mihov, and Van-Zandt (2011) find that the WTO influences extensive product margin of trade rather than intensive margin; members increase the goods that they trade with each other rather than trading higher volumes of the same goods. Helpman, Melitz, and Rubinstein (2008) show that nearly 50 percent of possible dyadic ties are lost if ties between states that do not trade with each other at all are excluded from analysis. However, studies that incorporate these new insights into a reexamination of the debate continue to arrive at varying conclusions. For example, Liu (2009) and Chang and Lee (2011) find WTO membership associated with large boosts to bilateral trade, while Eicher and Henn (2011) and Barigozzi, Fagiolo, and Mangioni (2011) find little effect of membership on trade. Using a network model of trade, De Benedictis and Tajoli (2011) find that WTO members are closer trading partners than are non-WTO members.

Beyond direct linkages between membership and trade, authors focus on how trade benefits accrue to developed and developing country trade regime members. Gowa and Kim (2005) show that trade benefits accrued to the five largest member states at the time of GATT establishment: the United States, Great Britain, Germany, France, and Canada. While many studies emphasize benefits of the regime accruing to developed countries, others emphasize benefits for developing countries. Developing country members who appear to benefit most from the regime are those who have alliances such that the trade rules reinforce concessions granted to them on the basis of a strong political relationship (Gowa 2010). In contrast, Carnegie (2014) emphasizes the value of the regime to those states that have *weak* political ties, because these states need the regime as protection against having trade interests held up in exchange for foreign policy concessions.

Other scholars analyze whether the trade regime provides stability of trade as distinct from the volume of trade. This line of reasoning follows closely the logic within the GATT that even a high fixed tariff is to be preferred over discretionary administrative measures. Mansfield and Reinhardt (2008) emphasize *sustainable* trade flows. They propose that members may seek lower trade volatility rather than higher trade levels and show that membership in the GATT/WTO lowers trade-policy volatility and trade-export volatility. Their finding counters Rose (2005), who finds no significant difference in trade volatility of members and nonmembers. As there is no standard method to calculate trade volatility, Mansfield and Reinhardt attribute the conflicting findings to the differences in how their study operationalizes the dependent variable. They apply four separate measures of annual trade volatility, in contrast to Rose's use of one measure based on a country's standard deviation of trade over twenty-five-year panels. Dreher and Voigt (2011) examine the impact of membership in international organizations on country risk ratings and find that the GATT/WTO has a statistically significant impact on lowering perceived risk by investors. In summary, membership—both formal and informal—is often used to identify the regime's effects on trade flows, but the literature has not reached a consensus. There is need for further research to reach more conclusive answers to this basic question.

Do Members Benefit from Multilateral Enforcement?

A strong legal framework that underlies third-party dispute settlement is a central benefit of membership. All members of the GATT/WTO have standing to file complaints under the Dispute Settlement Understanding when they allege that another member has a policy in violation of the agreement. The process begins with the filing of a formal complaint, which initiates a consultation period. If settlement is not achieved through consultation, the complainant may request a panel of third parties to rule on the legal status of the challenged policy. This process has remained largely consistent across both the GATT and WTO, although reforms of the Uruguay Round Agreements codified a more robust process. Key reforms included the automatic right to panel and the introduction of an appellate body of standing judges to hear appeals as an additional legal layer. The dispute process offers enforcement authority that is important to resolve the specific disputes and to deter future violations.

Within the set of cases filed under the dispute settlement process, compliance with consultative agreements and panel rulings has been generally good. Hudec (1993), in the first attempt to tally dispute outcomes, found that the large majority of the early GATT panels resolved the dispute. Busch and Reinhardt (2003, 725) find that GATT/WTO disputes produce substantial concessions in 50 percent of cases and partial concessions for another 20 percent of cases. Interest in upholding the overall credibility of the system of rules leads countries to comply with most rulings (Kovenock and Thursby 1992; Jackson 1997; Hudec 2002).[3] The director of the WTO legal affairs division, Bruce Wilson, acclaims members specifically for high compliance with rulings (Wilson 2007). Further, the direct costs of authorized retaliation and the potential reputational costs from noncompliance increase the incentives to cooperate (Bagwell and Staiger 1999, 2002; Maggi 1999).

Critics argue that developing countries benefit less from multilateral enforcement than other members, because they lack legal capacity and retaliatory power. Evidence from filed complaints suggests that developing countries gain fewer trade benefits from winning cases (Bown 2004a, 2004b), suffer from weak legal capacity (Busch, Reinhardt, and Shaffer 2009), and may be less willing to impose countermeasures if the defendant refuses implementation (Bagwell, Mavroidis, and Staiger 2007). However, these studies are motivated by the question of whether a developing country WTO member that files a legal complaint would get more from the system if it had more resources, which is different from asking whether the developing country would get a better outcome *in the absence* of the WTO dispute settlement process. The latter is the relevant question when considering the benefits of membership, which provides access to WTO dispute settlement. Davis (2006) compares the negotiation process for Peru and Vietnam in two "all else being equal" disputes over fish labeling policies based on nearly identical legal terms on technical barriers to trade. Peru used its rights as a WTO member to file a legal complaint at the WTO against Europe, while Vietnam pursued bilateral negotiations with the United States because it had not yet completed the WTO accession process. The divergent outcomes are quite stark—Peru won concessions, while Vietnam got nothing. Officials in Vietnam saw this case as further motivation to continue its negotiations to join the WTO. Once Vietnam joined the WTO, it used the dispute settlement process to bring two cases against the United States. Small countries would do even better if they were larger and if institutions were revised to auction countermeasures or to implement collective retaliation. Yet this does not detract from the reality that WTO dispute settlement under the multilateral trade regime offers small states greater leverage against large states than they would otherwise have outside the regime in asymmetrical negotiations.

To assess the effectiveness of dispute settlement, it is important to include counterfactual outcomes of trade disputes that were *not* addressed through adjudication. Davis (2012) compares outcomes of similar trade barrier disputes raised in negotiations to those adjudicated through a WTO complaint. On average, barriers that were also challenged through a WTO complaint were more likely to show progress toward removal of the trade barrier than those that were not subject to a formal WTO complaint.

Others challenge whether "victory" in a dispute matters in the sense of bringing observable changes to trade flows. The findings of Goldstein, Rivers, and Tomz (2007), who show that nonmember participants experience the same or even larger trade benefits from the regime than formal members, imply that the dispute system does not play a large role in protecting trade flows; nonmember participants shared all rights with formal members, with the exception of the right to use the dispute settlement process. In recent work, Chaudoin, Kucik, and Pelc (2013) and Hofmann and Kim (2013) find little evidence that a WTO ruling produces increased exports to the market that has been found in violation. If true, this raises the question of why states use the dispute process. It may be that they are more interested in political signals sent by dispute actions to actors both at home and abroad. Other work, however, does find a positive effect between dispute settlement and increased trade flows (Bechtel and Sattler forthcoming).

Even though all members have a right to use the dispute system, the structure of government institutions influences how frequently countries use it (Rickard 2010; Davis 2012). Governments push harder in dispute actions on behalf of key interest groups (Fattore 2012; Rosendorff, this volume), and complainants select the timing of disputes against the United States during election years, which could bring more pressure for compliance (Chaudoin forthcoming). Looking at trade partners and products beyond those directly at stake in the specific dispute, governments may seek a deterrent effect, as winning one case could prevent future disputes. Deterrence of cheating counts as a benefit that accrues to members from their access to a legal dispute system.

There are many quantities of interest for assessing the effectiveness of the trade regime. Any single study highlights one aspect of how the regime may benefit members, such as increasing bilateral trade with other members or resolving trade disputes. Each of these outcomes may have varying importance to different members. Where one state seeks more trade, another wants to avoid negative trade linkages with foreign policy or excessive volatility. The average effect of membership may be less relevant than the effect conditional on characteristics of states that influence what they need from membership. A fuller appreciation of regime benefits would need to take into account all dimensions across which the regime serves its members.

Different levels of analysis—beyond dyads and individual states—suggest broader trade regime effects. For example, Oatley (2011) emphasizes that an institution such as the trade regime is a systemic factor that affects outcomes, because political decisions on a range of issues are made conditional upon the context provided by the multilateral regime. Another approach is to compare how states respond to crises. Davis and Pelc (forthcoming) suggest that the ability of the regime to restrain protection must be understood within the context of different types of economic crises that give rise to new demands for protectionist policies. In contrast to local crises in which only one or a few states have incentives to increase trade protection, during pervasive crisis—when many members *simultaneously* face hard economic times—the trade regime establishes a focal point and coordinates a collaborative response to limit the increase in protection. Cao (2012) analyzes trade flows within a network analysis and establishes how trade similarity, not trade flows, is associated with domestic regulatory convergence. Economic researchers have also begun to analyze trade at the network level (e.g., De Benedictis and Tajoli 2011). These new perspectives that move beyond dyadic analysis emphasize the importance for scholars of specifying clear counterfactuals.

The Problem of Using Membership to Identify Regime Effectiveness

GATT/WTO membership status is central to empirical analyses about the effects of the trade regime. In the research discussed in the previous section, membership is used as an identification strategy whereby the effect of membership is inferred from analysis that compares policy outcomes for members and nonmembers. The average effect of membership is taken to reflect the regime's effect as a whole. It is necessary to flag the limitations that arise from using membership to identify institutional effects.[4]

This approach assumes that membership is exogenously given and has no spillover effects. These two assumptions may be problematic. First, selection bias is a concern, given that the process generating membership in the trade regime is not random. Thus, these studies capture the different performance between members and nonmembers but neglect the prior question of what leads countries to join or stay outside of the trade regime in the first place. Second, spillover effects are likely because the policy changes related to being a member of the trade regime are often comprehensive. For example, domestic laws that have been reformed to enhance protection of intellectual property rights will offer this protection equally to members and nonmembers. Even tariff changes are often implemented through MFN policies without exclusively privileging members. Other functions of the regime may induce stability at the systemic level through reducing the volatility of trade flows and supporting open markets during economic crises.

Theories about regime formation and the effects of membership must take into account the endogenous nature of institutions, which are created to serve the interests of members (Martin and Simmons 2001). Downs, Rocke, and Barsoom (1996) highlight that if states accept rules that already reflect their preferences, compliance is not a meaningful concept. From this perspective, liberalization is driven by an exogenous process that leads to preference changes. Hence states should pursue gradual expansion of membership to include new members as they become more liberal (Downs, Rocke, and Barsoom 1998). Theories about why states join the institution need to be connected to the empirical debate about the extent to which the trade regime has been responsible for liberalization of trade flows and resolution of trade disputes.

Decisions to Join

Membership in any regime is voluntary. States must decide to join an institution, and the current members must be willing to accept the applicant. The organizational rules of the GATT and WTO support an inclusive mandate to achieve broad membership. Any country or territory with autonomous control over its trade policy is eligible to join. This section reviews the process of becoming a member and theories about the political and economic variables that shape when countries join. A brief case study of Mexico's accession to the GATT illustrates the factors that can influence decisions to join the regime.

The Accession Process

Under the GATT, two accession processes existed. The standard accession process outlined in GATT Article 33 was decentralized, with most details of accession delegated to the working party, a group of existing contracting parties that opted-in to oversee the accession process for a given applicant. The working party and applicant country held consultations and bargained over an initial tariff schedule, which was then presented to the GATT General Council. GATT Article 33 formally required a two-thirds majority vote to adopt the arrangement, although in practice few votes occurred. Nonmember countries meeting certain criteria, mostly former colonies, were eligible to join the GATT under a simpler accession process outlined in GATT Article 26, which granted membership on the basis of sponsorship (i.e., the written support) of its former colonial power and a note of intention to join the regime. Upon receipt of these notices, the GATT granted immediate membership, bypassing the negotiations required under GATT Article 33. This lowered the entry cost for countries eligible to accede under GATT Article 26 as compared to most countries that acceded under GATT Article 33.[5] Since the establishment of the WTO in 1995, a single process has governed accession. The WTO Article 12 process is formally the same as the GATT Article 33 accession process, but nonmember countries acceding through WTO Article 12 have a longer list of required agreements to negotiate (including GATS, TRIMS, and TRIPS) before gaining WTO membership. Further, trade rounds under the WTO are no longer associated with negotiating entry of applicants, which means that there are few opportunities for reciprocity during WTO Article 12 negotiations. Pelc (2011) highlights how asymmetrical bargaining shapes WTO accession negotiations, as applicants are forced to make concessions while members do not concurrently change their commitments. All applicant countries that were not contracting parties upon transition from the GATT to the WTO in 1995 must complete the WTO Article 12 accession process. Observers have noted the prevalence of WTO-plus commitments, whereby the accession protocol of an applicant country goes beyond the obligations of WTO member countries. Although the rules for accession have not changed greatly between the GATT and WTO, there is a widespread perception that the WTO accession process is more demanding than the GATT accession process.

The accession process is a key moment of leverage when regime members can dictate entry terms for nonmembers. Jones (2009) establishes that the length of WTO accession negotiations has been increasing over time. As the scope of rules has become broader, new members must accept more obligations. The higher cost of being outside the growing regime also allows members to demand more of entrants. Kim (2010) argues that those who join the trade regime under WTO rules enjoy higher increases in trade than earlier entrants who joined under the GATT rules. Allee and Scalera (2012) demonstrate that states given a free ride to enter the regime without any negotiation, an accession option under the GATT available to the former colonies of members, receive the smallest trade gains. The more rigorous negotiation demands placed on other states bring more liberalization concessions that also lead to more trade gains. The demands placed on entrants also vary as a function of their economic size. Pelc (2011) identifies middle-income states—those not protected by norms of special and differential treatment and those whose export markets are not large enough to have strong bargaining power—as those that offer the most liberalization concessions during accession negotiations. Neumayer (2013) finds that trade interests determine which members opt into the GATT/WTO working party that negotiates accession terms. Members recognize the risks of competition from expanding membership and use the accession window to strategically delay accession and negotiate terms that will protect their key interests. This flexibility surrounding accession becomes a source of informal institutional power (Stone 2011).

The Economic and Political Determinants of Membership

New research directly models the economic, political, and legal factors that create differential costs and benefits for a country to join the trade regime. The interests of the members ultimately determine entry; these interests reflect not only their economic gains from an expanding membership in the trade regime, but also their broader foreign policy objectives. Applicants weigh a mix of economic risks and benefits from expanding market access and competition and may see the rules as a guarantor against arbitrary sanctions. Thus on both the supply and demand sides, one must examine multiple dimensions.

The largest draw of membership is market access. For states dependent on trade with GATT/WTO members, entry will lower their trade costs. In an innovative study, Copelovitch and Ohls (2012) examine the former colonies of members who were granted "free pass" entry under Article 26 provisions of GATT accession. Since these countries did not face any bargaining or policy reform conditions that could act as a barrier to entry, the study highlights the demand side of membership. They find that high trade dependence with members was an important factor in bringing some of these countries to join early after independence. In contrast, a country such as Vietnam waited until later—after expansion of the agreement terms under the WTO made accession more difficult—before it decided to join.

Ironically, the ability to protect sensitive industries under the trade regime is one important condition for accession into the institution. Kucik and Reinhardt (2008) provide evidence that states with stronger antidumping laws are more likely to join the trade regime and to liberalize more when they join. As described by Rosendorff (this volume), flexibility measures have been essential to allow free trade commitments by countries that want to be responsive to domestic political actors. A heterogeneous group of countries with mixed preferences on free trade has joined the institution because it does not demand rigid commitments to fully open markets. This in turn presents challenges for cooperation. India was among the founding members of the GATT and has also been among the most reluctant to open its markets, to the point where its demand for a special safeguard measure to protect its agricultural sector was given as one reason for the collapse of the Doha Round ministerial meeting in 2008. Former US Trade Representative Susan Schwab commented on the long deadlock in WTO negotiations: "No future multilateral negotiation will succeed, however, without addressing the very real differences in economic strength, prospects, and capabilities within the so-called developing world. It is worth recalling that one of the WTO's most important characteristics is the inclusion of these developing economies in governance and decision-making from its origins as the General Agreement on Tariffs and Trade in 1948" (2011, 117).

In addition to trade levels, geopolitical alignment and democracy appear to be equally important for determining membership. The GATT, negotiated as part of the ITO at the Bretton Woods conference, brought together twenty-three countries under the leadership of the United States and United Kingdom. Countries that subsequently joined were colonies and friends of these countries. The Cold War made it less likely that the Soviet Union or its allies would join (although the Soviet Union was invited to join the GATT, and Czechoslovakia was a founding member). Davis and Wilf (2014) argue that geopolitical ties between applicants and members provide a basis of common interest that draws states rapidly into the regime. The discretionary accession process has allowed members to use the GATT/WTO as a tool of statecraft, raising and lowering the bar for nonmember states to enter the organization. By modeling the timing of nonmember application—instead of formal accession year—Davis and Wilf avoid the endogeneity problem associated with many states' long accession processes. Their statistical analysis of applicants shows that the allies of members and democratic states are significantly more likely to join the regime. In some cases, members encourage the application of an ally or dependency, such as US sponsorship of Japan's application in 1952 or the US role in encouraging Iraq and Afghanistan to apply in 2004. When East European countries were being courted as part of foreign policy strategy, Poland, Hungary, and Romania were granted lenient accession terms so that they could join in the 1960s without substantial tariff liberalization or reforms of their state-planned economies.

Mexico's Debate over Membership

The case of Mexico illustrates a number of factors that can impact membership decisions. Economic preferences shape whether governments are willing to engage in trade liberalization, and both domestic political interests and the structure of the economy impact views about economic benefits from joining the regime. In addition, broader political concerns related to nationalism and relations with other countries shape the calculus of leaders.

Reluctance to embrace free trade delayed application and accession by Mexico. The first rejection of membership occurred in 1947, when the Mexican finance minister announced that the country would not ratify the Havana Charter to establish the International Trade Organization or participate in the GATT because the organization would ruin national industries (Ortiz Mena 2005, 217). Import substitution policies led to declining shares of trade as percent of GDP throughout the 1950s and 1960s and at first delivered strong economic growth. With economic downturn in the 1970s, however, the government began to experiment with different economic policies. Under pressure from the International Monetary Fund after receiving funds to help address the 1976 balance of payments crisis, the Mexican government launched a series of reforms, including steps to liberalize trade policies (Ortiz Mena 2005, 219). It appeared that Mexico was turning from import substitution to export promotion, and this shift in policy orientation explained the move to apply for GATT membership in 1979. The working group on accession met five times to produce an accession protocol that gave Mexico wide latitude to pursue its development strategies (Story 1982, 772–773).

At this point, Mexican President Lopez Portillo engaged in a remarkably open domestic debate on the merits of GATT accession. The deliberation process, with input from economic analysts and consultation with industry and labor groups, was covered in front-page media commentary. Ortiz Mena (2005, 221–222) notes the irony that this debate went forward entirely separate from the accession offer, which was negotiated with extremely favorable terms for Mexico. Rather than specific industries lobbying against import competition, attention focused on economic sovereignty and the development model writ large. The final vote of the cabinet in March 1980 opposed accession, and the government informed the GATT that it would postpone its application. Mexico had decided to remain committed to state intervention and oil exports. The push for economic reform was set aside as rising oil prices raised the prospect for a return to high growth.

The United States had actively lobbied Mexico on the need for it to join the GATT. Story (1982) contends that the desire to assert independence from the United States perversely pushed Portillo to decline joining. Portillo's relations with the Carter administration were poor at this time. Opponents of the GATT in Mexico portrayed accession as a move toward dependence on the United States. Portillo announced the postpone-ment of GATT accession on the 42nd anniversary of Mexico's expropriation of US oil companies, framing rejection of the GATT in terms of Mexican nationalism and anti-American policy (Story 1982, 775).

Caught by surprise when Mexico postponed its application in 1980, the United States began to impose higher countervailing duties against imports from Mexico (Lara-Fernandez 1987, 20). Export subsidies used as part of Mexican sectoral promo-tion strategies were seen as inimical to US interests. Friction between the countries was resolved under desperate circumstances. When the collapse of oil prices and spiral-ing cost of servicing debt obligations threw the Mexican economy into turmoil in the early 1980s, the United States used the Baker plan as leverage to encourage economic reforms in Mexico, including trade liberalization. The 1982 National Development Plan launched structural reforms to restore stable growth and improve competitiveness.

Mexico renewed its application to the GATT in 1985, stating its desire to improve market access and reduce its reliance on petroleum exports.[6] As domestic reforms had begun a process to liberalize its own markets, many urged the government to bargain for access rather than simply adopt unilateral liberalization (Ortiz Mena 2005, 225). Yet the government had not made a complete reversal in course. It only agreed to the accession protocol when assured that it would be allowed to continue sectoral promotion policies, exclude sensitive agricultural products, and retain its pricing system.

Mexico applied after its economic and geopolitical alignment became more similar to that of trade regime members. Its negotiations also displayed the willingness of mem-bers to let Mexico in with low conditionality. The accommodating stance of members, in combination with more interest in trade policy reform by Mexican leaders, led the country to finally accept entry into the organization in 1986 after having twice declined to join.

CONCLUSION

We have highlighted the role of membership in access to markets and dispute settle-ment. The gains to members, however, remain contested within the literature. The role of economic interests, geopolitical ties, and democracy in shaping member selection means that one needs to be cautious about using membership to identify the effective-ness of the institution. Furthermore, the commonly used dyadic framework neglects broader systemic impact from the regime. More attention needs to be given to discov-ering how membership benefits some countries in different ways from others or has changed over time.

As the trade regime reaches nearly universal membership, the comparison of mem-bers with nonmembers will become increasingly irrelevant. Indeed, the expansion of the regime had already become so inclusive at the time of establishing the WTO that it is very difficult to compare the effect of membership during the WTO period and during the earlier GATT period. By 1995, the year the GATT transitioned to the WTO, 128 countries (two-thirds of total countries in the world) had formally joined the regime, and outsiders were newly independent former Soviet Union countries and an unusual group of laggards. Only two nonmembers—China and Russia—individually held greater than 1 percent of world trade. Since then 32 countries—including China in 2001 and Russia in 2012—completed the accession process under the WTO, 23 countries are in the process of negotiating accession, and only a handful of countries are neither members nor formal applicants in the process of negotiating membership (as of 2013). The remaining outsiders are such a biased sample of countries that one could not generalize from analysis of this group of states.

Instead, attention is turning to the WTO-plus agreements being concluded among subsets of members. The proliferation of bilateral and regional agreements raises the question of how these overlapping memberships impact the benefits of membership in the WTO (Mansfield and Reinhardt 2003). Diversion of trade flows and fragmentation of legal obligations could erode benefits, but a competitive liberalization process could push broader and deeper commitments at both levels. A serious challenge lies in the imbalance of power across negotiation and enforcement of rules. The large membership of the WTO contributes to the stalled negotiations over new rules in the Doha Round, while more limited membership allows countries to forge ahead in the rapid conclusion of bilateral and regional trade agreements. Yet the asymmetrical nature of many bilateral and regional trade agreements weakens their enforcement power, while the multilateral system draws broader enforcement credibility from the wider membership. Increasingly, progress to negotiate new rules occurs outside of the WTO, while enforcement issues continue to be taken up largely within the WTO.

Notes

1. See Irwin, Mavroidis, and Sykes (2008) on the founding of the GATT.
2. Rose's (2004) analysis includes multiple specifications of the model, and in his conclusion he identifies a number of factors that could drive his finding. In cross-section analysis, he found a positive effect of early trade rounds and a negative effect of later rounds. See Hicks and Gowa chapters in this volume.
3. See Busch and Pelc, in this volume, for a full review.
4. See also Hicks, in this volume.
5. At the beginning of a wave of decolonization in 1960, the GATT determined that each territory eligible to become a contracting party under the GATT Article 26 accession process would gain "de facto" status within the GATT while the territory deliberated about whether or not to accede to the regime. Goldstein, Rivers, and Tomz (2007, 42) treat these nonmember states as participants because de facto participants received MFN treatment and could observe GATT proceedings. These states, however, could not participate in decision making or dispute settlement and lacked status as formal members.
6. GATT, November 27, 1985, L/5919.

REFERENCES

Allee, Todd L., and Jamie E. Scalera. 2012. The Divergent Effects of Joining International Organizations: Trade Gains and the Rigors of WTO Accession. *International Organization* 66 (2): 243–276.

Bagwell, Kyle, Petros Mavroidis, and Robert Staiger. 2007. Auctioning Countermeasures in the WTO. *Journal of International Economics* 73: 309–332.

Bagwell, Kyle, and Robert Staiger. 1999. An Economic Theory of GATT. *American Economic Review* 89 (1): 215–248.

Bagwell, Kyle and Robert Staiger. 2002. *The Economics of the World Trading System*. Cambridge, MA: MIT Press.

Barigozzi, Matteo, Giorgio Fagiolo, and Giuseppe Mangioni. 2011. Identifying the Community Structure of the International-Trade Multi-Network. *Physica A* 390 (11): 2051–2066.

Bechtel, Michael M., and Thomas Sattler. Forthcoming. What Is Litigation in the World Trade Organization Worth? *International Organization*.

Bown, Chad. 2004a. Developing Countries as Plaintiffs and Defendants in GATT/WTO Trade Disputes. *World Economy* 27 (1): 59–80.

Bown, Chad. 2004b. On the Economic Success of GATT/WTO Dispute Settlement. *Review of Economics and Statistics* 86 (3): 811–823.

Broda, Christian, Nuno Limao, and David E. Weinstein. 2008. Optimal Tariffs and Market Power: The Evidence. *American Economic Review* 98 (5): 2032–2065.

Busch, Marc, and Eric Reinhardt. 2003. Developing Countries and GATT/WTO Dispute Settlement. *Journal of World Trade* 37 (4): 719—735.

Busch, Marc, Eric Reinhardt, and Greg Shaffer. 2009. Does Legal Capacity Matter? A Survey of WTO Members. *World Trade Review* 8 (4): 559–577.

Cao, Xun. 2012. Global Networks and Domestic Policy Convergence: A Network Explanation of Policy Changes. *World Politics* 64 (3): 375–425.

Carnegie, Allison. 2014. States Held Hostage: Political Hold-Up Problems and the Effects of International Institutions. *American Political Science Review*. 108 (1): 54–70.

Chang, Pao-Li, and Myoung-Jae Lee. 2011. The WTO Trade Effect. *Journal of International Economics* 85 (1): 53–71.

Chaudoin, Stephen. Forthcoming. Information Transmission and the Strategic Timing of Trade Disputes. *International Organization*.

Chaudoin, Stephen, Jeff Kucik, and Krzysztof Pelc. 2013. Do WTO Disputes Actually Increase Trade? Unpublished manuscript: University of Pittsburgh, University College London and McGill University.

Copelovitch, Mark S., and David Ohls. 2012. Trade, Institutions, and the Timing of GATT/WTO Accession in Post-Colonial States. *Review of International Organizations* 7 (1): 81–107.

Davis, Christina. 2003. *Food Fights Over Free Trade: How International Institutions Promote Agricultural Trade Liberalization*. Princeton, NJ: Princeton University Press.

Davis, Christina. 2006. Do WTO Rules Create a Level Playing Field for Developing Countries? Lessons from Peru and Vietnam. In *Negotiating Trade: Developing Countries in the WTO and NAFTA*, edited by John Odell, 219–256. Cambridge, UK: Cambridge University Press.

Davis, Christina L. 2012. *Why Adjudicate? Enforcing Trade Rules in the WTO*. Princeton, NJ: Princeton University Press.

Davis, Christina, and Meredith Wilf. 2014. Joining the Club? Accession to the GATT/WTO. Unpublished manuscript, Princeton University.

Davis, Christina L., and Krzysztof J. Pelc. Forthcoming. Cooperation in Hard Times: Self Restraint of Trade Protection. Journal of Conflict Resolution.

De Benedictis, Luca, and Lucia Tajoli. 2011. The World Trade Network. World Economy 34 (8): 1417–1454.

Downs, George, David Rocke, and Peter Barsoom. 1996. Is the Good News about Compliance Good News about Cooperation? International Organization 50 (3): 379–406.

Downs, George, David Rocke, and Peter Barsoom. 1998. Managing the Evolution of Multilateralism. International Organization 52 (2): 397–419.

Dreher, Axel, and Stefan Voigt. 2011. Does Membership in International Organizations Increase Governments' Credibility? Testing the Effects of Delegating Powers. Journal of Comparative Economics 39: 326–348.

Dutt, Pushan, Ilian Mihov, and Timothy Van-Zandt. 2011. Does WTO Matter for the Extensive and the Intensive Margins of Trade? Unpublished manuscript, INSEAD.

Eicher, Theo S., and Christian Henn. 2011. In Search of WTO Trade Effects: Preferential Trade Agreements Promote Trade Strongly, But Unevenly. Journal of International Economics 83: 137–153.

Fattore, Christina. 2012. Interest Group Influence on WTO Dispute Behaviour: A Test of State Commitment. Journal of World Trade 46 (6): 1261–1280.

Gilligan, Michael. 1997. Empowering Exporters: Reciprocity, Delegation, and Collective Action in American Trade Policy. Ann Arbor: University of Michigan Press.

Gilpin, Robert. 2001. Global Political Economy: Understanding the International Economic Order. Princeton, NJ: Princeton University Press.

Goldstein, Judith, and Robert Gulotty. 2014. America and Trade Liberalization: The Limits of Institutional Reform. International Organization 68 (2): 263–295.

Goldstein, Judith, Miles Kahler, Robert O. Keohane, and Anne-Marie Slaughter. 2000. Introduction: Legalization and World Politics. International Organization 54 (3): 385–399.

Goldstein, Judith, Douglas Rivers, and Michael Tomz. 2007. Institutions in International Relations: Understanding the Effects of the GATT and the WTO on World Trade. International Organization 61 (1): 37–67.

Gowa, Joanne. 2010. Alliances, Market Power, and Postwar Trade: Explaining the GATT/WTO. World Trade Review 9 (3): 487–504.

Gowa, Joanne, and Soo Yeon Kim. 2005. An Exlusive Country Club: The Effects of the GATT on Trade, 1950–94. World Politics 57 (4): 453–478.

Helpman, Elhanan, Marc Melitz, and Yona Rubinstein. 2008. Estimating Trade Flows: Trading Partners and Trading Volumes. Quarterly Journal of Economics 123 (2): 441–487.

Hofmann, Tobias, and Soo Yeon Kim. 2013. Does Trade Comply? The Economic Effect(ivenes)s of WTO Dispute Settlement. Unpublished manuscript, National University of Singapore.

Hudec, Robert. 2002. The Adequacy of WTO Dispute Settlement Remedies: A Developing Country Perspective. In Development, Trade, and the WTO, edited by Bernard Hoekman, Aaditya Mattoo, and Philip English, 81–91. Washington, DC: The World Bank.

Hudec, Robert. 1993. Enforcing International Trade Law: The Evolution of the Modern GATT Legal System. Salem, NH: Butterworth.

Imai, Kosuke, and In Song Kim. 2013. On the Use of Linear Fixed Effects Regression Estimators for Causal Inference. Unpublished manuscript, Princeton University.

Irwin, Douglas, Petros Mavroidis, and Alan Sykes. 2008. The Genesis of the GATT. Cambridge, UK: Cambridge University Press.

Jackson, John H. 1997. *The World Trading System: Law and Policy of International Economic Relations*. 2nd ed. Cambridge, MA: The MIT Press.

Johnson, Harry. 1953–1954. Optimum Tariffs and Retaliation. *Review of Economic Studies* 21: 142–153.

Jones, Kent. 2009. The Political Economy of WTO Accession. *World Trade Review* 8 (2): 279–314.

Keohane, Robert. 1982. The Demand for International Regimes. *International Organization* 36 (2): 325–355.

Kim, Soo Yeon. 2010. *Power and the Governance of Global Trade: From the GATT to the WTO*. Ithaca, NY: Cornell University Press.

Kindleberger, Charles P. 1986. *The World in Depression*. Berkeley: University of California Press.

Kovenock, Dan, and Marie Thursby. 1992. GATT, Dispute Settlement and Cooperation. *Economics and Politics* 4 (2): 151–170.

Krasner, Stephen D. 1976. State Power and the Structure of International Trade. *World Politics* 28 (3): 317–347.

Kucik, Jeffrey, and Eric Reinhardt. 2008. Does Flexibility Promote Cooperation? An Application to the Global Trade Regime. *International Organization* 62 (3): 477–505.

Lake, David. 2009. *Hierarchy in International Relations*. Ithaca, NY: Cornell University Press.

Lara-Fernandez, Martha. 1987. Mexico's Accession to the GATT: A Turning Point in Mexican Foreign Trade Policy and Its Possible Implications. Geneva: Institut universitaire de hautes etudes internationales.

Liu, Xuepeng. 2009. GATT/WTO Promotes Trade Strongly: Sample Selection and Model Specification. *Review of International Economics* 17 (3): 428–446.

Maggi, Giovanni. 1999. The Role of Multilateral Institutions in International Trade Cooperation. *American Economic Review* 89 (1): 190–214.

Maggi, Giovanni, and Andres Rodriquez-Clare. 1998. The Value of Trade Agreements in the Presence of Political Pressures. *Journal of Political Economy* 106 (3): 574–601.

Mansfield, Edward D., and Eric Reinhardt, 2003. "Multilateral Determinants of Regionalism: The Effects of GATT/WTO on the Formation of Preferential Trading Arrangements." International Organization 57(4): 829--862.

Mansfield, Edward D., and Eric Reinhardt. 2008. International Institutions and the Volatility of International Trade. *International Organization* 62: 621–652.

Martin, Lisa. 1992. Interests, Power, Multilateralism. *International Organization* 46 (3): 765–792.

Martin, Lisa, and Beth Simmons. 2001. Theories and Empirical Studies of International Institutions. In *International Institutions: An International Organization Reader*, edited by Lisa Martin and Beth Simmons, 437–465. Cambridge, MA: The MIT Press.

Morrow, James. 1994. The Forms of International Cooperation. *International Organization* 48 (3): 387–423.

Neumayer, Eric. 2013. Strategic Delaying and Concessions Extraction in Accession Negotiations to the World Trade Organization: An Analysis of Working Party Membership. *World Trade Review* 12 (4): 669–692.

Oatley, Thomas. 2011. The Reductionist Gamble: Open Economy Politics in the Global Economy. *International Organization* 65: 311–341.

Ortiz Mena, Antonio. 2005. Mexico. In *The World Trade Organization: Legal, Economic and Political Analysis, Volume 3*, edited by Patrick F. J. Macrory, Arthur E. Appleton, and Michael G. Plummer, 217–247. New York: Springer.

Pelc, Krzystof. 2010. Constraining Coercion? Legitimacy and its Role in U.S. Trade Policy, 1975–2000. *International Organization* 64: 65–96.

Pelc, Krzysztof J. 2011. Why Do Some Countries Get Better WTO Accession Terms Than Others? *International Organization* 65 (4): 639–672.

Rickard, Stephanie. 2010. Democratic Differences: Electoral Institutions and Compliance with GATT/WTO Agreements. *European Journal of International Relations* 16 (4): 711–729.

Rose, Andrew K. 2004. Do We Really Know That the WTO Increases Trade? *American Economic Review* 94 (1): 98–114.

Rose, Andrew K. 2005. Does the WTO Make Trade More Stable? *Open Economies Review* 16 (1): 7–22.

Rosendorff, Peter. 2005. Stability and Rigidity: Politics and Design of the WTO's Dispute Settlement Procedure. *American Political Science Review* 99 (3): 389–400.

Rosendorff, Peter, and Helen Milner. 2001. The Optimal Design of International Trade Institutions: Uncertainty and Escape. *International Organization* 55 (4): 829–857.

Ruggie, John Gerard. 1982. International Regimes, Transactions, and Change: Embedded Liberalism in the Postwar Economic Order. *International Organization* 36 (2): 379–415.

Schoppa, Leonard. 1997. *Bargaining With Japan: What American Pressure Can and Cannot Do.* New York: Columbia University Press.

Schwab, Susan. 2011. After Doha: Why the Negotiations are Doomed and What We Should Do About It. *Foreign Affairs* 90 (3): 104–117.

Staiger, Robert, and Guido Tabellini. 1999. Do GATT Rules Help Governments Make Domestic Commitments? *Economics and Politics* 2 (2): 109–144.

Steinberg, Richard. 2002. In the Shadow of Law or Power? Consensus-Based Bargaining and Outcomes in the GATT/WTO. *International Organization* 56 (2): 339–374.

Stone, Randall. 2011. *Controlling Institutions: International Organizations and the Global Economy.* Cambridge, UK: Cambridge University Press.

Story, Dale. 1982. Trade Politics in the Third World: A Case Study of the Mexican GATT Decision. *International Organization* 36 (4): 767–794.

Subramanian, Arvind, and Shang-Jin Wei. 2007. The WTO Promotes Trade, Strongly but Unevenly. *Journal of International Economics* 72 (1): 151–175.

Wilson, Bruce. 2007. Compliance by WTO Members with Adverse WTO Dispute Settlement Rulings: The Record to Date. *Journal of International Economic Law* 10 (2): 397–403.

....

CHAPTER 21

DISPUTE SETTLEMENT IN THE WTO

....

MARC L. BUSCH AND KRZYSZTOF J. PELC

INTRODUCTION

Not long ago, scholars had to justify studying litigation under the General Agreement on Tariffs and Trade (GATT). After all, the institution was derided as a "court with no bailiff."[1] Today, studying dispute settlement under the World Trade Organization (WTO) is very much in vogue, for good reason. There is no other instance of as many countries delegating as much decision making to an international legal body over the enforcement of binding commitments. Since its creation in 1995, the WTO's Dispute Settlement Understanding (DSU) has developed a sophisticated body of jurisprudence, leading many to agree with Bhala (1998–1999) that the institution features de facto binding precedent, meaning past rulings constrain current ones. Add to this that compliance with rulings is high, and it is little wonder that the WTO gets so much attention. But how far has the literature come since the old GATT days? And where should it go in the future?

Recent scholarship has delivered some impressive insights. For example, while the literature once took it as a matter of faith that developing countries were at a disadvantage in litigation because of their lack of *power*, it turns out that weak *legal capacity*—political, legal, and economic resources—matters more (Busch, Reinhardt, and Shaffer 2009; Davis and Bermeo 2009). Not only are the two variables only loosely correlated, the solutions to addressing this disparity differ dramatically. The record also reveals no disadvantage for developing countries in terms of winning verdicts or compliance from defendants. Rather, they trail rich complainants in *rates of settlement*: developing countries not only lack legal capacity, but tend to file disputes against large wealthy markets, which draw in other parties, making them harder to resolve in pretrial negotiations (Busch and Reinhardt 2003). These insights are not what the GATT-era literature expected.

We submit, however, that for all of its advances, the literature needs retooling. Three areas stand out. First, scholars have always struggled with the question of *selection*: Is there something different about the cases that get filed, in relation to the universe of all trade disputes? In the 1990s critics of GATT insisted that cases brought to Geneva were likely less contentious, or "easy," than those taken up as matters of high politics. This view fit with the prevailing debate over institutions more generally, forcing students of GATT to tease out implications of selection bias to show that these disputes mattered. In recent years more involved statistical methods have been used in making the point, and with some success, as relatively few pages are now devoted to the issue. Yet more can be done. Most important, there are data on so-called specific trade concerns (STCs) raised before the WTO's committees on technical barriers to trade (TBT) and sanitary and phytosanitary (SPS) measures. For example, on technical regulations, standards, and conformity assessment, which include some of the most contentious regulatory politics, the WTO's TBT committee has handled 379 STCs, versus 47 dispute settlement cases referencing this agreement. Similarly, the ratio of STCs to litigation on health and safety standards is almost 10:1. These STCs can shed new light on selection issues, especially because the data are coded according to the type of infraction alleged and whether there was a resolution reported to the WTO. Some scholars are already pursuing this lead (see, e.g., Horn, Mavroidis, and Wijkstrom 2013). GATT-era scholarship could not have imagined this treasure trove.

Second, much of the criticism of the institution's dispute settlement procedures (DSPs) has consisted of normative claims about a lack of transparency and unequal participation. In this telling, small countries are excluded not only from negotiations during multilateral rounds, but also from participation in disputes that may bear on their interests. These critics bemoan the lack of access to the room during consultations and litigation. They call for open hearings, such as take place in the European Court of Justice (ECJ), and greater access for nongovernmental organizations (NGOs). Yet these calls often ignore the means that members *do* have to participate, the full costs and benefits entailed, and the drivers of the decision to participate or not. The bottom line is that normative claims, such as the ones made about participation and transparency, carry empirical implications, and these implications can be tested. In doing so, scholars are likely to find the normative case more ambiguous than it appears at first blush. This matters, since it leads to divergent policy solutions.

Third, scholars give insufficient attention to the institution's words. For all the interest in the *acquis* of WTO case law, few studies unpack the content of the decisions rendered. It is as if the words matter only because members think they do, not because of the words themselves. But the words do matter. WTO verdicts are longer, and more complicated, than the GATT-era documents, and say things that the field should take seriously. There is, for starters, an inventory of legal precedents, called the *WTO Analytical Index*, which can guide scholars in making more use of these rulings. Indeed, if the WTO increases the predictability and stability of the global economy, it does so through precedent. The field of American politics has started to take the utterances of courts seriously, as should WTO scholars. It may be the case, for example, that precedent-heavy rulings bear on rates of compliance or settlement. Apart from these outcomes, moreover, WTO panel reports detail procedural aspects of cases that can be important, like the decision *not* to rule on certain legal claims, which can limit the scope of the resulting precedent. This practice, called *judicial economy*, is explicitly explained in panel reports and offers a crucial link between the interests of the wider membership and the dispute at hand (Busch and Pelc 2010). Given all of the new methodologies for doing content analysis, the words reasoned by the WTO merit a closer look. GATT-era scholarship could only have dreamed of allowing the institution to speak for itself.

This chapter first surveys some of the main themes in the literature on WTO dispute settlement and provides an apercu of the stages of a typical dispute. It then proposes tackling trade specific concerns, participation, and the WTO's words. Finally, the conclusion.

The Literature on WTO Dispute Settlement

The study of WTO dispute settlement is a multidisciplinary venture. Lawyers, economists, and political scientists have drawn on each other's research more in this than in most other areas of international affairs. Like many, we attribute this to Robert Hudec, a legal scholar by training but a political economist at heart. Hudec (2000) set a high standard, demanding that research be grounded in the institution's mechanisms, but sensitive to the "theater" he saw domestically and internationally, reflecting governments' efforts to curry favor at the ballot box. This same high standard is no less relevant today.

The defining feature of dispute settlement is that it is *decentralized*. This distinguishes the WTO from domestic courts or supranational enforcement, the latter of which, in the European context, boasts at least some centralized prosecutorial functions. In contrast, WTO disputes begin when a member considers that its rights have been impaired. Disputes are typically responses to domestic interest groups that lobby for better market access abroad (Davis 2012), although some are pursued for "systemic" interests, including cases over measures that have never been used.

In keeping with its decentralized character, the WTO has no enforcement power to speak of. It merely produces legal rulings, which are referred to as "recommendations" but considered binding on states. The WTO cannot force compliance; it cannot punish violators. The WTO can only authorize a complainant to "suspend concessions" to a defendant, by raising tariffs so that foreign exporters lobby for compliance.

In truth, retaliation never happens. Less than 1 percent of cases result in the suspension of concessions. In fact, only 40 percent of cases ever go to a panel. This is because most cases are solved or withdrawn in *consultation*, a mandatory sixty-day period preceding the request for a panel. Consultations are a holdover from the GATT days, when the system was (purportedly) more about diplomacy than law. Consultations are held behind closed doors, and this is essential to their success. Indeed, countries are more likely to reach an agreement if they do not need to pander to powerful domestic interest groups. The design of the WTO's DSU, more generally, reflects the fact that governments negotiate with domestic interest groups as much as they do with one another. Consultations, in particular, shield negotiators from these demands at home.

Consultations are not completely closed off to all comers, however. Other WTO members can enter as "third parties" if they have a substantial trade interest in the dispute at hand, such as when they are affected by the barrier at issue (Busch and Reinhardt 2006). Yet this only happens if both the complainant and the defendant agree to have those other countries present. Complainants welcome such third parties in about half of all cases, and defendants rarely block them, for the simple reason that a blocked third party can always bring a suit of its own, which leads to greater trouble for the defendant (Johns and Pelc 2014). The one most telling finding about the effect of privacy on negotiations is that the greater the number of third parties present, the less likely is a negotiated solution (Busch and Reinhardt 2006; Davey and Porges 1998). Indeed, third parties add voices and issues to the disputes, and they may also create an incentive on the part of litigants to posture, to "act tough" and demonstrate resolve, with an eye toward subsequent disputes (Stasavage 2004).

The high rate of settlement is good news. Litigation is an inefficient outcome (Gilligan, Johns, and Rosendorff 2010): it entails considerable legal and bureaucratic costs, and from the point of view of litigants, it throws a spotlight on the underlying issue. Litigants no longer enjoy insulation from domestic interests, since the outcome of litigation—the panel report—is made public, along with both litigants' full arguments. Governments can no longer claim that they wrought a "hard won deal" and misrepresent any losses as wins. The panel report lays it out for all to see. For these reasons, concessions on the part of the defendant are most likely to take place *prior* to the ruling. This is a sign of a functioning legal system: most of the action takes place in the shadow of the law.

These beliefs are empirically supported. On average, complainants are more likely to obtain concessions if they can reach a settlement than if the case moves on to litigation and results in a ruling, even if the complainant wins on all counts (Busch and Reinhardt 2001). Indeed, what pushes respondents to concede is the benefit of doing so privately, which allows governments to shape the perception of these concessions domestically. That, together with governments' desire to avoid the normative condemnation that comes with a ruling by the WTO, explains why the odds of agreement are greatest before the panel hands down a ruling. This, in short, is the institution's single greatest forte.

The trade regime effectively relies on self-enforcement. One reason this is achievable in international politics is that countries have a wealth of information about each other's behavior. When there is reason for ambiguity about the legality of a given country's policies, litigation is a means of resolving it. In this light, the main function of WTO verdicts is to clarify the meaning of the institution's rules, lending greater predictability and stability to the global economy.

Another reason self-enforcement is achievable is that governments continually interact with one another; the trade regime, after all, is nearly seventy years old. And while it remains the prerogative of a sovereign country to ignore a WTO ruling if it chooses, it does so at the risk that a subsequent ruling it wins may be spurned; that its demands will be less likely to be met; and that the concessions it offers during trade rounds will be devalued. In short, countries join the institution knowing that in some cases the rules will work against them, but on average, membership is a net benefit (Pelc 2010). This is also the reason why, despite the ability to block unfavorable rulings during the GATT, surprisingly few countries availed themselves of this option over the half century prior to the WTO's inception. Just as countries can spurn rulings now, they could block rulings then. In both cases, they avoid doing so for analogous reasons.

To avoid normative condemnation, defendants will dig in their heels once an unfavorable ruling is handed down. Indeed, there is little left to lose at that point. As Schelling (1960) noted, a threat that needs to be exercised has lost all potency; it is an ineffective threat. As a result, concessions are most likely to occur at the prelitigation stage. Of course, whether cases proceed to litigation and result in a panel report is not a random occurrence. Some cases stand little chance of settling early. Disputes like *US—Cotton* or *EC—Hormones* touch on such sensitive issues that the domestic political costs of conceding, even behind closed doors, would have been prohibitive (Heinisch 2006; Rountree 1998–1999; Shumaker 2007; Sien 2006–2007). Some disputes, in other words, are launched even though it is known that they will not settle. Moreover, it is likely that countries sometimes file cases not principally for the sake of the aggrieved domestic industry, but rather because they are seeking a favorable interpretation of the rules (Pelc 2013). This is why a country that "wins" at the panel stage may still appeal the verdict, looking to secure more favorable legal logic from a body new to the WTO: the Appellate Body (AB).

The AB is comprised of seven full-time jurists, three of whom hear any given case. Insofar as the WTO establishes precedent, this is the body that does it. The AB weighs the validity of the appealed portion of a contested panel report. It has no fact-finding power, in that it cannot collect additional information or ask questions, and it cannot send a case back to a panel to complete unfinished analysis. Some 70 percent of panel verdicts are appealed.

If the defendant loses its appeal, and the complainant perceives that the policy at fault has not been remedied, the next step is a compliance panel, where the same panelists from the panel report now address a single question: Has the defendant followed the panel's recommendations? If the defendant is found not to have complied, then the complainant can ask for the authorization to retaliate.

This final step, the DSU's last resort, has preoccupied much of the literature, despite its rarity. One thing is readily agreed on: retaliation serves no balancing function, because it does not remedy the harm done (Hudec 2000, 22). In economic terms, it amounts to shooting oneself in the foot. Indeed, it is worth reflecting on the apparent irony of a system built on the principle of free trade that allows aggrieved countries to respond to injury by raising tariffs in turn.

Adam Smith foresaw retaliation for what it was: economic folly in the service of potentially rational politics, belonging "not . . . so much to the science of a legislator, . . .

as to the skill of that insidious and crafty animal, vulgarly called a statesman or politician" (1937, 435). Although nearly 250 years old, this view is not out of date. As the representative from Ecuador put it recently, retaliation at the WTO "does not restore the balance lost, . . . but rather tends to inflict greater injury on the complaining party, as occurred in the banana dispute."[2] Indeed, retaliatory tariffs end up hurting end-users in the complaining country, who, as Ecuador further explains, "have nothing to do with the dispute. [N]ever mind consumers."[3] This is not the position of developing countries alone. The European Union (EU) has declared that "the use of suspension of trade concessions involves a cost not only for the defending party, but also for the economy of the complaining Member."[4]

Most important, however, the threat most likely to drive behavior is that of an unfavorable ruling, rather than the suspension of concessions, no matter how credible the latter may be. The GATT period, wherein the trade system successfully resolved trade conflicts, serves as good evidence on this count. Despite the lack of any credible threat of retaliation—since defendants could always block a case—the system worked. It did so because it led countries to settle their disagreements, to avoid being branded as violators.

SELECTION AND SPECIFIC
TRADE CONCERNS

The methodological challenge that has gnawed at WTO scholars most systematically is the issue of selection (see Rosendorff, this volume). While the problem of endogeneity plagues much of social science inquiry, selection is a particular obstacle for the study of courts, since disputes only become observable once they are officially launched, and observers rarely have any sense of what potential disputes were not acted on.

This has considerable consequences for empirical analysis. Imagine a research design that seeks to investigate whether panel recommendations that require legislative approval in the defendant country are less likely to be complied with. If we believe that WTO members are rational, we would then also expect them not to file such cases as complainants, or to file them with much less frequency. Those filed might have higher legal merit, making compliance more likely, all things being equal. What WTO scholars lack, in sum, is a sense of the disputes that are not filed: the proverbial nonbarking dogs.

A range of new statistical approaches has sought to deal with such selection effects, chief among them being the search for valid instrumental variables, which is of limited use in getting a sense of nonfiled disputes in the study of courts. Others have attempted to delve into the process of selection itself. Davis (2012), for example, looks at the step prior to dispute initiation in the United States by examining the petitions of industries for enforcement of trade rules in Congress.

In recent years another promising avenue for exploring the issue of selection has become available. Specifically, the WTO collects data on STCs reported to the TBT and SPS committees. The key is that these are not (yet) formal dispute settlement cases. Rather, they are complaints brought to the attention of the committee with the aim of seeking a resolution. The data are organized just as in a dispute settlement case: the member(s) raising the concern is identified; the member(s) implementing the measure at issue, and its description, are recorded; and the case's "status" is listed, including whether it was partially or fully resolved or an outcome was not reported. These data are instructive in thinking about selection issues.

The first thing that stands out about STCs is the numbers. With respect to TBT measures, there have been 379 STCs versus 47 dispute settlement cases. In terms of SPS, STCs outnumber instances of formal litigation by a wide margin: 350 to 40. So what exactly are STCs? Horn, Mavroidis, and Wijkstrom (2013, 1) describe them as an "*informal* form of resolution of trade conflicts" over TBT and SPS measures. These measures are complex because they involve regulatory politics. The stakes are thus often high, and the WTO invests in making these measures transparent. Since TBT and SPS measures can act as nontariff barriers, members are required to "notify" others of any changes in policy. Many STCs arise as a result of these notifications, but STCs can also be brought in reaction to measures that are not notified. As the WTO explains it, STCs "relate normally to the proposed draft measures . . . or to the implementation of existing measures" (WTO, 2011 Document G/TBT/1/Rev.10).

The point is that STCs are informal and cheap to bring, and there is little incentive for governments not to let them proceed. The bureaucratic processes that select disputes to initiate formally are not yet at play. Indeed, because the WTO equates notifications with transparency, governments are likely to err on the side of more, not fewer, STCs. Data on STCs can thus be expected to be rather inclusive, permitting a look at easy and hardest-test cases, and everything in between.

This brings us to the second aspect that stands out about STCs: the subject matter. Unsurprisingly, some are partly, or wholly, probative. Most basically, a member has a question about a measure(s) that has an impact on its trade. For example, in 261 STCs concerning TBT, one or more parties asked for "further information" on, or "clarification" of, the measure. But many STCs invoke the sort of language that one expects to read in a dispute settlement case. Staying with TBT, fully 100 STCs cite a measure's discriminatory effect; 151 question the rationale and/or legitimacy of a given measure; and 141 ask how the measure relates to international standards, the sine qua non of a case litigated under TBT Article 2.

Turning to SPS, Australia, Canada, and the United States brought the first STC on January 6, 1995, over Korea's shelf-life requirements. A day later the WTO recorded a partial resolution. A year later the EU brought an STC concerning Brazil's import requirements for wine. No resolution has been reported. These STCs are a window on the dogs that did not bark. True, STCs still involve a decision to go to Geneva. There is still a selection issue in that something motivated the EU to bring its worry to the SPS committee, even if it opted not to litigate this case right away. The point is that STCs help us understand why certain contentious trade conflicts, once brought to the WTO, go to litigation, but not others. It is in this sense that STCs flesh out the cases that *weren't*.

Then again, STCs sometimes precede cases that *were*. Returning to TBT, STC 42, raised on February 25, 2000, by Brazil, Mexico, and Egypt, concerns US dolphin-safe labeling. In 2008 Mexico requested consultations with the United States, commencing for formal dispute settlement. The case, *US—Tuna II*, is one of the most important TBT cases to date, involving core aspects of the agreement. There is little doubt that the STC was focused on these issues; in addition to requesting information and clarification, Brazil, Mexico, and Egypt focused on the non-product-related process and production methods that trigger the label "dolphin-safe." These measures are increasingly widespread and the subject of much debate. That this STC preceded formal litigation is not surprising. What is surprising is that Brazil and Egypt did *not* join as co-complainants, and only Brazil reserved its third-party rights. Moreover, all of this took place in full knowledge of what happened in the GATT-era case *US—Tuna I*. This suggests that STCs can offer insights into the politics and legal strategy leading up to the request for consultations.

STCs can teach us still more. Horn, Mavroidis, and Wijkstrom (2013), for example, find that the relationship between the number of STCs and dispute settlement cases is not obvious. Our instinct would be to match the content of STCs to the specific legal claims raised in dispute settlement cases, an effort that, to our knowledge, has yet to be undertaken. Not that this is easy. In the case where an STC precedes dispute settlement, a litigant is likely to learn from the responses to its initial inquiries and adjust its legal claims accordingly. This may make it difficult, at times, to directly map dispute settlement cases onto STCs. On the other hand, in cases like *US—Tuna II*, this mapping is fairly straightforward.

The payoff for doing the mapping promises to be significant. Not only will it give us a better sense for selection issues, but it will tell us new things about the protagonists. Horn, Mavroidis, and Wijkstrom (2013) observe that developing countries are disproportionately involved in STCs, relative to their trade volumes. Do STCs teach developing countries how to prosecute trade conflicts? Busch and Reinhardt (2006) suggest that the high rates of developing-country participation as third parties might be part of a "learning by watching" strategy. Perhaps the same is true of STCs. Or perhaps developing countries derive something quite different from bringing STCs.

To be sure, it would be a mistake to view STCs as just the prelude to litigation. The fact that they get the TBT and SPS committees involved in interpreting rules is tremendously valuable. This may be especially helpful for developing countries. One intriguing possibility is that STCs get the TBT and SPS committees to reflect on the implications of ongoing litigation. If so, lessons may be incorporated into a resolution faster than if members had to wait out the verdicts issued by the WTO's judicial bodies. Consider, for example, Cuba's involvement in the dispute over Australia's tobacco measures. Cuba filed this case in May 2013, joining the Dominican Republic, Honduras, and Ukraine, all of which filed in 2012. Interestingly, Cuba, the Dominican Republic, and Honduras, together with nine other developing countries, raised TBT STC 377 in March 2013 against EU measures on tobacco, including packaging restrictions. We submit that the TBT committee has some latitude to informally discuss the litigation, anticipate the politics of an outcome, and suggest the contours of a negotiated settlement in the shadow of the law. This is exactly the logic behind DSU Article 5, "Good Offices, Conciliation and Mediation," another informal provision to be used alongside formal dispute settlement, but one that is almost never used. Given the technical subject of TBT and SPS, and since STCs are not a part of formal dispute settlement per se, perhaps they fill in where DSU 5 has fallen short.

Studying STCs will not end concerns about selection bias, but it will go a long way in getting at the sources of potential bias. The data speak explicitly to those cases that look more like information gathering than allegations of discrimination. This in itself is a win that GATT-era scholars found elusive.

Finally, there are alternative means of addressing our inability to observe the cases that weren't. Imagine a typical empirical claim, drawn from the political economy of trade literature, that politically powerful industries get more enforcement of their grievances. The difficulty of testing such a claim rests in the same problem of selection. If we look at the cases filed and find that they disproportionately concern politically powerful industries, what are we to conclude? This could be a sign of domestic institutions favoring such industries, or it could be that, for example, the type of industry that is politically powerful is also more likely to be faced with WTO-inconsistent import barriers abroad. How are we to know if we cannot inspect the pool of potential cases from which disputes are drawn? One way of getting at such a story is to invert conditional hypotheses (Johns and Pelc 2014). If domestic institutions favor politically powerful cases, then conditional on such a case being filed, it should have on average lower legal merit than a case not favored for this reason. This institutional bias should then have observable effects at the settlement and ruling stages—all things being equal, cases representing politically powerful industries should result in less favorable panel rulings. If, instead, those cases are filed because the industries genuinely face more trade barriers abroad, then there should be no difference in panel outcomes.

In sum, the literature has reached the stage where it needs to take methodological concerns such as selection bias seriously. Although no one solution is a panacea, there are different ways of addressing these concerns. Selection effects can sometimes be identified by examining subsequent legal outcomes. Or scholars can examine the data that have emerged about that prior step, by looking at domestic petitions or STCs within the WTO itself.

PARTICIPATION

A significant portion of the literature on the WTO is made up of normative claims. This is not surprising, given how the institution brings together developed and developing countries under an agreement with common objectives that addresses increasingly sensitive political issues. One of these normative assessments has grown particularly salient: observers have claimed that developing countries are effectively excluded from the system.[5]

As with multilateral negotiations during trade rounds, most countries are kept outside of the room during WTO legal proceedings, even if their interests are at stake (Smythe and Smith 2006; Steinberg 2002; Heisenberg 2007). And neither domestic interest groups nor NGOs have any access to DSU hearings.[6] As the literature has begun addressing these claims empirically, some unexpected conclusions have emerged.

It is worth noting that in many respects the WTO's level of transparency compares favorably with that of other international organizations. Public access to adopted panel reports, by itself, constitutes a unique window on decision making in the institution, the likes of which does not exist in the sister Bretton Woods institutions. The comparison is less favorable with other courts, such as the European Court of Justice, where hearings are open to the public. And there is far from a harmony of interests among participation advocates. The often-overlooked truth is that while developing countries demand greater representation in negotiations and greater access to legal proceedings, they also seek to prevent opening up the process to NGOs, such as through the acceptance of amicus briefs, submissions from "friends of the court." Now that they are engaged in the process of governance, developing countries resist the entrance of another set of actors that would dilute their influence (Kahler 2004). In other words, every increase in participation also holds distributional effects.

The institution offers opportunities for empirical assessment of the claims underlying the participation debate. Indeed, the WTO has championed the option of third-party participation during disputes. Third-party status, whereby nonlitigant countries can join a dispute from its very beginning, is one means of allowing developing and least-developed countries to be in the room when an issue in which they may have a stake is being negotiated. It is also a means for countries to learn the intricacies of trade law and build their legal capacity (Busch, Reinhardt, and Shaffer 2009).

There is also evidence that the presence of third parties has a positive effect on the *content* of settlements. Whereas complainants are found to capture a disproportionate portion of gains from settlement when consultations are conducted entirely in private, this is not the case when third parties are present (Kucik and Pelc 2013). In those instances, the complainant, on average, gains no more than the remainder of the membership. Third parties, in other words, perform an unwitting enforcement function, by ensuring that the gains reached in a settlement are extended to the remainder of the membership, per DSU rules.[7] Naturally countries do not join as third parties out of altruism; above and beyond the desire to have their views recorded and building legal capacity, countries join as third parties to ensure that they are not left out of an otherwise private settlement.

Indeed, countries that choose not to sign on as third parties run the risk of being left out of potential concessions if the parties reach early settlement (Nakagawa 2007; Alschner 2014; Bown 2009). When parties settle before proceeding to the panel stage, the terms of the settlement remain private. Defendants wary of increasing market access across the board can carefully design concessions to appease the complainant, while limiting benefits to the broader membership. Such discriminatory settlements are prohibited by the rules of the DSU. Nevertheless, the secrecy surrounding settlements makes this difficult to enforce (Nakagawa 2006). A country that has an interest in the dispute but elects not to sign on as a third party may find itself out in the cold unless it follows up by filing a new dispute. In sum, third parties join to ensure that they get their share of a settlement, yet in doing so, they also have a positive effect on the equity of the deal for everyone else.

There is a catch. These beneficial effects of third parties pertain to those disputes in which a settlement is reached. Yet it turns out that the presence of third parties also affects the odds of such a settlement being reached in the first place. Despite all the benefits of third-party participation, this step toward greater inclusivity thus comes at a cost. The presence of an audience makes settlement significantly less likely (Busch and Reinhardt 2006; Davey and Porges 1998; Stasavage 2004). There is enough incentive to posture for the sake of these other member states that the odds of reaching agreement between the litigants decline precipitously as the number of other countries in the room rises. In fact, beyond five third parties, the odds of agreement are effectively nil (Busch and Reinhardt 2006). In other words, if settlement is the goal of the system, then greater inclusiveness through third-party participation exerts a cost. And this is the case even when the audience in the room is made up of other countries, rather than NGOs and domestic interest groups.

The effect of third parties on the odds of prelitigation settlement, it turns out, is a special concern for developing countries. Herein lies one of the true cleavages between rich and poor countries in dispute settlement. It is not found in the odds of winning a case, which are statistically indistinguishable for rich versus poor countries. The true difference is that, on average, developed countries settle, and developing countries litigate. This happens for two reasons. First, developing countries tend to file cases against large, rich countries with whom countless others trade, meaning that third parties are more likely to join, with their participation undermining the prospects for early settlement (Busch and Reinhardt 2006). Second, developing countries generally lack the legal capacity to make the most of consultations (Busch, Reinhardt, and Shaffer, 2009), further reducing these odds.

Wider participation, as in other fora, also has the effect of politicizing outcomes (see Rosendorff, this volume). It takes away from the unambiguous legal condemnation that is intended to drive country behavior. Courts are intended to shift disputes and decision making from the political to a legal arena. These bodies can promote cooperation by creating a "functional domain to circumvent the direct clash of political interests" (Burley and Mattli 1993, 44). Third-party participation achieves the opposite. And such repoliticization has distributional effects: the ambiguity it generates over legal rulings helps the losing party in a dispute and hurts the party that prevails on the legal merits (Johns and Pelc 2014).

Yet the most striking aspect of third-party participation is that for all its benefits—voicing one's interests, building legal capacity, ensuring one is not left out of a settlement—relatively few countries avail themselves of the opportunity (Horlick 1998, 690). Despite its low cost, the average dispute counts about four third parties, while estimates suggest that based on countries' trade stakes, the number should be closer to fourteen (Johns and Pelc 2014). This outcome would seem to complicate the simple prescription of allowing for greater access: the option to participate exists, yet relatively few countries exercise it. The reason seems to be that countries take the aforementioned consequences of participation in settlement into account. Given that more countries in the room means lower odds of settlement, and litigation is an inefficient outcome for all involved, countries appear to exercise restraint. Rather than try to capture a larger slice of a potentially smaller pie, states strategically choose to settle for a potentially smaller slice of a larger pie. The literature until now has focused on how power considerations may deter participation: Elsig and Stucki (2012) describe in detail the reluctance of African countries to join the cotton dispute filed by Brazil against the United States, for fear of jeopardizing US aid. What these recent findings suggest, however, is that controlling for such power considerations, a greater driver of nonparticipation, on average, appears to be every country's interest in avoiding the negative consequences of overcrowding. The result is that paradoxically, every additional third party makes everyone else less likely to participate. In short, low rates of participation may be the result not of power plays and exclusionary rules, but of strategic country behavior.

In sum, cleavages between rich and poor countries exist. Yet they do not lie where we most often look for them. Success in dispute settlement hinges most of all on the ability to assess the legal merit of potential cases (Busch, Reinhardt, and Shaffer 2009) and to settle disputes in the shadow of the law, before a ruling is handed down. Developing countries are at a disadvantage in this respect, as they tend to settle less and litigate more. Yet scholars have shown that countries can rapidly learn to use dispute settlement (Davis and Bermeo 2009). Gaining legal capacity is more easily achievable than growing one's market power or retaliatory capacity. Finally, there are institutional solutions to the participation deficit. The option of joining as a third party is beneficial, as it allows poor countries to be present and participate in proceedings, to voice their views and potentially affect legal outcomes, and to protect their trade interests in so doing. Yet third-party participation also comes at a cost to the institution: as diplomats know, audiences make agreement less likely (Keohane and Nye 2001). There exists an observable trade-off between inclusiveness and the odds of settlement, meaning that there is no easy solution to the participation deficit. The challenge of the institution is to balance these competing objectives.

WORDS

With a wink and a nod at the role of precedent, economists and political scientists reduce WTO rulings to which country won or lost a case (e.g., Busch and Reinhardt 2001; Petersmann 1994). There is a sense that more predictable legal decisions, through precedent, make the system work, but there is seldom much attention paid to what the rulings actually say or the structure of the legal arguments rendered. Lawyers generally do a better job mulling over the references to past cases, but tend to focus on one or two disputes, offering little perspective on broader trends, which after all are at the heart of the matter. To capture these trends, we need to combine the wider accounting of economists and political scientists with the attention to detail of the lawyers, something the literature has yet to do. Put simply, we need both the forest and the trees if we are to measure the *extent* to which past rulings hold sway over present ones.

Law is a fundamentally rhetorical exercise. And while the rules have remained constant since the WTO's inception, their agreed-upon meaning has changed. This has taken place through rulings spanning the GATT and WTO periods.

The traditional search for sources of law falls short in trying to delimit between what binds countries and what does not. Despite DSU Article 3.2 explicitly stating that "recommendations and rulings of the DSB cannot add to or diminish the rights and obligations provided in the covered agreements," echoing Article 59 of the ICJ Statute, panel rulings plainly shape members' understanding of the meaning of the rules. Even *unadopted* GATT panel reports, such as the ones for the *Tuna—Dolphin* decision against the United States, have shaped the interpretation of subsequent WTO law concerning nontrade issues, taken up in some of the WTO's most important disputes (Venzke 2012). And this is in spite of having no actual legal standing whatsoever. Indeed, WTO rulings have had most to say about issues that countries find hard to arrive at a consensus on during negotiations. In this way, it is legal rulings that have created expectations about how policies addressing nontrade concerns must be "primarily aimed at" addressing these concerns (whereas the text of Article XX[g] merely states that they must be "related to" these policies) and that such measures must be "least trade restrictive" (whereas the text at issue in Article XX[d] states that the policy must be "necessary") (Venzke 2012). Where the legislative function of an institution falls short, judges often step in. The way they do so cannot be captured by looking at who wins and who loses.

Scholars lag behind policy makers in the realization that words affect the obligations that bind them. There is growing evidence that countries recognize the importance of words in their behavior. Countries sometimes appeal favorable rulings, because the particular language employed by the panelists does not suit their long-term interests. They have strong preferences about judges' use of judicial economy, even as it is meant to leave the final verdict unaffected (Busch and Pelc 2010). And they file some cases not with the typical goal of satisfying some export-oriented industry, but rather with a longer-term goal of modifying the meaning of the rules in a way that favors their interests (Pelc 2013).

The EU's pursuit of safeguards disputes successfully achieved such a change. Safeguards are the institution's quintessential escape clause. The EU, an infrequent safeguards user, filed a number of low-profile cases soon after the WTO's inception, targeting Korean skim powdered milk and Argentinean footwear—insignificant markets by any measure. It successfully argued for an interpretation of the new Agreement on Safeguards through its predecessor, GATT Article XIX. In doing so, it significantly raised the threshold for the use of safeguards, reenlisting the GATT's mention of "unforeseen developments" as a prerequisite for any exercise of a safeguard (Pelc 2009). As soon as this legal strategy bore fruit, the EU turned to bigger fish: it took on the United States in a series of safeguards cases that rank among the WTO's most important in terms of their commercial value. The United States lost these cases and immediately cut its reliance on safeguards. The rules did not change, but their meaning did, as the EU convinced the AB to adopt its interpretation of the text. Scholars need to recognize the importance of words: their ability to affect state behavior.

While this discussion emphasizes how words figure in countries' strategic behavior, the same can naturally be said of judges themselves. Judges have preferences: panelists would rather not have their rulings overturned on appeal; both panelists and AB judges would rather see compliance with their recommendations. More subtly, WTO judges may have some preferences about the evolution of the institution that differ from those of states. Words are the means by which judges act on these preferences. While the interplay between legislative politics and judicial decisions has been studied most closely in the European context (Burley and Mattli 1993), similar conclusions have obtained in other contexts. American legal scholars have recently shown that US Supreme Court judges write less "readable" opinions when they anticipate a hostile reaction in the House (Owens, Wedeking, and Wohlfarth 2013). All of this variation gets lost when one reduces rulings to wins or losses, as the literature has largely done up to now. The time is ripe for taking words seriously.

Conclusion

The literature on WTO dispute settlement has come a long way. It is richer and deeper in so many ways than its earliest contributors could have imagined. It is also more multidisciplinary than many would have predicted. But along the way, as issues like selection and participation have preoccupied scholars, some of the institution's most axiomatic features have been overlooked. As a matter of course, the literature controls for things like trade dependence or dummy SPS measures as being especially politically contentious. But it does not always ask about what the litigants argued or what the panel's verdict did or did not say. It has been a long time since the literature moved beyond the question of *whether* institutions matter and turned to the question of *why* they matter. If we are to take dispute settlement seriously, part of the answer to why they matter must be the words uttered in a panel or AB report, the calibration of legal arguments to key precedents, and the *acquis* of case law that extends the longest shadow on the decision to file in the first place. None of this will be as easy to code as variables like trade dependence. But then again, nothing was ever easy about coding GATT disputes back in the day. The methods and technology that we have today make it possible to be as creative as we are rigorous in studying WTO dispute settlement. It is an institution of laws that renders legal judgments. It is time to let the institution speak for itself.

ACKNOWLEDGEMENTS

Our thanks to Lisa Martin for comments on this chapter, and Amanda Kennard for her research assistance.

NOTES

1. Rossmiller (1994, 232).
2. Contribution of Ecuador to the Improvement of the Dispute Settlement System of the WTO, 2002, TN/DS/W/9. The dispute being referred to is *EC—Bananas*, WTO/DS27.
3. WTO, TN/DS/W/9.
4. WTO, TN/DS/W/1.
5. For instance, at a WTO meeting in 2011, the representatives of Bolivia, Cuba, Ecuador, and Nicaragua complained that "[i]n practice, the WTO has become an organization that is not led by its Members, in which decision-making based on facts is not governed by consensus, and negotiation meetings are not open to participation by all Members."
6. Oxfam International and WWF International, together with eight other NGOs, released a memo in 2003 claiming that the WTO features "proliferation of 'informal', undocumented and exclusive meetings, amounting to lack of transparency and inability of many countries to participate."
7. See Article 3.2 of the DSU.

REFERENCES

Alschner, W. 2014. Amicable Settlements of WTO Disputes: Recent Trends, New Concerns and Old Problems. *World Trade Review* 13: 65–102.

Bhala, Raj. 1998–1999. The Myth about Stare Decisis and International Trade Law (Part One of a Trilogy). *American University International Law Review* 14: 845–956.

Bown, Chad P. 2009. *Self-Enforcing Trade: Developing Countries and WTO Dispute Settlement.* Washington, DC: Brookings Institution Press.

Burley, Anne-Marie, and Walter Mattli. 1993. Europe before the Court: A Political Theory of Legal Integration. *International Organization* 47 (1): 41–76.

Busch, Marc L., and Eric Reinhardt. 2001. Bargaining in the Shadow of the Law: Early Settlement in GATT/WTO Disputes. *Fordham International Law Journal* 24 (1): 158–172.

Busch, Marc L., and Eric Reinhardt. 2003. Developing Countries and General Agreement on Tariffs and Trade/World Trade Organization Dispute Settlement. *Journal of World Trade* 37: 719–735.

Busch, Marc L., and Eric Reinhardt. 2006. Three's a Crowd: Third Parties and WTO Dispute Settlement. *World Politics* 58: 446–477.

Busch, Marc L., Eric Reinhardt, and Gregory Shaffer. 2009. Does Legal Capacity Matter? Explaining Dispute Initiation and Antidumping Actions in the WTO. *World Trade Review* 8: 559–577.

Busch, Marc L., and Krzysztof J. Pelc. 2010. The Politics of Judicial Economy at the World Trade Organization. *International Organization* 64: 257–279.

Davey, William J., and Amelia Porges. 1998. Comments on Performance of the System I: Consultations and Deterrence. *International Lawyer* 32: 695–707.

Davis, Christina. 2012. *Why Adjudicate? Enforcing Trade Rules.* Princeton, NJ: Princeton University Press.

Davis, Christina L., and Sarah Blodgett Bermeo. 2009. Who Files? Developing Country Participation in GATT/WTO Adjudication. *Journal of Politics* 71: 1033–1049.

Elsig, Manfred, and Philipp Stucki. 2012. "Low-income Developing Countries and WTO Litigation: Why Wake Up the Sleeping Dog?" *Review of International Political Economy* 19 (2): 292–316.

Gilligan, Michael, Leslie Johns, and B. Peter Rosendorff. 2010. Strengthening International Courts and the Early Settlement of Disputes. *Journal of Conflict Resolution* 54: 5–38.

Heinisch, E. L. 2006. West Africa Versus the United States on Cotton Subsidies: How, Why and What Next? *Journal of Modern African Studies* 44 (2): 251–274.

Heisenberg, Dorothee. 2007. Informal Decision-Making in the Council: The Secret of the EUs Success? In *Making History: European Integration and Institutional Change at Fifty,* edited by Sophie Meunier and Kathleen R. McNamara, 67–88. Oxford: Oxford University Press.

Horlick, Gary N. 1998. The Consultation Phase of WTO Dispute Resolution: A Private Practitioner's View. *International Lawyer* 32: 685–693.

Horn, H., P. C. Mavroidis, and E. N. Wijkstrom. 2013. In the Shadow of the DSU: Addressing Specific Trade Concerns in the WTO SPS and TBT Committees. *Journal of World Trade* 47 (4): 729–759.

Hudec, Robert E. 2000. *Broadening the Scope of Remedies in the WTO Dispute Settlement: Issues and Lessons from the Practice of Other International Court and Tribunals.* London: Cameron May.

Johns, Leslie, and Krzysztof J. Pelc. 2014. Who Gets to Be in the Room? Manipulating Participation in WTO Disputes. *International Organization* 68(3): 663-699.

Kahler, Miles. 2004. Defining Accountability Up: the Global Economic Multilaterals. *Government and Opposition* 39(2): 132–158.

Keohane, Robert, and Joseph S. Nye. 2001. The Club Model of Multilateral Cooperation and Problems of Democratic Legitimacy. In *Efficiency, Equity, and Legitimacy: The Multilateral Trading System at the Millennium,* edited by Roger B. Porter, Pierre Sauv, Arvind Subramanian, and Americo Beviglia Zampetti, Washington, DC: Brookings Institution Press, 264-294.

Kucik, Jeff, and Krzysztof J. Pelc. 2013. Measuring the Cost of Privacy: A Look at the Distributional Effects of Private Bargaining. McGill University and University College London Working Paper.

Nakagawa, J. 2007. "No More Negotiated Deals?: Settlement of Trade and Investment Disputes in East Asia." *Journal of International Economic Law* 10(4):837–867.

Owens, Ryan J., Justin Wedeking, and Patrick C. Wohlfarth. 2013. How the Supreme Court Alters Opinion Language to Evade Congressional Review. *Journal of Law and Courts* 1(1): 35–59.

Pelc, Krzysztof J. 2010. Constraining Coercion? Legitimacy and Its Role in U.S. Trade Policy, 1975–2000. *International Organization* 64: 65–96.

Pelc, Krzysztof J. 2009. Seeking Escape: The Use of Escape Clauses in International Trade Agreements. *International Studies Quarterly* 53 (2): 349–368.

Pelc, Krzysztof J. 2013. The Politics of Precedent in International Law: A Social Network Application. *American Political Science Review* 108(3): 1-18.

Petersmann, Ernst-Ulrich. 1994. The Dispute Settlement System of the World Trade Organization and the Evolution of the GATT Dispute Settlement System Since 1948. *Common Market Law Review* 31: 1157–1244.

Rossmiller, George E. 1994. Discussion. In *Agricultural Trade Conflicts and GATT: New Dimensions in US-European Agricultural Trade Relations*, edited by Giovanni Anania et al., Boulder, CO: Westview Press, 262–263.

Rountree, G. H. 1998–1999. Raging Hormones: A Discussion of the World Trade Organization's Decision in the European Union-United States Beef Dispute. *Georgia Journal of International and Comparative Law* 27: 607–634.

Schelling, Thomas C. 1960. *The Strategy of Conflict*. Cambridge, MA: Harvard University Press.

Shumaker, M. J. 2007. Tearing the Fabric of the World Trade Organization: United States-Subsidies on Upland Cotton. *North Carolina Journal of International Law and Commercial Regulation* 32: 548–604.

Sien, I. A. R. 2006–2007. Beefing up the Hormones Dispute: Problems in Compliance and Viable Compromise Alternatives. *Georgetown Law Journal* 95: 565–590.

Smith, Adam. 1937. *The Wealth of Nations (1776)*. New York: Modern Library.

Smythe, Elizabeth, and Peter J Smith. 2006. Legitimacy, Transparency, and Information Technology: The World Trade Organization in an Era of Contentious Trade Politics. *Global Governance: A Review of Multilateralism and International Organizations* 12 (1): 31–53.

Stasavage, David. 2004. Open-Door or Closed-Door? Transparency in Domestic and International Bargaining. *International Organization* 58: 667–703.

Steinberg, Richard H. 2002. In the Shadow of Law or Power? Consensus-based Bargaining and Outcomes in the GATT/WTO. *International Organization* 56: 339–374.

Venzke, I. 2012. *How the Practice of Interpretation Makes International Law: On Semantic Change and Normative Twists*. Oxford: Oxford University Press.

World Trade Organization. 2011. Decisions and Recommendations Adopted by the WTO Committee on Technical Barriers to Trade Since 1 January 1995. Committee on Technical Barriers to Trade, G/TBT/1/Rev.10, June 9.

PART VI

....

ISSUE LINKAGES

....

....

CHAPTER 22

TRADE AND WAR

....

ERIK GARTZKE AND JIAKUN JACK ZHANG

INTRODUCTION

THE relationship between trade and war has been both a cornerstone of statecraft and a subject of debate for centuries. In recent decades the conventional wisdom that commerce brings peace has had a major impact on American foreign policy toward a rising China and has served as an intellectual impetus behind the formation of the European Economic Community. The belief that heightened economic interdependence inhibits conflict rests on a widely cited empirical literature that documents the pacifying effect of trade at the cross-national level. Yet the causal mechanisms that drive the empirical relationship between economic interdependence and reduced military conflict have yet to be fully established. Existing empirical studies suffer from important shortcomings related to endogeneity and the measurement of key constructs. Much of this literature has been motivated by, and framed in terms of, stylized debates between and among traditional paradigms in international relations. Only in the last decade have researchers begun to establish a common set of microfoundations. Our analytical understanding of trade and war has also progressed from the system level, to dyad, and more recently to network-based theories. Considerable room remains for theoretical and empirical development. Scholarship on interdependence can be improved through adoption of common assumptions about the causes of war and through better understanding of the domestic sources of trade and foreign policy.

This chapter begins by outlining the bargaining theory of war in order to offer a set of working assumptions about the nature of conflict initiation that can guide future research on war and trade. Because many theoretical priors used in the existing literature come from paradigms, the following section reviews and critiques the ways in which liberals, realists, Marxists, and others have approached the relationship between trade and war. The next section surveys the methodology and empirical findings of the existing literature. Moving beyond paradigmatic approaches, the authors advocate that future work focus on theory development and empirical tests of three broad mechanisms that could potentially link trade with war and/or peace: constraints, information, and the transformation of actors' preferences. The chapter concludes with a discussion of how these three broad mechanisms are likely to benefit future research.

A Theory of War

A discussion on the relationship between trade and war must begin with a theory of conflict. Theories that are intended to explain how a given process is thought to modify conflict behavior must function by interacting with the underlying conflict process, whatever it might be. Simply being explicit about why nations are believed to fight will go a long way toward whittling down the number of possible ways that trade is likely to have an impact on decisions about war and peace.

Advances in the study of interstate conflict have produced a theoretical perspective in tension with the logic and validity of established theories of war. Once-dominant structural explanations asserting that balances of power promote peace and imbalances lead to conflict have come under particular scrutiny (Niou et al. 2007). The problem with using indicators of power as determinants of war and peace is that the conflicts they might produce are resolvable through negotiation; theories of war fall short if they fail to take into consideration the role and effect of endogenous bargaining as a more efficient way of resolving who gets what (Powell 1999). Warfare is only one way in which states can pursue their interests. Leaders who negotiate and obtain the settlements before fighting begins are better off than those who must pay the high costs of war (Wagner 2007). It is thus not simply the distribution of power that determines war and peace, but the degree to which power and benefits overlap or correspond in the global system. Nations compete not because of power imbalances, but because of imbalances between the distribution of power and the distribution of benefits.

Even then, it is not power relations per se that lead to conflict, but the incompatibility of actors' perceptions of them. Fearon (1995) places in a rationalist and internally consistent framework Blainey's (1988) basic insight that the causes of war reside not in disparities of power but in incompatible beliefs about power. Rationalist explanations assume purposive action on the part of leaders when they are considering the use of force. Opponents have incentives to feign strength and conceal weakness. Because information about an opponent's resolve or capabilities is generally incomplete, rational leaders must make decisions in an environment of uncertainty. The centrality of uncertainty to rationalist explanations for war means that the advent of war is itself stochastic (Gartzke 1999). Reasoning leaders generally are trying to avoid war because it is a costly outcome. But they can still find themselves at war, for three reasons.

First, war can occur as competitors mistake relative resolve or capabilities, and because competition generates incentives for actors to conceal true information about these variables. In an uncertain world, egoistic leaders can benefit by bluffing. This "asymmetric information" argument encourages researchers to seek ways that states or other actors may be able to communicate more or less credibly (Schultz 2001), though this is difficult.

Second, actors can fight because they face a "commitment problem" created by time inconsistency. If power relations are shifting over time, so that one actor is declining in power relative to another, then agreements between them are unstable, as the rising power will often have an incentive to insist on better terms in the future, when it becomes more capable. The declining power in turn has incentives to blunt the ascent of the rising state. Since fighting a winning war today may be better than losing one tomorrow, commitment problems can cause conflict. Powell (2006) shows that large, rapid shifts in the distribution of power can lead to war in three classes of commitment problems: preventive war, preemptive attacks due to offensive advantage, and conflicts produced by bargaining over issues that affect future bargaining power.

Finally, actors can fight over issues because those at stake are not readily divisible. This "indivisibility problem" appears to be an infrequent cause of war, as it is typically possible to fashion bargains through side payments that resolve this motive for war. However, the fact that indivisibility problems can be resolved does not mean that actors invariably have an interest in resolving them; competitors may choose to retain or even develop indivisibility problems for strategic advantage. This in turn could lead to fighting in a chicken-type scenario if actors are unable to unravel previous indivisibilities.

THE THEORIES OF TRADE

The literature on trade and war has remained paradigmatic and is not yet well integrated with the evolution in thinking about the nature of conflict, such as the bargaining theory of war. Though various unresolved debates in the paradigmatic literature might well prove important, they are somewhat less likely to generate the most innovative future research agendas. The next section discusses the literature on trade and war, using the paradigmatic framework to present arguments and evidence. We then offer a nonparadigmatic approach in the subsequent section.

Liberal theories have dominated discourse on economic interdependence. But liberalism is not without its theoretical rivals. Realists and Marxists make starkly contrasting predictions about the effects of trade on war and peace. Whereas liberals believe that trade creates virtuous interdependencies that tend to dampen down conflict tendencies, realists view trade more harshly, believing that it creates vulnerabilities and imbalances of power, both of which make war more likely. Marxists contradict the realist perspective on the relationship between trade and war at the level of major powers, believing instead that class and power collude to suppress and rule. At the same time, Marxists are in agreement with realists on the more general point that trade tends to increase conflict at the systemic level, mostly between the core and the periphery.

Liberalism

The view that trade has a dampening effect on war is almost a liberal article of faith. As such, it is in some tension with the liberal perspective's emphasis on rationality and evidence-based inference. Advocacy of a commercial peace appears prominently in the writings of Montesquieu, Rousseau, Kant, Adam Smith, Thomas Paine, and other Enlightenment figures. Classical liberal political economy espoused policies that would restrict the war-making power of the aristocratic elite and increase the autonomy of the commercial classes. The key mechanisms driving liberal trade theories about peace involve opportunity costs, domestic interest groups, and constitutional republicanism. Commerce is seen as creating bonds of mutual benefit between countries that are costly to sever. War threatens to disrupt these beneficial ties, and so the liberal logic predicts that with increased trade, the incentives to fight will recede. In modern economic terms, trade raises the opportunity cost of war. A notable articulation of this logic can be found in Norman Angell's *The Great Illusion* (1910), in which he criticized the jingoistic nationalism of turn-of-the-century Europe and argued that war, even when victorious, was socially and economically futile, because wealth in the modern era is tied to credit and commercial contracts, not to war.

The view that trade increases the opportunity costs of fighting has been revived in recent years to account for the statistical linkage between trade interdependence and conflict (Copeland 1996; Oneal et al. 1996; Oneal and Russet 1997, 1999; Oneal et al. 2003; Hegre et al. 2010). According to the classical liberal account, however, the accumulation of commercial interest groups with increasing levels of economic interdependence provides a check on sovereigns who are otherwise inclined to go to war. Trading states become populated with commercial interests, which seek to prevail on leaders to refrain from resorting to force (Bentham 1781; Cobden 1867). Schumpeter (1962) in particular emphasizes the role of democracy in facilitating the expression of commercial interests in national politics, an approach also championed by Doyle (1983, 1986), and for which Mousseau (2000, 2003, 2010) provides further theoretical and empirical justification.[1]

The channel through which commercial interests express themselves could be greater in democracies. As Immanuel Kant emphasized in *Perpetual Peace*, economic interdependence may dampen the risk of war between states if the governments of those states are responsive to, and representative of, wider rather than narrower social interests. For Kant, "republican constitutions," "a commercial spirit," and a federation of interdependent republics would provide the basis for "perpetual peace." Oneal and Russett have provided much of the systematic empirical justification for the "Kantian peace." Gelpi and Grieco (2003, 2008) apply the logic of selectorate theory (De Mesquita and Smith 2005), appearing to show that trade and democracy are each contingent upon the other.

While it is plausible on its face, there are at least three reasons to believe that the impact or applicability of the classical perspective may be limited. First, to deter conflict, potential trade losses must be substantial relative to the (subjective) valuations nations place on issues or resources in dispute. War is already a highly costly enterprise, while the portion of trade forfeit in a contest will often be modest in scale. Where commercial losses can be expected to be small relative to the value of the issues at stake, there is no reason to believe that interdependence will achieve what amounts to mutual deterrence. Second, conflict is strategic. The most immediate effect of increasing the cost of warfare for one actor is to make it more appealing for opponents to behave more aggressively toward the state that is inhibited. States vary in their dependence on trade; if trade makes war too costly for one actor, then political competitors—even states also dependent on trade—have incentives to behave aggressively and to seek further concessions. Whether raising the cost of fighting leads to cooperation or conflict depends on whether states can capitalize on the leverage created by trade to achieve more satisfactory diplomatic solutions, or whether the additional friction that results from increased leverage spills over from economic to political and military conflict. Interdependence can make war less, or more, likely depending on other factors (Morrow 1999). Some actors with limited aims may choose to enjoy increased leverage in the form of a more stable peace, but others will not, given that most conflicts involve actors with considerable differences in preferences or interests. Again, mutual linkages will best deter conflict where the incentives to fight are already marginal from the outset.

Finally, conflict is highly competitive by its nature. The very point of competition is to take advantage of the vulnerabilities of an opponent. The fact that vulnerabilities are mutual does not in itself ensure peace, any more than common mortality guarantees that humans never fight. As such, trade is not only compatible with, but sufficient for, practicing conflict. Nations contemplating war are already anticipating considerable harm and inconvenience. The additional burden of economic loss must be substantial before this can do more than marginally affect the willingness to fight. The notion that nations will avoid war because trade is valuable ignores the fact that war itself involves imposing and suffering substantial loss. It is the search for value that ignites competition and the destruction of value that makes war coercive. Indeed, war in modern times typically involves economic conflict, as well as the forfeiture of human life.

Realism

The realist perspective on trade is no less venerable. Thucydides attributed the origins of the Peloponnesian War to the rise of Athens as a commercial empire and the alarm that this inspired in Lacedaemon. One can point to many other wars that have been fought over trade. Liberal theory makes a strong case that nations are better off trading than fighting. Yet history is replete with examples in which nations appeared to prefer fighting to trading. The Anglo-Dutch wars of the seventeenth and eighteenth centuries witnessed two trading states with republican governments fighting for control of European and world commerce. The Anglo-French wars of the eighteenth and nineteenth centuries shared many of the same dynamics of commercial rivalry that did not appear to be mitigated by the rise of republicanism in France. While these and other historical examples are familiar to contemporary researchers, fighting over trade has hardly been reconciled with liberal theory.

Realist theories of war rely on economic development as the primary internal mechanism for increasing state power. The connection is indirect; economic growth allows for more internal balancing and the accumulation of military power (Morgenthau 1948; Waltz 1959; Mearsheimer 2001). Trade is generally believed to increase economic efficiency and therefore the size of the surplus. To the degree that commerce augments the resources available to a state, commercial powers should be more capable and—depending on variables like system structure, the local or regional balance, or other relationships—trading states may then be better equipped for foreign adventures. The realist view of trade dates back to Jean-Baptiste Colbert, Alexander Hamilton, and Frederich List, and has been closely identified with mercantilism, protectionism, and statism.

Realists view the effects of interdependence as at odds with the competitive logic of politics under anarchy (Carr 1964; Krasner 1976; Waltz 1979; Mastanduno 1998). Kenneth Waltz maintains that "close interdependence means closeness of contact and raises the prospect of at least occasional conflict" (1970, 250). Elsewhere, Waltz argues that the rise of globalization has widened inequalities between rich and poor states, producing dependencies rather than interdependencies. "A world in which a few states can take care of themselves quite well and most states cannot hope to do so is scarcely an interdependent one" (1979, 159). To realists like Waltz, states differ from each other primarily in terms of power. Trade has the effect of exacerbating imbalances by changing relative capabilities, usually in favor of those states that already wield disproportionate influence in world affairs. Operating under anarchy, states worry that a partner today can become a threat in the future. Building on this logic, Gowa (1989) shows that economic ties between countries can have large security-related consequences because the real income from trade is a source of security externalities.

More recent research challenges key assumptions and findings of realist scholarship. As discussed earlier in the chapter, realist theories do not provide logically coherent mechanisms for how differences in relative capabilities or shifts in the balance of power lead to war. More generally, realists have had trouble explaining the broader empirical correlation between trade and peace. In addition, the logic of relative gains (Grieco 1988, 1990; Mastanduno 1991) has been criticized by Snidal (1991) and Powell (1991), who show that concerns about relative gains break down as the number of actors involved grows. In a world with many states, preoccupation with relative gains within one pair of states (a dyad) disproportionately advantages third parties. Finally, recent scholarship (Gartzke and Lupu 2012) challenges the realist account of World War I, the most often cited case of the failure of interdependence to maintain peace. The "Great War" began in the Balkans, where trade was local and vestigial and where disputes regularly flared into open warfare. Fighting then spread to states where trade had played an important role in managing previous conflict, but where commitments to the warring factions took precedence.

Marxism

Marxists and realists both view trade as exacerbating political competition. However, Marxism (and radicalism in general) focuses on imbalances of power not among great powers but between weak states and the powerful centers of trade (core and periphery). Marxists see the modern industrial state as captured by expansionist capitalist interests. At first blush, the history of European colonialism seems to validate the Marxist perspective. The nations of Europe spent a considerable portion of the sixteenth through the eighteenth centuries fighting over the very lucrative East Asia trade or fighting with indigenous groups to impose mercantilist commercial systems. Private commercial firms created armies and navies and fought wars to consolidate markets, protect their profits, and prevent foreign competition. These efforts were then augmented by hybrid "crown companies" that drew sovereigns directly into private enterprise. Crown companies were later eclipsed by the power of sovereign governments that had grown rich on global commerce.

Socialists (Hobson 1905) and Marxists (Lenin 1916) believed that the capitalist need for markets propelled class warfare abroad. Hobson (1905) argued that imperialism results from the structural problem of overproduction and underconsumption. As capitalists continue to reinvest their wealth in production, they soon exhaust demand for goods in their domestic markets and must look for foreign markets to absorb the surplus goods and capital that they can't use at home. Lenin (1916) built on Hobson's idea of excess production to argue that capitalism is the primary source of international wars, as more powerful nations exploit weaker ones for economic gains. Marxists point to World War I as an example of a capitalist war, in which business interests prospered from the war while millions of ordinary people lost their lives in the trenches. Paradoxically, imperialism was also used to explain delay in the advent of revolution in Europe, since foreign trade and investment put off the crisis between domestic class interests.

Reacting to modernization theory, dependency theorists (Santos 1970; Wallerstein 1974) revived Marxist arguments during the Cold War. Dependency theory has since been heavily criticized on economic and historical grounds. Exploitation of peripheral countries by the core exists, but appears more uneven than dependency theory would imply. More important, successful economic modernization in East Asia, and the manifest failure of import-substituting industrialization (ISI) in Latin America appeared to refute many of the policy recommendations of dependency theory. Gilpin argues that developing countries are dependent because they are "weak in a world of the strong," suffering not from external dependence but from internal inefficiency (Gilpin 2011). Marxism was also discredited by the collapse of the Soviet empire. However, normative concerns about the capture of state policy by business interests as well as the role of international capital in war suggest the need for, and value of, further inquiry.

EMPIRICAL AND FORMAL
THEORETICAL FINDINGS

Debate over the effects of trade on conflict has generated a tremendous amount of scholarship. A large volume of empirical work in the 1990s and 2000s produced contradictory findings; various scholars demonstrated positive, negative, and indeterminate relationships between trade and war. The liberal view that trade pacifies conflict dominates contemporary thinking, even though it has proven difficult to find definitive evidence for the mechanisms proposed by available theories.

Realists have used similar data in an attempt to demonstrate that trade actually increases conflict (Barbieri 1996, 2002). It is also possible that trade has no net effect on warfare (Gartzke et al. 2001; Gartzke and Li 2003; Gartzke 2007), or that the effect of commerce is ambiguous, given contrasting incentives and the impact of rational expectations in conditioning trade prior to actual fighting (Morrow 1999). Ambiguity about trade and conflict stems from the very forces highlighted by available perspectives. States in competition have motives to fight, while trade provides a rationale for restraint, or at least for moderation in managing tensions. The net effect of these contrasting effects is difficult to divine. States enmeshed in intense trading relationships may find that these present a costly or informative barrier to conflict. Other states may fight, despite trading ties, if the issues at stake are sufficiently important. Still other nations will find that trade, though valuable, is seldom sufficiently important in any given relationship to interrupt the path to war. Table 22.1 offers a summary of available findings in the current empirical literature.

The first section in the table lists studies finding that increased trade decreases conflict. Central to this set of studies is the finding that increased levels of trade are associated with a significant reduction in interstate disputes. Polachek's (1980) pioneering empirical work first documents a negative statistical correlation between dyadic trade and peace. Oneal and colleagues (1996, 1997, 1999, 2003, 2010) approach interdependence from the perspective of the Kantian peace. Their analysis shows that higher levels of trade and democracy tend to lead to peace. They argue that the mechanism behind the pacifying effect of trade is the classical liberal expectation that state participation in interstate conflict is motivated by expected utility; trade increases the benefits of refraining from war and decreases incentives to fight.

The second section reviews studies finding that trade increases conflict among states. Realists contradict the Kantian peace findings with empirical results that seem to show that heightened trade increases the likelihood of country dyads engaging in militarized interstate disputes but has no influence on the occurrence of wars (Barbieri 1996, 2002; Barbieri and Levy 1999). Barbieri argues that there is a curvilinear relationship between interdependence and conflict; low to moderate degrees of interdependence reduce the likelihood of dyadic disputes, and extensive economic linkages increase the probability of disputes.

Table 22.1 Summary of Empirical Findings on the Trade–War Relationship

Main Findings	Author(s)	Methodology and Unit of Analysis
Trade Decreases Warfare	Lupu and Traag (2012)	Regression, network
	Dorussen and Ward (2010)	Regression, network
	Hegre, Oneal, and Russett (2010)	Regression, dyads
	Oneal and Russett (2003)	Regression, PRD
	Oneal and Russett (1999)	Regression, PRD
	Polachek, Robst, and Chang (1999)	Regression, dyads
	Oneal and Russett (1997)	Regression, PRD
	Oneal and Ray (1997)	Formal model, regression, dyads
	Polachek (1997)	Regression, PRD
	Oneal, Oneal, et al. (1996)	Regression, PRD
	Copeland (1996)	Case study, system
	Mansfield (1994)	Regression, dyads
	Gasiorowski and Polachek (1982)	Granger causality, system
	Polachek (1980)	Regression, dyads
Trade Increases Warfare	Barbieri (2002)	Regression, dyads
	Barbieri and Levy (1999)	Regression, dyads
	Barbieri (1996)	Regression, dyads
	Domke (1988)	Case study, system
Indeterminate or No Effect	Li and Reuveny (2011)	Regression, dyads
	Ward and Hoff (2007)	Prediction, network
	Ward, Siverson, and Cao (2007)	Bayesian model, dyads
	Keshk, Pollins, and Reuveny (2004)	Regression, dyads
	Gartzke and Li (2003)	Replication, dyads
	Gartzke (2007)	Regression, dyads
	Gartzke, Li, and Boehmer (2001)	Regression, dyads
	Dorussen (1999)	Formal model, >2 actors
	Morrow (1999)	Formal model, 2 actors
	Dorussen (1999)	Granger causality, dyads
	Reuveny & Kang (1996)	Formal model, 2 actors
	Gowa (1994)	Regression, dyads
	Gasiorowski (1986)	

PRD = Politically relevant dyads.

A final section of Table 22.1 deals with studies whose findings are inconclusive or in which only the null hypothesis (that there is no relationship between trade and conflict) is substantiated. We discuss these nonrelationships more extensively in the next subsection.

Artifacts of Variable Selection

Dyad level quantitative studies from the 1990s on the effects of trade on conflict appear to yield discrepant findings. However, these differences may just be the result of features inherent in the variable selection used by the competing approaches (Gartzke and Li 2001). Oneal and Russet (1997) operationalize interdependence as whether a particular trade relationship matters relative to a state's overall economic performance (trade/GDP—trade salience), while Barbieri (1996) operationalizes interdependence as a function of whether trade is valuable relative to other trade relationships (trade/ trade—trade share). Gartzke and Li show that the effect of trade share is inversely related to the consensus measure of openness (monadic trade interdependence). In effect, the Barbieri measure captures disconnectedness from the world economy or dependency aspects of trading relations. Table 22.2 illustrates the steps for constructing each dyadic measure.

Gartzke and Li show that *trade share* is inversely related to trade *openness*. *Trade share* thus tends to reflect a country's *lack* of integration into the world economy. Hence, the positive effect of *trade share* and the negative effect of *openness* do not necessarily

Table 22.2 Comparisons of Two Measures of Trade Interdependence

Studies	Measure
Barbieri (1995, 1996, 1998b)	(1) $tradeshare_i = \dfrac{\left(imports_{ij} + exports_{ij}\right)}{\left(imports_i + exports_i\right)} = \dfrac{trade_{ij}}{trade_i}$
	(2) $trade\,salience_{ij} = \sqrt{trade\,share_i * trade\,share_j}$
	(3) $tradesymmetry_{ij} = 1 - \left\| trade\,share_i - trade\,share_j \right\|$
	(4) $trade\,interdependence_{ij} = trade\,salience_{ij} * trade\,symmetry_{ij}$
Oneal & Russett (cf. 1997, 1999)	(5) $trade\,dependence_{ij} = \dfrac{\left(imports_{ij} + exports_{ij}\right)}{GDP_i} = \dfrac{trade_{ij}}{GDP_i}$
	(6) $trade\,dependence_{ji} = \dfrac{\left(imports_{ji} + exports_{ji}\right)}{GDP_j} = \dfrac{trade_{ji}}{GDP_j}$
	(7) trade interdependence$_{ij}$ = lower of (dependence$_{ij}$ and dependence$_{ji}$)
	(8) trade asymmetry$_{ij}$ = higher of (dependence$_{ij}$ and dependence$_{ji}$)

indicate inconsistencies in theory, data, or other sources. Instead, it is possible to attribute the discrepancy to variable construction alone. The inverse relationship between *trade share* and *openness* helps to resolve the puzzle of why Barbieri and Oneal and Russett and others achieve discrepant findings. There need be no theoretical contradiction between the positive correlation of the *trade share* measure and the negative correlation of the *trade dependence* measure in analyzing interstate disputes, at least not at the dyadic level. More economic linkages correlate with fewer disputes.

Problems of Endogeneity

Much of the empirical literature relies on cross-national time series data and does not effectively deal with endogeneities between trade and conflict. While a robust correlation exists between dyadic trade and interstate disputes, it is difficult to determine causality. It is plausible that trade reduces war as the liberals claim, but it is equally likely that peace leads to an increase in trade. Formal theoretical work pays more attention to the issue of endogeneity than existing empirical research. James Morrow (1999) points out that the endoegeneity problem in interdependence has been overlooked by empiricists and links interdependence to conflict bargaining. Outcomes of peace and conflict hinge on information decision makers have about each other's relative bargaining positions. Because actual trade flows (and, by inference, other observable economic relations) only provide a sliver of relevant information about players' relative resolve, Morrow finds economic links have an indeterminate effect on conflict. The failure to endogenize decision makers' choice to trade is a critical shortcoming of empirical studies. If trading states are integrated because they anticipate the likelihood of peace, then one would expect to find a correlation between trade and peace even without a causal connection (Benson and Niou 2007).

Beyond Dyads

Maoz and Russett (1993) started a trend of dyad year designs using militarized interstate dispute (MID) data that has been widely adopted in subsequent literature (see column 2 in Table 22.1). However, the empirical relationships established using this mode of analysis have been challenged by studies that point out problematic assumptions about spatial and/or temporal independence (Beck et al. 1998; Ward et al. 2007). Because these observations are temporally dependent—a peaceful dyad today is likely to persist in being peaceful tomorrow—Beck and colleagues advocate using a grouped duration model over logit or probit regressions. Ward and colleagues show that the statistical association in the literature stems from three components: (1) geographical proximity, (2) dependence among MIDs with the same initiator or target, and (3) higher order dependences in dyadic data. They conclude that the Kantian peace tripod loses its predictive power once these factors are controlled for statistically.

Other scholars have pushed the analysis of interdependence beyond dyads. Commercial enterprises can generally continue through third parties, even when conflicts interfere with direct bilateral ties. Recognition of this fact has led to attempts to estimate the demand elasticity of substitution present in sourcing goods and services elsewhere (Polachek et al. 1999; Crescenzi 2003). Others have tried to model the effects of trade networks on whether states fight (Ward and Hoff 2007; Dorussen and Ward 2008, 2010; Lupu and Traag 2012; Ward et al. 2013), suggesting that it is the cumulative indirect effects of trade and conflict that are most important. The network approach makes more realistic theoretical assumptions about trade and allows for a better test of interdependence. At the same time, however, it obscures particular tendencies, making causal inference even harder.

RETHEORIZING INTERDEPENDENCE

As Beth Simmons notes, "the empirical project has largely been stylized as a 'realist' versus 'liberal' horse race. When formulated in this way, scholars are missing rich opportunities to specify the nature of state-society relations that link private profiteering with national foreign (even military) policy" (Simmons 2003, 32). Focusing on mechanisms rather than paradigms allows for a more eclectic research agenda capable of resolving inconsistencies found in existing empirical work. Borrowing from Scott Kastner (2009), we outline three ways in which trade can interact with war. Interdependence can constrain, inform, or transform political relationships.

Trade Constrains

Much of the literature relies on constraint as the key mechanism behind commercial peace. Scholars in this tradition view trade as generating efficiency gains. Constraint mechanisms begin with the assumption that military conflict disrupts valuable commercial ties between economic partners that happen to be sovereign, independent states. Because the disruptions caused by military conflict are costly for domestic actors (export-oriented firms and consumers), these groups appeal to their government to refrain from escalating crises to open conflict or war.

Constraints, also referred to as "opportunity costs," are the mechanism most frequently used by liberal scholars to account for commercial peace (Levy 2003). The theory is often tied to democracy, since popular rule is reasonably believed to be more sensitive to the needs of domestic constituents. As with the Kantian conception of liberal political restraint on warlike monarchs, leaders may still want to go to war, for territorial or nationalistic reasons. However, the disruption of commerce associated with war leads domestic constituents to oppose these other objectives (McDonald 2009). As a result, the leader avoids or de-escalates fighting, despite his or her initial preferences. The argument suggests in particular that one should see evidence of considerable lobbying at the firm level against war and associated with crises or escalation.

While opportunity costs could inhibit conflict, they need to be large enough to alter the calculus of war. Marginal increases in the overall cost of fighting can at most have a marginal effect on whether conflict occurs. At the same time, factors that increase war costs create leverage that opponents, even trade partners, can use to extract additional concessions or increase the odds that an adversary concedes rather than fighting. Having more reasons *not* to fight makes it easier for other states, even other trade partners, to make more extractive demands, since the nominal risk that the opponent will refuse is lower. Finally, introducing domestic politics further complicates the constraint argument. Some economic actors will favor peace, but others may prefer to fight (Brooks 2013). Indeed, the practice and study of tariffs and other trade barriers suggests that import-competing factors or sectors might favor using military force under some circumstances. War can act as a tariff, allowing import-competing industries and workers to receive higher returns on their inputs to production. The net effect of these tendencies is again unclear.

Trade Informs

A second set of mechanisms focuses on the role of information and attempts to explain the relationship between commerce and conflict within a bargaining framework (Fearon 1995; Gartzke 1999; Morrow 1999; Powell 2002). As discussed previously in this chapter, wars often arise due to bargaining failures driven by uncertainty about an opponent's resolve or capabilities. In these models, military disputes result when leaders misjudge the relative commitment of their opponents. Both sides benefit from overstating the level of their commitment, hoping that the opponent will back down. Wars result when at least one side underestimates an adversary's commitment, assuming that the adversary is bluffing when in fact he is resolved. To overcome the problem of incomplete information, leaders must demonstrate their commitment through costly acts such as tying hands or sinking costs (Fearon 1997). Costly signals avoid the cheap talk problem, backing up words with action.

Cutting off trade is one way that leaders can communicate resolve during crises. Without economic interdependence, threats have relatively little cost until one side escalates to military violence. Economic interdependence creates a middle step in the escalation ladder between war and peace. Making threats or taking actions that harm commerce is costly to both parties in an interdependent relationship. Therefore, as the degree of economic interdependence increases, the costs involved in threatening war rise as well (as merchants and investors abandon markets when and where war becomes more likely), ensuring that leaders more credibly communicate resolve. Economies that are well integrated into the global markets face the risk of capital flight when conflict is on the horizon. Markets are thus a credible mechanism for revealing information, because they offer leaders a way to signal resolve that is costly but also short of military violence.

A few scholars have studied the informational effects of trade on conflict (Gartzke et al. 2001; Gartzke 2007). However, the foundations of this mechanism remain undertheorized and in need of additional empirical support. This is thus a fertile area for future work. At the same time, the impact of informational effects of interdependence may (also) be marginal, as the reduction in uncertainty will at most be partial, and there are many reasons that states do not fight.

Trade Transforms

A final set of mechanisms involves the potential for economic ties to transform the preferences of political actors. Transformation is at the core of Richard Rosecrance's (1986) notion of the trading state, in which he argues that changes in the world economy have led modern states to become less reliant on territory than on commerce. A related argument notes that trade is more efficient than military conquest as a way to acquire goods and services, just as buying things at the store is often more efficient than stealing them, even for thieves and bank robbers.

Whereas the first two mechanisms treat the interests of leaders as exogenous and fixed, the transformation predicts that heightened economic exchange will change not just the payoffs, but also the preferences of decision makers. In other words, economic integration harmonizes the goals and interests of interdependent states. The most salient example of this is the integration of Europe after World War II. In advancing the Marshall Plan, American policy makers argued for rebuilding Germany's economy alongside the rest of Western Europe, in order to tie German interests to peace and prosperity in the West. Together, the Marshall Plan and the rise of European economic and political institutions transformed European geopolitics. Economic integration ensured development and growth, enabled economic cooperation, reduced strategic mistrust, and created bonds of common interest between historical rivals. International commerce catalyzed fundamental changes to the culture, civil society, and political institutions of these states. As the exchange of capital, goods, people, and ideas across borders increases, the preferences of leaders are said to change, such that conquest is no longer considered a legitimate tool of foreign policy. Indeed, despite recent turmoil in the Eurozone, European leaders and their populations would find another continental war like those of the twentieth century inconceivable.

The transformation interpretation of trade and conflict scores points for being optimistic and appearing to offer the potential for dramatic change. However, both Rosecrance's view and later arguments leave it unclear whether preferences or payoffs are changing. In a sense the latter is a better option, since this does not require the changing of hearts and minds, but only the filling of pockets. It would, for example, be easier to imagine that stability in Asia is possible because most states benefit intensely from trade, than to argue that preferences must converge and that nations such as China, Japan, and the Koreas are no longer willing even to contemplate the use of force.

DIRECTIONS FOR FUTURE RESEARCH AND INQUIRY

The relationship between trade and war remains an important and appealing area for future research. Despite considerable attention and a substantial amount of plausible conjecture and speculation, there is much that remains in doubt. Growing consensus about the theory of war can play a critical role in building consensus about cause and effect. Trade is most likely to impact peace where it most closely influences the causes of war. Explanations of the effects of trade on conflict that do not address a coherent theory of conflict must thus be held in some doubt. This creates an opportunity for refining theory by evaluating existing claims in terms of causal logic.

The study of interdependence can also be improved by more rigorous assessment of trade at different levels of analysis. Earlier studies measure the cross-national effects of trade on war, but existing causal mechanisms make unsubstantiated assumptions about the preferences of domestic actors. Scholars can begin to better understand the domestic microfoundations of interdependence by incorporating the latest research on public opinion, firm level preferences toward trade, and distributional effects of trade on local politics. Rather than rely on national level measures of trade share or trade salience, scholars may choose to examine the behavior of key domestic political actors for evidence of causal mechanisms. Evidence that firms are not significantly harmed by conflict would cast doubt on the assumption that export-oriented firms constrain conflict by lobbying for peace. Eliminating mechanisms with no empirical grounding at the subnational level would allow scholars to hone in on the drivers of commercial peace.

Existing theories must also be shaped through dialogue with other strands of research. Current thinking on trade and peace pays very little attention to the best information about trade economics, corporate strategy, or political economy research. Assumptions in existing studies tend to be crude and the models of trade and politics tend to be overly simplistic. For example, much of the literature uses aggregate bilateral trade to make claims about the preferences of private actors rather than studying these actors directly. Studies of interdependence must engage more with emerging scholarship in the international political economy literature using firm-level and product-level data.

As Kastner (2009) points out, an understanding of interdependence requires a thorough understanding of the domestic determinants of trade policy. However, existing studies of trade and conflict rarely focus on domestic actors and their preferences. Michael Plouffe, in this volume, presents an analysis of the political economy of trade emphasizing the political role of heterogeneity in firm preferences. Firms' preferences over trade policy are dictated by their ability to engage foreign markets. His data show that in comparative advantage industries, low productivity firms pursue import protection, while in comparative disadvantage industries, high productivity firms seek trade liberalization. Both of these firm level behaviors contradict classical models of trade politics, which ignore firm level differentiation within industries. These firm-level differences matter for interdependence because conflict would disrupt trade for some firms more than others. Whether or not the constraint mechanism works should therefore depend on which set of firms can sway policy in their favor.

The literature on the domestic determinants of foreign policy is also informative. To establish common microfoundations for trade and war, the preferences of relevant domestic actors (policy makers, firms, consumers, etc) must be linked with foreign policy outcomes. This is easier to do for some types of outcomes, particularly in democracies. Kleinberg and Fordham (2013) investigate whether domestic distributional effects of trade affect support for hostile foreign policies toward China in the U.S. Congress.

They find that the export orientation and import dependency of congressional districts influence many members' decisions to take a tough stance against China in cosponsorship and roll-call voting. More work is needed to examine the influence of economic interests arising from trade on other aspects of the foreign-policy-making process. The role that domestic politics play in the decisions made by chief executives, foreign ministries, and militaries is not systematically understood. But because trade clearly has important domestic distributional consequences the interdependence literature should incorporate domestic politics to help better understand how, and when, trade is able to constrain, inform, or transform conflict.

In summary, students of interdependence will benefit by being more explicit about the unit of analysis and the agency of relevant actors. Existing research take the nation-state as the unit of analysis and does not often account for the agency of domestic actors, be they trading firms or policymakers,. However, as other chapters in this volume indicate, scholars of trade are turning increasingly to consumer, firm, and product level data. The challenge ahead for the trade and war literature is to make sense of these new findings about trade at the sub-national level and connect them to foreign policy at the international level.

Conclusion

Existing paradigmatic approaches to economic interdependence remain underspecified and the causal mechanisms untested. Too much of the literature consists of empirical findings intended to resolve theoretical debates, but since the evidence is inconclusive, and theories are imprecise, less has been learned than many would like. As Mansfield and Pollins noted in their review of the literature over a decade ago, "existing research has focused too much on addressing whether there is a relationship between interdependence and conflict and too little on identifying the underlying micro-foundations of any such relationship" (2003). This chapter has argued that future work can improve upon the existing literature by adopting common assumptions about the causes of war and building a better understanding of the domestic sources of trade and foreign policy. A microfoundations approach will unify these two disparate literatures and offer new insights about the nature of trade and war. Three basic mechanisms—constraints, information, and transformation—appear to be likely candidates as drivers of the key findings in the literature. The chapter also offered some ideas about how to operationalize and test these mechanisms, and their strengths and weaknesses.

It should also be noted that the existing literature has focused largely only on the impact of economic interdependence on conflict onset. Studying the effects of trade within a rationalist framework can open up new areas for research. The bargaining perspective promises to link war onset, initiation, prosecution, termination, and consequences into a single overarching theoretical framework. The role of trade could also be examined in each of these stages (not just onset).

Looking beyond trade, future research might also examine other dimensions of commerce and their effects (positive and negative) on war and peace. Rosecrance and Thompson (2003) argue that foreign direct investment (FDI) represents a link that is more costly than trade to break; thus FDI links between countries are more likely to reduce conflict than trading links. Other interdependencies such as capital markets (equity, bond, forex, etc.) may play even greater roles in constraining state discretion (Gartzke 2007). After all, investment is much more volatile than the exchange of goods and services, and the volume of exchange is also much larger.

Finally, while this chapter has focused on the positive impact of trade on war and peace, disruptions to the flow of commerce also merit study. The role of economic sanctions, such as those deployed by the Western powers against Russia in 2014, and consumer boycotts, such as those organized in China against Japanese goods in 2012, in conflict are other areas ripe for further research. Examining the role of commerce in war, not just the positive impact of trade, greatly broadens the potential for future study.

NOTE

1. For a discussion of the role of international economic institutions in this process, see Gowa chapter in this volume.

REFERENCES

Angell, S. N. 1910. *The Great Illusion*. New York: The Knickerbocker Press.

Barbieri, K. 1996. Economic Interdependence: A Path to Peace or a Source of Interstate Conflict? *Journal of Peace Research* 33 (1): 29–49.

Barbieri, K. 2002. *The Liberal Illusion: Does Trade Promote Peace?* Ann Arbor: University of Michigan Press.

Barbieri, K., and J. S. Levy. 1999. Sleeping with the Enemy: The Impact of War on Trade" *Journal of Peace Research* 36 (4): 463–479.

Beck, N., J. N. Katz, et al. 1998. Taking Time Seriously: Time-Series-Cross-Section Analysis with a Binary Dependent Variable. *American Journal of Political Science* 42 (4): 1260–1288.

Benson, B. V., and E. M. Niou. 2007. Economic Interdependence and Peace: A Game-Theoretic Analysis. *Journal of East Asian Studies* 7 (1): 35–59.

Blainey, G (1988). *Causes of War*. New York: Simon and Schuster.

Brooks, S. G. 2013. Economic Actors' Lobbying Influence on the Prospects for War and Peace. *International Organization* 67 (04): 863–888.

Carr, E. H. 1964. *Twenty Years' Crisis, 1919–1939*. New York: Harper Perennial.

Copeland, D. C. 1996. Economic Interdependence and War: A Theory of Trade Expectations. *International Security* 20 (4): 5–41.

Crescenzi, M. J. 2003. Economic Exit, Interdependence, and Conflict. *Journal of Politics* 65 (3): 809–832.

De Mesquita, B. B., and A. Smith. 2005. *The Logic of Political Survival*. Cambridge, MA: MIT Press.

Domke, W. K. 1988. *War and the Changing Global System*. New Haven, CT: Yale University Press.

Dorussen, H. 1999. Balance of Power Revisited: A Multi-country Model of Trade and Conflict. *Journal of Peace Research* 36 (4): 443–462.

Dorussen, H., and H. Ward. 2008. Intergovernmental Organizations and the Kantian Peace A Network Perspective. *Journal of Conflict Resolution* 52 (2): 189–212.

Dorussen, H., and H. Ward. 2010. Trade Networks and the Kantian Peace. *Journal of Peace Research* 47 (1): 29–42.

Doyle, M. W. 1983. Kant, Liberal Legacies, and Foreign Affairs. *Philosophy & Public Affairs* 12 (3): 205–235.

Doyle, M. W. 1986. Liberalism and World Politics. *American Political Science Review* 80(4): 1151–1169.

Fearon, J. D. 1995. Rationalist Explanations for War. *International Organization* 49: 379–379.

Fearon, J. D. (1997). Signaling Foreign Policy Interests Tying Hands versus Sinking Costs. *Journal of Conflict Resolution*, 41(1): 68–90.

Gartzke, E. 2007. The Capitalist Peace. *American Journal of Political Science* 51 (1): 166–191.

Gartzke, E. 1999. War Is in the Error Term. *International Organization* 53 (3): 567–587.

Gartzke, E., and Q. Li. 2003. Measure for Measure: Concept Operationalization and the Trade Interdependence-Conflict Debate. *Journal of Peace Research* 40 (5): 553–571.

Gartzke, E., Q. Li, et al. 2001. Investing in the Peace: Economic Interdependence and International Conflict. *International Organization* 55 (02): 391–438.

Gartzke, E., and Y. Lupu. 2012. Trading on Preconceptions: Why World War I Was Not a Failure of Economic Interdependence. *International Security* 36 (4): 115–150.

Gasiorowski, M., and S. W. Polachek. 1982. Conflict and Interdependence East-West Trade and Linkages in the Era of Detente. *Journal of Conflict Resolution* 26 (4): 709–729.

Gasiorowski, M. J. 1986. Economic Interdependence and International Conflict: Some Cross-National Evidence. *International Studies Quarterly* 30 (1): 23–38.

Gelpi, C., and J. M. Grieco. 2003. Economic Interdependence, the Democratic State, and the Liberal Peace. *Economic Interdependence and International Conflict: New Perspectives on an Enduring Debate*: 44–59.

Gelpi, C. F., and J. M. Grieco. 2008. Democracy, Interdependence, and the Sources of the Liberal Peace. *Journal of Peace Research* 45 (1): 17–36.

Gilpin, R. 2011. *Global Political Economy: Understanding the International Economic Order*. Princeton, NJ: Princeton University Press.

Gowa, J. 1989. Bipolarity, Multipolarity, and Free Trade. *American Political Science Review* 83 (4): 1245–1256.

Grieco, J. M. 1988. Realist theory and the problem of international cooperation: analysis with an amended prisoner's dilemma model. *The Journal of Politics* 50 (3): 600-624.

Grieco, J. M. 1990. *Cooperation among nations: Europe, America, and non-tariff barriers to trade*. New York: Cornell University Press.

Hegre, H., J. R. Oneal, et al. 2010. Trade Does Promote Peace: New Simultaneous Estimates of the Reciprocal Effects of Trade and Conflict. *Journal of Peace Research* 47 (6): 763–774.

Hobson, J. A. 1905. *Imperialism: A Study*. Great Britain: Spokesman Books.

Kastner, S. L. 2009. *Political Conflict and Economic Interdependence across the Taiwan Strait and Beyond*. Stanford, CA: Stanford University Press.

Keshk, O. M., B. M. Pollins, et al. 2004. Trade Still Follows the Flag: The Primacy of Politics in a Simultaneous Model of Interdependence and Armed Conflict. *Journal of Politics* 66 (4): 1155–1179.

Kleinberg, K. B., and B. O. Fordham. 2013. The Domestic Politics of Trade and Conflict. *International Studies Quarterly.*

Krasner, S. D. 1976. State Power and the Structure of International Trade." *World Politics* 28 (3): 317–347.

Lenin, V. I. 1916. *Imperialism: The Highest Stage of Capitalism.* Australia: Resistance Books.

Levy, J. S. 2003. Economic Interdependence, Opportunity Costs, and Peace. *Economic Interdependence and International Conflict: New Perspectives on an Enduring Debate*: 127–147.

Li, Q., and R. Reuveny. 2011. Does Trade Prevent or Promote Interstate Conflict Initiation? *Journal of Peace Research* 48 (4): 437–453.

Lupu, Y., and V. Traag. 2012. Trading Communities, the Networked Structure of International Relations and the Kantian Peace. *Journal of Conflict Resolution.* doi: 10.1177/0022002712453708

Mansfield, E. D. (1994). *Power, Trade, and War.* Princeton, NJ.: Princeton University Press.

Mansfield, E. D., and B. M. Pollins. 2003. *Economic Interdependence and International Conflict: New Perspectives on an Enduring Debate.* Ann Arbor: University of Michigan Press.

Maoz, Z., and B. Russett. 1993. Normative and Structural Causes of Democratic Peace, 1946–1986. *American Political Science Review* 87 (3): 624–638.

Mastanduno, M. 1991. Do relative gains matter? America's response to Japanese industrial policy. *International Security* 16 (1): 73-113.

Mastanduno, M. 1998. Economics and Security in Statecraft and Scholarship. *International Organization* 52 (4): 825–854.

McDonald, P. J. 2009. *The Invisible Hand of Peace: Capitalism, the War Machine, and International Relations Theory.* Cambridge, UK: Cambridge University Press.

Mearsheimer, J. J. 2001. *The Tragedy of Great Power Politics.* United States of America: W.W. Norton.

Morgenthau, H. J. 1948. *Politics Among Nations: The Struggle for Power and Peace.* New York: Alfred Knopf.

Morrow, J. D. 1999. How Could Trade Affect Conflict? *Journal of Peace Research* 36 (4): 481–489.

Mousseau, M. 2010. Coming to Terms with the Capitalist Peace. *International Interactions* 36 (2): 185-213.

Mousseau, M. 2000. Market Prosperity, Democratic Consolidation, and Democratic Peace. *Journal of Conflict Resolution* 44 (4): 472–507.

Mousseau, M. 2003. The Nexus of Market Society, Liberal Preferences, and Democratic Peace: Interdisciplinary Theory and Evidence. *International Studies Quarterly* 47 (4): 483–510.

Niou, E. M., P. C. Ordeshook, et al. 2007. *The Balance of Power: Stability in International Systems.* Cambridge, UK: Cambridge University Press.

Oneal, J., and B. Russett. 1999. The Kantian Peace. *World Politics* 52 (1): 1–37.

Oneal, J. R., F. H. Oneal, et al. 1996. The Liberal Peace: Interdependence, Democracy, and International Conflict, 1950-85. *Journal of Peace Research* 33 (1): 11–28.

Oneal, J. R. and J. L. Ray. 1997. New Tests of the Democratic Peace: Controlling for Economic Interdependence, 1950-85. *Political Research Quarterly* 50 (4): 751–775.

Oneal, J. R., and B. Russett. 1999. Assessing the Liberal Peace with Alternative Specifications: Trade Still Reduces Conflict. *Journal of Peace Research* 36 (4): 423–442.

Oneal, J. R., and B. M. Russet. 1997. The Classical Liberals Were Right: Democracy, Interdependence, and Conflict, 1950–1985. *International Studies Quarterly* 41 (2): 267–294.

Oneal, J. R., B. Russett, et al. 2003. Causes of Peace: Democracy, Interdependence, and International Organizations, 1885–1992. *International Studies Quarterly* 47 (3): 371–393.

Polachek, S. W. 1980. Conflict and Trade. *Journal of Conflict Resolution* 24 (1): 55–78.

Polachek, S. W. (1997). Why Democracies Cooperate More and Fight Less: The Relationship between International Trade and Cooperation. *Review of International Economics* 5 (3): 295–309.

Polachek, S. W., J. Robst, et al. 1999. Liberalism and Interdependence: Extending the Trade-Conflict Model. *Journal of Peace Research* 36 (4): 405–422.

Powell, R. 1991. Absolute and Relative Gains in International Relations Theory. *American Political Science Review* 85 (4): 1303–1320.

Powell, R. 2002. "Bargaining Theory and International Conflict. *Annual Review of Political Science* 5 (1): 1–30.

Powell, R. 1999. *In the Shadow of Power: States and Strategies in International Politics.* Princeton, NJ: Princeton University Press.

Powell, R. 2006. War as a Commitment Problem. *International Organization* 60 (01): 169–203.

Reuveny, R., and H. Kang. 1996. International Trade, Political Conflict/Cooperation, and Granger Causality. *American Journal of Political Science* 40 (3): 943–970.

Rosecrance, R., and P. Thompson. 2003. Trade, Foreign Investment, and Security. *Annual Review of Political Science* 6 (1): 377–398.

Rosecrance, R. 1986. *The Rise of the Trading State: Commerce and Conquest in the Modern World.* New York: Basic Books.

Santos, T. D. (1970). The structure of dependence. *The American Economic Review.* 60 (2): 231-236.

Schultz, K. A. (2001) *Democracy and Coercive Diplomacy.* Vol. 76. United Kingdom: Cambridge University Press.

Schumpeter, J. A. 1962. *Capitalism, Socialism and Democracy.* New York: Harper & Row.

Simmons, B. (2003). 'Pax Mercatoria and the Theory of the State'. *Economic Interdependence and International Conflict: New Perspectives on an Enduring Debate*: 31–43.

Snidal, D. 1991. Relative Gains and the Pattern of International Cooperation. *American Political Science Review* 85 (3): 701–726.

Wagner, R. H. 2007. *War and the State.* Ann Arbor: University of Michigan Press.

Wallerstein, I. (1974). The rise and future demise of the world capitalist system: concepts for comparative analysis. *Comparative studies in society and history* 16(4): 387-415.

Waltz, K. 1970. The Myth of National Interdependence. In *The International Corporation,* edited by C. P. Kindleberger, Cambridge, MA: MIT Press.

Waltz, K. N. 1959. *Man, the State, and War: A Theoretical Analysis.* New York: Columbia University Press.

Waltz, K. N. 1979. *Theory of International Politics.* New York: McGraw-Hill.

Ward, M. D., J. S. Ahlquist, et al. 2013. Gravity's Rainbow: A Dynamic Latent Space Model for the World Trade Network. *Network Science* 1 (01): 95–118.

Ward, M. D., and P. D. Hoff. 2007. Persistent Patterns of International Commerce. *Journal of Peace Research* 44 (2): 157–175.

Ward, M. D., R. M. Siverson, et al. 2007. Disputes, Democracies, and Dependencies: A Reexamination of the Kantian Peace. *American Journal of Political Science* 51 (3): 583–601.

CHAPTER 23

TRADE AND ENVIRONMENT

J. SAMUEL BARKIN

THIS chapter examines two of the ways in which international trade is linked to the natural environment in the literatures on both trade and environment. The first way addresses the question of whether trade in general is good or bad for the environment. At the general level, there is no clear answer to this question. The answer depends on the specific version of the question asked and on the counterfactual posited. Nonetheless, reviewing the manners in which the question can be asked and what the counterfactuals might be is a useful exercise in thinking about the mechanisms through which international trade affects the natural environment.

The second way looks more specifically at the relationship between international trade institutions and environmental regulation. This is the terrain onto which much of the politics of the relationship between trade and environment has been mapped. Critics of globalization claim that these institutions constrain the ability of national governments to make environmental policy. Furthermore, they fear that international trade rules will undermine the use of trade sanctions to enforce multilateral environmental agreements (MEAs). However, a careful look at the restrictions that international trade institutions and agreements place on environmental regulation, whether national or international, suggests a more nuanced reading. International rules do indeed constrain national autonomy to use trade restrictions, but in ways that do not necessarily undermine effective environmental regulation. And while there is no proof that these rules will not undermine MEAs, there is also no evidence that they are likely to.

The third section of this chapter looks at the politics of current negotiations over the trade and environment relationship. There is little movement in these negotiations, as has been the case since the beginning of this century. This is so both in trade negotiations, such as the Doha Round negotiations, and (to a lesser extent) in the creation of new environmental rules that have potential trade-restricting effects. This relative stasis has happened in part because of the structure of the relevant international institutions, which are biased toward the trade status quo. In large part, however, the stasis reflects the current state of international politics. North-South tensions hinder change in the trade-environment relationship, and there are too few states interested in prioritizing international environmental regulation to overcome these tensions to create major new regulatory mechanisms.

THE POLITICAL ECONOMY OF TRADE AND THE ENVIRONMENT

The effects of international trade on the natural environment are complicated. At first glance, the question of what these effects are might seem to be one purely of economics and environmental science. But the question itself is a political one; what kind of trade is considered and how, what environmental effects are focused on, and what counterfactuals are chosen are all political statements. Proponents of international trade argue that it makes economies more efficient and therefore results in more efficient uses of the natural environment (Bhagwati 2000). Opponents argue that since trade increases economic activity, and economic activity in turn degrades the environment, trade contributes to environmental crisis (Princen, Maniates, and Conca 2002). Both positions are simplistic (and most scholars of the relationship recognize that it is more nuanced). But at the same time, both contain some truth.

One way to disaggregate the environmental effects of trade on the natural environment is to look at two distinctions. The first is between pollution and resource use. In economic terms, resource use is a primary economic activity, and pollution is a negative externality. Resources, furthermore, can be both renewable and nonrenewable. Somewhat counterintuitively, renewable resources are more prone to be overexploited. As nonrenewable resources become scarcer, their price increases, leading to less quantity demanded and greater investment in new sources and new technologies for extraction. The system, in other words, self-equilibrates. Renewable resources, however, can be exploited too quickly, undermining their ability to reproduce themselves. Fish and forests, in other words, are easier to use up than are iron or petroleum.

The second distinction is between local and global effects. Trade can relieve the pressure on a resource base in a particular place by generating access to resources from afar, for example by making food available in places that are suffering from drought. Or it can add to pressure on a local resource base by allowing a global market access to those resources. Allowing international trade in American shale gas, for instance, would increase both extraction rates and prices in the United States. Similarly, trade can affect global pollution levels by increasing levels of emissions of pollutants such as carbon dioxide. But it can also have the effect of moving pollution from place to place, making some places (usually richer ones) cleaner and others (usually poorer ones) dirtier.

The key argument that increasing international trade is benign or even actively beneficial for the environment is based on the efficiency gains from trade. Trade allows production to happen where it can be done most cost-efficiently. Some of this efficiency comes from different comparative advantages, both natural and infrastructural, and from efficiencies of scale. Therefore, for any given level of economic activity, production is likely to happen more resource-efficiently the greater the level of international trade (Bhagwati 2007). This argument clearly applies more directly to problems of resource use than to pollution.

A related argument is that the economic growth that is generated by increasing levels of international trade will lead countries to clean up their local environments. This argument takes as its starting point what is called the environmental Kuznets curve, which suggests that there is an inverted U-shaped relationship between national levels of economic activity and pollution. As countries develop from lower- to middle-income status, local pollution levels tend to get worse. But they level off in the middle-income levels, and as countries develop from there they tend to focus more on cleaning up their local environments. To the extent that international trade generates economic growth, therefore, increases should be expected to make poor countries dirtier, but middle-income countries cleaner. It should be noted, however, that this relationship applies primarily to local pollution levels, such as soil pollution or smog. More global forms of pollution, such as greenhouse gas emissions, do not seem to follow an environmental Kuznets curve (Dinda 2004).

A final potential mechanism for trade to have positive environmental effects is through the application of consumer power. On the one hand, international trade allows consumers to affect the behavior of corporations or governments abroad. Examples range from organized consumer boycotts of Chilean sea bass to opposition among European consumers to genetically modified food crops. In the former case the boycott helped force fishers in the southern oceans, generally not from the boycotting countries, into international regulatory mechanisms (Jacquet et al. 2010). In the latter case, the aversion has kept some producers in commercial agriculture outside of Europe from using such crops, when they otherwise would likely have adopted them (Paarlberg 2009). While consumer power can be effective in specific instances, however, it is not viable as a systematic mechanism for generating global environmental governance.

On the other hand, increasing international trade might hurt the environment in a number of ways. Broadest among them is the possibility of limits to growth. This argument begins with the key selling point of international trade, the equation between increased trade and economic growth. Both the planet's natural resource base and its ability to absorb pollution are finite. To the extent that increased economic activity uses more resources and generates more pollution, there must eventually be limits to economic growth (Meadows et al. 1972). To the extent that increased trade, or freer trade, generates increased economic activity, it brings us closer to those limits. This argument is part of a broader critique of modernization in critical environmental thinking and is distinct from the arguments (discussed below) that identify the regulation of economic activity, rather than the activity itself, as the problem (Eckersley 1992).

A final argument that links increases in international trade with environmental degradation focuses on the process of trade rather than production and final consumption, and in particular on the transportation of goods between countries. Simply put, international trade generally means shipping goods greater distances than would be the case with domestic production (e.g., Gallagher 2005). This argument has made its way into the popular discourse, most notably in the local food movement, which speaks of "food miles," the distance any particular bit of food has traveled between its original source and the table, as necessarily bad, in part because transportation over greater distances leads to higher levels of carbon emissions in transportation (e.g., MacGregor and Vorley 2007).

Which of these various arguments is right? There have been many empirical studies of the effects of trade on the natural environment, but the conclusions of these studies tend to be quite sensitive to the precise question being asked and specification of the model being tested (Frankel and Rose 2005). In other words, the world is complicated enough that one can generally find some evidence for most arguments linking trade and the environment if one looks in the right places. More broadly, both the economic efficiency and the limits to growth arguments are right, in different ways. International trade in all likelihood does make the global use of resources more efficient, other things being equal. But it also increases the aggregate level of economic activity. So resources can be used more efficiently and more intensively at the same time.

The efficiency argument is focused on the resource-use part of the environmental effects of trade. It does not speak as clearly to the pollution effects. Furthermore, it depends on what kinds of effects one is speaking of. Local economic activity can cause critical levels of local pollution absent international trade, and in many instances there is no clear connection between increased trade and pollution even when they covary (Frankel and Rose 2005). However, it is also the case that local pollution from industrial activities in various places can cause global effects. For example, the global climate in the middle of the twentieth century was probably kept cooler than would otherwise have been the case because of the accumulated effects of localized particulate pollution.

The evidence with respect to the transportation effects of trade, such as it is, is similarly equivocal. The relationship between the distance goods travel from point of production to point of consumption and the amount of pollution generated in transportation is not linear. Different forms of transportation have very different levels of fuel efficiency per amount transported—shipping goods by sea between ports half a world apart can use less fuel than trucking those goods a few hundred miles within a country (Barkin 2003). And the efficiency gains, energy and otherwise, generated by international trade can more than offset the effects of additional transportation. For example, growing tomatoes in North Africa in winter and shipping them to northern Europe can be more energy efficient than growing those same tomatoes in a greenhouse next door to the point of consumption (on food miles more broadly, see Weber and Matthews 2008).

Ultimately, economic modernization and industrialization are driving general global levels of resource use and pollution. The amount of, and rules of, international trade may affect these levels at the margins, but they are not the driving force behind the economic expansion of the last two centuries and its attendant environmental effects. By the same token, changing levels of and rules governing international trade can exacerbate or mitigate the environmental effects of global economic activity at the margins but are unlikely to change basic patterns of pollution or resource exploitation. There are exceptions to this generalization, as discussed below, but these tend to be for specific pollutants or resources, not for more general patterns of economic activity.

One exception to the generalization is the possibility that increased trade inhibits national environmental regulation. This can happen through both regulatory races to the bottom and pollution havens. The regulatory race to the bottom argument is that trade puts pressure on countries to attract investment in a globalized market. One way that governments can attract investment is by lowering regulatory costs. This should lead states to compete with each other to lower these costs, and the more open the international economy becomes, the greater this competition should be. Arguments about regulatory races to the bottom can be found with respect to a variety of international standards, including labor as well as environmental (Rodrik 1997).

Rather than a generalized pattern of laxer environmental regulation in response to international trade, the pollution haven argument posits that increased economic globalization generally, and international trade specifically, will generate dramatically increased pollution (or, in some instances, unsustainable levels of resource extraction) in specific sites (e.g., Clapp 2002). By this logic, international trade allows the negative externalities of economic activity to be concentrated in those locations that are either most desperate or have the least effective regulatory structures: the poorest and least well governed of countries.

How big are these regulatory effects? The evidence here is, again, mixed. Evidence for environmental regulatory races to the bottom, in which increased international trade or globalization more generally causes a generalized reduction in environmental standards across countries, is scarce (Drezner 2001). Environmental compliance is generally a small enough proportion of companies' total costs that regulatory competition on this front is not an effective strategy for states to attract investment. There is even some evidence of the opposite effect, in which globalization leads transnational corporations to push local regulatory standards up toward international norms, as the corporations seek regularization of regulatory levels across countries where they operate (e.g., Garcia-Johnson 2000).

Pollution havens, conversely, are a real problem, as poorer countries accept the rich world's industrial detritus, either for disposal or for recycling (Clapp 2001). Examples of this effect can be found with used electronic equipment and parts sent to China, retired ships sent to India, or toxic chemicals sent to West Africa. A similar effect can be found with some forms of resource use, such as depleting forests for the international market, as has happened, and continues to happen, in Southeast Asia. It should be noted, however, that while pollution havens are an effect of international trade, they are not necessarily an effect of freer trade.

This distinction, between the effects of international trade in general and the effects of freer trade in particular on the natural environment, is an important one. Many of the most environmentally damaging aspects of international trade are those least covered by free trade agreements, particularly primary products such as agricultural goods, minerals, and fuels. This is ironic inasmuch as much of the criticism of trade from an environmental perspective happens within the context of trade institutions such as the World Trade Organization (WTO) and North American Free Trade Agreement (NAFTA). These agreements in turn have been much more effective at freeing trade in manufactured than in primary products.

And yet much of the environmental harm related to international trade is generated by trade in primary products, such as natural resources and agricultural products. International demand for petroleum or timber, for example, can lead to a far greater level of exploitation of these resources in countries with poor environmental regulation. The widespread deforestation in countries such as the Philippines would likely not have happened absent international trade, and far less oil would have been spilled in the Niger delta without an international market. In both cases, the culprit is incompetent government, as is made clear by recent improvements in regulatory standards in these two countries and a resultant decrease in environmental externalities (although standards in both countries could still do with considerably more improvement).

In both of these cases, the architecture of international trade governance is more or less irrelevant. The goods in question are often sold on a global market and are difficult to trace, making it difficult for foreign governments to force up environmental standards in producer countries, either unilaterally or through collective governance. Effective reduction in the environmental externalities of trade in primary products is more likely to happen through efforts to improve governance in source countries than through changes in international trade rules. And as was the case in the broader efficiency-versus-limits-to-growth argument, the real driving factor behind these sorts of examples of environmental degradation is modernization and global economic expansion generally, rather than the freeing of international trade more specifically.

A final category of international trade that has environmental effects is illegal trade. This category encompasses illicit movements of goods that are not themselves contraband, as well as trade in contraband goods. Illicit movement of legal goods can result in extraction processes that are less well regulated than those in the legal trade. Examples include minerals such as coltan, luxury goods like diamonds, and food resources such as fish (Nest 2011; Bieri 2010; DeSombre 2005). It can also include the export of waste. In these cases, the illicit activity can result from efforts to avoid the costs of environmental regulation (as with fish caught outside of regulatory agreements) or the need to pay royalties to governments (as with conflict diamonds). Trade in illicit goods is likely as a general rule to generate greater negative environmental externalities than legal trade because the goods are extracted or produced in a manner specifically designed to avoid effective regulation. Even when it is not environmental regulation that is being intentionally avoided, it seems unlikely that producers and traders of illicit goods will pay as much attention to such regulation as producers and traders of licit goods.

From an environmental perspective, as well as from a trade governance perspective, the most effective remedy to the negative externalities of illicit international trade is to bring as much of it as possible into the formal international trade system. This can be done by improving governance at the point of extraction or production and by using markets to force as much of the trade as possible into the legal system. Improving governance at the point of extraction generally means improving capacity in poor, weak, or underperforming governments and improving cooperative international governance for resources extracted in the international commons, such as is sometimes the case with fisheries. Using markets to force trade within the legal system means having governments of countries whose markets account for a significant proportion of the trade of the good in question take measures to prevent the importation of illicit goods. In the case of diamonds, many of the world's countries have done this through the Kimberly process (Wright 2004). In the case of fish, it is being done through various catch documentation schemes (DeSombre 2005). This use of market access to affect environmental behavior abroad might seem to be an interference in international trade that would run into difficulties with WTO rules. But as discussed in the next section, this is not the case. Multilateral cooperation to enforce environmental standards is an accepted use of market access policy.

Whereas illicit trade is illegal trade in goods that are themselves legal, illegal trade is trade in goods that are themselves illegal (or illegal to trade internationally). Illegal trade can have a negative impact on the natural environment through a number of routes. The cultivation of illegal crops, such as cocaine in South America, is generally done outside of regulatory control and in a manner that does not prioritize environmental sustainability. Efforts by governments to control or eradicate those crops can also be environmentally harmful, particularly if these efforts involve large-scale use of herbicides. The exportation of certain toxic chemicals and waste products, trade in which is banned by international law, leads directly to toxic pollution, generally in those countries least well placed to clean it up. Other chemicals such as chlorofluorocarbons (CFCs), while not themselves toxic, are banned for other environmental damage that they do. The illegal trade in CFCs, for example, hurts efforts to restore the earth's ozone layer (DeSombre 2000). And finally, the process of trading illegal goods can undermine governance and therefore effective environmental governance, not only in source and destination countries, but also in the countries through which the goods transit. This problem is particularly acute with the narcotics trade.

International Trade Institutions and the Environment

Whereas many of the effects of trade on the environment occur, and can be remediated, independently of international trade institutions, much of the politics of the relationship between trade and the environment is focused specifically on those institutions. On a broad historical scale it is patterns of economic development generally rather than levels and forms of international trade specifically that drive most anthropogenic environmental effects. But the specific rules of international trade can affect both the ability of governments to make effective environmental policy and the forms that such policy takes. And opposition to the growth of international trade from an environmental perspective often focuses on the institutions of, rather than general patterns of, international trade (e.g., Eckersley 2004).

The WTO, as the only site for global authoritative rule-making on international trade, is clearly a central institution for the discussion of trade and environment. Its rules allow for exceptions to both general principles such as nondiscrimination and specific national commitments in support of environmental policy. These exceptions, which are discussed in more detail below, are limited and are adjudicated by the WTO's Dispute Settlement Mechanism (DSM), which has heard several environment-related complaints. The WTO has a standing committee on trade and environment, and several environment-related issues are on the Doha Round negotiating agenda, for example the reduction of fisheries subsidies (Grynberg 2003).

Environmental concerns played a bigger role in the creation of NAFTA's rules and institutional structures than those of the WTO (Steinberg 1997). NAFTA itself incorporates the WTO's environmental exceptions (NAFTA 1993, Article 2101), but from an environmental perspective does not go much beyond them. However, the agreement was signed in conjunction with the North American Agreement on Environmental Cooperation, which has two key features in this context. The first is a legally binding commitment by all three signatory governments to actually enforce their existing environmental rules and to allow interested parties from within the NAFTA area to sue if those rules are not being enforced (NAAEC 1993, Article 24). This commitment was designed to discourage a regulatory race to the bottom in effective environmental standards.

The second key feature is the creation of the Commission for Environmental Cooperation (CEC). The CEC's remit is to encourage environmental cooperation among the three NAFTA signatories by encouraging information-sharing and making recommendations for environmental action and regulation both on transborder and continental issues and on the enforcement of existing laws. The CEC is also charged with "considering on an ongoing basis the environmental effects of the NAFTA" (NAAEC 1993, Article 10[6]). In practice this has meant a set of reports over time compiling existing research on the environmental effects of NAFTA, as well as commissioning original research on the question.

This research has generally concluded that NAFTA has not had a systematically negative effect on the North American environment (e.g., CEC 2008). It has had locally negative effects, however, particularly in places where the local enforcement of environmental policy has not been able to keep up with NAFTA-driven economic change (this is particularly true of the maquiladoras on the Mexican side of the border with the United States). NAFTA may nevertheless have had a dampening effect on the creation of new environmental policy in some cases. This is particularly true of the effects of its Chapter 11, which allows companies to sue governments for compensation for the costs of unexpected policy changes. This particular rule has been the object of much environmentalist ire (e.g., Mann and Von Moltke 1999). Although Chapter 11 rulings cannot require changes to existing policy (as can WTO DSM rulings), the costs of settlement can be high. Although few large settlements related to environmental policy have in practice been ordered, the threat of Chapter 11 may nonetheless have an intimidating effect on governments.

NAFTA is an important case not only in its own right, but also because it serves as a template for other bilateral agreements that the United States negotiates. As a result, these agreements often have stricter environmental controls than other trade agreements and often have specific environmental requirements. For example, the bilateral trade agreement between the United States and Peru has the strongest environmental controls of any US trade agreement, which has in turn had a positive effect on the implementation of environmental regulation in Peru (e.g., Jinnah 2011).

The European Union (EU) is not usually thought of as primarily a trade institution, but it does have a common market at its core. Unlike other free or managed trade areas, however, the EU also has a common environmental policy. As such, the primary environmental complaint concerning trade agreements, that they can lead to competition among governments to promote trade by reducing environmental standards, does not apply. Nor does the fear that international trade rules will interfere with the creation of more stringent environmental rules at the national level, for the same reason. In a way, it makes more sense to think of the EU as more akin to commerce across states within the United States than to international trade (although the reality is of course more complicated; see, e.g., Jordan and Lenschow 2000).

One can still ask what effects the increased trade that has resulted from the creation of the common market and a common environmental policy within the EU has had on environmental outcomes. The overall answer is that it has probably improved outcomes, through two mechanisms. The first is efficiency gains from trade, which probably outweigh increased consumption in this case. The second is that the EU has had a ratcheting-up effect on environmental policy in most of its member states. This is certainly not true across the board—the Common Fisheries Policy, for example, has from an environmental perspective been a complete disaster (Khalilian et al 2010). It is perhaps most true with respect to the Central and Eastern European countries that have joined the EU since the beginning of the twenty-first century (Carmin and VanDeveer 2005).

The relationship between international trade agreements generally and the environment has changed significantly over the years. While mechanisms for environmental exceptions to trade rules were built into the original General Agreement on Tariffs and Trade (GATT) in 1947 (as discussed below), the application of these exceptions did not really become a political issue until the early 1990s. Mexico brought a complaint against the United States to the GATT dispute resolution mechanism, arguing that US rules designed to protect dolphins that prevented the importation of Mexican-caught tuna broke GATT rules. The arbitration panel that heard the case ruled against the United States, although Mexico decided not to pursue the ruling for fear of derailing then-ongoing negotiations for NAFTA. The following year the European Economic Community (EEC) launched a second case against the same US practice. The panel ruled in the EEC's favor, but the ruling was not adopted by the GATT. Both sets of rulings were notable, among other things, for not recognizing protection of the global environmental commons as a legitimate use of national trade policy (DeSombre and Barkin 2002).

By the time the tuna-dolphin issue had played out, however, the institutions of international trade had begun to adopt a more formal environmental consciousness. The agreement establishing the WTO has the goal of sustainable development written into the first paragraph of its preamble and created a committee on trade and the environment. NAFTA created the CEC as part of its institutional structure. The tuna-dolphin decisions represent a low-water mark for environmental consciousness in the interpretation of international trade rules, and the situation has changed significantly in the past two decades. Whether or not it has made any difference in practice, the language of sustainable development has come to pervade the discourse on international trade. What has made a difference in practice is a significant change in interpretation by international trade tribunals, particularly the WTO's DSM, of the legitimacy of environmental protection as a role for trade policy.

The key basis for DSM decisions on environmental exceptions to the WTO's trade rules is Article XX of the original GATT, "General Exceptions." The introduction to this article (called the "chapeau" in international legal parlance) allows member states to adopt and enforce several categories of measures, as long as "such measures are not applied in a manner which would constitute a means of arbitrary or unjustifiable discrimination between countries where the same conditions prevail, or a disguised restriction on international trade." The two relevant categories for environmental purposes are in Article XX (b), measures "necessary to protect human, animal or plant life or health," and (g), measures "relating to the conservation of exhaustible natural resources if such measures are made effective in conjunction with restrictions on domestic production or consumption" (GATT 1947, Article XX).

Further guidance on environmental exceptions to trade rules can be found in the Agreements on Sanitary and Phytosanitary Measures (SPS) and on Technical Barriers to Trade (TBT), both of which are among the Uruguay Round agreements that are the legal basis of the WTO. These agreements commit member states to ensuring that measures related to human, animal, and plant health that interfere with trade be based on science, and that where possible, environmental measures that interfere with trade be based on international standards. Member states, in other words, can take measures to protect the environment that interfere with trade and/or discriminate against other members of the WTO, as long as they can make a plausible case that the environmental or health goal is real, that the discrimination is necessary for that goal, and that it is compatible with international standards, where these exist and are applicable.

Disagreements about how these exceptions should work in practice are adjudicated by the DSM in much the same way as other disputes within the WTO, as discussed by Busch and Pelc (this volume). Several cases related to the environment have been heard, the best known of which was a complaint launched by four South and Southeast Asian states concerning US rules requiring that shrimp imported into the United States be caught only with nets that contained turtle-excluder devices (TEDs), which are basically holes in shrimp nets that allow marine turtles to escape. The original panel ruling, in 1998, went against the United States and became a bit of a cause célèbre among environmentalists. For example, several environmental protestors in the big protests against the WTO in Seattle in 1999 wore turtle hats, expecting that television audiences would understand the reference (DeSombre and Barkin 2002).

The case eventually went through five panel rulings, including two at the appellate level, between 1998 and 2001. The first two rulings went against the United States on the basis that its rules as applied to the complainants were arbitrary, that they did not sufficiently take into account attempts by the complainants to protect turtles other than through TEDs, and that the United States had made no good-faith effort to address turtle protection multilaterally rather than unilaterally. A second round of rulings, responding to claims by the complainants that the United States had not adequately addressed the first round, found that the United States had made some of the necessary changes, but not enough of them. The third round, in 2001, found largely in favor of the United States: that its revised rules interfered with the international trade in shrimp no more than was necessary to protect turtles.

A clear set of precedents came out of this case, which has since been reinforced by a variety of other rulings by the DSM on the trade-environment relationship. The most notable of these is that the protection of the global environmental commons is an accepted basis for national laws that interfere with international trade, even if the environmental good in question is abroad. In other words, the DSM's interpretation of the WTO's rules is that trade does not trump the environment. The environment trumps trade, subject to a set of specific conditions, which were clearly articulated in the shrimp-turtle findings and have been reinforced by other DSM panels since then. These conditions are there to ensure that states are not using environmental protection as an excuse to favor domestic industry over imports (DeSombre and Barkin 2002).

There are three such conditions. A Mexican complaint about US tuna import restrictions designed to protect dolphins has (perhaps ironically, given the history of the issue) served to reinforce these conditions. Mexico launched the complaint in 2008, leading to an appellate panel report in 2012 that referenced all three as accepted precedent (WTO 2012). The first condition is that the mechanisms of the policy be clearly related to, and effective in achieving, the environmental goal. An innovation of the first appellate panel in the shrimp-turtle case was that it heard testimony from turtle conservation experts and other interested parties about whether the US rules were actually an effective means of saving turtles in South and Southeast Asia (Appleton 1999).

The second condition is that the policy must be applied in a fair and nondiscriminatory manner. There are a number of ways in which environmental rules can be unfair or discriminatory. In the shrimp-turtle example, US rules required that the complainant states be certified by the State Department as having TEDs installed throughout their fleets, but the State Department did not have the personnel necessary to do the certifying. The panel found this to be unfair, because it left the complainants unable to comply with the rules through no fault of their own. In another case, brought by Brazil against the United States and relating to pollution levels from refineries, the rules in question allowed many US refineries to be dirtier than what was required for Brazilian refineries

(WTO 1996). There was no environmental logic for this distinction—it was simple protectionism. In both cases the DSM accepted the goal of the environmental regulations but required that they be applied in a fairer way that would nonetheless leave their environmental effectiveness intact.

The third condition is that states make a good-faith effort to address environmental issues in the global commons multilaterally prior to, or at minimum concurrent with, taking unilateral actions that affect trade. Thus, the United States was taken to task in the first set of shrimp-turtle rulings for not attempting to negotiate turtle conservation efforts with the complainant states, even though US law mandated efforts to do so (DeSombre and Barkin 2002). The corollary of this condition is that DSM precedent is to accept multilateral environmental cooperation on an issue as prima facie evidence that environmental action on that issue is legitimate. In the shrimp-turtle case, the fact that some of the species of turtle that the United States was trying to protect were listed as endangered by the Convention on International Trade in Endangered Species of Wild Fauna and Flora (CITES) was taken by the panel to obviate further discussion of the issue.

This discussion of multilateralism leads to one final concern of many environmentalists, about the relationship between the WTO and MEAs (e.g., Palmer and Tarasofsky 2007). Some MEAs explicitly use trade mechanisms to enforce environmental commitments by member states or to coerce nonmembers either to join or to accept MEA rules anyway. CITES, for example, explicitly bans international trade in those species it lists as endangered and limits trade in those species listed as threatened. Other MEAs, such as the Rotterdam and Basel Conventions, restrict international trade in hazardous chemicals and waste. A complete ban on international trade in certain categories of hazardous waste has been negotiated under the auspices of the Basel Convention, although it has not yet come into force (on the hazardous chemicals regime complex, see Selin 2010).

Another type of MEA uses restrictions on trade in particular goods to encourage nonmembers to participate in production limits on those goods. Examples range from ozone-depleting substances to fish. The Montreal Protocol on Substances that Deplete the Ozone Layer allows member states to prohibit the importation from nonmembers of a wide range of goods that use CFCs and other ozone-depleting chemicals (DeSombre 2000). A number of regional fisheries management organizations, such as the Convention for the Conservation of Antarctic Marine Living Resources (CCAMLR) and the International Convention for the Conservation of Atlantic Tunas (ICCAT), use catch documentation schemes to identify fish caught legally and within quotas and require members to prevent the importation of undocumented fish (DeSombre 2005). Since these mechanisms in effect call for embargoes on imports of certain kinds of goods from states that are not members of the relevant MEA, even if they are members of the WTO, these rules are clearly discriminatory.

But at the same time, all of these MEA trade mechanisms fit well into the three conditions for environmental restrictions to trade rules. They are clearly related to the environmental issues at hand. They are not needlessly discriminatory—nonmember states are welcome to join the relevant MEAs, and once they have joined, they can reasonably be expected to follow the rules. And they are (by definition) multilateral. DSM panels have tended, without recent exception, to defer to MEAs on environmental issues and to accept MEAs as evidence in and of themselves that the environmental issues that they deal with are appropriate objects of environmental policy, even if such policy interferes with trade. There has been no indication in the history of DSM jurisprudence that the dispute resolution body would rule against an MEA, and precedent suggests that it is highly unlikely that it will do so in the future. This particular fear about the WTO and the environment is misplaced.

THE POLITICS OF TRADE AND ENVIRONMENT

In fact, much of the criticism of the institutions of international trade from an environmental perspective is misplaced. There are certainly some specifics of particular treaties that may in particular cases have a dampening effect on environmental policy making, such as NAFTA's Chapter 11. But there is little evidence that this effect is widespread. Meanwhile, changes in production patterns caused by trade agreements do affect pollution patterns. Where the changes move production from developed to developing countries, the net effect, at least in the short term, can be an increase in levels of pollution. But trade agreements also often have the effect of ratcheting up environmental standards in less well-regulated countries toward those in better-regulated countries. Furthermore, the patterns of international trade that tend to cause the most environmental damage are those that are least well-regulated by international trade institutions. This includes a range of products from primary goods to illegal goods. Whether increased environmental harm results from inadequate governance at the national or the international level, the answer to environmental harm from trade is likely to be better governance rather than less cooperation.

Better governance can better manage the environmental effects of economic growth. If one's complaint about trade institutions is that they promote economic growth and therefore necessarily promote increased pollution and resource use, then a focus on trade specifically, and even more so on the institutions of international trade, misses the core of the problem. International trade should generate more efficient use of resources for any given level of economic activity and should not necessarily increase pollution. The core problem in this view is with an economic system that is based on an ethic of constant expansion rather than with particular patterns of trade within this system, and a focus on trade will do little to change the system (Princen, Maniates, and Conca 2002).

Improving environmental governance at the national level is beyond the scope of this chapter, beyond noting that efforts to do so are included in some international trade agreements, and that the use of trade mechanisms to force improvements in environmental governance in other countries is allowed within the rules of the WTO, particularly when done through MEAs. Improving environmental governance at the international level can only be done multilaterally. Preventing changes in existing trade institutions, or preventing the creation of new ones, leaves us with the existing status quo. It does not allow governments to address weaknesses in the current rules and therefore can hinder environmental cooperation rather than help it.

Preventing change in the existing institutional structure is, however, easily done. There are two key stumbling blocks to improving international cooperation at the trade-environment nexus: political structure and a waning of interest by states in international environmental cooperation. As a result of these two obstacles, there is little movement on trade and environment issues at the multilateral level. The major exception to this generalization is cases in which major importing nations can use their market power to coerce participation in new environmental rules. Examples of such coercion include bilateral trade deals between the United States and smaller countries and the use of trade mechanisms in MEAs (which tend to be effective only when supported by the largest market economies, particularly the United States).

Beyond these examples of market power supporting the creation of new forms of regulation at the trade-environment nexus, progress is often stifled by the structure of international law in general and of existing institutions in particular. International law in general binds only those countries that explicitly agree to new regulation, meaning that it is easy for a minority of countries to undermine negotiations for new agreements. This is a problem particularly with pollution issues, for which the explicit cooperation of major polluters is needed for cooperation to be effective. Absent effective coercion by importers, there is often little incentive for polluters to cooperate. This pattern of behavior can be clearly seen, for example, in climate change negotiations. The United States will not agree to anything that does not put it on an equal footing with China, and China will not agree to anything that puts it on the same footing as the United States. The result has been almost two decades of deadlock.

Existing institutions, particularly the WTO, often have rules requiring unanimous agreement for effective change in rules. In the case of the WTO, this requirement has left the Doha Round of negotiations stalled, with no successful end in sight. Since WTO practice is for comprehensive rather than piecemeal changes in the rules, change in environmental rules, beyond changes driven by the adjudication process of the DSM, are held hostage to negotiations about issues that have nothing to do with the environment. Other institutions deal with unanimity requirements by adopting voluntary guidelines rather than rules, or in other words soft law rather than hard law. For example, negotiations toward reducing subsidies to fishers are being negotiated, or have recently been negotiated, in a number of international forums. But the talks at the WTO are held hostage to the broader failure of the Doha Round. An agreement at the UN's Food and Agriculture Organization is voluntary, and separate talks under the auspices of the Organisation for Economic Co-operation and Development and the Convention on Biological Diversity failed outright (Barkin and DeSombre 2013).

This failure connects with the second key stumbling block to multilateral cooperation at the trade-environment nexus, a waning of interest by states in prioritizing multilateral environmental cooperation (Thomas 2004). In part, this change reflects a decline of environmental issues in the international priorities of the global North. While different parts of the North remain committed to international action on different environmental issues, the range of such issues on which the developed world as a whole agrees and is willing to pursue aggressively through trade measures has shrunk since the high point of international environmental cooperation in the last quarter of the twentieth century.

In part, a subset of a broader North-South tension in international politics (Neumayer 2004) has hampered progress at the WTO's Committee on Trade and Environment since its inception. The simple version of this tension is that the global North argues that the environment is worth protecting for its own sake, and the global South worries that environmental regulation, whatever the intensions of the North, will in practice become a disguised form of protectionism. Most parties accept the principle of "common but differentiated responsibilities," the idea that all countries much participate in environmental governance, but the developed world should pay a greater share of the costs of doing so (e.g., Stone 2004). But the gulf in interpretation can be unbridgeable, with countries of the North arguing that effective environmental governance requires active participation by the global South (or at least its larger and richer members), and countries of the South arguing that development must be prioritized over managing the global commons.

The good news is that existing international trade institutions are likely to continue to defer to MEAs on environmental issues and to defer to national environmental policy making when rules are not unnecessarily discriminatory or unilateral. A potential source of worry is new trade agreements. Bilateral agreements between the United States and the EU on the one hand and smaller markets on the other will likely follow existing models, but this is less clear with respect to regional multilateral negotiations. More broadly, the state of the global environment will be affected much more by patterns of multilateral environmental cooperation and of international economic development than by details of trade agreements, whether existing or new.

CONCLUSION

The relationship between trade and environment is complex and multifaceted. Trade can be beneficial for the natural environment to the extent that it contributes to economic efficiency and generates preferences for stricter environmental policy. However, increased global consumption and production may stress finite resources and the ability of natural systems to absorb pollutants. Meanwhile, the institutions that govern international trade and those that address global environmental protection are not, as many have assumed, inherently at odds. To the extent that they have seemed to be so, it has often been because trade policies used environmental protection as a cover for intentionally protectionist measures. International trade institutions allow a wide scope for environmental policy, particularly if it is multilateral and not unnecessarily discriminatory.

References

Appleton, Arthur E. 1999. Shrimp/Turtle: Untangling the Nets. *Journal of International Economic Law* 2: 477–496.

Barkin, J. Samuel. 2003. The Counterintuitive Relationship between Globalization and Climate Change. *Global Environmental Politics* 3: 8–13.

Barkin, J. Samuel, and Elizabeth R. DeSombre. 2013. *Saving Global Fisheries: Reducing Fishing Capacity to Promote Sustainability*. Cambridge, MA: MIT Press.

Bhagwati, Jagdish. 2007. *In Defense of Globalization*. With a New Afterword. New York: Oxford University Press.

Bhagwati, Jagdish. 2000. On Thinking Clearly about the Linkage between Trade and the Environment. *Environment and Development Economics* 5: 483–529.

Bieri, Franziska. 2010. *From Blood Diamonds to the Kimberley Process: How NGOs Cleaned up the Global Diamond Industry*. London: Ashgate Publishing.

Carmin, JoAnn, and Stacy D. VanDeveer. 2005. *EU Enlargement and the Environment: Institutional Change and Environmental Policy in Central and Eastern Europe*. New York: Routledge.

Clapp, Jennifer. 2001. *Toxic Exports: The Ttransfer of Hazardous Wastes from Rich to Poor Countries*. Ithaca, NY: Cornell University Press.

Clapp, Jennifer. 2002. What the Pollution Havens Debate Overlooks. *Global Environmental Politics* 2: 11–19.

Commission for Environmental Cooperation (CEC). 2008. *Environmental Assessment of NAFTA: Lessons Learned from CEC's Trade and Environment Symposia*. Montreal: Secretariat of the Commission for Environmental Cooperation.

DeSombre, Elizabeth R. 2000. The Experience of the Montreal Protocol: Particularly Remarkable, and Remarkably Particular. *UCLA Journal of Environmental Law & Policy* 19: 49–81.

DeSombre, Elizabeth R. 2005. Fishing under Flags of Convenience: Using Market Power to Increase Participation in International Regulation. *Global Environmental Politics* 5: 73–94.

DeSombre, Elizabeth R., and J. Samuel Barkin. 2002. Turtles and Trade: The WTO's Acceptance of Environmental Trade Restrictions. *Global Environmental Politics* 2: 12–18.

Dinda, Soumyananda. 2004. Environmental Kuznets Curve Hypothesis: A Survey. *Ecological Economics* 49: 431–455.

Drezner, Daniel W. 2001. Globalization and Policy Convergence. *International Studies Review* 3: 53–78.

Eckersley, Robyn. 2004. The Big Chill: The WTO and Multilateral Environmental Agreements. *Global Environmental Politics* 4: 24–50.

Eckersley, Robyn. 1992. *Environmentalism and Political Theory: Toward an Ecocentric Approach*. London: UCL Press.

Frankel, Jeffrey A., and Andrew K. Rose. 2005. Is Trade Good or Bad for the Environment? Sorting Out the Causality. *Review of Economics and Statistics* 87: 85–91.

Gallagher, Kevin P. 2005. International Trade and Air Pollution: Estimating the Economic Costs of Air Emissions from Waterborne Commerce Vessels in the United States. *Journal of Environmental Management* 77: 99–103.

Garcia-Johnson, Ronnie. 2000. *Exporting Environmentalism: US Multinational Chemical Corporations in Mexico and Brazil.* Cambridge, MA: MIT Press.

General Agreement on Tariffs and Trade (GATT). 1947.

Grynberg, Roman. 2003. WTO Fisheries Subsidies Negotiations: Implications for Fisheries Access Arrangements and Sustainable Management. *Marine Policy* 27: 499–511.

Jacquet, Jennifer, John Hocevar, Sherman Lai, Patricia Majluf, Nathan Pelletier, Tony Pitcher, Enric Sala, Rashid Sumaila, and Daniel Pauly. 2010. Conserving Wild Fish in a Sea of Market-based Efforts. *Oryx* 44: 45–56.

Jinnah, Sikina. 2011. Strategic Linkages: The Evolving Role of Trade Agreements in Global Environmental Governance. *Journal of Environment & Development* 20: 191–215.

Jordan, Andrew, and Andrea Lenschow. 2000. "Greening"the European Union: What Can Be Learned from the "Leaders" of EU Environmental Policy? *European Environment* 10: 109–120.

Khalilian, Setareh, Rainer Froese, Alexander Proelss, and Till Requate. 2010. Designed for Failure: A Critique of the Common Fisheries Policy of the European Union. *Marine Policy* 34: 1178–1182.

MacGregor, James, and Bill Vorley. 2007. *"Fair Miles": The Concept of "Food Miles" Through a Sustainable Development Lens.* London: International Institute for Environment and Development.

Mann, Howard, and Konrad Von Moltke. 1999. *NAFTA's Chapter 11 and the Environment: Addressing the Impacts of the Investor-State Process on the Environment.* Winnipeg, MB: International Institute for Sustainable Development.

Meadows, Donella H., Donella H. Meadows, Jorgen Randers, and William W. Behrens. 1972. *The Limit s to Growth: A Report to The Club of Rome.* New York: New American Library.

North American Agreement on Environmental Cooperation (NAAEC). 1993.

North American Free Trade Agreement (NAFTA). 1993.

Nest, Michael. 2011. *Coltan.* Cambridge, UK: Polity.

Neumayer, Eric. 2004. The WTO and the Environment: Its Past Record Is Better Than Critics Believe, but the Future Outlook Is bleak. *Global Environmental Politics* 4: 1–8.

Paarlberg, Robert. 2009. *Starved for Science: How Biotechnology Is Being Kept Out of Africa.* Cambridge, MA: Harvard University Press.

Palmer, Alice, and Richard Tarasofsky. 2007. *The Doha Round and Beyond: Towards a Lasting Relationship between the WTO and the International Environmental Regime.* London: Chatham House.

Princen, Thomas, Michael Maniates, and Ken Conca. 2002. *Confronting Consumption.* Cambridge, MA: MIT Press.

Rodrik, Dani. 1997. *Has Globalization Gone Too Far?* Washington, DC: Peterson Institute.

Selin, Henrik. 2010. *Global Governance of Hazardous Chemicals.* Cambridge, MA: MIT Press.

Steinberg, Richard H. 1997. Trade-Environment Negotiations in the EU, NAFTA, and WTO: Regional Trajectories of Rule Development. *American Journal of International Law* 91: 231–267.

Stone, Christopher D. 2004. Common But Differentiated Responsibilities in International Law. *American Journal of International Law* 98: 276–301.

Thomas, Urs P. 2004. Trade and the Environment: Stuck in a Political Impasse at the WTO after the Doha and Cancún Ministerial Conferences. *Global Environmental Politics* 4: 9–21.

Weber, Christopher L., and H. Scott Matthews. 2008. Food-miles and the Relative Climate Impacts of Food Choices in the United States. *Environmental Science & Technology* 42: 3508–3513.

World Trade Organization (WTO). 2012. *United States—Measures Concerning the Importation, Marketing and Sale of Tuna and Tuna Products*. Report of the Appelate Body, WT/DS381/AB/R. Geneva: World Trade Organization.

World Trade Organization (WTO). 1996. *United States—Standards for Reformulated and Conventional Gasoline*. Report of the Appellate Body, WT/DS2/AB/R. Geneva: World Trade Organization.

CHAPTER 24

BRIDGING THE SILOS

Trade and exchange rates in international political economy

MARK S. COPELOVITCH
AND JON C. W. PEVEHOUSE

INTRODUCTION

THE inextricable link between trade and exchange rates is a central feature of the international economy. Any traveler who crosses a border considers the effect of exchange rate levels on a decision to purchase goods. As the cost of traversing international borders has decreased, as production of goods has become globalized, and as exchanging currencies has become easier, the effect of exchange rates on the price of goods and services has become more visible to the average citizen. Trade and financial liberalization are both key components of globalization, and they are intimately linked through the conduit of exchange rates.

The vital connection between trade and exchange rate policies is also illustrated by a variety of well-known historical and contemporary examples. The question of whether or not to adhere to the gold standard mobilized tradable goods producers and dominated political debates about economic policy in the United States and elsewhere during both the pre-World War I and interwar periods (Eichengreen 1992; Frieden 1993; Simmons 1994). Similarly, the large current US account deficits in the late 1960s and early 1970s, coupled with concerns of American exporters about the loss of competitiveness vis-à-vis Europe and Japan, heavily influenced the Nixon administration's decision to close the "gold window" and end the Bretton Woods era (Odell 1982; Gowa 1983). In the mid-1980s the trade-related implications of the dollar's 50 percent appreciation relative to the West German deutsche mark and Japanese yen were a major factor leading to the Plaza and Louvre Accords, in which G-7 central banks engaged in coordinated foreign exchange intervention to stabilize their exchange rates (Destler and Henning

1989; Frankel 1994). Over the last decade the extensive academic and policy debate about Chinese currency undervaluation has further illustrated the relationship among exchange rate regimes, levels, and trade flows (Bergsten 2006, 2010).

Despite this widespread acknowledgment of the links between trade and exchange rates, international political economy (IPE) scholars have largely treated the two policy areas as analytically distinct realms of inquiry. A large literature discusses the political determinants of states' trade policy and trade flows, focusing on a host of international and domestic political factors.[1] Likewise, a robust literature examines the determinants and effects of the choice of exchange rate policies.[2] Yet in the vast majority of the writings in both areas, there is little discussion of exchange rates as determinants of trade policy and of trade policy as a predictor of exchange rate and monetary policy choices. We defer our discussion of why this "silo-ing" of IPE has developed to our final section. For now, we simply note that while the political economy literature on the nexus between trade and exchange rates is certainly not an empty set, it is substantially smaller than one might expect given the widespread economic understanding of the intimate linkages between trade and exchange rates.

This chapter highlights some of the existing work that has begun to explore these linkages between trade and exchange rate policies, takes stock of the state of our knowledge about the overlap between these policies, and suggests fruitful avenues for future research. We begin our review of existing work on the relationship between trade and exchange rates by examining how trade policy and trade flows may influence exchange rates and monetary policy. We then discuss how monetary and exchange rate policy choices may influence trade policy, briefly reviewing an extensive number of studies that have examined this question. Finally, we consider how research might better address these policies together and bridge the "silos" of trade, money, and finance to better understand the complex and interactive relationship between these policies in the contemporary global economy.

Trade as a Determinant of Exchange Rates

Economists have long been aware of the trade implications of exchange rate regimes, exchange rate levels, and monetary policy choices. Indeed, while more recent work has focused on the adoption of fixed exchange rates as a nominal anchor for monetary policy (Svensson 1999; Calvo and Vegh 1994), the canonical literature in economics on exchange rates emphasizes the reduction of exchange rate risk—and the corresponding increase in cross-border trade and financial flows—as one of the key reasons that countries choose fixed exchange rates over more flexible regimes (Mundell 1961; McKinnon 1962; Kenen 1969). In developing the theory of optimum currency areas (OCA), Mundell emphasized trade ties as the first of four key criteria determining whether it is optimal for countries to share a common currency. McKinnon encapsulates this logic nicely: "[T]here is less need for independent monetary policies within the bloc and a strong case to be made for imposing the uniform discipline that a common currency system would provide" (1973, 86). Independent national policies are neither necessary nor desirable if exchange rate changes can upset carefully negotiated tariff, tax, and pricing policies.

Building on this body of work in economics, the IPE literature on interest groups and exchange rates also emphasizes the importance of trade as a reason that some actors favor fixed exchange rates over floating regimes. Pegging the exchange rate is generally favored by tradables producers and international investors, since it reduces or eliminates exchange rate risk and facilitates cross-border trade and exchange (Frieden 1991). In contrast, currency volatility creates uncertainty about cross-border transactions, adding a risk premium to the price of traded goods and international assets (Frieden 2008). At the same time, the level of the exchange rate also has important implications for trade, as it affects the relative price of traded goods in both domestic and foreign markets. Fluctuations in exchange rates can have substantial effects on domestic producers' competitiveness in world markets: "In the case of a real appreciation, domestic goods become more expensive relative to foreign goods; exports fall and imports rise as a result of the change in competitiveness. Real depreciation has the opposite effects, improving competitiveness" (Frieden and Broz 2001, 331). Consequently, exchange rate movements have significant domestic distributional consequences. All else being equal, exporters and import-competing industries lose from currency appreciation, while the nontradables sector and domestic consumers gain (Frieden 1991). Currency depreciations have the opposite effect, helping exporters and import-competing firms at the expense of consumers and the nontradables sector (Frieden and Broz 2001). The degree to which firms and interest groups are sensitive to exchange rate movements and levels, however, depends heavily on the degree of exchange rate "pass-through": the degree to which prices of goods respond rapidly to exchange rate fluctuations (Campa and Goldberg 2005; Goldberg and Knetter 1997; Devereaux and Engel 2002). In general, standardized products and commodities exhibit more pass-through than highly differentiated, more specialized products (Frieden and Broz 2006). At the same time, exporters' preferences regarding the level of the exchange rate also depend on the degree to which they import intermediate inputs of production; when firms are more heavily dependent on such inputs, the benefits to competitiveness of a more depreciated currency may be more than offset by the higher cost of factors of production purchased from overseas providers (Campa and Goldberg 1999). Although firm-level tests of the political economy hypotheses are limited, the evidence to date suggests that producers' preferences about currency stability and depreciation fall broadly in line with these expectations (Broz, Frieden, and Weymouth 2008).

More recent work (Walter 2008, 2013) shows that firms' and households' balance sheet exposure to foreign currencies also creates domestic constituencies for or against devaluation or depreciation. Thus, the trade side of the equation, though important, is only "one half of the story" (Walter 2013). When firms and consumers have assets and liabilities denominated in foreign currency—such as interbank loans or home mortgages—these financial linkages also influence preferences regarding exchange rate regime choice and macroeconomic policies. These societal preferences, Walter argues, strongly influence policy makers' decisions to delay macroeconomic adjustments and to defend (or abandon) currency pegs. Drawing on both qualitative and quantitative analyses of the Asian financial crisis and the global economic crisis, Walter finds substantial evidence that these firm- and consumer-level balance sheet considerations also influence governments' exchange rate policy choices. Further research into how domestic actors and governments weigh the relative importance of the trade and financial aspects of their interests is a promising route forward for scholars.

Beyond Flows: Trade Policy, Trade Institutions, and Exchange Rates

Thus, the relationship between trade *flows* and exchange rate regimes and levels is widely understood. A less well-understood and more interesting political question, however, involves the effect of trade *policy* and international trade *institutions* on monetary and exchange rate policy choices. Here the literature is far less developed. A good starting point is the literature on economic regionalism. Within this body of work, studies focusing on questions involving sequencing in regional integration directly address the issue of linkages between trade and exchange rate policy. The foundational work of Balassa (1961) identified five stages of regional integration: 1) a free trade area (among members only); 2) a customs union (establishing a common external tariff); 3) a common market (including free movement of labor and capital); 4) an economic union (which includes harmonization of national economic policies); and finally 5) a political union, including the unification of social, fiscal, and monetary policies. Balassa argued that significant supranational political institutions would be needed to facilitate these final stages of integration. To coordinate the adoption and enforcement of trade, social, and monetary integration, states would have to agree to an extensive set of common rules and regulations. These in turn would require the establishment of legal and political institutions at the supranational level. In Balassa's early formulation, the form, timing, and impetus for cooperation were largely assumed or left implicit. However, work by neofunctionalist scholars of European integration identified several causal mechanisms driving the move from one stage of regional integration to another (Haas 1958; Schmitter 1969): spillover (frustration in one issue area leading to efforts in cognate areas); externalization (the need to deal with third parties and the externalities arising from cooperation); and politicization (the mobilization of domestic actors in response to more controversial integration efforts). In the neofunctionalist view, any or all of these factors could lead to an expansion (or contraction) of cooperative efforts from one area (trade) to another (monetary policy).

In contrast to the OCA literature in economics, the logic underlying this approach is not simply economic efficiency. Rather, the political and economic interests of private economic agents and supranational bureaucrats play a critical role in determining when and why trade cooperation and regional trade agreements evolve into broader monetary cooperation (Haas 1958; Sandholtz and Stone Sweet 1998). Clearly the European Union (EU) is the most illustrative case of these stages of regional integration and the linkage between trade institutions and monetary integration. Indeed, of the eight cases of regional trade integration leading to extensive monetary cooperation identified by Cooper (2007, 631), three are related to the European Monetary Union (EMU) and its two predecessors: the Snake agreement under the EEC and the EMS agreement under the EC. Given Europe's unique success (at least until 2008) in the realm of monetary integration, this is not surprising. Nonetheless, there are and have been other cases of regional monetary integration (e.g., the CFA Franc zone in West Africa, the East Caribbean dollar zone, the German Zollverein, the Latin and Scandinavian monetary unions).

Moreover, given the vast growth in bilateral and regional agreements in the last two decades (Mansfield and Milner 1999), the broader question of the relationship between trade policies/institutions and exchange rates applies to many more countries than those within the EU. Indeed, Mansfield and Pevehouse (2013) show that every region has experienced an expansion in regional trade agreements of various types since World War II, with nearly every country now involved in at least one such agreement. Moving from trade cooperation to institutionalized monetary cooperation, however, has been relatively rare. Cooper (2007) hypothesizes several reasons for the difficulty in moving from trade to money; most involve the higher costs to governments of losing monetary policy autonomy as well as the comparative difficulty in reversing monetary versus trade cooperation. Moreover, as McNamara (1999) has argued, the roots of monetary policy lie not only in interest-based factors, but also in ideas. Without significant ideational convergence among policy makers, states are unlikely to give up the ability to print their own money—an important sign of national sovereignty.

While the literatures on regionalism and European integration offer important insights into the relationship between trade and exchange rate policies, another important starting point is the literature on "exchange rate protection" (Corden 1982), the manipulation of the exchange rate as a substitute for trade policies that are prohibited under a country's international trade commitments in the General Agreement on Tariffs and Trade (GATT)/World Trade Organization (WTO) or preferential trade agreements (PTAs). The logic here starts from the observation that a real currency depreciation is tantamount to both a tax on imports and an export subsidy for domestic producers (McKinnon and Fung 1993). In other words, a currency depreciation alters the terms of trade in precisely the same way as protectionist trade policies. Coupled with the large body of research that has demonstrated the correlation between flexible exchange rates and both nominal and real depreciation (International Monetary Fund 1997; Frieden 2002; Blomberg, Frieden, and Stein 2005), this logic suggests that countries that have tied their hands more on trade policy through international trade agreements will be more likely to engage in competitive devaluations or depreciations to enhance the competitiveness of domestic exporters. Recent empirical work strongly supports this conjecture. Copelovitch and Pevehouse (2013a) argue that PTAs influence both a country's choice of exchange rate regime and its propensity to allow its currency to depreciate. They find that countries that have signed a PTA with their "base" country—the country most likely to be their anchor currency based on current and past experience with fixed exchange rates, regional proximity, and trade ties (Klein and Shambaugh 2006)—are less likely to adopt a fixed exchange rate and tend to have more depreciated/devalued currencies (Copelovitch and Pevehouse 2013a).

These results suggest that the linkages between exchange rate and trade policies present policy makers with a trade-off. On the one hand, fixed exchange rates and trade liberalization are complementary, as articulated in the logic of regionalism and Balassa's stages of integration. On the other, flexible exchange rates and competitive devaluation may allow a government to circumvent its commitments to liberalize trade by pursuing monetary policies that are close substitutes and cater to the interests of domestic actors (e.g., import-competing sectors) hurt by the policies imposed under PTAs. These "conflicting interests"—to stabilize exchange rates to stimulate further trade or to retain monetary and exchange rate policy autonomy to influence the competitiveness of domestic export interests—are ever more salient, given the proliferation of bilateral, regional, and multilateral trade institutions in the global economy (Pomfret and Pontines 2013). This could be yet another explanation for the finding that trade agreements rarely move into monetary cooperation: if trade and monetary policy are substitutes, policy makers will want to keep some policy autonomy to respond to domestic pressures for adjustment during difficult economic times.

And while IPE scholars have only begun to examine the relationship between trade and monetary institutions, further work will no doubt assess how specific elements of these trade institutions affect countries' exchange rate and monetary policy choices. For example, how might the presence or absence of escape clauses (Rosendorf and Milner 2001) influence a government's desire to use monetary policy to respond to pressures, given the ability to temporarily get relief within the trade realm? Will the presence of dispute settlement mechanisms (Busch 2007) in trade institutions deter leaders from undertaking exchange rate protectionism, given an institution to adjudicate accusations of such behavior from other members? (See also Pelc and Busch, this volume.)

EXCHANGE RATES AND TRADE POLICY

Thus far we have focused on the influence of trade and trade policy on exchange rates. However, much of the existing empirical literature reverses the causal arrow and explores the effects of exchange rates and monetary policy choices on trade. Most of this work has been done in economics, where scholars have extensively studied the effects of exchange rate regime choice on the level and volatility of trade flows (IMF 1984, 2004; De Grauwe 1988; Baccheta and van Wincoop 2000; Rose 2000; Lopez-Cordova and Meissner 2003; Klein 2005; Bahmani-Oskooee and Hegerty 2007; Auboin and

Ruta 2011; Klein and Shambaugh 2006, 2010; Huchet-Bourdon and Korinek 2011). The theoretical predictions and empirical results of this literature are largely indeterminate and highly sensitive to assumptions about price elasticities and model specification, as well as to the specific time period or country sample selected (Auboin and Ruta 2011; Pomfret and Pontines 2013).

A subset of this literature specifically explores the effects of currency unions on trade. Frankel and Rose (2002) find that countries that share a currency trade three times more than similarly related countries that do not; Engel and Rogers (1996) found that US states (specifically North and South Dakota) trade *twenty-two* times more with each other than with neighboring Canadian provinces. These results, and the logic underlying them—permanently eliminating currency risk through the adoption of a single currency—provided a clear economic rationale and aspiration for European monetary union and are the driving force behind other regional experiments with monetary integration.

In spite of this extensive literature in economics on the effects of exchange rates on trade *flows*, work on the specific link between exchange rate and trade *policies* is far less extensive. One productive line of research in this vein focuses on the link between exchange rate regime choice and trade policy. In an influential article and book, Eichengreen and Irwin (2010) and Irwin (2012) show that the degree to which countries engaged in protectionist trade policies during the Great Depression was driven primarily by their exchange rate policies. Those countries that remained on the gold standard—thereby foregoing the opportunity to employ monetary and fiscal policy to stimulate domestic employment and growth—were more likely to impose protectionist trade policies and capital controls as "a second-best macroeconomic tool" (Eichengreen and Irwin 2010, 872). Thus, with their hands tied on monetary policy by the commitment to a fixed exchange rate regime, Depression-era governments resorted to trade protection as an imperfect substitute for macroeconomic adjustment policies. This historical finding may also have contemporary relevance. In preliminary work, Copelovitch and Pevehouse (2013b) find a similar phenomenon within the WTO. Drawing on Eichengreen and Irwin's logic and linking it to the Mundell-Fleming "trilemma," we find that governments are more likely to impose legalized protectionist measures (e.g., safeguards, antidumping duties) within the WTO when they have adopted fixed exchange rates and liberalized their capital accounts. As a consequence, such countries are also more likely to find themselves named by other member states as defendants in WTO disputes.

A second line of research focuses on the impact of exchange rate levels and fluctuations on trade policy choices. This work indicates that protectionism has been greatest at the regional level during periods of sharp exchange rate fluctuations, such as the 1992–1993 European Monetary System (EMS) crisis and the 1999 Brazilian real devaluation within Mercosur (Fernandez-Arias et. al. 2004; Eichengreen 1993; Pearce and Sutton 1985).[3] Similarly, Frieden (1997) shows that protectionist demands in the United States during the nineteenth century correlated closely with the strength of the dollar. In addition, a number of studies suggest that real exchange rate appreciations have led to increases in antidumping filings in the United States and other industrialized countries (Oatley 2010; Niels and Francois 2006; Irwin 2005; Knetter and Prusa 2003; Grilli 1988; Bergsten and Williamson 1983). Broz and Werfel (2013) extend this work to the firm level, arguing that several industry-specific characteristics determine the protectionist response to changes in the exchange rate, including the degree of exchange-rate pass-through, the level of import penetration, and the share of imported intermediate inputs in total industry inputs. Jensen, Quinn, and Weymouth (2013) go further, showing that currency undervaluation promotes demands for protection in some cases but not others. They find clear differences in the international investment positions and the composition of trade flows among US firms that file antidumping petitions and those that do not: firms with vertical foreign direct investment (FDI) and high related-party trade with host countries are less likely to initiate antidumping disputes against those countries when their currencies are undervalued (Jensen, Quinn, and Weymouth 2013). In short, undervaluation's effects are mediated through a firm's investments in the undervalued currency or its imports from the country with the undervalued exchange rate. Thus, at both the country and firm levels, there appears to be a strong link between exchange rate levels and trade protection.

Trade and Exchange Rate Policy: Moving Beyond the "Silos" of IPE

As this brief review of the existing literature illustrates, we now know quite a lot about the political economy of trade and exchange rates, albeit less about the precise relationship between policy choices in each issue area. And yet in many ways we have only scratched the surface of the possibilities, particularly within IPE. Vast swathes of the trade literature within the subfield, for example, ignore exchange rates and monetary policy entirely. The burgeoning literature on mass public opinion and trade policy preferences (e.g., Scheve and Slaughter 2001; Hainmueller and Hiscox 2006; Mansfield and Mutz 2009; Kuo and Naoi, this volume) has not, to our knowledge, addressed the issue of the trade-exchange rate nexus. Likewise, the sizeable literature on the determinants of WTO disputes completely ignores exchange rate levels and regime choices as possible determinants of conflict between member states (e.g., Bown 2005; Busch and Reinhardt 2000).[4] Finally, the rich literature on the design and effects of bilateral and regional trade agreements (e.g., Haftel 2013; Kucik 2012) also does not incorporate exchange rate regime choices or levels into the analysis. We single out these specific bodies of research not because they are exceptional, but because they are representative. Despite widespread general recognition of the inextricable relationship between these two policy areas, the vast majority of IPE scholars continue to act as if trade policy and exchange rate/monetary policy can be analyzed separately in "silos."

To some extent, this strategy is not particularly surprising. The literature on the political economy of trade policy has developed largely from cases and data within the United States, where exchange rates are substantially less salient as a political issue than in smaller, more open economies and in those countries whose money is not the global reserve currency.[5] On the other hand, the literature on the political economy of exchange rates over the last decade has focused far more extensively on the adoption of fixed exchange rates as a solution to the time-inconsistency problem confronting monetary policy makers (e.g., Bernhard, Broz, and Clark 2002; Hallerberg 2002; Keefer and Stasavage 2003; Guisinger and Singer 2010), rather than on the trade implications of regime choice and exchange rate levels. The recent shift back toward a focus on the trade policy implications, as discussed earlier, is a welcome and overdue adjustment in the literature. Thus, the first step to moving beyond the current silos of IPE is to more closely incorporate the "other" policy area into existing lines of research in the field. Trade scholars need to take more seriously the exchange rate preferences of domestic actors, as well as the domestic and international monetary commitments of governments. At the same time, monetary scholars need to pay closer attention to trade institutions—particularly PTAs and the WTO— and how they might affect governments' choices of monetary policy and exchange rate regimes.

Bridging the trade/monetary silos, however, raises a second issue in need of further research: the direction of causality. As discussed above, there is substantial evidence from existing work that the causal arrow points in both directions (trade policy determining exchange rate policy; exchange rate regime choice and monetary policy influencing trade policy). Clarifying the conditions under which each relationship holds presents both theoretical and empirical challenges, yet this must be a critical area of focus for future work. One potential way to do this is to work toward developing a typology of policy "baskets" (combinations of trade, monetary, and exchange rate policies), rather than adopting the usual strategy of holding one policy or institution constant while seeking to explain variation in the other.

Another way forward is to more closely look at lobbying on monetary policy and exchange rates to see whether the same actors are involved in pressuring governments for both types of policies and whether these actors view trade and exchange rate policies as complements or substitutes. Clearly there is an extensive empirical literature on lobbying and trade policy (e.g., Gawande and Hoekman 2006; Baldwin and Magee 2000; Busch and Reinhardt 2000), yet even much of that literature makes strong assumptions about lobbying as necessarily correlated with the location of industry or congressional votes as evidence of lobbying. And although there are good reasons to believe that domestic actors will lobby less extensively on monetary issues (Gowa 1988), such domestic pressure is the bread-and-butter of many political economy models of exchange rate policy choice (e.g., Leblang 2003), and more work is clearly warranted in this arena. Indeed, early researchers of exchange rate policies were quite puzzled by the lack of open lobbying (Odell 1982), especially given that extant models predicted the preferences of firms for various exchange rate policies under various political and economic circumstances. More recently, such lobbying behavior has become more visible. For example, the US Congress spent two years debating the Currency Reform for Fair Trade Act, meant to cajole China into easing its peg on the Renminbi.[6] This bill had more than two hundred cosponsors in the House and was the subject of intense lobbying, meant to link US trade policy to currency issues. These types of instances are among those that could allow IPE scholars to closely assess the presence and effectiveness of lobbying on exchange rate policy.

A third way forward for the literature is to focus more clearly on the bureaucratic agencies and actors involved in trade and monetary policy making. The trend toward micro-level experimental approaches and the focus on legislative votes in the trade literature masks the fact that—as has long been the case with monetary and exchange rate policy, where central bankers play a major role in policy making—trade policy is increasingly made by officials in executive agencies (e.g., the US Trade Representative's office, the European Commission). Yet we know almost nothing about the political economy of these actors' behavior. Instead, the vast majority of our domestic politics models of trade and exchange rates continue to adopt a simple "Grossman-Helpman" style policy-making model, in which office-seeking elected officials trade off the interests of the median voter against those of organized sectors or lobbies ("votes for campaign contributions") (Grossman and Helpman 1994; for a clear summary see Goodhart, this volume). A better understanding of the relationships between trade and monetary policy-making bureaucrats—as well as the potential conflicts these actors have within the executive branch—would substantially improve our understanding of the ways in which these two sets of policies are complementary or in conflict with each other in particular countries. A focus on agencies and bureaucrats could also answer the "puzzle" of why so little lobbying has appeared visible to scholars to date (see Frieden and Broz 2001, 333): if lobbying occurs between private agents and bureaucrats, there would be much less chance of discovering this behavior.

Finally, the longer-term goal in terms of bridging the silos of IPE needs to be not just linking the study of trade policy with that of exchange rates, but rather to move toward simultaneously modeling trade, monetary policies, and financial policies. In recent years IPE scholars have reached a broad consensus on the use of the Mundell-Fleming "trilemma" or "impossible trinity" (Mundell 1960; Fleming 1962) as the workhorse framework for analyzing the political economy of monetary policy and exchange rate regime choice in an open economy. According to this framework, countries can achieve only two of three policy goals simultaneously: a fixed exchange rate, full capital mobility, and domestic monetary policy autonomy—the ability to adjust interest rates in reaction to exogenous shocks or domestic economic downturns. The logic is straightforward: in a world of mobile capital, a discrepancy between domestic and world interest rates causes capital to flow toward higher returns. Under floating exchange rates, capital inflows will lead to an exchange rate appreciation, while outflows will result in depreciation. Under fixed exchange rates, however, interest rate differentials will be arbitraged away by these capital flows. Consequently, the combination of capital mobility and fixed exchange rates makes it impossible for a government to adopt an independent monetary policy.

The trilemma has proven enormously useful in identifying the trade-offs facing macroeconomic policy makers in a world of global finance. And yet IPE scholars have not really fully explored the implications of the trilemma. Rather, the common assumption is to take full capital mobility as a given and analyze the political economy of the remaining dilemma: the choice between monetary policy autonomy and fixed exchange rates. Since the onset of the global financial crisis in 2007–2008, however, a wide range of countries have imposed capital controls in an attempt to stem currency appreciation, capital outflows, or capital inflows (e.g., Brazil, Iceland), and the International Monetary Fund (IMF) has even revised its long-standing blanket opposition to the use of controls. These developments make clear that capital account openness is also a policy choice, and that policy makers around the world evaluate the pros and cons of financial liberalization differently.

Of course there are nontrivial challenges in combining the study of trade and exchange rates. First is the question of timing and time horizons. Exchange rates fluctuate daily, and while large market-driven devaluations may take time, these changes still happen more quickly than most legislative or bureaucratic processes. Thus, to discuss how shifts in exchange rates influence government behavior, it is helpful to think about timing. Changes in trade policy require legislation or administrative hearings. World Trade Organization disputes involve complex legal procedures. Will the proposed policy actually help provide relief fast enough for those lobbying for it? How quickly does the proposed policy take to enact?

The answers to such questions clearly depend on the causal mechanisms and the model of politics employed. For example, if the trade policy remedy arising from exchange rate fluctuations is enacted to provide actual relief to aggrieved parties, one should probably focus on remedies arising out of the executive branch or emergency relief policies. If the remedy is enacted to provide political cover—that is, so it appears the government is "doing something" in response to lobbying—timing may be less important. These two causal processes, however, are very different: in the former political actions are the means, whereas in the latter political actions are the ends. Both of these mechanisms also ignore the other states: Are tariffs raised as a bargaining chip in international negotiations? The inevitable two-level game involving competing governments and their domestic constituencies becomes all the more complex once one theorizes about multiple policy levers and domestic constituencies.

This leads to a second challenge: what we label the "blunt instrument" problem. Trade policy can be narrowly tailored. In theory, tariffs can be placed on a very small or very large number of goods—as specific as the six-digit product code in the Harmonized System of Codes. Thus, political actors could respond to lobbying by aggrieved parties with very focused trade policy measures. Adopting a new exchange rate policy or even attempting to intervene in a managed float exchange rate system influences terms of trade for *all* goods. Would a government alter exchange rate policy or intervene in exchange markets due to strong complaints from important exporters even if those policies would impose costs on all domestic actors through currency devaluation? Is the cure worse than the disease?

Third is a question of political agency. Governments set tariff and exchange rate policies. Firms trade and lobby for trade policy. State actors and private actors (firms and individuals) engage in currency exchange. Markets determine exchange rate levels in floating exchange rate regimes; government agents do so in pegged and (to a lesser extent) in managed float regimes. In the trade realm, it is largely assumed that state policies will change the behavior of economic actors. But in the monetary realm, states must compete with actors who, in the aggregate, possess resources that are stronger than those of all but the largest states. Indeed, the size of transaction flows in each area is significantly different: $18 trillion of goods are exported in a year; over $5 trillion per *day* changes hands in FOREX markets. Can governments undertake policies, short of major exchange rate regime changes, to influence monetary policy? While this is not a new question in IPE, its implications for questions of trade and exchange rate policy are significant: one reason governments may want to pull trade policy levers in response to noncompetitive currency positions is their inability to influence their currency without very costly interventions or policy changes. Still, any theory of linkages between trade and exchange rate policies must confront the varying ability of states to influence trade policy versus monetary policy change.

Fourth, if the causal story linking trade and monetary policy involves lobbying, finding evidence of such lobbying can be difficult (Bearce 2003). As previously discussed, while there are a myriad of papers on lobbying in the trade policy realm, few tackle the difficult question of whether it is the lobbying that influences votes or simply economic fundamentals. Put differently, with lobbying in any issue area, it is difficult to show the counterfactual: that without lobbying a government or legislator would behave differently. Demonstrating that a legislator behaved consistently with her or his district's economic interests in a vote on tariffs is not evidence of lobbying, but simply the recognition of the interests within that legislator's district.

We have a final point on the opportunities and challenges of integrating the literatures on trade policy and exchange rates. Note that empirically, the most voluminous work exists on questions involving trade and monetary *flows*. This is particularly true in the economics literature, where politics is often considered a nuisance or exogenous. And this state of affairs is hardly surprising: armed with a theory of firm behavior, holding constant policy and changes in policy, one can find how firms that create flows respond to the incentives created by policy. Moving forward, empirically assessing the relationship between trade and monetary *policies* requires a careful theory of political actors, their preferences, and an aggregation mechanism to move from firm or constituent demands to policy. In other words, economics has provided us with a common theory of the firm from which a set of expectations about behavior flows. We have no equivalent theory of politics, nor is such a theory desirable: it is exactly the variations in politics that make policy outcomes interesting to study and that is the comparative advantage of political science.

CONCLUSION

For consumers and firms, the relationship between the trade in goods and exchange rates has long been apparent. Unfortunately, most scholars of international political economy have developed theories and models of each largely in isolation from the another. This chapter reviewed the many ways in which trade and exchange rate policies as well as trade and monetary flows influence one another.

We first examined the implications of trade policy for exchange rates and exchange rate regime choice. While the least amount of work has occurred in this area, it is certainly not an empty set. In particular, exploration of the evolution of trade integration agreements to encompass monetary policy stands out as an important strand of literature examining this question. Yet given that so few trade agreements evolve into monetary agreements, there is unfortunately a paucity of systematic empirical work on this question.

More common are studies reversing the causal arrow: the influence of exchange rate regimes on trade. Here, economists have dominated the study of the linkages between finance and trade, yet little consensus has been reached on when exchange rate regimes influence trade flows. A new set of research has recently emerged examining fluctuations in exchange rates as determinants of trade policy choices such as targeted protection. This newer literature is a promising avenue to link finance to trade policy.

Finally, we outlined some of the problematic aspects of integrating theories of trade policy and exchange rate choices. While these hurdles are surmountable, they are not trivial, involving problems of blunt policy instruments, preference aggregation, and political agency. Efforts to integrate the worlds of trade and finance should be undertaken with care, paying equal attention to the many levers that can be pulled by policy makers in each area.

As globalization continues to bring together actors in high-frequency interactions across the trade and finance world, it is incumbent on IPE scholars to explore the linkages between actions taken by political actors to regulate and govern those interactions. Here we have outlined several avenues that we think can be fruitful for exploring the relationship between trade and finance.

NOTES

1. See Milner (1999); Frieden and Martin (2002); and Lake (2009) for reviews of this vast literature.
2. See Frieden and Broz (2001, 2006) and Frieden (2008) for reviews.
3. Such episodes of currency instability and protectionism were precisely why Europeans pushed for completion of the single market in the 1992 Maastricht Treaty and moved toward economic and monetary union in 1999. Within the Southern Cone, tensions arising from the Brazilian devaluation, the subsequent Argentine protectionist response, and the ensuing financial crises in Argentina and Uruguay nearly led to the collapse of Mercosur in the early 2000s.

4. See Copelovitch and Pevehouse (2013b) for a preliminary attempt to address this gap in the literature.
5. Indeed, it is not an accident that initial theories of trade and exchange rates were pioneered by Robert Mundell, a Canadian economist!
6. Evans-Pritchard (2010).

References

Auboin, M., and M. Ruta. 2011. The Relationship between Exchange Rates and International Trade: A Review of Economic Literature. WTO Staff Working Paper ERSD-2011-17.

Baccheta, P., and E. van Wincoop. 2000. Does Exchange Rate Stability Increase Trade and Welfare? *American Economic Review* 93: 42–55.

Bahmani-Oskooee, M., and S. Hegerty. 2007. Exchange Rate Volatility and Trade Flows: A Review Article. *Journal of Economic Studies* 34 (3): 211–55.

Baldwin, Robert E., and Christopher S. Magee. 2000. Is Trade Policy for Sale? Congressional Voting on Recent Trade Bills. *Public Choice* 105 (1–2): 79–101.

Bearce, David H. 2003. Societal Preferences, Partisan Agents, and Monetary Policy Outcomes. *International Organization* 57 (2): 373–410.

Belassa, Bela. 1961. Towards a Theory of Economic Integration. *Kyklos* 14 (1): 1–17.

Bergsten, C. Fred. 2010. Correcting the Chinese Exchange Rate: An Action Plan. http://www.voxeu.org/index.php?q=node/4876.

Bergsten, C. Fred. 2006. The US Trade Deficit and China. Testimony at the Hearing on US-China Economic Relations Revisited. Committee on Finance, United States Senate, March 29. http://www.iie.com/publications/papers/paper.cfm?ResearchID=611.

Bergsten, C. Fred, and John Williamson. 1983. Exchange Rates and Trade Policy. In *Trade Policy in the 1980s*, edited by William R. Cline, 99–120. Washington, DC: Institute for International Economics.

Bernhard, William, J. Lawrence Broz, and William Roberts Clark. 2002. The Political Economy of Monetary Institutions. *International Organization* 56 (4): 693–723.

Blomberg, S. Brock, Jeffry Frieden, and Ernesto Stein. 2005. Sustaining Fixed Rates: The Political Economy of Currency Pegs in Latin America. *Journal of Applied Economics* 8 (2): 203–225.

Bown, Chad P. 2005. Participation in WTO Dispute Settlement: Complainants, Interested Parties, and Free Riders. *World Bank Economic Review* 19 (2): 287–310.

Broz, Lawrence, Jeffry Frieden, and Stephen Weymouth. 2008. Exchange Rate Policy Attitudes: Direct Evidence from Survey Data. *IMF Staff Papers* 55 (3): 417–444.

Broz, Lawrence, and Seth Werfel. 2013. Exchange Rates and Industry Demands for Trade Protection. *International Organization* 68 (2): 393–416.

Busch, Marc. 2007. Overlapping Institutions, Forum Shopping, and Dispute Settlement in International Trade. *International Organization* 61 (4): 735–761.

Busch, Marc, and Eric Reinhardt. 2000. Bargaining in the Shadow of the Law: Early Settlement and GATT/WTO Disputes. *Fordham International Law Journal* 24: 158–165.

Calvo, Guillermo, and Carlos Vegh. 1994. Inflation Stabilization and Nominal Anchors. *Contemporary Economic Policy* 12 (2): 35–45.

Campa, Jose Manuel, and Linda Goldberg. 2005. Exchange Rate Pass-Through into Import Prices. *Review of Economics and Statistics* 87 (4): 679–690.

Campa, Jose Manuel, and Linda Goldberg. 1999. Investment, Pass-through, and Exchange Rates: A Cross-Country Comparison. *International Economic Review* 40 (2): 287–314.

Cooper, Scott. 2007. Why Doesn't Regional Monetary Cooperation Follow Trade Cooperation? *Review of International Political Economy* 14 (4): 626–652.

Copelovitch, Mark S., and Jon C. W. Pevehouse. 2013a. Ties That Bind? Preferential Trade Agreements and Exchange Rate Policy Choices. *International Studies Quarterly* 57 (2): 385–399.

Copelovitch, Mark S., and Jon C. W. Pevehouse. 2013b. The Trilemma and Trade Policy: Exchange Rates, Financial Openness, and WTO Disputes. Unpublished manuscript, University of Wisconsin.

Corden, W. Max. 1982. Exchange Rate Protection. In The International Monetary System Under Flexible Exchange Rates—Global, Regional, and National: Essays in Honor of Robert Triffin, edited by Richard Cooper, Peter Kenen, Jorge Braga de Macedo, and Jacques Van Ypersele, 17–34. Cambridge, MA: Ballinger.

De Grauwe, P. 1988. Exchange Rate Variability and Slowdown in International Trade. *IMF Staff Papers* 35: 63–84.

Destler, I. M., and C. Randall Henning. 1989. *Dollar Politics: Exchange Rate Policymaking in the United States*. Washington, DC: Institute for International Economics.

Devereaux, M. B. and Charles Engel. 2002. Exchange Rate Pass-Through, Exchange Rate Volatility and Exchange Rate Disconnect. *Journal of Monetary Economics* 49 (5): 913–940.

Eichengreen, B. 1992. *Golden Fetters: The Gold Standard and the Great Depression, 1919–1939*. Oxford, UK: Oxford University Press.

Eichengreen, B. 1993. The Crisis in the EMS and the Transition to EMU: An Interim Assessment. CIDER Working Paper C93-022. University of California–Berkeley.

Eichengreen, B., and D. Irwin. 2010. The Slide to Protectionism in the Great Depression: Who Succumbed and Why? *Journal of Economic History* 70 (4): 871–97.

Engel, Charles, and John Rogers. 1996. How Wide Is the Border? *American Economic Review* 86: 1112–1125.

Evans-Pritchard, Ambrose. 2010. Currency Wars Are Necessary If All Else Fails. *The Telegraph*, October 10. http://www.telegraph.co.uk/finance/comment/ambroseevans_pritchard/ 8054 066/Currency-wars-are-necessary-if-all-else-fails.html.

Fernández-Arias, Eduardo, Ugo Panizza, and Ernesto Stein. 2004. Trade Agreements, Exchange Rate Disagreements. In *Monetary Unions and Hard Pegs: Effects on Trade, Financial Development, and Stability*, edited by Volbert Alexander, George M. von Furstenberg, and Jacques Melitz, 135–150,. New York: Oxford University Press.

Fleming, Marcus. 1962. Domestic Financial Policies under Fixed and under Floating Exchange Rates. *IMF Staff Papers* 9: 369–380.

Frankel, Jeffrey. 1994. The Making of Exchange Rate Policy in the 1980s. In *American Economic Policy in the 1980s*, edited by Martin Feldstein, 293–341. Chicago: University of Chicago Press.

Frankel, Jeffrey, and Andrew Rose. 2002. An Estimate of the Effect of Common Currencies on Trade and Income. *Quarterly Journal of Economics* 117 (2): 437–466.

Frieden, Jeffry. 1991. *Debt, Development and Democracy: Modern Political Economy and Latin America 1965–1985*. Princeton, NJ: Princeton University Press.

Frieden, Jeffry. 1993. The Dynamics of International Monetary Systems: International and Domestic Factors in the Rise, Reign, and Demise of the Classical Gold Standard. In *Coping with Complexity in the International System*, edited by Jack Snyder and Robert Jervis, 137–162. Boulder, CO: Westview Press.

Frieden, Jeffry. 2008. Globalization and Exchange Rate Policy. In *The Future of Globalization*, edited by Ernesto Zedillo, 344–357. New York: Routledge.

Frieden, Jeffry. 1997. Monetary Populism in Nineteenth-Century America: An Open-Economy Interpretation. *Journal of Economic History* 57 (2): 367–395.

Frieden, Jeffry. 2002. Real Sources of European Currency Policy: Sectoral Interests and European Monetary Integration. *International Organization* 56: 831–860.

Frieden, Jeffry A., and J. Lawrence Broz. 2006. The Political Economy of Exchange Rates. In *Oxford Handbook of Political Economy*, edited by Barry Weingast and Donald Wittman, 587–600. New York: Oxford University Press.

Frieden, Jeffry A., and J. Lawrence Broz. 2001. The Political Economy of International Monetary Relations. *Annual Review of Political Science* 4: 317–343.

Frieden, Jeffry A., and Lisa L. Martin. 2002. International Political Economy: Global and Domestic Interactions. In *Political Science: The State of the Discipline*, edited by Ira Katznelson and Helen Milner, 118–146, New York: W.W. Norton.

Gawande, Kishore, and Bernard Hoekman. 2006. Lobbying and Agricultural Trade Policy in the United States. *International Organization* 60 (3): 527–561.

Goldberg, Pinelopi, and Michael Knetter. 1997. Goods Prices and Exchange Rates: What Have We Learned? *Journal of Economic Literature* 35: 1243–1292.

Gowa, Joanne. 1983. *Closing the Gold Window: Domestic Politics and the End of Bretton Woods*. Cornell Studies in Political Economy. Ithaca, NY: Cornell University Press.

Gowa, Joanne. 1988. Public Goods and Political Institutions: Trade and Monetary Processes in the United States. *International Organization* 42 (1): 15–32.

Grilli, Enzo. 1988. Macroeconomic Determinants of Trade Protection. *World Economy* 11 (3): 313–326.

Grossman, Gene M., and Elhanan Helpman. 1994. Protection for Sale. *American Economic Review* 84 (4): 833–850.

Guisinger, Alexandra, and David Andrew Singer. 2010. Exchange Rate Proclamations and Inflation-Fighting Credibility. *International Organization* 64 (1): 313–337.

Haas, Ernst B. 1958. *The Uniting of Europe*. Notre Dame, IN: Notre Dame Press.

Haftel, Yoram. 2013. Commerce and Institutions: Trade, Scope, and the Design of Regional Economic Organizations. *Review of International Organizations* 8: 389–414.

Hainmueller, Jens, and Michael Hiscox. 2006. Learning to Love Globalization: Education and Individual Attitudes Toward International Trade. *International Organization* 60 (2): 469–498.

Hallerberg, Mark. 2002. Veto Players and Monetary Commitment Technologies. *International Organization* 56 (4): 775–802.

Huchet-Bourdon, M., and J. Korinek. 2011. To What Extent Do Exchange Rates and Their Volatility Affect Trade? OECD Trade Policy Papers No. 119. Paris: OECD. http://dx.doi.org/10.1787/5kg3slm7b8hg-en.

International Monetary Fund. 2004. Exchange Rate Volatility and Trade Flows—Some New Evidence. IMF Occasional Paper 235.

International Monetary Fund. 1984. Exchange Rate Volatility and World Trade. IMF Occasional Paper 30.

International Monetary Fund (IMF). 1997. *World Economic Outlook*. Washington, DC: International Monetary Fund.

Irwin, Douglas A. 2005. The Rise of U.S. Anti-Dumping Activity in Historical Perspective. *World Economy* 28 (5): 651–668.

Irwin, Douglas A. 2012. *Trade Policy Disaster: Lessons from the 1930s*. Cambridge, MA: MIT Press.

Jensen, J. Bradford, Dennis Quinn, and Stephen Weymouth. 2013. Global Supply Chains, Currency Undervaluation, and Firm Protectionist Demands. NBER Working Paper No. 19239.

Keefer, Philip, and David Stasavage. 2003. Checks and Balances, Private Information, and the Credibility of Monetary Commitments. *International Organization* 56 (4): 751–774.

Kenen, Peter. 1969. The Theory of Optimum Currency Areas: An Eclectic View. In *Monetary Problems in the International Economy*, edited by Robert Mundell and Alexander Swoboda, 41–60. Chicago: University of Chicago Press.

Klein, Michael W. 2005. Dollarization and Trade. *Journal of International Money and Finance.* 24 (6): 935–43.

Klein, Michael W., and Jay Shambaugh. 2010. *Exchange Rates in the Modern Era*. Cambridge, MA: MIT Press.

Klein, Michael W., and Jay Shambaugh. 2006. Fixed Exchange Rates and Trade. *Journal of International Economics* 70 (2): 359–383.

Knetter, Michael M., and Thomas J. Prusa. 2003. Macroeconomic Factors and Antidumping Filings: Evidence from Four Countries. *Journal of International Economics* 61: 1–17.

Kucik, Jeffrey. 2012. The Domestic Politics of Institutional Design: Producer Preferences over Trade Agreement Rules. *Economics and Politics* 24 (2): 95–118.

Lake, David A. 2009. Open Economy Politics: A Critical Review. *Review of International Organizations* 4: 219–244.

Leblang, David. 2003. To Devalue or to Defend? The Political Economy of Exchange Rate Policy. *International Studies Quarterly* 47 (4): 533–560.

López-Córdova, Jose Ernesto, and Christopher M. Meissner 2003. Exchange-Rate Regimes and International Trade: Evidence from the Classical Gold Standard Era. *American Economic Review* 93(1): 344–353.

Mansfield, Edward D., and Helen Milner. 1999. The New Wave of Regionalism. *International Organization* 53 (3): 589–627.

Mansfield, Edward D., and Diana Mutz. 2009. Support for Free Trade: Self-Interest, Sociotropic Politics, and Out-Group Desire. *International Organization* 63 (3): 425–457.

Mansfield, Edward D., and Jon C. W. Pevehouse 2013. The Expansion of Preferential Trade Agreements. *International Studies Quarterly* 57 (3): 592–604.

McKinnon, Ronald I. 1973. The Dual Currency System Revisited. In *The Economics of Common Currencies*, edited by H. G. Johnson and A. K. Swoboda, 85–92,. Cambridge, MA: Harvard University Press.

McKinnon, Ronald I. 1962. Optimum Currency Areas. *American Economic Review* 53: 717–725.

McKinnon, Ronald I., and K. C. Fung. 1993. Floating Exchange Rates and the New Interbloc Protectionism. In *Protectionism and World Welfare*, edited by Dominick Salvatore, 221–244. Cambridge, UK: Cambridge University Press.

McNamara, Kathleen. 1999. *The Currency of Ideas: Monetary Politics in the European Union*. Princeton, NJ: Princeton University Press.

Milner, Helen. 1999. The Political Economy of International Trade. *Annual Review of Political Science* 2: 91–114.

Milner, Helen V., and B. Peter Rosendorff. 2001. The Optimal Design of International Institutions: Uncertainty and Escape. *International Organization* 55 (4): 829–857.

Mundell, Robert. 1960. The Monetary Dynamics of International Adjustment under Fixed and Flexible Exchange Rates. *Quarterly Journal of Economics* 74: 227–50.

Mundell, Robert. 1961. A Theory of Optimum Currency Areas. *American Economic Review* 51: 657–664.

Niels, Gunnar, and Joseph Francois. 2006. Business Cycles, the Exchange Rate, and Demand for Antidumping Protection in Mexico. *Review of Development Economics* 10 (3): 388–399.

Oatley, Thomas. 2010. Real Exchange Rates and Trade Protectionism. *Business and Politics* 12 (2): 1–17.

Odell, John. 1982. *US International Monetary Power: Markets, Power, and Ideas as Sources of Change*. Princeton, NJ: Princeton University Press.

Pearce, Joan, and John Sutton. 1985. *Protection and Industrial Policy in Europe*. London: Routledge & Kegan Paul.

Pomfret, M., and V. Pontines. 2013. Exchange Rate Policy and Regional Trade Agreements: A Case of Conflicted Interests? ADBI Working Paper 436. Tokyo: Asian Development Bank Institute. http://www.adbi.org/working-paper/2013/10/08/5909.exchange.rate.policy.trade.agreements/.

Rose, Andrew. 2000. One Money, One Market: The Effect of Common Currencies on Trade. *Economic Policy: A European Forum* 30: 7–33.

Sandholz, Wayne, and Alec Stone Sweet, eds. 1998. *European Integration and Supranational Governance*. Oxford: Oxford University Press.

Scheve, Kenneth, and Matthew Slaughter. 2001. What Determines Individual Trade Policy Preferences? *Journal of International Economics* 54 (2): 267–292.

Schmitter, Phillipe C. 1969. Three Neo-functional Hypotheses About International Integration. *International Organization* 23 (1): 161–166.

Simmons, Beth. 1994. *Who Adjusts? Domestic Sources of Foreign Economic Policy During the Interwar Years*. Princeton, NJ: Princeton University Press.

Svensson, Lars E. O. 1999. Inflation Targeting as a Monetary Policy Rule. *Journal of Monetary Economics* 43 (3): 607–654.

Walter, Stefanie. 2008. A New Approach for Determining Exchange-Rate Level Preferences. *International Organization* 62 (3): 405–438.

Walter, Stefanie. 2013. *Financial Crises and the Politics of Macroeconomic Adjustment*. Cambridge, UK: Cambridge University Press.

CHAPTER 25

....

TRADE AND DEVELOPMENT

....

MARK S. MANGER AND
KENNETH C. SHADLEN

INTRODUCTION

....

SINCE the latter years of the twentieth century developing countries have become increasingly integrated in international trade. There is near consensus that engagement in international trade is a necessary condition for economic development, reduction of poverty, and improved living standards. But what steps should countries undertake to increase their participation in international trade? Under what terms should countries engage? These questions remain debated. In this chapter we attempt to shed light on the political underpinnings of the trade policy choices that countries face regarding these issues.

The chapter is organized around two themes. First is the role of trade in development policy, and in particular the relationships between trade, industrialization strategy, and economic development. We maintain that trade needs to be understood in the context of broader constellations of economic policies, and that scholars need to keep in mind the overarching commonalities with regard to the role of the state in late development. Importantly, we suggest that not enough work has gone into analyzing the political economy conditions that underpin variants of state intervention and "developmental" trade policies.

The second theme is the challenges developing countries face when they adopt more explicitly export-oriented strategies to secure greater integration into the global trade regime. Here we emphasize that following a period of rapid, unilateral liberalization in the aftermath of major economic crises, many developing countries have chosen a particular route of trade opening: preferential trade agreements between North and South. While accession to the World Trade Organization (WTO) is often a laborious process (see Davis and Wilf, this volume), nearly all countries have decided to go this route. By contrast, with whom to negotiate a preferential trade agreement (PTA) and what liberalization to agree to in doing so is a policy choice that varies across countries.

Before we address these two themes, we highlight three overarching issues that give the politics of trade a distinct flavor in developing countries: the relative importance of trade to national economies, the importance of trade taxes as a source of government revenue, and a set of structural characteristics that complicate expected patterns of adjustment to changing trade flows. These conditions arguably make trade more prominent in policy debates in developing than developed countries, and often more salient in the minds of citizens.

First and foremost, trade typically makes up a large share of gross domestic product (GDP) for smaller, developing economies. In 2011 the total of exports and imports was equal to more than 30 percent of GDP in every developing country (World Bank 2013). For nearly a third of countries, combined exports and imports exceeded GDP. Even during the period of most restrictive import policies in the 1960s, larger developing economies like Argentina and Mexico had trade shares in GDP around 15 percent, a figure the United States did not attain until the mid-1970s. The archetype of a small trading state, the Netherlands, only reached a trade-to-GDP share greater than 100 percent in 1980. Individual developing countries may contribute little to global trade, but they are nonetheless buffeted by the winds of trade. At the same time, this means that export growth can potentially contribute more to national income than in larger, less open, and more mature economies.

Likewise, taxes on external trade make up a much larger share of government revenue in developing countries, with an average of 10 percent in 2011. Least-developed countries relied on tariffs on imports and exports for up to 30 percent, and this figure is probably understated given that many of the poorest countries do not report any data. By comparison, the average for Organisation for Economic Co-operation and Development (OECD) countries was a mere 0.85 percent. Trade liberalization thus has manifestly different effects on the revenue stream of developing country governments, with important implications for trade policy choices (see Kono, this volume). Economic growth, gains from trade, and the generation of new sources of tax revenue could of course more than compensate for lost tariff revenues, but this presupposes the capacity of states to tax the economy by means other than tariffs. This has historically been—and remains—a challenge for most developing countries.

Trade liberalization, in addition to compelling states to find new sources of revenue, also requires societal actors (firms, workers) to adjust. Yet in settings marked by lower levels of education and human capital development, poorer infrastructure, less mature financial and credit systems, and, in general more recurrent market failures—all distinguishing characteristics of developing countries—adjustment becomes complex and difficult. Rarely is adjusting to international trade a simple and smooth process, but the abilities of actors to redeploy their resources in other sectors where they are more productive should be regarded as at least in part a function of these structural and institutional characteristics that may systematically differ in developing countries. This is not to deny the welfare gains that can be generated by adjustment and resource redeployment; the point is simply that trade liberalization raises different and potentially more complex political challenges in developing countries. A prominent argument in political economy is that the welfare state has expanded in industrialized countries in response to trade opening—but in developing countries, welfare states, where they exist, have tended to be primarily accessible for urban citizens employed in the formal sector, placing greater burdens of adjustment on those outside. Moreover, the presence of a large pool of reserve labor can keep wages at minimal levels (the classic argument by Lewis 1954) and lead to an erosion of existing welfare states as a consequence of trade opening (Rudra 2002). In short, the social and economic costs of trade liberalization in developing countries are often enormous, with little state capacity to soften the blow—and there remains insufficient research on the relationship between trade policy and social protection aside from the important contributions by Rudra (2004) and Fernández de Córdoba and Laird (2006).

TRADE, INDUSTRIALIZATION, AND DEVELOPMENT

Throughout much of the post–World War II era the contribution of trade policy to economic development has been seen through the prism of competing approaches to the challenges of industrialization. The vast majority of developing countries started out as commodities exporters and, as postulated by development economists such as Raúl Prebisch (1949) and Hans Singer (1950), the terms of trade for such countries were perceived to be continuously worsening and subject to endemic volatility, necessitating sustained efforts at industrialization. This premise, the empirical accuracy and substantive effects of which were subject to considerable debate (Spraos 1980), has continued to frame policy making and inspire efforts to diversify exports in many developing countries. The dominant question, then, was not so much the relationship between trade and development directly, but rather indirectly, via trade's effects on the industrialization process.

To build their own industries, most developing countries aimed to replace imports with domestically produced goods and to structure their economic relationships with the developed world to facilitate such industrialization strategy efforts; otherwise, it was feared, developing countries would continue to specialize in primary commodity exports and remain vulnerable to declining and volatile terms of trade. Thus, virtually all developing countries' industrialization efforts began with efforts to substitute imports, a characteristic that makes patterns of "late-late industrialization" (Hirschman 1968) distinct from the experience of "late industrialization" described by Gerschenkron (1962).

Key elements of "import-substitution industrialization" (ISI) strategies included tariffs and nontariff measures (NTMs) to shield local producers of consumer goods from international competition, along with subsidies and tax incentives to encourage investment in industry. In its initial phases, ISI tended to focus on producing basic consumer goods, for which demand existed and which did not require significant capital expenditure or technological prowess and thus were within reach of local investors.[1] Capital goods that could not (yet) be produced in developing countries would have to be imported, however, and with only the earnings from commodity exports available to pay for said imports, balance-of-payments difficulties were sure to arise (Chenery 1958; Diaz-Alejandro 1965). In response, many countries made efforts to "deepen" their industrial structures, sometimes referred to as moving to "secondary" stages of ISI, and produce more complex producer goods, capital goods, and capital-intensive consumer durables locally. To do so, the array of trade policies (e.g., tariffs and NTMs, tax incentives, subsidies) introduced in the early phases of ISI were extended to new sectors.

Importantly, policies to regulate imports were also supplemented by a broad complex of "industrial policy" instruments. By imposing local content requirements on foreign investors, for example, many developing countries sought to compel transnational firms to source more of their inputs locally and thus increase demand for domestically manufactured goods (and also increase foreign firms' incentives to work with and raise the quality of local suppliers). Countries often conditioned foreign investors' participation in the local market on forming joint ventures with local partners, sharing technology, reinvesting revenues in the domestic economy, and employing nationals in key management positions.[2] Beyond regulating the activities of foreign investors, "strategic" sectors were often reserved outright for national firms. Many countries also had significant levels of state ownership in key sectors (e.g., energy, electricity, finance) to provide local firms with critical inputs. Preferential treatment of national firms in government procurement was often used as a tool to promote local industry. States actively regulated technology markets, often requiring licensing and technology transfer agreements to be registered with and approved by trade and industry officials. Many countries introduced lax intellectual property (IP) regimes that made patents difficult to obtain (and, where obtainable, difficult to assert), to facilitate local actors' efforts to access and reverse-engineer foreign technologies. Obviously developing countries displayed important differences in the relative priorities and emphases given to different instruments. The point of this brief—and by no means exhaustive—review of industrial policy instruments is to drive home a frequently overlooked point that development policies in this period included both "trade" and a multitude of "trade-related" industrial policies. Industrial policy was not only about reserving markets for local firms, "infant industry" protection, but about creating incentives for investment and capabilities in new productive sectors.

Notwithstanding broad commonalities in trade and industrial policy instruments, they were often deployed toward different ends. While the prevailing tendency in Latin America (particularly in the larger countries in the region) was to utilize these instruments toward deepening of ISI, the tendency in East Asia was to complement ISI with efforts to promote manufactured exports (Gereffi and Wyman 1990; Haggard 1990). East Asian countries (most notably South Korea and Taiwan) also sought to deepen their industrial structures through the promotion of local manufacturing capabilities, but industries that benefited from government promotion were encouraged to achieve export proficiency. They were often *required* to do so: according to Amsden's (1989) prominent account of Korea, meeting export targets was the quid pro quo for receiving state support. Indeed, the enforcement of "reciprocal control mechanisms" (Amsden 2001) was the hallmark of successful "developmental states" (Woo-Cumings 1999; Wong 2004). In these countries ISI and export-led growth became not opposites, as typically portrayed, but flip sides of a coin.

As the discussion above reveals, countries across the developing world tended to actively attempt to direct resources into particular sectors, utilizing not just trade policies per se but also investment, technology transfer, IP, and other "trade-related" instruments to create new capabilities. What distinguished countries from each other was not so much whether they were "liberal" or "statist," but the extent to which state interventions included measures to create and sustain export-competitive firms and sectors. Though the extent of the differences must not be exaggerated, as even the archetypal ISI poster children, large Latin American countries such as Argentina, Brazil, and Mexico, were putting significantly greater efforts into manufactured exports in the 1970s, all in all it is clear that the array of policy tools to support the local manufacturing base and generate industrial exports was deployed in systematically different ways across regions (Gereffi and Wyman 1990). The result of these two different trajectories is that industrialization in Latin America was more prone to balance-of-payments deficits and thereby became more dependent on external financing (which ultimately contributed to debt crises in the 1980s), whereas industrialization in East Asia was more balanced as imported inputs needed for subsequent industrialization could more easily be financed from manufactured export revenues.[3]

Understanding the political conditions underlying these different trajectories is essential. Why were some countries, particularly in East Asia, so much more able to combine policies designed to promote rapid industrial development with greater engagement in global trade? Attributing East Asian dynamics to the existence of "strong states" that allegedly were insulated from societal pressures and thus able to manage trade and other economic policies effectively is unsatisfactory without an explanation of the social and political underpinnings of state strength (Robinson 2011).

Scholars of the political economy of trade have proffered many explanations for the differences. Some focus on distinct external conditions, such as different forms of foreign aid and financing available (Stallings 1990) and the imperatives that conditions of "systemic vulnerability" provided East Asian governments to construct more efficacious state institutions to promote industrial upgrading and export-competitive firms (Doner, Ritchie, and Slater 2005). Scholars have also suggested that Latin American countries' earlier period of economic development and wealth had the perverse effect of making shifts of the sort witnessed in Asia more challenging, either because of the greater attractiveness of local markets for transnational firms seeking to deepen ISI (Maxfield and Nolt 1990) or because greater wealth and union density would have made the costs of shifting economic strategies politically prohibitive (Mahon 1992).

Another explanation has to do with the effects of large-scale land reforms (Kay 2002; Schrank 2007). Late-late industrialization requires significant resource transfers from the rural sector (agriculture, natural resources) to the urban sector. In countries that had land reforms that weakened agricultural elites, the transfer of resources could be made directly via taxation. In contrast, in countries without significant land reforms, where entrenched landlords or agricultural elites could resist direct taxation of this sort, intersectoral transfers tended to be achieved indirectly, via overvalued exchange rates (Hirschman 1968). The pernicious effects on industrial development of persistently overvalued exchange rates are well known and need not be elaborated on here. We simply add that, in as well as providing industrialists with strong disincentives against trying to engage in exports, the environment created by overvalued real exchange rates (RERs). Overvalued RERs made it more difficult for governments to establish the sorts of institutional arrangements and enforce the array of performance requirements and reciprocal control mechanisms that were the cornerstone of developmental states (Amsden 2001). Quite simply, intervention to promote local industry in the context of overvalued exchanges must depend more on tariffs, but because tariffs also serve a purpose of providing governments with sources of revenue, threats to withdraw the support (i.e., to enforce the performance requirement) are less credible. Subsidies and tax incentives, in contrast, impose costs on the public purse, and thus the threat of removal ("meet this export target within five years or the subsidy will no longer be available") is more credible.

The debt crises in the 1980s set off a sea change in trade policy. With lack of access to external finance making acquisitions of key imports virtually impossible, many countries' trade and industrialization strategies became unsustainable. Unprecedented debt-servicing obligations for many countries made generating foreign exchange revenues through increased exports an imperative. At the same time, technological change that facilitated the fragmentation of production created new opportunities for countries to participate in international trade networks. Thus, the 1980s and 1990s witnessed shifts, throughout the developing world, toward new strategies of economic development based on more liberalized trade and export orientation, with a principal objective of trade and industrialization strategies to build capabilities to integrate into global value chains (GVCs).

New and shifting economic environments—internal in terms of the sustainability of prevailing models of development and external in terms of new opportunities and challenges created by technological change and the emergence of GVCs—were accompanied by changes in the nature of international economic regimes—that is, the formal and informal rules and regulations that structure the global trading system. These changes include, of course, a new approach toward trade, industrialization, and development promoted by the World Bank, other international financial institutions, and foreign donors (Woods 2007)—what has been called the "Washington Consensus," with an emphasis on liberalization and reliance on international price signals to allocate resources within economies. So, for example, countries that turned to international financial institutions such as the International Monetary Fund and World Bank for support during episodes of debt restructuring were typically subject to "structural adjustment" conditionalities that included, among other things, trade liberalization and deregulation of foreign investment.

This period also witnessed the conclusion of the Uruguay Round and the creation of the WTO to supplant the General Agreement on Tariffs and Trade (GATT). The WTO introduced a significant expansion in the scope of international trade governance. In contrast to the GATT, which had a narrow remit focused largely on tariffs of manufactured goods and left most policy areas unaffected and not subject to international constraints,[4] the WTO includes a multitude of agreements affecting a nearly all aspects of international trade. Agreements on tariff levels for manufactured goods are supplemented by rules on, for example, subsidies, health and safety measures, product standards, agricultural trade, and customs valuation. Moreover, the WTO now includes rules that affect national policies in a range of other areas, such as services (shipping, telecommunications, finance, movement of people), regulation of foreign investment, and IP. In the simplest terms, this is a shift from an international trade regime designed to facilitate "shallow integration" to one that attempts to dismantle barriers to "deep integration" (Lawrence 1996).

Changes in the nature of production and trade and in the international rules governing trade go hand in hand. After all, the construction of GVCs based on fragmented and modularized production is only feasible to the extent that barriers—both "trade" and "trade-related"—to markets and restrictions on economic activity are eliminated or reduced. Technological change creates opportunities for the creation of integrated production networks and GVCs, but to go further, to make production networks truly integrated (to put the global in GVCs), national rules and regulations regarding the entry of firms to markets and the activities that firms undertake in markets must be addressed. Firms creating GVCs may seek to take advantage of cost and locational advantages and thus source different stages of production in different settings (directly or via subcontracting); to conduct different elements of R&D or design in different countries; to locate billing, finance, and customer service operations in yet other locations; and so forth. But the ability to take these steps depends on national policies. Thus, firms creating (or seeking to create) GVCs become concerned not just with developing countries' tariffs and NTMs that directly affect imports, but with regulations and policies that affect investment, IP, services, and other areas that affect interfirm relations. In short, broadening of the scope of the international trade regime—from shallow integration to deep integration—creates the political underpinnings to facilitate the globalization of production and the expansion of GVCs.

At the same time that the GATT/WTO's rules became more expansive, they also became more popular. Prior to the 1980s membership in the GATT was far from universal, but the new emphasis on exports and, relatedly, attracting efficiency-seeking foreign investors to help integrate national economies in GVCs, made countries much more concerned with the international trade regime. After all, only as members of the GATT/WTO can countries be assured that their exports will benefit from most-favored nation (MFN) treatment in developed countries' markets. Thus, with more countries now members of an international organization with such a wide remit as the WTO, virtually the entire array of trade and "trade-related" policies that had constituted countries' economic development strategies became subject to new sets of international rules. The establishment of a new complex of rules on both "trade" and "trade-related" issues was controversial, and their existence presents developing countries with a new international environment. The following section examines the political economy of trade and development policies in the contemporary international context.

DEVELOPMENT AND TRADE POLICY CHOICES

Until the late 1990s, developing countries had very little influence on the institutions of the global trade regime, and they had to accept its rules upon joining. While many former colonies availed themselves of GATT provisions in Article XXVI:5(c) that allowed automatic accession with very little liberalization, others delayed accession until after the creation of the WTO and thus faced arduous negotiations (Copelovitch and Ohls 2012). Late entrants had to liberalize their trade policies and dismantle other regulatory policies much more deeply and rapidly than founding members. And yet while the WTO certainly places constraints and limitations on developing countries' policy choices, eliminating some important tools from the arsenal of available measures, most analysts tend to agree that strategies to promote key sectors, build new capabilities, and upgrade industries remain feasible for WTO members (Amsden and Hikino 2000; Shadlen 2005).[5]

Much more constraining than the WTO, however, are the disciplines in North-South PTAs, which have multiplied at a rapid pace. Indeed, following the unilateral changes in the trade policy of developing countries in the late 1980s and early 1990s, subsequent policy changes have almost exclusively been the cause and consequence of PTA negotiations. While "deep integration" (see Kim, this volume) is becoming common among PTAs in general, at least for agreements among developed countries this appears as a response to slow progress at the WTO. Although, for example, the Australia-US PTA covers much more than tariffs and trade in goods, the required policy changes were limited. Since the turn of the millennium, South-South PTAs have also become more common, but these sorts of agreements typically do not entail much liberalization: The "Enabling Clause" agreed upon in the 1979 Tokyo Round of the GATT allows developing countries to postpone liberalization or exclude whole sectors. Some South-South agreements may be meaningful (e.g., most PTAs involving the ASEAN countries), but others (e.g., Morocco-Pakistan) neither cover much trade nor prescribe any tariff reductions. By contrast, North-North and North-South PTAs fall under GATT Article 24 and thus participating states have to eliminate nearly all barriers on trade within ten to fifteen years.

Given this context, North-South PTAs often require the creation of regulation from scratch and transform long-standing policies in developing countries.[6] In a sense the exchange implicit in many North-South PTAs might be regarded as asymmetrically enhanced versions of the WTO. Developing countries receive somewhat improved market access to developed countries' markets, in that they receive better than MFN treatment on more stable terms than would be available otherwise (e.g., through the Generalized System of Preference, GSP), though many developing countries' exports remain encumbered under the WTO (e.g., agriculture) and are not covered in PTAs. At the same time, developing countries commit to undertaking reforms, in both trade and trade-related realms, beyond what is required by the WTO.

Notwithstanding these asymmetries, North-South PTAs have proliferated in recent decades. Developing countries have sought PTAs with developed countries for a number of (not mutually exclusive) reasons. And yet, especially the literature in economics has long remained attached to a focus on trade in goods as the driver of trade policy even in developing countries. This contrasts with accounts that, in particular in Latin America, the initial motivation was to attract foreign direct investment (Cameron and Tomlin 2000, 59–63). PTAs support this goal in two ways: first, by committing the developing country to a specific set of trade policies that cannot be overturned without abrogating the agreement, and second, by facilitating a coalition that can implement further trade policy reforms. PTAs with big, developed economies are obviously attractive because these countries remain the most important sources of foreign direct investment (FDI) and offer large export markets, but North-South PTAs also have political advantages: The bigger and more powerful the partner, the more capable it is of monitoring and policing compliance with the rules of a PTA. This applies in particular to the European Union (EU) and the United States. Baccini and Urpelainen (2014) provide rich evidence that developing countries have implemented much "deeper" PTAs with these two actors, often changing trade policy prior to, during, or shortly after the conclusion of negotiations.

Two key issues need to be understood in discussing the proliferation of North-South PTAs. First, we need to understand the reasons countries want to sign such agreements. Second, we need to understand the distinct nature of the politics of trade (and in particular the politics of PTAs) within developing countries.

One reason developing countries seek PTAs is to secure stable and preferential market access. One of the cornerstones of the global trade regime regulating North-South trade has been the GSP, whereby on a unilateral, nonreciprocal basis, developed countries can offer better market access to developing countries than is granted under MFN status. The GSP originated in United Nations Conference on Trade and Development (UNCTAD) demands for such nonreciprocal concessions in the 1960s. By the mid-1970s most developed economies offered such programs. Since then, several countries have implemented related programs that make more goods eligible for preferential treatment and higher tariff preference margins. The United States supplements GSP with the Caribbean Basin Initiative (CBI), the Caribbean Basin Trade Partnership Act (CBPTA), the Andean Trade Promotion and Drug Eradication Act (ATPDEA),[7] and the African Growth and Opportunity Act (AGOA). The EU's preferential programs include a GSP+ scheme and the "Everything But Arms" initiative for least developed countries.

While the GSP itself excludes textiles and apparel, related schemes permit their export, so that they make up a large share of trade under the GSP+ programs. Production of light manufactured goods is generally the first step on the ladder toward industrialization, so that prima facie the GSP and related schemes should be ideal complements to a development-friendly trade policy. Less appreciated is that reliance on preferential schemes can induce considerable dependence on access to individual markets, which in turn leads to a phenomenon we have elsewhere referred to as "political trade dependence" (Manger and Shadlen 2014).[8] Although the GSP and related schemes are preferential and do not require reciprocal *trade* concessions, they are by no means nonreciprocal or unconditional. Developed countries retain nearly complete discretion with regard to the design and implementation of these schemes. Virtually all aspects of the schemes' design and implementation—which products are covered, how large quotas are, what ceilings (if any) are imposed, what procedures are used to waive ceilings, and so on—are determined by the importing country. Eligibility is often explicitly linked to a range of political criteria. The United States, for example, makes GSP preferences conditional on the enforcement of labor and environmental standards, improvements in the protection of IP rights, participation in the "War on Drugs" in the form of drug eradication, and other, often less explicit forms of foreign policy cooperation (Mason 2004, 524–525). The EU requires the ratification of international human rights conventions and compliance with a variety of other governance standards as a precondition for GSP+ and other programs. Both make decisions on compliance unilaterally and internally, with authority respectively lying with the US Trade Representative and the European Commission.

Most problematic in terms of economic development is that the establishment of a competitive, successful export industry is often rewarded with the withdrawal of trade preferences. In the case of the United States, "competitive need limitations" automatically limit preferences at the request of import-competing industries. In the EU, member states can at any time request the reintroduction of MFN tariffs. Because the GSP and enhanced preferential schemes are unilateral concessions, developing countries have no recourse if they lose market access in this way. In particular, they cannot access the WTO dispute settlement procedures, unlike in the case of trade remedies that temporarily suspend MFN.

To avail themselves of the tariff benefits of these schemes in the first place, exporters often have to comply with onerous documentation requirements. In the case of the EU, some studies estimate that half of the tariff preferences go unused because of complex rules of origin (Brenton 2003). Exporters therefore have to make investments that are specific to the relationship; that is, to the market access to a particular country. Yet they do so in industries such as apparel where capital is mobile, barriers to entry are low, and production is quickly redeployed across the globe. Developing countries that use preferential schemes can therefore become particularly dependent on their continued existence, because it is difficult to sustain any other advantage over competing locations. In our own research (Manger and Shadlen 2014), we have found evidence that in response, they often seek fully reciprocal PTAs with the countries whose markets they also have access to through the GSP and other programs. Although PTA negotiations are unlikely to yield further tariff reductions, whatever is implemented in a PTA is at least locked in and no longer completely at the discretion of the importing country.

The Central American countries provide examples of this dependence. Prior to the conclusion of the Dominican Republic-Central American Free Trade Agreement (DR-CAFTA) with the United States, a majority of exports to the United States were textiles and apparel under preferential schemes. While some import-competing industries opposed the agreement in the Dominican Republic, well-organized exporters in the apparel sector provided much of the political support for the country's accession (Schrank 2008). As we discuss below, export interests in developing countries are often acutely aware of trade policy developments, politically mobilized, and able to attain their political goals.

Political trade dependence contributes to the larger issue of asymmetrical interdependence in a trade relationship. Simply put, only the largest developing countries have much leverage in bilateral negotiations to extract tariff concessions from developed countries, insofar as trade negotiations aim at opening export markets. In this case, asymmetry is simply a function of market size, or more specifically the size of the economy, income per capita, and expectations of future growth. While for the United States not much is lost from walking away from the table when negotiating with a small country, this is not true for the other side. Consequently, in particular in North-South PTAs, developing countries have therefore accepted many of the "deep integration" clauses in return for limited market access gains.

Discussion of how trade structure affects countries' desire for PTAs needs to be complemented by analysis of domestic politics. Analysis of trade policy since the 1980s is by and large a story of the dismantling of many of the policies and institutions introduced during the postwar period of state-led industrialization. As indicated, under the rubric of "reform," most developing countries followed the prescriptions of the "Washington Consensus" to tear down barriers. A plethora of research has studied this process, with particularly insightful contributions by Rodrik (1994), who argues that trade liberalization is inherently difficult because it results in enormous redistribution for very limited overall efficiency gains. However, the situation can be different in situations of profound macroeconomic crisis, such as high levels of inflation, where liberalization becomes more broadly perceived as part of the solution to right the economy (e.g., Pastor and Wise 1994). Trade reform is thus most likely to occur when it takes place concurrently with economic stabilization programs. This helps explain why such extensive trade liberalization in developing countries took place in the aftermath of debt crises.

Moving from the politics of trade per se to the politics of PTAs requires yet another shift. Most of the literature on trade builds on a standard model in which the likely beneficiaries of liberalization are expected to be unaware of their potential gains, geographically diffuse, and unorganized, while those who stand to be adversely affected are expected to be keenly aware of their likely fate, concentrated, and organized (Destler 1995; Haggard 1998). The result, then, is that trade liberalization according to this model occurs more or less in spite of politics—it requires mobilization of "silent majorities" who may be in a position to secure privileges ex post but are unlikely to mobilize to push for policy change in the first place, or of politicians who hope for the overall economic growth that trade liberalization promises to generate (Grossman and Helpman 1994). These are the political underpinnings of a "status quo" bias (Fernandez and Rodrik 1990), and only a few authors have underscored how trade policy is influenced by export interests (Milner 1988; Dür 2010; Gilligan 1997).

Research on the politics of trade in developing countries reveals different patterns of political organization and mobilization. Potential beneficiaries are often exceptionally well-organized, actively mobilized, and politically influential (Solís 2013; Shadlen 2008; Thacker 2006). For example, exporters organized in associations in export-processing zones (EPZs) are likely to be keenly and acutely aware of the benefits to be gained from securing a PTA. At the same time, because trade policy reform (i.e., liberalization, PTA formation) often occurs in the wake of economic crisis, where import-competing producers are already suffering on account of diminished purchasing power in the domestic market, the potential losers tend to be already weakened and politically disarticulated. In sum, we witness a distinct model of trade politics in developing countries, where the actors who stand to benefit directly from liberalization are better positioned politically than those who stand to lose.

The structure of trade and investment also affect trade politics in profound ways. As developing countries engage in trade negotiations with the aim to attract FDI, the interests and lobbying of investing multinational firms change the relationship, and as stages of manufacturing are located in developing countries, new coalitions emerge that span the North-South divide. Using Dunning's (2002) well-established typology, foreign investors may seek markets, assets, or efficiency. If a developing country is primarily a market, barriers to FDI matter as much as tariffs. If, on the other hand, FDI aims at efficiency gains—mostly in manufacturing industries—then the endowments of a developing country, its human capital, and its geographic location may give it leverage in trade negotiations.

Consider the case of Mexico. Geographic proximity to the United States, long seen as more of a burden than a boon, made the country attractive for foreign investment in manufacturing with the goal to serve an integrated North American market. In particular after the entry into force of NAFTA, Mexico therefore gained leverage in trade negotiations with the EU and Japan—both under pressure from multinational firms that sought to establish parity with US firms in the conditions for foreign investment in Mexico and in the export of intermediate and capital goods to facilitate this (see respectively Dür 2007; Manger 2005)—and obtained market access concessions that went considerably beyond existing GSP and GSP+ preferences.

Furthermore, Mexico is an example of the growing integration of middle-income developing countries into global manufacturing networks. While the notion of GVCs is often more metaphor than substantiated by data, the "processing trade" with the United States in EPZs, in the Mexican case called "maquiladoras," created substantial support for trade talks with Mexico in the United States (Cameron 1997; Chase 2003).

FDI then subsequently led to the production of goods for sale in developed markets, a process that is called vertical specialization in intra-industry trade (Krugman 1981). Less sophisticated goods are produced in developing countries, while highly capital-intensive, high-value-added goods are produced in developed economies. In both countries, however, such manufacturing efforts are characterized by economies of scale, so that a developed and a developing country can negotiate mutual tariff reductions by "exchanging" market access concessions for these specialized goods (see Milner 1997, for the original statement; also Manger 2012 for PTAs and vertical specialization). As the same firms undertake manufacturing FDI and trade, we no longer observe the traditional split along industry lines predicted by specific-factor models (Alt et al. 1996). General Motors, its labor force, and its suppliers are as much actors in Mexico's political economy as in the United States, much like Panasonic in Japan and Thailand. A renewed interest in the role of multinational firms in issues of trade and development could yield plentiful research.

Finally, it is worth noting how the second issue we have discussed here—the domestic politics of PTAs—reinforces the first—the proliferation of such agreements. While the first North-South PTA in general requires profound adjustment in the developing country, the coalition of PTA supporters only has to overcome opposition in initial negotiations. Not only does the existence of trade officials whose mission is to negotiate such agreements and already-mobilized business organizations create inertia for additional trade agreements, but subsequent PTAs become easy to negotiate: each additional PTA may add to market access but not require much more domestic adjustment.

The New International Political Economy of Trade and Development

While ISI was a more or less universal strategy pursued by developing countries, the various exit paths of developing countries represent different challenges and attempts to harness trade for developmental purposes. We close this chapter with a typology of developing countries that we hope will generate future research that fills the gap between small-N, within-region comparisons and the broad sweep of large-N studies.

First, small countries with limited market potential never stood much chance of developing "national" industries primarily serving a domestic market. While the dynamics of change vary across time and space, in general the move toward more open and export-oriented economic strategies is hardly surprising. Yet smaller countries' integration into the global trade regime creates particular development challenges: there simply are many—perhaps too many—countries whose comparative advantage is low labor cost. Individually, each country has little influence on the global trade regime and is generally a rule-taker rather than rule-maker. Asymmetrical interdependence therefore often leads to trade policy choices that closely approximate the Washington Consensus.

These countries move from first-stage ISI to an export-oriented trade policy based on foreign direct investment. Yet there are precious few examples of countries (among them Mauritius) that have managed to "upgrade" technologically, moved up the value chain, or diversified their exports away from textiles and apparel (Heron 2012). Whether the causes for this stagnation lie in the lack of domestic capabilities, as in the domain of traditional development economics, or in international or domestic political economy remains an unanswered question that we hope future research will address.

Second, the "East Asian" trade policy rested on decisive steps to complement ISI with the deliberate promotion of exports by key manufacturing industries. This policy was the more successful, the fewer alternatives there were; Taiwan did better than Malaysia, perhaps because Malaysia had agricultural products and natural resources to export. While these states relied to some extent on foreign aid or foreign capital, they generally did not focus on attracting FDI. And yet the demonstrated role of the state and the remarkable success in combining rapid economic growth with relatively low income inequality points to the continuing importance of the East Asian model. Indeed, for many developing countries, efforts to reinvent industrial policy remain inspired by the Asian experience.

Third, some countries moved through a second stage of ISI, but with domestic markets that are big enough to attract market-seeking FDI. Archetypal examples are Brazil, India, and Turkey. Compared to our first type, they often retain much higher trade barriers (with the exception of Turkey, due to its 1996 customs union with the EU), but have undertaken considerable efforts at liberalizing their domestic markets. Aside from being in a less asymmetrical position in trade negotiations, we do not have many accounts for why these countries are more reluctant to liberalize than smaller economies, especially if the benefits of increased trade might be considerable.

Finally, we submit that no discussion of trade and development is complete without special reference to China. Several of our categories map onto Chinese provinces and Chinese policies in different times. One the one hand, the coastal region successfully industrialized based on FDI for export, turning whole provinces into the equivalent of export-processing zones. Simultaneously, the growing sizable Chinese market provides the Chinese government with enough leverage to require local content quotas, joint ventures, and technology transfer to an extent not seen since the heyday of ISI. The Chinese state is authoritarian and has been called strong, yet corruption is rampant. None of this is usefully explained with existing categories of the developmental state literature. We do not believe that China is a case sui generis—but comparisons need to dig deeper than is possible in large-N studies.

Neither is it the case that research in general has ignored these questions. In particular Rodrik's work (as a sample, consider Rodrik 1994, 2006; Hausmann, Hwang, and Rodrik 2007) offers rich inspiration but has not been taken up sufficiently by political economy scholars. Political economy has an inherent tendency to endogenize all forces, with the result that accounts appear to describe the inevitable—and yet choices clearly matter for development outcomes.

Notes

1. It is worth noting that in many countries ISI began not as a policy choice but as a result of supply shortages during the 1940s, as industrial plants in developed countries were oriented toward war efforts.

2. These requirements were often imposed informally, in terms of inspectors or tax authorities treating foreign investors differently depending on their relationships with local suppliers.

3. Note that industrialization in South Korea, the archetypal East Asian "export-oriented" state, also relied heavily on financing from commercial lenders in the 1970s (Frieden 1981), but because of a greater ability to generate revenues through manufactured exports, Korea could borrow on fixed rates. The result is that the substantial increase in international interest rates of the early 1980s did not translate into higher debt-servicing obligations.

4. The GATT did include additional agreements that expanded beyond tariffs, particularly following the Tokyo Round of the 1970s, but most of these were in the form of optional "codes."

5. For a contrarian view, which depicts the WTO as placing severe limits on policy choices and thus essentially freezing the international division of labor, see Wade (2003).

6. Though not the focal point of this chapter, it is worth underscoring here that the prominence of deep integration in PTAs means that conventional metrics used to assess the relative costs and benefits of such agreements may be misleading. That is, most analyses aim to estimate the relative differences between trade creation and diversion, yet the flow of goods and services may be just a part (and a small part) of what matters in these agreements.

7. The ATPDEA replaced the Andean Trade Preference Act (ATPA) in 2002.

8. The broader point that the manipulation of asymmetrical trading relations can function as an instrument of coercion was anticipated in Hirschman (1945).

References

Alt, James E., Jeffry A. Frieden, Michael Gilligan, Dani Rodrik, and Ronald Rogowski. 1996. The Political Economy of International Trade: Enduring Puzzles and an Agenda for Inquiry. *Comparative Political Studies* 29 (6): 689–717.

Amsden, Alice H. 1989. *Asia's Next Giant: South Korea and Late Industrialization*. New York: Oxford University Press.

Amsden, Alice H. 2001. *The Rise of "the Rest": Challenges to the West from Late-Industrializing Economies*. New York: Oxford University Press.

Amsden, Alice H., and Takashi Hikino. 2000. The Bark Is Worse Than the Bite: New WTO Law and Late Industrialization. *Annals of the American Academy of Political and Social Science* 570 (4): 104–114. doi: 10.2307/1049243

Baccini, Leonardo, and Johannes Urpelainen. 2014. International Institutions and Domestic Politics: Can Preferential Trading Agreements Help Leaders Promote Economic Reform? *Journal of Politics* 76 (1): 195–214. doi: 10.1017/S0022381613001278

Brenton, Paul. 2003. Integrating the Least Developed Countries into the World Trading System: The Current Impact of European Union Preferences under "Everything but Arms". *Journal of World Trade* 37 (3): 623–646.

Cameron, Maxwell A. 1997. North American Trade Negotiations: Liberalization Games Between Asymmetric Players. *European Journal of International Relations* 3 (1): 105–139.

Cameron, Maxwell A., and Brian W. Tomlin. 2000. *The Making of NAFTA: How the Deal Was Done.* Ithaca, NY: Cornell University Press.

Chase, Kerry A. 2003. Economic Interests and Regional Trading Arrangements: The Case of NAFTA. *International Organization* 57 (1): 137–174.

Chenery, Hollis B. 1958. The Role of Industrialization in Development Programmes. In *The Economics of Underdevelopment*, edited by A. N. Agarwala and S. P. Singh, 450–471. Oxford: Oxford University Press.

Copelovitch, Mark S., and David Ohls. 2012. Trade, Institutions, and the Timing of GATT/WTO Accession in Post-Colonial States *Review of International Organizations* 7 (1): 81–107. doi: 10.1007/s11558-011-9129-2

Destler, I. M. 1995. *American Trade Politics.* 3rd ed. Washington, DC: Peterson Institute.

Diaz-Alejandro, Carlos F. 1965. On the Import Intensity of Import Substitution. *Kyklos* 18 (3): 495–511. doi: 10.1111/j.1467-6435.1965.tb00986.x

Doner, Richard F., Bryan K. Ritchie, and Dan Slater. 2005. Systemic Vulnerability and the Origins of Developmental States: Northeast and Southeast Asia in Comparative Perspective. *International Organization* 59 (02): 327–361.

Dunning, John H. 2002. Theories and Paradigms of International Business Activity. Edited by John H. Dunning. The Selected Essays of John H. Dunning vol. 1. Cheltenham, UK: Edward Elgar.

Dür, Andreas. 2007. EU Trade Policy as Protection for Exporters: The Agreements with Mexico and Chile. *Journal of Common Market Studies* 45 (4): 833–855.

Dür, Andreas. 2010. *Protection for Exporters: Power and Discrimination in Transatlantic Trade Relations, 1930–2010.* Ithaca, NY: Cornell University Press.

Fernandez, Raquel, and Dani Rodrik. 1990. Why Is Trade Reform so Unpopular? On Status Quo Bias in Policy Reforms. NBER Working Paper No. 3269. Cambridge, MA: National Bureau for Economic Research. http://www.nber.org/papers/w3269.

Fernández de Córdoba, Santiago, and Sam Laird. 2006. *Coping with Trade Reforms: A Developing Country Perspective on the WTO Industrial Tariff Negotiations.* Houndmills, Basingstoke, UK: Palgrave Macmillan.

Frieden, Jeffry A. 1981. Third World Indebted Industrialization: International Finance and State Capitalism in Mexico, Brazil, Algeria, and South Korea. *International Organization* 35 (3): 407–431. doi: 10.2307/2706430

Gereffi, Gary, and Donald L. Wyman. 1990. *Manufacturing Miracles: Paths of Industrialization in Latin America and East Asia.* Princeton, NJ: Princeton University Press.

Gerschenkron, Alexander. 1962. *Economic Backwardness in Historical Perspective.* Cambridge, MA: Belknap Press.

Gilligan, Michael J. 1997. *Empowering Exporters: Reciprocity, Delegation, and Collective Action in American Trade Policy.* Ann Arbor: University of Michigan Press.

Grossman, Gene M., and Elhanan Helpman. 1994. Protection for Sale. *American Economic Review* 84 (4): 833–850.

Haggard, Stephan. 1990. *Pathways from the Periphery: The Politics of Growth in the Newly Industrializing Countries.* Ithaca, NY: Cornell University Press.

Haggard, Stephan. 1998. The Political Economy of Regionalism. In *The Post-NAFTA Political Economy: Mexico and the Western Hemisphere*, edited by Carol Wise, 302–338. University Park: University of Pennsylvania Press.

Hausmann, Ricardo, Jason Hwang, and Dani Rodrik. 2007. What You Export Matters. *Journal of Economic Growth* 12 (1): 1–25.

Heron, Tony. 2012. *The Global Political Economy of Trade Protectionism and Liberalization: Trade Reform and Economic Adjustment in Textiles and Clothing*. Milton Park, Abingdon, Oxford (UK): Routledge.

Hirschman, Albert O. 1945. *National Power and the Structure of Foreign Trade*. Expanded ed. The Politics of the International Economy. Berkeley and Los Angeles: University of California Press.

Hirschman, Albert O. 1968. The Political Economy of Import-Substituting Industrialization in Latin America. *Quarterly Journal of Economics* 82 (1): 1–32. doi: 10.2307/1882243

Kay, Cristóbal. 2002. Why East Asia Overtook Latin America: Agrarian Reform, Industrialisation and Development. *Third World Quarterly* 23 (6): 1073–1102. doi: 10.1080/0143659022000036649

Krugman, Paul R. 1981. Intraindustry Specialization and the Gains from Trade. *Journal of Political Economy* 89 (5): 959–973.

Lawrence, Robert Z. 1996. *Regionalism, Multilateralism, and Deeper Integration*. Integrating National Economies. Washington, DC: Brookings Institution.

Lewis, W. Arthur. 1954. Economic Development with Unlimited Supplies of Labour. *Manchester School* 22 (2): 139–191. doi: 10.1111/j.1467-9957.1954.tb00021.x

Mahon, James E., Jr. 1992. Was Latin America Too Rich to Prosper? Structural and Political Obstacles to Export-led Industrial Growth. *Journal of Development Studies* 28 (2): 241–263. doi: 10.1080/00220389208422231

Manger, Mark S. 2005. Competition and Bilateralism in Trade Policy: The Case of Japan's Free Trade Agreements. *Review of International Political Economy* 12 (5): 804–828. doi: 10.1080/09692290500339800

Manger, Mark S. 2012. Vertical Trade Specialization and the Formation of North-South PTAs. *World Politics* 64 (4): 622–658.

Manger, Mark S., and Kenneth C. Shadlen. 2014. Political Trade Dependence and North-South Trade Agreements. *International Studies Quarterly* 58 (1): 79-91. doi: 10.1111/isqu.12048

Mason, Amy M. 2004. The Degeneralization of the Generalized System of Preferences (GSP): Questioning the Legitimacy of the US GSP. *Duke Law Journal* 54 (2): 513–547.

Maxfield, Sylvia, and James H. Nolt. 1990. Protectionism and the Internationalization of Capital: U.S. Sponsorship of Import Substitution Industrialization in the Philippines, Turkey and Argentina. *International Studies Quarterly* 34 (1): 49–81. doi: 10.2307/2600405

Milner, Helen V. 1997. Industries, Governments, and the Creation of Regional Trade Blocs. In *The Political Economy of Regionalism*, edited by Edward D. Mansfield and Helen V. Milner, 77–106. New York: Columbia University Press.

Milner, Helen V. 1988. *Resisting Protectionism: Global Industries and the Politics of International Trade*. Princeton, NJ: Princeton University Press.

Pastor, Manuel, and Carol Wise. 1994. "The Origins and Sustainability of Mexico Free-Trade Policy." *International Organization* 48 (3): 459–489.

Prebisch, Raúl. 1949. O Desenvolvimento Econômico Da América Latina E Seus Principais Problemas. *Revista Brasileira de Economia* 3 (3): 47–1111.

Robinson, James A. 2011. Industrial Policy and Development: A Political Economy Perspective. In *Annual World Bank Conference on Development Economics Global 2010: Lessons from East Asia and the Global Financial Crisis*, edited by Justin Yifu Lin and Boris Pleskovic, 61–79. Washington, DC: The World Bank.

Rodrik, Dani. 1994. The Rush to Free Trade in the Developing World: Why So Late? Why Now? Will It Last? In *Voting for Reform: Democracy, Political Liberalization, and Economic Adjustment*, edited by Steven B. Webb and Stephan Haggard, 61–88. New York: Oxford University Press.

Rodrik, Dani. 2006. What's So Special about China's Exports? *China & World Economy* 14 (5): 1–19.

Rudra, Nita. 2002. Globalization and the Decline of the Welfare State in Less-Developed Countries. *International Organization* 56 (2): 411–445.

Rudra, Nita. 2004. Openness, Welfare Spending, and Inequality in the Developing World. *International Studies Quarterly* 48 (3): 683–709. doi: 10.1111/j.0020-8833.2004.00320.x

Schrank, Andrew. 2007. Asian Industrialization in Latin American Perspective: The Limits to Institutional Analysis. *Latin American Politics & Society* 49 (2): 183–200. doi: 10.1353/lap.2007.0025

Schrank, Andrew. 2008. Export Processing Zones in the Dominican Republic: Schools or Stopgaps? *World Development* 36 (8): 1381–1397.

Shadlen, Kenneth C. 2005. Exchanging Development for Market Access? Deep Integration and Industrial Policy under Multilateral and Regional-Bilateral Trade Agreements. *Review of International Political Economy* 12 (5): 750–775.

Shadlen, Kenneth C. 2008. Globalisation, Power and Integration: The Political Economy of Regional and Bilateral Trade Agreements in the Americas. *Journal of Development Studies* 44 (1): 1–20.

Singer, Hans W. 1950. The Distribution of Gains between Investing and Borrowing Countries. *American Economic Review* 40 (2): 473–485. doi: 10.2307/1818065

Solís, Mireya. 2013. Business Advocacy in Asian PTAs: A Model of Selective Corporate Lobbying with Evidence from Japan. *Business and Politics* 15 (1): 87–116. doi: 10.1515/bap-2012-0045

Spraos, John. 1980. The Statistical Debate on the Net Barter Terms of Trade Between Primary Commodities and Manufactures. *Economic Journal* 90 (357): 107–128. doi: 10.2307/2231659

Stallings, Barbara. 1990. The Role of Foreign Capital in Economic Development. In *Manufacturing Miracles: Paths of Industrialization in Latin America and East Asia*, edited by Gary Gereffi and Donald L. Wyman, 55–89. Princeton, NJ: Princeton University Press.

Thacker, Strom C. 2006. *Big Business, the State, and Free Trade: Constructing Coalitions in Mexico*. Cambridge, UK: Cambridge University Press.

Wade, Robert H. 2003. What Strategies Are Viable for Developing Countries Today? The World Trade Organization and the Shrinking of "Development Space". *Review of International Political Economy* 10 (4): 621–644.

Wong, Joseph. 2004. The Adaptive Developmental State in East Asia. *Journal of East Asian Studies* 4 (3): 345–362.

Woo-Cumings, Meredith. 1999. *The Developmental State*. Ithaca, NY: Cornell University Press.

Woods, Ngaire. 2007. *The Globalizers: The IMF, the World Bank, and Their Borrowers*. Ithaca, NY: Cornell University Press.

World Bank. 2013. *World Development Indicators*. Washington, DC: The World Bank.

CHAPTER 26

A MATCH MADE IN HEAVEN? THE WEDDING OF TRADE AND HUMAN RIGHTS

SUSAN ARIEL AARONSON

As long and men and women have traded, they have wrestled with questions of human rights. Not surprisingly, throughout history policy makers have tried to marry trade and human rights policies throughout history. For example, archaeological evidence shows that ancient civilizations traded at great risk to their freedoms. According to economist Peter Temin (2003), the ancients shipped a wide range of goods, from wheat to wine. But these traders often lived in fear; when they engaged in trade they risked being captured, sold as slaves, or enslaved by pirates. The sea may bring contact with strangers who could enhance national prosperity, but these same strangers might threaten the security of the nation and its people.

Many years later, during the Age of Exploration, theologians, scholars, and royal advisors debated whether they had the right to exploit the land and wealth of indigenous populations. The economic historian Douglas Irwin notes that Vitoria, one of the "founders of international law," contended that the right to trade is "derived from the law of nations. . . . Foreigners may carry on trade, provided they do no hurt to citizens."[1]

The truth is that although scholars, policy makers, and activists have long debated the relationship between trade and human rights, scholars today still know very little about that relationship or about causality. Do trade and human rights make an effective and enduring match? Figure 26.1 shows the big questions that scholars should be asking about the relationship between trade and human rights. This chapter discusses whether scholars have asked and answered these questions and whether they have examined why countries are demanding and accepting such human rights provisions. It also considers whether scholars have examined the "so what" question: Have these provisions led to changes in human rights policies, conditions, and the ability of citizens to demand their rights?

The chapter is organized in three sections. The first defines human rights and discusses human rights language within existing trade agreements. In the second, I discuss the state of scholarship on the relationship between trade and human rights. Many

1. Does expanded trade stimulate or undermine government responsibility for respecting human rights?	2. Does expanded trade encourage or discourage public demand for specific human rights?	3. Does the protection of specific human rights make trade liberalization or specific trade agreements possible (e.g., property rights protection)?

4. Do governments use trade agreements to promote a particular human right, and is that strategy effective (conditionality)?	5. Do governments use human rights conditions to justify trade agreements or relationships (or nonrelationships)? Should they be linked?

FIG. 26.1 The Big Questions in the Complex Relationship between Trade and Human Rights.

scholars have used empirical tools to examine the trade and human rights relationship, but have paid little attention to what trade agreements actually say about human rights. Moreover, as I will show, when scholars use empirical tools to examine the effects of trade on human rights, they tend to focus on one grouping of human rights: personal integrity. Personal integrity rights include freedom from physical abuse by authorities, such as torture, arbitrary imprisonment, or rape. I argue that although this scholarship has reached a critical mass in scale and scope, academics may not be asking the right questions.[2] Scholars have asked whether trade leads to human rights improvements, whether governments use trade to promote specific human rights, and whether policy makers use human rights conditions to justify trade agreements. But they are not asking if expanding trade empowers people to demand their rights. Nor are they asking whether government respect for specific human rights (an aspect of good governance) might be a precondition for trade liberalization; for example, establishing the protection of property rights. From my vantage point, while past studies have provided new insights, they often seem disconnected from the real world where policy makers are increasingly linking trade and specific human rights (although these officials are not linking trade and personal integrity rights).

The third section offers some conclusions as to why governments are increasingly linking trade and human rights, whether such links are effective, and whether these policy unions will thrive. I then make suggestions for further research.

THE RIGHTS AND RESPONSIBILITIES OF STATES AND WHAT THEY MEAN FOR TRADE POLICY

Under international law, states are supposed to do everything in their power to respect, promote, and fulfill human rights. But advancing human rights is not easy. As noted previously, many states are unable or unwilling to meet all of their "international" human rights responsibilities. Moreover, few officials win or maintain office on the basis of their efforts to promote the human rights of non-citizens.

Not surprisingly, most policy makers do not make human rights a top priority for trade policy making. In most countries, they develop trade policies as if these policies were strictly commercial policies. These officials weigh the interests of their producers and consumers, and although they may consider national security or political concerns, they rarely introduce the interests of the global community into such deliberations. Although policy makers are well aware of the human rights consequences of some of their trade decisions, they have few incentives to ensure that trade policies advance the human rights outlined under the Universal Declaration of Human Rights. Moreover, trade policy makers are generally not charged with ensuring that trade policies or flows do not undermine specific human rights at home or abroad. In trade negotiations, governments are charged with pursuing national commercial interests, not global interests (Commission on Human Rights 2004; 3D 2005; Aaronson and Zimmerman 2007).

However, many people are not comfortable knowing that other human beings lack basic rights in their own countries or live in countries where government officials undermine human rights. These individuals may demand that policy makers take action to protect human rights in other countries. Trade policy is not the best means of extending such protection, but policy makers have few options short of military force for changing the behavior of leaders in other countries. Hence, when a country such as the United States wants to affect human rights in another country such as Syria (not a member of the World Trade Organization [WTO]), it can use access to its markets as leverage.

A Brief Overview of the Rules Governing Trade and Its Intersection

Policy makers first began to regulate state behavior regarding trade and human rights in the nineteenth century. In some instances they used the incentive of trade expansion; at other times they used trade sanctions—the disincentive of lost trade—to punish officials from other countries that undermined human rights. For example, after the United Kingdom and the United States outlawed the slave trade in 1807, the United Kingdom signed treaties with Denmark, Portugal, and Sweden to reinforce its own ban. When the United States banned goods manufactured by convict labor, Australia, Canada, and the United Kingdom followed with similar measures. These efforts stimulated international cooperation, and in 1919 the signatories of the Treaty of Versailles formed the International Labour Organization (ILO) to establish fair and humane rules regarding the treatment of labor producing goods for trade (Aaronson 2001).

Although policy makers had long used trade policy to affect human rights conditions abroad, it was not until the twentieth century that trade diplomats first negotiated specific human rights language within trade agreements. In the 1980s and 1990s, US and European Union (EU) officials began to include human rights conditionality clauses in their preference programs, which were justified as a waiver to WTO rules (Charnovitz 2005, 29, n. 103–105). The 1993 North American Free Trade Agreement (NAFTA), signed by Canada, Mexico, and the United States, included language on labor rights provisions in a side agreement. More than 131 countries (some 70 percent of all countries) participated in a trade agreement containing human rights language or requirements (Aaronson 2011, 443). Moreover, as Table 26.1 illustrates, trade agreements today cover a diverse range of human rights.

While some of these human rights provisions are aspirational and simply expressed in hortatory language in a preamble, other human rights are delineated in actionable provisions in the body of a trade agreement. As Table 26.2 show, some governments even make their human rights commitments disputable—in other words, they may challenge a country that fails to live up to the obligations in a trade dispute. Finally, middle-income and developing-country governments such as Chile, Brazil, and Uruguay have included human rights provisions in their free trade agreements (FTAs).

Some analysts see these provisions as "legal inflation" and assert that governments are using trade agreements to globalize their social policies or regulatory approaches. Many argue that trade agreements are not the right place to address human rights issues, and they point out that trade agreements do not need to have explicit human rights language to have positive human rights spillovers.

But others argue that trade policy makers pay insufficient attention to human rights, which are necessary to achieve sustainable development (Sen 1999). Sen asserts that governments must actively provide citizens with public goods such as education, property rights, credit, and justice; these public goods allow citizens to meet their potential and in turn to act in ways that grow the economy (UNDP 2000).

Trade and human rights is not only a controversial development issue; even Western policy makers disagree about how to protect human rights and what human rights should be discussed in trade agreements. In July 2013 the twenty-eight nations of the EU and the United States began negotiating a free trade agreement. These twenty-nine nations include the world's most technologically advanced and richest democracies, which have made steady progress on human rights. Yet stakeholders on both sides of the Atlantic have expressed concern that the potential trade agreement could actually undermine human rights and are worried that the agreement has no chapter on human rights.[3] Moreover, the negotiations were colored by revelations that the United States had not adequately protected personal online data that it had gathered. Many EU politicians complained that EU privacy rights were not respected by the United States; some officials even threatened to cancel the trade talks to illustrate how important privacy rights are to the EU populace.[4]

Table 26.1 Human Rights Embedded in Free Trade Agreements and the Countries Embedding Them

Labor Rights	Democratic Rights	Access to Affordable Medicines	Right to Cultural Participation	Freedom of Movement	Indigenous Minority Rights	Political Participation and Due Process	Privacy
Canada	The Members of Mercosur	Costa Rica	Canada	The Members of EFTA/EEA	Canada	Canada	Canada
Chile		United States	New Zealand	The Members of CARICOM	New Zealand	EU	

Note: CARICOM = Caribbean Community; EEA = European Economic Area; EFTA = European Free Trade Agreement; EU = European Union; Mercosur = Southern Cone Common Market (Mercado Común del Sur).

Table 26.2   Aspirational vs. Binding Language in Free Trade Agreements: Comparing the EFTA, the EU, the United States, and Canada

	EFTA	EU	United States	Canada
Strategy	Universal human rights	Universal human rights and specific rights	Specific human rights	Specific human rights
Which rights?		Labor rights, transparency, due process, political participation, and privacy rights	Transparency, due process, political participation, access to affordable medicines, and labor rights	Transparency, due process, political participation, labor rights, privacy rights, cultural and indigenous rights
How enforced?	No enforcement	Human rights violations lead to dialogue and possible suspension depending on nature of violation.	Since 2007 (e.g., in Colombia), labor rights can be disputed under dispute settlement body affiliated with the agreement. Process begins with bilateral dialogue to resolve issues.	Only labor rights (monetary penalties). Use dialogue first.
Any challenge?			First challenge: Guatemala Review of Jordan	

Source: Aaronson (2011).
Note: EEA = European Economic Area; EFTA = European Free Trade Agreement; EU = European Union.

GATT and WTO Provisions on Human Rights

From 1948 to 1995 the General Agreement on Tariffs and Trade (GATT) governed multilateral trade relations. GATT grew from 23 nations in 1948 to 128 in 1995. In 1995 the members of the GATT agreed to join a new international organization, the WTO, which contains the GATT agreement and has a stronger system of dispute settlement. Today, the 160 GATT/WTO members must adhere to two key principles: most favored nation (MFN) principle, and national treatment principle. The MFN principle requires that the best trading conditions extended to one member by a nation must be extended automatically to every other nation. The national treatment principle provides that once a product is imported, the importing state may not subject that product to regulations less favorable than those that apply to like products produced domestically. The GATT/WTO does not explicitly prohibit countries from protecting human rights at home or abroad, but its rules do constrain the behavior of governments. The WTO (and the GATT) require that when member states seek to promote human rights at home or abroad, they must not unnecessarily or unduly distort trade by discriminating among producers and products as noted above. Hence, member states are not supposed to use trade to distinguish among those nations that may undermine the human rights of their citizens and those that strive to advance these rights.

The GATT/WTO do not directly address how governments relate to their own citizens, and they say very little about human rights. But human rights are seeping into the workings of the WTO (Aaronson 2007). Some WTO members have used the GATT/WTO exceptions to advance human rights abroad or to protect human rights at home. Under Article XX, nations can restrict trade when necessary to "protect human, animal, or plant life or health" or to conserve exhaustible natural resources. This article also states that governments may restrict imports relating to the products of prison labor. Although it does not refer explicitly to human rights, the public morals clause of Article XX is widely seen as allowing GATT/WTO members to put in place trade bans in the interest of promoting human rights at home or abroad (Howse 2002; Charnovitz 2005).

The national security exception, Article XXI, states that WTO rules should not prevent nations from protecting their own security. Members are not permitted to take trade action to protect another member's security or to protect the citizens of another member. If, however, the United Nations Security Council authorizes trade sanctions because of human rights violations, WTO rules allow countries to comply with such authorizations, such as when sanctions were instituted against South Africa's apartheid regime in the 1980s (Levy 1999; Aaronson and Zimmerman 2007, 19).

Members of the GATT/WTO can use other avenues to protect human rights at home and within other member states (see Table 26.3). In recent years member states have used temporary waivers of GATT rules to promote human rights. For example, after the United Nations (UN) called for a ban on trade in conflict diamonds, WTO member states agreed to temporarily waive WTO rules to allow trade in only those diamonds certified by the Kimberly process to be free of conflict (Aaronson and Zimmerman 2007, 43). In addition, some members bring up human rights during accessions, when new members are asked to make their trade and other public policies transparent, accountable, and responsive. They have also discussed human rights issues at trade policy reviews, when member states review the trade and governance performance of other member states. Finally, WTO members have discussed some human rights issues during recent trade negotiations; examples include food security, intellectual property rights (IPRs), and public health (Aaronson 2007; Aaronson and Abouharb 2011).

Although the GATT/WTO contains no explicit human rights provisions, it does refer to human rights implicitly. Some of these provisions relate to economic rights, such as the right to property, while others refer to democratic and political rights. For example, under GATT/WTO rules, member states give economic actors "an entitlement to substantive rights in domestic law including the right to seek relief; the right to submit comments to a national agency, or the right to appeal adjudicatory rulings" (Charnovitz 2001). Member states must also ensure that "[m]embers and other persons affected, or

Table 26.3 Examples of Avenues and Actions at the WTO Related to Human Rights, 2003–2013

Avenue	Human Right Affected
Accessions	Labor rights, access to information, due process (Vietnam, Saudi Arabia, Cambodia) 2003–present
Trade policy reviews	Members discussed labor rights, women's rights, access to medicines 2003–present
Disputes	Right to health (*Brazil tires*) 2005–2009 Public morals (*Antigua gambling*) 2003–2013 Freedom of speech, access to information (*China-Audiovisual Services* case) WTO, 2007–2010
Negotiations	Access to safe, affordable food 2003–present. Access to medicines, 2003–present

Source: Aaronson (2007), updated.

likely to be affected, by governmental measures imposing restraints, requirements and other burdens, should have a reasonable opportunity to acquire authentic information about such measures and accordingly to protect and adjust their activities or alternatively to seek modification of such measures."[5] These rules can be rephrased as promoting due process and access to information, or more generally as "political participation rights."

Although these provisions in the GATT/WTO were not directly intended to advance human rights per se, these provisions could have important human rights spillovers (indirect effects). Under WTO rules, member states must apply the same rules and privileges to domestic and foreign actors. These provisions may prod policy makers to provide access to information and enforce rights to public comment in countries where governance is not transparent and participatory. In repressive states, WTO rules may empower domestic market actors (consumers and taxpayers, as well as producers) who may not have been able to use existing domestic remedies to obtain information, influence policies, or challenge their leaders (Aaronson and Abouharb 2011). In WTO countries without a strong democratic tradition, member states may make these changes because they want to signal investors that they can be trusted to enforce property rights; uphold the rule of law; and act in an evenhanded, impartial manner (Dobbin, Simmons, and Garrett 2007; Büthe and Milner 2008; Mansfield and Pevehouse 2008, 273).

In sum, the WTO regime is not hostile to human rights, and human rights discussions are clearly part of the trade agenda. Trade policy makers have become more willing to accommodate human rights as the public became more aware of their human rights and more demanding of policies that advance and protect those rights.

An Overview of the Literature
on Trade and Human Rights

At first glance, this might be the golden age of scholarship on the marriage of trade and human rights. Economists, political scientists, philosophers, and law professors have joined the discussion and at times have transcended traditional academic boundaries. Moreover, they have examined the trade and human rights relationship from many angles with a variety of tools, from empirical analysis to case studies.

Some academics have focused on the long run, arguing that trade is a means to the end of improving human welfare. They note that when trade contributes to economic activity, more people can improve their quality of life (Dollar 1992; Sachs and Warner 1995). As trade expands, individuals exchange ideas, technologies, processes, and cultural norms and goods. With more trade, people in countries with fewer rights and freedoms become aware of conditions elsewhere, and with such knowledge they may demand greater rights (van Hees 2004). Still others argue that trade stimulates an export-oriented middle class, which will use its increasing economic clout to demand political freedoms and press for openness and good governance (Rodrik: 2000). Blanton and Blanton conclude that there is a "mutually reinforcing relationship between trade openness and human rights. Trade openness contributes to societal changes conductive to respect for human rights ... conversely, respect for human rights enables states to better compete in the global trading order" (2008, 93). Some scholars directly assert that trade may help to encourage guarantees of civil and political liberties. In this regard, law professor Joel Paul cites the example of Mexico, where greater trade with Canada and the United States helped the country mature into a multiparty democracy (Paul: 2003). Thus, many of these scholars conclude that policy makers need not include human rights provisions in trade agreements (Bhagwati 1996, 1; Sykes 2003, 2–4). However, other analysts disagree; they believe that human rights are trade issues and cite history and the increasing number of human rights provisions in preferential trade agreements (PTAs) as evidence for their perspective.

However, others have a less benign view of the marriage of trade and human rights. As an example, some gender rights scholars argue that because the WTO restricts the ability of member states to adopt protectionist policies, these states are less able to protect their citizens, especially women, from harm. They also believe that because many women are small farmers who can't compete effectively with farmers from middle income and industrialized nations, they are effectively penalized by the WTO (Seguino and Grown 2006). Moreover, women often find it harder to compete with men for skilled jobs created by trade (Korinek 2005, 11).

But trade and trade agreements can also increase access to resources and opportunities for women. In both developing and industrialized states, trade-related globalization may provide more and better jobs for some citizens, but job loss for others—both women and men. Scholars don't yet know if job loss can be attributed solely to globalization or if unemployment and underemployment are caused by other factors such as technological progress.[6] Whatever the reason, given demographic changes, many countries will need to find strategies to encourage lasting female participation in the workforce.[7] Hence, countries with rapidly aging populations and relatively low female workplace participation may benefit by gaining a broader understanding of how to make their labor, gender, and trade policies more coherent (Jansen and Lee 2007, 90).

Although growing numbers of scholars are examining gender and trade and other topics, the bulk of scholarship has focused on one subset of human rights: physical integrity rights such as the right to life and the inviolability of the human person. President Franklin Roosevelt first enunciated this concept in his "Four Freedoms" speech (1941) when he mentioned freedom from fear. Although Roosevelt was referring directly to freedom from the fear caused by war and violence, personal integrity rights are a subset of human rights that include freedom from rape, torture, and arbitrary imprisonment. Apodaca (2001, 597–598) and Harrelson-Stephens and Callaway (2003, 151–152) argue that increased trade enhances government respect for physical integrity rights, even after substituting *country exports* for trade openness. Harrelson-Stephens and Callaway conclude that "increases in *both* imports and exports have a substantial impact on human rights performances of a state" (2003, 152). Hafner-Burton and Tsutsui (2007) and Hafner-Burton (2005) find that trade and/or foreign direct investment is positively related to stronger respect for physical integrity rights. Hafner-Burton (2009, 160–164) finds that about 82 percent of the countries that have a PTA with the EU improve their human rights protection, as opposed to 75 percent of countries without a trade agreement. Wesley Milner also finds that trade openness enhances physical integrity rights (2002, 90–91). In an intriguing study, Brian Greenhill finds that membership in an international organization such as a trade agreement may "socialize" policy makers and encourage them to respect human rights (Greenhill 2010).

Political scientists Cao, Greenhill, and Prakash (2013) sought to test whether trade can improve human rights standards. They hypothesized that if a country trades with another country that has strong human rights practices, it may be encouraged to adopt stronger standards itself. They also posited that there may be a tipping point at which outside pressure (from business, governments, nongovernmental organizations [NGOs], trade unions, and consumer groups) can prod a government with a relatively poor human rights record to improve its performance. Although many of their qualitative examples relate to labor rights (2013, 135–141), Cao, Greenhill, and Prakash tested their hypothesis using physical integrity rights. They conclude that "trading relationships can, under certain conditions, serve as 'transmission belts' for the diffusion of human rights standards," but only at a certain tipping point. They note that trade not only connects firms, but also "connects the practices of importing jurisdictions to those of the governments of exporting states." Therefore, they conclude that scholars should pay greater attention to such norm diffusion, and activists should see trade as a tool to help developing countries improve governance (Cao, Greenhill, and Prakash 2013, 154–155). This phenomenon was evident in Bangladesh in 2013. After a series of fires and a building collapse killed over a thousand garment workers who toiled in unsafe conditions, activists pressed the US government to suspend trade preferences and several companies organized to do a better job monitoring work conditions among their suppliers.[8]

Although these studies have helped us better understand the marriage of trade and human rights, many of these analyses have two important flaws. First, they conflate physical integrity rights with human rights in general. As a result, they assert broader human rights effects than they are actually finding. Hafner-Burton and Ron (2009, 365–366) essentially argue that scholars have little choice; using personal integrity rights makes sense because they allow scholars to study "the state's actual treatment of its population . . . Personal integrity rights are vital . . . [because] states are obliged under international treaties to immediately cease and desist from their abuse." Second, scholars who rely on personal integrity data don't explain how trade or trade agreements affect physical integrity rights directly or indirectly. We can find no trade agreements that mention physical integrity rights, so scholars need to map out how, when, and why trade agreements and policies affect personal integrity rights. To put it differently, how does enhanced trade or a specific trade agreement affect whether or when states torture, rape, or use arbitrary imprisonment? Until scholars can show the mechanism of transmission, it seems strange that they are examining personal integrity rights to illuminate how trade affects human rights, rather than other human rights directly affected by or mentioned in trade agreements, such as labor, freedom of speech, access to information, or due process.

Scholars can increasingly choose from other data sets.[9] CIRI, as an example, has data on women's rights, political and civil liberties, and labor rights for the bulk of the world's countries.[10] The Social and Economic Empowerment Rights Initiative (SERF) has two years of useful data examining country performance on the fulfillment of economic and social rights obligations.[11] Global Integrity, an NGO that works on anticorruption counterweights, prepares an annual survey that looks at various democratic rights in principle and in practice, including access to information and freedom of speech and assembly. The information is comparable and has been available since 2004, but not for every country in every year.[12] Finally, the World Bank has good data on property rights,[13] while UNCTAD has the Human Development Index and the Multidimensional Poverty Index, which examine the many dimensions of how people experience development and poverty, respectively.[14]

Some scholars are trying to examine human rights that are directly affected by trade and/or mentioned in trade agreements. In contrast with those working on physical integrity rights, scholars working on the trade-labor rights relationship have an easier time showing why they chose to examine labor rights. In a survey, Elliott and Freeman (2003) demonstrate that labor rights can improve under globalization. Mosley and Uno (2007) hypothesize that the impact of globalization on labor rights depends not only on the overall level of economic openness, but also on how a country participates in global production networks. They find that although foreign investment inflows are positively and significantly related to the rights of workers, trade competition generates downward "race to the bottom" pressures on collective labor rights. The authors also find that domestic institutions and labor rights in neighboring countries are important correlates of workers' rights. Mosley (2008) examines the specific case of Costa Rica, finding that local conditions influence its ability to improve labor standards. Greenhill, Mosley, and Prakash (2009) examine whether high trade standards in the importing country prod the developing country to improve labor conditions. They conclude that labor standards in developing countries are influenced by the labor standards of their exporting destinations, not by their overall levels of trade openness. Instead of exporters pushing down labor standards of the importing countries, as the race to the bottom literature suggests, importers can influence—positively or negatively—the collective labor laws and practices of trade partners. They also find it is not trade openness per se that matters for labor standards in the developing world, but rather the status of activism and labor standards in the importing country.

Other scholars have tried to understand the trade-human rights relationship by examining the activists who have pushed for greater balance between trade and human rights objectives. Cambridge law professor Andrew Lang believes activists have taught policy makers that they must pay greater attention to human rights. Hebrew University professor Tomer Broude (2013), in contrast, believes activists have finally realized that the WTO is not directly causing human rights problems. He stresses that during "the Battle in Seattle" in 1999, activists blamed the WTO for human rights abuses, but during "Occupy Wall Street" some ten years later, the WTO was rarely, if ever, mentioned. The Occupy protestors blamed the banks and complicit governments. He concludes that activists now recognize that member states, which make WTO decisions, are the problem.[15] Shareen Hertel (2005) has a very different take. She believes that protestors made human rights arguments against WTO rules, but did not have a clear argument or understanding of human rights. For example, she stresses that labor rights and human rights were discussed in separate spheres, as if labor rights are not human rights.[16]

In lieu of reviewing activism, other scholars have decided to follow the money—to examine the role of business as a human rights actor conducting trade (Spar 1998; Ottoway 2001; Elliott and Freeman 2003; Aaronson and Higham 2013). University of Memphis professors Robert Blanton and Shannon Blanton have done several studies that examined how human rights conditions might affect business and trade relationships (Blanton and Blanton 2001). They argue that repressive states are tricky trade partners. Because corporations are conscious of their image, executives may seek locales where there is good governance and respect for human rights. Clearly a growing number of firms have been under pressure to monitor how their practices affect human rights, especially in nations with inadequate governance (Cassel 2001; Chandler 2003). Blanton and Blanton argue that "respect for human rights may be the foundation for a 'virtuous cycle' in which citizens have both the skills and motivation to succeed in the global economy" (2008, 103). However, many citizens around the world may feel that globalization is undermining the value of their skills and expertise, and that the cycle is less virtuous than vicious.

The Effects of the Marriage of PTAs and Human Rights: Are Human Rights Conditions Improving?

Although the wedding of trade and human rights in specific trade agreements is a new policy phenomenon, it seems the marriage has been consummated. Policy makers in a growing number of countries are changing how they think about human rights. As a result, more policy makers are respecting human rights norms, as Hafner-Burton (2009) and Bartels (2005a, 2008) have noted.

Mauritania

Mauritania provides an example of how the EU used an FTA to ensure that a government met its commitments to civil and political rights. In 2005, after the military seized power in a coup, the European Commission warned the new government that its behavior had breached that country's commitments under the Cotonou Agreement, the most comprehensive partnership agreement among seventy-nine developing countries in Africa, the Caribbean, and the Pacific. Soon thereafter the new Mauritanian regime pledged to hold free and fair elections and initiated a process to establish an independent National Commission for Human Rights. In 2007 the government held free and fair elections. Political scientist Hafner-Burton concludes that these provisions gave the EU leverage over the government's progress toward reforms (Hafner-Burton 2009, 151–160).

Thailand

Thailand provides a good example of how citizens are monitoring policy makers' adherence to international human rights norms when they make trade policy. In 2003 Thailand began negotiating an FTA with the United States. In 2005 the Thailand National Human Rights Commission drafted a report on the human rights implications of the proposed agreement. Thailand was the first country to do a thorough human rights review of an FTA, expressing concern about traditional knowledge and intellectual property rights. Traditional knowledge can be defined as a knowledge system embedded in the cultural traditions of regional or indigenous communities. It can include knowledge about hunting or agriculture, midwifery, ethnobotany, or ecological knowledge. In recent years indigenous peoples have sought to prevent the patenting of traditional knowledge and resources where they have not given explicit consent. The commission concluded that if the FTA was approved, Thailand might undermine its citizens' human rights.[17] As the report was publicized, growing numbers of Thai citizens began to oppose the agreement. The Thai prime minister pledged to ensure greater public involvement in the negotiating process to shape the agreement.[18] However, the negotiations ended after a military coup on September 19, 2006. In recent years, as Thailand's neighbors have become active participants and demandeurs of FTAs, Thailand has become more willing to negotiate these agreements with the EU, EFTA, and United States. Various NGOs, including human rights NGOs, are closely monitoring these efforts and plan to make sure policy makers pay attention to the human rights implications for Thailand, should FTA negotiations recommence.[19]

Mexico

Mexico provides a real-world example of how trade agreements may encourage policy makers to accept human rights norms. Since joining NAFTA, Mexican trade policy has become more responsive to public concerns about labor rights. For example, the Mexican government, which was long chided for its unwillingness to respect labor rights, began to work internationally to protect its citizens' labor rights. In September 2009 Mexican consulates attempted to educate Mexican guest workers in the United States regarding their labor rights. Moreover, NAFTA leaders meet regularly, and human rights and the rule of law have become important parts of their discussions. Thus, at their meeting in August 2009 the leaders of the three NAFTA countries discussed public health, border controls, and public safety—all issues relating to human rights.[20]

NEXT STEPS: WHAT SHOULD SCHOLARS EXAMINE?

1. While policy makers have examined how some human rights are affected by trade and how some trade agreements affect some human rights, they do not yet know how protecting human rights may facilitate trade or what human rights should be in place to encourage trade. Policy makers should ask whether respect for human rights, such as property rights, needs to be in place for trade to be conducted.
2. While scholars have extensively studied trade and personal integrity rights, workers' rights, and gender, they have paid little attention to other important rights such as privacy or access to information, which are directly affected by trade agreements. In fact, the United States has struggled to balance Internet freedom, the need to surveil Internet users to protect national security and the competitive advantage of its Internet firms to find an effective balance between expanding trade and respecting human rights.

Edward Snowden's revelations about US (and other governments') surveillance of cross-border communications has undermined international efforts to balance privacy, public security, and information flows. Given the importance of the Internet as a platform for trade as well as a medium to enhance human rights, we find it surprising that so few scholars have examined this area where trade and human rights intersect.

When individuals exchange information across borders, they are trading. As citizens, consumers, and producers of information, individuals have a right to privacy when their personal information is exchanged between third parties. Citizens also have the right to have their data be protected from theft or misuse. The EU, Canada, Australia, and New Zealand, among other countries, have strong privacy laws. The EU and Canada include privacy regulations in their trade agreements, although that language is aspirational and not binding.

However, under authority delineated in the USA Patriot Act of 2001, the US National Security Agency routinely examines communications between foreign citizens and US citizens when officials suspect possible links to terrorist activity. In so doing, the United States has violated the privacy of these foreign citizens without their knowledge or permission. American officials claim they are trying to protect human security by monitoring the Internet for terrorists. Although other democracies have acted in a similar manner (monitoring their citizens' online communications),[21] many American allies have not responded positively to Snowden's revelations. For example, some Canadian agencies have refused to send information to the United States through e-mail or data flows; they are concerned that such outsourcing could undermine Canada's security.[22] Several Canadian provinces including British Colombia (BC) and Nova Scotia have enacted legislation to restrict the disclosure of personal information outside Canada and expanded the scope of personal liability and sanctions for contraventions this legislation.[23]

Meanwhile, the United States has become a strong advocate for including language encouraging the free flow of information in its new trade agreements, the Trans-Pacific Partnership (TPP) and the Trans-Atlantic Trade and Investment Partnership (TTIP) (Aaronson and Maxim, forthcoming). The United States wants its trade partners to eliminate barriers to the free flow of information across borders such as restrictions on server location, egregious privacy standards, or censorship and filtering. The United States is the largest source of Internet services and seeks to maintain its comparative advantage. Should it succeed in including these policies in these new trade agreements, the country could simultaneously enhance access to information, facilitate freedom of expression, and maintain the market power of the American Internet industry. However, international support for these provisions seems shaky in light of Snowden's revelations. Other nations are determined to protect their citizens from US surveillance but they also may see an opportunity to gain market share by developing regulations that require information be housed in local servers or maintained by domestic firms.

While other governments have become more determined to protect their citizens' online privacy, US policy makers (at the behest of major firms) have become increasingly concerned that privacy protections can undermine both the free flow of information and Internet industry competitiveness. For example, in its 2013 report on foreign trade barriers, the US Trade Representative (USTR) argued that British Columbia's and

Nova Scotia's privacy laws discriminate against US suppliers because they require that personal information be stored and accessed only in Canada.[24] The USTR claims these laws prevent public bodies from using US services when personal information could be accessed from or stored in the United States.[25] In its 2012 report the United States also cited Australia's approach to privacy, noting Australia's unwillingness to use US companies for hosting due to concerns about privacy violations.[26] In 2013 the USTR noted that negative messaging about US privacy is on the decline, but has not disappeared.[27] The US government also complained about Japan's uneven approach to privacy and Vietnam's unclear approach.[28] Ironically, the United States also argues that China's failure to enforce its privacy laws stifles e-commerce.[29]

The US government is also concerned that some governments have restricted information flows to the United States because of the Patriot Act.[30] However, because of the National Security Agency privacy leaks, the United States may struggle to convince other governments and its own citizens that it fully respects foreigners' privacy rights.

Finally, the US government is closely monitoring how some countries regulate the Internet and the effects of such domestic policies on Internet freedom. For example, in December 2012 the United States extended normal trade relations to Russia and Moldova. The law contains a provision added by the House of Representatives that would expand the scope of the Special 301 report issued by the Office of the US Trade Representative each year. This provision mandates that the report include a description of laws, policies, or practices by the Russian Federation that deny "fair and equitable treatment" to US digital trade.[31]

To some observers, the US approach to digital trade and human rights appears contradictory and ineffective. On the one hand, the United States is pushing for language in trade agreements to facilitate the free flow of information, which could enable more people access to more information. American officials have been forceful and vocal advocates of Internet freedom. Yet at the same time, the United States tries to name and shame governments that are developing data localization policies or local server requirements in the interest of protecting their citizens' privacy. In so doing, the US may encourage other governments to enact policies that favor local firms which respect local privacy standards. Finally, Snowden's revelations have led to distrust among netizens and doubt about U.S. efforts to promote digital rights.

3. Surprisingly, although the WTO's GATT is the main international trade agreement, very few scholars have examined how WTO rules may have direct or indirect human rights spillovers. Moreover, there are few studies that examine how WTO membership affects the behavior of governments regarding human rights.

Mary C. Cooper tried to test the relationship between WTO membership and democratization (as opposed to protecting a particular human right) for the period 1947–1999. She could not determine whether democratic states were more likely to join the WTO or WTO membership makes countries more likely to become or remain democratic (Cooper 2003). Aaronson and Abouharb (2011) tested whether WTO norms, which replicate civil and political rights, due process, access to information (what the WTO calls transparency), and nondiscrimination (evenhandedness) spill over into the polity of member states. Although today policy makers seem more focused on their bilateral and regional FTAs, they are still working with the WTO. We need more information on its influence on human rights.

4. We need a greater understanding of how trade disputes may facilitate greater governmental respect for human rights (or empower individuals to demand their rights).

In 2010 European Commission vice president Neelie Kroes said that China's Internet censorship qualified as a trade barrier that could be challenged in a trade dispute. China's Web filtering and firewall act as trade barriers, and they aren't applied in a uniform and impartial way. In late 2011 the US government sent a letter to the Chinese government asking it to explain inconsistencies in its Internet policies. Under paragraph 4 of Article II of the General Agreement on Trade in Services (GATS), the United States asked China to explain why some foreign sites were inaccessible in China, who decides if and when a foreign website should be blocked, and if China has an appeal procedure for such blockage. Although China is required to respond under the GATS, the US government supposedly did not receive a formal reply. The US Trade Representative has also researched whether it could challenge Chinese Internet restrictions as a violation of WTO rules.[32] However, the United States is unlikely to take this route, as policy makers would not want to create precedents that could limit its or its allies' ability to restrict access to the Internet for national security reasons.[33] Tomer Broude and Holger Hestermeyer (forthcoming) conclude that a trade dispute would not be a good idea, as it is unclear what specific WTO rules have been breached by such censorship. Scholars might provide new insights into whether trade disputes should be utilized in this manner, and if so, how.

5. Is the strategy of linking trade and human rights supportive of internationally accepted human rights? Here again the United States provides a contradictory case study.

On the one hand, it prioritizes certain human rights and makes adherence binding in the trade agreement. On the other hand, it undermines a central ethos of the human rights community: that human rights are universal and indivisible. The EU approach is more supportive of human rights as universal and indivisible, but it appears less effective at achieving human rights improvements. Scholars should examine the pros and cons of each approach.

Moreover, by focusing on specific human rights in its FTAs, the United States ignores the internationally accepted notion that human rights are universal and indivisible, yet it works hard to promote specific human rights and now makes some of these rights binding. In this sense, the United States does more than any other government to link

FTAs and human rights. However, it is essentially saying to its partner nations: make the rights we value top priorities. In this way, the US strategy for linking human rights is insensitive toward other cultures that may have different human rights priorities. This strategy may inspire US trade partners to do more to advance some human rights, but it is unlikely to inspire these governments to devote more resources to human rights in general.

In contrast, the EU includes language supportive of universal human rights as delineated in the Universal Declaration. It requires its developing-country trade partners to accept a clause stipulating that human rights be protected to receive trade benefits. If its partners don't adhere, the EU can suspend trade concessions and reduce foreign aid. However, the EU seems reluctant to use the power inherent in these agreements. It rarely suspends trade concessions, because policy makers believe that the process of dialogue can change hearts and minds (Aaronson and Zimmerman 2007).

6. Countries have a wide range of views about whether they should accept human rights provisions in trade agreements. Scholars should examine what is behind these differing attitudes.

Some nations, such as Australia, have actually refused to negotiate trade agreements with human rights provisions. Yet China has accepted human rights provisions in its PTAs with Chile and New Zealand. How do we explain these differences? Some countries are comfortable using their economic power to promote political change, some are neutral and noninterventionist, and others may be using their acceptance of these provisions to signal investors and funders. Perhaps China sees adopting these provisions as a way to signal foreign investors that it is evenhanded and is attempting to promote the rule of law. Scholars should endeavor to explain why countries respond so differently to the marriage of trade and human rights.

7. Scholars don't know if trade-related incentives work better than disincentives to encourage policy makers to respect and advance human rights. What do incentives or disincentives do for the ability of citizens to demand their rights?

Some countries have decided to use disincentives such as trade sanctions or fines as a means of advancing the human rights embedded in particular trade agreements. However, sanctions or fines can do little to build demand for human rights or to train government officials or factory managers in how to respect such rights. Isolating a government or punishing it will do little to increase the targeted country's commitment to human rights over time. Other countries rely on dialogue to prod changes, but dialogue may do little to encourage a country to change its behavior. Still others rely on incentives. Scholars can do more to help policy makers understand whether these incentives are really effective, and if so, when such incentives should be offered.

8. Human rights provisions in trade agreements have costs as well as benefits.

The world and its people benefit when more governments protect, respect, and realize human rights. Yet some human rights provisions are expensive for developing countries to implement. These governments often have few resources, yet under many recent trade agreements they are tasked with protecting intellectual property, providing access to affordable medicines, and investing in education, among other goals. Often developing-country governments cannot achieve all of these goals and instead must prioritize them. Trade agreements may prod policy makers to turn the human rights priorities of their trade partners into their own human rights priorities. We don't know if this strategy ultimately increases the supply of, and demand for, human rights. To gain better understanding of the costs and benefits of the association of trade and human rights, scholars, policy makers, and activists could use qualitative studies, empirical studies, or human rights impact assessments. Human rights impact assessments are relatively new; they are designed to measure the potential impact of a trade agreement on internationally accepted human rights standards. Trade and human rights policy makers should collaborate with scholars, NGOs, and others to develop a clear and consistent methodology for evaluating such impacts (3D 2009; Walker 2009).

9. We have little insight into whether governments use human rights conditions to justify a trade agreement or relationship.

Some scholars tried to make this case for China, when that country sought to become a member of the WTO. Did human rights improve in China as a result of expanded trade? Which human rights? How did membership in the WTO directly or indirectly affect the ability of Chinese citizens to demand their rights, or the government's willingness to respect particular rights (such as due process or access to information)? Or has expanded trade perpetuated a repressive regime?

Conclusion

Scholars have made great progress in trying to understand the relationship of trade and human rights, but we don't know if it is an enduring match made in heaven, or a match in name only. Scholars have asked and attempted to answer only some of the big questions. They have not researched whether expanded trade encourages (or discourages) public demand for specific human rights. They have not done much work on whether the protection of specific human rights facilitates trade and trade agreements (such as property rights). Moreover, we have little insight into whether governments use human rights conditions to justify a trade agreement or relationship. Empirical scholars need to move beyond labor rights, women's rights, and physical integrity rights to examine other human rights such as privacy, property rights, and access to information. Moreover, because a growing number of countries are linking human rights and trade objectives, scholars need to pay greater attention to what governments are actually doing and which strategies work.

In the world beyond the ivy tower, more countries are joining trade and human rights. If this marriage is to be sustainable, we need greater understanding of whether this union is effective and can or should endure.

ACKNOWLEDGMENT

I am grateful to Rob Maxim and K. Daniel Wang for their editing and research assistance and to Lisa Martin for her advice on this chapter.

NOTES

1. Irwin (1996, 14–16, 21).
2. I asked my research assistant, K. Daniel Wang, to do a general count of articles and books on the trade and human rights relationship since 2001. He found approximately one hundred books and articles.
3. European Commission (2013); Remarks of Industrial Trade Union, p. 5 (http://trade.ec.europa.eu/doclib/docs/2013/july/tradoc_151656.pdf).
4. Reaching for the Clouds, *The Economist*, July 20, 2013, http://www.economist.com/news/europe/21582015-europe-wants-tougher-data-privacy-rules-deter-american-snooping-reaching-clouds.
5. Paragraph 2(a) General 319, GATT Analytical Index, http://www.wto.org/english/res_e/booksp_e/analytic_index_e/gatt1994_04_e.htm#articleXA.
6. International Monetary Fund (2007, 169–172); Jansen and Lee (2007).
7. OECD Secretariat (2005, 3, 9); OECD (2002, 2003, 2004, 2005).
8. On Bangladesh, see Bose (2013) and Greenhouse (2013).
9. Some of these options are listed at http://www.law.harvard.edu/library/research/databases/international-relations.html   and   http://classguides.lib.uconn.edu/content.php?pid=30942&sid=330266.
10. http://www.humanrightsdata.org/faq.asp#2.
11. http://www.serfindex.org/data/ and http://www.serfindex.org/research/.
12. http://www.globalintegrity.org/report.
13. http://www.doingbusiness.org/about-us.
14. http://hdr.undp.org/en/statistics/hdi/.
15. The "Battle in Seattle" refers to the protests that took place during the WTO's Third Ministerial Conference, held in Seattle, Washington, in November–December 1999.
16. Hertel (2005); Compa and Diamond (1996).
17. http://www.measwatch.org/autopage/show_page.php?t=5&s_id=3&d_id=7.
18. PM Calls for More Public Participation in FTA Deals, *MCOT News*, http://www.bilaterals.org/article.php3?id_article=953&var_recherche=public+information (accessed August 3, 2006).
19. http://www.bilaterals.org/spip.php?rubrique117;   http://www.ftawatch.org/;   http://www.ustr.gov/sites/default/files/US--Thailand%20TIFA.pdf;   http://www.ustr.gov/about-us/press-office/press-releases/2013/january/US-Thailand-engagement, all last searched 8/18/2013.

20. US Trade Representative (2009).

21. See for example, Britain, at http://www.theguardian.com/technology/2013/jun/07/ uk-gathering-secret-intelligence-nsa-prism?guni=Article:in%20body%20olink, or France, at http://www.nytimes.com/2013/07/05/world/europe/france-too-is-collecting-d ata-newspaper-reveals.html.

22. Information Technology Association of Canada, Shared Services Canada Takes National Security Exception, http://itac.ca/news/shared_services_canada_takes_national_security_ exception.

23. Jason Young, BC Attempts to Regulate Outsourcing of Personal Information," November 4, 2004, http://www.dww.com/?page_id=1052; Cate (2008, 1–2); and Fred H. Cate, "Provincial Canadian Geographical Restrictions on Personal Data in the Public Sector, Center for Information Leadership, Hunton and Williams, http://www.hunton.com/files/ Publication/2a6f5831-07b6-4300-af8d-ae30386993c1/Presentation/PublicationAttachme nt/0480e5b9-9309-4049-9f25-4742cc9f6dce/cate_patriotact_white_paper.pdf. And Cate, "Private Data in Public Hands," and http://www.hunton.com/files/Publication/ caa02b36-10f1-41eb-8237-90699b4d0777/Presentation/PublicationAttachment/ d63a384c-c51f-47ee-a660-bb9dd470f232/Private_Data_in_Public_Hands.pdf.

24. US Trade Representative (2013, 60–61).

25. USTR Flags Procurement, Data Flow Issues as New Barriers in Canada, *Inside US Trade*, April 27, 2012, http://insidetrade.com/Inside-US-Trade/Inside-US-Trade-04/27/2012/ ustr-flags-procurement-data-flow-issues-as-new-barriers-in-canada/menu-id-710.html.

26. US Trade Representative (2012).

27. US Trade Representative (2013, 31).

28. US Trade Representative (2012, 216).

29. US Trade Representative (2012, 96).

30. US Trade Representative (2012, 166).

31. Sec. 203—Reports on Laws, Policies, and Practices of the Russian Federation That Discriminate Against United States Digital Trade," Russia and Moldova Jackson-Vanik Repeal and Sergei Magnitsky Rule of Law Accountability Act of 2012, Public Law 112-208, http://www.gpo.gov/fdsys/pkg/PLAW-112publ208/html/PLAW-112publ208.htm.

32. Obama Acts on FAC Petition against China's "Great Firewall," *FAC*, October 19, 2011, http://www.firstamendmentcoalition.org/2011/10/obama-acts-on-fac-petition-against-chinas-Internet-censors/.

33. Brendan Greeley and Mark Drajem, China's Face- book Copycats Focus US on Trade as Well as Rights, *Bloomberg/BusinessWeek*, March 10, 2011; letter from Ambassador Michael Puncke, US Ambassador to the WTO, to Ambassador Yi Xiaozhun, Chinese Ambassador to the WTO, and attachment, October 17, 2011, http://insidetrade.com/iwpfile.html?file=0 ct2011%2Fwto2011_2996a.pdf.

REFERENCES AND RECOMMENDED READING

Aaronson, Susan A. 2011. Human Rights. In *Preferential Trade Agreement Policies for Development: A Handbook*, edited by Jean-Pierre Chauffour and Jean-Christophe Maur,. Washington, DC: World Bank Publications, pp. 443–466.

Aaronson, Susan Ariel. 2007. Seeping in Slowly: How Human Rights Concerns Are Penetrating the WTO. *World Trade Review* 6 (3): 413–449.

Aaronson, Susan Ariel. 2002. *Taking Trade to the Streets: The Lost History of Public Efforts to Shape Globalization.* Ann Arbor. University of Michigan Press.

Aaronson, Susan Ariel, and M. Rodwan Abouharb. 2011. Unexpected Bedfellows: The GATT, the WTO and Some Democratic Rights. *International Studies Quarterly* 55 (2): 379–408.

Aaronson, Susan Ariel, and Ian Higham. 2013. "Re-righting Business": John Ruggie and the Struggle to Develop International Human Rights Standards for Transnational Firms. *Human Rights Quarterly* 35 (2): 333–364.

Aaronson, Susan Ariel, and Robert Maxim. Forthcoming. "Trade and the Internet." In *International Political Economy of Trade*, edited by David Deese, Edward Elgar.

Aaronson, Susan Ariel, and Jamie M. Zimmerman. 2007. *Trade Imbalance: The Struggle to Weigh Human Rights Concerns in Trade Policymaking.* Cambridge, U.K. Cambridge University Press.

Apodaca, Clair. 2001. Global Economic Patterns and Personal Integrity Rights after the Cold War. *International Studies Quarterly* 45 (4): 587–602.

Bagwell, Kyle, and Robert W. Staiger. 1998. Will Preferential Agreements Undermine the Multilateral Trading System? *Economic Journal* 108: 1162–1182.

Bartels, Lorand. 2008. *The Application of Human Rights Conditionality in the EU's Bilateral Trade Agreements and Other Trade Arrangements with Third Countries.* Brusel: Evropský parlament.

Bartels, Lorand. 2005a. *Human Rights Conditionality in the EU's International Agreements.* Oxford: Oxford University Press.

Bartels, Lorand. 2005b. The Legality of the EC Mutual Recognition Clause under WTO Law." *Journal of International Economic Law* 8 (3): 691–720.

Bhagwati, Jagdish. 1996. The Demands to Reduce Domestic Diversity among Trading Nations." *Fair Trade and Harmonization: Prerequisites for Free Trade* 1: 9–40.

Blanton, Robert G., and Shannon L. Blanton. 2008. Virtuous or Vicious Cycle? Human Rights, Trade, and Development. In *North and South in the World Political Economy*, edited by Rafael Reuveny and William R. Thompson, 91–103. Malden, MA; Oxford: Blackwell Publishing.

Blanton, Robert. G., and Shannon Lindsey Blanton. 2001. Democracy, Human Rights, and US-Africa Trade. *International Interactions* 27 (3): 275–295.

Bose, Nandita. 2013. Stronger Labor Law in Bangladesh after Garment Factory Collapse. *Reuters,* July 13. http://www.reuters.com/article/2013/07/15/us-bangladesh-labour-idUSBRE 96E05R20130715.

Broude, Tomer. 2013. From Seattle to "Occupy": Trade, Human Rights and the Shifting Focus of Social Protest. in Daniel Drache and Les Jacobs, eds., The Changing Global Landscape for International Trade and Human Rights Linkages (app. 16 pages) (forthcoming) (Oxford: Routledge, 2013).

Broude, Tomer, and Holger P. Hestermeyer. Forthcoming. The First Condition of Progress? Freedom of Speech and the Limits of International Trade Law. *Virginia Journal of International Law.* (Abstract at http://ssrn.com/abstract=2260969.)

Büthe, Tim, and Helen V. Milner. 2008. The Politics of Foreign Direct Investment into Developing Countries: Increasing FDI Through International Trade Agreements? *American Journal of Political Science* 52 (4): 741–762.

Cao, Xun, Brian Greenhill, and Aseem Prakash. 2013. Where Is the Tipping Point? Bilateral Trade and the Diffusion of Human Rights. *British Journal of Political Science* 43 (1): 133–156.

Cassel, Douglass. 2001. Human Rights and Business Responsibilities in the Global Marketplace. *Business Ethics Quarterly:* 261–274.

Cate, Fred H. 2008. Provincial Canadian Geographic Restrictions on Personal Data in the Public Sector. Centre for Information Policy Leadership, Submitted to the Trilateral Committee on Transborder Data Flows.

Cate, Fred H. 2010, "Private Data in Public Hands," Speech to 11th Annual Privacy and Security Conference," Victoria, British Columbia.

Chandler, Geoffrey. 2003. The Evolution of the Business and Human Rights Debate." In *Business and Human Rights: Dilemmas and Solutions*, edited by Rory Sullivan, 22–32. Greenleaf Publishing.

Charnovitz, Steve. 2005. The Labor Dimension of the Emerging Free Trade Area of the Americas. In *Labor Rights as Human Rights*, edited by Philip Alston, Oxford: Oxford University Presspp. 143–176.

Charnovitz, Steve. 2001. The WTO and the Rights of the Individual. *Intereconomics* 36 (2): 98–108.

Compa, Lance, and Stephen Diamond, eds. 1996. *Human Rights, Labor Rights and International Trade*. Philadelphia: University of Pennsylvania Press.

Cooper, Mary Comerford. 2003. International Organizations and Democratization: Testing the Effect of GATT/WTO Membership. Asia Pacific Research Center, April. http://www.kenanflagler.unc.edu/KI/kiWashington/humanRightsAndTrade/hrtLibrary.

Dobbin, Frank, Beth Simmons, and Geoffrey Garrett. 2007. The Global Diffusion of Public Policies: Social Construction, Coercion, Competition, or Learning? *Annual Review of Sociology* 33: 449.

Dollar, David, 1992. "Outward-Oriented Developing Economies Really Do Grow More Rapidly: Evidence from 95 LDCs, 1976-1985," *Economic Development and Cultural Change*, University of Chicago Press, 40(3), pp. 523–44.

Elliott, Kimberly Ann, and Richard B. Freeman. 2003. *Can Labor Standards Improve under Globalization?* Washington: D.C. Peterson Institute Press/All Books.

European Commission. 2013. Update on the Transatlantic Trade and Investment Partnership (TTIP)—First Negotiation Round. *Civil Society Dialogue*, July 16.

Greenhill, Brian. 2010. The Company You Keep: International Socialization and the Diffusion of Human Rights Norms. *International Studies Quarterly* 54 (1): 127–145.

Greenhill, Brian, Layna Mosley and Aseem Prakash 2009 "Trade-Based Diffusion of labor rights: A Panel Study, 1986-2002. *American Political Science Review* 103 (4): 669–691.

Greenhouse, Stephen. 2013. Bangladesh Adopts New Labor Law. *New York Times*, July 16. http://www.nytimes.com/2013/07/17/world/asia/under-pressure-bangladesh-adopts-new-labor-law.html?_r=0.

Hafner-Burton, Emilie. 2009. *Forced to Be Good: Why Trade Agreements Boost Human Rights*. Ithaca, NY: Cornell University Press.

Hafner-Burton, Emilie M. 2005. Right or Robust? The Sensitive Nature of Repression to Globalization. *Journal of Peace Research* 42 (6): 679–698.

Hafner-Burton, Emilie M., and James Ron. 2009. Seeing Double: Human Rights Impact Through Qualitative and Quantitative Eyes. *World Politics* 61 (2): 360–401.

Hafner-Burton, Emilie M., and Kiyoteru Tsutsui. 2005. Human Rights in a Globalizing World: The Paradox of Empty Promises. *American Journal of Sociology* 110 (5): 1373–1411.

Harrelson-Stephens, Julie, and Rhonda Callaway. 2003. Does Trade Openness Promote Security Rights in Developing Countries? Examining the Liberal Perspective. *International Interactions* 29 (2): 143–158.

Hertel, Shareen. 2005. What Was All the Shouting About: Strategic Bargaining and Protest at the WTO Third Ministerial Meeting. *Human Rights Review* 6 (3): 102–118.

Howse, Robert. 2002. Human Rights in the WTO: Whose Rights, What Humanity? Comment on Petersmann. *European Journal of International Law* 13 (3): 651–659.

International Monetary Fund. 2007. Chapter 5: The Globalization of Labor. *World Economic Outlook* (October). http://www.imf.org/external/pubs/ft/weo/2007/01/pdf/c5.pdf.

Irwin, Douglas A. 1996. *Against the Tide: An Intellectual History of Free Trade.* Princeton, NJ: Princeton University Press.

Jansen, Marion, and Eddy Lee. 2007. *Trade and Employment: Challenges for Policy Research; A Joint Study of the International Labour Office and the Secretariat of the World Trade Organization.* International Labour Organization.

Korinek, Jane. 2005. *Trade and Gender: Issues and Interactions.* OECD Trade Policy Working Paper No. 24. Paris, France: OECD Publishing.

Lang, Andrew T. F. 2007. The Role of the Human Rights Movement in Trade Policy-Making: Human Rights as a Trigger for Policy Learning. *NZJPIL* 5: 77–102.

Levy, Philip I. 1999. Sanctions on South Africa: What Did They Do? Yale Economic Growth Center, Discussion Paper No. 796.

Mansfield, Edward D., and Jon C. Pevehouse. 2008. Democratization and the Varieties of International Organizations." *Journal of Conflict Resolution* 52 (2): 269–294.

Milner, Wesley T. 2002. Economic Globalization and Rights. In *Globalization and Human Rights*, edited by Alison Brysk,. Oakland: CA. University of California Press.

Mosley, Layna. 2008. Workers' Rights in Open Economies Global Production and Domestic Institutions in the Developing World. *Comparative Political Studies* 41 (4–5): 674–714.

Mosley, Layna, and Saika Uno. 2007. Racing to the Bottom or Climbing to the Top? Economic Globalization and Collective Labor Rights. *Comparative Political Studies* 40 (8): 923–948.

OECD. 2002. *Babies and Bosses: Reconciling Work and Family Life.* Volume 1, *Reconciling Work and Family Life in Australia, Denmark and the Netherlands.* Paris: OECD. (Volume 1, 2002; Volume 2, 2003; Volume 3, 2004; Volume 4, 2005).

OECD Secretariat. 2005. Aging Populations: High Time for Action. Background Paper Prepared for the Meeting of G-8 Employment and Labour Ministers, London, 10–11 March. http://www.oecd.org/dataoecd/61/50/34600619.pdf.

Ottaway, Marina. 2001, "Reluctant Missionaries. http://www.foreignpolicy.com/articles/2001/07/01/reluctant_missionaries.

Paul, Joel R. 2003. Do International Trade Institutions Contribute to Economic Growth and Development. *Virginia Journal of International Law* 44: 285.

Rodrik, Dani. 2000. *Trade Policy Reform as Institutional Reform.* Cambridge, MA: Harvard University Press.

Roosevelt, Franklin D. 1941. Four Freedoms Speech: Annual Message to Congress on the State of the Union, January 1. http://www.fdrlibrary.marist.edu/pdfs/fftext.pdf.

Sachs, Jeffrey D., and Andrew M. Warner. 1995. *Economic Convergence and Economic Policies.* No. 5039. Cambridge: MA., National Bureau of Economic Research.

Seguino, Stephanie, and Caren Grown. 2006. Gender Equity and Globalization: Macroeconomic Policy for Developing Countries. *Journal of International Development* 18 (8): 1081–1104.

Sen, Amartya. 1999. *Development as Freedom.* Oxford University Press.

Spar, Debora L. 1998. The Spotlight and the Bottom Line: How Multinationals Export Human Rights. *Foreign Affairs* 77, 2: 7–12.

Sykes, Alan O. 2003. *"International Trade and Human Rights: An Economic Perspective."* Law and Economics Working Paper No 188, University of Chicago Law School.

Temin, Peter. 2003 Mediterranean Trade in Biblical Times. In *Eli Heckscher, International Trade, and Economic History*, edited by Ronald Findlay, 141–156.

3D. 2009. Insights on Human Rights Impact Assessments of Trade Policies and Agreements. Geneva. http://www.humanrights.ch/upload/pdf/100607_09_HRIA_3D_berblick.pdf.

US Trade Representative. 2009. Joint Statement of the 2009 NAFTA Commission Meeting. http://www.ustr.gov/about-us/press-office/press-releases/2009/october/joint-statement-2 009-nafta-commission-meeting.

US Trade Representative. 2012. 2012 National Trade Estimate Report of Foreign Trade Barriers. http://www.ustr.gov/sites/default/files/NTE Final Printed_0.pdf.

US Trade Representative. 2013. 2013 National Trade Estimate Report on Foreign Trade Barriers. March. http://www.ustr.gov/sites/default/files/2013%20NTE.pdf.

van Hees, Floris. 2004. *Protection V. Protectionism: The Use of Human Rights Arguments in the Debate for and Against the Liberalisation of Trade*. Åbo akademi Turku, Finland.

Walker, Simon. M. 2009. The Future of Human Rights Impact Assessments of Trade Agreements. *School of Human Rights Research Series* 35: (2009).

World Trade Organization. 2013. General Agreement on Tariffs and Trade 1994. Geneva: WTO *WTO Analytical Index*.

CHAPTER 27

··

TRADE AND MIGRATION

··

MARGARET E. PETERS

As citizens, policy makers, and scholars, we do not often think about trade and migration as linked: trade in goods seems to be an activity of profit-motivated firms, whereas migration is an act of people for a myriad of economic and personal reasons. Yet from some of our earliest models of trade, trade and migration have been linked through their effects on prices for goods and the returns to the factors of production (people and capital). In the Stolper-Samuelson (1948) model of trade and factor mobility, trade leads to the equalization of goods prices and from there to the equalization of factor prices. Likewise, factor mobility leads to the equalization of factor prices and from there to the equalization of goods prices. Mundell (1957) argues that under this model, free trade should decrease the demand for migration—if wages are the same in two countries there would be little reason to migrate—and migration should dampen the demand for trade—as migration would lead to more equal wages and more equal goods prices. Further trade barriers should stimulate factor mobility, assuming the factors can move, and barriers to the movement of capital or people should lead to increased trade, assuming there are few barriers to trade. Thus, our classic economic models of trade suggest that it is deeply tied to issues of both capital mobility and migration.

These classic models, of course, rely on many assumptions about the nature of trade between two countries, some of the most important assumptions being that the countries have identical technologies; consumers in both countries have identical preferences driven by cost rather than love of variety; production is characterized by perfect competition; and there are no domestic economic distortions (e.g., taxes, subsidies) in either country (Markusen 1983, 342). Markusen argues that when we relax these assumptions, we find that trade and factor movements can be complements instead of substitutes. Similarly, theories of intra-industry trade (e.g., Melitz 2003) argue that consumers gain from trade due to an increase in variety instead of simply from decreased prices of goods. Other scholars (e.g., Gould 1994) argue that a desire for variety can also make migration and trade complementary. I discuss below when it is likely that greater trade leads to more migration, when it leads to less migration, and vice versa.

While scholars have devoted considerable attention to the issues of trade and capital mobility (see Copelovitch and Pevehouse 2014 in this volume Should there be a link to the Copelovitch and Pevehouse piece and should it be listed at 2015?), they have devoted less attention to connections between trade and migration. This lacuna is due in part to the lack of attention paid to migration in the international political economy (IPE) literature in general. For example, Keohane and Milner note that "since labor moves much less readily across national borders than goods or capital, we have not considered migration as part of internationalization.... [I]n future work, serious attention should be given to including migration in the analysis of internationalization" (1996, 258). Lake's (2009) review of open economy politics (OEP) mentions "trade" seventy-eight times, "capital" twelve times, and "immigration" three times. Oatley's (2011) critique of OEP mentions tariffs, monetary and exchange rate policies, and investment flows, but not migration.

Migration has been relatively understudied because it was not seen as an important policy issue when the field of IPE began in the 1960s and 1970s. At the time migration was at historically low levels for several reasons: emigration was restricted from the Communist bloc countries; most of Western Europe was relatively wealthy, giving Europeans few reasons to migrate; and most of the rest of the world was still poor enough, given transportation costs, to make migration almost impossible. Today, of course, migration has become a much larger issue as the flows of migrants have increased.

In response to the increased attention paid to migration by policy makers and the public, scholars have also increased their study of migration. There are three main areas of study that have linked trade and migration. The first seeks to understand public opinion on trade and immigration. Given that trade and immigration should have similar effects on the wages people earn and the prices they pay for goods, many have argued that public opinion on these two flows should be similar. The literature has consistently found that this is not the case and has explored two main explanations: the fiscal effects of immigrants (Hanson, Scheve, and Slaughter 2007) and the cultural effects of immigrants (Hainmueller and Hiscox 2007, 2010).

Second, scholars have sought to understand how trade and immigration policy affect each other. They have found that trade policy and immigration policy are substitutes. Hatton and Williamson (2005, 2007) focus on how individual level preferences, driven by the fiscal costs of immigrants and/or immigrants' effects on inequality, lead to policy change. Peters (2014, 2015) examines how trade affects business preferences for immigration. Closed trade leads to an increase in businesses that use much immigrant labor, and open trade leads to the closure of these businesses. Trade policy thus affects the average business demand for immigration openness. Similarly, immigration policy may affect trade policy: businesses that are uncompetitive internationally can be made more competitive using immigrant labor (Peters 2014, 2015). This makes these firms more supportive of trade openness than they would have been in the absence of immigration openness.

Finally, scholars have examined how immigration and trade flows affect each other. It has long been hoped by policy makers that open trade will lead to decreased migration. Here, it is thought that open trade will lead to increased trade flows, which in turn will lead to increased development and a lower demand for migration. This logic was used to help sell the North American Free Trade Agreement (NAFTA) as a way to decrease Mexican migration (Uchitelle 2007). Similarly, European policy makers have often opened trade with new members of the European Union (EU) prior to opening their labor markets to migration in hopes that open trade would increase development in new member states and decrease migration (Geddes and Money 2011). While this may be true in the long run, scholars have found that in the short run trade can be disruptive to local economies, paradoxically resulting in more migration (Bacon 2012; Sassen 1988).

Scholars have also studied how increased migration can increase trade flows (e.g., Gould 1994). In this line of research, it is argued that migrants can increase trade because they want goods from home that are not available in their new country, which increases imports, and are parts of networks that can facilitate overseas trade, increasing both imports and exports.

Trade and migration thus are linked in important ways: at times they act as a substitute for each other, and at times they are complements. These different effects can influence how the public perceives these flows; how interest groups, including firms, approach these flows; and how policy makers respond to these flows. The first section of this chapter discusses the classic approaches to trade and migration from economics. I then review the public opinion literature on trade and migration. In the third section I examine how trade and migration policies can interact. The fourth section discusses how trade and migration flows affect each other. Finally, I conclude with some thoughts on new areas for research.

Standard Approaches to Trade and Migration

Trade and migration have been linked by economists through the Stolper-Samuelson model of trade (e.g., Samuelson 1948). In this model, there are two countries (A and B) and two factors of production, capital and labor (or land and labor). One country (Country A) is relatively abundant in capital but scarce in labor, and the other (Country B) is relatively abundant in labor but scarce in capital. The important thing to note is that the countries are relatively abundant or scarce in the factors; one country may have an absolute advantage in both labor and capital. Because Country A is relatively abundant in capital, capital is relatively cheap and labor is relatively expensive (wages are high); similarly, because Country B is relatively abundant in labor, labor is relatively cheap (wages are low) and capital is relatively expensive. Goods made with capital (labor) are relatively cheap (expensive) in Country A, and goods made with labor (capital) are relatively cheap (expensive) in Country B.

If the two countries were to open migration, people would migrate from Country B to Country A, because the wages in Country A are higher than they are in Country

B. Wages would decrease in Country A as the supply of labor increased; wages would increase in Country B as the supply of labor decreased. People would continue to move until wages equalized. At this point, both countries would have the same ratio of capital to labor, the same wages, and the same returns to capital. Goods would be the same price, as the inputs—capital and labor—would cost the same in the two countries.

If the two countries were to open trade instead, goods made mostly with labor (*labor-intensive goods*) would be exported from Country B to Country A, since they are cheaper in Country B, and goods made mostly with capital (*capital-intensive goods*) would be exported from Country A to Country B, since they are relatively cheaper in Country A. Because labor-intensive goods imported from Country B are cheaper than those made in Country A, companies in Country A that make labor-intensive goods would go out of business (or reinvest their capital in the production of the capital-intensive good) and lay off their workers. This would increase the supply of workers in Country A relative to the number of jobs, leading to a decrease in wages. In Country B, the reverse would happen. Because companies that make labor-intensive goods are increasing production to export goods to Country A, their demand for labor would go up. This would decrease the supply of workers in Country B relative to the number of jobs, leading to an increase in wages. Trade would therefore eventually lead to the equalization of wages.

Under the Stolper-Samuelson model, trade and migration have the same effect on wages and prices. Opening trade or migration decrease wages in Country A and increases wages in Country B, leading to equalization of the prices of goods. Closing trade and migration has the reverse effect: wages increase in Country A and decrease in Country B, and prices would diverge.

Given these similar effects, Mundell (1957) argued that closing trade could spur factor movements, assuming that factors are allowed to move. Although he examined the effect of trade and capital movement, his argument could easily apply to migration. If trade is closed, wages in Country A will be higher than in Country B. Assuming that there is no impediment to moving, people should move from Country A to Country B until wages equalize. Thus, if a country closes trade, it should expect more migration—emigration if it is relatively labor abundant and immigration if it is relatively labor scarce. Over time, wages will tend to converge. At this point, trade would decrease regardless of the country's openness to it. In this model, to produce one capital-intensive widget takes the same amount of capital and labor in Country A as in Country B; similarly, it takes the same amount of labor and capital to produce one labor-intensive widget in both countries. Because the costs of labor and capital are the same in both countries, the prices of the capital- and labor-intensive goods are equal in both countries. Note, however, that these results rely on the assumptions that goods are made with the same technology in both countries, so that the equal price of inputs leads to equal costs; that production has constant returns to scale, so that having one country specialize in the production of one good does not lead to cost savings; and that there is perfect competition in each country, so that marginal price equals the marginal cost. Under these strong assumptions, there is no reason to trade. In practice, wages will tend to converge over the long run, but it is unlikely that there would be no trade, because these assumptions do not hold fully.

Similarly, if a state closes migration, trade should increase, assuming that there are no impediments to trade. Labor-intensive goods would be exported from Country B to Country A, and capital-intensive goods would be exported from Country A to Country B. Wages would eventually equalize; at this point the two states could remove any barriers to migration without their removal leading to much migration, as wages would be the same. Thus, in the Mundell model trade and migration are substitutes.

While the Stolper-Samuelson model and the Mundell model are helpful for understanding much of the relationship between trade and migration, the results of these models rely on several assumptions that may or may not hold. Markusen (1983) provides several reasons why trade and migration might be complements instead of substitutes; among the most important are different production technologies, production taxes, monopolies, economies of scale, and distortions in the factor (labor or capital) markets. In each case, one industry has a special advantage when it comes to trade that it would not otherwise have. For example, if labor-intensive goods have a special advantage in Country A, say due to technology that leads to increased productivity, it will export those goods instead of capital-intensive goods. Factor mobility will lead to more inputs going into the sector with the special advantage instead of the disadvantaged sector. In the example above, migration will lead to increased labor in the labor-intensive sector in Country A, decreasing the price of labor-intensive goods further and leading to more trade.

Similarly, as long as consumers like variety, states with similar factor endowments trade goods in the same industry (intra-industry trade). For example, the United States and Germany, both relatively capital abundant states, trade Fords for Volkswagens. Migration could be a complement to trade if, as we will see below, migration leads to a desire for a greater variety of products. Thus, there are numerous reasons why trade and migration would be complements rather than substitutes.

The importance of this discussion is that whether trade and migration are substitutes or complements is likely to affect the politics of these two flows differently, as we will see below.

OPINIONS ON TRADE AND MIGRATION

One area of research that examines the interplay of trade and migration is public opinion. Most scholars start from the Stolper-Samuelson model, which suggests that respondents should view trade and migration similarly. In many of these studies, the model relies on a different set of factors of production than the canonical model; namely, high-skill and low-skill labor, instead of capital and labor, as the main factors of production. Nonetheless, the results are the same: in states that are high-skill labor abundant (developed states), opening trade or migration should lead to an increase in wages for high-skill labor and a decrease in wages for low-skill labor. In states that are low-skill labor abundant (developing states), opening trade or migration should lead to an increase in wages for low-skill labor and a decrease in wages for high-skill labor.

Survey respondents should favor trade and/or immigration based on these effects, and their responses on these two issue areas should be similar. In a country like the United States, high-skill survey respondents should favor open trade and open immigration for low-skill workers and immigration restrictions for high-skill workers. Low-skill survey respondents should favor restrictions on trade and low-skill immigration and favor openness for high-skill immigration. However, the survey data do not show this (Goldstein and Peters 2014; Hainmueller and Hiscox 2007, 2010; Hanson, Scheve, and Slaughter 2007; Malhotra, Margalit, and Mo 2013; Mayda 2008). Instead, high-skill respondents tend to like trade and immigration of both high- and low-skill immigrants more than low-skill respondents. Further, over the entire population, trade, even with developing countries, is usually greatly preferred to immigration, especially low-skill immigration.

Scholars have posited several different reasons for this difference on opinions between trade and immigration. Hanson, Scheve, and Slaughter (2007) argue that the difference is caused by the fiscal effects of immigrants. Unlike goods, immigrants use the social welfare system. Thus, high-skill natives may oppose low-skill immigration to a greater degree than trade, because low-skill immigrants are more likely to use the social welfare system, leading to an increase in taxes. Low-skill natives may also dislike low-skill immigrants for their use of the social welfare system, as it may lead to crowding out. Nonetheless, trade may also have these effects: increased trade may lead to fewer job opportunities and increasing natives' use of social welfare programs, leading to crowding out or increased taxation.

Mayda (2008) argues that the difference in views is driven by the difference in exposure to trade and immigration in the labor market. She finds that respondents who work in nontradable sectors are more pro-free trade than people who work in tradable sectors. Because these respondents do not face job competition from trade, they view trade more positively, as consumers who benefit from it. In contrast, immigrants can penetrate all sectors of the economy, which leads to the greater fear of labor market competition from immigrants and greater opposition to immigration. Yet immigration also does not have an impact on most respondents. While in the United States the overall share of the foreign born population is 12 percent, immigrants are disproportionately represented in a few industries, including agriculture, construction, textiles, and low-skill services. Similar patterns of employment are found in European countries. Moreover, many studies have found that immigration leads natives to up-skill, giving them more economic opportunity than they had before (e.g., Strauss 2012). Many natives thus face little labor market competition from immigration or trade, making their divergence on these issues puzzling.

Hainmueller and Hiscox (2007, 2010) argue that it is probably differences in the cultural costs of trade and immigration that lead to the differences in responses. They argue that education, usually used to measure skill level, also measures tolerance. As part of education, we are also taught tolerance; thus, those respondents who are more educated will express more tolerance, or at least be unwilling to express intolerance. Thus it is the cultural animus of the less educated that is driving their different preferences for immigration and trade.

Recently, two studies have taken a more nuanced view. Malhotra, Margalit, and Mo (2013) show that cultural animus and economic threat are both a factor. They find that information technology (IT) workers are more likely to oppose immigration of other IT workers but are no more opposed to immigration of other immigrants than other similarly skilled natives. Goldstein and Peters (2014) argue that cultural animus can affect the baseline preferences people have about immigration, but that shocks to economic circumstances can lead to changes in opinion. They examine a six-year panel survey conducted during the Great Recession to see how opinions change with large shocks to the economic system. As expected, those who have suffered during the Great Recession are more anti-immigrant than those who did not. Thus, it is likely that both cultural animus (or tolerance) and economic threat affect opinions on immigration and, to a lesser extent, on trade.

In all, the puzzle of why survey respondents are more anti-immigrant than anti-trade has not yet been resolved. Yet perhaps it does not matter what opinions respondents hold on these issues if their opinions do not affect policy outcomes. While there is some research on whether/when public opinion affects policy (Peters and Tahk 2011), there is much room for more research on this topic as well.

Ties Between Trade and Migration Policy

Researchers have also focused on the link between trade and migration policies in developed countries. Immigration and trade policy in developed countries have tended to move in opposite directions: trade closure was paired with immigration openness prior to World War II, and trade openness has been paired with immigration restrictions since World War II. These policy combinations are somewhat surprising from a political standpoint. The Stolper-Samuelson model shows that openness (closure) to trade or immigration will lead to lower (higher) wages for low-skill labor and higher (lower) wages for high-skill labor and higher (lower) returns to capital. Thus, if a policy maker wants to protect native low-skill labor, she or he should restrict both trade and immigration. On the other hand, if the policy maker wants to help native high-skill labor and capital, she or he could open either or both flows. By this logic, states' choices of policy should be idiosyncratic, or all should open in tandem, since opening any one flow would lead to the same distributional consequences as opening the other. Yet empirically, trade and immigration policy are rarely opened together, nor do states seem to choose these policies idiosyncratically. To explain the patterns of policy, scholars have focused on three explanations: the rise of the welfare state, the extension of the franchise, and the effects of trade on firms.

Hatton and Williamson (2005, 2007) focus on two explanations for the pattern of trade and immigration openness: the rise of the welfare state and the expansion of the franchise. The rise of the welfare state argument is similar to that of the fiscal costs argument in the public opinion literature. Once states had welfare systems, immigrants became costly to society, as immigrants are (or are thought to be) more likely than natives to use the welfare system. Natives opposed immigration more because they feared having to pay higher taxes or face crowding out. There are two problems with this argument. First, as noted above, trade has also caused much, if not more, job dislocation, leading to increased use of the welfare system by natives. Thus, if natives are concerned about the costs of the welfare system or crowding out, they should also oppose trade openness. Second, there were concerns about immigrants' use of the social welfare system as early as the colonial period in the United States. Neuman (1993) argues that many US states passed laws against immigration in part due to immigrants' use of poor relief. Thus, immigrants' use of the welfare system was nothing new in the mid-twentieth century, when many of the new restrictions on immigration were put into place and trade was opened.

Hatton and Williamson's (2005, 2007) second argument focuses on how immigration increases inequality and how that, combined with the increase in the franchise, leads to immigration restrictions. As the franchise expanded, those who competed directly with immigrants were more likely to vote for immigration restrictions, and/or middle-class voters did not like the increasing inequality from immigration and voted for immigration restrictions as well. Again, the problem with this argument is that trade also causes inequality in developed countries and may have increased inequality to a greater degree than immigration. Thus, if voters are worried about inequality, they should also have been against free trade.

Hatton and Williamson's (2005, 2007) research, like the public opinion literature, is based on how individuals perceive trade and immigration; however, they apply a median voter model to these opinions to say something about policy. Instead of focusing on how trade and migration affect individuals, Peters (2014, 2015) examines how trade and migration affect firms and in turn, how this affects firm lobbying on these two issues.

Peters (2014, 2015) also uses Stolper-Samuelson as a starting point. In labor scarce states, opening trade would lead to the export of capital-intensive goods and the import of labor-intensive goods. Labor-intensive industries would then shrink in size as they could not compete with the imported goods. As the Stolper-Samuelson model predicts, these industries would lay off their workers, which would not be absorbed entirely by the export industries. These layoffs would lead to a decrease in wages across society.

Overall, as the demand for labor in open labor-scarce states decreases, so too does the incentive for firms to lobby for immigration. Some labor-intensive firms that had lobbied for open immigration no longer exist, having been forced to close due to trade pressure. These firms lay off their workers, which decreases the wage that all other firms have to pay. Existing firms may in general want increased immigration, but they have limited resources to spend on lobbying; money (effort) spent on lobbying could always be spent in other aspects of the business or spent lobbying on other, now more pressing issues. As their labor costs decrease due to the layoffs caused by increased trade, firms decrease their lobbying on immigration. Given the existence of groups that oppose immigration, the decrease in lobbying allows policy makers to restrict immigration.

Similarly, closure to trade would lead to an increase in support for immigration and immigration openness. Closure to trade increases the size of the import-competing sector, as consumers can no longer buy imported goods and instead turn to domestically produced goods. The import-competing sector is labor intensive and will thus increase the overall economy's demand for labor, pushing up wages throughout the economy. As demand for labor increases, so too should lobbying for immigration by firms, which leads policy makers to open immigration (Peters 2014, 2015).

Immigration may also affect support for trade, at least in the short run. Immigration makes import-competing firms in labor-scarce states more competitive, by driving down labor costs. This may make import-competing firms more supportive of free trade, as it is less likely that they will be forced out of business with trade openness (Peters 2015).

While an open immigration policy may support free trade in the short run, free trade will likely undermine open immigration in the long run. As trade opens further—either through decreasing tariffs and nontariff barriers more or decreasing them on more goods—immigration would have to open further to keep import-competing firms competitive. In order to keep firms competitive as trade opens, policy makers would have to open immigration enough so that, eventually, wages would equalize. As discussed above, immigration is not politically popular for several reasons, which makes it hard for policy makers to open immigration enough to keep firms competitive. At this point, some firms will close, reducing the economy-wide need for labor and allowing the policy maker to restrict immigration (Peters 2015).

This experience of immigration policy supporting trade policy may help explain why Western European countries were able to open their economies to trade after World War II. Many of these countries, notably West Germany, France, and the Netherlands, had guest worker programs that allowed their firms to hire thousands of foreign workers. Many of these migrants worked in sectors that were relatively uncompetitive. Even with the immigrant labor, many of these industries closed, as they could not compete as trade opened further. At this point, support for immigration declined, and labor migration was largely curtailed throughout Europe (Peters 2015).

Thus the empirical regularity we see of open immigration, closed trade and open trade, closed immigration is driven by firms. Firms are affected by trade, which in turn affects their preferences for immigration. The level of trade openness affects the average firm-level demand for immigration and the amount of lobbying by firms for immigration. Immigration policy may also affect trade policy by making relatively uncompetitive firms more competitive, but it is unlikely that immigration will be able to support all uncompetitive firms, especially as trade opens further.

TRADE AND MIGRATION FLOWS

Finally, we can consider how trade and migration flows affect one another. The Stolper-Samuelson model predicts that increased trade flows should lead to less migration and vice versa. Increased trade flows should lead to equalization of wages across borders, reducing much of the demand to migrate, and increased migration flows should lead to the equalization of prices, reducing the demand to trade most goods. Yet the data are inconsistent with the Stolper-Samuelson model to some extent. In the short run, trade flows seem to lead to more migration, but in the long run trade flows do seem to lead to equalization of wages and less migration. In contrast, so far the data suggest that migration leads to increased trade in the short and long runs.

In the short run, trade flows affect the desire and ability of potential migrants to emigrate by disrupting the traditional economy and removing the cost constraint on migrating. Trade flows often disrupt the traditional economy. One recent example of this was Mexico's decision, due to its commitments under NAFTA, to reduce its tariffs on US corn. This decision severely disrupted small-scale agriculture in Mexico, resulting in a loss of jobs for agricultural laborers (Bacon 2012). These laborers, then, were forced to find employment elsewhere, including migrating to the United States.

This phenomenon has not been limited to Mexico. World systems scholars, most notably Sassen (1988), have argued that increased globalization has led to increased immigration. Trade, as in the Mexican case, leads to the displacement of workers who were employed in the import-competing sector in developing countries. This increases the benefits of migration, as there are fewer economic opportunities at home. Further, increased trade also often comes with increased foreign direct investment in many developing countries. These investments, often in factories, lead to "stepping-stone migration." Poor migrants from the countryside first move to cities within their country (or a neighboring developing country) to work in the factories; once they have enough money saved for the journey to a developed state, they migrate internationally. For example, rural Mexicans have long migrated first to the factories on the border with the United States and then to the United States, once they have saved enough money for the journey (Fernandez-Kelly 1983).

In addition to disrupting the traditional economy, trade can also increase the resources that potential migrants have for migrating. Lopez and Schiff (1998) focus on how trade can release the cost constraint on migration. Migration is relatively costly for most potential migrants. They have to have the funds to pay the cost of transportation to the new location, the cost of a visa if they migrate legally or the cost of smuggling if they migrate illegally, and the cost of supporting themselves both during the journey and in their new location until they get a new job. Further, potential migrants often live in countries that are credit constrained; as such, many migrants have to save for their journey before they can migrate. Trade helps to release the cost constraint by providing an increase in income for low-wage workers in developing nations, which allows them to save more and have a greater ability to migrate (Lopez and Schiff 1998). Thus, trade may increase the desire to migrate by reducing job opportunities in the traditional economy in developing countries as well as increasing the ability to migrate by releasing the cost constraint.

In the long run, however, there is evidence that trade helps to decrease the incentives to migrate, as predicted by the Stolper-Samuelson Model. Hatton and Williamson (1998, 2005) and O'Rourke and Williamson (1999) provide evidence that European wages increased throughout the late nineteenth and early twentieth centuries, converging to American and other New World country wages. Part of the convergence was driven by migration, which drastically lowered unemployment and underemployment, and part of it was driven by development of European economies, which in turn was driven in part by trade. Thus, trade and migration helped lead to the convergence of wages in the Atlantic economy.

Policy makers, using the Stolper-Samuelson model and the evidence of convergence in wages in the Atlantic economy, have often sold free trade as a way to decrease immigration. For example, it was argued by US policy makers that NAFTA would help curb Mexican migration to the United States (Uchitelle 2007). While Mexican migration increased directly after NAFTA, recently it has been falling and now is at net-zero levels. Part of the reason for the decline in Mexican migration has been the poor state of the US economy in recent years, but the other part has been the growth of the Mexican economy, in part driven by increased trade. Similarly, the EU has always kept restrictions on freedom of movement from new, poorer member states longer than restrictions on free trade. It was argued in the EU case that free trade (and free capital movement) would help these new EU members develop, leading to less migration once the borders were opened (Geddes and Money 2011). In the case of the EU, migration too has often increased in the short term but has decreased over time as new members have become more developed, thanks in part to trade.

Migration flows have also been found to increase trade flows (e.g., Dunlevy and Hutchinson 1999; Dunlevy 2006; Felbermayr and Jung 2009; Felbermayr and Toubal 2012; Gould 1994; Hatzigeorgiou 2010; Head and Ries 1998; Herander and Saavedra 2005; Rauch and Trindade 2002). There are two main reasons why migration increases trade: preferences for home goods and increased information. Migrants bring with them preferences for goods that are only produced at home. Once they migrate, they increase demand for these goods, which increases imports in the country that they migrated to and exports from their home country. This effect decreases as the migrant network ages—the longer migrants have been in the immigrant-receiving country, the less they import goods from home (Dunlevy and Hutchinson 1999). Instead they may find other sources of them in the immigrant receiving country, create sources of these products in the receiving country, or simply lose their taste for them.

The second, and likely the more important reason, is the informational mechanism. Trade requires information about arbitrage opportunities, language, preferences in both their home and host countries, business contacts, business norms and practices, and the legal framework, as well as trust. Migrants thus can increase intra-industry trade by identifying varieties of goods from the home (host) country that would appeal to consumers in the host (home country). Migrants can also increase trade more generally by making trade contracts more secure. Many trade contracts rely on a difference in time (and space) between delivery of goods and payment. For trade to occur, merchants in one country must find trustworthy partners in other countries. Migrant networks have been able to overcome these informational and trust problems for a long time. For example, Greif (2006) shows how, in the Middle Ages, the Maghrabi traders, who were migrants, used their networks to facilitate trade and punish those who did not abide by their contracts. Similarly, Rauch and Trindade (2002) argue that ethnic Chinese migrants play a similar role today. Further, several empirical studies show a robust link between migration flows and trade flow creation (Felbermayr and Toubal 2012; Gould 1994; Head and Ries 1998; Rauch and Trindade 2002).

Migrant networks are especially important in facilitating trade in situations where enforcement of contracts is likely to be weak or where more knowledge about goods is needed. For example, Dunlevy (2006) finds that the effect of migration is greater for those countries with relatively high levels of corruption. Migrant networks can help circumvent the problems associated with corrupt governments by providing information about the business environment and providing trustworthy trading partners. Rauch and Trindade (2002) find that the effect of migration networks on trade is stronger for differentiated goods. It is relatively easy to gain knowledge about prices and demand for homogeneous goods, such as raw materials. It is more difficult to gain information about prices and demand for differentiated goods, as they typically have a smaller market. Thus migrant networks help fill in these informational gaps and increase trust between trading partners, leading to increased trade.

CONCLUSION

Trade and migration have long been linked. Since the Middle Ages, migrants have often been traders because they were the ones who had information about market opportunities and had the trustworthy contacts to make trade over long distances possible. Within the study of international trade, trade and migration have also long been linked through one of the canonical trade models: the Stolper-Samuelson model. While there are many reasons the Stolper-Samuelson model may not hold, it has provided scholars with a useful framework from which to examine the ties between trade and migration.

In the last two decades scholars have begun to examine the relationships between trade and migration empirically and with new formal models. They have focused on three main areas of study: pubic opinion, policy, and flows. The literature has started to make headway, at least in establishing some empirical regularities: trade is preferred by most survey respondents to immigration; trade policy and immigration policy appear to be substitutes, with only one open at any given time in labor-scarce countries; trade flows at first increase but later decrease migration; and migration flows increase trade flows. As discussed above, scholars have given many different reasons for these empirical regularities but have also converged on a few causal mechanisms.

The results on public opinion have engendered some of the most scholarly debate. Scholars have posited that it is the fiscal effects of migrants, their effects on the labor market, and their cultural effects that drive the relationship between opinions on trade and those on migration. Recent studies focus on teasing out these effects. Malhotra, Margalit, and Mo (2013) use a carefully designed sample with oversampling of technology workers to show that cultural animus against migration often serves as a baseline for opinions on immigration, but that direct labor market competition can lead to intense anti-immigrant sentiment. Similarly, Goldstein and Peters (2014), using a panel survey during the Great Recession and the recovery, show that respondents also have a baseline of cultural animus toward immigrants but that their support for immigration is affected by their economic situation. Finally, Helbling and Kriesi (2014) use carefully designed survey experiments to tease out how exactly the fiscal effect and cultural animus may play out in different institutional environments.

More research on the differences in public opinion on trade and on migration could be done. For example, instead of examining population averages, scholars could examine more closely which respondents favor (oppose) trade and migration and which have differing opinions. What differences are there between these two groups? Further, like Helbling and Kriesi (2014), they could undertake more careful analysis of the different hypotheses in various institutional environments.

In addition to these empirical puzzles, scholars should examine why the dislike of foreigners affects immigration more than it affects trade, why some groups are more disliked than others, and why the dislike of foreigners is more salient at some times than at others. For example, we know that American survey respondents dislike both Chinese trade and Mexican immigration (Goldstein and Peters 2014), yet the effect of culture seems to influence overall levels of support for immigration more than trade. Why does nativism have a greater effect on immigration than nationalism does on trade? Similarly, we know that respondents in the United States currently dislike Indian immigration more than they dislike German immigration, and Chinese trade is more disliked than German trade (Goldstein and Peters 2014). Yet while there are more Indian immigrants, both Indian and German immigrants pose a threat to high-skill natives, and both Germany and China have been running large trade surpluses at the expense of the United States. So why then do Americans dislike Indian immigrants or Chinese goods more than German immigrants or goods? Is it just racism, or is there an economic logic to the opposition to these flows? Finally, how do we explain the salience of cultural threat? For example, in the early 1900s an increase in nativism helped lead to passage of the Literacy Act and the 1921 and 1924 quota acts in the United States and anti-Asian immigrant acts in Australia and Canada, and increased nationalism led to beggar-thy-neighbor trade and exchange rate policies during the Great Depression. Increased nativism and nationalism during the Great Recession has not had the same effect on either migration or trade. Why was nativism/ nationalism more effective in the past than today? Is it the case that the public is less nativist/ nationalist, or that norms against nativism/ nationalism prevent policy makers from using it as a way to frame the debate (see Freeman 1995), or are their other factors that have made nativism/ nationalism less salient?

Moreover, there is a missing link between opinion and policy that public opinion scholars should examine. Peters and Tahk (2011) offer one of the few studies to examine whether public opinion translates to policy, finding little link between opinion on immigration and policy. However, they only examine the United States and Canada. It could be that these two countries are relatively special institutional environments and that opinion links to policy in other countries. However, we do not know. Scholars should examine whether opinion affects policy, as well as why or why not.

While scholars have found that trade and migration policy are substitutes in labor-scarce countries, little research has been done on whether trade and emigration are substitutes or complements in labor-abundant countries. Many developing countries, for example the former Communist countries but also Japan before 1868, kept both trade and emigration relatively restricted. Some countries, like India and Mexico until recently, tacitly or explicitly encouraged emigration while maintaining trade barriers. Others, like China, have opened trade but discouraged emigration, especially high-skill emigration. Finally, some countries, like South Korea in the 1960s and 1970s, encouraged both trade and emigration. What explains these divergent patterns? If a labor-abundant country keeps trade closed, it may restrict emigration to keep a cheap supply of labor for capitalists or for security reasons. On the other hand, it may encourage emigration to decrease unemployment or serve as a safety valve against revolution. Similarly if a labor-abundant country opens trade, it may restrict emigration as a way to keep its low labor costs or may encourage emigration as another way to help the country develop or as a way to decrease unrest during times of trade-related economic dislocation. Thus, it is an open puzzle how trade and emigration policy might affect each other in developing countries.

Finally, the scholarship on migration and trade flows has tended to focus on individual market actors and not on how political leaders might respond to those market actors. Yet if trade and migrant flows affect each other, we should expect that there would be some political ramifications from these effects. For example, it appears that Mexico used the issue of Mexican migration to the United States to help gain support for NAFTA; do other emigrant-sending states use the issue of migration to lobby for preferential trade access in immigrant- receiving states? Are they successful? What about lobbying by migrants themselves? Bermeo and Leblang (2012) find that migrants are relatively successful in lobbying for foreign aid. Are they also successful in lobbying for trade openness with their home country? Or would this openness cut at their advantage over other groups, making them less likely to lobby? In general, how do migrant networks protect their advantages in the world economy, if they do at all?

Stolper and Samuelson long ago argued that trade and migration are linked, yet this scholarship was largely ignored in favor of studying trade and migration separately. In large part this was because when the field of IPE began in the 1960s and 1970s, trade was relatively open—at least in comparison to the interwar years—whereas migration was relatively restricted, resulting in low levels of migration. Globalization, then, was defined as the movement of goods and capital, but not people. In contrast, the nineteenth century was a time of high levels of migration as well as trade and capital movements; globalization, as defined in this period by Keynes (1919), was the movement of goods, capital, and people. Today, however, migration is becoming a more important topic in the policy world and in scholarship as well. Scholars have begun studying the ties between trade and migration, returning to the Stolper-Samuelson model and examining when and where it holds. This line of inquiry is still in its infancy but promises to be a fruitful one for scholars.

References

Bacon, David. 2012. How US Policies Fueled Mexico's Great Migration. *The Nation*, January 23.

Bermeo, Sarah Blodgett, and David A. Leblang. Forthcoming. Migration and Foreign Aid. *International Organization*.

Dunlevy, James A. 2006. The Influence of Corruption and Language on the Pro-trade Effect of Immigrants: Evidence from the American States. *Review of Economics and Statistics* 88 (1): 182–186.

Dunlevy, James A., and William K. Hutchinson. 1999. The Impact of Immigration on American Import Trade in the Late Nineteenth and Early Twentieth Centuries. *Journal of Economic History* 59 (4): 1043–1062.

Felbermayr, Gabriel J., and Benjamin Jung. 2009. The Pro-trade Effect of the Brain Drain: Sorting Out Confounding Factors. *Economic Letters* 104: 72–75.

Felbermayr, Gabriel J., and Farid Toubal. 2012. Revisiting the Trade-Migration Nexus: Evidence from New OECD Data. *World Development* 40 (5): 928–937.

Fernandez-Kelly, Maria Patricia. 1983. Mexican Border Industrialization, Female Labor Force Participation and Migration. In *Women, Men, and the International Division of Labor*, edited by June C. Nash and Fernandez-Kelly, Maria Patricia, 205–223. Albany: State University of New York Press.

Freeman, Gary P. 1995. Modes of Immigration Politics in Liberal Democratic States. *International Migration Review* 29 (4): 881–902.

Geddes, Andrew, and Jeannette Money. 2011. Mobility Within the European Union. In *Migration, Nation States, and International Cooperation*, edited by Randall Hansen and Jobst Koehler, 31–43. New York: Routledge.

Goldstein, Judith L., and Margaret E. Peters. 2014. Nativism or Economic Threat: Attitudes Toward Immigrants During the Great Recession. *International Interactions*. 40 (3): 1–26.

Gould, David M. 1994. Immigrant Links to the Home Country: Empirical Implications for U.S. Bilateral Trade Flows. *Review of Economics and Statistics* 76 (2): 302–316.

Greif, Avner. 2006. *Institutions and the Path to the Modern Economy: Lessons from Medieval Trade*. Cambridge, UK: Cambridge University Press.

Hainmueller, Jens, and Michael J. Hiscox. 2010. Attitudes Toward Highly Skilled and Low-skilled Immigration: Evidence from a Survey Experiment. *American Political Science Review*: 1–24.

Hainmueller, Jens, and Michael J. Hiscox. 2007. Educated Preferences: Explaining Attitudes Toward Immigration in Europe. *International Organization* 61 (2): 399–442.

Hanson, Gordon H., Kenneth Scheve, and Matthew J. Slaughter. 2007. Public Finance and Individual Preferences Over Globalization Strategies. *Economics & Politics* 19 (1): 1–33.

Hatton, Timothy J., and Jeffrey G. Williamson. 1998. *The Age of Mass Migration: Causes and Economic Impact*. New York: Oxford University Press.

Hatton, Timothy J., and Jeffrey G. Williamson. 2007. "A Dual Policy Paradox: Why Have Trade and Immigration Policies Always Differed in Labor-Scarce Economies?" In *The New Comparative Economic History*, edited by Hatton, Timothy J., Kevin H. O'Rourke, and Alan M. Taylor, Chapter 9, 217–240. Cambridge, MA: MIT Press.

Hatton, Timothy J., and Jeffrey G. Williamson. 2005. *Global Migration and the World Economy*. Cambridge, MA: MIT Press.

Hatzigeorgiou, Andreas. 2010. Migration as Trade Facilitation: Assessing the Links Between International Trade and Migration. *B.E. Journal of Economic Analysis & Policy* 10 (1): Article 24.

Head, Keith, and John Ries. 1998. Immigration and Trade Creation: Econometric Evidence from Canada. *The Canadian Journal of Economics/Revue Canadienne d'Economique* 31 (1): 47–62.

Helbling, Marc, and Hanspeter Kriesi. 2014. Why citizens prefer high-over low-skilled immigrants. Labor market competition, welfare state and deservingness", *European Sociological Review*. (forthcoming).

Herander, Mark G., and Luz A. Saavedra. 2005. Exports and the Structure of Immigrant-Based Networks: The Role of Geographic Proximity. *Review of Economics and Statistics* 87 (2): 323–335.

Keohane, Robert O., and Helen V. Milner. 1996. *Internationalization and Domestic Politics*. Cambridge, UK: Cambridge University Press.

Keynes, John Maynard. 1919. *The Economic Consequences of the Peace*. New York: Harcourt, Brace and Howe.

Lake, David A. 2009. Open Economy Politics: A Critical Review. *Review of International Organizations* 4: 219–244.

Lopez, Ramon, and Maurice Schiff. 1998. Migration and the Skill Composition of the Labour Force: The Impact of Trade Liberalization in LDCs. *Canadian Journal of Economics/Revue Canadienne d'Economique* 31 (2): 318–336.

Malhotra, Neil, Yotam Margalit, and Cecilia Mo. 2013. Economic Explanations for Opposition to Immigration: Distinguishing Between Prevalence and Conditional Impact. *American Journal of Political Science* 57 (2): 391–410.

Markusen, James R. 1983. Factor Movements and Commodity Trade as Complements. *Jounral of International Economics* 14 (3–4): 341–356.

Mayda, Anna Maria. 2008. Why Are People More Pro-trade Than Pro-migration? *Economic Letters* 101: 160–163.

Melitz, Marc J. 2003. The Impact of Trade on Intra-Industry Reallocations and Aggregate Industry Productivity. *Econometrica* 71 (6): 1695–1725.

Mundell, Robert A. 1957. International Trade and Factor Mobility. *American Economic Review* 47 (3): 321–335.

Neuman, Gerald L. 1993. The Lost Century of American Immigration Law (1776–1875). *Columbia Law Review* 93 (8): 1833–1901.

Oatley, Thomas. 2011. The Reductionist Gamble: Open Economy Politics in the Global Economy. *International Organization* 65 (2): 311–341.

O'Rourke, Kevin H., and Jeffrey G. Williamson. 1999. *Globalization and History: The Evolution of a Nineteenth-Century Atlantic Economy*. Cambridge, MA: MIT Press.

Peters, Margaret E. 2015. Open Trade, Closed Borders: Immigration in the Era of Globalization. *World Politics.* 67 (1). 114-154.

Peters, Margaret E. 2014. "Trade, Foreign Direct Investment and Immigration Policy Making in the US." *International Organization* 68 (4): 811–844.

Peters, Margaret E., and Alexander M. Tahk. 2011. Are Policy Makers Out of Touch with Their Constituencies When It Comes to Immigration? Working Paper. University of Wisconsin—Madison and Yale University.

Rauch, James E., and Vitor Trindade. 2002. Ethnic Chinese Networks in International Trade. *Review of Economics and Statistics* 84 (1): 116–130.

Samuelson, Paul A. 1948. International Trade and the Equalisation of Factor Prices. *The Economic Journal* 58 (230): 163–184.

Sassen, Saskia. 1988. *The Mobility of Labor and Capital: A Study in International Investment and Labor Flow.* Cambridge, UK: Cambridge University Press.

Strauss, Jack. 2012. Does Immigration, Particularly Increases in Latinos, Affect African American Wages, Unemployment and Incarceration Rates? Working Paper. University of Denver—Reiman School of Finance.

Uchitelle, Louis. 2007. NAFTA Should Have Stopped Illegal Immigration, Right? *New York Times*, February 18, The Nation section. http://www.nytimes.com/2007/02/18/weekinreview/18uchitelle.html.

INDEX

CPSIA information can be obtained
at www.ICGtesting.com
Printed in the USA
BVHW070857211021
618933BV00001B/1

9 780190 077785